T0304477

Market Risk Analysis
Volume III

Pricing, Hedging and Trading
Financial Instruments

Market Risk Analysis
Volume III

Pricing, Hedging and Trading
Financial Instruments

Carol Alexander

John Wiley & Sons, Ltd

Published in 2008 by   John Wiley & Sons Ltd, The Atrium, Southern Gate, Chichester,
West Sussex PO19 8SQ, England

Telephone (+44) 1243 779777

Email (for orders and customer service enquiries): cs-books@wiley.co.uk
Visit our Home Page on www.wiley.com

Other Wiley Editorial Offices

John Wiley & Sons Inc., 111 River Street, Hoboken, NJ 07030, USA

Jossey-Bass, 989 Market Street, San Francisco, CA 94103-1741, USA

Wiley-VCH Verlag GmbH, Boschstr. 12, D-69469 Weinheim, Germany

John Wiley & Sons Australia Ltd, 42 McDougall Street, Milton, Queensland 4064, Australia

John Wiley & Sons (Asia) Pte Ltd, 2 Clementi Loop #02-01, Jin Xing Distripark, Singapore 129809

John Wiley & Sons Canada Ltd, 6045 Freemont Blvd, Mississauga, Ontario, Canada L5R 4J3

Wiley also publishes its books in a variety of electronic formats. Some content that appears in print may
not be available in electronic books.

British Library Cataloguing in Publication Data

A catalogue record for this book is available from the British Library

ISBN 978-0-470-99789-5 (HB)

Typeset in 10/12pt Times by Integra Software Services Pvt. Ltd, Pondicherry, India
Printed and bound in Great Britain by Antony Rowe Ltd, Chippenham, Wiltshire
This book is printed on acid-free paper responsibly manufactured from sustainable forestry
in which at least two trees are planted for each one used for paper production.

C9780470997895_120224

To Jacques Pézier

Contents

List of Figures

List of Tables

List of Examples

Foreword

How many children dream of one day becoming risk managers? I very much doubt little Carol Jenkins, as she was called then, did. She dreamt about being a wild white horse, or a mermaid swimming with dolphins, as any normal little girl does. As I start crunching into two kilos of Toblerone that Carol Alexander-Pézier gave me for Valentine's day (perhaps to coax me into writing this foreword), I see the distinctive silhouette of the Matterhorn on the yellow package and I am reminded of my own dreams of climbing mountains and travelling to distant planets. Yes, adventure and danger! That is the stuff of happiness, especially when you daydream as a child with a warm cup of cocoa in your hands.

As we grow up, dreams lose their naivety but not necessarily their power. Knowledge makes us discover new possibilities and raises new questions. We grow to understand better the consequences of our actions, yet the world remains full of surprises. We taste the sweetness of success and the bitterness of failure. We grow to be responsible members of society and to care for the welfare of others. We discover purpose, confidence and a role to fulfil; but we also find that we continuously have to deal with risks.

Leafing through the hundreds of pages of this four-volume series you will discover one of the goals that Carol gave herself in life: to set the standards for a new profession, that of market risk manager, and to provide the means of achieving those standards. Why is market risk management so important? Because in our modern economies, market prices balance the supply and demand of most goods and services that fulfil our needs and desires. We can hardly take a decision, such as buying a house or saving for a later day, without taking some market risks. Financial firms, be they in banking, insurance or asset management, manage these risks on a grand scale. Capital markets and derivative products offer endless ways to transfer these risks among economic agents.

But should market risk management be regarded as a professional activity? Sampling the material in these four volumes will convince you, if need be, of the vast amount of knowledge and skills required. A good market risk manager should master the basics of calculus, linear algebra, probability – including stochastic calculus – statistics and econometrics. He should be an astute student of the markets, familiar with the vast array of modern financial instruments and market mechanisms, and of the econometric properties of prices and returns in these markets. If he works in the financial industry, he should also be well versed in regulations and understand how they affect his firm. That sets the academic syllabus for the profession.

Carol takes the reader step by step through all these topics, from basic definitions and principles to advanced problems and solution methods. She uses a clear language, realistic illustrations with recent market data, consistent notation throughout all chapters, and provides a huge range of worked-out exercises on Excel spreadsheets, some of which demonstrate analytical tools only available in the best commercial software packages. Many chapters on advanced subjects such as GARCH models, copulas, quantile regressions, portfolio theory, options and volatility surfaces are as informative as and easier to understand than entire books devoted to these subjects. Indeed, this is the first series of books entirely dedicated to the discipline of market risk analysis written by one person, and a very good teacher at that.

A profession, however, is more than an academic discipline; it is an activity that fulfils some societal needs, that provides solutions in the face of evolving challenges, that calls for a special code of conduct; it is something one can aspire to. Does market risk management face such challenges? Can it achieve significant economic benefits?

As market economies grow, more ordinary people of all ages with different needs and risk appetites have financial assets to manage and borrowings to control. What kind of mortgages should they take? What provisions should they make for their pensions? The range of investment products offered to them has widened far beyond the traditional cash, bond and equity classes to include actively managed funds (traditional or hedge funds), private equity, real estate investment trusts, structured products and derivative products facilitating the trading of more exotic risks – commodities, credit risks, volatilities and correlations, weather, carbon emissions, etc. – and offering markedly different return characteristics from those of traditional asset classes. Managing personal finances is largely about managing market risks. How well educated are we to do that?

Corporates have also become more exposed to market risks. Beyond the traditional exposure to interest rate fluctuations, most corporates are now exposed to foreign exchange risks and commodity risks because of globalization. A company may produce and sell exclusively in its domestic market and yet be exposed to currency fluctuations because of foreign competition. Risks that can be hedged effectively by shareholders, if they wish, do not have to be hedged in-house. But hedging some risks in-house may bring benefits (e.g. reduction of tax burden, smoothing of returns, easier planning) that are not directly attainable by the shareholder.

Financial firms, of course, should be the experts at managing market risks; it is their métier. Indeed, over the last generation, there has been a marked increase in the size of market risks handled by banks in comparison to a reduction in the size of their credit risks. Since the 1980s, banks have provided products (e.g. interest rate swaps, currency protection, index linked loans, capital guaranteed investments) to facilitate the risk management of their customers. They have also built up arbitrage and proprietary trading books to profit from perceived market anomalies and take advantage of their market views. More recently, banks have started to manage credit risks actively by transferring them to the capital markets instead of warehousing them. Bonds are replacing loans, mortgages and other loans are securitized, and many of the remaining credit risks can now be covered with credit default swaps. Thus credit risks are being converted into market risks.

The rapid development of capital markets and, in particular, of derivative products bears witness to these changes. At the time of writing this foreword, the total notional size of all derivative products exceeds $500 trillion whereas, in rough figures, the bond and money markets stand at about $80 trillion, the equity markets half that and loans half that again. Credit derivatives by themselves are climbing through the $30 trillion mark. These derivative markets are zero-sum games; they are all about market risk management – hedging, arbitrage and speculation.

This does not mean, however, that all market risk management problems have been resolved. We may have developed the means and the techniques, but we do not necessarily understand how to address the problems. Regulators and other experts setting standards and policies are particularly concerned with several fundamental issues. To name a few:

1. How do we decide what market risks should be assessed and over what time horizons? For example, should the loan books of banks or long-term liabilities of pension funds be marked to market, or should we not be concerned with pricing things that will not be traded in the near future? We think there is no general answer to this question about the most appropriate description of risks. The descriptions must be adapted to specific management problems.
2. In what contexts should market risks be assessed? Thus, what is more risky, fixed or floating rate financing? Answers to such questions are often dictated by accounting standards or other conventions that must be followed and therefore take on economic significance. But the adequacy of standards must be regularly reassessed. To wit, the development of International Accounting Standards favouring mark-to-market and hedge accounting where possible (whereby offsetting risks can be reported together).
3. To what extent should risk assessments be 'objective'? Modern regulations of financial firms (Basel II Amendment, 1996) have been a major driver in the development of risk assessment methods. Regulators naturally want a 'level playing field' and objective rules. This reinforces a natural tendency to assess risks purely on the basis of statistical evidence and to neglect personal, forward-looking views. Thus one speaks too often about risk 'measurements' as if risks were physical objects instead of risk 'assessments' indicating that risks are potentialities that can only be guessed by making a number of assumptions (i.e. by using models). Regulators try to compensate for this tendency by asking risk managers to draw scenarios and to stress-test their models.

There are many other fundamental issues to be debated, such as the natural tendency to focus on micro risk management – because it is easy – rather than to integrate all significant risks and to consider their global effect – because that is more difficult. In particular, the assessment and control of systemic risks by supervisory authorities is still in its infancy. But I would like to conclude by calling attention to a particular danger faced by a nascent market risk management profession, that of separating risks from returns and focusing on downside-risk limits.

It is central to the ethics of risk managers to be independent and to act with integrity. Thus risk managers should not be under the direct control of line managers of profit centres and they should be well remunerated independently of company results. But in some firms this is also understood as denying risk managers access to profit information. I remember a risk commission that had to approve or reject projects but, for internal political reasons, could not have any information about their expected profitability. For decades, credit officers in most banks operated under such constraints: they were supposed to accept or reject deals a priori, without knowledge of their pricing. Times have changed. We understand now, at least in principle, that the essence of risk management is not simply to reduce or control risks but to achieve an optimal balance between risks and returns.

Yet, whether for organizational reasons or out of ignorance, risk management is often confined to setting and enforcing risk limits. Most firms, especially financial firms, claim to have well-thought-out risk management policies, but few actually state trade-offs between risks and returns. Attention to risk limits may be unwittingly reinforced by regulators. Of course it is not the role of the supervisory authorities to suggest risk–return trade-offs; so supervisors impose risk limits, such as value at risk relative to capital, to ensure safety and fair competition in the financial industry. But a regulatory limit implies severe penalties if breached, and thus a probabilistic constraint acquires an economic value. Banks must therefore pay attention to the uncertainty in their value-at-risk estimates. The effect would be rather perverse if banks ended up paying more attention to the probability of a probability than to their entire return distribution.

With *Market Risk Analysis* readers will learn to understand these long-term problems in a realistic context. Carol is an academic with a strong applied interest. She has helped to design the curriculum for the Professional Risk Managers' International Association (PRMIA) qualifications, to set the standards for their professional qualifications, and she maintains numerous contacts with the financial industry through consulting and seminars. In *Market Risk Analysis* theoretical developments may be more rigorous and reach a more advanced level than in many other books, but they always lead to practical applications with numerous examples in interactive Excel spreadsheets. For example, unlike 90% of the finance literature on hedging that is of no use to practitioners, if not misleading at times, her concise expositions on this subject give solutions to real problems.

In summary, if there is any good reason for not treating market risk management as a separate discipline, it is that market risk management should be the business of *all* decision makers involved in finance, with primary responsibilities on the shoulders of the most senior managers and board members. However, there is so much to be learnt and so much to be further researched on this subject that it is proper for professional people to specialize in it. These four volumes will fulfil most of their needs. They only have to remember that, to be effective, they have to be good communicators and ensure that their assessments are properly integrated in their firm's decision-making process.

Jacques Pézier

Preface to Volume III

A *financial instrument* is a legal contract between two or more parties that defines conditions under which the various parties incur costs and receive benefits. A cost or benefit need not be a monetary amount; it could be a commodity, for instance. The simplest type of financial instrument is a *financial asset*, which is a legal claim on a real asset such as a company, a commodity, cash, gold or a building. A *financial security* is a standardized form of financial asset that is traded in an organized market. For instance, equity securities (shares on a company's stock) are traded on exchanges and debt securities such as bonds and money market instruments (including bills, notes and repurchase agreements) are traded in brokers' markets.

A *derivative contract*, usually called a 'derivative' for short, is another type of financial instrument which is a contract on one or more *underlying* financial instruments. The underlying of a derivative does not have to be a traded asset or an interest rate. For instance, futures on carbon emissions or temperature have started trading on exchanges during the last few years. Derivatives are the fastest-growing class of financial instruments and the notional amount outstanding now far exceeds the size of ordinary securities markets. For instance, in 2007 the Bank for International Settlements estimated the total size of the debt securities market (including all corporate, government and municipal bonds and money market instruments) to be approximately US$70 trillion. However, the amount outstanding on all interest rate derivatives was nearly $300 trillion.

The most common types of financial derivatives are futures and forwards, swaps and options, and within each broad category there are numerous subcategories, so there is a huge diversity of financial derivatives. For instance, the vast majority of the trading in swaps is on interest rate swaps, but credit default swaps and cross-currency basis swaps are also heavily traded. Other swaps include variance swaps, covariance swaps, equity swaps and contracts for differences. But the greatest diversity amongst all derivative instruments can be found in the category of options. Options can be defined on virtually any underlying contract, including options on derivatives such as futures, swaps and other options. Many options, mostly standard calls and puts, are traded on exchanges, but there is a very active over-the-counter (OTC) market in non-standard options. Since the two parties in an OTC contract are free to define whatever terms they please, the pay-off to the holder of an OTC option can be freely defined. This means that ever more exotic options are continually being introduced, with pay-off profiles that can take virtually any shape.

A *portfolio* is a collection of financial instruments. An investor holds a portfolio with the aim of obtaining a particular return on his investment and to spread his risk. The more differences between the financial instruments available to the investor, the better he can diversify his risk. Risk can be substantially reduced in large, well-diversified portfolios, but there can never be zero risk associated with any return above the risk free rate, and some investors are more averse to taking risks than others. The main reason for the terrific number of different financial instruments is that the risk–return profiles of different investors are not the same. Each new type of instrument is introduced specifically because it purports to provide its own unique profile of risk and return.

AIMS AND SCOPE

This book is designed as a text for advanced university and professional courses in finance. It provides a pedagogical and complete treatment of the characteristics of the main categories of financial instruments, i.e. bonds, swaps, futures and forwards, options and volatility. Given the tremendous diversity of financial instruments, it is not surprising that there are many books that deal with just one type of financial instrument. Often the textbooks that cover fixed income securities alone, or just futures and forwards, or swaps or options, are large books that go into considerable details about specific market conventions. Some present each subcategory of instrument in its own unique theoretical framework, or include all mathematical details. By contrast, this book adopts a general framework whenever possible and provides a concise but rigorous treatment of only the essential mathematics.

To cover all major financial instruments (excluding credit derivatives) in one volume, one has to be very selective in the material presented. The reason why I have decided to exclude credit derivatives is that this book series is on market risk and not credit risk. Also I have not set up the background in Volume I, *Quantitative Methods in Finance*, to be able to cover credit derivatives in the same detail as I can analyse swaps, futures, options and volatility. Also we do not have a chapter specifically devoted to cash equity in this volume. This material naturally belongs in the Econometrics volume of *Market Risk Analysis*. A large part of Volume II, *Practical Financial Econometrics*, concerns cash equity portfolios, including the regression factor models that are used to analyse their risk and return and more advanced equity trading strategies (e.g. pairs trading based on cointegration).

Readers will appreciate the need to be concise, and whilst a mathematically rigorous approach is adopted some detailed proofs are omitted. Instead we refer readers to tractable sources where proofs may be perused, if required. My purpose is really to focus on the important concepts and to illustrate their application with practical examples. Even though this book omits some of the detailed arguments that are found in other textbooks on financial instruments, I have made considerable effort not to be obscure in any way. Each term is carefully defined, or a cross-reference is provided where readers may seek further enlightenment in other volumes of *Market Risk Analysis*. We assume no prior knowledge of finance, but readers should be comfortable with the scope of the mathematical material in Volume I and will preferably have that volume to hand. In order to make the exposition accessible to a wide audience, illustrative examples are provided immediately after the introduction of each new concept and virtually all of these examples are also worked through in interactive Excel spreadsheets.

This book is much shorter than other general books on financial instruments such as Wilmott (2006), Hull (2008) and Fabozzi (2002), one reason being that we omit credit derivatives. Many other textbooks in this area focus on just one particular category of financial instrument. Thus there is overlap with several existing books. For instance, Chapter 3 on *Options* covers the same topics as much of the material in James (2003). A similar remark applies to Gatheral (2006), which has content similar to the first 75 pages of Chapter 4, on *Volatility* but in Gatheral's book this is covered in greater mathematical depth.

The readership of this volume is likely to be equally divided between finance professionals and academics. The main professional audience will be amongst traders, quants and risk managers, particularly those whose work concerns the pricing and hedging of bonds, swaps, futures and forwards, options and volatility. The main academic audience is for faculty involved with teaching and research and for students at the advanced master's or PhD level in finance, mathematical finance or quantitative market risk management. There are only five (extremely long) chapters and each aims to provide sufficient material for a one-semester postgraduate course, or for a week's professional training course.

OUTLINE OF VOLUME III

Chapter 1, *Bonds and Swaps*, begins by introducing fundamental concepts such as the compounding of interest and the relationship between spot and forward rates, by providing a catalogue of fixed and floating coupon bonds by issuer and maturity and by performing a basic analysis of fixed coupon bonds, including the price–yield relationship, the characteristics of the zero coupon spot yield curve and the term structure of forward interest rates. We cover duration and convexity for single bonds and then for bond portfolios, the Taylor expansion to approximate the change in portfolio price for a parallel shift in the yield curve, and the traditional approach to bond portfolio immunization. Then we look at floating rate notes, forward rate agreements and interest rate swaps and explain their relationship; we analyse the market risk of an interest rate swap and introduce the PV01 and the dollar duration of cash flow. Bootstrapping, splines and parametric yield curve fitting methods and convertible bonds are also covered in this chapter.

Chapter 2, *Futures and Forwards*, gives details of the futures and forward markets in interest rates, bonds, currencies, commodities, stocks, stock indices, exchange traded funds, volatility indices, credit spreads, weather, real estate and pollution. Then we introduce the no arbitrage pricing argument, examine the components of basis risk for different types of underlying contract, and explain how to hedge with futures and forwards. Mean–variance, minimum variance and proxy hedging are all covered. We illustrate how futures hedges are implemented in practice: to hedge international portfolios with forex forwards, stock portfolios with index futures, and bond portfolios with portfolios of notional bond futures. The residual risk of a hedged portfolio is disaggregated into different components, showing which uncertainties cannot be fully hedged, and we include an Excel case study that analyses the book of an energy futures trader, identifying the key risk factors facing the trader and providing simple ways for the trader to reduce his risks.

Chapter 3, *Options*, introduces the basic principles of option pricing, and the options trading strategies that are commonly used by investors and speculators; describes the characteristics of different types of options; explains how providers of options hedge their risks; derives and interprets the Black–Scholes–Merton pricing model, and a standard trader's adjustment to this model for stochastic volatility; explains how to price interest rate options and how to calibrate the LIBOR model; and provides pricing models for European exotic options. It begins with a relatively non-technical overview of the foundations of option pricing theory, including some elementary stochastic calculus, deriving the principle of risk neutral valuation and explaining the binomial option pricing model. The scope of the chapter is very broad, covering the pricing of European and American options with and without path-dependent pay-offs, but only under the assumption of constant volatility. 'Greeks' are introduced and analysed thoroughly and numerical examples show how to hedge the risks of trading options. For interest rate options we derive the prices of European caps, floors and swaptions and survey the family of mean-reverting interest rate models, including a case study on the LIBOR model. Formulae for numerous exotics are given and these, along with more than 20 other numerical examples for this chapter, are all implemented in Excel.

Chapter 4, *Volatility*, begins by explaining how to model the market implied and market local volatility surfaces and discusses the properties of model implied and model local volatility surfaces. A long case study, spread over three Excel workbooks, develops a dynamic model of the market implied volatility surface based on principal component analysis and uses this to estimate price hedge ratios that are adjusted for implied volatility dynamics. Another main focus of the chapter is on option pricing models with stochastic volatility and jumps. The model implied and local volatility surfaces corresponding to any stochastic volatility model are defined intuitively and several stochastic volatility models, including their applications to options pricing and hedging, are discussed. We cover a few specific models with jumps, such as the Heston jump model (but not Lévy processes) and introduce a new type of volatility jump model as the continuous version of Markov switching GARCH. We explain why the models for tradable assets (but not necessarily interest rates) must be scale invariant and why it does not matter which scale invariant model we use for dynamic delta–gamma hedging of virtually any claim (!). Then we describe the market and the characteristics of variance swaps, volatility futures and volatility options and explain how to construct a term structure of volatility indices, using for illustration the Vftse, a volatility index that is not currently quoted on any exchange. At 94 pages, it is one of the longest and most comprehensive chapters in the book.

Chapter 5, *Portfolio Mapping*, is essential for hedging market risks and also lays the foundations for Volume IV, *Value-at-Risk Models*. It begins by summarizing a portfolio's risk factors and its sensitivities to these factors for various categories of financial instruments, including cash and futures or forward portfolios on equities, bonds, currencies and commodities and portfolios of options. Then it covers present value, duration, volatility and PV01 invariant cash flow mapping, illustrating these with simple interactive Excel spreadsheets. Risk factor mapping of futures and forward portfolios, and that of commodity futures portfolios in particular, and mappings for option portfolios are covered, with all technical details supported with Excel spreadsheets. Mapping a volatility surface is not easy and most vega bucketing techniques are too crude, so this is illustrated with a case study based on the Vftse index. Statistical techniques such as regression and principal component analysis are used to reduce the dimension of the risk factor space and the chapter also requires some knowledge of matrix algebra for multivariate delta–gamma mapping.

ABOUT THE WEBSITE

Virtually all the concepts in this book are illustrated using numerical and empirical examples which are stored in Excel workbooks for each chapter. These may be found on the accompanying website in the folder labelled by the chapter number. Simply search for the book on wiley.com and select 'Related Resources' to access the material. Within these spreadsheets readers may change parameters of the problem (the parameters are indicated in *red*) and see the new solution (the output is indicated in *blue*).

Rather than using VBA code, which will be obscure to many readers, I have encoded the formulae directly into the spreadsheet. Thus the reader need only click on a cell to read the formula and it should be straightforward to tailor or extend most of the spreadsheets to suit the reader's particular problems. Notably, they contain formulae for exotic option prices, not only barrier options and Asians but also pricing formulae for many other exotics. Matlab code, written by my PhD student Andreas Kaeck, is provided for calibrating option pricing models. Several case studies, based on complete and up-to-date financial data, and all graphs and tables in the text are also contained in the Excel workbooks on the website.

For teaching purposes, the Excel spreadsheets are designed so that the course tutor can set an unlimited number of variations on the examples in the text as exercises. Also the graphs and tables can be modified if required, and copied and pasted as enhanced metafiles into lecture notes (respecting the copyright notice that is included at the end of the book).

ACKNOWLEDGEMENTS

One of the problems with being an author is that to be truly original one should minimize contact with related textbooks. But if one possesses books only to consult them briefly, for instance to verify a formula, how does one learn? Reading academic research papers is very important of course, but most of the practical knowledge of finance and risk management that I bring to this textbook has been gained through discussions with my husband, Jacques Pézier. We share a passion for mathematical finance. The first two presents he gave me were paperweights with shapes resembling a volatility surface and a normal mixture copula density. When I met Jacques I was a mere econometrician having some expertise with GARCH models, but because of him I have moved into mainstream quantitative finance, a change that has been continually fuelled by our frequent discussions. I can honestly say that without Jacques my state of knowledge would not warrant writing this book and it gives me enormous pleasure to dedicate it to him.

Jacques spent twenty-five years working in the City as a consultant and a financial risk manager, helping to set up LIFFE and to build risk management groups for several major banks. And his hand-written documents for the original version of Reuters 2000 software in 1994 formed the basis of the exotic option spreadsheets included on the website. Five years ago I eventually persuaded him to return to academic life, and now we work side by side at the ICMA Centre with a large and wonderful quantitative finance research group. I would like to thank Professor John Board, Director of the Centre, and the two past directors, Professors Brian Scott-Quinn and Chris Brooks, for creating an environment in which this is possible.

I would like to thank my very careful copyeditor, Richard Leigh, who has been good-humoured and patient with my last minute changes to the text. It helps so much to have a specialist mathematical copyeditor who can spot errors in equations, and Richard is also an excellent linguist. He is very much appreciated, not only by me but also by Viv Wickham, whom I would like to thank for the lightening speed and efficiency with which she published these books, and all her staff on the production side at Wiley.

Since the first printing I have been working very closely with Philippe Derome and Ronnie Barnes. These two readers, who are using all four books to broaden their already-considerable education, have taken a special interest in correcting typos and requesting brief clarifications. To paraphrase an early email from Phillipe, 'a fine meal deserves the finest service'. I would like to say a *huge* "thank you" to Ronnie and Philippe.

Like most academics, I choose research problems because I want to learn more about a certain area, and it is so much more pleasurable to walk the path of learning accompanied by a student. My PhD students have played a very important role in the advancement of my knowledge and I have been lucky enough to supervise a succession of excellent students at the ICMA Centre. All of these students, past and present, have contributed significantly to my understanding of mathematical finance and quantitative risk management. Those whose research relates to this book deserve a special mention. My research with Dr Ali Bora Yigitbaşıoğlu, who now works at Lehman Brothers in London, contributed to my understanding of convertible bond pricing and hedging models. I learned how to build yield curves and calibrate the LIBOR model with Dr Dmitri Lvov, now at JP Morgan Chase in London. With Dr Andreza Barbosa, who is also working at JP Morgan Chase, I learned about exchange traded finds and minimum variance hedging with futures. And with Aanand Venkatramanan, who is now in the third year of his PhD, I learned about commodity markets and about multi-asset option pricing.

Two of my past PhD students are now highly valued colleagues at the ICMA Centre. These are Dr Emese Lazar and Dr Leonardo Nogueira. Emese and I continue to work together on the continuous limit of GARCH models, where her confidence, perseverance and meticulous calculations have led to some important breakthroughs. In particular, we have derived two new GARCH diffusions, the numerous advantages of which have been described in Chapter 4. And Leonardo's expansive vision, energy and enthusiasm for new research problems have led to some far-reaching results on hedging options. Our papers on scale invariance have cut through a considerable research effort on finding the best hedging model, since we have shown that all appropriate models for hedging any options on tradable assets have the same hedge ratios! Working with Leonardo, I learned a considerable amount about volatility modelling.

My good friends Dr Hyungsok Ahn of Nomura, London and Moorad Choudhry of KBC financial products, have shared many insights with me. I am also privileged to count the two top academics in this field amongst my friends, and would like to extend my thanks to Professor Emanuel Derman of Columbia University and Dr Bruno Dupire of Bloomberg, for their continuous support and encouragement.

Finally, I would like to express my sincere gratitude to three of my present PhD students who have been of invaluable assistance in preparing this book. Joydeep Lahiri has prepared all the three dimensional graphs in these volumes. Stamatis Leontsinis and Andreas Kaeck have spotted several errors when reading draft chapters, and Andreas has very kindly allowed readers access to his option pricing calibration code. My students count amongst their many talents an astonishing capacity for computational and empirical work and their assistance in this respect is very gratefully acknowledged.

Discussion forums and other resources for the Market Risk Analysis series are available at **www.marketriskanalysis.com**.

III.1
Bonds and Swaps

III.1.1 INTRODUCTION

A financial *security* is a tradable legal claim on a firm's assets or income that is traded in an organized market, such as an exchange or a broker's market. There are two main classes of securities: primitive securities and derivative securities. A *primitive security* is a financial claim that has its own intrinsic price. In other words, the price of a primitive security is not a function of the prices of other primitive securities. A *derivative security* is a financial claim with a pay-off that is a function of the prices of one or more primitive securities.

This chapter focuses on *interest rate sensitive securities* that are traded in the debt markets, and on bonds and swaps in particular. We are not concerned here with the very short term debt markets, or *money markets* which trade in numerous interest rate sensitive instruments with maturities typically up to 1 year.[1] Our focus is on the market risk analysis of bonds and swaps, and at the time of issue most swaps have maturities of 2 years or more.

Virtually all bonds are primitive securities that are listed on exchanges but are traded by brokers in over-the-counter (OTC) markets. The exception is *private placements* which are like transferable loans. Since there is no secondary market, private placements are usually accounted for in the *banking book*, whereas most other interest rate sensitive securities are *marked to market* in the *trading book*. Forward rate agreements and swaps are derivative securities that are also traded OTC but they are not listed on an exchange.

By examining the relationships between bonds, forward rate agreements and swaps we explain how to value them, how to analyse their market risks and how to hedge these risks. Developed debt markets simultaneously trade numerous securities of the same maturity. For instance, for the same expiry date we may have trades in fixed and floating coupon bonds, forward rate agreements and swaps. Within each credit rating we use these instruments to derive a unique term structure for *market interest rates* called the *zero coupon yield curve*. We show how to construct such a curve from the prices of all liquid interest rate sensitive securities.

Bond futures, bond options and swaptions are covered in Chapters III.2 and III.3. However, in this chapter we do consider bonds with embedded options, also called *convertible bonds*. Convertible bonds are *hybrid securities* because they can be converted into the common stock of the company. These claims on the firm's assets share the security of bonds at the same time as enjoying exposure to gains in the stock price. The bond component makes them less risky than pure stock, but their value depends on other variables in addition to the stock price.

The outline of this chapter is as follows. In Section III.1.2 we introduce fundamental concepts for the analysis of bonds and associated interest rate sensitive securities. Here

---

[1] Money market instruments include Treasury bills and other discount bonds, interbank loans, sale and repurchase agreements, commercial paper and certificates of deposit. Exceptionally some of these instruments can go up to 270 days maturity.

we explain the difference between *discrete* and *continuous compounding* of interest and show how to translate between the two conventions. Then we introduce the terminology used for common types of market interest rates, describe the distinction between *spot* and *forward* interest rates and show how to translate between the spot curve and the forward curve.

Section III.1.3 begins with a brief catalogue of the different types of bonds that are commonly traded. We can distinguish bonds by the type of issuer, type of coupon (i.e. fixed or floating) and the bond maturity (i.e. the time until the claim expires) and we make the distinction between *fixed coupon bonds* and *floating rate notes*. Section III.1.4 examines the relationship between the price of a fixed coupon bond and its yield, and introduces the *zero coupon yield curve* for a given credit rating. We also examine the characteristics of the zero coupon spot yield curve and the *term structure of forward interest rates*.

Section III.1.5 examines the traditional measures of market risk on a single bond and on a bond portfolio. We introduce bond *duration* and *convexity* as the first and second order bond price sensitivities to changes in yield. These sensitivities allow us to apply Taylor expansion to approximate the change in bond price when its yield changes. Then we show how to approximate the change in value of a bond *portfolio* when the zero coupon curve shifts, using the *value duration* and the *value convexity* of the portfolio. Finally, we consider how to *immunize* a bond portfolio against movements in the yield curve.

Section III.1.6 focuses on bonds with semi-annual or quarterly coupons and floating rate notes. Section III.1.7 introduces *forward rate agreements* and *interest rate swaps* and explains the relationship between these and floating rate notes. We demonstrate that the market risk of a swap derives mainly from the fixed leg, which can be analysed as a bond with coupon equal to the swap rate. Examples explain how to fix the rate on a standard fixed-for-floating swap, and how the cash flows on a cross-currency basis swap are calculated. Several other types of swaps are also defined.

Section III.1.8 examines a bond portfolio's sensitivities to market interest rates, introducing the *present value of a basis point* (PV01) as the fundamental measure of sensitivity to changes in market interest rates.[2] We are careful to distinguish between the PV01 and the *dollar duration* of a bond portfolio: although the two measures of interest rate risk are usually very close in value, they are conceptually different.

Section III.1.9 describes how we *bootstrap* zero coupon rates from money market rates and prices of coupon bonds of different maturities. Then we explain how splines and parametric functions are used to fit the zero coupon yield curve. We present a case study that compares the application of different types of yield curve fitting models to the UK LIBOR curve and discuss the advantages and limitations of each model. Section III.1.10 explains the special features of *convertible bonds* and surveys the literature on convertible bond valuation models. Section III.1.11 summarizes and concludes.

III.1.2   INTEREST RATES

The future value of an investment depends upon how the interest is calculated. *Simple interest* is paid only on the principal amount invested, but when an investment pays *compound interest* it pays interest on both the principal and previous interest payments. There are two methods

---

[2] One *basis point* equals 0.01%.

of calculating interest, based on *discrete compounding* and *continuous compounding*. Discrete compounding means that interest payments are periodically accrued to the account, such as every 6 months or every month. Continuous compounding is a theoretical construct that assumes interest payments are continuously accrued, although this is impossible in practice. Both simple and compound interest calculations are possible with discrete compounding but with continuous compounding only compound interest rates apply.

Interest rates are divided into spot rates and forward rates. A *spot rate* of maturity T is an interest rate that applies from now, time 0, until time T. A *forward rate* is an interest rate starting at some time t in the future and applying until some time T, with $T > t > 0$. With forward interest rates we have to distinguish between the *term* (i.e. the time until the forward rate applies) and the *tenor* (i.e. the period over which it applies). The aim of this section is to introduce the reader to discretely compounded and continuously compounded spot and forward interest rates and establish the connections between them.

Since they are calculated differently, continuously compounded interest rates are different from discretely compounded interest rates and it is common to use different notation for these. In this text we shall use lower-case r for continuously compounded spot rates and capital R for discretely compounded spot rates. We use lower-case f for continuously compounded forward rates and upper-case F for discretely compounded forward rates. When we want to make the maturity of the rate explicit we use a subscript, so for instance R_T denotes the discretely compounded spot rate of maturity T and f_{nm} denotes the continuously compounded forward rate with *term* n and *tenor* m (i.e. starting at time n and ending at time $n + m$). For instance, the forward rate $f_{t,T-t}$ starts at time t and ends at time T and has tenor $T - t$.

The debt market convention is to quote rates in discretely compounded terms, with compounding on an annual or semi-annual basis. Since each market has its own *day count convention* the analysis of a portfolio of debt market instruments can be full of tedious technical details arising from different market conventions. For this reason banks convert market interest rates into continuously compounded interest rates because they greatly simplify the analysis of price and risk of debt market instruments.

III.1.2.1 Continuously Compounded Spot and Forward Rates

The *principal N* is the nominal amount invested. It is measured in terms of the local currency, e.g. dollars. The *maturity T* is the number of years of the investment. Note that T is measured in years so, for instance, $T = 0.5$ represents 6 months; in general T can be any finite, positive real number. Let r_T denote the continuously compounded T-maturity interest rate. Note that this is always quoted as an *annual* rate, for any T. Finally, let V denote the continuously compounded value of the investment at maturity.

It follows from Section I.1.4.5 and the properties of the exponential function (see Section I.1.2.4) that

$$V = N \exp(r_T T). \qquad (III.1.1)$$

Conversely, the *present value* of an amount V paid at some future time T is

$$N = V \exp(-r_T T). \qquad (III.1.2)$$

Formally, $\exp(r_T T)$ is called the *continuous compounding factor* and $\exp(-r_T T)$ is called the *continuous discount factor* for maturity T.

We now show how continuously compounded spot and forward rates are related. Let $r_1 \left(\equiv f_{0,1} \right)$ denote the continuously compounded spot interest rate that applies for one period, from time 0 until time 1. Let us say for simplicity that one period is 1 year, so the spot 1-year rate applies from now and over the next year. Then the 1-year forward interest rate $f_{1,1}$ is the 1-year rate that will apply 1 year from now. Denote by $r_2\ (\equiv f_{0,2})$ the spot interest rate, quoted in annual terms, which applies for two periods (i.e. over the next 2 years in this example). The value of the investment should be the same whether we invest for 2 years at the current 2-year spot rate, or for 1 year at the 1-year spot rate and then roll over the investment at the 1-year spot rate prevailing 1 year from now. But the fair value of the 1-year spot rate prevailing 1 year from now is the 1-year forward interest rate. Hence, the compounding factors must satisfy $\exp(2r_2) = \exp(r_1)\exp(f_{1,1})$. In other words,

$$r_2 = \frac{r_1 + f_{1,1}}{2}. \tag{III.1.3}$$

This argument has a natural extension to k-period rates. The general relationship between continuously compounded spot and forward compounding factors is that the k-period spot rate is the arithmetic average of the one-period spot rate and $k-1$ one-period forward interest rates:

$$r_k \equiv f_{0,k} = \frac{f_{0,1} + f_{1,1} + \cdots + f_{k-1,1}}{k}. \tag{III.1.4}$$

III.1.2.2 Discretely Compounded Spot Rates

The discretely compounded analogue of equations (III.1.1) and (III.1.2) depends on whether simple or compound interest is used. Again let N denote the principal (i.e. the amount invested) and let T denote the number of years of the investment. But now denote by R_T the discretely compounded T-maturity interest rate, again quoted in annual terms. Under simple compounding of interest the future value of a principal N invested now over a period of T years is

$$V = N(1 + R_T T). \tag{III.1.5}$$

However, under compound interest,

$$V = N(1 + R_T)^T. \tag{III.1.6}$$

Similarly, with simple interest the present value of an amount V paid at some future time T is

$$N = V(1 + R_T T)^{-1}. \tag{III.1.7}$$

but with compound interest it is

$$N = V(1 + R_T)^{-T}. \tag{III.1.8}$$

Simple interest is usually only applied to a single payment over a fixed period of less than 1 year. For a period T of less than 1 year the *discretely compounded discount factor* is

$$\delta_T = (1 + R_T T)^{-1}, \tag{III.1.9}$$

and when T is an integral number of years it is

$$\delta_T = (1 + R_T)^{-T}. \tag{III.1.10}$$

When T is greater than 1 year but not an integral number of years the discretely compounded discount factor for maturity T is

$$\delta_T = (1 + R_T)^{-[T]}(1 + (T - [T])R_T)^{-1}, \tag{III.1.11}$$

where $[T]$ denotes the integer part of T.

Remarks on Notation

1. In this chapter and throughout this book we shall be discounting a sequence of cash flows at a set of future dates. Usually at least the first date occurs within 1 year, and frequently several dates are less than 1 year. The cash flow payments almost never occur in exactly integer years. Hence, the formula (III.1.11) should be used for the discount factor on these payment dates. However, to specify this will make the formulae look more complex than they really are. Hence, we shall assume that cash flows occur annually, or semi-annually, to avoid this burdensome notation. This is not without loss of generality, but all the concepts that we focus on can be illustrated under this assumption.

2. We remark that some authors use the notation B_T instead of δ_T for the discretely compounded discount factor of maturity T, because this also is the price of a pure *discount bond* of maturity T and redemption value 1. We shall see in the next section that a discount bond, which is also called a *zero coupon bond* or a *bullet bond*, is one of the basic building blocks for the market risk analysis of cash flows.

3. When market interest rates are quoted, the rate is specified along with type of rate (normally annual or semi-annual) and the frequency of payments. In money markets discretely compounded interest rates are quoted in annual terms with 365 days. In bond markets they are quoted in either annual or semi-annual terms with either 360 or 365 days per year. To avoid too many technical details in this text, when we consider discretely compounded interest rates we shall assume that all interest rates are quoted in annual terms and with 365 days per year, unless otherwise stated.

The frequency of payments can be annual, semi-annual, quarterly or even monthly. If the annual rate quoted is denoted by R and the interest payments are made n times each year, then

$$\text{Annual compounding factor} = \left(1 + \left(\frac{R}{n}\right)\right)^n. \qquad \text{(III.1.12)}$$

For instance, $(1 + \tfrac{1}{2}R)^2$ is the *annual* compounding factor when interest payments are semi-annual and R is the 1 year interest rate. In general, if a principal amount N is invested at a discretely compounded annual interest rate R, which has n compounding periods per year, then its value after m compounding periods is

$$V = N\left(1 + \frac{R}{n}\right)^m. \qquad \text{(III.1.13)}$$

It is worth noting that:

$$\lim_{n \to \infty}\left(1 + \frac{R}{n}\right)^n = \exp(R), \qquad \text{(III.1.14)}$$

and this is why the continuously compounded interest rate takes an exponential form.

EXAMPLE III.1.1: CONTINUOUS VERSUS DISCRETE COMPOUNDING

Find the value of \$500 in 3.5 years' time if it earns interest of 4% per annum and interest is compounded semi-annually. How does this compare with the continuously compounded value?

SOLUTION

$$V = 500 \times \left(1 + \frac{0.04}{2}\right)^7 = \$574.34,$$

but under continuous compounding the value will be greater:

$$V = 500 \times \exp(0.04 \times 3.5) = \$575.14.$$

III.1.2.3 Translation between Discrete Rates and Continuous Rates

The discrete compounding discount factor (III.1.11) is difficult to work with in practice since different markets often have different day count conventions; many practitioners therefore convert all rates to continuously compounded rates and do their analysis with these instead. There is a straightforward translation between discrete and continuously compounded interest rates.

Let R_T and r_T denote the discretely and continuously compounded rates of maturity T. R_T and r_T are equivalent if they provide the same return. Suppose there are n compounding periods per annum on the discretely compounded rate. Then equating returns gives

$$\exp(r_T T) = \left(1 + \frac{R_T}{n}\right)^{nT},$$

i.e. $\exp(r_T) = (1 + R_T/n)^n$, and taking logarithms of both sides gives the continuously compounded rate that is equivalent to R_T as

$$r_T = n \ln\left(1 + \frac{R_T}{n}\right). \tag{III.1.15}$$

For instance, the continuously compounded equivalent of a semi-annual rate of 5% is $2\ln(1.025) = 4.9385\%$.

Similarly, the discretely compounded rate that is equivalent to r_T is

$$R_T = n\left(\exp\left(\frac{r_T}{n}\right) - 1\right). \tag{III.1.16}$$

III.1.2.4 Spot and Forward Rates with Discrete Compounding

Recall that we use F_{nm} to denote an m-period discretely compounded forward interest rate starting n periods ahead, that is, n is the term and m is the tenor of the rate. For instance, if the period is measured in months as in the example below, then $F_{6,9}$ denotes the 9-month forward rate 6-months ahead, i.e. the interest rate that applies between 6 months from now and 15 months from now.

The argument leading to the relationship (III.1.3) between continuously compounded forward and spot rates also extends to discretely compounded forward and spot rates. Measuring periods in 1 year, we have

$$(1 + R_2)^2 = (1 + R_1)(1 + F_{1,1}) \tag{III.1.17}$$

and in general

$$(1 + R_k)^k = (1 + F_{0,1})(1 + F_{1,1}) \cdots (1 + F_{k-1,1}). \tag{III.1.18}$$

The relationship (III.1.18) allows forward rates of various terms and tenors to be calculated from the spot rate curve, as the following examples show.

EXAMPLE III.1.2: CALCULATING FORWARD RATES (1)

Find the 1-year and 2-year forward rates, given that the discretely compounded annual spot interest rates are 5%, 6% and 6.5% for maturities 1 year, 2 year and 3 years, respectively.

SOLUTION

1-year forward rate, $F_{1,1} = \dfrac{1.06^2}{1.05} - 1 = 7.0\%$

2-year forward rate, $F_{2,1} = \dfrac{1.065^3}{1.06^2} - 1 = 7.5\%$

A variety of forward rates can be computed from any given spot rate curve, as shown by the following example.

EXAMPLE III.1.3: CALCULATING FORWARD RATES (2)

Given the spot rates in Table III.1.1, calculate a set of discretely compounded 3-month forward rates for 3 months, 6 months and 9 months ahead. Also calculate $F_{6,6}$, the 6-month forward rate that applies 6 months ahead.

SOLUTION

Table III.1.1 Discretely compounded spot and forward rates

Maturity (months)	Spot rates	Forward rates	
3	4.5%	$F_{0,3}$	4.5%
6	4.3%	$F_{3,3}$	4.05%
9	4.2%	$F_{6,3}$	3.92%
12	4.0%	$F_{9,3}$	3.30%

The 3-month forward rates are shown in Table III.1.1. Note that in the table, the forward rate matures at the time specified by the row and starts 3 months earlier. The forward rate from 0 months to 3 months is the same as the spot rate, and this is entered in the first row. Denote the spot and forward rates as above. Since the rates are quoted in annual terms, we have:

$$\left(1 + \frac{F_{0,3}}{4}\right)\left(1 + \frac{F_{3,3}}{4}\right) = \left(1 + \frac{F_{0,6}}{2}\right).$$

Thus the 3 month forward rate at 3 months (i.e. effective from 3 months to 6 months) is given by:

$$F_{3,3} = 4 \times \left[\left(1 + \frac{F_{0,6}}{2}\right)\left(1 + \frac{F_{0,3}}{4}\right)^{-1} - 1\right]$$

$$= 4 \times \left[\left(1 + \frac{0.043}{2}\right)\left(1 + \frac{0.045}{4}\right)^{-1} - 1\right] = 0.0405 = 4.05\%.$$

This is the forward rate in the second row. Similarly, the 3-month forward rate at 6 months is given by the relationship

$$\left(1 + \frac{F_{0,6}}{2}\right)\left(1 + \frac{F_{6,3}}{4}\right) = \left(1 + \frac{3F_{0,9}}{4}\right).$$

Substituting in for the spot rates $F_{0,6}$ and $F_{0,9}$ and solving for the forward rate gives $F_{6,3} = 3.92\%$. Similarly,

$$\left(1 + \frac{3F_{0,9}}{4}\right)\left(1 + \frac{F_{9,3}}{4}\right) = \left(1 + F_{0,12}\right),$$

and this gives $F_{9,3} = 3.30\%$. And finally, $F_{6,6} = 3.62\%$ is found by solving

$$\left(1 + \frac{F_{0,6}}{2}\right)\left(1 + \frac{F_{6,6}}{2}\right) = \left(1 + F_{0,12}\right).$$

III.1.2.5   LIBOR

LIBOR stands for 'London Inter Bank Offered Rate'. It is the interest rate charged for short term lending between major banks. It is almost always greater than the *base rate*, which is the rate that banks obtain when they deposit their reserves with the central bank. LIBOR is published each day (between 11.00 and 11.30) by the British Bankers' Association (BBA). The BBA takes a survey of the lending rates set by a sample of major banks in *all* major currencies. Thus the LIBOR rates refer to funds not just in sterling but also in US dollars and all the major currencies. The terms for the lending rates are usually overnight, 1 week, 2 weeks, 1 month, and then monthly up to 1 year. The shorter rates up to 3 or 6 months are very precise at the time they are measured, but the actual rates at which banks will lend to one another continue to vary throughout the day.

London is the main financial centre in the world and so LIBOR has become the standard *reference rate* for discounting short term future cash flows to present value terms. It is used to find the fair (or theoretical) value of forwards and futures, forward rate agreements and swaps, bonds, options, loans and mortgages in all major currencies except the euro. For the euro the usual reference rates are the EURIBOR rates compiled by the European Banking Federation. Also emerging economies such as India are now developing their own reference rates, such as MIBOR in Mumbai.

III.1.3   CATEGORIZATION OF BONDS

The *principal* or *face value* of the bond is the amount to be repaid to the bond holder at maturity (if the bond is issued at a discount or premium, the principal is not the amount invested). The *coupon* on a bond determines the periodic payment to the bond holder by the issuer until the bond expires. The amount paid is equal to the coupon multiplied by the face value. When we price a bond we assume that the face value is 100.[3] If the price is 100 we say the bond is priced *at par*; bonds are *below par* if their price is below 100 and *above par* if their price is above 100. On the *expiry date* of the bond, the bond holder *redeems* the bond with the issuer. The *redemption value* of the bond is often but not always the same as the face value.[4] The *issuer* of a bond raises funds by selling bonds in the *primary market*.[5] This is called *debt financing*. Between issue and expiry, bonds may be traded in the *secondary market* where trading is usually OTC.[6]

The bond market is a very old market that has evolved separately in many different countries. Each country has different conventions, and even within a country there are numerous variations on bond specifications. In the following we provide only a very general summary of the different types of straight bonds that are commonly traded, categorizing

---

[3] Depending on the currency unit, bonds usually have a minimum amount invested much greater than 100. For instance, the minimum amount one can buy of Fannie Mae bonds is $1,000. Nevertheless their market prices are always quoted as a percentage of the face value, i.e. based on the face value of 100.

[4] For instance, there could be a bonus payment at maturity, in addition to payment of the face value.

[5] Usually bonds are underwritten by banks and placed with their investors.

[6] But some government bonds are exchange traded.

them by issuer and the type of coupon paid. Readers seeking more specific details are recommended to consult the excellent books by Fabozzi (2005) or Choudhry (2005, 2006).

III.1.3.1 Categorization by Issuer

Bonds are divided into different categories according to the priority of their claim on the issuer's assets, if the issuer becomes insolvent. For instance, *senior* bond holders will be paid before *junior* bond holders and, if the bond is issued by a company that has also sold shares on its equity, all bond holders are paid before the equity holders. This gives bonds a security not shared by stocks and so investing in bonds is less risky than investing in equities. This is one of the reasons why bond prices are typically less volatile than share prices.

Almost all bonds have a *credit rating* which corresponds to the perceived probability that the issuer will default on its debt repayments. The best credit rating, corresponding to an extremely small probability of default, is labelled AAA by Standard & Poor's and Aaa by Moody's. Only a few bonds, such as G10 government bonds and some corporate bonds, have this credit rating. Standard & Poor's credit ratings range from AAA to C, and the C rating corresponds to a 1-year default probability of 20% or more. Any bond rated below *investment grade* (BBB) is called a *junk bond*.

Table III.1.2 sets out the common types of bond issuers ordered by the size of the markets in these bonds, stating the terminology used when we refer to these bonds and listing some specific examples of each type of bond.

Table III.1.2   Examples of bonds

Issuer	Examples					
	Issuer	Currency	Maturity	Coupon	Yield[a]	Rating
Financial institutions	HBOS	GBP	Apr. 2008	5.50%	6.23%	AA
(banks, insurance	Goldman Sachs	USD	Nov 2014	4.25%	6.01%	AA−
companies and	Deutsche Fin.	EUR	Jul. 2009	1.75%	4.33%	AA
financial companies)	KFW Int. Fin.	JPY	Mar 2010	6.38%	1.00%	AAA
Governments (called	Australia	AUS	Feb. 2017	6.00%	5.96%	AAA
sovereign, Treasury or	Greece	EUR	Jul 2017	4.30%	4.58%	A
government bonds)	Brazil	GBP	Mar 2015	7.88%	5.96%	BB+
Government agencies	Fannie Mae	USD	Jun 2017	5.375%	5.53%	AAA
(agency bonds[b])	Freddie Mac	USD	Nov 2017	5.125%	5.14%	AAA
Towns/regions	Dutchess County	USD	Sep 2050	5.35%	3.53%	AA
(municipal bonds)	NYSU Dev. Corp.	USD	Jan 2025	5.00%	3.13%	AA−
Corporations (corporate	General Motors	USD	Nov 2031	8.00%	7.46%	BB+
bonds)	Tokyo Motor	JPY	June 2008	0.75%	0.90%	AAA
	Boots	GBP	May 2009	5.50%	8.65%	BBB

[a] Yields quoted as of 25 August 2007, reopening auctions.
[b] The main suppliers of agency bonds are the US housing associations that issue bonds backed by mortgages. See www.fanniemae.com and www.freddiemac.com for further details.

Bonds can be further categorized as follows:

- *Domestic bonds* are issued in the country of domicile of the issuer. In other words, they are issued by a domestic borrower in their local market and they are denominated in the local currency.

- *Foreign bonds* are issued by a foreign borrower in the local currency. For instance, a US issuer can issue a sterling denominated bond in the UK market (this is called a *Yankee*).
- *Eurobonds* are *bearer bonds* that are issued on the international market in any currency.[7] This is a broker's market with a self-regulatory body called the *International Capital Markets Association* (ICMA).[8]

III.1.3.2 Categorization by Coupon and Maturity

The coupon payments on a bond are usually made at regular intervals. Often they are made once every year, in which case we say the bond has *annual coupons*, or every 6 months for a *semi-annual coupon* bond. If the coupons are semi-annual then half of the coupon payment is made every 6 months.[9]

The majority of bonds pay a *fixed coupon*: for instance, a 5% annual 2015 bond pays the bond holder 5% of the face value every year until 2015. However, some bonds, called *floating rate notes* or *floaters* for short, have a variable coupon. The periodic payment is based on a reference rate such as the LIBOR rate prevailing at the time that the coupon is paid.[10] For instance, a semi-annual floater pays 6-month LIBOR plus spread, and a quarterly floater pays 3-month LIBOR plus spread.

Bonds are further divided into *short term bonds* (2–5 years), *medium term bonds* (5–15 years) and *long term bonds* (over 15 years) where the numbers in parentheses here refer to the time between issue and expiry.[11] Interest rate sensitive securities that have less than 2 years to expiry at issue are generally regarded as money market instruments. Most money market instruments such as *US Treasury bills* pay no coupons. They are just priced at a discount to their par value of 100. If they are held until expiry the profit is guaranteed. For instance, if a US Treasury bill is purchased at 95 and held until expiry the return is $5/95 = 5.26\%$.[12] Even though very few bonds pay no coupon it is convenient to work with hypothetical zero coupon bonds of different maturities and different credit ratings.[13] In particular, for reasons that will become evident in Section III.1.4.3, the yields on zero coupon bonds are used as *market interest rates* for different credit ratings.

III.1.4 CHARACTERISTICS OF BONDS AND INTEREST RATES

In the following we begin by using market interest rates to price a bond. We do not question how these interest rates have been derived. Then we explore the relationship between the price of a bond and the yield on a bond and show that two bonds with the same maturity but different coupons have different yields. However, all zero coupon bonds of the same maturity have the same yield. This *zero coupon yield* is the *market interest rate* of that maturity. But

---

[7] Bearer bonds are like banknotes – they belong to the person who holds the bond in his hand. But the owners of other types of bonds must be registered.

[8] The ICMA Centre also hosts the MTS bond database. See http://www.mtsgroup.org/newcontent/timeseries/ and http://www.icmacentre.ac.uk/research_and_consultancy_services/mts_time_series for further details.

[9] Some bonds also have quarterly payments, but these are usually floating rate notes.

[10] LIBOR is usually greater than the *base rate*, which is the remuneration rate when banks make deposits with the central bank. See Section III.1.2.5 for further details.

[11] This varies according to the country: for example, the longest Italian bonds are around 10 years to expiry.

[12] Of course, the same applies to any fixed income security: if it is held to expiry the return is locked in. This does not, however, mean that fixed income securities have no interest rate risk! See Section III.1.8.3 for further details.

[13] We also call zero coupon bonds *discount bonds* for obvious reasons.

we are in a typical 'chicken and egg' situation. We could use the market interest rates to price bonds, and then derive the market interest rates from bond prices. So which come first, the bond prices or the market interest rates?

The prices of bonds in the secondary market are determined by supply and demand. They are *not* priced using a formula. Just because we start this section with a formula that relates the fair price of a bond to market interest rates, this does *not* imply that such a formula is actually used by brokers to price bonds. Of course, brokers might use this formula if the market is not very liquid, but in general they set their prices by supply and demand.[14]

In the following we shall characterize a bond of maturity T_n by a sequence of non-negative cash flows, starting with a sequence of regularly spaced coupon payments $C_{T_1}, \ldots, C_{T_n-1}$ and finishing with a cash flow C_{T_n} which consists of the redemption value plus the coupon paid at time T_n. We shall price the bond assuming that the coupon payments and redemption value are both based on a face value of 100. In other words, a coupon of 5% paid at time t means that $C_t = 5$ and the redemption value is 100. However, coupon payments are, in reality, based on the principal amount invested and the redemption value could be different from the principal, for instance if bonus payments are included.

III.1.4.1   Present Value, Price and Yield

Denote the sequence of cash flows on the bond by $\{C_{T_1}, \ldots, C_{T_n}\}$. Since we assume these are based on the face value of 100 the cash flows on a fixed annual coupon bond of maturity T_n years paying a coupon of c percent are:

$$C_{T_i} = \begin{cases} 100c, & \text{for } i = 1, \ldots, n-1, \\ 100(1+c), & \text{for } i = n. \end{cases} \tag{III.1.19}$$

Suppose we have a set of discretely compounded spot market interest rates, $\{R_{T_1}, \ldots, R_{T_n}\}$, where R_{T_i} is the rate of maturity T_i for $i = 1, \ldots, n$. That is, the maturity of each spot rate matches exactly the maturity of each cash flow. Then we can calculate the present value of a cash payment at time T_i as the payment discounted by the discretely compounded T_i-maturity interest rate.

The *present value* of a bond is the sum of the discounted future cash flows. If based on a face value of 100 it is

$$PV = \sum_{i=1}^{n} C_{T_i}(1+R_{T_i})^{-T_i}. \tag{III.1.20}$$

More generally the present value is

$$PV = \frac{N}{100} \sum_{i=1}^{n} C_{T_i}(1+R_{T_i})^{-T_i}, \tag{III.1.21}$$

where N is the principal amount invested.

The difference between the present value (III.1.20) and the *market price, P* of a bond is that the present value is a fair or theoretical value, whereas the market price of the bond is set by supply and demand. The market price of a bond is always quoted relative to a face value of 100.

The market interest rates on the right-hand side of (III.1.20) will not normally be the same. There is likely to be a *term structure* of interest rates, i.e. where short rates are not the same as long rates (see Figure III.1.6 below, for instance). Nevertheless, provided that all the cash

---

[14] A similar comment applies to any liquid market. For instance, the prices of standard European calls and puts are *not* set by the Black–Scholes–Merton formula. We use this formula, yes, but not to price options unless they are illiquid. And even then, we usually adjust the formula (see Section III.3.6.7).

flows are positive, we can find a *single* discount rate that, when applied to discount every cash payment, gives the market price of the bond. In other words, we can find y such that

$$P = \sum_{i=1}^{n} (1+y)^{-T_i} C_{T_i}. \qquad (\text{III.1.22})$$

This y is called the discretely compounded *yield*, or *yield to redemption*, on the bond. It is a single number that represents the *internal rate of return* on the bond.[15] In other words, it is the return that an investor would get if he held the bond until expiry.

Similarly, given a set of continuously compounded interest rates $\{r_{T_1}, \ldots, r_{T_n}\}$, the continuously compounded yield is found by solving

$$\sum_{i=1}^{n} \exp(-r_{T_i} T_i) C_{T_i} = \sum_{i=1}^{n} \exp(-yT_i) C_{T_i} \qquad (\text{III.1.23})$$

assuming the bond is fairly priced.

EXAMPLE III.1.4: CALCULATING THE PRESENT VALUE AND YIELD OF FIXED COUPON BONDS

Consider two bonds that pay coupons annually. Bond 1 has coupon 5% and maturity 3 years and bond 2 has coupon 10% and maturity 5 years. Suppose the market interest rates are as shown in Table III.1.3. Find the present value and, assuming this present value is also the market price, find the yield on each bond.

Table III.1.3   Market interest rates

Maturity (years)	1	2	3	4	5
Interest rate	4.0%	4.25%	4.5%	4.25%	4.20%

SOLUTION   Table III.1.4 sets out the cash flow for each bond, which is then discounted by the relevant interest rate to give the present values in column 4 (for bond 1) and column 6 (for bond 2). The sum of these discounted cash flows gives the price of the bond, i.e. 101.42 for bond 1 and 125.59 for bond 2. Bond prices reflect the coupon rate. For instance, if bond 2 had a coupon of only 5% then its price would be only 103.5, as readers can verify using the spreadsheet for this example.

Table III.1.4   Bond prices

Maturity	Interest rate	Cash flow	Present value	Cash flow	Present value
1	4.0%	5	4.81	10	9.62
2	4.25%	5	4.60	10	9.20
3	4.5%	105	92.01	10	8.76
4	4.25%	0	0	10	8.47
5	4.20%	0	0	110	89.55
		Price bond 1	**101.42**	Price bond 2	**125.59**

---

[15] Loans normally have all positive cash flows, i.e. the interest payments on the loan, but interest rate swaps do not. Hence. we cannot define the yield on a swap, but we can define the yield on a loan.

Although bond 2 has a much higher price than bond 1, this does not mean that investing in bond 2 gives a lower, or higher, return than investing in bond 1. The rate of return on a bond is given by its yield, and this is mainly determined by the interest rate at the bond maturity because the redemption payment has the most effect on the yield.

Table III.1.5 Bond yields

Maturity	Yield	Cash flow	Present value	Yield	Cash flow	Present value
1	4.48%	5	4.79	4.22%	10	9.60
2	4.48%	5	4.58	4.22%	10	9.21
3	4.48%	105	92.05	4.22%	10	8.83
4	4.48%	0	0	4.22%	10	8.48
5	4.48%	0	0	4.22%	110	89.48
		Price bond 1	**101.42**		Price bond 2	**125.59**

Table III.1.5 takes the bond price as given in Table III.1.4 and uses an iterative method to back out the value of the yield so that the sum of the cash payments discounted by this single yield is equal to the bond price.[16] We find that the yield on bond 1 is 4.48% and the yield on bond 2 is 4.22%. This reinforces our comment above, that the coupon rate has little effect on the bond yield. For instance, if bond 2 had a coupon of only 5% then its yield would still be close to 4.2%, because this is the 5-year spot rate. In fact, it would be 4.21%, as readers can verify using the spreadsheet.

III.1.4.2 Relationship between Price and Yield

The price of bond 1 in Example III.1.4 is 101.42 and its yield is 4.48%. What would the price be if its yield changed by 1%? If the yield increased to 5.48% the price would decrease by 2.73 to 98.69; and if the yield decreased to 3.48% its price would increase by 2.83 to 104.25. The price increases when the yield decreases, and conversely, so the price and yield have a negative relationship. And since the price does not change by the same absolute amount when the bond yield increases and decreases, the price and yield have a *non-linear* negative relationship. The *price–yield curve* is the set of all points (y, P) determined by the price–yield relationship (III.1.22). In other words, it is a convex decreasing curve which gives the price of a fixed coupon bond as a function of its yield.

EXAMPLE III.1.5: THE EFFECT OF COUPON AND MATURITY ON THE PRICE–YIELD CURVE

Plot the price–yield curve for the following annual coupon bonds:

(a) coupon 5%, maturity 3 years;
(b) coupon 10%, maturity 3 years;
(c) coupon 10%, maturity 5 years.

SOLUTION Figure III.1.1 illustrates the price–yield curve, i.e. the relationship (III.1.22) between the price and the yield, for each bond. It verifies the following:[17]

---

[16] In the Excel spreadsheet for this example we have done this using the RATE function in Excel. However the bond yield could also be found using the Excel Solver.
[17] These properties of the price–yield relationship may also be proved algebraically from (III.1.22).

- *An increase in coupon increases the price at each yield.* For instance, fixing the yield at 6.5%, the 3 year 5% coupon bond has price 96.03 but the 3 year 10% coupon bond has price 109.27.
- *When the yield equals the coupon the bond price is* 100. And we say it is priced at *par*. For instance, if the yield is 10% then both of the 10% coupon bonds have price 100.
- *An increase in maturity increases the steepness and convexity of the price–yield relationship.* And, comparing the curves for the 10% coupon bonds (b) and (c), the price at a given yield increases for yields below the coupon and decreases for yields greater than the coupon.

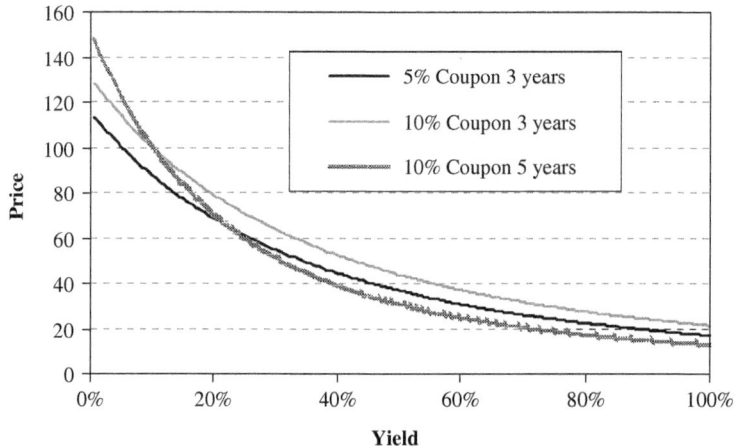

Figure III.1.1   Price–yield curves

III.1.4.3   Yield Curves

Now we consider the 'chicken and egg' situation that we referred to at the beginning of this section. We can replicate fair bond market prices using market interest rates, but the market interest rate of some given maturity is derived from a bond yield of the same maturity, which in turn is derived from the bond price. But two bonds with the same maturity but different coupons have different yields. So which bond yield should we use to derive the market interest rate? The next example illustrates how to break this circular construction.

EXAMPLE III.1.6: COMPARISON OF YIELD CURVES FOR DIFFERENT BONDS

Consider three sets of bonds. Each set contains 20 bonds with the same coupon but different maturities, and the maturities are 1, 2, . . . , 20 years. The coupons are 0% for the first set, 5% for the second set and 10% for the third set. The market interest rates are given in Table III.1.6.

(a) Draw a graph of the fair prices of each set of bonds, against the maturity.
(b) Draw a graph of the yields of each set of bonds, against the maturity.

Indicate the market interest rates on each graph.

Table III.1.6 Some market interest rates

Maturity (years)	1	2	3	4	5	6	7	8	9	10
Market interest rate	6.00%	6.50%	7.00%	7.20%	7.20%	6.60%	6.00%	5.60%	5.40%	5.25%
Maturity (years)	11	12	13	14	15	16	17	18	19	20
Market interest rate	5.25%	5.20%	5.20%	5.00%	5.10%	5.00%	4.90%	4.90%	4.80%	4.80%

SOLUTION   The spreadsheet for this example calculates the prices using (III.1.20) and then, given each bond price it uses the Excel RATE function to back out the yield from the formula (III.1.22). The resulting graphs (a) and (b) are shown in Figures III.1.2 and III.1.3. The market interest rates from Table III.1.6 are added to each graph and in Figure III.1.2 we use the right-hand scale for these.

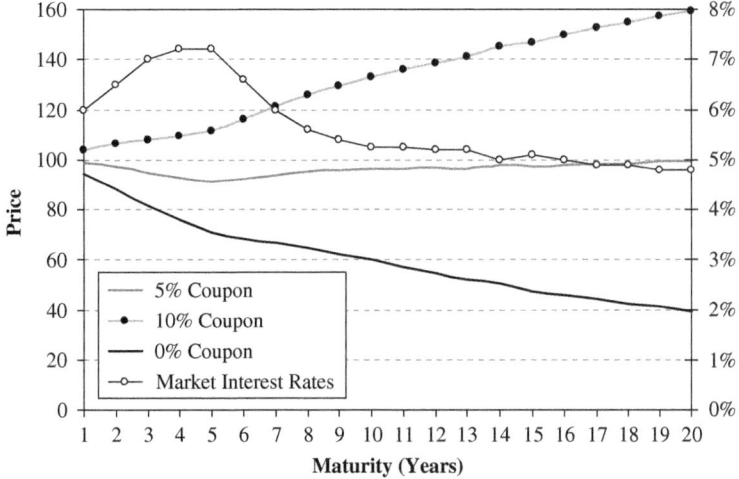

Figure III.1.2   Bond price versus maturity

Figure III.1.2 shows that the bonds with coupon above the market interest rate are priced above par, and those with coupon below the market interest rate are priced below par. We already know this from the preceding subsection. But Figure III.1.2 gives us some additional information: the price of a bond increases with maturity if the coupon is above the market interest rates and decreases with maturity if the coupon is below the market interest rates.

A *yield curve* is a graph of bond yield versus maturity, keeping the coupon fixed. Bonds with different coupons have different yield curves, and this is illustrated by Figure III.1.3. Here we depict three *different* yield curves, one for each set of bonds, i.e. the bonds with coupons 0%, 5% and 10% and varying maturities. We also show the market interest rates, but these are identical to the *zero coupon yield curve*.

It is this set of zero coupon yields that we use as the basic set of interest rates for pricing interest rate sensitive instruments. Whenever we refer to 'the' yield curve, as in *the BBB yield curve*, we mean the zero coupon yield curve. The zero coupon yield curve

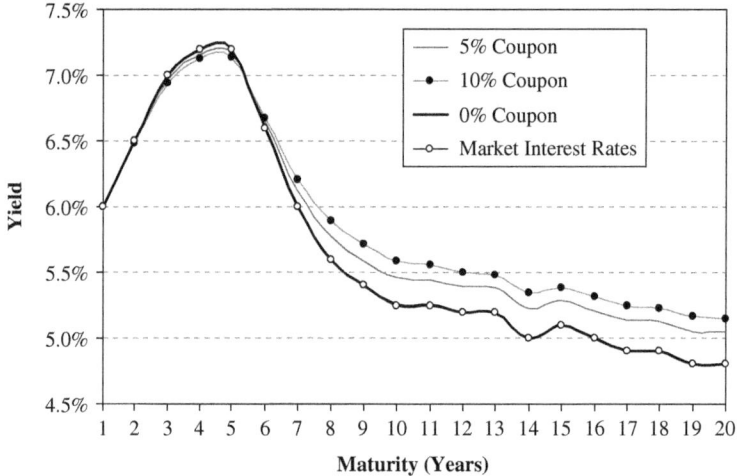

Figure III.1.3 Bond yield versus maturity

is a term structure, i.e. a set of yields of different maturities on zero coupon bonds of the same credit rating category (AAA, BBB, etc). For each credit rating we have a different yield curve (i.e. a different set of market interest rates). The other two yield curves shown in Figure III.1.3, which are derived from market prices of coupon bearing bonds, are called *par yield curves*. There is one par yield curve for each coupon and for each credit rating.

Now let us return to the 'chicken and egg' problem. *If* we could observe the market price of a zero coupon bond, then we could use this market price to derive the market interest rate of maturity equal to the bond maturity. The price of a zero coupon bond of maturity T is just 100 times the T *period discount factor:*

$$\delta_T = (1+y_T)^{-T},\qquad\qquad\text{(III.1.24)}$$

where y_T is the discretely compounded zero coupon yield with maturity T years. So if we observe the market price P_T of a zero coupon bond with maturity T we can back out the market interest rate as y_T from the formula

$$P_T = 100\,(1+y_T)^{-T}.\qquad\qquad\text{(III.1.25)}$$

That is, we simply set:

$$y_T = \left(\frac{100}{P_T}\right)^{1/T} - 1.\qquad\qquad\text{(III.1.26)}$$

But we cannot observe the price of a zero coupon bond in the market for every T. Although there are many discount (i.e. zero coupon) instruments that are traded in the money markets, these rarely have maturity beyond 1 year, or 18 months at the most. Hardly any zero coupon bonds are traded with maturities longer than this. Hence, to obtain a complete set of market interest rates covering all maturities we must use a model for fitting a zero coupon yield curve using the prices of *coupon* bearing instruments. These *yield curve fitting models* are described in Section III.1.9.

III.1.4.4 Behaviour of Market Interest Rates

We examine the time series properties of a single interest rate, and for this we choose the US Treasury 3-month spot rate. Figure III.1.4 shows a daily time series of the 3-month US Treasury spot rate from January 1961 to December 2006.[18] After reaching a high of over 14% in the early 1980s, US dollar interest rates declined sharply. In 2003 the 3-month rate reached an historic low, dipping below 2% for the first time since the 1950s. After this time rates rose steadily to above 4% by mid 2006.

Figure III.1.4   US Treasury 3-month spot rate, 1961–2006

In continuous time we model the short rate as a *mean-reverting* stochastic process. But if we use a very long term average rate then the rate of mean reversion is extremely slow, as is evident just by looking at the time series in Figure III.1.4. To confirm this view, we estimate a general mean-reverting stochastic process of the form[19]

$$dr(t) = \varphi(\theta - r(t))dt + \sigma r(t)^\gamma \, dW, \qquad (\text{III.1.27})$$

where r is the US Treasury 3-month rate. The parameter φ is called the *rate of mean reversion* and the parameter θ is the long term average value of r. Of course what is 'long term' depends on the data used to estimate the parameters. If we use the entire sample of interest rates shown in Figure III.1.4 the long term value will be close to 6.53%, since this is the average rate over the entire sample. And the speed of reversion to this long term average, if indeed there *is* a mean reversion to this average, will be very slow indeed. There might be a 40-year cycle in Figure III.1.4, so we are going to test for this below. Interest rates increased from 4% in 1961 to almost 16% in 1981, then returned to 4% in 2001. Estimating the simple one-factor model (III.1.27) will yield parameters that reflect this single, long cycle if it exists.

---

[18] Available from http://www.federalreserve.gov/releases/h15/data.htm.
[19] See Sections I.3.7 and II.5.3.7 for more details about mean-reverting stochastic processes and see Section III.3.8.4 for more details about their application to short term interest rate models.

The estimated coefficients and standard errors, based on the entire sample between 1961 and 2006, are shown in Table III.1.7.[20] Using the parametric form

$$dr(t) = (\alpha + \beta r(t))\, dt + \sigma r(t)^\gamma\, dW(t), \qquad (\text{III.1.28})$$

we have:

- long term interest rate, $\theta = -\alpha\beta^{-1}$;
- mean reversion rate, $\varphi = -\beta$;
- characteristic time to mean-revert, $\varphi^{-1} = -\beta^{-1}$.

Table III.1.7   Estimates and standard errors of one-factor interest rate model

	Coefficient	Est. s.e.
α	0.00262	0.0024
β	−0.00039	0.0006
γ	1.06579	1.8799
σ	0.00864	0.2141
Long term interest rate	6.76%	
Mean reversion rate	0.00039	
Characteristic time to mean-revert	10.30 years	
Volatility	13.66%	

Note that the estimate of γ is very close to 1, with a large standard error, so we may as well set this to 1 and assume that interest rates follow a *geometric* process rather than an arithmetic process. The interest rate volatility is assumed constant, and it is estimated as 13.66%. As expected, the long term interest rate is 6.76%, which is close to the sample average. And it takes a very long time to mean-revert. The characteristic time to mean-revert is $(0.00039)^{-1} = 2754$ days. But note that the estimated standard error (s.e.) on β is 0.0006 so we cannot reject the null hypothesis that $\beta = 0$, i.e. that the series is integrated.[21] In short, our estimation of the general model (III.1.27) using the entire sample leads to the conclusion that the 3-month US Treasury rate follows a standard geometric Brownian motion and there is no mean reversion in these interest rates!

We can try to detect other cycles in interest rates at different frequencies using a two-factor model of the form

$$dr(t) = \varphi_1(\theta(t) - r(t))dt + \sigma_1 r(t)^{\gamma_1}\, dW_1(t),$$
$$d\theta(t) = \varphi_2(\omega - \theta(t))dt + \sigma_2 \theta(t)^{\gamma_2}\, dW_2(t). \qquad (\text{III.1.29})$$

In this model the level to which interest rates mean-revert is not assumed to be constant. Instead it is a mean-reverting process itself. This way we can try to detect a shorter cycle in interest rates if it exists. Again we estimate the models in a form that allows us to test for the presence of mean reversion. That is, we could estimate

$$dr(t) = (\alpha(t) + \beta_1 r(t))\, dt + \sigma_1 r(t)^{\gamma_1} dW_1(t),$$
$$d\alpha(t) = (\lambda + \beta_2 \alpha(t))\, dt + \sigma_2 \alpha(t)^{\gamma_2} dW_2(t), \qquad (\text{III.1.30})$$

---

[20] Many thanks to my PhD student Stamatis Leontsinis for providing these estimates, based on a generalized methods of moments algorithm.
[21] A careful discussion on this point is given in Section II.5.3.7.

and set

- mean reversion level of interest rate, $\theta(t) = -\alpha(t)\beta_1^{-1}$;
- characteristic time to mean-revert, $\varphi_1^{-1} = -\beta_1^{-1}$;
- long term level of interest rate, $\omega = -\lambda\beta_2^{-1}$;
- characteristic time to mean-revert, $\varphi_2^{-1} = -\beta_2^{-1}$.

III.1.4.5   Characteristics of Spot and Forward Term Structures

We also examine the properties of a cross-section of interest rates of different maturities (i.e. a *term structure* of interest rates) at a specific point in time, and for this we choose the term structures of UK spot rates and the associated term structure of UK forward rates. Data are provided by the Bank of England.[22]

Figure III.1.5 shows how the UK spot rate curve evolved between 4 January 2000 and 31 December 2007. On 4 January 2000 the 1-year rate was 6.32% and the 25-year rate was 4.28%. During the whole of 2000 and until mid 2001 the short rates were higher than the long rates. A downward sloping yield curve indicates that the market expects interest rates to fall. If the economy is not growing well and inflation is under control, the government may bring down base rates to stimulate economic growth. From the end of 2001 until mid 2004 the (more usual) upward sloping term structure was evident, after which the term structure was relatively flat until the beginning of 2006. Notice the downward sloping term structure persisted throughout 2006, so the market was expecting interest rates to fall during all this time. In the event it turned out that they were not cut until August 2007, when the UK followed the US interest rate cuts that were necessitated by the sub-prime mortgage crisis.

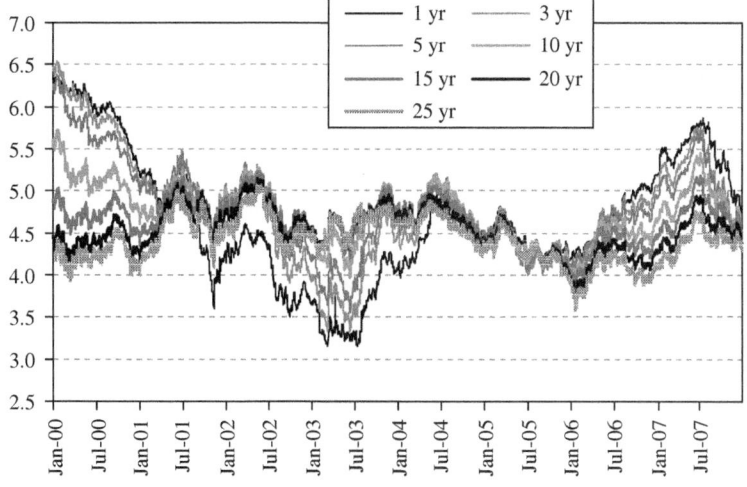

Figure III.1.5   UK spot rate curve, January 2000 to December 2007

---

[22] The Bank provides daily data on the UK government and LIBOR yield curves for maturities between 6 months and 25 years, based on zero coupon gilts, and a separate short curve to use for risk free interest rates up to 5 years' maturity. The short curve is based on sterling interbank rates (LIBOR), yields on instruments linked to LIBOR, short sterling futures, forward rate agreements and LIBOR-based interest rate swaps. More information and data are available from http://www.bankofengland.co.uk/statistics/yieldcurve/index.htm

Taking a vertical section though Figure III.1.5 on any fixed date gives the term structure of spot interest rates on that day. As is typical of interest rate term structures, the UK spot rates fluctuate between a downward sloping term structure, where short rates are above long rates (e.g. during 2000–2001 and 2006–2007) and an upward sloping term structure, where short rates are below long rates (e.g. during 2002–2003). By definition, the forward rates will be greater than spot rates when the spot curve is upward sloping, and less than spot rates when the spot curve is downward sloping. To illustrate this, Figure III.1.6 compares the term structure of UK spot rates with that of 6-month forward rates on (a) 2 May 2000 and (b) 2 May 2003.

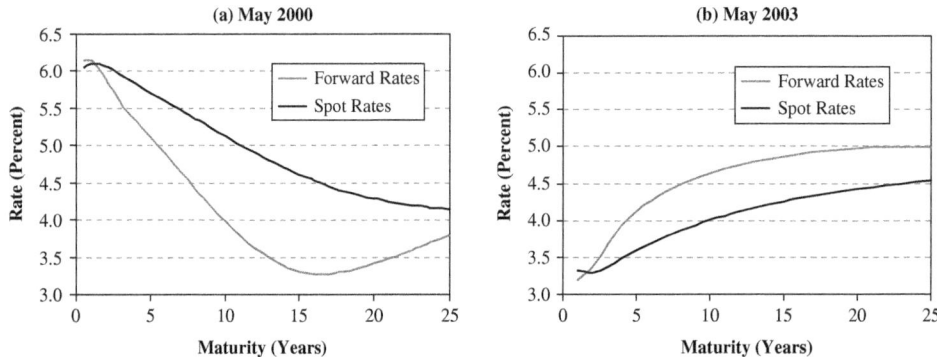

Figure III.1.6   UK government spot and 6-month forward rates on (a) 2 May 2000 and (b) 2 May 2003

We conclude this section by referring to two chapters in *Market Risk Analysis*, Volume II, with detailed analyses of the statistical properties of term structures of interest rates. Specifically:

- the characteristics of different covariance and correlation matrices of US Treasury interest rates are analysed in Section II.3.5;
- the principal component analysis of the covariance and correlation matrices of UK spot and forward rates is discussed in Section II.2.3. In each case we analyse both the short curve of 60 different rates with monthly maturities up to 5 years, and the entire curve with 50 different maturities from 6 months to 25 years.

The website for Volume II contains all the data and results in Excel.

III.1.5   DURATION AND CONVEXITY

This section describes two traditional measures of a fixed coupon bond's price sensitivity to movements in its yield. The first order price sensitivity is called the *duration*, and we introduce the two most common duration measures: the *Macaulay duration* and the *modified duration*. The second order price sensitivity to changes in the yield is called the *convexity* of the bond. We explain how duration and convexity are used in first and second order Taylor approximations to the change in bond price when its yield changes, and how to obtain similar approximations to the profit and loss (P&L) of a bond portfolio when the yield curve shifts parallel.

The Macaulay duration is the maturity weighted average of the present values of the cash flows. It is measured in years and a zero coupon bond has Macaulay duration equal to its maturity. Under continuous compounding we show that the Macaulay duration is also a first order approximation to the percentage change in bond price per unit change in yield. However, under discrete compounding the first order approximation to the percentage change in bond price per unit change in yield is the modified duration. This is the Macaulay duration divided by the discrete compounding factor for the yield.

Duration increases with the maturity of the bond, and for two bonds of the same maturity the duration is higher for the bond with lower coupon, or for the bond with less frequent coupon payments. Since the price–yield relationship is non-linear, the duration also depends on the yield. The duration is related to the slope of the price–yield curve. In general, the lower the yield, the higher the duration. The bond convexity is the sensitivity of duration to changes in the bond yield. It measures the curvature of the price-yield curve. We conclude this section by explaining how modified duration and convexity are used to immunize a bond portfolio against interest rate changes.

III.1.5.1   Macaulay Duration

The Macaulay duration of a bond – or indeed of any sequence of positive cash flows – is the maturity weighted average of the present values of its cash flows,

$$D_M = \frac{\sum_{i=1}^n T_i P_{T_i}}{P}, \tag{III.1.31}$$

where P is the price of the bond and

$$P_{T_i} = (1+y)^{-T_i} C_{T_i}. \tag{III.1.32}$$

Here y is the yield and C_{T_i} are the coupon payments for $i = 1, \ldots, n-1$ and C_{T_n} is the redemption value which consists of the face value plus the coupon payment, all based on a face value of 100.[23]

Thus a zero coupon bond always has Macaulay duration equal to its maturity, by definition. In general the Macaulay duration provides a single number, measured in years, that represents an average time over which income is received. It can be shown (see Example III.1.8 below) that if the yield curve shifts down the Macaulay duration represents a 'break-even' point in time where the income lost through reinvestment of the coupons is just offset by the gain in the bond's value.

EXAMPLE III.1.7: MACAULAY DURATION

What is the Macaulay duration of a 4-year bond paying a coupon of 6% annually when the interest rates at 1, 2, 3 and 4 years are as shown in Table III.1.8? What would the Macaulay duration be if the coupon rate were 5%?

SOLUTION   The answer to the first part is also shown in Table III.1.8. The price of this bond is 103.62 and its yield is calculated using the Excel RATE function as usual, giving 4.98%. The Macaulay duration is therefore

$$D_M = 381.27/103.62 = 3.68 \text{ years.}$$

---

[23] We could calculate a time weighted average present value based on discounting by market interest rates, but it is easier to use the yield. For a bond we know the market price, and so also the yield, thus we can calculate D_M without having to construct the zero curve.

Although this is not shown in the table, using the spreadsheet for this example the reader can change the coupon rate to 5% and read off the Macaulay duration. When the coupon drops from 6% to 5% the Macaulay duration increases to 372.57/100.06 = 3.72 years.

Table III.1.8 Macaulay duration of a simple bond

Year	Spot rate	Cash flow	PV (Spot)	Yield	PV (Yield)	PV (Yield) × Year
1	4.5%	6	5.74	4.98%	5.72	5.72
2	4.75%	6	5.47	4.98%	5.44	10.89
3	4.85%	6	5.21	4.98%	5.19	15.56
4	5%	106	87.21	4.98%	87.28	349.10
Sum			**103.62**		**103.62**	**381.27**

This example has demonstrated that the duration and the coupon are inversely related. Thus if two bonds have the same maturity, the one with the higher coupon will have the smaller duration.

EXAMPLE III.1.8: MACAULAY DURATION AS A RISK MEASURE

Consider a 10-year bond with a 10% coupon and with the market interest rates as in Table III.1.9. Find the fair value of the bond at maturity, and at h years from now for $h = 9$, 8, 7, ... , 0 (the value at $h = 0$ being the present value of the bond). Now suppose that the yield curve shifts up by 2%. Re-evaluate the future value of the bond at the same points in time as before, and draw a graph of the bond values versus time under (a) the original yield curve in Table III.1.9, and (b) when the yield curve shifts up by 2%. At which point do the two value lines intersect? Does this point change if the shift in yield curve is different from +2%?

Table III.1.9 A zero coupon yield curve

Maturity	1	2	3	4	5	6	7	8	9	10
Spot rate	4.00%	4.25%	4.50%	4.25%	4.20%	4.15%	4.10%	4.00%	4.00%	4.00%

SOLUTION   In the spreadsheet for this example we calculate the bond's maturity value and then discount this value using the relevant forward rate. This gives the value of the bond h years from now. We do this both for the original interest rates shown in Table III.1.9 and then after shifting that yield curve up by 2%. The resulting graph is shown in Figure III.1.7. The reader may change the yield curve shift in the spreadsheet from 2% to any different value and will note that, whilst the grey line changes, the point of intersection remains constant at approximately 7.36 years. Then we show, using the Excel Solver, that the Macaulay duration of the bond is 7.36 years. That is, the point in time where the two lines intersect is always equal to the Macaulay duration. If interest rates increase the value of the bond (including all reinvested coupons) decreases, but the reinvestment income from the coupon stream

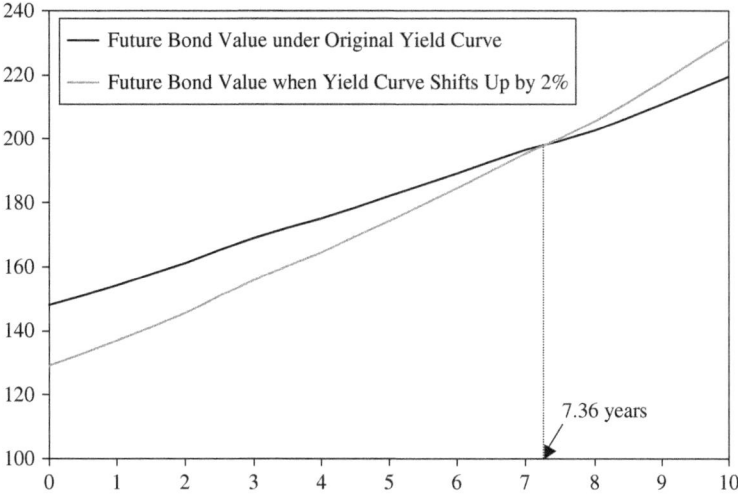

Figure III.1.7   Future value of a bond under two different yield curves

increases.[24] The Macaulay duration represents the future point in time where the loss from the fall in the bond price is just offset by the income gained from an increased interest on the coupon payments. This is why Macaulay duration has been used as a measure of sensitivity to market interest rates.

III.1.5.2   Modified Duration

The modified duration is the first order approximation to the *percentage price change per unit change in yield*, multiplied by −1 so that the modified duration is positive (since the price falls when the yield increases). For an *annual* bond the modified duration is the Macaulay duration divided by $1 + y$.

It can be shown that, under *continuous* compounding, the Macaulay duration is given by[25]

$$D_M = \text{Macaulay duration} = -\frac{1}{P}\frac{dP}{dy}.$$

But this is only the case under continuous compounding. Under discrete compounding, we have

$$D = \text{Modified duration} = -\frac{1}{P}\frac{dP}{dy} = \frac{D_M}{1+y}. \qquad \text{(III.1.33)}$$

Since discrete compounding is applied in the markets it is the modified duration, not the Macaulay duration, that is used as the first order approximation to the percentage change in bond price per unit change in yield.

---

[24] This analysis is based on the assumption that all realised spot rates (i.e. the spot rates at which coupons are reinvested) are equal to the current forward rates.

[25] With continuous compounding, $P = \sum_{T_i} P_{T_i} = \sum_{T_i} e^{-yT_i} C_{T_i}$ so $\frac{dP}{dy} = -\sum_{T_i} T_i P_{T_i}$ and $-\frac{1}{P}\frac{dP}{dy} = \frac{1}{P}\sum_{T_i} T_i P_{T_i} = D_M$.

III.1.5.3 Convexity

The duration gives a first order approximation to the percentage change in the bond price per unit change in yield. Thus it is related to the slope of the price–yield curve. Yet we know that the price and yield have a non-linear relationship. Hence an additional measure of interest rate sensitivity is often employed to capture the curvature of the price–yield relationship. We define

$$\text{Convexity} = \frac{1}{P}\frac{d^2P}{dy^2}. \tag{III.1.34}$$

For instance, we can use (III.1.34) to calculate the convexity for an *annual* bond of maturity T years, with T being an integer and so coupon payments are in exactly $1, 2, \ldots, T$ years. Then

$$\frac{d^2P}{dy^2} = \frac{2C_1}{(1+y)^3} + \frac{6C_2}{(1+y)^4} + \frac{12C_3}{(1+y)^5} + \ldots + \frac{T(T+1)C_T}{(1+y)^{T+2}}, \tag{III.1.35}$$

which follows on differentiating (III.1.22) twice with respect to y.

A *zero* coupon bond of maturity T has convexity

$$\text{Zero coupon bond convexity} = T(T+1)(1+y)^{-2}. \tag{III.1.36}$$

This can be proved by differentiating $P = (1+y)^{-T}$ twice and then dividing by P. For coupon bonds the convexity increases as the coupon payments become more spread out over time.

Convexity captures the second order effect of a change in yield on the price of a bond. The convexity of a bond is its second order price sensitivity to a change in the yield, i.e. convexity measures the sensitivity of modified duration to an absolute change in the yield. See Example III.1.9 below for a numerical illustration.

III.1.5.4 Duration and Convexity of a Bond Portfolio

Modified duration measures the percentage change in bond price per unit change in yield. Since these cannot be added, how do we measure duration when we have several bonds in a portfolio?

The *value duration* of a bond is the *absolute* change in bond price per unit change in yield:

$$\text{Value duration} = D^\$ = -\frac{dP}{dy}. \tag{III.1.37}$$

Similarly, the *value convexity* is defined in terms of absolute changes as

$$\text{Value convexity} = C^\$ = \frac{d^2P}{dy^2}. \tag{III.1.38}$$

The value duration and convexity derive their names from the fact that they are measured in the same currency unit as the bond.[26] The value duration is the modified duration multiplied by the bond price and the value convexity is the convexity multiplied by the bond price. Note that, like ordinary duration and convexity, they can be defined for *any* sequence of positive cash flows, so they can also be calculated for fixed income securities other than bonds.

It is useful to work with value duration and value convexity *because they are additive.* Suppose a portfolio has positions on k different fixed income securities and that the value

---

[26] Note that they are also commonly called the *dollar duration* and *dollar convexity*. But not all bonds are measured in dollars, so we prefer the terms value duration and value convexity.

durations for these positions are $D_1^\$, \ldots, D_k^\$$ and their value convexities are $C_1^\$, \ldots, C_k^\$$. Then the portfolio has value duration $D_P^\$$ and value convexity $C_P^\$$ given by the sum of the value durations for each position:

$$D_P^\$ = D_1^\$ + \ldots + D_k^\$ \tag{III.1.39}$$

and

$$C_P^\$ = C_1^\$ + \ldots + C_k^\$. \tag{III.1.40}$$

For instance, consider a long position of \$2 million with value duration \$400 and value convexity \$15 million, and a short position of \$1.5 million with value duration \$500 and value convexity \$25 million. Then the value duration of the total position is –\$100 and the value convexity is –\$10 million.

Since each bond in the portfolio has a different yield, the interpretation of the value duration and value convexity is tricky. For these to represent yield sensitivities we must assume that the yields on all the bonds in the portfolio move by the same amount. In other words, value duration and value convexity are the first and second order price sensitivities of the portfolio, measured in value terms, to an identical shift in the yields on all bonds in the portfolio. This is explained in more detail in the next subsection.

III.1.5.5   Duration–Convexity Approximations to Bond Price Change

Consider a second order Taylor approximation of the bond price with respect to its yield:[27]

$$P(y) \approx P(y_0) + \left.\frac{dP}{dy}\right|_{y=y_0} (y - y_0) + \tfrac{1}{2}\left.\frac{d^2P}{dy^2}\right|_{y=y_0} (y - y_0)^2.$$

Write $(y - y_0) = \Delta y$ and $P(y) - P(y_0) = \Delta P$, so ΔP is the change in bond price when the yield changes by Δy. Then the second order Taylor approximation may be written

$$\Delta P \approx \frac{dP}{dy}\Delta y + \tfrac{1}{2}\frac{d^2P}{dy^2}(\Delta y)^2. \tag{III.1.41}$$

So using the definitions of value duration and convexity above, we have

$$\Delta P \approx -D^\$\Delta y + \tfrac{1}{2}C^\$(\Delta y)^2. \tag{III.1.42}$$

Now suppose that we hold a bond portfolio and that we assume that all the yields on the bonds in the portfolio change by the same amount Δy. Then we can add up the approximations (III.1.42) over all the bonds in the portfolio to obtain

$$\Delta P \approx -D_P^\$\Delta y + \tfrac{1}{2}C_P^\$(\Delta y)^2, \tag{III.1.43}$$

where now ΔP denotes the change in portfolio value, i.e. the portfolio P&L, when all yields change by Δy.

Bond traders' limits are usually based on value duration and value convexity and traders often use (III.1.43) to approximate the effect of a change in *market interest rates* on their portfolio P&L. That is, they assume that *all the bond yields change by the same amount when the zero coupon yield curve shifts parallel.* They must assume this, otherwise (III.1.43) would

---

[27] See Section I.1.6 for an introduction to Taylor approximation.

not hold, but of course when the zero curve shifts parallel different bond yields change by different amounts.

Another duration–convexity approximation, this time for a single bond, follows on dividing (III.1.41) by P, giving

$$\frac{\Delta P}{P} \approx \frac{1}{P}\frac{dP}{dy}\Delta y + \frac{1}{2P}\frac{dP}{dy}(\Delta y)^2.$$

When we compare the above with the definitions (III.1.33) and (III.1.34) we see that we have obtained an approximation to the percentage change in bond price for a given change in yield. That is:

$$\frac{\Delta P}{P} \approx -\text{Modified Duration} \times \Delta y + \tfrac{1}{2} \times \text{Convexity} \times (\Delta y)^2. \qquad \text{(III.1.44)}$$

Notice that the signs on modified duration and convexity are opposite. Hence, for two cash flows with the same modified duration, the one with the higher convexity has a value that is less sensitive to adverse interest rate movements. That is, its value decreases less if interest rates increase and increases more if interest rates fall. Hence, a large and positive convexity is a desirable quality.

EXAMPLE III.1.9: DURATION–CONVEXITY APPROXIMATION

Find the modified duration and convexity of the two bonds in Example III.1.4. Hence, for each bond, use the duration–convexity approximation to estimate the change in bond price when the yield increases by 1%. Compare this estimate to the full valuation of each bond's price based on the new yield.

SOLUTION   We already know the price and the yield of the bonds from Example III.1.4. Now, using the formulae derived above, first we obtain the Macaulay duration (as the maturity weighted average of the present value of the cash flows) and then we divide this by $1+y$ to obtain the modified duration. For the convexity we use (III.1.35) and (III.1.34). Finally, the approximate change in price of each bond is obtained on applying (III.1.44) with $\Delta y = +1\%$. The actual percentage price change is calculated using the exact relationship (III.1.22) for the original yield and the yield $+1\%$. The solution is summarized in Table III.1.10.

Table III.1.10   Duration-convexity approximation

	Bond 1	Bond 2
Macaulay duration	2.86	4.27
Modified duration	2.74	4.09
Convexity	10.31	22.24
Duration–convexity approximation		
Yield change	1%	1%
Percentage price change	−2.686%	−3.982%
Actual percentage price change	−2.687%	−3.985%

III.1.5.6   Immunizing Bond Portfolios

Bond portfolio managers often have a view about interest rates. For instance, they might believe that short rates will increase. Portfolio managers aim to balance their portfolios so that they can profit from the movements they expect, and will make no losses from other common types of movements in interest rates. One of the most common movements is an approximately parallel shift in the yield curve, i.e. all interest rates change by approximately the same absolute amount.

Thus a portfolio manager who aims to 'immunize' his portfolio from such movements will hold a portfolio that has both zero duration and zero convexity. On the other hand, if he wants to take advantage of a positive convexity he will structure his portfolio so that the convexity is large and positive and the duration is zero.

EXAMPLE III.1.10: IMMUNIZING BOND PORTFOLIOS

Consider again the two bonds in Examples III.1.4 and III.1.9. Suppose the principal amount invested in bond 1 is $1.5 million and the principal of bond 2 is $1 million.

(a) Calculate the value duration and value convexity of each bond.[28]
(b) Find the value duration and value convexity of a portfolio that is long bond 1 and short bond 2.
(c) Immunize this portfolio using bonds 3 and 4 with characteristics in Table III.1.11.

Table III.1.11   Two bonds[29]

	Bond 3	Bond 4
Principal ($)	1,000	10,000
Present value ($)	1,200	10,780
Value duration ($)	5	2
Value convexity ($)	20,000	100,000

SOLUTION   The solution to parts (a) and (b) is given in the spreadsheet and summarized in Table III.1.12.

Table III.1.12   Value duration and value convexity

	Bond 1	Bond 2	Portfolio
Value duration ($)	416.41	514.00	−97.59
Value convexity ($)	15,687,184	27,938,173	−12,250,989

For part (c) we therefore seek (w_1, w_2) such that

$$\text{zero duration} \Rightarrow 5w_1 + 2w_2 - 97.59 = 0.$$

$$\text{zero convexity} \Rightarrow 20,000\, w_1 + 100,000\, w_2 - 12,250,989 = 0.$$

[28] Note that we have computed value durations here as the actual price change for a 1 *basis point* change in yield, rather than with respect to a 1% change in yield. This is so that the value duration and the PV01 have similar orders to magnitude, as demonstrated by Table III.1.17.
[29] Recall that the present value is the bond price times the principal amount invested divided by 100. Hence, bond 3 has price 120 and bond 4 has price 107.8.

The solution is

$$\begin{pmatrix} w_1 \\ w_2 \end{pmatrix} = \begin{pmatrix} 5 & 2 \\ 20{,}000 & 100{,}000 \end{pmatrix}^{-1} \begin{pmatrix} 97.59 \\ 12{,}250{,}989 \end{pmatrix} = \begin{pmatrix} -32.05 \\ 128.92 \end{pmatrix},$$

which means

- selling $32.05 \times \$1200 = \$38{,}459$ of bond 3. Since its price is 120 this is equivalent to selling the principal amount of $\$32{,}049$ in bond 3, and
- buying $128.92 \times \$10{,}780 = \$1{,}389{,}755$ of bond 4. Since its price is 107.8 this is equivalent to buying the principal amount of $\$1{,}289{,}198$ in bond 4.

The resulting portfolio, whose value is approximately invariant to parallel shifts in the yield curve, is summarized in Table III.1.13.

Table III.1.13   An immunized bond portfolio

Portfolio	Bond 1	Bond 2	Bond 3	Bond 4
Principal ($)	1,500,000	−1,000,000	−32, 049	+1,289,198

We remark that a disadvantage of using the traditional sensitivities for hedging the risk of a bond portfolio is that duration and convexity hedging is limited to *parallel* movements of the zero coupon yield curve. More advanced bond portfolio immunization techniques based on *principal component analysis* are introduced and demonstrated in Section II.2.4.4. The advantage of these is that we can:

- hedge the portfolio against the *most common* movements in the yield curve, based on historical data;
- quantify how much of the historically observed variations in the yield curve we are hedging.

Hence, these techniques provide better hedges than standard duration–convexity hedges.

III.1.6   BONDS WITH SEMI-ANNUAL AND FLOATING COUPONS

For simplicity all the numerical examples in Sections III.1.4 and III.1.5 were based on fixed coupon annual bonds. When a bond does not have an annual coupon, the coupon is usually paid every 6 months, and it is called a *semi-annual bond*. For instance, a semi-annual bond with coupon 6% pays 3% of the principal amount invested every 6 months. The first part of this section extends the general formulae for the price, yield, duration and convexity of a bond to semi-annual bonds, and then we generalize the formulae to a fixed coupon *quarterly bond* (i.e. coupons are paid every 3 months).

Fixed coupon quarterly bonds are rare, but *floating rate notes*, which are bonds that have variable coupons, are usually semi-annual or quarterly. The characteristics of floating rate notes, or *floaters* as they are commonly termed, are different from the characteristics of fixed coupon bonds. For instance, if the coupon on a semi-annual floater, which is set six months in advance, is just the 6-month LIBOR rate at the time the coupon is set then the duration of the floater is very short. In fact a semi-annual floater has a duration of no more than 6 months, as we shall demonstrate in this section. Thus by adding long or short positions in floaters, bond traders can change the duration of their bond portfolios, for instance to stay within their trading limits. In addition to straight floaters we have reverse floaters, capped floaters, floored floaters and many other floaters that can have complex option-like features.

III.1.6.1 Semi-Annual and Quarterly Coupons

When dealing with semi-annual bonds the only thing to keep in mind is that the definitions are stated in terms of the *semi-annual yield*, which is one-half the value of the annual yield. In terms of the annual yield y and annual coupon c percent, the price–yield relationship (III.1.22) for a bond with maturity $T/2$ years becomes:

$$P = \sum_{t=1}^{T} \left(1 + \frac{y}{2}\right)^{-t} C_t,$$
(III.1.45)

where

$$C_t = \begin{cases} 100 \times c/2, & \text{for } t = 1, \ldots, T-1, \\ 100\,(1 + c/2), & \text{for } t = T. \end{cases}$$
(III.1.46)

Note that we now use t to index the cash flows. Hence $t = 1, \ldots, T$, but t is *not* the time in *years* when the cash flows are paid. These times are $T_1 = \frac{1}{2}$, $T_2 = 1$, $T_3 = 1\frac{1}{2}$, $\ldots$, $T_n = \frac{1}{2}T$.

EXAMPLE III.1.11: YIELD ON SEMI-ANNUAL BOND

A 3-year semi-annual bond pays an 8% coupon and has a price of 95. Find its semi-annual yield and its annual equivalent yield.

SOLUTION   We use the Excel RATE function to back out the semi-annual yield from the formula (III.1.45) with $P = 95$, $T = 6$ and semi-annual coupons of 4%. This gives the semi-annual yield $\frac{1}{2}y = 4.98\%$ so the annual equivalent yield y is 9.96%.

The duration and convexity are calculated using slight modifications of the formulae given in Section III.1.5. For instance, the Macaulay duration on a semi-annual bond of maturity $T/2$ is[30]

$$D_M = \frac{\frac{1}{2}\sum_{t=1}^{T} tP_t}{P},$$
(III.1.47)

where P is the price of the bond and

$$P_t = \left(1 + \frac{y}{2}\right)^{-t} C_t,$$
(III.1.48)

with y the annual equivalent yield on the bond.

The modified duration of a semi-annual bond is the Macaulay duration divided by $1 + \frac{1}{2}y$. That is, we divide the Macaulay duration by the compounding factor for the *semi-annual* yield and not the annual yield on the bond. This way, the modified duration is still defined as the percentage change in bond price for a unit change in the *annual equivalent* yield. Thus for a semi-annual bond (III.1.33) becomes

$$D = -\frac{1}{P}\frac{dP}{dy} = \frac{D_M}{1 + y/2}.$$
(III.1.49)

---

[30] We use t to represent the payment number, i.e. $t = 1, 2, \ldots, T$, but the times these payments are made are $t/2 = \frac{1}{2}, 1, \ldots, T/2$. Hence the factor of $\frac{1}{2}$ in the formula (III.1.47).

The convexity of a semi-annual bond is still defined as the second derivative of the bond price with respect to the annual equivalent yield, so (III.1.34) still applies. Thus, for a semi-annual bond,

$$\text{Convexity} = \frac{1}{P}\frac{d^2P}{dy^2}, \tag{III.1.50}$$

But when the coupons are paid semi-annually the formula (III.1.35) for the second derivative of the bond price with respect to a change in the annual equivalent yield y needs to be modified to

$$\frac{d^2P}{dy^2} = \frac{C_1/2}{(1+y/2)^3} + \frac{3C_2/2}{(1+y/2)^4} + \frac{3C_3}{(1+y/2)^5} + \ldots + \frac{(T(T+1)/4)C_T}{(1+y/2)^{T+2}}$$

$$= \sum_{t=1}^{T}\frac{(t(t+1)/4)C_t}{(1+y/2)^{t+2}}, \tag{III.1.51}$$

with the semi-annual cash flows defined by (III.1.46).

EXAMPLE III.1.12: DURATION AND CONVEXITY OF A SEMI-ANNUAL BOND

Find the Macaulay duration, modified duration and convexity of a 3-year semi-annual bond that pays an 8% coupon and has a price of 95.

SOLUTION   This is the bond for which we found the semi-annual yield of 4.98% in the previous example. In (III.1.47) and (III.1.48) we have $P = 95$, $P_t = 4 \times (1.0498)^{-t}$ for $t = 1, 2, \ldots, 5$, and $P_6 = 104 \times (1.0498)^{-6}$. The spreadsheet for this example sets out the calculation for the Macaulay duration, and we obtain $D_M = 2.718$. Then we find the modified duration using (III.1.49), so we divide D_M by 1.0498, and this gives the modified duration $D = 2.589$. Finally, the spreadsheet implements (III.1.50) and (III.1.51) with $T = 6$, giving the convexity 8.34.

For reference, the formulae for price, duration and convexity of a fixed coupon *quarterly* bond are summarized below:

$$P = \sum_{t=1}^{T}PV_t$$

$$PV_t = \left(1+\frac{y}{4}\right)^{-t}C_t$$

$$C_t = \begin{cases} 100 \times c/4. & \text{for } t = 1, \ldots, T-1 \\ 100(1+c/4) & \text{for } t = T \end{cases}$$

$$D_M = \frac{\left(\sum_{t=1}^{T}tP_t\right)/4}{P} \tag{III.1.52}$$

$$\frac{d^2P}{dy^2} = \sum_{t=1}^{T}\frac{(t(t+1)/16)C_t}{(1+y/4)^{t+2}}$$

$$D = -\frac{1}{P}\frac{dP}{dy} = \frac{D_M}{1+y/4}$$

$$\text{Convexity} = \frac{1}{P}\frac{d^2P}{dy^2}$$

III.1.6.2 Floating Rate Notes

A floating rate note (FRN) or *floater* is a bond with a coupon that is linked to LIBOR or some other reference interest rate such as a treasury zero coupon rate. A typical floater pays coupons every 3 months or every 6 months, but coupon payments are sometimes also monthly or annual.[31] When a coupon payment is made the next coupon is set by the current reference rate, and the period between the date on which the rate is set and the payment date is referred to as the *lock-out period*.

Usually the maturity of the reference rate is the time between coupon payments. So, for example, the next coupon payment on a semi-annual floater is equal to the 6-month reference rate prevailing at the last coupon payment date plus a spread; for a quarterly floater the next coupon payment is equal to the 3-month reference rate at the time of the last coupon plus a spread. The spread depends on the credit quality of the borrower. For instance, since LIBOR is rated AA any borrower with a rating less than AA will have a positive spread over LIBOR and this spread increases as the borrower's credit rating decreases. Also, to account for the possible deterioration in the credit quality of the borrower over time, the spread increases with maturity of the floater, so that a 10-year floater has a larger spread than a 2-year floater.

We now demonstrate how to price a floater. It is slightly easier to write down the mathematics by assuming the coupons are paid annually, so we shall make that assumption merely for simplicity; it does not alter the concepts in the argument. Suppose we are at time zero and the next coupon, which has been fixed at c on the last coupon payment date, is paid at time t, measured in years. Also suppose there are T further annual coupon payments until the floater expires. So the subsequent payments are at times $t+1, t+2, \ldots, t+T$ and the final payment at time $t+T$ includes the principal amount invested, N.

Denote the 1-year reference rate at time t by R_t and for simplicity assume this is also the discount rate, i.e. the LIBOR rate. Denote the fixed spread over this rate by s. Thus the coupon payment at time $t+n$ is $100(R_{t+n-1} + s)$. Now the price of a floater may be written

$$P_{t+T}^s = \left(B_{t+T}^s - B_{t+T}^0\right) + 100\,(1 + c - s)\,(1 + tR_0)^{-1}, \qquad \text{(III.1.53)}$$

where P_m^s is the price of the floater with spread s and maturity m, B_m^s is the price of a bond with fixed coupon $100s$ and maturity m and R_0 is the t-period discount rate at time 0.

To prove (III.1.53) we decompose the coupon payments into two parts: the payments based on the reference rate and the payments based on the fixed spread s over this reference rate. First consider the fixed coupon payments of $100s$ on every date, including the last. What is the discounted value of the cash flows $100\{s, s, \ldots, s, s\}$ at times $t, t+1, \ldots, t+T$? Let us temporarily add 100 to the final payment, recalling that the discounted value of a cash flow of 100 at time $t+T$ is the value of a zero coupon bond expiring at time $t+T$. Adding this zero bond, the cash flows become $100\{s, s, \ldots, s, 1+s\}$. These are the cash flows on a bond with maturity $t+T$ and fixed coupon s. Hence, discounting the cash flows $100\{s, s, \ldots, s, s\}$ to time zero gives $B_{t+T}^s - B_{t+T}^0$, which is the first term in (III.1.53).

Now consider the floating part of the payments. Working backwards from the final payment, we discount to time t all the floating coupon payments at $t+1, t+2, \ldots, t+T$, plus 100 at $t+T$, assuming the spread is zero. At time $t+T$ the payment of $100(1 + R_{t+T-1})$ is discounted to time $t+T-1$ using the reference rate R_{t+T-1}, so the discounted value is 100.

---

[31] However, Fed funds floaters, for instance, can reset coupons daily because the reference rate is an overnight rate, while T-bill floaters usually reset weekly following the T-bill auction.

Similarly, at time $t+T-1$ the coupon payment added to the discounted value of 100 of the final payment is $100(1+R_{t+T-2})$. This is discounted to time $t+T-2$ using the reference rate R_{t+T-2}, so the discounted value is again 100. Continuing to discount the coupon payment plus the discounted values of future payments until we reach time t gives 100. Note that this is independent of the interest rates. Now we have a cash flow of $100(1+c)$, where c is the coupon fixed at the previous payment date, at time t. Discounting this to time zero gives the second term in (III.1.53).

EXAMPLE III.1.13: PRICING A SIMPLE FLOATER

A 4-year FRN pays annual coupons of LIBOR plus 60 basis points. The 12-month LIBOR rate is 5% and the 2-, 3- and 4-year discount rates are 4.85%, 4.65% and 4.5%, respectively. Find its price.[32]

SOLUTION   To calculate the first term in (III.1.53) we need to find the price of a 4-year bond paying annual coupons of 60 basis points and the price of a 4-year zero bond. These are based on (III.1.20) and are found in the spreadsheet as 86 for the coupon bond and 83.866 for the zero bond. Hence, the fixed part of the floater, i.e. the first term in (III.1.53), is 2.144. Since we are pricing the floater on a coupon payment date, the floating part of the floater, i.e. the second term in (III.1.53), is 100. This is because the payment in 1 year is discounted using the coupon rate, c.[33] Hence the price of the floater is 102.144.

The yield on a floater is the fixed discount rate that gives the market price when all cash flows are discounted at the same rate. Since a floater with zero spread is equivalent to an instrument paying 100 at the next coupon date, in present value terms, we can calculate the yield y on an annual floater using the formula[34]

$$P_{t+T}^s = 100\left(\sum_{\tau=t}^{t+T-1} s(1+y)^{-\tau} - (1-s)(1+y)^{-t+T} + (1+c-s)(1+y)^{-t}\right). \qquad (\text{III.1.54})$$

We can thus back out the yield from the price using a numerical algorithm such as the Excel Solver. The Macaulay and modified durations are then calculated using the usual formulae (III.1.31) and (III.1.33).

EXAMPLE III.1.14: YIELD AND DURATION OF A SIMPLE FLOATER

Calculate the yield and the Macaulay and modified durations of the annual floater of the previous example. How would these quantities change if the floater paid 100 basis points over LIBOR?

SOLUTION   The Solver is set up in the spreadsheet to back out the yield from (III.1.54) based on a price of 102.114, found in the previous example. The result is a yield of 4.98%, and then the usual formulae for the durations give a Macaulay duration of 1.03 years and a modified duration of 0.981. When we change the spread to 1% in the spreadsheet and repeat the exercise, the yield changes considerably, to 4.98%. However, the modified duration changes very little. The Macaulay duration becomes 1.049 years but the modified duration is 0.999, only 0.028 greater than it was for the floater with a spread of 60 basis points.

---

[32] The solution assumes the 60bp spread is not a reflection of a lower than AA credit rating. If it is, then discounting should be not at LIBOR but at LIBOR + 60bp and the price would simply be 100.
[33] But note that the floating part would not be 100 if the floater were priced *between* coupon dates, because the cash flow of 100 $(1+c)$ would be discounted at a rate different from c, as it is in (III.1.53).
[34] To avoid awkward notation here we assume t and T are measured in years, as in our examples.

This example illustrates the fact that the duration of a floater is approximately equal to the time to the next coupon payment, in the case 1 year because we considered an annual floater priced on a coupon payment date. But floaters are typically monthly, quarterly or semi-annual, and are of course priced between coupon payments. Their duration is *always* approximately equal to the time to the next coupon payment. Hence, floaters have very short duration and are therefore often used by traders to change the duration of their bond portfolios.

The pricing formula (III.1.53) has important implications. It means that the market risk of a principal amount N invested in a floater has two components:

- The market risk on a portfolio where we buy a notional N of a bond with coupon s and are short N on a zero bond. This part of the market risk is often very low because the spread s is typically quite small. For instance, an AA borrower on a 5-year floater might pay 20–50 basis points over LIBOR.
- The market risk on a single cash flow at the next coupon date, which is equal to principal N plus the coupon payment on N, i.e. $N(1+c-s)$. As with any cash flow, the market risk is due to fluctuations in the discount rate, because the present value of $N(1+c-s)$ will fluctuate as spot rates change.

Hence, a floater has virtually no market risk beyond the first coupon payment. Clearly floaters with longer reset periods are more vulnerable to market risks.

III.1.6.3   Other Floaters

The simple floaters considered in the previous section were easy enough to price because the coupon payments were based on a spread over a discount rate of the same maturity as the time between coupons. But many floaters are not linked to a market interest rate of the same maturity as the coupon period. For instance, a quarterly floater could have coupons linked to a 12-month LIBOR rate. The valuation of these floaters is complex since it depends on the volatilities and correlations between interest rates. For instance, to value a quarterly floater with coupons linked to a 12-month LIBOR rate, we would need to estimate the volatilities of the 3- and 12-month LIBOR rates and their correlation.

A *reverse floater* has a coupon equal to a fixed rate *minus* the reference rate. For instance, the coupon could be 10% – LIBOR or 12.5% – 2 × LIBOR. Of course, no coupon is paid if the reverse floater coupon formula gives a negative value and since we cannot have negative coupons it is rather complex to price reverse floaters. The constraint that the coupon is non-negative imposes an embedded option structure on their price. Other floaters with embedded options are *capped floaters*, which have coupons that cannot rise above the level of the cap, and *floored floaters*, which have coupons that cannot fall below the level of the floor. Hence, a reverse floater is a special type of floored floater with the floor at zero.

III.1.7   FORWARD RATE AGREEMENTS AND INTEREST RATE SWAPS

This section introduces two related interest rate products that are very actively traded in OTC markets: forward rate agreements (FRAs) and interest rate swaps. Since these fixed income instruments are not exchange traded, their trading needs to be accompanied by legal documentation. In 1992 the International Swaps and Derivatives Association (ISDA) issued standard terms and conditions for the trading of FRAs and swaps. Since then these markets have grown considerably, and the ISDA Master Agreement was thoroughly revised in 2002. The Bank for International Settlements estimate that by December 2006 the total notional value outstanding on interest rate swaps and FRAs was about 250 trillion US dollars, with a mark-to-market value of \$4.2 trillion.[35] The vast majority of this trading is on interest rate swaps rather than FRAs.

III.1.7.1   Forward Rate Agreements

A *forward rate agreement* is an OTC agreement to buy or sell a forward interest rate. For instance, a company entering into an FRA may wish to buy or sell the 3-month forward 3-month LIBOR rate, $F_{3,3}$. Consider an example of a company that has a loan of \$100 million from bank A on which it pays a floating interest rate, with interest payments every 3 months. As each interest payment is made the next payment is fixed based on the current 3-month spot LIBOR rate plus a spread. For instance, the payment due in 6 months will be determined by the spot rate in 3 months' time.

If the company is concerned that interest rates could rise over the next 3 months it may prefer to *fix* the payment that is due in 6 months *now*. This can be accomplished by exchanging the floating rate, which is whatever the 3-month spot LIBOR rate will be in 3 months' time, for a fixed rate which is determined when the FRA is purchased. Let us suppose the company buys this FRA from bank B when $F_{3,3} = 5\%$.[36] With this FRA, in 3 months' time the company and the bank make an exchange of interest rates. The company pays 5% and receives R_3, i.e. the 3-month spot LIBOR rate in 3 months' time. So in effect, the company only pays 5% interest on its loan (plus the spread). In 6 months' time, when the interest on the loan is due, there is a single settlement to the company of

$$\tfrac{1}{4}\left(R_3 - 5\%\right) \times \$100\text{m},$$

which could of course be either positive or negative, depending on R_3. However, this payment is actually made in 3 months' time, i.e. as soon as R_3 becomes known. So, discounted to that date, the payment is

$$\left(1 + \frac{R_3}{4}\right)^{-1} \times \tfrac{1}{4}\left(R_3 - 5\%\right) \times \$100\text{m}. \tag{III.1.55}$$

For instance, if the 3-month spot LIBOR rate R_3 turned out to be 5.6%, the company would gain on the FRA, because they pay only 5% when the floating payment would have been 5.6%. In this case the payment to the company 3 months from now would be:

$$1.014^{-1} \times \tfrac{1}{4} \times 0.006 \times \$100\text{m} = 1.014^{-1} \times \$150,000 = \$147,929.$$

Note that there is no exchange of principal. The only cash flows are the interest payments on some notional principal amount.

---

[35] See the Statistical Annex to the *BIS Quarterly Review*, available from www.BIS.org

[36] Being a market rate this is quoted in annual terms, and so the equivalent interest rate over 3 months is 1.25%. Hence, the company knows now that it will pay interest of 1.25% on its loan (plus the spread, which is not swapped in the FRA) in 6 months' time. Also bank A and bank B could be the same bank.

III.1.7.2 Interest Rate Swaps

Most of the interest rate swaps market is in short term interest rate swaps. Bid–ask spreads on the swap rate are just a few basis points and swap rates serve as reference for AA fixed rates. They are used to manage interest rate risks without inflating the balance sheet,[37] and without creating large credit risks. They are often combined with ordinary debt instruments to form *structured products* that provide a match between the specific needs of borrowers and objectives of investors.

In a standard or *vanilla* interest rate swap, one party pays LIBOR and receives a fixed rate, the swap rate, from the other party over an agreed period. When interest payments are matching in time only one net payment is made on each payment date. There is no exchange of principal. The swap rate is set so that the initial value of the swap is zero.

For example, a typical short-rate vanilla interest rate swap could be to

- receive a fixed rate F,
- pay a floating rate of 3-month LIBOR
- on a notional principal of $10 million
- for a duration of 1 year, with four quarterly exchanges of payments.

The fixed rate F at which the swap is struck is called the *swap rate*. When a swap is struck, the swap rate is found by setting the net present value of the cash flows to zero. At each payment date the floating rate for the next payment is fixed according to the current spot rates. For this reason the floating leg payment dates are often called the *reset* or *fixing dates*.

This is an example of a standard *fixed-for-floating* interest rate swap, which is the most common interest rate hedging instrument. We have shown in Section III.1.6.2 that floaters have very short duration and hence very little market risk. By contrast, long bonds with fixed coupons have significant market risks. So fixed-for-floating swaps allow investors to alter the market risk profile of their portfolio.

In the following we show that a fixed-for-floating interest rate swap can be regarded as a series of FRAs where net interest rate payments are made at regular intervals but without necessarily the same periodicity on the fixed and floating legs. Financial markets are full of idiosyncrasies that make calculations just that little bit more complex. In the case of swaps, the fixed and floating leg payments are usually based on different frequencies and day count conventions: the fixed leg is based on the bond market convention and the floating leg is based on the money market convention.[38] To keep track of two different day count conventions is necessary in practice, but not useful for illustrating the main concepts. We therefore assume in the next example that all payments are at quarterly intervals.

EXAMPLE III.1.15: VALUING A SWAP

Consider a $10 million 1-year receive fixed pay floating swap with quarterly payments where the floating rate is 3-month LIBOR. Suppose the swap rate is 6% and that we are 1 month into the swap. The LIBOR rates are currently at 5%, 5.5%, 6% and 6.5% at the 2-, 5-, 8- and 11-month maturities, respectively. The first payment on the floating leg was fixed 1 month

---

[37] Swaps are traded OTC and are therefore *off-balance sheet* instruments, in the sense that the notional does not appear on the balance sheet. However, under the EU accountancy standards IAS 39, all derivatives are marked-to-market on the balance sheet.

[38] So the fixed leg may have semi-annual or yearly payments, and these are based on bond market day count conventions, whilst the floating leg is usually based on LIBOR (or some other standard short term reference rate) and may have more frequent payments which are based on the money market day count convention.

ago, based on the (then) current 3-month forward rate of 5.5%. Find the value of the swap now. If we were to fix the swap rate now, what would be its fair value?

SOLUTION   Although the floating payments are determined by the spot LIBOR at the previous fixing date, for valuation purposes we can assume that realised spot rates are equal to current forward rates. Consider Table III.1.14. The current spot interest rates are as given in the column headed LIBOR, the interest payments corresponding to a swap rate of 6% are given in the column headed 'Receive 6%' and their value discounted to today is given in the next column. The present value of the fixed leg is the sum of these discounted values, $0.57852 million.

Table III.1.14   The value of a vanilla swap

Months	LIBOR	Receive 6%	Discounted	Forward rates		Pay Floating	Discounted
2	5%	0.15	0.14876	$F_{-1,3}$	5.50%	0.13750	0.13636
5	5.5%	0.15	0.14664	$F_{2,3}$	5.79%	0.14463	0.14139
8	6%	0.15	0.14423	$F_{5,3}$	6.68%	0.16701	0.16058
11	6.5%	0.15	0.14157	$F_{8,3}$	7.53%	0.18830	0.17771
Present value			0.58120				0.61605

The floating leg payments are shown on the right-hand side of the table. The payment in 2 months' time was fixed last month, at 5.5%. For the other floating leg payments we use (III.1.18) to obtain the relevant forward rates from the current LIBOR curve. These are shown in the column headed 'Forward rates'. When all the floating payments are discounted (using the spot rates) and summed we obtain the present value of the floating leg as $0.61605 million. Thus, based on a swap rate of 6%, the net present value of the swap is $0.58120m − $0.61605m, i.e. −$34,851.

If we were to set the swap rate now, we would find the value of the swap rate F so that the present value of the swap was zero. The swap rate only affects the fixed leg payments, so using the Excel Solver (or Goal Seek) we find the fixed rate that makes the net present value of the fixed leg equal to $0.61605 million. It turns out to be 6.36%.

III.1.7.3   Cash Flows on Vanilla Swaps

The above example considered an *on-the-run swap*, i.e. one with standard vertices as payment dates. These are often used for hedging swaps portfolios because they have a liquid market. But in a typical swaps portfolio the swaps have payment dates at various times in the future. For this reason the cash flows need to be mapped to a fixed set of vertices. We deal with the principles of cash flow mapping in Section III.5.3. But before we can map the cash flows on an interest rate swap we need to know how to represent these cash flows.

A *vanilla swap* is a swap where the floating payments at the end of a certain period depend only on the forward rate prevailing over that period. We now show that we can decompose the cash flows on a vanilla swap into two series: a series of cash flows on a coupon bearing bond and a single cash flow at the first payment date. Figure III.1.8 illustrates the cash flows on the swap considered in Example III.1.15 with one modification: we have supposed there is an exchange of the notional principal at maturity. This is marked in grey on the figure. Such an exchange of principal does not actually happen in a vanilla swap, but by assuming this hypothetical exchange it becomes easier to decompose the cash flows on the

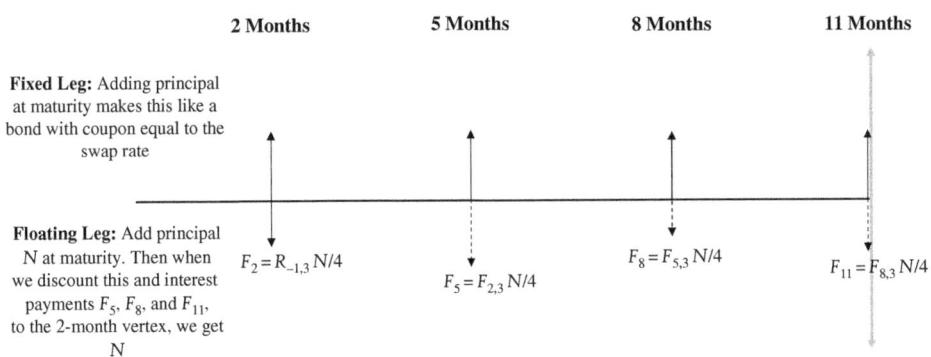

Figure III.1.8 Cash flows on a vanilla swap

swap. Since there is both a positive and a negative cash flow of N when we exchange the principal, this does not affect the value of the swap.

The fixed leg payments are shown above the line as positive cash flows and the floating leg payments are shown below the line as negative cash flows. Note that the first floating payment in Figure III.1.8, denoted F_2, is already fixed by the three month spot rate at the time of the last payment, denoted $R_{-1,3}$ in the figure. So we use a solid arrow to depict this, whereas the subsequent floating payments have yet to be determined, and we use dotted arrows to depict these.

The floating payments at 5, 8 and 11 months, plus the principal at 11 months, all discounted to the 2-month vertex, together have value $10 million. In other words, at the next reset date the value of the remaining floating leg payments plus principal, discounted to this reset date, is equal to the principal. This follows using the same logic as we used when valuing FRNs in Section III.1.6.2.[39] This is not a special case: it is *always* true that the principal plus floating payments after the first payment date, discounted to the first payment date, together have value equal to the principal, in this case $10 million.

The implication is that there is no market risk on the floating leg payments after the first payment date. It does not matter how interest rates change between now and the first payment date, the discounted value of the future payments plus principal will always be equal to the principal. Hence, the only market risk on the floating leg of a swap is the risk from a single cash flow at the first payment date, equal to the notional N plus the first interest payment on N, i.e. $N(1 + R/4)$ where R is the fixed interest rate applied to the first interest payment. The market risk on the floating leg is due only to fluctuations in the discount rate as we move towards the next reset date, because the present value of $N(1 + R/4)$ will fluctuate as spot rates change.

Finally, consider the fixed leg in Figure III.1.8, where we have fixed payments determined by the swap rate (6%) and a payment of $10 million principal at 11 months. This is equivalent to a face value of $10 million on a hypothetical bond with coupon rate 6% paid quarterly. We conclude that the market risk of the fixed leg of a swap can be analysed as the market risk of a bond with coupon equal to the swap rate.

---

[39] At 11 months the payment of $10.18830 million discounted to the 8-month vertex must have value $10 million, because it will be discounted using the forward rate $F_{8,3}$ which is exactly the same as the forward rate used to calculate the interest payment of $0.18830 million. So we have $10.16701 million to discount from 8 months to 5 months, i.e. at the rate $F_{5,3}$ which is the same as the rate used to calculate the interest in the first place, and so the value discounted to 5 months is $10 million. Now we have $10.14463 million to discount to 2 months, which has value $10 million.

III.1.7.4 Cross-Currency Swaps

A *basis swap* is an interest rate swap where two floating rates are exchanged on each payment date. These floating rates may be of different maturities, or they may be denominated in different currencies. In the latter case, if we add exchanges of principal, in the opposite direction to interest rate flows initially and in the same direction at maturity, we have the standard or *vanilla* cross-currency swap, also called a *cross-currency basis swap*. It can be regarded as two FRNs in different currencies, as illustrated in the following example.

EXAMPLE III.1.16: A CROSS-CURRENCY BASIS SWAP

On 6 July 2004 bank A entered into a 3-year floating basis swap with bank B based on a notional principal of $100 million. Bank A pays 6-month US dollar LIBOR (actual/360) and receives 6-month sterling LIBOR (actual/365). Both LIBOR rates are set 6 months in advance. For instance, the interest rates for the payments on 6 July 2005 are fixed at the spot 6-month LIBOR rates on 6 January 2005. It is now 7 July 2007. We can look back over the past 3 years, recording the LIBOR rates and the exchange rate on the payment dates, and they are as shown in Table III.1.15. Explain the mechanisms of this *cross-currency basis swap* and calculate the net payments on each payment date.[40]

Table III.1.15   USD and GBP 6-month LIBOR rates and spot USD/GBP exchange rate

Date	$LIBOR	£LIBOR	USD/GBP
06/07/04	1.68%	4.73%	1.8399
06/01/05	2.63%	4.57%	1.8754
06/07/05	3.41%	4.39%	1.7578
06/01/06	4.39%	4.36%	1.7718
06/07/06	5.31%	4.60%	1.8365
08/01/07	5.13%	5.22%	1.9347
06/07/07	5.01%	5.86%	2.0131

SOLUTION   In effect, bank A is borrowing $100 million from bank B to make an investment in sterling LIBOR. Bank A will pay the interest on the $100 million to bank B based on USD LIBOR and will finance these payments (hoping to make a profit) from the income it receives from its investment in sterling LIBOR. At the end of the 3-year period bank A pays back $100 million to bank B.

The payments from the perspective of bank A are set out in Table III.1.16, where a negative number means a payment and a positive number means money is received. Thus on 6 July 2004, bank A receives $100 million and, based on the spot exchange rate of 1.8399, invests £(100/1.8399) million = £54,350,780 at sterling 6-month LIBOR. On 6 January 2005 it makes its first payment to bank B on this loan, of:

$$\$\left(100 \times 0.0168 \times \frac{184}{360}\right) m = \$858,667.$$

---

[40] Note that 6 January 2007 was a Saturday.

But the same day its investment in UK LIBOR pays to bank A:

$$£\left(54,350,780 \times 0.0473 \times \frac{184}{365}\right) = £1,295,961.$$

The spot exchange rate on 6 January 2005 was 1.8754. Hence the net sum received by bank A on that date, in US dollars, is $-858,667 + 1,295,961 \times 1.8754 = 1,571,778$. This is shown in the last column of Table III.1.16.

Table III.1.16 Payments on a cross-currency basis swap

Date	Days	$ LIBOR	Pay ($m)	£ LIBOR	Pay (£m)	GBP/USD	Net payment ($)
06/07/04		1.68%	100	4.73%	−54.350780	1.8399	0
06/01/05	184	2.63%	−0.858667	4.57%	1.295961	1.8754	1,571,778
06/07/05	181	3.41%	−1.322306	4.39%	1.231708	1.7578	842,790
06/01/06	184	4.39%	−1.742889	4.36%	1.202805	1.7718	388,241
06/07/06	181	5.31%	−2.207194	4.60%	1.175109	1.8365	−49,108
08/01/07	186	5.13%	−2.743500	5.22%	1.274042	1.9347	−278,611
06/07/07	179		−102.550750		55.742130	2.0131	9,663,732

We continue to calculate the payments on the $100 million loan and the receipts on the £54,350,780 investment using the 6-month LIBOR rates that are fixed 6 months before the payment dates, and then calculating the net dollar payment by bank A. In fact, bank A did very well on the deal, since it only had to make a net payment on 6 July 2006 and on 8 January 2007.

It is very common that the main cash flow in a cross-currency swap arises from the change in the exchange rate over the period of the swap. And it is indeed the case here. The US dollar weakened considerably over the 3-year period, so bank A had an advantage holding sterling when it came to repaying the loan on 6 July 2007. On that date, it received interest of

$$£\left(54,350,780 \times 0.0522 \times \frac{179}{365}\right) = £1,391,350$$

and it received its principal of £54,350,780. Based on the exchange rate of 2.0131, it received $112,214,482. After paying back the loan of $100 million and the last interest payment on that of:

$$\$\left(100 \times 0.0513 \times \frac{179}{360}\right) m = \$2,550,750,$$

bank A receives $112,214,482 − $102,550,750 = $9,663,732 when the swap terminates.

In a cross-currency basis swap exchanges of principal take place initially and at maturity. The swap is therefore equivalent to an exchange of two FRNs, one in each currency. For instance, in Example III.1.16 the cash flows corresponded to the positions

- short a $100 million 3-year floater with 6-month $LIBOR coupons and
- long a £54,350,780 three-year floater with 6-month £LIBOR coupons.

The value of the swap is therefore equal to the difference in value of these two floaters, as illustrated in the example above.

Cross-currency basis swaps allow borrowers and investors to seek markets where they have a comparative advantage, including foreign markets. For instance, multinational companies with production costs and sales revenues in various countries might use a cross-currency basis swap to convert these cash flows into different currencies. They do not have to be based on two FRNs: for instance, the cash flows could be based on fixed interest rates in either currency.[41]

III.1.7.5   Other Swaps

In some interest rate swaps the floating payments at the end of a certain period are not determined only by the forward rate prevailing over that period. For instance, the payments could be based on a rate that has a tenor different than the time between payments. It may also be that the reset dates are not equal to the payment dates. Since it is no longer true that discounting the floating payments plus principal to next payment date always gives the value of the principal, the valuation of these swaps is much more complex. The swap rate will depend on the volatilities and correlations of the forward rates with tenor equal to the time between payments, and the interest rates used to determine the floating payments.

Another popular type of swap is a *total return swap*, in which two parties exchange returns on one asset for returns on another, including the capital gains or losses at every payment date. Two common types of total return swaps are the contract for difference and equity swap:

- A *contract for difference* is a short term total return swap on a share versus an interest rate. Here there is a single terminal payment linked to a principal N where the price appreciation of an investment of N in the share, plus any dividend, is swapped for the (fixed) interest on N.
- An *equity swap* is a long term total return swap on a share versus an interest rate, but now there are regular settlements. For instance, at time $t+1$ the equity payer pays the total return on N_t invested in a share to the rate payer, who in return pays a floating rate plus a spread on N_t where N_t is the market value of the equity position at the beginning of the time interval.

These swaps are used by institutions, such as hedge funds, that require short equity positions. Alternatively, a fund manager may simply wish to hedge shares that he cannot sell against a fall in price. This second application is illustrated in the following example.

EXAMPLE III.1.17: A SIMPLE TOTAL RETURN SWAP

A UK fund manager thinks the price of Tesco shares will drop over the next month. So he borrows funds to buy 1 million shares in Tesco for 1 month. He uses this holding to enter a contract for difference with a bank. Tesco is currently quoted at 330–331p per share, LIBOR rates are flat at 4.5%, and the bank quotes 1-month LIBID at $+40/-50$ basis points.[42] After a month, Tesco is quoted at 320–321p. How much did the fund manager make on the contract?

---

[41] In which case that leg of the swap is valued like a normal fixed coupon bond. In this case we have a cross-currency swap without basis risk.

[42] Interest payments in contracts for difference are at the *London Interbank Bid Rate* (LIBID) which is quoted at LIBOR plus a spread for the buyer and minus a spread for the seller. So the UK fund manager, the seller of the contract, will receive interest of 4.5% less 50 basis points, i.e. 4.0%, in this case.

SOLUTION The principal is based on 1 million shares at 330p, hence $N = £3.3$ million. Hence the interest received over the 1-month period is $£3.3$ million $\times 0.04/12 = £11,000$. In return the fund manager pays the bank the total return on the shares, but since they fell in price, the bank must pay the fund manager this negative return. Selling 1 million shares at 330p and buying back at 321p makes a profit of $£90,000$ for the fund manager. So far, his total profit on the contract is $£101,000$, but we still have to subtract the funding cost for buying 1 million shares for 1 month. Assuming borrowing at LIBOR, the funding cost of the initial position is $£3.3$ million $\times 0.045/12 = £12,375$. So the net gain to the fund manager was $£88,625$.

Many other non-standard interest rate swaps are traded, for instance:

- *constant maturity swap* – between a LIBOR rate and a particular maturity swap rate;
- *constant maturity treasury swap* – between a LIBOR rate and a particular maturity treasury bond yield;
- *extendable/putable swaps* – one party has the option to extend or terminate the swap;
- *forward starting swap* – interest payments are deferred to a future date;
- *inflation linked swap* – between LIBOR and an inflation index adjusted rate;
- *LIBOR in arrears swap* – LIBOR fixings are just before each interest payment;
- *variable principal swap* – principal changes during the life of the swap;
- *yield curve swap* – between rates for two maturities on the yield curve;
- *zero coupon swap* – between a fixed or floating rate and a fixed payment at maturity.

Readers are recommended to consult Flavell (2002) for further details.

III.1.8 PRESENT VALUE OF A BASIS POINT

There is no such thing as a yield on a swap. That is, it is not possible to back out a unique discount rate which, when applied to all the cash flows, gives the present value of the swap. A unique yield exists only when all the cash flows are positive, but the cash flows on a swap can be negative. And since we cannot define the yield, we cannot define duration or convexity for a swap. So what should we use instead as a measure of sensitivity to interest rates?

In this section we introduce an interest rate sensitivity called the present value of a basis point move, or 'PV01' or 'PVBP' for short. It is the change in the present value of a sequence of cash flows when the yield curve shifts down by one basis point, i.e. when all zero coupon rates are decreased by one basis point. So the PV01 of a bond portfolio is almost, but not quite, the same as its value duration. The importance of PV01 is that it can be used for *any* sequence of cash flows, positive or negative. After explaining how to calculate PV01, including useful approximations under discrete and continuous compounding of interest rates, we end the section with a discussion on the nature of interest rate risk.

III.1.8.1 PV01 and Value Duration

In the case of a single bond, the PV01 measures *the absolute change in the value of the bond for a fall of one basis point in market interest rates*. More generally, we can define the PV01 for *any* sequence of cash flows given an associated set of spot rates of maturities matching these cash flows. We use the vector notation

$$\mathbf{c} = \left(C_{T_1}, \ldots, C_{T_n}\right)' \text{ and } \mathbf{r} = \left(R_{T_1}, \ldots, R_{T_n}\right)'$$

for the cash flows and for the interest rates, respectively. Denote the present value of the cash flows $\mathbf{c}$ based on the discount rates $\mathbf{r}$ by $PV(\mathbf{c},\mathbf{r})$. Let $\mathbf{r}^- = \mathbf{r} - 0.01\% \times \mathbf{1}$ where $\mathbf{1}$ is the vector with all elements equal to 1. That is, $\mathbf{r}^-$ denotes the interest rates when each rate is shifted down by one basis point. Now we define:

$$PV01(\mathbf{c},\mathbf{r}) = PV(\mathbf{c}, \mathbf{r}^-) - PV(\mathbf{c},\mathbf{r}). \tag{III.1.56}$$

For a single bond, the PV01 is similar to the value duration, which is the absolute change in the present value of the bond per unit absolute change in the bond *yield*. For a single bond, the PV01 and the value duration will only differ in the fifth decimal place or so. But when a cash flow corresponds to an entire portfolio of bonds, there is a subtle difference between value duration and the PV01. The PV01 is the *exact* cash flow sensitivity to a parallel shift in the zero coupon yield curve, whereas value duration is the *approximate* cash flow sensitivity to a parallel shift in the zero curve. The two would only coincide if a shift in the zero curve caused the yields on all the bonds in the portfolio to change by the same amount. Clearly this is very unlikely, so for a bond portfolio PV01 is a more precise measure of interest rate sensitivity than its value duration.

Moreover, value duration is not a concept that can be extended to cover all interest rate sensitive instruments other than bonds.[43] By contrast, the PV01 is very easy to calculate for *any* portfolio. We merely have to represent each instrument as a series of cash flows, net these cash flows, and then we can find the PV01 using the simple method described below. In short, PV01 is a more accurate and more general measure of interest rate sensitivity than value duration.

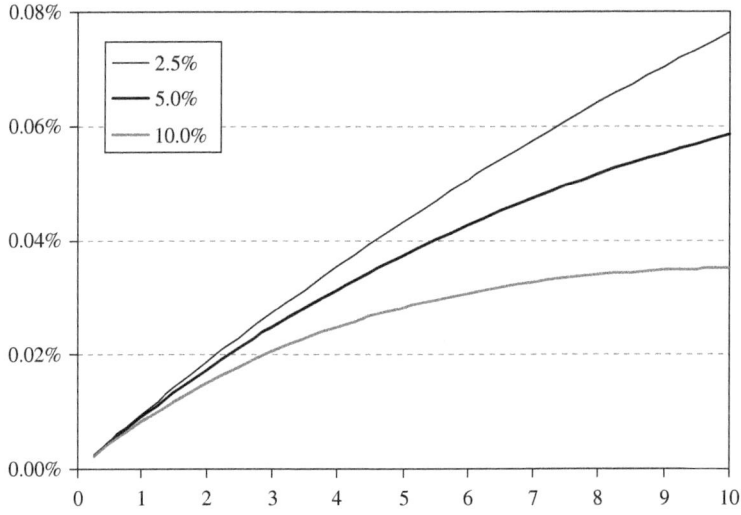

Figure III.1.9 $\delta01$ as a function of maturity

Consider a single cash flow at time T, where R_T is the associated discount rate. For simplicity we assume that T is an integral number of years, but the extension to non-integer values of T should be obvious from our definitions in Section III.1.2.2. We define $\delta01$, the *basis point sensitivity of the discount factor*, as

$$\delta01_T = \left[(1 + R_T - 0.01\%)^{-T} - (1 + R_T)^{-T}\right]. \tag{III.1.57}$$

---

[43] In some cases it can be extended, for instance we can define a discrete approximation called the *effective duration* for a convertible bond.

This is the change in the discount factor when its associated interest rate falls by one basis point. Figure III.1.9 depicts $\delta 01_T$ as a function of T for different levels of $\mathbf{r}$, in each curve assuming the term structure of interest rates is flat. This shows that typically, $\delta 01$ will be less than 10 basis points, that $\delta 01$ increases with maturity and that this increase is more pronounced for low levels of interest rates (e.g. 2.5%) than for high levels of interest rates (e.g. 10%).

Using this notation, we can express the PV01 of a cash flow C_T at time T as

$$\text{PV01}_T = C_T \times \delta 01_T,$$

and the total PV01 of all the cash flows is the sum of these,

$$\text{PV01} = \sum_{i=1}^{n} C_{T_i} \times \delta 01_{T_i}. \tag{III.1.58}$$

EXAMPLE III.1.18: CALCULATING THE PV01 OF A SIMPLE BOND

Calculate the PV01 for £1 million notional in a 6% 4-year annual bond when the zero coupon rates are 4.5%, 4.75%, 4.85% and 5% at maturities of 1, 2, 3 and 4 years, respectively. Compare this with the value duration of the bond.[44]

SOLUTION   This bond was examined in Example III.1.7, where we computed its price, yield and Macaulay duration. Table III.1.17 extends the calculations of Table III.1.8 to compute the PV01 and the value duration of the bond. For the PV01, the present value of each cash flow is calculated twice, first based on the zero coupon yield curve and then again based on the same curve shifted down one basis point. The PV01 is the difference between the two values, i.e. £36,312.75. This tells us that if *zero coupon rates* were to shift down by one basis

Table III.1.17   PV01 for a bond

Years to maturity	Cash flow (£m)	Interest rate	Present value	Interest rate	Present value	PV01
1	6	4.5%	5.7416	4.49%	5.7422	549.49
2	6	4.75%	5.4682	4.74%	5.4692	1,044.19
3	6	4.85%	5.2053	4.84%	5.2068	1,489.64
4	106	5%	87.2065	4.99%	87.2397	33,229.42
			103.6216		103.6579	36,312.75

Years to maturity	Cash flow (£m)	Bond yield	Present value	Bond yield	Present value	Value duration
1	6	4.98%	5.7154	4.97%	5.7160	544.49
2	6	4.98%	5.4443	4.97%	5.4454	1,037.37
3	6	4.98%	5.1861	4.97%	5.1876	1,482.32
4	106	4.98%	87.2757	4.97%	87.3090	33,262.41
			103.6216		103.6579	36,326.59

[44] Note that we have computed value durations here as the actual price change for a 1 *basis point* change in yield, rather than with respect to a 1% change in yield. This is so that the value duration and the PV01 have similar orders of magnitude, as demonstrated by Table III.1.17.

point the bond price would rise by 0.03631, i.e. from 103.6216 to 103.6579, and we would make a profit of £36,312.75 per million pounds invested in the bond.

We also calculate the value duration by shifting the bond's *yield* down by one basis point. In Example III.1.7 we found that the bond had yield 4.98% based on a price of 103.62. The present value is calculated again, now based on a yield of 4.97%, and the value duration is the difference between the original value and the new value, i.e. £36,326.59. This tells us that if the *bond yield* were to fall by one basis point then the price of the bond would rise by 0.03633, i.e. from 103.6216 to 103.6579, and we would make £36,326.59 per million pounds invested in the bond.

This verifies that, for a single bond, the PV01 and the value duration are almost exactly the same. However, for reasons made clear above, PV01 is the preferred interest rate sensitivity measure.

III.1.8.2   Approximations to PV01

In this subsection we derive a first order approximation to $\delta 01$ that allows one to approximate the PV01 very quickly. If T is an integral number of years, the discount factor is $\delta_T = (1+R_T)^{-T}$ and so

$$\delta 01_T \approx -\frac{d\delta_T}{dR_T} \times 10^{-4} = T(1+R_T)^{-(T+1)} \times 10^{-4}.$$

This shows that a useful approximation to the PV01 of a cash flow C_T at time T, when T is an integral number of years, is

$$\text{PV01}_T \approx T\,C_T(1+R_T)^{-(T+1)} \times 10^{-4}. \tag{III.1.59}$$

Similar first order approximations can be derived when T is not an integral number of years. For instance, when T is less than 1 year,

$$\delta_T = (1+TR_T)^{-1}$$

and

$$\delta 01_T \approx T(1+TR_T)^{-2} \times 10^{-4}. \tag{III.1.60}$$

This is simple enough, but the expression becomes a little more complex when T is greater than 1 year but not an integer.

Because of the unwanted technical details associated with working with discretely compounded rates it is common practice to price fixed income instruments and futures with continuously compounded rates using the relationship between discretely and continuously compounded rates derived in Section III.1.2.3. An approximation that is equivalent to (III.1.59) but that applies for continuously compounded interest rates of *any* maturity is derived by differentiating the continuous discounting factor $\delta_T = \exp(-r_T T)$ with respect to the continuously compounded interest rate r_T of maturity T. Thus

$$\delta 01_T \approx -\frac{d\delta_T}{dr_T} \times 10^{-4} = T\exp(-r_T T) \times 10^{-4} = T\delta_T \times 10^{-4}. \tag{III.1.61}$$

Hence, a simple approximation to the PV01 for a cash flow at *any* maturity, under continuous compounding, is

$$\text{PV01}_T \approx T\,C_T \exp(-r_T T) \times 10^{-4}. \tag{III.1.62}$$

EXAMPLE III.1.19: CALCULATING PV01

Suppose a cash flow has been mapped to vertices at 1 and 2 years with €10 million mapped to the 1-year vertex and €5 million mapped to the 2-year vertex. Suppose the 1-year zero rate is 4% and the 2-year zero rate is 4.5%. Use the above approximation to calculate the PV01 at each vertex and hence find the total PV01 of the mapped cash flow.

SOLUTION   From (III.1.59),

$$PV01_1 \approx 10^{-4} \times 10 \times 10^6 \times (1.04)^{-2} = 1000 \times (1.04)^{-2} = 924.56,$$

$$PV01_2 \approx 10^{-4} \times 2 \times 5 \times 10^6 \times (1.045)^{-2} = 1000 \times (1.045)^{-2} = 876.30,$$

so the total PV01 is approximately €1800.86. For comparison we also compute the exact solution, which is summarized in Table III.1.18. With the original interest rates the present value of the cash flow is €14.194 million, but if interests fall by one basis point the present value will become €14.1958 million. Hence, the exact PV01 of the cash flow is €1801.07.

Table III.1.18   PV01 for a cash flow

Maturity (years)	Cash flow (€m)	Interest rate	δ	PV (€m)	Interest rate	δ	PV (€m)	PV01(€)
1	10	4.0%	0.9615	9.6154	3.99%	0.9616	9.6163	924.65
2	5	4.5%	0.9157	4.5786	4.49%	0.9159	4.5795	876.42
		Totals		14.1940			14.1958	1801.07

In the above example the approximation error from using (III.1.59) instead of exact valuation is only 0.01%. These approximations are clearly very accurate and they will prove useful later when we show how to perform a PV01 invariant cash flow mapping, in Section III.5.3.

III.1.8.3   Understanding Interest Rate Risk

Consider a cash flow of C_T dollars at time T. We know the present value of this cash flow today: it is just C_T dollars discounted to today using the appropriate discount rate, i.e. the spot zero coupon rate of maturity T. We also know its present value when we receive the cash at time T, as this requires no discounting. But at any time t between now and maturity, we do not know the present value exactly. There is an uncertainty on this future discounted value that depends on (a) how much the discount rate changes and (b) how sensitive the value is to changes in the discount rate. How do we assess these?

(a) The standard deviation of the discount rate represents the possible changes in the future discount rate, as seen from today. If σ denotes the volatility of this forward rate then, assuming changes in the forward rate are *independent and identically distributed*, we may use the square-root-of-time rule to find the t-period standard deviation of the forward rate as $\sigma_{t,T-t}\sqrt{t}$.[45]

---

[45] The square-root-of-time rule is explained in Section II.3.1.

(b) The best forecast of the appropriate discount rate at time t is the forward zero coupon rate $F_{t,T-t}$ starting at time t with tenor $T - t$. The expected discounted value at time t of the cash flow at time T is C_T dollars discounted by this forward rate. The sensitivity of this value at time t to movements in the forward rate is measured by the PV01 that is given (approximately) by (III.1.59) with maturity $T - t$, assuming T and t are integers, i.e.

$$PV01_{t,T} \approx 10^{-4} C_T \left(1 + F_{t,T-t}\right)^{-(T-t+1)} (T - t).$$

The interest rate risk of a cash flow of C_T dollars at time T refers to the uncertainty about the discounted value of this cash flow at some future time t. It can be measured by the standard deviation of this future discounted value, which is the product of (a) and (b) above. It is easier to express this assuming continuous compounding, since then for *any* values of T and t:

$$StDev(PV_t) \approx 10^{-4} \sigma_{t,T-t} \sqrt{t} \, (T - t) \, C_T \exp\left(-f_{t,T-t}(T - t)\right). \tag{III.1.63}$$

where $\sigma_{t,T-t}$ is the volatility of the continuously compounded forward rate, $f_{t,T-t}$.

EXAMPLE III.1.20: STANDARD DEVIATION OF FUTURE PV

The current zero-coupon forward rates, starting in m months and ending in 12 months, and their volatilities are as shown in Table III.1.19 for $m = 1, 2, \ldots, 11$. Calculate the discounted value in m months' time of a cash flow of £5 million received in 1 year. Also calculate the standard deviations of these discounted values.

Table III.1.19   Forward rates and their volatilities (in basis points)

m (months)	1	2	3	4	5	6	7	8	9	10	11
Forward rate (%)	4.70	4.75	4.80	4.85	4.80	4.85	4.80	4.75	4.70	4.65	4.60
Volatility (bps)	15	18	20	25	30	35	35	35	40	40	40

SOLUTION   The expected discounted values of the cash flow in m months time are calculated by discounting at the appropriate forward rate, given in the second row of Table III.1.19. For instance the expected discounted value of the cash flow in 3 months' time is $5 \times \exp(-0.048 \times 0.75) = £4.82$ million, since there are 9 months of discounting. The corresponding PV01 is calculated using the approximation (III.1.62) and this is shown in the third row of Table III.1.20. For instance:

PV01 of expected value in 3 months $= 100 \times 0.75 \times 5 \exp(-0.048 \times 0.75) = £362$.

Note that we multiply by 100 because the cash flow is measured in millions and the PV01 refers to a movement of one basis point. Now the standard deviation of the future discounted value of the cash flow is PV01 $\times \sigma \sqrt{t}$ where σ denotes the volatility of the forward rate. For instance:

Standard deviation of value in 3 months $= 362 \times 20 \times \sqrt{0.25} = £3617$.

Equivalently, to calculate the standard deviation directly we could have used (III.1.63) with $t = 1, 2, \ldots, 12$. Take care to multiply the result by 100 to obtain the correct units of measurement, as we did for the PV01. Either way, we obtain the standard deviations of the future discounted values that are shown in the last row of Table III.1.20.

Table III.1.20   Expectation and standard deviation of future PV

Time (months)	1	2	3	4	5	6	7	8	9	10	11
Expected value (£m)	4.79	4.81	4.82	4.84	4.86	4.88	4.90	4.92	4.94	4.96	4.98
PV01 (£)	439	400	362	323	284	244	204	164	124	83	42
StDev of value (£)	1901	2943	3617	4658	5492	6039	5459	4688	4280	3019	1509

In Figure III.1.10 we use $\pm 1.96 \times$ StDev to obtain approximate 95% confidence limits for the value of the cash flow in the future. Note that there is no uncertainty about the discounted values now, and when we receive the cash flow. But between now and the time that the cash flow is received (shown on the horizontal axis) there is an uncertainty that arises from possible changes in the discount rate that will apply in the future, when we calculate the cash flow's present value. This is interest rate risk.

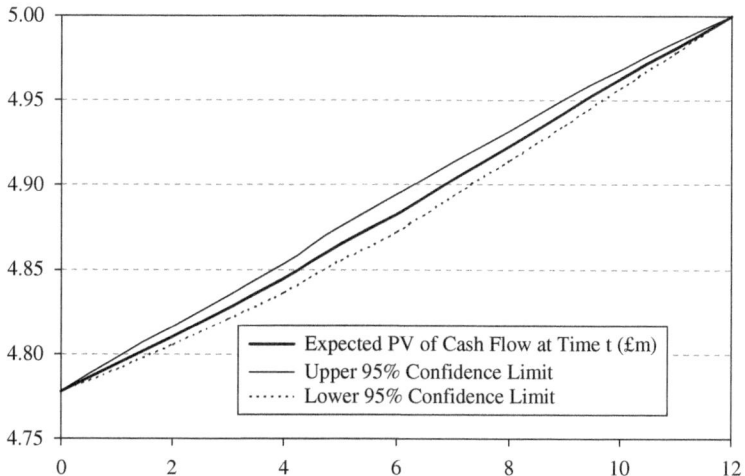

Figure III.1.10   Uncertainty about future values of a single cash flow

In general, the interest rate risk of a fixed income portfolio is the uncertainty about the discounted value of all the portfolio's future cash flows, where this value is measured at some future date – the *risk horizon*. The uncertainty arises from unpredictable movements in the discount rate between now and the risk horizon, i.e. we do not know exactly what the discounted value of the cash flows will be in the future, because we do not know what the discount rate will be at some future point in time.

Our perception of interest rate risk depends on whether the interest is fixed or floating and it also depends upon the accounting framework. Fixed income instruments are entered into the trading book at their mark-to-market value. Their interest rate risk depends on the evolution of discount rates, as explained above. But if entered into the banking book, where accrual accounting is applied, fixed income instruments are *not* marked to market. Cash flows are valued at the time of payment, so fixed income instruments have no interest rate risk in accrual accounting. On the other hand, floating rate instruments have virtually no interest rate risk in mark-to-market accounting, as we have shown in Section III.1.6.2. But they do have interest rate risk in accrual accounting, because the cash flow on any future payment date is uncertain.

Hence, the perceptions of interest rate risk of fixed and floating instruments differ depending on the accounting framework. In accrual accounting floaters are risky but fixed rates are not, whilst the opposite is true under mark-to-market accounting. It is this difference that drives the swap market.

III.1.9   YIELD CURVE FITTING

In this section we review the techniques that can be used to obtain a yield curve from the market prices of fixed income instruments such as short term discount bonds, FRAs and swaps. Section III.1.9.1 discusses the suitability of each type of instrument for yield curve fitting, and thereafter we focus on the influence that the chosen fitting technique has on the statistical properties of spot and forward interest rates. The simplest way to obtain a yield curve is to use a *bootstrap*. Section III.1.9.2 demonstrates how securities prices can be used to bootstrap the yield curve using a simple empirical example. The problem with bootstrapping is that even a small amount of noise in these securities prices can result in large spikes in the forward curve, especially at longer maturities. Therefore if the yield curve is to be used to make inferences on the volatility and correlation structure of interest rates it is better not to derive the yield curve using the bootstrap technique.

Sections III.1.9.3 and III.1.9.4 describes the semi-parametric and parametric models for yield curve fitting that are used by the Bank of England,[46] the European Central Bank[47] and the US Federal Reserve.[48] These techniques are also applied to the LIBOR market, as discussed in the comprehensive and excellent book by James and Webber (2000). LIBOR rates for a number of currencies are provided on the BBA CD-ROM.[49] The case study in Section III.1.9.5 demonstrates how the volatilities and correlations of forward LIBOR rates depend very much on whether we obtain the yield curve using natural splines, cubic splines or a parametric yield curve model.

III.1.9.1   Calibration Instruments

The US government short curve is obtained from the prices of Treasury bills, FRAs, swaps and liquid coupon bearing bonds in the AA rating category. The UK government curves are derived from UK government bonds (also called *gilts*), gilt sale and repurchase transactions (*gilt repos*), interbank loans, short sterling futures, FRAs and swaps. A LIBOR yield curve is usually constructed using a combination of spot LIBOR rates, FRAs, futures and swap rates. One would typically use the 1-month to 12-month LIBOR rates to estimate the short end of the curve. But LIBOR rates are not available for maturities longer than 1 year so other instruments with the same credit risk and liquidity as LIBOR rates need to be used for

---

[46] See http://www.bankofengland.co.uk/statistics/yieldcurve/index.htm.
[47] See http://www.ecb.int/stats/money/yc/html/index.en.html.
[48] See http://www.federalreserve.gov/releases/h15/update/.
[49] See http://www.bba.org.uk.

building the longer end of the LIBOR curve. To fit LIBOR rates in the medium and long range we could use interest rate futures, FRAs and/or swaps.

There are many combinations of bonds, futures, FRAs and swaps that can be used to construct a yield curve. Of course, if the data were perfect and markets were arbitrage free, the choice of instruments should not matter. However, given the inevitable noise in market data, the choice of securities *does* have an impact on the shape of the yield curve. We now discuss the relative advantages and disadvantages of using futures, FRAs and swaps for yield curve fitting.

Interest rate futures and FRAs typically cover a period up to 2 years. Both kinds of contracts enable an investor to lock in a rate of return between two dates and therefore provide information about the corresponding forward LIBOR rates. The main difference between these contracts is that the settlement on an FRA occurs at the contract maturity, while futures positions are marked to market on a daily basis, resulting in a stream of cash flows between the parties along the whole life of the contract. Since these cash flows are a function of the prevailing level of the LIBOR rate, futures provide *biased* information about forward rates. The bias results from the fact that the short party experiences a cash outflow in the event of an interest rate increase and a cash inflow in the event of a fall in interest rates. Therefore the short party will systematically seek financing when interest rates rise and invest the cash flows from marking to market as interest rates fall. The opposite is true about the long party on the futures contract. Thus the equilibrium futures price will be biased upward, in order to compensate the short party. The importance of the bias depends on the length of the contract and the LIBOR rate volatility expectations. Strictly speaking, one would need to use an interest derivative pricing model to value a futures contract. From this perspective, the use of futures as an input to a yield curve fitting model should be avoided.

Unlike futures, FRAs could be seen as instruments providing unbiased information about the forward LIBOR rates. However, the liquidity of FRAs is typically lower than that of the LIBOR rates and futures. Therefore, FRA quotes may be stale and fail to reflect the changes in the yield curve. Consequently, neither futures nor FRAs are ideal instruments to use for LIBOR yield curve estimation.

The information about the long end of the yield curve can be obtained from interest rate swaps, since these are liquid instruments that extend up to 30 years. For the purposes of yield curve fitting we decompose a swap into an exchange of a fixed coupon bond for a floating bond paying prevailing LIBOR rates.[50] At initiation the value of a swap is 0 and the value of a floater is equal to the notional, which means that the price of the fixed rate bond paying the swap rate must be 100 at the initiation of the swap. In other words, the swap rate can be regarded as a coupon rate on a par-coupon bond of a corresponding maturity, as shown in Section III.1.7.3.

III.1.9.2   Bootstrapping

Bootstrapping is the term we apply to an iterative coupon stripping technique, which is illustrated in the following example.[51]

---

[50] As explained in Section III.1.7.
[51] See Miron and Swannell (1991) for further details.

EXAMPLE III.1.21: COUPON STRIPPING

Calculate zero coupon rates from the market prices of four zero coupon bonds and two coupon bearing bonds shown in Table III.1.21.

Table III.1.21   Six bonds

Maturity	1 month	2 months	3 months	12 months	2 years	3 years
Coupon	0	0	0	0	6%	10%
Market price	99.5	99.1	98.7	95	101	112

SOLUTION   Dividing the price of a zero bond by 100 gives the discount factor and then putting $y_n = n^{-1}(\delta_n^{-1} - 1)$ when $n \le 1$, gives the zero coupon yields shown in Table III.1.22.

Table III.1.22   Bootstrapping zero coupon yields

Maturity	1 month	2 month	3 month	12 months	2 years	3 years
Coupon	0	0	0	0	6%	10%
Price	99.5	99.1	98.7	95	101	112
Discount factor	0.995	0.991	0.987	0.95	0.90	0.85
Zero coupon yield	6.03%	5.45%	5.27%	5.26%	5.46%	5.56%

This table also shows zero coupon yields for the 2-year and 3-year maturities. These are obtained via a bootstrapping procedure as follows:

1. The price, cash flows and discount factors on the 2-year bond are related as

$$101 = 6 \times \delta_1 + 106 \times \delta_2.$$

   We know δ_1 from the 12-month zero bond, so we can obtain δ_2.
2. Moving on to the 3-year bond, now we have

$$112 = 10 \times \delta_1 + 10 \times \delta_2 + 110 \times \delta_3$$

   which, knowing δ_1 and δ_2, gives δ_3.
3. Once we know the discount factors we can obtain the zero coupon yields, using

$$y_n = \delta_n^{-1/n} - 1$$

We can generalize the method used in the above example to state a general algorithm for bootstrapping a yield curve as follows:

1. Take a set of T liquid instruments.
2. Map the cash flows to a set of T standard maturities (see Section III.5.3).
3. Denote the mapped cash flows on the kth instrument by $\mathbf{c}_k = (C_{k1}, \ldots, C_{kT})'$ and let $\mathbf{C}$ be the $T \times T$ matrix of cash flows, with kth column $\mathbf{c}_k$.
4. Take the market price of each instrument and label the $T \times 1$ vector of market prices $\mathbf{p} = (P_1, P_2, \ldots, P_T)'$.

5. Denote the discount factor at maturity i by δ_i and let $\boldsymbol{\delta} = (\delta_1, \delta_2, \ldots, \delta_T)'$ be the $T \times 1$ vector of discount factor.
6. Then $\mathbf{p} = \mathbf{C}\boldsymbol{\delta}$ or equivalently, $\boldsymbol{\delta} = \mathbf{C}^{-1}\mathbf{p}$. Hence, the market prices and cash flows of the instruments together determine the discount factor.

This algorithm has two shortcomings:

- It is restricted to using the same number of instruments as maturities in the yield curve.
- We only obtain zero coupon yields at the same maturities as the instruments, so we cannot price instruments with other maturities.

The second problem, that we only obtain discount rates at maturities for which liquid instruments exist, can be solved by proceeding as follows:

7. Interpolate between the discount factors (e.g. using splines, as explained in the next subsection) to obtain discount rates for every maturity.
8. Obtain the zero coupon yield of any maturity n as described above.

But still the bootstrap has tendency to *overfit* the yield curve so any noise in the original data is translated into the bootstrapped forward rates. This often results in spikes in the forward curve, especially at longer maturities, which gives a misleading indication about the volatility and correlation structure of forward rates.

When fitting a yield curve we should take into account the market prices of *all* liquid instruments having the same credit rating as the curve, and typically there will be more than one instrument for each maturity. In practice, more instruments than maturities are used for yield curve construction. In that case the inverse cash flow matrix $\mathbf{C}^{-1}$ cannot be found exactly and instead of bootstrapping we must use a best fitting technique, such as minimizing the root mean square error (RMSE) between the prices based on the fitted curve and the market prices. We describe the two most popular yield curve fitting methods in the following subsections.

III.1.9.3 Splines

Spline-based yield curve techniques fit a curve to the data, and this curve is composed of many segments that can move almost independently between the fixed *knot points*, save for some constraints imposed to ensure that the overall curve is smooth. To limit the number of parameters used it is important to use a low order polynomial to model the curve between the knot points, hence the popularity of *cubic splines* which were first applied to yield curve fitting by McCulloch (1975). Cubic spline interpolation was introduced and applied to interpolate between interest rates of different maturities in Section I.5.3.3.[52]

Cubic splines may also be applied to fit a yield curve by fitting the corresponding discount factors, or by fitting the market prices of all securities in the calibration set. The discount factors are linear in the parameters and the calibration can be done by a simple regression where the objective is to minimize the weighted squared differences between the model prices of the securities in the calibration set and their market prices. However, the most straightforward spline fitting method, natural cubic splines, are commonly found to be numerically unstable.[53]

---

[52] See also Lancaster and Salkauskas (1986).
[53] See Anderson and Sleath (1999) for further details.

An alternative is to use *basis splines* (B-splines), as in Steely (1991), where each segment of the yield curve between the knot points $\{x_1, \ldots, x_m\}$ is built using a linear combination of some fundamental curves. To define these fundamental curves, which are called *basis functions*, we set:

$$B_{i,1}(\delta) = \begin{cases} 1, & \text{if } x_i \leq \delta < x_{i+1}, \\ 0, & \text{otherwise}, \end{cases}$$

for $i = 1, \ldots, m - 1$. Then the nth order basis functions, for $n = 2, 3, \ldots, N$, are obtained by setting

$$B_{i,n}(\delta) = \left(\frac{\delta - x_i}{x_{i+n-1} - x_i} \right) B_{i,n-1}(\delta) + \left(\frac{x_{i+n} - \delta}{x_{i+n} - x_{i+1}} \right) B_{i+1,n-1}(\delta), \tag{III.1.64}$$

where δ denotes the discount factor.

Clearly the order of the basis functions used to fit the curve between knot points can be smaller when there are many knot points than when there are only a few knot points. But as the number of knot point increases, the smoothness of the fitted yield curve will deteriorate. Hence, there is a trade-off between using enough knot points to ensure a good fit with low order basis functions and using so many knot points that the fitted curve is not smooth. However, it is possible to impose a roughness penalty on the optimization algorithm,[54] and our case study below demonstrates why this is essential.

III.1.9.4   Parametric Models

Introduced by Nelson and Siegel (1987) and later extended by Svensson (1994), parametric yield curve fitting models impose a functional form on the instantaneous forward rate curve that captures its typical 'humped' shape. The *Nelson and Siegel model* assumes that the instantaneous forward rate of maturity n is parameterized as

$$f(n; \beta_0, \beta_1, \beta_2, \tau) = \beta_0 + \left(\beta_1 + \beta_2 \left(-\frac{n}{\tau} \right) \right) \exp \left(-\frac{n}{\tau} \right). \tag{III.1.65}$$

The curve (III.1.65) has only one 'hump', which reflects the typical shape of the interest rate term structure. However, sometimes the term structure develops *two* humps, and in that case the parameterization (III.1.65) is too restrictive. The *Svensson model* has two additional parameters, which allow for an additional hump, with

$$f(n; \beta_0, \beta_1, \beta_2, \beta_3, \tau_1, \tau_2) = \beta_0 + \left(\beta_1 + \beta_2 \left(-\frac{n}{\tau_1} \right) \right) \exp \left(-\frac{n}{\tau_1} \right)$$
$$+ \beta_3 \left(-\frac{n}{\tau_2} \right) \exp \left(-\frac{n}{\tau_2} \right). \tag{III.1.66}$$

In both (III.1.65) and (III.1.66) the short rate is $\beta_0 + \beta_1$ and the curve is asymptotic to β_0 at the long end. The discount factors are non-linear in the parameters and the model calibration requires a non-linear least squares algorithm. In the case study below we have used the Levenberg–Marquardt algorithm, described in Section I.5.4.1, with the objective of minimizing the sum of the squared differences between the model and the market prices of the instrument calibration set.

---

[54] See Fisher et al. (1995), Waggoner (1997) and Anderson and Sleath (1999).

The Federal Reserve Board has made available to the public the entire US Treasury yield curve from 1961.[55] The spot curve is estimated daily using the Svensson model, and spot and forward rates, monthly up to 30 months, are provided. The Excel spreadsheet also gives the Svensson parameter estimates for each day so that users can infer rates of any maturities from the key rates at monthly maturities.

III.1.9.5   Case Study: Statistical Properties of Forward LIBOR Rates[56]

In this study we compare the applications of B-splines and the Svensson model, for calibration of the UK LIBOR yield curve. Both yield curve fitting models were applied to 703 daily observations on UK LIBOR rates, FRAs and swap rates between October 1999 and June 2002[57]. For each day all the available market instruments were used to build the discount curve and the associated spot curve. These were then used to obtain model LIBOR rates, FRAs and swap rates. The model rates were then compared to the market data to obtain the RMSE.

Figures III.1.11 and III.1.12 compare the yield curves calibrated using the two procedures. There are noticeable differences between the two curves, especially at the long end and especially when rates are volatile (for instance, during the last 6 months of 2001). At the short end, where LIBOR rates are observed in the market, the differences are usually tiny and of the order of 5–10 basis points, but at the very long end where the market instruments consist of only a few long term swaps, the differences can exceed 50 basis points at times, as shown in Figure III.1.13.

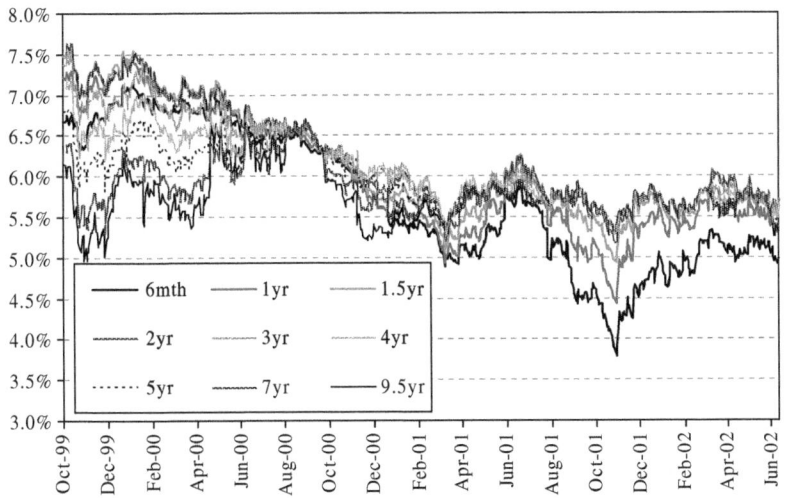

Figure III.1.11   UK LIBOR curve (Svensson model)

[55] See Gurkaynak et al. (2006) and http://www.federalreserve.gov/pubs/feds/2006/200628/200628abs.html.
[56] Many thanks to my PhD student Dmitri Lvov for providing these results.
[57] The following contracts were used: 1-month to 12-month LIBOR rates; 3-month FRAs starting in 2, 3, . . . , 9 months; 6-month FRAs starting in 1, 2, . . . , 6, 12 and 18 months; 9-month FRA starting in 1 month; 12-month FRAs starting in 2, 3, 6, 9 and 12 months; and swap contracts maturing in 2, 3, . . . , 10 years.

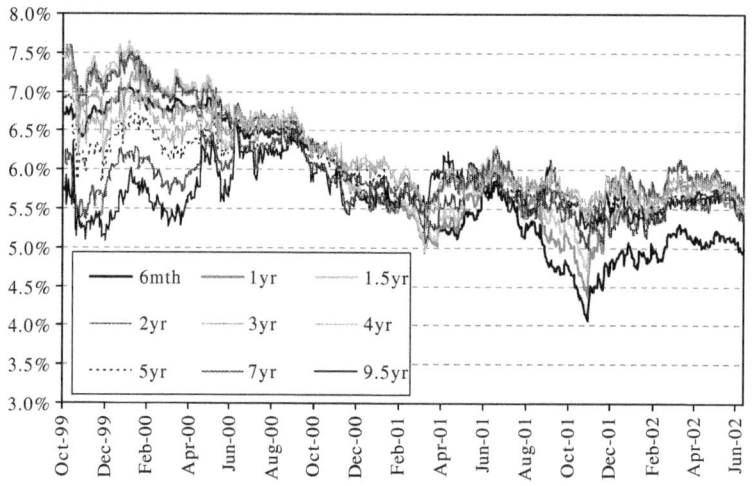

Figure III.1.12   UK LIBOR curve (B-splines)

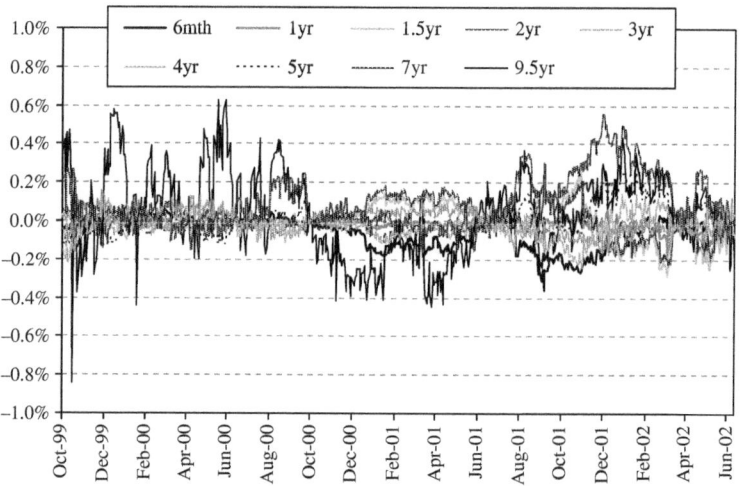

Figure III.1.13   Difference between Svensson rates and B-spline rates

Comparison of the Models' Goodness of Fit

The average RMSE over the entire sample period were very similar: 2.59 for the B-spline and 2.55 for the Svensson model. However, the time series plots of these RMSEs reveal some interesting characteristics. Figure III.1.14 compares the RMSE obtained from the two models for every day during the sample.[58] The lowest errors occurred during the year

---

[58] We tested several different B-spline and natural cubic spline procedures with different choices of knot points. When the knot points were the same, all splines on discount factors produced virtually identical RMSE on every day during the sample. So henceforth we present results for the B-spline on discount factors, and the optimal choice of knots had several at the medium to long maturity.

2000 and greater errors were experienced during the latter half of 2001, when interest rates were unusually volatile, especially using the Svensson model. In view of this time variation it is difficult to draw general conclusions about the relative performance of in-sample fit from the two yield curve fitting procedures. However, further information can be obtained from the historical volatilities and correlations of daily changes in log forward LIBOR rates, as these differ considerably depending on the choice of the technique used to fit the yield curve.

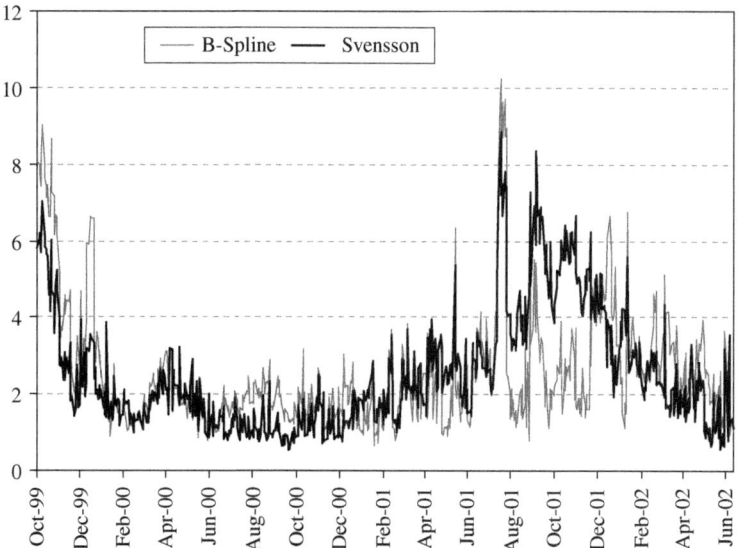

Figure III.1.14   RMSE errors from the model calibrations

The Influence of Yield Curve Model on Forward Rate Volatilities

In the LIBOR model forward rates are usually assumed to follow correlated *geometric* processes and so we estimate historical forward rate volatilities using log returns, not changes in forward rates.[59] Figure III.1.15 depicts the historical forward rate volatility term structures estimated using the entire sample based on the two yield curve models.

The implied volatilities of forward rates that are backed out from cap prices often display a hump shape, with maximum volatility usually lying somewhere between the 1- and 2-year maturities. So the empirical evidence on historical forward rates does not appear to support traders' views on interest rates at all. The short maturity forward rates tend to be *less* volatile than long maturity rates. However, to a large extent this is due to the presence of measurement errors, which are greater for longer maturity rates since one observes relatively few data points, and these measurement errors are compounded when spot rates are translated into discrete forward rates. The net result is an increasing volatility of forward rates with respect to maturity.

---

[59] See Section III.3.8.5 for further details about the LIBOR model.

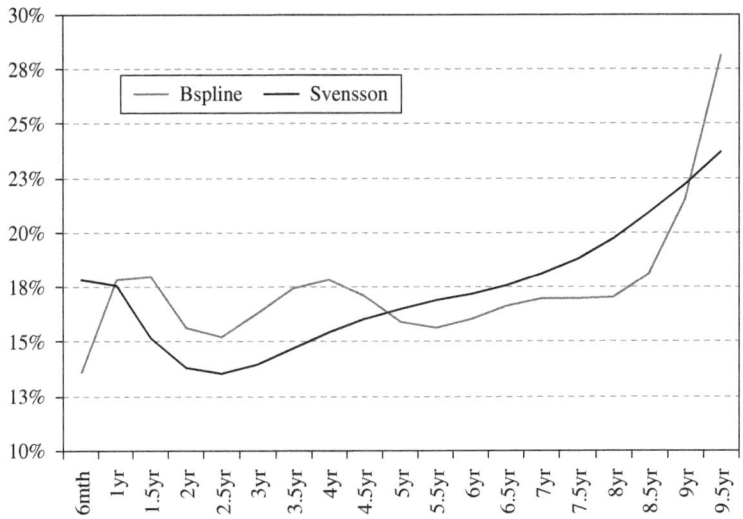

Figure III.1.15 Forward rate volatility estimates based on B-splines and Svensson

The forward rates have different volatility characteristics depending on the yield curve fitting model used.

- The Svensson forward rate volatilities are influenced by the quality of fit of a two-hump parametric form. Further analysis that the reader may wish to apply using the data in the case study work book shows that the Svensson model produced highly volatile long rates at the end of 2001, when the goodness-of-fit statistics implied that the Svensson model was giving the worst in-sample fit.
- The B-spline forward rate volatilities are constrained to be lower at the knot points (in order to maximize the goodness of fit, several knots were placed between the 5-year and 8-year maturities). Although the McCulloch natural spline volatilities are not shown, they have similar characteristics to the B-spline volatilities, again being dominated by the choice of knot points.

The Influence of Yield Curve Fitting on Forward Rate Correlations

The correlation structure of the semi-annual forward rates obtained from the Svensson model is related to the functional form imposed on the instantaneous forward rates. The 'hump' shape of the Svensson forward rate curve induces correlations between short and long maturity forward rates that can be higher than correlations between medium and long maturity forward rates. Forward rate correlations do not necessarily decrease monotonically with the maturity spread, nevertheless the Svensson model imposes exactly this sort of smooth pattern on the forward rate correlations. The empirical correlations between Svensson semi-annual forward rates of different maturities are shown in Figure III.1.16 based on equal weighting over the entire sample period. The empirical correlations have a less structured pattern when the yield curve is fitted using a spline model, and the B-spline correlations are shown in Figures III.1.17. Here, correlations are distorted and very much depend on the knot points chosen.

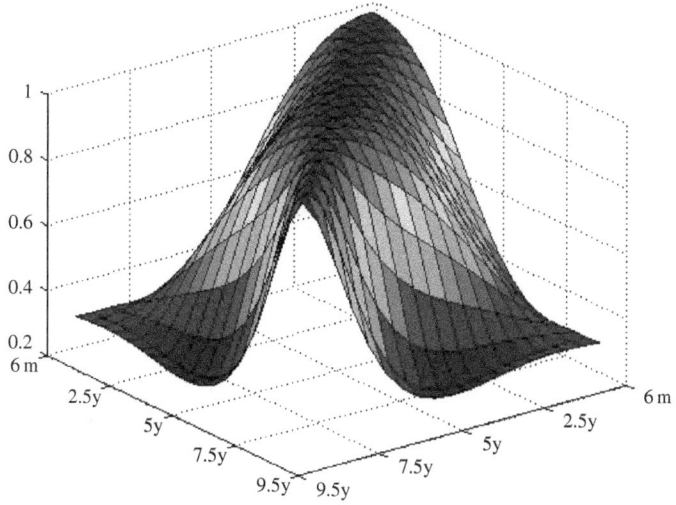

Figure III.1.16 Forward rate correlation estimates (Svensson model). (See Plate 1)

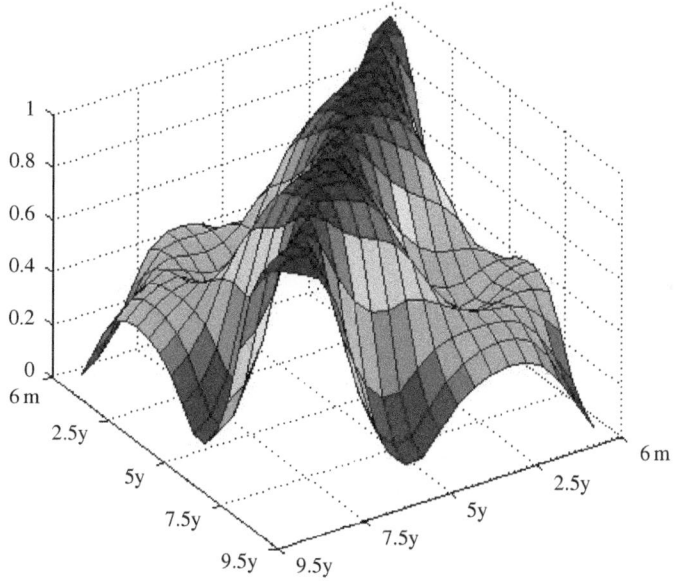

Figure III.1.17 Forward rate correlation estimates (B-spline model). (See Plate 2)

Comparison with Bank of England Forward Rate Curves

Daily and monthly data on UK government and commercial liability yield curves for maturities between 6 months and 25 years, and the short curve for monthly maturities from 1 month to 5 years are available from the Bank of England.[60] The curves are fitted using a cubic B-spline algorithm with robustness penalty, as explained in Anderson and Sleath (1999).

---

[60] See http://www.bankofengland.co.uk/statistics/yieldcurve/index.htm

The robustness penalty has the effect of smoothing the curve between the knot points, thus reducing the possibility for ill-behaved volatilities and correlations such as those obtained above from the B-spline procedure. The short forward curve, which contains 60 monthly maturities up to 5 years, is very well behaved: the forward rate volatilities exhibit a humped shape and the forward rate correlations are very smooth. However the entire forward curve, containing semi-annual rates up to 25 years, still has quite a rough volatility and correlation structure, despite the smoothing in their algorithm.

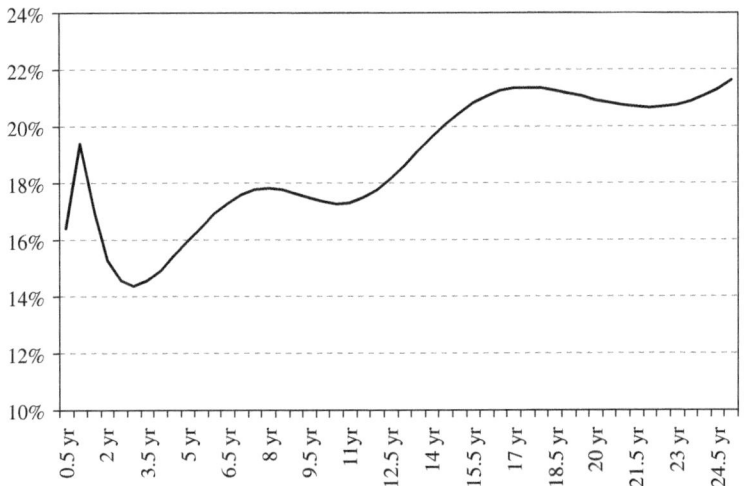

Figure III.1.18   Bank of England forward curve – volatilities

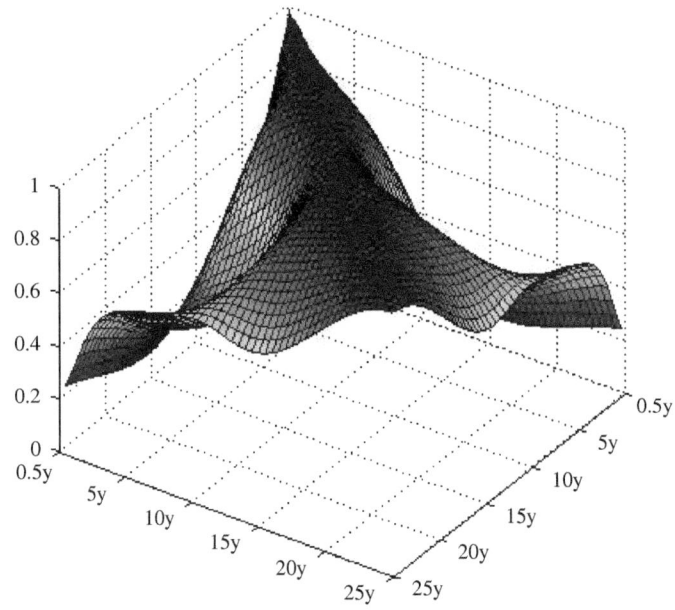

Figure III.1.19   Bank of England forward curve – correlations. (See Plate 3)

For instance, Figures III.1.18 and III.1.19 show the term structure of forward rate volatilities and correlations respectively, based on daily log returns over the period January 2005 to September 2007. As before the volatilities and correlations are based on equally weighted averages of returns and cross products over the entire sample. The robustness penalty does provide some smoothing, but the irregular features in volatility and correlation that result from the use of a B-spline are still apparent.

Conclusions

Goodness-of-fit criteria are inconclusive as to the best fitting yield curve model because this varies over time. We have presented some empirical evidence indicating that B-splines may fit better during volatile periods, but otherwise the Svensson model provides a very close fit. The important learning point to take away from this study is that forward rate volatilities and correlations inherit their structure from the yield curve fitting model: the Svensson forward rate volatilities and correlations are the best behaved since their structure is determined by the exponential functional form of the model; by contrast, in spline methods, volatilities and correlations are distorted by the choice of knot points.

Whilst implied forward rate volatilities that are backed out from the market prices of caps often exhibit a humped shape, we have found no empirical support for hump-shaped volatility term structures in historical forward rates, except at the very short term where the rates are anyway observed in the market. The lack of liquid market instruments of medium to long maturities introduces significant measurement error in calibrated forward rates, so that historical volatilities increase with maturity whatever yield curve fitting model is applied.

Likewise, when historical forward rate correlations are used to calibrate the lognormal forward rate model, their correlation matrix is usually assumed to have a simple parameterization where correlation decreases monotonically with the maturity gap between the futures.[61] Such a parameterization is more appropriate for forward rate correlations that are derived from the Svensson yield curves than those derived from B-spline fitting procedures, since the choice of knot points has a marked effect on forward rate correlations when the yield curve is fitted using spline functions.

III.1.10   CONVERTIBLE BONDS

Convertible bonds are hybrid derivative instruments that simultaneously offer the potential upside of equities and a limited downside, since the investor holds a bond. The pay-off to holding a convertible bond is asymmetric, in that the increase in the bond's value corresponding to an increase in the stock price is greater than the decrease in the bond's value corresponding to an equivalent decrease in the stock price. Another reason why convertible bonds offer attractive investment opportunities is their inherent diversification. A convertible bond offers exposure to equity volatility as well as to equities, interest rates and credit spreads. This diversification benefit is significant since volatility is negatively correlated with share prices and credit spreads, especially during periods of market crisis. Thus convertible

---

[61] See Alexander (2003).

bonds are a growing asset class and at the time of writing the global market has an estimated notional size of over \$613 billion.[62] Over half of this is in US bonds, over \$150 billion is in European bonds and \$62 billion is in Japanese bonds.

III.1.10.1   Characteristics of Convertible Bonds

The purchaser of a convertible bond has the option to convert it into shares in the same company, usually after a certain *lock-in period*.[63] The *conversion ratio* is

$$\text{Conversion ratio} = \frac{\text{Face value of bond}}{\text{Conversion price of share}}. \qquad (\text{III.1.67})$$

For instance, if the face value is \$1000 and the conversion price of the share is \$50 then the conversion ratio is 20. That is, 20 shares are received for each bond redeemed. Often, but not always, the conversion ratio is fixed at the time the bond is issued.

The decision whether to convert depends on the conversion ratio, the current prices of the bond and the share and the credit risk of the issuer. Convertible bonds carry a significant credit risk for two reasons. First, they are often issued by growth firms, i.e. firms that may not have a high credit rating but whose share prices are thought likely to rise in the future. These firms can issue a convertible bond with a relatively low coupon, thus limiting their payments, but the conversion option still makes them attractive to investors. Secondly, convertible bonds are frequently classed as junior or subordinated debt.

The conversion feature provides a floor for the bond price, which varies with the stock price. For example, suppose a bond with face value \$1000 may be converted at any time to 20 shares, and that the stock is currently trading at a price of \$52.50. Then the value of the bond cannot be less than \$52.50 × 20 = \$1050 so the price of the bond cannot fall below 105 at this time.

Most convertibles have a *put feature* whereby the bond holder has the right to return the bond to the issuer at a fixed *put price*, which is usually well below par. This provides a fixed floor for the price of the convertible, which does not vary over time. For instance, if the put price of the above convertible is 85, then the price can never fall below 85 (otherwise the bond holders would put the bond back to the issuer). Similarly, most convertibles are also *callable* by the issuer on certain dates, at which times the issuer has a right to buy back the convertible at a given *call price* which is usually well above par.[64] This price provides a fixed cap on the bond price. For instance, if the call price is 125 then the bond price can never exceed this, otherwise the issuer would call the bond. If a convertible is called the bond holder is usually given a *call notice period* of between 15 days and several months during which the bond holder can elect to convert at any time.

Call features are attractive to issuers for several reasons: they cap investors' profits from a rise in share price; they lessen the uncertainty about issuers' future liabilities; and they are a means to force conversion, typically when the firm can refinance at a cheaper rate. On the other hand, call features make the bond less attractive to prospective investors. For this reason the contract usually specifies that the bond is not callable for the first few years

---

[62] See www.ubs.com/2/e/us_library/gis/white_papers/Benefits_of_Convertible_Bonds.pdf.
[63] For instance, a 10-year convertible bond may only be convertible after 5 years. And some bonds are only convertible on specific *conversion dates*.
[64] The effective call price is the clean call price, which is fixed in the bond's covenant, plus accrued interest.

after issue (the *hard call protection* period) and following this there may also be *soft call protection*, where the bond can only be called if the share price exceeds a certain threshold that is typically significantly greater than the call price. Another form of soft call protection is a *make-whole provision*.[65] Call protection is designed to increase the attraction of the bond to investors.

According to Grimwood and Hodges (2002), the most common type of US convertible bond contract in the MTS database at the ICMA Centre has a maturity of 15.0 years, pays a 6% semi-annual coupon and is hard-callable for the first time within 3 years. Of these contracts, 72% have a hard no-call period, and 53% have a put clause. There are many Japanese convertibles in the database, of which 88% have a hard no-call period, 91% have a soft no-call period, 23% have a put clause, 78% are cross-currency and 56% have a conversion ratio re-fix clause.

III.1.10.2   Survey of Pricing Models for Convertible Bonds

The option to convert into shares creates a premium for convertibles, so that the price of a convertible bond is never less than the equivalent straight bond price. But the price of a convertible bond is very difficult to calculate because it depends on so many factors other than interest rates and credit spreads. The price also depends on the conversion ratio, the probability of default, the recovery rate, the stock price behaviour in the event of default, and the dynamics of the stock price. Of all these highly uncertain quantities the stock price dynamics and default behaviour are perhaps the most important.[66]

With so many uncertain factors affecting the price of a convertible bond, the pricing of these securities has been the subject of considerable academic research. Ingersoll (1977a) derived a closed-form pricing formula for callable convertible bonds but this is based on very simple assumptions about the evolution of the risk factors and can only be applied to bonds having very simple features. McConnell and Schwartz (1986) observed that when the stock price is modelled as a diffusion the discount rate must be adjusted, otherwise there is no possibility of default. This observation inspired several *blended discount* approaches to convertible bond valuation. Notably, Derman (1994) considered a stock price binomial tree where the discount rate at each time step is a weighted average of the risky discount rate and the risk free rate, with weight determined by the probability of conversion. In this framework the default event is not explicitly modelled; however, compensation for credit risk is included through a credit-adjusted discount rate.

One of the most important papers, by Tsiveriotis and Fernandes (1998), provided a rigorous treatment of Derman's ideas by splitting the bond value into equity and bond components, each discounted at different rates. This approach has since been extended to include interest rate and foreign exchange risk factors by Landskroner and Raviv (2003a, 2003b), who applied a blended discount model to price domestic and cross-currency inflation-linked convertible bonds.

All these papers assume that the stock price will not jump if the issuer announces that it is bankrupt, which is of course rather unrealistic. The most recent convertible bond valuation models developed by Davis and Lischka (1999), Takahashi et al. (2001), Ayache et al. (2003), Bermudez and Webber (2003) and Andersen and Buffum (2004) include a stock

---

[65] For instance, if a call is made between coupon payments then the accrued interest on the coupon will be paid to the bond holder.
[66] See Grimwood and Hodges (2002).

price jump on default. Most of these models incorporate *equity-linked hazard rates* that are driven by the stock price diffusion and are calibrated to the initial term structure of interest rates, often via the Hull and White (1990) model.

Some of the most interesting research on convertible bonds seeks to explain the issuer's call policy after the call protection period. During the call notice period the issuer effectively gives the investor a put on the share. Thus the optimal call price (i.e. the share price at which it becomes optimal for the issuer to call) should be such that the conversion price is just greater than the effective call price plus the premium on the put. However, it is quite possible that the stock price will decline during the call notice period and the investors will choose to receive the cash instead of converting. Since the issuer typically calls because it wants to give out stock, it will call only when the stock is very far above the effective call price. Thus issuers often wait until the conversion price is significantly higher than the optimal call price before issuing the call.

Many reasons have been proposed for this *delayed call* phenomenon. These include stock price uncertainty during the call notice period and the issuer's aversion to a sharp stock price decline (Ingersoll, 1977b; Butler, 2002; Asquith, 1995; Altintiğ and Butler, 2005; Grau et al., 2003); the preferential tax treatment of coupons over dividends, which acts as an incentive to keep the convertible bonds alive (Constantinides and Grundy, 1987; Campbell et al., 1991; Asquith and Mullins, 1991; Asquith, 1995); signalling effects, whereby convertible bonds calls convey adverse information to shareholders that management expects the share price to fall (Harris and Raviv, 1985; Mikkelson, 1985); and issuers preferring to let sleeping investors lie (Dunn and Eades, 1984; Constantinides and Grundy, 1987).

Although the stock price dynamics are more important for the bond valuation than those of the interest rate or credit spread, relatively few papers incorporate realistic stock price dynamics into the pricing model. Most of the literature on convertible bond valuation assumes that equity volatility is constant. An exception is Yigitbaşioğlu and Alexander (2006) who obtain arbitrage-free price bounds and hedge ratios for convertible bonds when there is uncertainty about the long term stock volatility. Their results also explain the delayed call feature of issuer's call policies.

III.1.11   SUMMARY AND CONCLUSIONS

This chapter introduces the theory and practice of pricing, hedging and trading standard interest rate sensitive instruments. Only a basic knowledge of finance is assumed, and although the treatment is concise several numerical examples and empirical studies have been provided, with accompanying interactive Excel spreadsheets on the website.

We began by introducing the fundamental concepts of *discrete compounding* and *continuous compounding* of interest. International bond and money markets use different *day count conventions* for accruing interest under discrete compounding, and so banks usually convert all discretely compounded rates to equivalent continuously compounded rates, which are easier to deal with mathematically. *Spot* interest rates are those that apply from now, and *forward* interest rates apply from some time in the future. Given a curve of spot interest rates of different maturities, we can find the corresponding forward rate curve; conversely, given a forward rate curve and the one-period spot rate, we can find the spot rate of other maturities. The standard reference curve for spot and forward rates is the London Interbank Offered Rate or LIBOR curve.

Bonds may be categorized by maturity, coupon and type of issuer. Bonds are issued by financial institutions, governments, government agencies, municipalities and corporates. Almost all bonds have a credit rating which corresponds to the perceived probability that the issuer will default on its debt repayments. Bonds are further categorized by the priority of their claim on the assets in the event of the issuer's default, and according to the domicile of the issuer. The majority of bonds pay a *fixed coupon*, but some bonds, called *floating rate notes* or *floaters*, have a variable coupon based on a reference rate such as LIBOR. In addition to straight floaters we have reverse floaters, capped floaters, floored floaters and many other floaters that can have complex option-like features. Bonds are further divided into *short, medium and long term* bonds and those that have less than 2 years to expiry at issue are generally regarded as *money market* instruments. Most of these pay no coupons, but are priced at a discount to their *par value* of 100. Very few bonds pay no coupon but the yields on hypothetical zero coupon bonds are used as *market interest rates* for different credit ratings.

The prices of liquid bonds are set by supply and demand, and their fair prices correspond to the present value of all the cash flows on the bond when discounted using market interest rates. Given *any* set of positive cash flows we can define a unique yield as the constant discount rate that, when applied to these cash flows, gives the market price of the bond. The price of a bond has a convex, decreasing relationship with the yield, and when the yield is equal to the coupon the bond is priced at par.

The *Macaulay duration* is the time-weighted average of the present value of the cash flows on the bond and, under continuous compounding, the Macaulay duration is also the first order sensitivity of the bond price to a unit change in its yield. Under discrete compounding this sensitivity is called the *modified duration*. We can use a second order Taylor expansion, the *duration–convexity approximation*, to approximate the change in present value of the cash flows when the yield changes by a small amount. When expressed in nominal terms we call these sensitivities the *value duration* and *value convexity*. Value durations can be added to obtain a single duration measure for a bond portfolio, which represents the change in portfolio value when all the bond yields change by the *same* amount. Similarly, value convexity is also additive over all bonds in the portfolio.

Floating rate notes have very short duration. Thus by adding long or short positions in floaters, bond traders can easily adjust the duration of their bond portfolios. But the problem with duration and convexity hedging, where a bond portfolio is constructed having zero value duration and zero value convexity, is that it only hedges against *parallel* movements of the zero coupon yield curve. It does not hedge the portfolio against the most common movements in the yield curve, based on historical data. For this we need to base bond portfolio immunization on *principal component analysis*.

A *forward rate agreement* is an OTC agreement to buy or sell a forward interest rate. In a standard *interest rate swap* one party pays LIBOR and receives a fixed rate, the swap rate, from the other party over an agreed period. This may be regarded as a sequence of forward rate agreements. A *vanilla swap* is a swap where the floating payments at the end of a certain period depend only on the interest rate prevailing over that period. We can decompose the cash flows on a vanilla swap into two series: the fixed leg of a vanilla swap can be regarded as a bond with coupon equal to the swap rate and the floating leg can be regarded as a single cash flow at the first payment date.

A *basis swap* is an interest rate swap where two floating rates are exchanged on each payment date. These floating rates may be of different maturities, or they may be denominated in different currencies. Unlike interest rates swaps, a *cross-currency basis swap* involves exchanges of principal. It can be regarded as two floating rate notes in different currencies. Another popular type of swap is a *total return swap*, in which two parties exchange returns on one asset for returns on another, including the capital gains or losses at every payment. Many other non-standard interest rate swaps are traded.

It is not possible to calculate the yield or duration of a swap. However, the *present value of a basis point* (PV01) applies to all types of cash flows. The PV01 is the sensitivity of the present value of the cash flow to a shift of one basis point in market interest rates. That is, the whole zero coupon yield curve shifts parallel by one basis point. The PV01 should be distinguished from the value duration, which measures the price sensitivity when the yields on all the bonds in the portfolio change by the same amount. The *interest rate risk* of a cash flow refers to the uncertainty about the discounted value of this cash flow at some future time t. It can be measured by the standard deviation of this future discounted value. This is the product of the standard deviation of the discount rate, in basis points,' and the interest rate sensitivity of the expected discounted value of the cash flow at time t, which is approximately equal to its PV01. Hence, at time t the interest rate risk of a cash flow at time T is approximately equal to the PV01 of the cash flow times the standard deviation of the forward rate of term t and tenor $T-t$.

We have reviewed the *yield curve fitting* techniques that can be used to obtain a zero coupon yield curve from the market prices of fixed income instruments. We discussed the suitability of each type of instrument for yield curve fitting, and focused on the influence that the chosen fitting technique has on the statistical properties of spot and forward interest rates. A case study compared the application of *basis splines* with the *Svensson model* for the calibration of the UK LIBOR yield curve. We showed that forward rate volatilities and correlations inherit their structure from the yield curve fitting model: the Svensson forward rate volatilities and correlations are the best behaved since their structure is determined by the exponential functional form of the model; by contrast, in spline methods, volatilities and correlations are mainly determined by the choice of knot points, even after imposing a roughness penalty.

Convertible bonds are hybrid derivative instruments that simultaneously offer the potential upside of equities and a limited downside since the investor holds a bond. A convertible bond offers exposure to equity volatility as well as to equities, interest rates and credit spreads. Most convertible bonds have *call features* that protect the issuer, but call protection policies and *put features* increase their attraction for investors. The price of a convertible bond is very difficult to calculate because it depends on so many factors other than interest rates and credit spreads. Perhaps the most important risk factors for convertible bonds are the stock price dynamics and the stock price behaviour in the event of an issuer default. We concluded the chapter with a survey of the very considerable academic literature on pricing models for convertible bonds.

III.2

Futures and Forwards

III.2.1 INTRODUCTION

A futures contract is an agreement to buy an underlying asset (or an interest rate) at a fixed date in the future, called the contract's *expiry date*, at a price agreed now. Futures are exchange traded contracts, so they have virtually no credit risk, and bid and ask market prices for a futures contract are quoted by market makers every few seconds throughout the trading day.[1] The buyer pays only a fraction of the contract price – the *margin* – and this is rebalanced daily as the futures price changes. At the time of expiry the futures price is equal to the spot price.[2]

The vast majority of futures contracts are on *notional bonds* such as the 2-, 5-, 10-year and long bond futures. Most of these are in the US, Europe and Japan. There are also some heavily traded futures contracts on money market interest rates, such as the 3-month eurodollar, eurosterling and EURIBOR contracts. The Bank for International Settlements (BIS) estimates that in June 2007 the notional size of the global bond and interest rate futures market was over $30 trillion. The BIS estimates for other futures contracts in December 2006 were: over $3 trillion on commodities; over $1 trillion on stock index futures; $200 billion on foreign exchange rates; and only a small amount in single stock futures. The total global turnover of futures contracts during 2006 was over $1,250 billion.[3]

A *forward* contract is essentially the same as a futures contract except that it is traded over the counter (OTC) and requires no margining. The only costs associated with trading forwards are transactions costs.[4] Since forward contracts are virtually costless to enter they must represent a *fair bet*. That is, if any investor expects the price of a forward contract to increase he will buy the forward. Likewise if any investor expects the price of a forward contract to decrease he will sell the forward. The price of any liquid instrument is fixed by balancing investors' supply and demand. Hence, there is never any reason to expect that the market price of a forward contract will change tomorrow, or at any other time in future. Put into technical terms, this means that every forward contract is a *martingale*.[5] We often assume the same about futures, even though there are small margin costs associated with trading them.

Whilst futures contracts tend to have a fixed expiry date, such as the third Friday of the month, most liquid forwards are traded at fixed *maturities,* such as 1 month, 2 months,

---

[1] The *ask price* or *offer price* is the price a dealer quotes when selling the contract, and the *bid price* is the price he is prepared to pay when buying the contract.
[2] The *spot price* or *cash price* of an asset is the price for immediate delivery.
[3] See the Statistical Annex to the *BIS Quarterly Review*, available from http://www.bis.org/statistics/extderiv.htm.
[4] *Transactions costs* are determined by the *bid–ask spread* (also called the *bid–offer spread*). This is the difference between the bid price and the ask or offer price. Generally speaking, the more liquid the market, the narrower the bid–ask spread. Transactions costs also include any brokers' fees and commissions.
[5] A *martingale* is a stochastic process in which the discounted expectation of any future value is the value today.

and so on. There is much more trading on forwards than on futures.[6] BIS estimates for the notional size of the global OTC markets in December 2006 were: $230 trillion on interest rate swaps; almost $20 trillion on foreign exchange forwards and forex swaps; over $18 trillion in FRAs; over $10 trillion in currency swaps; over $7 trillion in equity-linked forwards and swaps; and almost $3 trillion in commodity forwards and swaps.

There is a long history of forward trading in agricultural commodities, with farmers seeking to hedge their risks by fixing in advance the price they obtain for their crop. The first forward contract dates back to the seventeenth century, where the price of rice for future delivery was fixed in Japan. But it was not until the nineteenth century that forward contracts evolved into futures contracts, becoming standardized and traded on exchanges. At the beginning futures were bought and sold by *open outcry* on the trading floor. But gradually futures exchanges are replacing the trading floor with an *electronic trading system*. These are believed to be faster, more accurate and cheaper than broker-dealer trading, so transactions costs are reduced and liquidity is increased.

Increased liquidity has the effect of reducing the *basis*, i.e. the difference between the market prices of the spot and the futures contract. There will always be a difference between the spot price and futures price, or between the spot price and the forward price, before expiry. This is because holders of the spot contract receive dividends if the contract is for a stock index or stock, or coupons if the contract is for a bond, and pay transportation, insurance or storage costs (collectively termed *carry costs*) if the contract is for a commodity. However, the holder of a forward or futures contract receives none of the benefits and incurs none of the costs associated with the spot contract. At expiry of the forward or futures contract the price quoted is the price for delivery now, so it is equal to the spot price by definition. But prior to expiry the basis is not zero, except by chance.

Usually the futures contract is more liquid than the spot. Indeed, the spot contract is not even a traded instrument in the case of bond futures, volatility futures and weather futures. Even when the spot contract can be traded it is often relatively illiquid compared with the futures. For instance, it used to be relatively difficult to trade on a stock index because all the stocks in the index had to be traded in the same proportion as the index.[7] By contrast, index futures are very easy to trade. Futures can be sold short, traded on margin and, most importantly, by trading *notional* futures as we do for bonds we avoid squeezing the market, because many different underlying contracts[8] can be delivered against a notional futures contracts.

Players in futures and forward markets can be divided into two types: the *hedgers* use futures to hedge their existing risk, and they pass it on to the *speculators* who are happy to accept the risk in the hope that they will make abnormally large returns. With so much speculative trading, and with futures prices often playing the dominant price-discovery role, exchanges see the benefit of limiting the amount of speculative trading that can occur in any one day. For this reason they set daily limits on the change in the futures price. If the price change reaches that limit, trading stops for the remainder of the day.

There are many detailed conventions that apply to different markets, but these will not be addressed in this chapter. Our purpose here is to introduce the important concepts

---

[6] As you can see from the BIS figures, most forward contracts take the form of forward rates agreements (FRAs) or swaps, which may be regarded as a sequence of FRAs. An FRA is an OTC agreement to buy or sell a forward interest rate. See Section III.1.7.

[7] This was before the launch of i-shares and index exchange traded funds, both of which trade like shares on the index.

[8] We often refer to the underlying contract simply as the *underlying*.

for pricing and hedging with futures and forwards that are essential for the market risk analysis of these positions. Section III.2.2 begins with a description of the different types of futures and forwards markets. We explain the individual characteristics of the futures and forward markets in interest rates, bonds, currencies, commodities, stocks, stock indices, exchange traded funds, volatility indices, credit spreads, weather, real estate and pollution.

The next two sections deal with the pricing of futures and forwards. First we derive a fundamental no arbitrage relationship that determines the *theoretical value* (also called the *fair value*) of a forward contract. In Section III.2.3 we focus on the relationship between the market price of the spot and the fair value of the forward or futures contract.[9] A general treatment of the no arbitrage pricing relationship is followed by examples of this relationship for different types of underlying. We shall explain how dividends, coupons, interest rate differentials, carry costs and convenience yields determine the difference between the market price of the spot and the fair value of the futures or forward. The empirical behaviour of the market prices of futures on different types of underlying is examined in Section III.2.4. Here we analyse the components of *basis risk*, i.e. the uncertainty associated with the difference between market prices of spot and futures. The ability to trade the spot reduces basis risk and so commodities, where it is not possible to short the spot, or instruments whose spot cannot be traded at all, such as temperature, typically have the greatest basis risk.

The rest of the chapter describes how to hedge different positions using futures or forward contracts. The theoretical results on hedging with futures or forwards are derived in Section III.2.5, and we also illustrate these with some simple numerical examples. The *mean–variance* approach to hedging, which assumes that hedgers have a speculative element to their behaviour, is contrasted with the traditional 'insurance' approach to hedging. Then the *minimum variance hedge ratio* is derived. When there is *maturity mismatch* or a *proxy hedge* must be used, the minimum variance hedge ratio need not be 1. That is, it may be better to buy or sell more futures than we have of the underlying cash exposure, to minimize the risk of the hedged portfolio. But when the hedge is held until expiry of the contract and the hedging instrument is exact, the minimum variance hedge ratio must be 1. We also analyse the residual *position risk* that results when we cannot purchase the number of futures contracts that is recommended by an optimal hedge ratio.

Section III.2.6 examines how futures hedges are implemented in practice. We consider how to hedge international portfolios with forex forwards, stock portfolios with index futures, and bond portfolios with portfolios of notional bond futures. We decompose the risk of the hedged portfolio into different components, showing that not all the uncertainties can be fully hedged, and include a case study that analyses the book of an energy futures trader, identifying the key risk factors facing the trader and explaining how easy it is for the trader to reduce his risks. Section III.2.7 critically examines the use of futures or forwards for the specific problem of *short term hedging*, such as overnight or over a few days. The empirical academic literature introducing advanced econometric models that purport to provide superior estimates of minimum variance hedge ratios for short term hedging is vast. But many of these studies are misconceived, flawed or out of date. Section III.2.8 summarizes and concludes.

---

[9] Or, and more relevantly since the futures or forward is often the more liquid instrument, the relationship between the market price of the futures or forward and the fair value of the spot price.

III.2.2   CHARACTERISTICS OF FUTURES AND FORWARDS

At any time prior to expiry, the futures or forward contract can be traded at the current price of the contract, just like any other tradable instrument. The difference between the cash or spot price and the forward or futures price is called the *basis*. Prior to expiry the basis is non-zero in general, but at expiry the price of the futures is equal to the spot price, since both prices are for immediate delivery.

Almost all futures contracts are closed before expiry, but if held until expiry they involve either *cash settlement* or *physical delivery*.

- Most futures contracts, with the exception of emissions futures and many commodities, are cash-settled. That is, there is a transfer of cash between the holder of the futures and the exchange. This cash transfer depends on the *settlement price* for the future. When the futures contract is on a bond, a stock or a stock index the settlement price is just the cash price of the notional bond, stock or stock index at the time that the contract expires. However, interest rate and commodity futures have more complex rules for calculating the settlement price.
- Many commodities have physical delivery, including metals and energy (excluding electricity) that are traded on the New York Metal Exchange (NYMEX) and grains and livestock traded on the Chicago Board of Trade (CBOT) and the Chicago Mercantile Exchange (CME). Soft commodities (milk, butter, orange juice, etc.) are usually cash-settled but some exchanges allow physical delivery. When delivery is of the physical asset the exchange specifies the type and grade of the commodity and the locations of the delivery. See Section III.2.2.4 for further details.

This section provides a general overview of the different types of futures and forward contracts. We explore the very different characteristics of the established markets on interest rates, bonds, stock indices and commodities and introduce some of the newer futures markets in exchange traded funds, volatility, credit spreads, weather and pollution.

III.2.2.1   Interest Rate and Swap Futures

An interest rate futures contract is just the exchange-traded version of an FRA. But there are two important differences between an interest rate futures contract and an FRA:

- An interest rate futures contract has a fixed expiry *date*, whereas an FRA is to buy or sell a forward interest rate with fixed time to expiry, i.e. with a fixed *term*. For instance, eurodollar futures expire on the standard *quarterly cycle* of March, June, September and December plus the four nearest contract months, whereas you can buy an FRA on the US Treasury 3-month rate starting 6 months from now.
- Three-month interest rate futures are quoted as 100 minus the 3-month LIBOR rate. By contrast, the FRA is simply quoted as the current value of the forward interest rate.

One of the most liquid interest rate futures contracts is for *eurodollar* futures, i.e. futures on US interest rates, traded on the International Money Market (IMM) of the CME. The vast majority of eurodollar futures are traded on the CME's electronic platform. The contract is based on a principal value of $1 million invested in the 3-month US Treasury bill. The standard increment or tick for a eurodollar futures quote is one basis point. Hence the *point value*, i.e. the dollar value of one tick, is[10]

$$\$1,000,000 \times 0.0001 \times \frac{90}{360} = \$25.$$

Like all interest rate futures contracts, eurodollar futures are cash-settled. So if I buy the contract at 98 and then close my position when the settlement price is 99, then the exchange will pay me \$2,500. The final settlement price is the British Bankers' Association (BBA) interest settlement rate, determined using an average of several different banks' quotes on the 3-month US Treasury bill on the day of expiry. Since the eurodollar futures contract's inception, it has become one of the most versatile investment vehicles offered on the listed markets. CME also offer options on eurodollar futures, and simultaneous trades on various portfolios of eurodollar futures.

The CME also has active futures contract on the 1-month US dollar LIBOR,[11] based on a principal of \$3 million. As always, the tick for a futures quote is one basis point. Hence, the point value is the same as for the other money market futures, i.e.

$$\$3,000,000 \times 0.0001 \times \frac{30}{360} = \$25.$$

Whilst eurodollar futures and LIBOR futures are specifically designed to hedge cash positions in market interest rates, the CME's futures on *swaps* are used for hedging interest rates with longer maturities.[12] The contracts are on the 2-year, 5-year and 10-year USD swap rates and each contract size is equivalent to a point value of \$100. For instance, the futures on the 5-year USD swap rate has a notional of \$200,000 since

$$\$200,000 \times 0.0001 \times 5 = \$100.$$

Similarly, the 2-year swap futures contract has a notional of \$500,000 and the 10-year swap futures has a notional of \$100,000. CME also trades interest rates on other currencies (e.g. *euroyen*). All contract specification details are available on the CME CD-ROM.[13]

The CBOT has 5-year, 10-year and 30-year swap futures on a notional swap that, at the time of writing, exchanges semi-annual interest payments at a 6% per annum fixed rate for floating interest rate payments based on three-month LIBOR. In each case the principal is based on a point value of \$1000. The CBOT also has actively traded interest rate futures contracts, for instance on the 30-day Fed Funds rate.[14]

The European equivalent to the eurodollar futures contract is the EURIBOR futures contract, which is traded on the Eurex exchange. The contract is for a notional size of €1 million on the 3-month European Interbank Offered Rate on the standard quarterly cycle. The price quotation is in percent, with three decimal places, expressed as 100 minus the traded rate of interest. The minimum price change is 0.005 percent, equivalent to a value of €12.50. The final settlement price is based on an average of several different banks' quotes on the 3-month EURIBOR rate.

---

[10] Money markets have an actual/360 day count convention. The minimum increment is 1/4 tick, representing \$6.25 per contract.
[11] See Section III.1.2.5.
[12] See Section III.1.7.
[13] See, for instance, http://www.cme.com/trading/prd/ir/libor.html
[14] See www.cbot.com for further details.

III.2.2.2   Bond Futures

Very few individual bonds have futures contracts, although some are traded on the CBOE. The vast majority of bond futures contracts are on government bonds that are based on a *notional* bond having a fixed coupon and maturity. For instance, futures on notional US Treasury notes of 2-year, 5-year and 10-year maturities and a notional 30-year long bond are traded on the CBOT for the standard quarterly cycle. At the time of writing the coupon on these notional bonds is 6%, having been reduced from 8% in March 2000.

Table III.2.1 shows the prices on 19 October 2007 of the most liquid bond futures with December 2007 and March 2008 expiry.[15] For instance, on 19 October 2007 the 10-year US Treasury note futures contract maturing in December 2007 closed at $110\frac{18}{32}$, the number of contracts traded on that day was 1,408,473 and the open interest on the contact at market close on 18 October was 2,389,385.[16] The *open interest* is the total number of outstanding contracts at the end of the day. The average number of days that a contract is held is the open interest divided by the daily trading volume. Hence, on 19 October the average time that a 10-year US Treasury note futures is held is approximately $2,389,385/1,408,473 = 1.69$. So the estimated turnover time is less than 2 days.

Table III.2.1   Bond futures prices, volume and open interest, 19 October 2007

Futures contract	Exchange	Expiry	Close	Est. vol.	Open int.	Est. turn. time
Euro 3mth bond	Eurex	Dec-07	113.39	1,417,937	1,453,162	1.025
US Tsy 10yr bond	CBOT	Dec-07	110-18	1,408,473	2,389,385	1.696
US Tsy 5yr bond	CBOT	Dec-07	107-265	592,638	1,633,990	2.757
US Tsy long bond	CBOT	Dec-07	113-07	383,710	943,798	2.460
Long gilt	LIFFE[a]	Dec-07	107.6	93,961	356,973	3.799
Japan 10yr bond	TSE[b]	Dec-07	135.7	52,776	134,831	2.555
US Tsy 10yr bond	CBOT	Mar-08	110-04	13,731	132,317	9.636
US Tsy 5yr bond	CBOT	Mar-08	107-210	1,041	12,008	11.535
US Tsy long bond	CBOT	Mar-08	113-07	331	8,506	25.698
Euro 3mth bond	Eurex	Mar-08	113.83	722	6,904	9.562

[a]LIFFE is a subsidiary of the new consolidated exchange, NYSE Euronext.
[b]Tokyo Stock Exchange.

Like all futures contracts, positions in bond futures are usually closed and cash-settled before expiry. The point value on the US bond futures is $1000. So if I buy a bond futures contract at 100 and sell it at 101, the exchange pays me $1000. However, if the contract is held until expiry the counterparty that is short the futures can deliver one or more bonds from a basket of bonds at any time during the delivery month. This basket of possible deliverable bonds is specified in the futures contract. For example, at the time of writing the *deliverable grades* of the 10-year US Treasury note futures contract on the CBOT are US Treasury notes maturing in at least $6\frac{1}{2}$ years but not more than 10 years from the first day of the delivery month.[17]

---

[15] Available from www.ft.com/bonds&rates. Source: Reuters.
[16] US bond prices are generally listed in increments of 1/32 point, but futures may have price differentials as low as 1/64 since the bid–ask spreads are extremely narrow.
[17] To take another example, the deliverable grades for the 30-year bond futures traded on the CBOT are US Treasury bonds that, if callable, are not callable for at least 15 years from the first day of the delivery month or, if not callable, have a maturity of at least 15 years from the first day of the delivery month.

The exact bonds in the basket of deliverables change every month because these bonds have fixed expiry dates. Each bond in the basket has a *conversion factor* that is used to determine its value relative to the notional bond. The conversion factor is the price of the deliverable bond based on the notional yield divided by 100. The exchange delivery settlement price is the futures settlement price times the conversion factor plus accrued interest.[18] The quoted futures price is multiplied by the conversion factor to take into account the difference between the coupon of the notional contract and the coupon of the deliverable bond.

For example, the 10-year US Treasury note futures contract has a notional yield of 6%, so if the US Treasury note that is delivered has a coupon of 6% then the conversion factor is 1. Otherwise we can determine the conversion factor by examining the price–yield relationship.

EXAMPLE III.2.1: FINDING THE CONVERSION FACTOR AND DELIVERY PRICE

What is the conversion factor against the 10-year US Treasury note futures contract for a US Treasury note with coupon 5% that has a maturity of exactly 7 years on the first trading day of the delivery month? If the bond has 90 days of accrued interest on that day and the settlement price for the 10-year US Treasury note futures is 105, calculate the delivery price for the bond.

SOLUTION   The price–yield relationship for the deliverable bond is shown in Figure III.2.1.[19] In the spreadsheet we can see that at a yield of 6% the bond price is 94.35.[20] Hence, the conversion factor is 0.9435. The delivery price of this bond, based on a settlement price of 105 and 90 days' accrued interest, is

$$P(0.05, 7) = 105 \times 0.9435 + \frac{90}{182} \times 2.5 = 100.31.$$

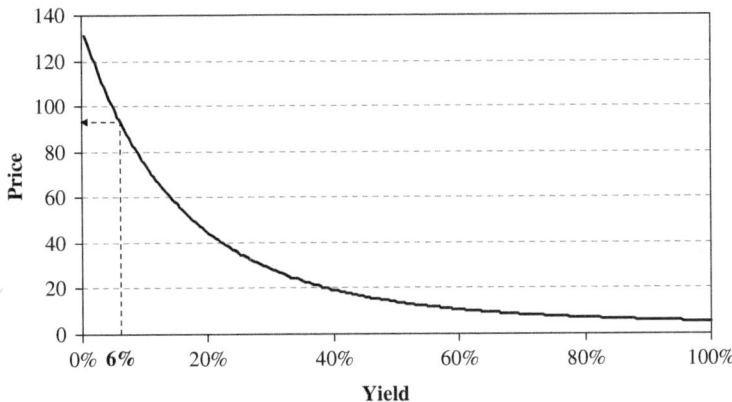

Figure III.2.1   Price–yield relationship for 5% semi-annual bond with maturity 7 years

---

[18] The *exchange delivery settlement price* for any futures is the settlement price for any futures contract. It is described in the contract specification.
[19] The bonds are semi-annual (so each coupon payment is 2.5% in this example) with day count convention actual/365. But for this example we have assumed the time between coupons is always exactly 0.5 years, for simplicity.
[20] That is, $94\frac{11}{32}$ using the standard notation for US bond quotations.

Conversion factors are published by the exchanges and updated on a regular basis. Table III.2.2 shows the conversion factors, as of 27 September 2007, for the bonds that are deliverable against the 10-year US Treasury note futures contracts expiring in December 2007, and March, June, September and December 2008.

Table III.2.2 Conversion factors for 10-year US Treasury note futures

Coupon	Maturity	Dec. 2007	Mar. 2008	Jun. 2008	Sep. 2008	Dec. 2008
4	15/02/2015	0.8870	0.8902	0.8937	–	–
$4\frac{1}{8}$	15/05/2015	0.8910	0.8941	0.8971	0.9003	–
$4\frac{1}{4}$	15/08/2014	0.9069	–	–	–	–
$4\frac{1}{4}$	15/11/2014	0.9040	0.9069	–	–	–
$4\frac{1}{4}$	15/08/2015	0.8955	0.8983	0.9012	0.9040	0.9069
$4\frac{1}{2}$	15/11/2015	0.9080	0.9105	0.9128	0.9153	0.9177
$4\frac{1}{2}$	15/02/2016	0.9058	0.9080	0.9105	0.9128	0.9153
$4\frac{1}{2}$	15/05/2017	0.8946	0.8968	0.8990	0.9013	0.9034
$4\frac{5}{8}$	15/11/2016	0.9074	0.9095	0.9115	0.9136	0.9157
$4\frac{5}{8}$	15/02/2017	0.9054	0.9074	0.9095	0.9115	0.9136
$4\frac{3}{4}$	15/08/2017	0.9105	0.9122	0.9140	0.9158	0.9177
$4\frac{7}{8}$	15/08/2016	0.9259	0.9275	0.9293	0.9310	0.9328
$5\frac{1}{8}$	15/05/2016	0.9436	0.9450	0.9463	0.9478	0.9491

In the basket of deliverables there is usually one bond that is *cheapest to deliver*. The bond futures price quoted at any time is based on supply and demand of the deliverable – as is, of course, the case for any liquid exchange traded contract. Hence, the bond futures price will track the price of the cheapest-to-deliver bond. In other words, we must determine which bond is the cheapest to deliver before we can determine the price of the futures contract on any day. For instance, if the bond that is currently the cheapest to deliver has a conversion factor of 0.92 and this bond has price 98 with no accrued interest, then the current price of the futures contract is $98/0.92 = 106.52$.

Figure III.2.2 compares the price–yield relationship for two (hypothetical) bonds that could be delivered against the 10-year US Treasury note futures contract. One bond is the 7-year US Treasury note with a 5% coupon considered in the previous example, and the other is a US Treasury note with 5.5% coupon and exactly 10 years to maturity on the first trading day of the delivery month. Which bond is the cheapest to deliver depends on the yields on the two bonds at the delivery time. The cheapest bond to deliver is marked on the figure. The choice of the cheapest-to-deliver bond at any time before expiry, and hence the price of the bond futures contract at this time, depends on our forecasts of the yields on the bonds in the delivery basket on the delivery date. But note that to construct the figure we assumed that:

- delivery will be made on the first day of the delivery month, and
- both bonds have the same yield on this day.

However, the delivery date could be at any time during the month of delivery and the two bonds will *not* have identical yields on the delivery date.[21]

---

[21] It is, however, usual that the basket of deliverables contains bonds that have similar yields.

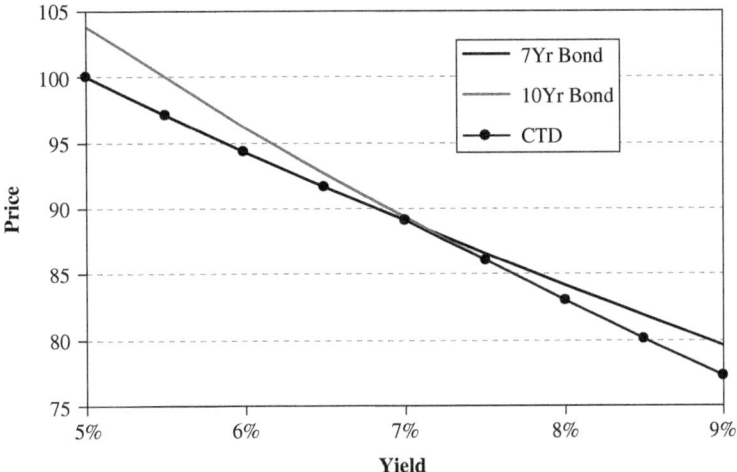

Figure III.2.2   Cheapest to deliver as a function of yield

III.2.2.3   Currency Futures and Forwards

A currency forward, also called a *forex forward*, is a forward contract on the forex market that locks in an exchange rate that is agreed today. The buyer of a currency forward buys a forward on the domestic value of a unit of foreign currency. If held until expiry the buyer receives the foreign currency at the forward exchange rate that was fixed when entering the contract, i.e. the currency forward rate. Similarly, being short a currency forward contract on the expiry date means that you deliver the foreign currency at the forward exchange rate that was fixed when you entered the contract.

Currency *futures* contracts are less liquid than the OTC traded currency forwards. Currency futures are only traded on some of the larger exchanges such as the CME. The most active futures contracts are on the euro, sterling, Canadian dollar, yen and Swiss franc, all against the US dollar. But most of the trading is on the currency forwards in OTC markets. Being OTC contracts, these are much more flexible than currency futures, which are all of a fixed notional size, are against the US dollar, and have only standard maturity dates. In OTC markets you can trade cross-currency forwards that do not involve the US dollar, of virtually any size. The currency forward market is one of the most liquid markets of all, especially up to 1-year maturities. The standard maturities quoted are overnight, 1 week, 2 weeks, 1 month, 2 months, 3 months, 6 months, 9 months and 12 months.

According to the *BIS Quarterly Review*, September 2007, at the end of December 2006 there was nearly $20 billion notional amount outstanding in currency forwards and swaps, with a gross market value of $467 billion. For major currency pairs the normal contract size is $1 million and the bid–ask spread is extremely small. In other words, the market is very highly liquid. A typical bid–ask spread for the USD/GBP 3-month forward at the time of writing is 2.0002–2.0004. This spread is much smaller than the no arbitrage range, so the basis risk on currency futures for major currencies is tiny.[22]

---

[22] See Section III.2.4 for further details on the no arbitrage range and basis risk.

III.2.2.4   Energy and Commodity Futures

Energy and commodities futures are actively traded on several exchanges such as CME, NYMEX, the US Commodities Exchange (Comex), the International Petroleum Exchange (IPE) and, for agricultural commodities such as softs and livestock, the NYSE Intercontinental Exchange (ICE), CBOT and NYSE Euronext.[23] The OTC markets in commodity forwards are also relatively liquid.

Traders in energy and commodity futures and forwards are divided into two groups:

- *Hedgers*. These are commercial traders, i.e. the producers and consumers of the energy or commodity who seek to lock in the price they receive or pay at some time in the future by hedging with the future or forward.
- *Speculators*. These are typically short term investors who take directional positions on the futures or forward price.

The Commodity Futures Trading Commission in the US provides a weekly 'Commitment of Traders' report that details the open positions taken by hedgers and speculators on different commodities in several US commodity exchanges.[24]

Whilst commodity futures over several different expiry dates are available, most of the liquidity is concentrated on the prompt futures. The *prompt futures* or *near futures* contract is the futures contract that is the first to expire. Hence, when commodity futures are used for long term hedges of the spot price it is normal to apply a *stack and strip* hedge. That is, we stack up all the exposures to futures up to many years ahead on to the prompt futures and then, just before expiry, we roll over the position to the next futures. This is called *rolling the hedge*. The problem with rolling a hedge is not the cost, since the transaction or 'spread cost' will usually be very small. But there is a basis because the market price of the next futures in the hedge is different from the price of the previous futures. There is no cost associated with this basis, but the basis *risk* can be considerable when stack and strip hedging is used.

If held until expiry, a commodity futures (or forward) contract may be settled either in cash or by physical delivery. If cash-settled the payment is determined by the difference between

- the futures price that was fixed when the contract was bought or sold, and
- the settlement price, which is usually determined as an average of spot prices over some period prior to expiry.

When commodity futures allow for physical delivery the quality of the product delivered and the location and time of the delivery are specified in the contract. For instance, Table III.2.3 shows the details of the French corn futures contract traded on NYSE Euronext. This contract specifies, among other things, the quality of the deliverables and the possible delivery locations.

The characteristics of commodity futures contracts vary enormously, depending on the nature of the underlying. Each market has different seasonal characteristics, different carry costs and a different *convenience yield*, which is a measure of the benefit of holding the spot commodity.[25] Carry costs and convenience yields are highly uncertain and extremely difficult to measure. Hence, if we try measure the market risk of a portfolio of commodity

---

[23] Every few months there are mergers and acquisitions between exchanges, so by the time this book is in print this list may be out of date!
[24] This can be downloaded from http://www.cftc.gov/cftc/cftccotreports.htm.
[25] See Section III.2.3.5 for further details.

Table III.2.3   Contract specifications for French corn futures

Unit of trading	50 tonnes
Origins tenderable	France
Quality	Yellow and/or red corn, class A1, of sound, fair and merchantable quality of a specified standard
Delivery months	January, March, June, August, November
Quotation	Euros per tonne
Minimum price movement	€0.25 per metric tonne
Value per tick	€12.50
Last trading day	18.30 on the fifth calendar day of the delivery month
Notice day/tender day	The first business day following the last trading day
Tender period	Any business day from the last trading day to the end of the specified delivery month
Delivery	Designated ports: Bordeaux-Blaye, Bayonne, La Pallice
Trading hours	10.45–18.30

futures using the spot commodity price as the market risk factor, we are left with the carry cost risk and convenience yield risk, and these are almost impossible to measure.

We shall see in Section III.5.4.2 that when measuring the risk of commodity futures portfolios, *constant maturity futures* can be useful time series to use as risk factors.[26] Constant maturity futures are not traded instruments. However, a time series of constant maturity commodity futures can be obtained by *concatenation* of adjacent futures prices. For instance, a time series for a constant maturity 1-month futures price can be obtained by taking the prompt futures with expiry less than or equal to 1 month and the next futures with expiry greater than 1 month and linearly interpolating between the two prices. So if the prompt futures contract with price P_1 has maturity $T_1 \leq 1$ month and the futures contract with price P_2 is the next to expire with maturity $T_2 > 1$ month, and T_1 and T_2 are measured in years, then the concatenated 1-month futures price is[27]

$$P = \frac{(T_2 - \frac{1}{12})P_1 + (\frac{1}{12} - T_1)P_2}{(T_2 - T_1)}.$$

Another advantage of using constant maturity futures is that they provide a long time series of futures prices that can be used to assess the market characteristics. These characteristics vary considerably from market to market. Prices are determined by unpredictable demand and supply factors such as the weather and the economic climate. For instance, the weather affects the supply of corn and the demand for gas and the outbreak of war affects the price of oil. But prices may also be affected by speculative trading, and the 'herding' behaviour of speculative investors can lead to prolonged price trends in futures prices that have nothing to do with demand and supply of the actual commodity.

Figures III.2.3–III.2.8 illustrate just how different are the empirical price characteristics of three energy markets and three commodity futures markets. In each case we show time series for the hypothetical constant maturity futures expiring each month, up to 6 months ahead.[28] First, Figure III.2.3 shows a very long series of NYMEX West Texas Intermediate (WTI) sweet crude oil futures prices between January 1985 and August 2006, where prices

---

[26] See Section III.2.6.3 for an empirical example.
[27] This is simple linear interpolation – see Section I.5.3.1 for further details.
[28] Graphs abstract from Alexander and Venkatramanan (2008a) with permission from Wiley.

are measured in US dollars per barrel. Oil prices are dominated by global economic events, and particularly by political turmoil in the Middle East. The inset figures show how prices rose steadily, on growing fears of an outbreak of war in Iran, from about $40 per barrel in January 2005 to nearly $80 per barrel in August 2006. As this book goes to press, the spot price has just exceeded $100 per barrel.

The term structure is extremely highly correlated because crude oil is one of the few commodities futures contracts where trading remains liquid beyond the first few maturities.

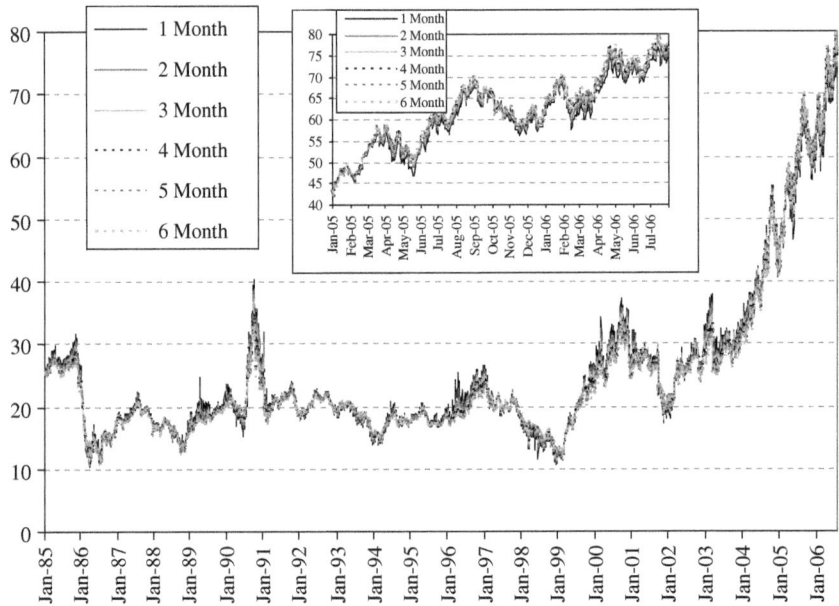

Figure III.2.3   WTI crude oil constant maturity futures prices

Figure III.2.4 shows Henry Hub natural gas futures prices in US dollars per million British thermal units. Natural gas futures are much less highly correlated than oil futures prices, and swings between backwardation and contango are seasonal.[29] Prices are dominated by hedging behaviour rather than speculation or politics. Backwardation tends to occur during winter months when short term futures prices can jump upward. Contango is more likely during summer months. A strong contango in the term structure was evident during the summer of 2006. There is a large basis risk with spot price spikes arising during unexpected cold snaps. Down spikes may also occur in the summer when storage is full to capacity.

Figure III.2.5 shows the PJM electricity futures prices in US dollars per megawatt-hour.[30] Since electricity cannot be stored spot prices are excessively variable, seasonal and rapidly mean-reverting, especially for futures that expire during summer months when the air conditioning required during heatwaves increases demand. The term structure is very different than the term structure of other commodity futures prices. Since the contracts are for

---

[29] *Backwardation* is the term given to a downward sloping term structure of futures prices and *contango* refers to an upward sloping term structure.
[30] See www.PJM.com. Prices are for futures traded on NYMEX.

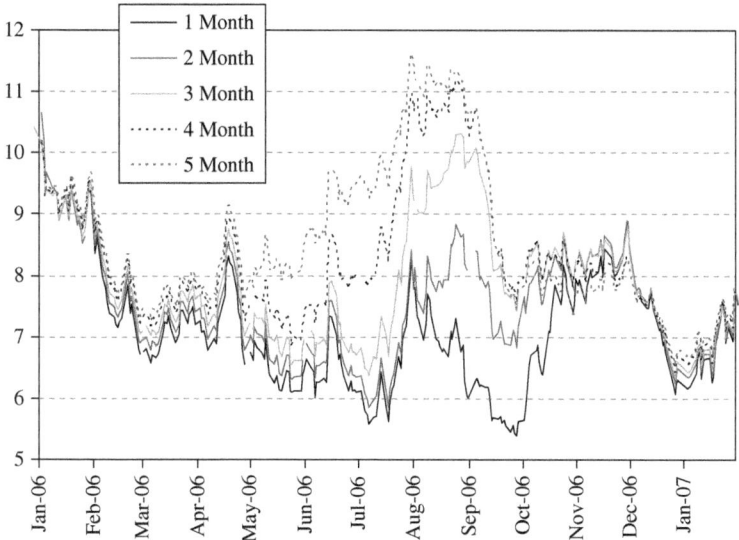

Figure III.2.4   Henry Hub natural gas constant maturity futures prices

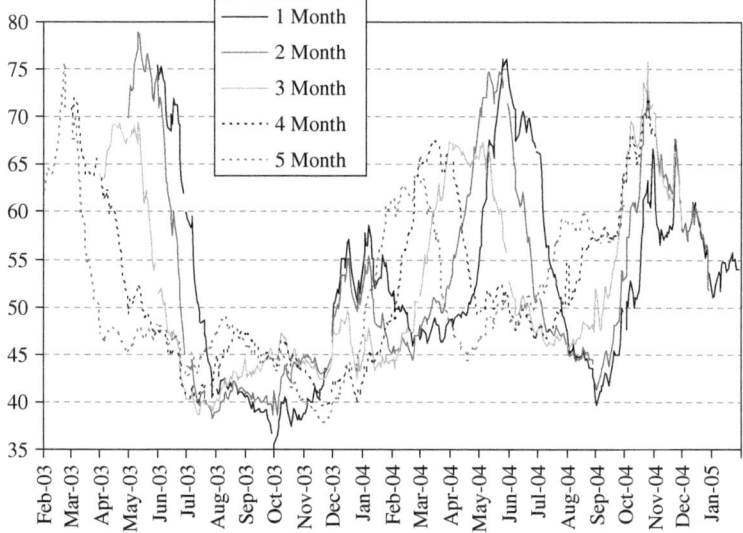

Figure III.2.5   PJM electricity constant maturity futures prices

physical delivery there is a very strong seasonal pattern and futures that expire in July, January and February have much higher prices than the futures that expire in spring and autumn.

Moving on to the traditional commodities, Figure III.2.6 shows the Comex silver futures prices in US dollars per troy ounce. The market is narrower than the gold market because there are less reserves of silver. On the demand side, silver is used in industrial processes (e.g. silver plating and electronics) but there is no inherent seasonality in these. Hence, the term structure is quite flat and movements are very highly correlated indeed, basis risk is small, and prices display no seasonality. The prices are dominated by speculative trading, as is evident from the long trends and the frequent spikes and jumps.

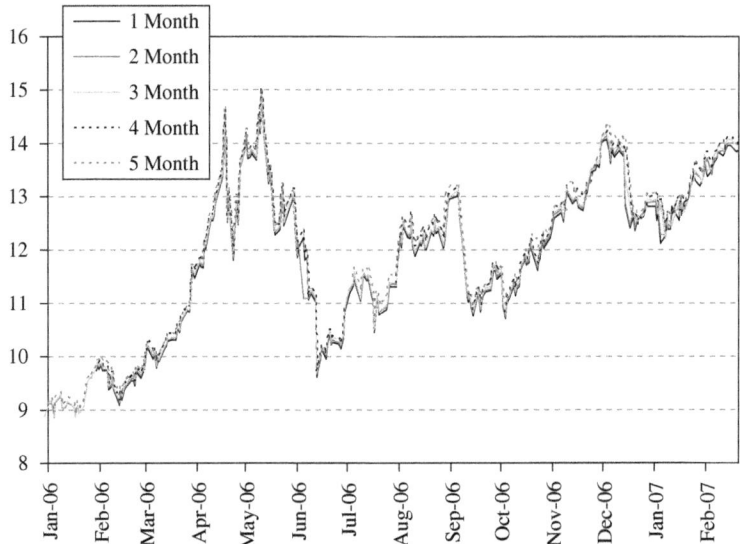

Figure III.2.6   Silver constant maturity futures prices

Figure III.2.7 illustrates the CBOT No.2 Yellow corn futures price in cents per bushel. Prices can jump at the time of the US Department of Agriculture crop production forecasts and in response to news announcements. A recent example of this was the reaction to President Bush's announcement of plans to increase ethanol production, clearly visible in January 2007.

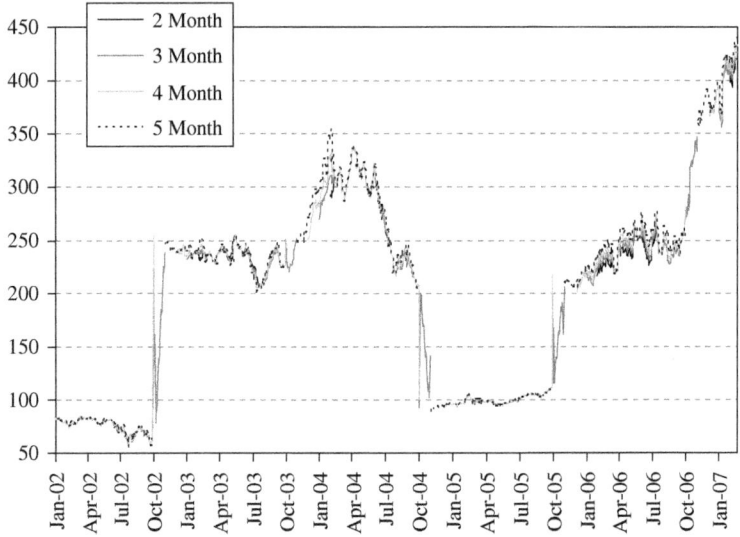

Figure III.2.7   Yellow corn constant maturity futures prices

Figure III.2.8 shows the CME lean hogs futures price in US dollars per pound. Futures prices display low correlation across different maturities, with winter futures prices being noticeably lower than summer futures prices. The market is characterized by a relatively flat demand and an inelastic supply that is set by farmers deciding to breed 10 months previously. High prices induce producers to retain more sows for breeding, thus pushing the price even higher, and prices tend to peak in the summer months when the supply of live hogs is usually at its lowest. Price jumps may correspond to the US Department of Agriculture 'Hogs and Pigs' report on the size of the breeding herd.

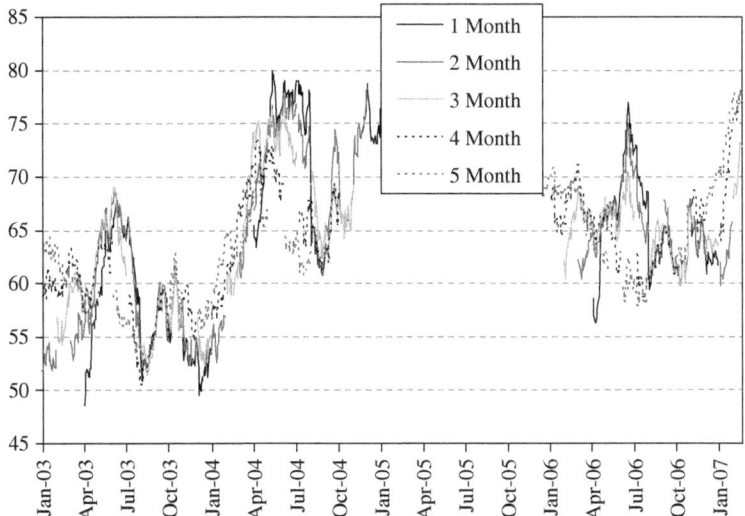

Figure III.2.8   Lean hogs constant maturity futures prices

III.2.2.5   Stock Futures and Index Futures

Stock index futures are traded on the CME, LIFFE and on the futures exchanges in Mexico, Brazil, Hong Kong, Singapore, Sydney, Johannesburg, India and many other countries. Individual stock futures are also traded on many futures exchanges, but the volume of trade is very small compared with that on index futures. Both stock and index futures are cash-settled. If an investor is long (short) the futures then he receives (pays) a cash amount equal to the difference between the settlement price and the futures price that was fixed on the contract date. Clearly this can be positive or negative, and in the latter case the long futures holder must pay the cash to the exchange.

Most of the major stock indices have futures contracts. Futures on broad market equity indices such as the S&P 500 and FTSE 100 are particularly liquid. On these *index futures* the expiry date is the third Wednesday of each month, which coincides with the expiry of the corresponding index options. The cash settlement on the S&P 500 futures is for $250 per point and that for the FTSE 100 is for £10 per point. For instance, if I buy one FTSE futures at 6000 the value of my position is £60,000, and if the FTSE futures price is at 6500 when I close out my position then I would make a profit of £5000.

Although both stock futures and index futures fall into the same broad class of equity futures, there is a fundamental difference between index futures and stock futures. A stock is a traded asset that can be bought or sold, but it is not easy to buy and sell a stock index since the replicating portfolio must be continually rebalanced so that the weight on each stock is always in proportion to its market capitalization.[31] If the underlying can be sold short then the no arbitrage range is fairly symmetric about the spot price, but it is particularly difficult to sell a stock index short.[32] Hence, the lower boundary of the no arbitrage range can be very low and as a result the spot price could be far above the futures price of the index. However, most stock indices now have an i-share or an index exchange traded fund (see below) and these cash assets will improve the pricing efficiency in the index futures market enormously. As a result the bid–ask spread on index futures is now a small fraction of the spreads we experienced before the introduction of an exchange traded fund.

III.2.2.6   Exchange Traded Funds and ETF Futures

An *exchange traded fund* (ETF) is an instrument for investment in a basket of securities. It is similar to an open-ended fund, but it can be transacted at market price at any time during the trading day. Market makers in index ETFs buy and sell securities to replicate an index, and then make a market in shares on the ETF itself. An ETF that replicates a stock index is similar to an *i-share* and both can be thought of as a share where the 'company' is the weighted average of companies in the index. ETFs can be bought and sold just like any other share with short selling, stop-loss and limit orders.[33]

The market makers in ETFs publicly quote and transact firm bid and offer prices, making money on the spread, and buy or sell on their own account to counteract temporary imbalances in supply and demand. Shares can only be created and redeemed at the fund's net asset value at the end of the trading day.[34] Daily net creation or redemption demands can be huge, especially around the time of dividend payments, when the tax treatment of dividends on ETF investments significantly increases trading volume.[35] There is a very active secondary market in index futures and, since the holder of the futures receives no dividends, there can be a considerable degree of *tax arbitrage* between the spot and the futures, or the ETF and the futures, around the time of dividend payments.

ETFs are becoming extremely popular investment vehicles. They offer investors relatively low trading costs and management fees, diversification, liquidity and tax efficiency. ETFs are now traded on most of the stock exchanges in developed markets, including the American Stock Exchange (AMEX), the National Association of Securities Dealers Automatic Quotations (NASDAQ) exchange, NYSE, CME, CBOE the London Stock Exchange (LSE), NYSE Euronext, and the stock exchanges in Mexico, Brazil, Hong Kong, Singapore, Sydney, Johannesburg and many more.[36] Stock exchanges have a huge interest in the development of the ETF markets to increase trading volume and thus commissions and brokerage fees.

---

[31] Assuming the index is cap weighted.

[32] Each stock in the index would have to be sold on a 'sale and repurchase agreement' or *repo*.

[33] In fact the short selling of a US index using the ETF is further facilitated because ETFs are exempt from the *up-tick rule* preventing short selling except after an up-tick.

[34] The net asset value is determined by the total value of the portfolio and other assets, less all liabilities including accrued expenses and dividends payable.

[35] The holder of the ETF on the ex-dividend date is entitled to receive the dividends, no matter how long the share has been held. But if the share is sold during the ex-dividend period the registered investor loses the dividends and any tax advantage or disadvantage related to it. Moreover, ETFs traded on the secondary market do not include the dividend or cash components.

[36] The NASDAQ exchange was originally a network of dealers but brokers introduced an electronic communications network during 1996–1997 and, by 2002, even super-montage consolidated quotes had been introduced. In this sense the NASDAQ is more efficient than both the London and New York stock exchanges.

Liquidity of ETFs, however, is not determined by the supply and demand of the ETF but rather by the liquidity of the underlying securities that compose the benchmark index.

Table III.2.4 shows the assets under management (AUM) and number of ETFs around the world. European ETFs have more flexibility than the American ETFs under European regulations. Also the European market has more fragmentation, with different currencies and different tax regimes. It is thus a fertile ground for innovation: for instance, commodity ETFs and fixed income ETFs were first launched in Europe. ETF market makers in Europe are also allowed to use more sophisticated tracking strategies, including index swaps.

Table III.2.4 ETFs in the United States, Europe and the world

	USA		Europe		World	
Year	AUM	No. Funds	AUM	No. Funds	AUM	No. Funds
2000	65,585	80	680	6	74,340	92
2001	82,993	102	5,660	71	104,800	202
2002	102,143	113	10,690	118	141,620	280
2003	150,983	119	20,440	104	212,020	282
2004	226,205	151	33,970	114	309,80	336
2005	296,022	201	54,920	165	416,810	453
2006	422,550	359	76,710	255	504,510	669

Source: Investment Company Institute and Morgan Stanley Investment Strategies.

Major providers of ETFs and i-shares currently include Vanguard (in the US) and Barclays Global Investors (in Europe and the rest of the world).[37] The oldest and largest index ETF in the US is called the *Spider*, which tracks the S&P 500 index.[38] It was first listed on the AMEX in 1993 and it remains by far the largest index ETF with over $60 billion under management at the time of writing (October 2007). The Spider share price corresponds to one-tenth of the S&P500 index value and the trust issues and redeems shares in creation units of 50,000. The other index ETFs and i-shares that are very actively traded in the US are the *Cubes*, an ETF that tracks the NASDAQ 100 index; the *Diamond*, an ETF that tracks the Dow Jones Industrial Average (DJIA) index; and the Russell 2000 iShare.[39] Other index ETFs track many other broad based market indices, sector indices, international and country-specific indices, style funds, commodities and fixed income funds and, more recently, leveraged funds and funds with short exposure.

ETFs are used for both speculation and hedging and offer many advantages over futures. Short selling ETFs implies borrowing ETF shares and paying interest on the borrowed amount,[40] a cost that is absent when shorting futures. But futures incur margin costs and extra commissions and spread costs when rolling the hedge. Many indices do not have

---

[37] Barclays was the first large scale provider of i-shares. However, the Vanguard Group, which is the second largest mutual fund manager in the US, was reluctant to enter the ETF market. At the time of the launch of its first ETF series, named *Viper* (Vanguard Index Participation Equity Receipts), Vanguard published a fact sheet questioning the lower expense ratios and tax efficiency of ETFs. Currently Vanguard has a significant market share of ETFs and has launched a number of innovative products. See www.vanguard.com and www.ishares.co.uk.

[38] The name Spider derives form Standard and Poor's Depository Receipts.

[39] The Cubes share price is approximately one-fortieth of the NASDAQ 100 index value, the Diamond share price is approximately one-hundredth of the DJIA index value and the Russell iShare price corresponds to one-tenth of the Russell 2000 index value.

[40] So investors who are long ETFs can benefit from lending revenue which can cover the expense ratio.

futures contracts and for those that do the contract size and margin requirements are often inaccessible to the average investor. ETFs have a smaller size than futures contracts, cover many indices that have no futures and are not subject to the same regulatory requirements.[41]

Following the introduction of an i-share or index ETF an existing index futures market will become much more efficient.[42] This is because ETFs can easily be sold short and trading ETFs is also much less expensive than index replication. So when the ETF is traded in place of the constituent stocks of the index, two-way arbitrage becomes not only possible but relatively inexpensive. Hence, the ETF has the effect of significantly reducing the no arbitrage range for the index future.

Price discovery is the process by which a transaction price for a given quantity of a security (or commodity) is arrived at. Prices are determined by basic supply and demand factors related to the market. The price discovery mechanism depends on market microstructure, including the characteristics of the buyers and sellers, the market information and timeliness of reporting trades, and the methods used to price the assets. Typically, the volume of trading on index futures far exceeds the total volume of trades on the stocks in the index. Hence, it is the futures contract that usually plays the important price discovery role. Academic research based on ultra high frequency data demonstrates that the price of the index futures usually moves before the ETF price, which itself moves before the index price. Nevertheless both ETF and index prices adjust very rapidly following a change in the futures price.[43]

At the end of the trading day ETF market makers decide whether to create or redeem shares, to lend or borrow shares from other market makers, to keep an open position on their own account, or to hedge their position overnight. Often they choose to hedge, since the net creation demand on the following day could be opposite to that today. The demand from market makers to hedge their positions had led to the recent introduction of futures contracts on ETFs. ETF futures have been traded on Eurex since 2002, but the CME started listing ETF futures only in June 2005. Trading volume on ETF futures remains very much lower than it is on the corresponding index futures and most of the hedging activity by stock and ETF market markers and investors is still concentrated on the index futures contract rather than the ETF futures contract.

III.2.2.7   New Futures Markets

In this subsection we provide a brief overview of the futures contracts on volatility, credit spreads, weather and pollution that have recently been launched on several exchanges. The underlying of these new futures contracts need not be a traded instrument. For instance, the *heating degree days* (HDD) weather contract is not a traded asset, but there is an active futures market on HDD. It need not even be the case that the underlying of the futures contract is the same as the spot. For instance, a volatility futures contract is to buy or sell volatility over a 1-month period that *commences* at the time that the futures expires. However, the spot volatility index is the volatility over a period starting now and ending in 1 month. For this reason the concepts of no arbitrage pricing and basis risk that we introduce in Sections III.2.3.1 and III.2.4.3 do not necessarily apply to pricing these new futures contracts. When there is no no-arbitrage range for the futures price the bid–ask spreads can become

---

[41] Because ETFs are not considered derivatives, they are not subject to the same regulatory restrictions as derivatives trading nor do they have expensive reporting and collateral management requirements.

[42] See for instance Switzer et al. (2000), Chu and Hsieh (2002) and Alexander and Barbosa (2007).

[43] See Chu et al. (1999).

very large. For instance the typical bid–ask spread on a volatility futures contract at the time of writing is about 50 basis points!

Volatility Futures

A volatility index is an average of the implied volatilities of all the fixed maturity options that are traded on the same underlying.[44] The only way to trade the spot volatility index is to buy (or sell) all the options in the correct proportions to the index and continually rebalance, which is very expensive. So the spot volatility index not a tradable asset in its own right and volatility index futures contracts offer a relatively cheap and easy way to buy or sell implied volatility.

The spot index at time t refers to an average implied volatility of all options with 30 days to expiry at time t, but the futures contract on this index of maturity T refers to an average implied volatility of all options with 30 days to expiry at time T. So the only time when the spot and the futures refer to the same underlying is when $t = T$. That is, the underlying of a volatility futures contract is *not* the spot volatility index, except on the expiry date of the futures.

This fundamental point about volatility indices differentiates them from traditional instruments with spot and futures contracts. It means that volatility futures are much less variable than the spot. Volatility index futures are like futures on temperature. Suppose that in July you buy a January temperature futures contract in Russia. The price of this futures contract will not change that much over its lifetime, whereas a spot temperature contract in Russia changes considerably between summer and winter months. A detailed description of volatility indices is given in Section III.4.7. There we explain how to price them and their applications to risk management and volatility trading.

At the time of writing four volatility futures contracts are traded on CBOE, with most of the trading on the Vix futures.[45] Also three volatility futures are traded on Eurex. The contract specifications are as follows.[46]

- Expiry: three near-term serial months and three additional months on the February quarterly cycle
- Based on 30-day volatility index and cash-settled at special opening quotation on CBOE and as an average of final ticks on Eurex
- Minimum contract size: 10
- Volatility percentage point value:
  - CBOE: $1000
  - Eurex: 1000 EUR or CHF
- Minimum price interval:
  - CBOE: 1 basis point (or $10 per tick)
  - Eurex: 5 basis points (or 50 EUR or CHF per tick).

Figure III.2.9 shows how the volume of contracts traded on the Vix futures increased from inception in March 2004 until May 2007.[47] They are still relatively illiquid compared

---

[44] The volatility index construction is based on the replication of a variance swap rate. See Section III.4.7 for further details.

[45] The Vix is the volatility index derived from the prices of S&P 500 index options.

[46] See http://www.cboe.com/micro/volatility/introduction.aspx, http://www.cboe.com/vix and http://www.eurexchange.com/trading/products/VOL_en.html.

[47] Trading volume is on the right-hand scale and open interest is on the left-hand scale.

with other futures. Nevertheless, exchange traded futures contracts on volatility indices have drawn considerable attention to volatility as a very attractive asset class in its own right. The high negative correlation between the volatility index and the underlying equity index means that volatility offers investors substantial diversification potential. They are also being used for hedging volatility exposures that arise from writing options or variance swaps.

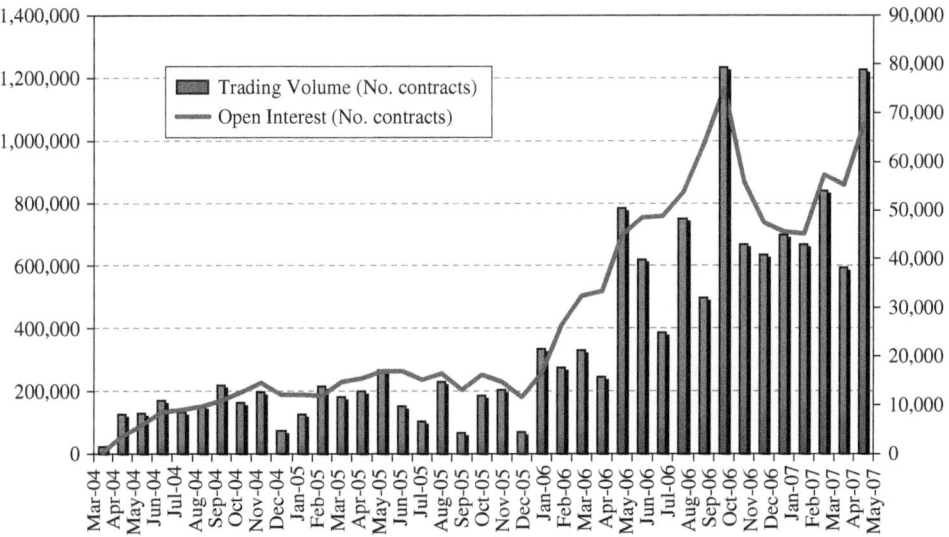

Figure III.2.9   Volume and open interest on all Vix futures traded on CBOE

Figure III.2.10 shows the price of the Vix December 2007 futures contract between issue in March 2007 and October 2007 (left-hand scale) and the open interest (number of contracts) at the end of each day (right-hand scale). The average turnover time on Vix December 2007 futures was about 40 days, and over all Vix futures it is currently about 15–20 days. This low turnover indicates that Vix futures are not, at present, being used for speculative purposes, possibly because the trading costs are so high.

Futures on Emissions Allowances

Environmental protection agencies in the US and in countries that have signed the Kyoto agreement aim to limit the amount of pollution that can be produced by power plants, refineries and factories. These producers are collectively termed *sources of emissions*. Each source of emissions has an annual emissions allowance and often the government imposes severe penalties for exceeding this allowance. The three main types of pollution that are regulated by the environmental protection agency are carbon dioxide, sulfur dioxide and nitrous oxide emissions.

But allowances can be traded, thus permitting some sources to produce far more (or less) pollution than originally allocated by their environmental protection agency. Allowances may be traded by anyone: brokers, corporations, municipalities, and even private individuals.

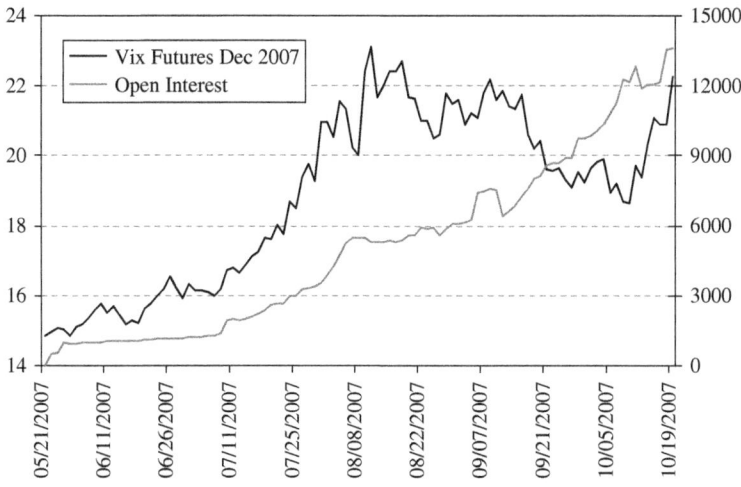

Figure III.2.10   Vix December 2007 futures prices and open interest

Counterparties do not need to be a source of emissions to trade in emission allowances, and the prices of allowances are set by supply and demand, just like any other asset. Carbon emissions can be traded on several exchanges in different countries. Amongst the first exchanges to deal in carbon emissions was the Chicago Climate Exchange (CCX) which launched its trading platform in 2003. In 2005, CCX launched the European Climate Exchange (ECX), and this is now the leading exchange operating in the European Union emissions trading.

The Chicago Climate Futures Exchange (CCFE) lists several futures contracts on sulfur and nitrous oxide emissions allowances and in August 2007 it became the first US exchange to list carbon futures. All emissions allowance futures contracts have physical delivery of the allowances. NYMEX have been listing futures contracts for sulfur and nitrous oxide emissions since 2005. The contract specifications may be summarized as follows.

- Expiry: Monthly cycle up to 4 years ahead
- Trading unit: 2000 lbs of emissions allowances
- Minimum contract size: 10
- Minimum price fluctuation: $25 per ton ($250 per contract).

Many other climate exchanges around the world are now offering futures on carbon, sulfur and nitrous oxide emissions allowances. For instance, the Australian Climate Exchange launched futures contracts on carbon emissions in July 2007, the Multi Commodity Exchange of India is in discussions with CCX on launching a futures carbon trading exchange in India and the Montreal Exchange in Canada has just filed to offer carbon futures at the time of writing.

Weather Futures

Weather derivatives are used to hedge the risks associated with adverse weather conditions. For instance power companies can be adversely impacted by summers that are cooler or winters that are warmer than anticipated. Weather derivatives are based on temperature, rainfall, frost, snowfall and hurricanes.

Weather futures are a type of weather derivative that obligates the buyer to purchase the value of an underlying weather index at a future date. For instance, the *cooling degree days* (CDD) weather index is related to a base temperature K.[48] For each day that the temperature rises above K keep a cumulative count of the difference between the average daily temperature on that day and K. On the CME the settlement price of the CDD weather index is equal to the value of the relevant month's CDD, multiplied by $20.[49]

For example, suppose a power company buys a CDD futures for January. If January is warmer than expected this will cause an unanticipated loss for the company, but the loss will be offset because the company will receive a positive value for January's CDD from the exchange. This way, weather futures allow companies whose profits depend on weather conditions to smooth their earnings.

Weather derivatives began trading OTC in 1997 and the CME started listing weather futures and options in 1999.[50] At the time of writing CME lists weather derivative contracts for nearly twenty cities in the United States, nine in Europe, six in Canada and two in Japan. Most of these futures and options contracts track HDD or CDD indices but recent additions track frost days, monthly/seasonal snowfall and, for insurance companies, hurricanes.

For instance, the contract specifications for the CME hurricane index futures are as follows.

- Trade unit: $1000 times the respective Carvill Hurricane index (CHI)
- Point descriptions: 1 point $= 1.00$ CHI index point $= \$1000$
- Contract listing: For each of the five regions listed, hurricane index contracts will be listed initially for the first hurricane to make landfall and second hurricane to make landfall. Thereafter, new hurricane index futures and options contracts are created only in the case where an event (landfall in one of the designated regions) occurs. When a hurricane hits in a region (e.g. first hurricane to make landfall), the next eligible contract (e.g., third hurricane to make landfall) for that region will be listed for trading.

Credit Index Futures

Credit index futures offer a liquid form of protection against corporate credit events, such as credit downgrade, failure to pay and bankruptcy. Eurex started trading in credit index futures in 2006 and now lists three futures contracts based on three i-Traxx indices of 5-year credit default swap (CDS) rates.[51] The indices themselves are only traded OTC and the composition of each i-Traxx index changes every 6 months, so only the composition of the underlying for the near futures contract is known.

---

[48] For instance in the UK the base temperature is often but not always taken as 15.5°C.
[49] Full details of the contract specifications are at http://www.cme.com/trading/prd/weather/us-month-heat_FCS.html. The HDD futures contract is defined similarly, except that for each day that the temperature falls below K we keep a cumulative count of the difference between K and the average daily temperature on that day.
[50] See http://www.cme.com/trading/prd/weather/index.html.
[51] These are the main Europe, HiVol and Crossover indices. The main *i-Traxx Europe index* is an equally weighted portfolio of the 125 most liquid European investment grade CDS entities. The *i-Traxx HiVol index* is an equally weighted portfolio of the 30 entities with the highest spread from the i-Traxx Europe index, while the *i-Traxx Crossover index* is an equally weighted portfolio of 45 European sub-investment grade entities. For further details on the contract specifications see http://www.eurexchange.com/trading/products/CRD_en.html.

CME began trading futures on its Credit Index Event (CIE) in 2007. The contracts are based on an index of North American investment grade high volatility CDS entities. At the time of writing there are plans to introduce high yield and Crossover indices also. Like the i-Traxx indices, new CIE series are introduced every 6 months. The futures are cash-settled according to the following general formula for the final settlement value (FSV):

$$FSV = N \times \sum_{i=1}^{n} 1_i w_i f_i \qquad (III.2.1)$$

where N is the notional, n is the number of companies in the index, 1_i is the credit event indicator for entity i which takes the value one if the credit event occurs and zero otherwise, w_i is the index weight of the company in the index and f_i is the company's final settlement weight that is specified by the exchange. At the time of writing the credit event is either bankruptcy or failure to pay, $n = 32$, all companies carry equal weight (so $w_i = 1/32$) and they all have the same final settlement weight of 0.6. So for instance, if there are two bankruptcies amongst the 32 companies before expiry of the futures then the final settlement value owed to the purchaser of the futures contract is:

$$\$100{,}000 \times \tfrac{1}{16} \times 0.6 = \$3750.$$

Real Estate Futures

Real estate futures provide protection against falls in real estate values; however, at the time of writing these derivatives are extremely new and they remain rather illiquid at the time of writing. In May 2006 the CME launched cash-settled housing futures, based on 11 home price indices, at \$250 per index point on the February quarterly cycle. They currently have plans to launch similar futures on commercial real estate including a US national composite index, five geographic regional indexes, and four national property type indexes. CBOT already list a futures contract on the Dow Jones US Real Estate index.

III.2.3 THEORETICAL RELATIONSHIPS BETWEEN SPOT, FORWARD AND FUTURES

This section describes the theoretical relationships between spot and forward prices, which may be extended to spot and futures prices. We present the general theory using continuous compounding and forward prices rather than discrete compounding and/or futures prices, because the analysis is easier to follow.[52]

III.2.3.1 No Arbitrage Pricing

If the same financial asset trades in two markets and the prices are not the same in both, then market makers and other *arbitrageurs* will sell the asset at the higher price and buy it at the lower price, thus making an instantaneous profit if the price difference exceeds the transaction costs. The ability to arbitrage prices in different markets implies that there is a unique market price for a tradable asset. This is called the *law of one price*.

---

[52] Although market interest rates are discretely compounded they are very cumbersome to work with. Indeed most practitioners convert all market rates into continuously compounded form. See Section III.1.2.3.

The *no arbitrage valuation principle* states that it is not possible to make an instantaneous profit on a riskless portfolio.[53] Put another way, if two investments are equally risky then they must offer the same return. In this section we use the no arbitrage principle to derive the fair value of a forward contract on a traded asset. A no arbitrage condition holds between spot and forward prices on the assumption the spot asset can be purchased. This provides a fair value for the forward price that is related to the market price of the spot.

We now define our notation. In Chapter III.1 we used the notation F_{nm} to denote an m-period discretely compounded forward interest rate starting n periods ahead, that is, n is the *term* and m is the *tenor* of the rate. But in this chapter we are not dealing specifically with a forward interest rate. We consider a general forward contract to buy or sell and asset (or an interest rate, or a swap, etc.) at a certain time T in the future. We shall suppose that the forward price is fixed at some time $t < T$ when the forward contract is purchased and we want to derive a theoretical relationship between the spot price and the forward price at this time. So the expiry date of the forward is fixed at T, the current time is t and we denote the current price of the spot asset by $S(t)$. The price that we agree at time t for the forward contract expiring at time T is denoted $F(t, T)$, with $S(T) = F(T, T)$.

There are two ways that we can own the asset at time T:

(a) borrow an amount $S(t)$ and buy the asset now, or
(b) buy the forward at the agreed price $F(t, T)$ now.

First assume there are no transactions costs and no cash flows such as dividends or carry costs on the asset during the life of the contract. Also assume we can borrow and lend at the continuously compounded risk free zero coupon rate $r(t, T)$ of maturity $T - t$ at time t. As usual this zero coupon rate is expressed in annual terms and time is measured in years. Then the value of strategy (a) at time T will be

$$S(T) - S(t)\exp(r(t, T)(T - t)). \qquad \text{(III.2.2)}$$

In strategy (b) we would at time T hold a contract that has value $S(T)$ for which we have agreed to pay $F(t, T)$, hence the value of strategy (b) at time T will be

$$S(T) - F(t, T). \qquad \text{(III.2.3)}$$

These two strategies lead to identical outcomes. Hence their values should be the same, otherwise there would be an arbitrage possibility.

The *fair value* or *theoretical value* of the forward at time t is the value of the forward contract that equates (III.2.2) and (III.2.3). We shall denote this value $F^*(t, T)$, and the no arbitrage argument above yields

$$F^*(t, T) = S(t)\exp(r(t, T)(T - t)). \qquad \text{(III.2.4)}$$

This shows that the fair value of long forward position is equivalent to a long position in a zero coupon bond with maturity equal to the maturity of the forward and with nominal equal to the value of the spot.

III.2.3.2   Accounting for Dividends

If the underlying asset is a dividend paying stock or a coupon paying bond then strategy (a) brings benefits that we have ignored in the above analysis. In particular, we need to take into

---

[53] A riskless portfolio only makes returns over a period of time: discounted to today (using the risk free rate), the return is zero.

account any *dividend payments*, between now and the expiry of the future; or if the asset is a bond we should include in the benefits to strategy (a) any *coupon payments* between now and the maturity of the future. The following analysis assumes the underlying asset is a stock with known dividend payments, but applies equally well when the asset is a fixed coupon bond.

The annual *dividend yield* on a stock is the present value of the annual dividends per share, divided by the current share price. Note that if dividends are reinvested then the present value should include the reinvestment income. The continuously compounded dividend yield $y(t, T)$ over the period from time t until time T is defined as

$$y(t, T) = \frac{C(t, T)}{S(t)(T - t)}, \tag{III.2.5}$$

where $C(t, T)$ is the present value at time t of the dividends accruing between time t and time T, including any reinvestment income.

EXAMPLE III.2.2: CALCULATING THE DIVIDEND YIELD

Consider a US stock with quarterly dividend payments. We hold the stock for 6 months, i.e. $T = 0.5$. Let the current share price be \$100 and suppose that we receive dividends of \$2 per share in 1 months' time and again in 4 months' time. Assuming that the dividends are not reinvested, that the 1-month zero coupon interest rate is 4.75% and the 4-month zero coupon rate is 5%, calculate:

(a) the continuously compounded present value of the dividend payments; and
(b) the continuously compounded dividend yield over the 6-month period.

SOLUTION   For the present value of dividend payments we have:

$$C(0, 0.5) = 2\exp(-0.0475/12) + 2\exp(-0.05/3) = \$3.959.$$

Therefore the continuously compounded dividend yield is

$$y(0, 0.5) = \frac{3.959}{100 \times 0.5} = 7.92\%.$$

We now adjust formula (III.2.4) for the fair value of the forward to take account of the dividends that accrue to the stockholder between now and the expiry of the future. In the general case when dividends or coupons are paid, the value of strategy (a) is no longer (III.2.2) but equal to

$$S(T) - S(t)\exp((r(t, T) - y(t, T))(T - t)).$$

Hence the no arbitrage condition yields the fair value

$$F^*(t, T) = S(t)\exp((r(t, T) - y(t, T))(T - t)). \tag{III.2.6}$$

EXAMPLE III.2.3: FAIR VALUE OF A STOCK INDEX FUTURES CONTRACT (ZERO MARGIN)

On 19 December 2005 the FTSE 100 index closing price was 5531.63. The 3-month continuously compounded dividend yield on the index was 3.14% and the 3-month zero coupon continuously compound interest rate was 4.57%. Assuming the futures can be purchased on zero margins, what was the fair price of the FTSE 100 index futures expiring on 17 March 2006?

SOLUTION   Since there are three months to expiry, (III.2.6) gives the fair price as

$$5531.63 \times \exp((0.0457 - 0.0314) \times 0.25) = 5551.44.$$

III.2.3.3   Dividend Risk and Interest Rate Risk

The dividend risk inherent in a futures contract is the risk associated with uncertainty in dividend payments on the underlying stock or index between now and expiry of the contract. If a dividend payment at any time before the expiry of the contract changes, then this affects the dividend yield. Then the stock or index price and the futures price may diverge. For instance, suppose that we buy a 3-month stock futures contract today when its fair value is calculated assuming a dividend payment will be made in 1 month. However, next week there is an announcement that, contrary to expectations, no dividend payment will now be made. This will affect both the stock and the futures prices but it is likely to have a greater effect on the stock price, because the stockholder will no longer receive the dividend that they previously anticipated.

Similarly, futures contracts have an inherent interest rate risk that stems from the uncertainty in borrowing costs associated with holding the stock. In the no arbitrage pricing relationship (III.2.6) these costs accrue over the life of the futures contract, so the interest rate risk arises from our uncertainty about zero coupon rates at any time between the inception and expiry of the futures contract.[54]

An exposure to a stock futures or stock index futures can be decomposed into exposures to three fundamental risk factors: the underlying stock or index, the dividend yield of maturity and the zero coupon rate. To see this we take logarithms of (III.2.6), giving

$$\ln F^*(t, T) - \ln S(t) = (r(t, T) - y(t, T))(T - t). \qquad \text{(III.2.7)}$$

The one-period log return on the spot and the futures are

$$r_S(t) = \ln S(t) - \ln S(t - 1),$$
$$r_{F^*}(t, T) = \ln F^*(t, T) - \ln F^*(t - 1, T). \qquad \text{(III.2.8)}$$

Now combining (III.2.7) with (III.2.8) yields the following approximate relationship for the log returns on the theoretical value of the futures:[55]

$$r_{F^*}(t, T) \approx r_S(t) - r(t, T) + y(t, T). \qquad \text{(III.2.9)}$$

This shows that the return on the fair value of the futures is approximately equal to the total return on the underlying asset, i.e. including the cost of borrowing and the dividend yield.

We can thus decompose an exposure of a nominal amount N to the futures into:

(i)   an exposure N to the underlying asset;
(ii) an exposure $-N$ to the zero coupon rate of maturity $T - t$, with nominal sensitivity

$$PV01_r(t, T) = -N\,\delta01_r(t, T) \approx -N(T - t)\exp(-r(t, T)(T - t)) \times 10^{-4};$$

---

[54] See Section III.1.8.3 for further details on the nature of interest rate risk.
[55] The approximation arises because we assume (a) the fair value of the futures is the same as the fair value of the forward, and (b) there is no change in the interest rate or the dividend yield between time $t - 1$ and time t.

(iii) an exposure N to the dividend yield of maturity $T - t$, with nominal sensitivity

$$PV01_y(t, T) = N\delta 01_y(t, T) \approx N(T - t)\exp(-y(t, T)(T - t)) \times 10^{-4}.$$

In (ii) and (iii) we have used the approximation given in Section III.1.8.2 to the $\delta 01$.

EXAMPLE III.2.4: EXPOSURE TO STOCK INDEX FUTURES

On 19 December 2005 we invest £5-million in the FTSE 100 index futures. Assume the margin is zero and the price of the futures is at its fair value. Calculate the sensitivities of this position to the spot index, the 3-month dividend yield and the 3-month zero coupon rates.

SOLUTION   Our nominal exposure to the spot index is £5 million. From Example III.2.3 we know that the current zero coupon rate and dividend yield are $r(0, 0.25) = 4.57\%$ and $y(0, 0.25) = 3.14\%$. Hence, their nominal sensitivities are given by the above approximations as:

$$PV01_r(0, 0.25) \approx -500 \times 0.25 \times \exp(-0.0457 \times 0.25) = -£123.58,$$

$$PV01_y(0, 0.25) \approx 500 \times 0.25 \times \exp(-0.0314 \times 0.25) = £124.02.$$

We conclude that, compared with the risk associated with the spot index return, the dividend and interest rate risk components are negligible.

III.2.3.4   Currency Forwards and the Interest Rate Differential

Suppose an investor finances an investment of $S_f(t)$ in foreign assets by taking a foreign currency forward position. Here $S_f(t)$ is the spot price of the asset in foreign currency units.[56] Then he should buy $S_f(t)$ units of the foreign currency at a forward date T and sell $S_d(t)$ units of the domestic currency at a forward date T; the fair value of the foreign currency forward contract is

$$F_d(t, T) = S_d(t)\exp(r_d(t, T)(T - t)), \tag{III.2.10}$$

and of the domestic currency forward contract is

$$F_f(t, T) = S_f(t)\exp(r_f(t, T)(T - t)). \tag{III.2.11}$$

The spot exchange rate $S(t)$ is the spot foreign value of one unit of domestic currency, hence $S(t) = S_f(t)/S_d(t)$. The fair value of the forward exchange rate is therefore found by dividing (III.2.10) by (III.2.11). That is, the fair value of the forward exchange rate is

$$F^*(t, T) = S(t)\exp((r_f(t, T) - r_d(t, T))(T - t)). \tag{III.2.12}$$

From (III.2.12) we can deduce, using an argument similar to that in the previous section, that

$$r_{F^*}(t, T) \approx r_S(t) + r_f(t, T) - r_d(t, T). \tag{III.2.13}$$

That is, the difference between the returns on the spot exchange rate and the forward exchange rate is approximately equal to the continuously compounded *interest rate differential*, i.e. the domestic interest rate minus the foreign interest rate.

    The relationship (III.2.13) implies that a forward forex rate exposure can be decomposed into an exposure to the spot forex rate and an exposure to the zero coupon rates in the two

---

[56] We use the subscripts f and d to denote the prices and interest rates in foreign currency and domestic currency, respectively.

currencies. An exposure of N to a forward forex rate of maturity $T - t$ can thus be expressed in terms of equivalent exposures to three fundamental risk factors:

(i)   an exposure N to the spot exchange rate;
(ii) an exposure $-N$ to the domestic zero coupon rate of maturity $T - t$, with nominal sensitivity

$$PV01_d(t, T) = -N\, \delta 01_d(t, T) \approx -N(T - t)\exp(-r_d(t, T)(T - t)) \times 10^{-4};$$

(iii) an exposure N to the foreign zero coupon rate of maturity $T - t$, with nominal sensitivity

$$PV01_f(t, T) = -N\, \delta 01_f(t, T) \approx -N(T - t)\exp(-r_f(t, T)(T - t)) \times 10^{-4}.$$

In (ii) and (iii) we have used the approximation given in Section III.1.8.2 to the $\delta 01$.

EXAMPLE III.2.5: FORWARD FOREX EXPOSURE

A UK investor takes a short position of £30 million on the 6-month forward £/\$ exchange rate. The 6-month continuously compounded zero coupon rates in the US and the UK are 5.5% and 4.5%, respectively. Calculate the sensitivity of the position to the spot rate and to the US and UK 6-month zero coupon rates.

SOLUTION   The nominal sensitivity to the spot forex rate is £30 million. Using the approximations in (ii) and (iii) above, we have:

$$PV01_{UK} \approx 3000 \times 0.5 \times \exp(-0.045 \times 0.5) = 1500 \times 0.9294 = £1467,$$

$$PV01_{US} \approx -3000 \times 0.5 \times \exp(-0.055 \times 0.5) = -1500 \times 0.9228 = -£1459.$$

We conclude that, compared with the risk associated with the spot forex rate, the interest rate risk components are negligible.

III.2.3.5   No Arbitrage Prices for Forwards on Bonds

We return to the no arbitrage argument presented above, but now the underlying asset is a *notional* bond and there is a fixed basket of deliverable bonds each with a fixed conversion factor, such as that shown in Table III.2.2. For each bond in the basket of deliverables we can define the continuously compounded *coupon yield* $y(t, T)$ similarly to (III.2.5). Now $C(t, T)$ is the present value at time t of the income from all coupons received between the time t and the maturity of the forward, including accrued interest, with income being reinvested at the zero coupon rate. Then for each of these bonds we can calculate the fair value of a forward on this bond at time t, using the standard formula, i.e.

$$F_i^*(t, T) = S_i(t)\exp((r(t, T) - y_i(t, T))(T - t)), \qquad \text{(III.2.14)}$$

where $i = 1, \ldots, n$ and there are n possible bonds that can be delivered, and $S_i(t)$ and $y_i(t, T)$ are the current price and coupon yield on the ith bond.

Denote by CF_i the conversion factor for the ith bond and suppose that there is no uncertainty about the yield on the notional bond on the delivery date. Further, assume that the delivery date is known, instead of being at any time during a period of 1 month. Then the cheapest-to-deliver bond is the bond for which $CF_i \times F_i^*(t, T)$ has the minimum value. Suppose that

$$CF_k \times F_k^*(t, T) = \min\{CF_1 \times F_1^*(t, T), \ldots, CF_n \times F_n^*(t, T)\}.$$

Then $F_k^*(t, T)$ is the fair value of *all* the bonds in the deliverables basket.

However, as mentioned already in Section III.2.2.2, in practice the computation of the cheapest-to-deliver bond is complicated by the uncertainty about the delivery date and the uncertainty about the yield on the notional bond on the delivery date. Hence, it is not at all straightforward to derive the fair value of a bond forward or futures.

III.2.3.6   Commodity Forwards, Carry Costs and Convenience Yields

We now consider the no arbitrage argument when the underlying asset is a commodity. In this case we must reconsider strategy (a), i.e. buying the asset now, because in addition to funding costs there are other costs associated with this strategy. These costs, which are termed *carry costs*, include the transportation, insurance and storage costs associated with holding the physical commodity.

But there are also benefits associated with holding certain commodities. Gold and other precious metals are held primarily for investment purposes but most commodities are for consumption rather than investment. In this case there can be a benefit to holding the physical asset in times of short supply, and this benefit is called the *convenience yield*. The convenience yield often has considerable seasonal fluctuations. For instance, during winter months the convenience yield on energy commodities is high because when the weather is very cold we need an unusual amount of energy now, rather than in the future. The *net* convenience yield is the convenience yield less the carry costs. Usually it is negative.

A no arbitrage relationship of the form (III.2.6) can be derived, following an argument identical to that in Section III.2.3.1, i.e. by setting the value of two strategies (a) and (b) equal. We obtain

$$F^*(t, T) = S(t) \exp((r(t, T) - y(t, T))(T - t)), \qquad \text{(III.2.15)}$$

where $S(t)$ is the spot price of the commodity at time t, $F^*(t, T)$ is the fair value at time t of the forward price for delivery at time T, $r(t, T)$ is the continuously compounded risk free interest rate at time t, maturing at time T, and $y(t, T)$ denotes the present value of the net convenience yield associated with holding the commodity between time t and time T, expressed as a percentage of the current spot price of the commodity. With these definitions the no arbitrage relationship (III.2.15) applies just as well to commodities as it does to financial futures on stocks, bonds and stock indices. However, there are two important differences that should be observed when considering the fair value of a commodity future.

Firstly, when the underlying is a financial instrument there is a natural symmetry in the no arbitrage argument. That is, in Section III.2.3.1 we could have replaced strategies (a) and (b) by 'sell the spot asset' and 'sell the forward', respectively. For this reason the no arbitrage range for the market price of financial futures is quite symmetrical about the fair value of the futures. But with commodities we are limited to a *one-way arbitrage* because we cannot short a spot commodity as we can the underlying of financial futures. Because of this the market price of a commodity futures contract can fall very far below its fair price. See Section III.2.4.1 for further details.

Secondly, there are many more uncertainties about carry costs and convenience yields than there are about dividends or interest rates. Storage costs in particular can fluctuate widely depending on whether the usual storage is nearly full to capacity or empty. Hence, the carry costs are particularly uncertain in energy markets, where the normal supply–demand balance can be altered during unpredictable weather conditions. Companies usually risk-manage their commodity exposures by planning their requirements in advance and taking positions on futures, rather than buying on the spot market. Expiry dates are normally every month and any excess supply that is not used before the next month's delivery is held in storage if possible. Problems arise if there is an unanticipated high demand, such as in an exceptionally cold winter snap, when companies may need to purchase the spot commodity if their inventories are depleted. At these times the price of the spot can peak whilst the futures prices are less affected. Sometimes the excess demand is so great that the futures that are expiring soon also have a huge price spike. On the other hand, there can be an unanticipated low demand, where storage becomes full to capacity and additional storage may be relatively expensive or impossible. At these times the demand for the spot commodity is very low indeed and spot prices can fall far below the futures prices.

III.2.3.7   Fair Values of Futures and Spot

The above analysis is based on a 'no arbitrage' relationship that assumed there were no costs to implementing strategy (b) at the time of inception. The only payment on a forward is made when the contract is terminated. However, when trading futures it is necessary to make an up-front payment of the margin and periodic adjustments to the margin if the asset price changes by a certain amount. For this we need to include a borrowing cost at the currently prevailing risk free rate every time the margin is adjusted. Then the no arbitrage argument above can be extended to futures prices, but the technical details are complex.

It can be shown that the theoretical price of a futures contract is equal to the theoretical price of the equivalent forward contract if the zero coupon yield curve is flat (i.e. the same for all maturities) and does not change over time. Otherwise the difference between the fair value of the futures and the fair value of the corresponding forward depends on the correlation between changes in the zero coupon rates and the returns on the underlying asset. If this correlation is positive the futures price tends to be higher than the equivalent forward price, but if it is negative the opposite is the case. Differences can be significant if the maturity of the futures is more than a few months.

In this chapter we have followed the traditional route of theoretical finance, using a no arbitrage argument to derive the fair value for a forward contract from a market price of the spot. But does this really make sense? What I mean is that it is the forward or futures price that usually plays the leading price discovery role.[57] That is, the forward or futures market is usually much more liquid than the spot market, and it is the forward or futures market where the balance between demand and supply is struck. So really, it is the market price of the *forward* or *futures* that is the standard by which we should judge whether the spot market price is at *its* fair value!

Given a market price $F(t, T)$ of the forward we can derive the 'fair value' of the spot as

$$S^*(t) = F(t, T) \exp((y(t, T) - r(t, T))(T - t)), \qquad (\text{III.2.16})$$

where $y(t, T)$ denotes the net convenience coupon or dividend yield, depending on whether the market is for a commodity, bond, stock or stock index. And in the forex market we have

$$S^*(t) = F(t, T) \exp((r_f(t, T) - r_d(t, T))(T - t)) \qquad (\text{III.2.17})$$

for the fair value of the spot exchange rate. We shall return to this issue immediately below, when we describe what is really meant by the *mispricing* of an asset or interest rate.

---

[57] See Section III.2.2.6.

III.2.4   THE BASIS

The *basis* is the difference between the market prices of the spot and the futures. So at time t the basis is defined as

$$B(t, T) = S(t) - F(t, T). \qquad (\text{III.2.18})$$

Basis risk measures our uncertainty about the future value of the basis. This section begins by examining the behaviour of the basis, showing that we can decompose changes in the basis into three components: a *maturity effect* that is entirely deterministic, changes in the *fair value of the basis*, and changes due to fluctuations of the futures price around its fair value. We shall also show how basis risk relates to the correlation between the market prices of the spot and the forward (or future).

III.2.4.1   No Arbitrage Range

In a perfectly liquid market without transactions costs the market price of a forward would be equal to its fair value. However, market prices of forwards deviate from their fair value because there are transactions costs associated with buying both the underlying contract and the forward. Write the market price of the T-maturity forward at time $t < T$ as

$$F(t, T) = F^*(t, T) + x(t, T)S(t). \qquad (\text{III.2.19})$$

Equivalently, the difference between the market price and the fair price of the forward, expressed as a proportion of the spot price, is

$$x(t, T) = \frac{F(t, T) - F^*(t, T)}{S(t)}. \qquad (\text{III.2.20})$$

Many authors refer to (III.2.20) as the *mispricing* of the market price of the forward compared with its fair value. But, as we have noted in the previous section, it is usually the futures contract that is most actively traded and which therefore serves the dominant price discovery role. Thus it is really the spot that is mispriced relative to the futures contract, rather than the futures contract that is mispriced relative to the spot.

In practice it is only possible to make a profitable arbitrage between the spot and the futures contract if the mispricing is large enough to cover transactions costs. In commodity markets there can be considerable uncertainty about the net convenience yield. And in equity markets there can be uncertainties about the size and timing of dividend payments and about the risk free interest rate during the life of a futures contract. All these uncertainties can affect the return from holding the spot asset. As a result there is not just one single price at which no arbitrage is possible. In fact there is a whole range of futures prices around the fair price of the futures for which no arbitrage is possible. We call this the *no arbitrage range*.

EXAMPLE III.2.6: DIFFERENCE BETWEEN FAIR VALUE AND MARKET VALUE

Let us continue with the example of the 3-month FTSE 100 index futures contract, already considered in Examples III.2.3 and III.2.4. We know that on 16 December 2005 the futures had a fair value of 5551.44 based on the spot price of 5531.63. But the 3-month FTSE 100 futures actually closed at 5546.50. How do you account for this difference?

SOLUTION   The percentage mispricing based on (III.2.20) was

$$\frac{5546.50 - 5551.44}{5531.63} = -8.9\,\text{bps}$$

But the usual no arbitrage range for the FTSE index is approximately ± 25 bps because the transactions costs are very small on in such a liquid market. So the closing market price of the futures falls well inside the usual no arbitrage range.

However, calculations of this type can lead to a larger mispricing, especially in less efficient markets than the FTSE 100. Having said this it should be noted that:

- the prices should be contemporaneous. The spot market often closes before the futures, in which case closing prices are not contemporaneous. It is possible that the futures price changes considerably after the close of the spot market.
- the fair value of a futures contract is based on the assumption of a zero margin, so that the fair value of the futures is set equal the fair value of the forward. But in practice the exchange requires margin payments, and in this case a negative correlation between the returns on the spot index and the zero coupon curve (up to 3 months) would have the effect of decreasing the fair value of the futures.

Any apparent 'mispricing' of the futures relative to the spot index should always be viewed with the above two comments in mind.

Figure III.2.11 illustrates the no arbitrage range for a 1-year forward on a non-dividend-paying asset assuming that *two-way arbitrage* is possible, i.e. that the spot can be sold as

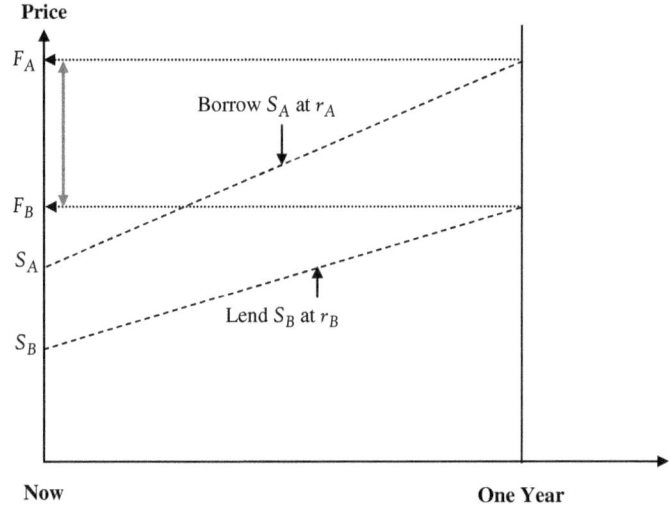

Figure III.2.11   The no arbitrage range for the market price of a financial future

well as bought. The subscripts A and B refer to 'ask' and 'bid' prices or rates.[58] Two no arbitrage strategies are depicted:

(1) Receive funds at r_B by selling the spot at S_B and buying the forward at F_B. By the no arbitrage condition (III.2.4), $F_B = S_B \exp(r_B)$.
(2) Borrow funds at r_A to buy the spot at S_A and sell the forward at F_A. By the no arbitrage condition (III.2.4), $F_A = S_A \exp(r_A)$.

The no arbitrage range for the forward price is marked on the diagram with the grey double-headed arrow. If the market bid price F_B^M or the market ask price F_A^M of the forward lies outside the no arbitrage range $[F_B, F_A]$ then we can make a profit as follows:

- if $F_A^M > F_A$ then sell the forward and buy the spot, or
- if $F_B^M < F_B$ then sell the spot and buy the forward.

III.2.4.2   Correlation between Spot and Futures Returns

Many exchanges in the US and Europe have highly developed electronic communications networks. Competition among dealers is high and bid–ask spreads are extremely narrow. Recently interest rates in these countries have also been low and stable, and so the no arbitrage range for market prices of futures is now very narrow indeed. In these circumstances the market prices of futures will be very highly correlated with spot prices.

To demonstrate this, Table III.2.5 reports the correlation between the daily log returns on the spot index and the near index futures (i.e. the futures contract that is the next to expire) for several stock indices. These are based on daily data from January 1997 to March 2006 and we have split the sample into two halves, to show that correlations were increasing over time.

Table III.2.5   Correlation between spot and futures returns: stock indices

Returns	NASD	SPX	FTSE	Hang Seng	Bovespa
Jan. 1997–Dec. 2000	0.967	0.961	0.967	0.948	0.911
Jan. 2001–Mar. 2006	0.976	0.980	0.981	0.960	0.954

We should note that on most exchanges the trading on stocks closes before the trading on the index futures. For instance, on the NYSE and LSE, stock trading closes 15 minutes before futures trading. Hence, the prices used to calculate these correlations are not even contemporaneous. If we had used contemporaneous prices the correlations shown in Table III.2.5 would have been even higher. Notice that the spot–futures correlations in Table III.2.5 are slightly higher for the more liquid stock markets. This is a general feature of spot and futures correlations: the more highly developed the trading mechanisms on the exchange and the higher the trading volume, the narrower the bid–ask spreads and hence the higher the spot–futures correlation.

---

[58] The *ask price* or rate is paid when an investor buys the asset or goes long an interest rate and the *bid price* or rate is paid when he sells an asset or goes short an interest rate. So the ask is greater than the bid.

In relatively illiquid futures markets, including the new futures markets described in Section III.2.2.7 and in some commodity futures markets, bid–ask spreads are very wide and the no arbitrage range for market prices of futures can fluctuate considerably about their fair value. We have also seen that there can be considerable uncertainty about the fair value itself, particularly in commodity markets where carry costs and convenience yields can be high and variable. In these situations the correlation between spot and futures returns may be low and quite variable over time.

In fact spot–futures correlations can become quite low even in liquid commodity markets. Figure III.2.12 shows the short term correlation between the spot price of light sweet crude oil and the NYMEX prompt futures price during an 11-year period from 1988 to 1999. The series shown is an exponentially weighted moving average (EWMA) correlation with a smoothing constant of 0.98.[59] The correlation is much less than 1, and varies considerably over time.

Figure III.2.12   Correlation between spot and futures prices: crude oil

III.2.4.3   Introducing Basis Risk

The *basis* is defined in (III.2.18) as the difference between the market prices of the spot and the futures (or forward). Since the futures or forward price converges to the spot price as $t \to T$, the basis is zero at expiry. In this section we demonstrate that prior to expiry there are three components to changes in the basis, due to:

(a) maturity;
(b) interest rates, dividends, carry costs and convenience yields; and
(c) fluctuation of the market price of the futures within its no arbitrage range.

Changes of type (a) are totally predictable and therefore do not constitute a risk, because risk is a measure of uncertainty. Changes of type (b) are unpredictable when the forward

---

[59] See Chapter II.3 for further information on exponentially weighted moving averages.

is on a commodity, because carry costs and convenience yields are difficult to predict. But for forwards on currencies, bonds, stocks, stock indices and ETFs changes of type (b) are a relatively minor component of basis risk. We shall now show that, whatever the underlying, the really important determinant of basis risk is the uncertainty due to changes of type (c).

We first illustrate how to isolate the first two components above by considering a forward on a stock with dividend yield $y(t, T)$ at time t. Note that we could illustrate this just as easily assuming the forward is on a bond, commodity, stock index or ETF, simply by changing our interpretation of $y(t, T)$. Denote by $b^*(t, T)$ the *fair value of the basis* at time t, as a proportion of the cash price. That is:

$$b^*(t, T) = \frac{S(t) - F^*(t, T)}{S(t)} = 1 - \exp((r(t, T) - y(t, T))(T - t)). \qquad \text{(III.2.21)}$$

Changes of type (a) and (b) result in changes to the fair value of the basis. These changes are illustrated in Figure III.2.13. The maturity effect (a) is completely predictable because the time to maturity $T - t$ appears on the right-hand side of (III.2.21) and as time varies between 0 and T, it declines linearly from T to 0. Hence, maturity changes give rise to the saw-tooth pattern shown by the bold black line in Figure III.2.13. Each time a futures contract expires and a new contract is issued, the fair value of the basis jumps up from zero and then declines towards zero again.

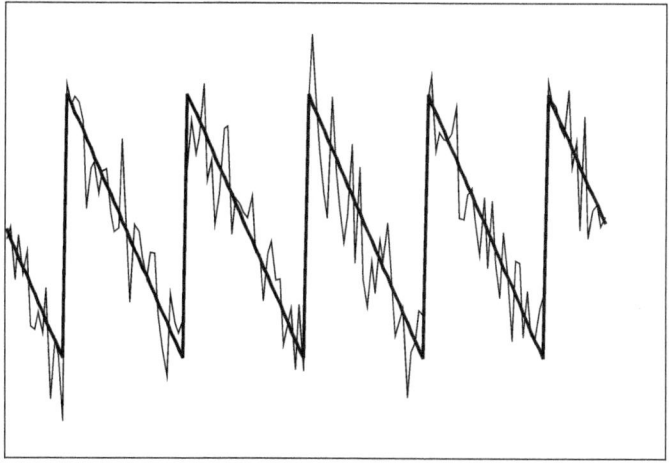

Figure III.2.13 The fair value of the basis over time

Superimposed on this line we have depicted the variation in the fair value of the basis due to changes in interest rates, dividend yields or net convenience yield. Dividends are often announced long in advance and therefore uncertainty in the dividend yield is minimal. It only arises if there are changes to dividends after the announcement. The equivalent variation for a fixed coupon bond, i.e. uncertainty in the coupon yield, is zero. This leaves the uncertainty about changes in interest rates, and convenience yield if the underlying is a commodity, as the major determinants of fluctuations in the fair value of the basis.

The two main contributions to basis risk are from:

- interest rate or, for a commodity, carry cost and convenience yield uncertainty, which affect the *fair* value of the basis, and
- the uncertainty in the mispricing series, i.e. the unpredictable fluctuations in the market price of the futures contract within its no arbitrage range.

We can distinguish these two effects by considering a cash position on a stock at time $t = 0$ with value $S(0)$ that is hedged by selling n contracts on futures with expiry date T and market price $F(0, T)$. We do not rebalance this hedge, so at any time t, with $0 < t < T$, the market value of the hedge position is

$$V(t) = S(t) - n(F(t, T) - F(0, T)).\qquad\text{(III.2.22)}$$

Now combining (III.2.20), (III.2.21) and (III.2.22) to eliminate $F(t, T)$ from the above expression yields, after come calculations,

$$V(t) = nF(0, T) + S(t)\left[1 - n(1 - b^*(t, T) + x(t, T))\right].\qquad\text{(III.2.23)}$$

In (III.2.23) the first term $nF(0, T)$ is known at time 0. But in the term in square brackets there are two sources of uncertainty that need to be hedged: the uncertainty about the fair value of the basis $b^*(t, T)$ and the uncertainty about the mispricing of the futures contract, $x(t, T)$. Of these two terms it is the mispricing uncertainty, about the market price of the futures between now and maturity, that is the main component of basis risk, except in commodities where the carry cost and convenience yield uncertainty can be large.

III.2.4.4   Basis Risk in Commodity Markets

Two-way arbitrage is not possible on commodities because we cannot sell the spot (unless we are a producer). This means that there is no lower bound to the no arbitrage range and the spot prices of commodities can rise very significantly above the market price of the futures. In some cases there is no spot market at all. This is the case for *weather derivatives* such as forwards on temperature. In that case the forward price can fluctuate within a very large range indeed, so these derivatives are amongst the most volatile and risky of all.

The decoupling of spot and futures prices is particularly evident in energy markets. Figure III.2.14 shows the daily spot prices of PJM electricity compared with the prices of different futures contracts during 2005 and the early part of 2006. Due to imbalances between demand and supply the spot price fluctuates excessively from day to day, so that they can be either far above or far below the futures prices. In fact spot electricity prices can even become negative! Negative electricity prices can occur because, unlike other energy commodities, electricity is almost impossible to store. Generally, electricity prices will be negative only for very short periods during the night. Most electricity generators must either run 24 hours a day or else huge shut-down and restart costs are incurred, so power supply can be considerably greater than demand. Negative prices are acceptable to power suppliers because the costs of a shut-down period are sometimes higher than the cost of off-loading the unwanted electricity. However, sometimes negative prices can last for long periods: this happened in the Netherlands in March 2003, for instance.

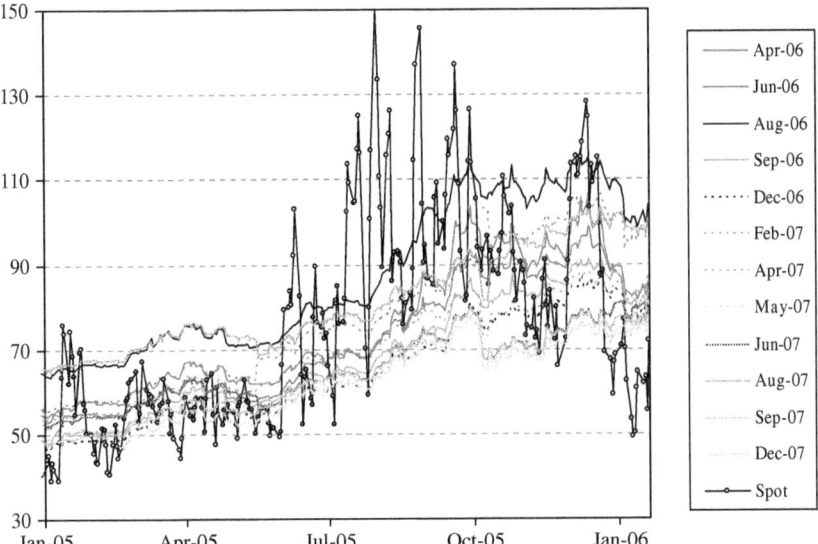

Figure III.2.14   Spot and futures price of electricity

III.2.5   HEDGING WITH FORWARDS AND FUTURES

This section is concerned with hedging a cash position with a forward or futures contract. What do we mean by 'hedging a cash position'? We should make clear from the outset that securing a price in the future by buying or selling a forward or futures contract now is equivalent to securing the *fair* spot price now, if the spot price exists. It is *this* cash position that is hedged. For instance, suppose we are to receive funds 3 months from now that we want to invest in the FTSE 100 index, but we believe that by the time we receive the funds the index will have increased substantially. We can buy the FTSE 100 futures contract now, paying only the margin. Suppose that the index is currently at 6000, that the 3-month FTSE 100 futures contract is at 6020 and the fair value of the 3-month basis (which is calculated using 3-month LIBOR and the dividend yield on the FTSE 100) is 30 index points. Then the current fair spot price is 5990. In other words, we have bought the index at the expiry of the futures at a fixed value of 6020 and this is equivalent to buying the spot now at 5990. So it is the *fair* value of the index that we have insured, not the actual value. The cost of this insurance is our margin cost on the futures.

The classical papers on hedging with forward and futures contracts go back more than half a century. The traditional view is that hedging with forward or futures contracts is used *only* for insurance and the aim of a hedge is only to minimize our uncertainty about a portfolio's value at some *future* time t, when the hedge is closed.[60] In this approach we are not concerned with the expected value of the portfolio; we are only concerned with minimizing our uncertainty about this value.

During the 1960s the *mean–variance* approach to hedging was introduced by Johnson (1960) and Stein (1961), and this was extended to proxy hedging by Anderson and Danthine

---

[60] The value of the portfolio at time t includes any costs or benefits accruing to the holder of the portfolio by time t.

(1981). These authors assume that hedging has an additional *speculative* element, so that hedgers are concerned about the expected returns as well as the risk of a hedged portfolio. We shall explain the mean–variance utility maximizing framework as it applies to hedging and show that the hedging problem becomes a standard portfolio allocation problem. In fact when hedging is approached from the mean–variance perspective it is equivalent to mean–variance portfolio optimization, which has already been introduced in Section I.6.3.

This section begins with a comparison of the traditional 'insurance' framework with the mean–variance hedging framework, explaining how the concept of *minimum variance hedging* fits into both of these approaches.[61] Then we present some numerical examples on minimum variance hedging, and in particular examine the residual risks that still exist in a hedged portfolio. Finally, we focus on the problems of hedging with an instrument that has a high, but less than perfect, correlation with the portfolio that is being hedged. This case arises in two situations: when the hedging instrument has a maturity that is different from the hedging horizon, which we call *maturity mismatch*, and when the hedging instrument is something other than the forward or futures contract on a spot asset for which we have a cash position, which we call *proxy hedging*.

We shall use the following definitions and notation throughout: N_S is the size of the spot position to be hedged at time 0, and N_F is the size of each futures contract. The futures contract has maturity T and the prices of the spot and the futures at time t are denoted $S(t)$ and $F(t, T)$, with $0 \leq t \leq T$. The number of futures contracts in the hedge is denoted n. This is determined at time 0 and held fixed until the hedge is closed. The *hedge ratio* $\beta(t)$ is the ratio of the value of the futures position to the value of the position on the underlying. Thus,

$$\beta(t) = \frac{n \times N_F \times F(t, T)}{N_S \times S(t)}. \tag{III.2.24}$$

III.2.5.1 Traditional 'Insurance' Approach

When a hedge is placed purely for insurance purposes the hedging criterion is to minimize our uncertainty about the value of the hedged portfolio *at the time that the hedge is closed*. But a spot exposure at time T is perfectly hedged by taking an equal and opposite position in the futures with expiry date T, if such a futures contract exists. At expiry the futures price is, by definition, equal to the spot price. Since the value of the hedge will exactly match the value of the underlying exposure, the value of the hedged portfolio at time T is zero and there is no uncertainty about this value. Thus, when a futures position is closed at maturity the optimal hedge ratio is always *one*.

For instance, consider the case of a power company that needs to purchase 10,000 barrels of heating oil on 31 March. Recently oil prices have been rising rapidly and the company is concerned that spot prices will increase, so it buys heating oil futures on NYMEX for delivery on 31 March at a price that is fixed today. Each heating oil futures contract is for 1000 barrels of oil, so the company's short exposure of 10,000 barrels in 1 month is perfectly insured by taking a long position of 10 heating oil March futures contracts. On 31 March

---

[61] When assessing the value of a hedged portfolio we should account for any costs or benefits associated with holding the spot asset, and with the margin costs of a futures position. But for simplicity we shall assume these costs or benefits are zero. Addition of these does not change the fundamental argument presented below.

the company will receive 10,000 barrels of heating oil at the price fixed today, i.e. at the current futures price.

Now suppose there is a maturity mismatch, so that the hedge position is closed at some time $t < T$, where T is the expiry date of the futures. The value of the hedged portfolio at time t is

$$P(t) = n \times N_F \times F(t, T) - N_S \times S(t). \tag{III.2.25}$$

The variance of this portfolio value is

$$V(P(t)) = n^2 N_F^2 V(F(t, T)) + N_S^2 V(S(t)) - 2nN_F N_S \text{Cov}(F(t, T) S(t)). \tag{III.2.26}$$

Note that if $nN_F = N_S$ as in the *one-for-one hedge* then

$$\text{StDev}(P(t)) = N_S \times \sqrt{V(F(t, T)) + V(S(t)) - 2\text{Cov}(F(t, T), S(t))}. \tag{III.2.27}$$

Our hedging criterion is to choose n at time 0 to minimize (III.2.26). Differentiating with respect to n and checking the second order condition gives the optimal number of contracts in the hedge as

$$n^* = \left(\frac{N_S}{N_F}\right) \times \beta^*, \tag{III.2.28}$$

where

$$\beta^* = \frac{\text{Cov}(F(t, T), S(t))}{V(F(t, T))}. \tag{III.2.29}$$

The ratio (III.2.29) is called the *minimum variance hedge ratio*.

This definition of the minimum variance hedge ratio, based on the variance and covariance of lognormal random variables, is standard in continuous time finance. It is used to derive delta hedges for options that are different from the standard 'partial derivative' delta hedges.[62] We have shown that it also applies to a minimum variance futures hedge ratio when the criterion for hedging is to minimize the uncertainty about the value of the hedged portfolio at the time that the hedge is closed.

In practice, when hedging a cash position with a forward or futures on the spot asset, we can estimate (III.2.29) without specifying the distribution of the spot price.[63] Since

$$S(t) = B(t, T) + F(t, T),$$

where $B(t, T)$ is the basis at time t, we have

$$\beta^* = 1 + \frac{\text{Cov}(F(t, T), B(t, T))}{V(F(t, T))} = 1 + \text{Corr}(F(t, T), B(t, T))\sqrt{\frac{V(B(t, T))}{V(F(t, T))}}. \tag{III.2.30}$$

The correlation between the futures and the basis is often negative and the basis usually has a much smaller volatility than the futures. So the minimum variance hedge ratio will, in general, be slightly less than 1. However, when the hedge is held until time T, the expiry date of the futures, the minimum variance hedge ratio is 1, because $B(T, T)$ is 0.

---

[62] See Section III.4.6.5.

[63] This is very useful because in some situations the spot bears no relation to the futures contract. This is the case, for instance, with volatility futures. It may even be that the spot does not even exist at the time of the hedge. This is the case for any perishable commodity for instance.

III.2.5.2 Mean–Variance Approach

The mean–variance view of hedging, introduced by Johnson (1960), assumes that as well as insuring our position we are interested in speculation. Johnson calls the standard deviation of the hedged portfolio P&L over the hedging period the *price risk* of the hedged portfolio. His hedging criterion is to minimize this price risk *and* to maximize the expected P&L over the hedging period.

Figure III.2.15 depicts the situation when there is a perfect hedge available. That is, there is a futures contract F on our initial portfolio S with a maturity that matches the hedging horizon exactly and whose price is perfectly correlated with the portfolio's price. The point S defines our initial portfolio, and its price risk and expected return are shown on the horizontal and vertical axes. The point F defines the risk and return on the futures contract which, in the case of a perfect hedge is just a leveraged position on S. It is very highly leveraged because the futures contract costs almost nothing to trade. By combining the portfolio with the hedge we can achieve any allocation along the straight line shown, just as we could in the classical mean–variance analysis described in Section I.6.3, by lending or borrowing at the risk free rate R and investing in S.

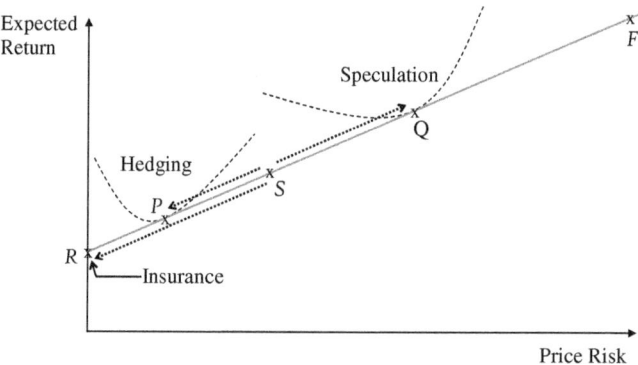

Figure III.2.15   Mean–variance hedging with perfect hedge

The traditional insurance view of hedging is to remove *all* risk from the hedged portfolio, thus attaining the risk free rate of return with zero risk. This is the minimum variance hedged portfolio. But we also show two utility functions of different investors in Figure III.2.15. These are represented by the indifference curves depicted by the two dotted curves. One investor is a 'hedger'. He sells the future in a sufficient amount to reduce his price risk, and hence also his expected return. But he does not necessarily reduce his price risk to zero, since he prefers the portfolio P to the risk free return. This type of mean–variance hedging is what we usually mean by hedging, i.e. the reduction of risk, so we shall call it simply *hedging*. The other investor is a 'speculator'. He buys the future to leverage his expected return, but he also increases his price risk at his optimal portfolio Q. We call this type of mean–variance hedging *speculation*.

Now suppose that a perfect hedge is not available. Either there is no forward or futures contract on the portfolio, or there is a forward or futures contract but it has a different maturity than the period over which we want to hedge. That is, we may use a proxy hedge or there may be a maturity mismatch. The mean–variance analysis is now depicted in Figure III.2.16. The hedging instrument is highly but not perfectly correlated with S, so by adding the hedging instrument F to S we can achieve all the portfolios lying along the grey curve. The minimum variance hedged portfolio is indicated by the point M. The mean variance optimal portfolios for two investors, a hedger and speculator, are also shown by the points P and Q respectively, assuming the risk free asset is available.

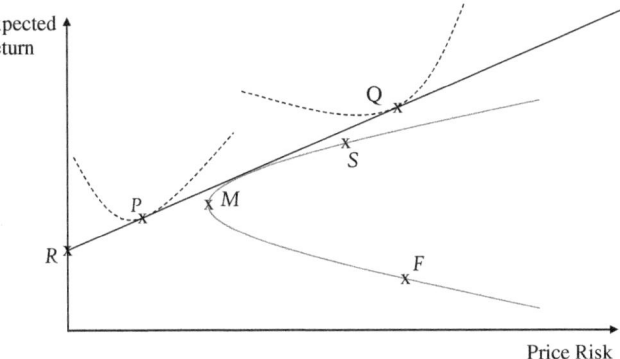

Figure III.2.16   Mean–variance hedging with proxy hedge or maturity mismatch

We now provide an algebraic description of the mean–variance framework. Suppose that the hedge is closed at time t with $0 < t \leq T$ and, for brevity write

$$\Delta P(t) = P(t) - P(0), \; \Delta S(t) = S(t) - S(0) \text{ and } \Delta F(t) = F(t, T) - F(0, T).$$

So $\Delta P(t)$, which is the change in value of hedged portfolio between time 0, when the hedge is placed, and time t, when the hedge is closed, is

$$\Delta P(t) = n \times N_F \times \Delta F(t) - N_S \times \Delta S(t). \tag{III.2.31}$$

Now we can calculate the expected P&L over the period of the hedge as

$$E(\Delta P(t)) = nN_F E(\Delta F(t)) - N_S E(\Delta S(t)), \tag{III.2.32}$$

and the price risk is the standard deviation of the P&L *about this expected value*, i.e. the square root of

$$V(\Delta P(t)) = n^2 N_F^2 V(\Delta F(t)) + N_S^2 V(\Delta S(t)) - 2nN_F N_S \text{Cov}(\Delta F(t), \Delta S(t)). \tag{III.2.33}$$

Note that if $nN_F = N_S$ as in the one-for-one hedge,

$$\text{StDev}(\Delta P(t)) = N_S \times \sqrt{V(\Delta F(t)) + V(\Delta S(t)) - 2\text{Cov}(\Delta F(t), \Delta S(t))}. \tag{III.2.34}$$

For instance, consider again the case of a power company that needs to purchase 10,000 barrels of heating oil on 31 March. Each heating oil futures contract is for 1000 barrels of oil, so the company's short exposure of 10,000 barrels in 1 month is perfectly insured by taking a long position of 10 heating oil March futures contracts. But if instead of insuring its exposure the company is also concerned about the profit and loss that it has on the hedge, then we may reach a different conclusion about the optimal hedge, and this optimal hedged portfolio will depend on the company's attitude to risk.

Suppose that the spot price of heating oil is $82 per barrel on 1 March and the hedger buys 10 heating oil futures contracts at $80 per barrel. At the time of taking out the hedge, the hedger believes that the spot and the futures returns have the same volatility of 25% and a correlation of 0.95. On 31 March when the hedge expires the spot price, which is by definition equal to the futures price, is \$85. The P&L of the hedged portfolio is

$$\$10,000\,[(85-80)-(85-82)]=\$10,000\times(82-80)=\$20,000.$$

Note that this is independent of the price at the time when the hedge expires.

The price risk is the standard deviation about this P&L. To quantify this we use the formula (III.2.34) with $N_S = 10,000$ and

$$\text{StDev}(\Delta F)=\$80\times 0.25\times 12^{-1/2}=\$5.77,$$

$$\text{StDev}(\Delta S)=\$82\times 0.25\times 12^{-1/2}=\$5.92,$$

$$\text{Cov}(\Delta F,\Delta S)=0.95\times 5.77\times 5.92=32.46.$$

The result is a price risk of

$$\$10,000\sqrt{5.77^2+5.92^2-2\times 32.46}=\$18,541.$$

Most of the recent literature on hedging with futures ignores the mean–variance criterion and simply focuses on the minimum variance criterion, i.e. the minimization of (III.2.33) without even considering the expected return. That is, the assumption is that the purpose of hedging is to achieve the minimum variance hedged portfolio. When a perfect hedge exists the minimum variance hedged portfolio is the risk free portfolio R in Figure III.2.15. Otherwise the minimum variance hedged portfolio is M in Figure III.2.16.

Minimizing (III.2.33) with respect to n gives the optimal number of contracts in the hedge,

$$n^* = \left(\frac{N_S}{N_F}\right)\times\beta^*, \qquad\qquad (\text{III.2.35})$$

where the minimum variance hedge ratio is

$$\beta^* = \frac{\text{Cov}(\Delta F(t),\Delta S(t))}{V(\Delta F(t))}. \qquad\qquad (\text{III.2.36})$$

For instance, the minimum variance hedge ratio for the heating oil hedging example is

$$\beta^* = \frac{32.46}{5.77^2}=0.97375. \qquad\qquad (\text{III.2.37})$$

Notice that this is not 1, even though the hedge is perfect in the heating oil hedging example, i.e. the futures is on the same commodity as the underlying and the hedge held to the expiry of the futures contract. But we have shown, using the traditional approach to hedging, that the minimum variance hedge ratio must be 1 when there is a perfect hedge. So where is the error this example? The next subsection gives the answer.

III.2.5.3 Understanding the Minimum Variance Hedge Ratio

It follows immediately on noting that both $F(0, T)$ and $S(0)$ are known at time 0 that the minimum variance hedge ratio (III.2.36) is identical to the minimum variance hedge ratio (III.2.29). That is,

$$\text{Cov}(\Delta F(t),\Delta S(t))=\text{Cov}(F(t,T),S(t)) \text{ and } V(\Delta F(t))=V(F(t,T)),$$

and so (III.2.36) and (III.2.29) are identical. When $t = T$, i.e. when the hedge is held until maturity,

$$\text{Cov}(\Delta F(T), \Delta S(T)) = \text{Cov}(F(T, T), S(T)) = V(S(T))$$

and

$$V(\Delta F(T)) = V(F(T, T)) = V(S(T)).$$

So it does not matter whether we use the traditional 'insurance' approach or the mean–variance approach, the minimum variance hedge ratio is always equal to 1 when there is a perfect hedge available. Of course, it may be different from 1 if there is a maturity mismatch and/or when we need to use a proxy hedge. If a hedge ratio of 1 *is* applied when there is a maturity mismatch and/or when a proxy hedging instrument is used, then we call this the *naïve hedge*.

We have just demonstrated that when a futures hedge is held to maturity the minimum variance hedge ratio must be 1. But in our heating oil example we calculated a minimum variance hedge ratio for a perfect hedge that was not equal to 1, so this example is clearly incorrect. We now show that the problem lay in the calculation of the price risk.

In Johnson's view price risk is based on the hedger's *beliefs*, at time 0, about the variances of the price changes in the spot and the futures over the hedging period. He did not impose any constraints on these beliefs. Any subjective probability distribution would do. This was fine because Johnson considered the mean–variance trade-off and did not ignore the expected P&L. But in the minimum variance framework, there *is* a constraint on the distribution of the hedged portfolio P&L because the minimum variance hedge ratio must be 1 when the hedge is held to maturity. This implies

$$\frac{\text{Cov}(\Delta F(T), \Delta S(T))}{V(\Delta F(T))} = \text{Corr}(\Delta F(T), \Delta S(T)) \sqrt{\frac{V(\Delta S(T))}{V(\Delta F(T))}} = 1,$$

and hence that

$$\text{Corr}(\Delta F(T), \Delta S(T)) = \sqrt{\frac{V(\Delta F(T))}{V(\Delta S(T))}}. \qquad \text{(III.2.38)}$$

In other words, under a perfect hedge, i.e. when a futures on the underlying asset is held until the futures expiry date, the hedger must believe that the P&L on the spot and futures has a correlation that is equal to the relative volatility of the futures with respect to the spot. This is a very strong constraint on the hedger's beliefs. For instance, in the heating oil example above the belief that the spot and the futures returns had the same volatility of 25% and a correlation of 0.95 was not possible, because the hedge was held until expiry of the futures.

If the hedge is closed before the futures expiry date, or a proxy hedge is used, the minimum variance hedge ratio is not usually equal to 1. As we explained in Section III.2.5.1, this is because there is a non-zero basis risk when the hedge is closed out before maturity or when a proxy hedging instrument is used. So in this case there are fewer constraints on the hedger's beliefs about the distribution of spot and futures over the period of the hedge. However, there *are* still constraints about the hedger's beliefs over any period. These constraints arise from the behaviour of the basis, which typically has a high negative autocorrelation.

Very often we express beliefs about the *returns* on the spot and futures over the period of the hedge, rather than beliefs on P&L. In this case we need to write (III.2.33) in the form

$$V(\Delta P(t)) = (N_S S \sigma_S)^2 + (n \, N_F F \sigma_F)^2 - 2nN_S N_F SF\varrho\sigma_S\sigma_F, \qquad \text{(III.2.39)}$$

where $S = S(0)$ is the spot price at time 0, $F = F(0, T)$ the futures price at time 0,

$$\sigma_S = \sqrt{V\big((S(t) - S(0)) \big/ S(0)\big)}$$

is the volatility of spot returns over the hedging period,

$$\sigma_F = \sqrt{V\big((F(t, T) - F(0, T)) \big/ F(0, T)\big)}$$

is the volatility of futures returns over the hedging period, and ϱ is the correlation between spot and futures returns.

Differentiating (III.2.39) with respect to n, setting this to zero and solving for n gives

$$n^* = \left(\frac{N_S}{N_F}\right)\left(\frac{S}{F}\right)\left(\varrho\frac{\sigma_S}{\sigma_F}\right). \tag{III.2.40}$$

This is the number of futures contracts in the hedge when we minimize the variance of the hedge portfolio. Note that when beliefs are expressed in terms of returns we normally express the minimum variance hedge ratio as

$$\tilde{\beta} = \varrho\frac{\sigma_S}{\sigma_F} \tag{III.2.41}$$

so that, according to the previous definition (III.2.35)

$$\beta^* = \left(\frac{S}{F}\right) \times \tilde{\beta}. \tag{III.2.42}$$

III.2.5.4   Position Risk

Very often it is not possible to buy exactly the right number of futures contracts that are recommended in the hedge. For instance, our hedge might recommend that we buy 10.45 futures contracts, as is the case in the example below. Since we can only buy 10 or 11 futures contracts there will be a residual risk in the hedge resulting from the mismatch of positions. If the optimal number of futures contracts recommended by the hedge is not a integral number of futures then we will over-hedge with the futures (if we round up the number of contracts) or under-hedge with the futures (if we round down). The computation of this *position risk* is best illustrated by a numerical example.

EXAMPLE III.2.7: PRICE RISK AND POSITION RISK OF NAÏVE AND MINIMUM VARIANCE HEDGES

Suppose a refinery needs to buy 10,450 barrels of crude oil and will hedge this exposure over a period of 1 month by buying crude oil futures. Each crude oil futures contract is for 1000 barrels of oil. Suppose that S is the current spot price of $100 per barrel, F is the current futures price of $102 per barrel, $\sigma_S = 40\%$ is the annual volatility of spot price returns, $\sigma_F = 35\%$ is the annual volatility of the futures returns, and $\varrho = 0.98$ is the correlation between spot and futures returns. What is the price risk before the hedge? Now consider the naïve hedge, and the minimum variance hedge. What is the price risk after the hedge and how much of this price risk is due to position risk? Now repeat your calculations on the assumption that the spot and futures returns are perfectly correlated.

SOLUTION   We first need to calculate the standard deviations and the covariance of the monthly P&L on the spot and futures. We have:

$$\text{StDev}(\Delta S) = \$100 \times 0.4 \times 12^{-1/2} = \$11.55,$$

$$\text{StDev}(\Delta F) = \$102 \times 0.35 \times 12^{-1/2} = \$10.31,$$

$$\text{Cov}(\Delta S, \Delta F) = 0.98 \times 11.55 \times 10.31 = 116.62.$$

The price risk before the hedge is $\$(10,450 \times 11.55) = \$120,666$.

Now consider the naïve hedge. Each crude oil futures contract is for 1000 barrels of oil, so ideally the refinery would buy 10.45 futures contracts with expiry date in one month. But this is impossible: either 10 or 11 futures contracts must be bought, and the closer of the two figures to the real naïve hedge ratio is to buy 10 contracts. Adding 10 futures contracts to his short spot exposure to 10,450 gallons gives the price risk of the naïve hedged portfolio as:

$$\sqrt{(10,000 \times 10.31)^2 + (10,450 \times 11.55)^2 - 2 \times 10,000 \times 10,450 \times 116.62} = \$28,417.$$

Part of this price risk is due to our inability to buy exactly the right number of contracts. The optimal number of contracts in the hedge was 10.45 and the residual exposure to the futures is 450 gallons. Hence, the position risk is $\$(450 \times 10.31) = \$4638$.

Now consider the minimum variance hedge. Since the spot is more variable than the futures, and they are highly correlated, the minimum variance hedge ratio (III.2.41) is greater than 1 in this case. In fact, it is

$$\tilde{\beta} = 0.98 \times \frac{0.40}{0.35} = 1.12.$$

Now (III.2.40) gives the optimal number of contracts in the hedge:

$$n^* = \frac{10,450}{1,000} \times \frac{100}{102} \times 1.12 = 11.4745.$$

So to minimize the variance of the hedged portfolio we buy 11 futures. The price risk of the hedged portfolio is now

$$\sqrt{(11,000 \times 10.31)^2 + (10,450 \times 11.55)^2 - 2 \times 11,000 \times 10,450 \times 116.62} = \$24,505.$$

But the optimal number of contracts in the hedge was 11.4745. There is a residual exposure to the futures of 474.5 gallons and the risk of this additional exposure to the futures is $\$(474.5 \times 10.31) = \$4890$. Hence \$4890 of the price risk is due to the position risk.

Finally, suppose that the correlation between the spot and the futures is 1. The reader can input this value to the spreadsheet and read off the revised calculations for the price and position risks of the naïve hedge and the minimum variance hedge. The price risk under the naïve hedge reduces to \$17,609, but some of this is position risk. Most importantly, notice that the minimum variance hedged portfolio *always* has a pure price risk of 0 when the spot and the futures are perfectly correlated. This is because we can choose the weights in the minimum variance portfolio of two perfectly correlated assets so that the portfolio has zero risk. However, there is still a position risk, which in this example is equal to \$3002. This position constitutes the entire price risk in the case where the spot and futures are perfectly correlated.

III.2.5.5 Proxy Hedging

In this section we consider the case of a company that needs to buy or sell an asset that has a spot market but no forward or futures market. In this case they can hedge their price risk from future exposures by purchasing futures on a correlated asset. For instance, a lemon producer in the US that sells frozen concentrated lemon juice might consider hedging its price using the actively traded cash-settled frozen concentrated orange juice futures on NYMEX, because no frozen lemon juice futures are available on US exchanges. However, in this case the hedge will not be perfect, even when there is no maturity mismatch or position risk.

EXAMPLE III.2.8: PROXY HEDGING

Suppose a lemon producer plans to sell 75,000 pounds of frozen concentrated lemon juice after the harvest in 6 months' time. He plans to hedge his risk using frozen orange juice futures. Let N_S be the size of spot exposure, 750,000 pounds of lemon juice solids; N_F the size of futures contract, 15,000 pounds of orange juice solids; S the current price of frozen concentrated lemon juice, $1.75 per pound; F the current price of frozen concentrated orange juice futures, $1.5 per pound; $\sigma_S = 40\%$ the volatility of spot price returns; $\sigma_F = 40\%$ the volatility of the futures returns; and $\varrho = 0.75$ the correlation between spot and futures returns. What is the price risk before the hedge? Now consider the naïve hedge, and the minimum variance hedge. What is the price risk after the hedge and how much of this price risk is due to position risk?

SOLUTION   We first need to calculate the standard deviations and the covariance of the 6-monthly P&L on the spot and futures. We have:

$$\text{StDev}(\Delta S) = \$1.75 \times 0.4 \times 2^{-1/2} = \$0.49,$$

$$\text{StDev}(\Delta F) = \$1.5 \times 0.4 \times 2^{-1/2} = \$0.42,$$

$$\text{Cov}(\Delta S, \Delta F) = 0.98 \times 0.49 \times 0.42 = 0.1575.$$

The price risk before the hedge is $(750,000 \times 0.49) = \$371,231$.

Each OJ futures contract is for 15,000 pounds of frozen orange juice, so the producer buys 50 futures contracts and has no position risk. The price risk of the naïve hedged portfolio is

$$750,000\sqrt{0.42^2 + 0.49^2 - 2 \times 0.1575} = \$248,747.$$

The minimum variance hedge ratio (III.2.41) is 0.75, since the spot and futures have the same volatility. The optimal number of contracts in the hedge is

$$n^* = \frac{750,000}{15,000} \times \frac{1.75}{1.5} \times 0.75 = 43.75.$$

So to minimize the variance of the hedged portfolio we buy 44 futures. The price risk of the hedged portfolio is now:

$$\sqrt{(660,000 \times 0.42)^2 + (750,000 \times 0.49)^2 - 2 \times 660,000 \times 750,000 \times 0.1575} = \$245,551.$$

of which the position risk is $\$(0.25 \times 15{,}000) = \$1591$.

Whilst the naïve hedge considerably reduces the price risk in this example, and in Example III.2.7, the further risk reduction resulting from the use of a minimum variance hedge ratio is fairly limited. We shall return to this point in Section III.2.7.2 when we review the academic literature on minimum variance hedging with futures.

III.2.5.6 Basket Hedging

The minimum variance hedge ratio (III.2.41) is related to the volatilities and correlations between the spot and futures returns. In fact, it is the ordinary least squares (OLS) estimate of the slope parameter β in a simple linear regression model,

$$r_{St} = \alpha + \beta r_{Ft} + \varepsilon_t, \tag{III.2.43}$$

where r_{St} and r_{Ft} denote the returns on the spot and on the futures at time t.[64] The use of regression allows one to extend the hedge to multiple hedging instruments. A multiple regression of the spot returns on the returns to various possible hedging instruments gives the minimum variance hedge ratio for each instrument as the OLS estimates of the relevant regression coefficient. The model is

$$r_{St} = \alpha + \beta_1 r_{F_1 t} + \beta_2 r_{F_2 t} + \ldots + \beta_k r_{F_k t} + \varepsilon_t. \tag{III.2.44}$$

The OLS minimum variance hedge ratios are

$$\hat{\boldsymbol{\beta}} = \left(\mathbf{X'X}\right)^{-1}\left(\mathbf{X'y}\right),$$

where

$$\mathbf{X} = \begin{pmatrix} \vdots & \vdots & \cdots & \vdots \\ 1 & r_{F_1} & \cdots & r_{F_k} \\ \vdots & \vdots & \cdots & \vdots \end{pmatrix} \quad \text{and} \quad \mathbf{y} = \begin{pmatrix} \vdots \\ r_S \\ \vdots \end{pmatrix}.$$

Then the number of futures contracts in each partial hedge is given by

$$n_i = \frac{N_S}{N_{F_i}} \times \frac{S}{F_i} \times \hat{\beta}_i, \quad i = 1, \ldots, k, \tag{III.2.45}$$

where S is the spot price and F_i is the price of the ith hedging instrument.

In a situation where a proxy hedge must be used, basket hedging should improve the performance of the hedge. But problems can arise when the futures used in the hedging basket are highly correlated. In that case multicollinearity can bias the hedge ratio estimates. Even without multicollinearity there can be a bias on the OLS estimates of the hedge ratios, and if present this will affect any measure of the performance of the hedge.[65] The best results are obtained using futures on quite different types of underlying, rather than futures on the same underlying with different maturities.[66]

---

[64] This fact rests on the relationship between the OLS regression beta and correlation – see Section I.4.2.2.
[65] See Lien (2006).
[66] See Chen and Sutcliffe (2007).

III.2.5.7 Performance Measures for Hedged Portfolios

Ederington (1979) introduced a simple measure of hedging effectiveness as the percentage reduction in variance achieved by the hedge. The *Ederington effectiveness* measure is

$$E = \frac{V_U - V_H}{V_U}. \tag{III.2.46}$$

For instance, if the volatility of the unhedged position is 25% and the volatility of the hedged position is 5%, then the hedge is 96% effective because

$$E = \frac{0.25^2 - 0.05^2}{0.25^2} = 96\%.$$

An alternative, but just as basic a measure of effectiveness is given by $\sqrt{1 - \varrho^2}$ where ϱ is the correlation between the spot returns on the hedging instrument. In the case of a basket hedge with hedge ratios estimated using OLS, ϱ^2 is the multiple R^2 of the regression. Hence, knowing only the correlation between the portfolio and the hedge returns, we can already estimate the efficiency of the hedge. The higher this correlation, the more efficient the hedge will be.

The correlation and the Ederington effectiveness are widely used even though they are known to be biased in favour of the OLS minimum variance hedge (see Lien, 2005). Also these performance criteria take no account of the effect of variance reduction on *skewness* and *kurtosis* in the hedged portfolio's returns. Minimum variance hedged portfolios are designed to have very low returns volatility and this could increase an investor's confidence to the extent that large leveraged positions are adopted. But a high kurtosis indicates that the hedge can be spectacularly wrong on just a few days and a negative skewness indicates that it would be losing rather than making money. Hence, several authors prefer to use an effectiveness criterion that penalizes negative skewness and positive kurtosis.[67]

During the 1980s there was a considerable debate about the best hedging effectiveness measure.[68] A veritable menagerie of performance measures for different types of hedged portfolio were introduced, each with different qualities and each applicable in different circumstances. However, most of these effectiveness measures are based on too few characteristics of the hedge portfolio returns distribution, do not take into account the risk attitude of the investor and may be justified only under very restrictive conditions.

For this reason Alexander and Barbosa (2008) and others employ the *certainty equivalent* (CE) that is derived from an exponential utility for the hedger.[69] The exponential utility function is defined as

$$U(x) = -\lambda \exp(-x/\lambda). \tag{III.2.47}$$

Here λ is the coefficient of risk tolerance, which defines the curvature of the utility function, and x is usually defined as wealth.[70] But in the context of measuring the performance of a hedge we can take x to represent the P&L on the hedged portfolio.

[67] See Cremers et al. (2004), Harvey et al. (2004), Patton (2004) and many others.
[68] See Howard and D'Antonio (1987) for instance.
[69] The CE is defined in Section I.6.2.1: It is the certain amount that gives the investor the same utility as the expected utility of an uncertain investment. Thus it depends on both the distribution of returns (or P&L) resulting from the investment and the utility function of the investor.
[70] Section I.6.2.3 explains how to determine the coefficient of risk tolerance for any investor.

In Section I.6.2.7 we derived the approximation

$$CE \approx \mu - \tfrac{1}{2}\gamma\sigma^2 + \frac{\tau}{6}\gamma^2\sigma^3 - \frac{(\kappa - 3)}{24}\gamma^3\sigma^4 \qquad (\text{III.2.48})$$

to the CE for an investor with an exponential utility function, where μ and σ are the mean and the standard deviation of the hedged portfolio P&L, and τ and κ are the skewness and kurtosis of the hedged portfolio P&L. Assuming the risk tolerance parameter $\lambda > 0$ the CE criterion (III.2.48) includes an aversion to risk associated with negative skewness and increasing kurtosis as well as increasing variance.

III.2.6   HEDGING IN PRACTICE

This section examines the hedging of international portfolios, stock portfolios, commodity portfolios and bond portfolios. First, we describe how to hedge an exposure to forward foreign exchange rates. Since there are liquid forward markets in most currencies, the hedging problem is particularly simple in this case. However, few stock portfolios have their own futures. We shall consider the case where a stock portfolio is tracking an index and we use the index futures for hedging. We then consider the problem of hedging a portfolio with positions in different commodity futures. A case study describes how best to characterize and hedge the key risk factors facing a trader in three different types of energy futures (crude oil, heating oil and gasoline). Finally, we explain how to hedge a bond portfolio using a bond futures or a basket of bond futures.

III.2.6.1   Hedging Forex Risk

International portfolios have an exposure to forward exchange rates. Suppose an amount N of domestic currency is invested in a foreign asset at time t and the investment is held until time T, during which the asset earns a known continuously compounded rate of return $r(t, T)$, expressed in annual terms. When the position is closed the asset will be worth $N \exp\left(r(t, T)\left(T - t\right)\right)$ in domestic currency, so this is our exposure to the forward exchange rate. Thus to hedge the forex risk at time t, i.e. when the investment is made, we must take a short position of this amount on the forward exchange rate with expiry T.

The short position on the forward exchange rate fully hedges the forex risk but a small uncertainty arises from that of the domestic discount rate, because we express the present value of the position in domestic currency. The following example illustrates the problem.

EXAMPLE III.2.9: INTEREST RATE RISK ON A HEDGED FOREIGN INVESTMENT

A UK investor buys £1 million of Australian dollars on the spot market to invest in an Australian asset that has a known annual continuously compounded return of 10% per annum. The investment is for 9 months and the forex risk is hedged by selling Australian dollar short based on the 9-month forward exchange rate. Suppose these are 2.50 Australian dollars per pound for the spot rate and 2.45 Australian dollars per pound for the 9-month forward rate. What is the return on our investment in present value terms? If the UK zero coupon continuously compounded 9-month spot rate is 5% what is the sensitivity to the UK zero coupon rate?

SOLUTION   The value of the investment at maturity is $2.5\exp(0.1 \times 0.75) = 2,694,710$ AUD. Hence to completely hedge the forex risk we must lock in this value by selling 2,694,710 AUD at the 9-month forward exchange rate of 2.45, providing a fixed sterling amount of £1,099,882 in 9 months. Since the UK discount rate is 5%, we have £1,059,400 in present value terms. But over the next 9 months the discount rate may change, so before we receive the cash we have an interest rate risk due to fluctuations in the discount rate. For instance, one month from now the 8-month discount rate is unknown, so the present value of the investment one month from now is uncertain. The current sensitivity to the discount rate is given by the PV01 of a cash flow in 9 months with present value £1,059,400. Using the approximation (III.1.62) we have:

$$PV01 \approx 109.9882 \times 0.75 \times \exp(-0.05 \times 0.75) = £\,79.45.$$

The situation becomes more complex if we do not know the return on the foreign asset with certainty. The minimum variance hedge ratio will depend on the volatilities and correlation between the exchange rate and the foreign asset.

III.2.6.2   Hedging International Stock Portfolios

The object of a futures hedge is to lock in the forward value of the portfolio so that there is no uncertainty about its value when the hedge matures. But hedging with futures (or forwards) introduces new risk factors into the portfolio. To see this, consider the simple case of hedging a stock with its futures. Suppose the futures contract is fairly priced. Then the log returns on the futures and the spot are approximately related as in (III.2.9).[71] Suppose there is no residual position risk, so the investor is fully hedged against variations in the spot price and this is no longer a risk factor. However, the hedged portfolio still has two – relatively minor – risk factors, which are the dividend yield and the zero coupon interest rate of maturity equal to the maturity of the future. But by far the largest component of basis risk stems not from dividend yields but from the possible mispricing of the spot relative to the market price of the future. This section aims to analyse *all* the risk factors of an international portfolio, before and after hedging, and to identify the most important risks.

A simple strategy for hedging the market risk of a stock portfolio is to take a short position on the index futures with hedge ratio β_I, the portfolio's market beta. This beta is usually calculated as described in Section II.1.2, i.e. using an OLS regression of the portfolio return on the *index* return. But in Section III.2.5.3 we showed that it is a regression of the portfolio return on the *futures* return (or on the return on any hedging instrument) that gives a minimum variance futures hedge ratio.

Hence, the market beta of a stock portfolio is not exactly equal to the minimum variance hedge ratio. In fact it is straightforward to show that the minimum variance hedge ratio $\tilde{\beta}$ may be derived from the market beta as follows:

$$\tilde{\beta} = \frac{\varrho_{PF}}{\varrho_{PI}} \times \frac{\sigma_I}{\sigma_F} \times \beta_I \tag{III.2.49}$$

where ϱ_{PF} is the correlation between the portfolio returns and the futures returns, ϱ_{PI} is the correlation between the index and the portfolio's returns, and σ_F and σ_I are the volatilities of the futures returns and of the index returns. We illustrate this in a series of examples.

---

[71] We shall ignore the margin costs.

EXAMPLE III.2.10: BETA AND THE MINIMUM VARIANCE HEDGE RATIO

A portfolio of stocks that aims to track the S&P 500 index has a market beta of 1. The correlation of the portfolio returns with the index returns is 0.9 and their correlation with the index futures returns is 0.81. Both the index and its futures returns have a volatility of 18%. Find the minimum variance hedge ratio for this portfolio and the portfolio volatility.

SOLUTION   Application of (III.2.49) gives

$$\tilde{\beta} = \frac{0.81}{0.9} = 0.9.$$

Using (III.2.41) with the minimum variance hedge ratio of 0.9, the futures correlation of 0.81 and the futures volatility of 0.18, we find that the portfolio volatility is 20%, since

$$\frac{0.9 \times 0.18}{0.81} = 0.20.$$

EXAMPLE III.2.11: HEDGING A STOCK PORTFOLIO

I have $1.8 million invested in the portfolio of the previous example. The S&P 500 index price is 1260, the index futures price is 1265 and the index point value of my portfolio is 1250. I want to hedge this portfolio with the index futures, and the futures contract is for $250 per index point. How many futures contracts are sold in the hedge?

SOLUTION   The optimal number of contracts to be sold is given by (III.2.40) as

$$\frac{1,800,000}{250 \times 1260} \times \frac{1250}{1265} \times 0.9 = 5.0819.$$

Hence we sell 5 futures contracts, and are slightly under-hedged. In fact we only hedge

$$\frac{5}{5.0819} = 98.39\%$$

of the position and 1.61% of the position remains unhedged.

EXAMPLE III.2.12: BASIS RISK IN A HEDGED STOCK PORTFOLIO

Assume that the 3-month dividend yield on the S&P 500 index is 4%, the 3-month US zero coupon rate is 5% (both continuously compounded) and that daily variations in the market price of the S&P 500 futures are normally within 2 index points of the spot price. Estimate the nominal daily sensitivities of the stock portfolio considered in the previous examples due to fluctuations in (a) the dividend yield, (b) the zero coupon rate and (c) the market price of the futures.

SOLUTION

(a) Using the decomposition described in Section III.2.3.4, the PV01 on a nominal exposure of $1.8 million due to changes in dividend yield is

$$-1,800,000 \times 0.25 \times \exp(-0.04 \times 0.25) \times 10^{-4} = -\$44.55.$$

(b) Similarly, the PV01 due to changes in interest rates is

$$1,800,000 \times 0.25 \times \exp(-0.05 \times 0.25) \times 10^{-4} = \$44.44.$$

(c) The proportion of the position that is hedged was found to be 98.39% in the previous example, so the daily basis risk due to changes in the market price of the futures is:

$$0.9839 \times \frac{2}{1260} = 15.62 \text{ bps.}$$

Thus the nominal sensitivity due to fluctuations in market price of the futures is:

$$1{,}800{,}000 \times 0.001562 = \$2811.$$

In this example we have expressed basis risk in daily terms. Note that basis risk does *not* scale with the square root of time, since the basis is usually highly negatively autocorrelated.

We now develop this example further to describe the other risks from this portfolio. If a stock portfolio tracks a stock index exactly then the equity risk may be almost fully hedged by taking a position on the index future, because the basis risk is usually very small indeed, as we have shown above. But if it does not track the index exactly only the *systematic* equity risk of the portfolio has been hedged and after the hedge we are still left with a *specific* equity risk due to the non-zero tracking error. How do we quantify this risk?

To examine the specific equity risk in more detail, let us suppose we invest a nominal amount N in a stock portfolio and we hedge the equity risk by taking a short position in the futures with hedge ratio β. Given the approximate relationship between the continuously compounded spot and futures returns (III.2.9), we may write the absolute return on the hedged portfolio as:

$$N(r(t, T) - \beta r_F(t, T)) \approx N(r(t, T) - \beta[r_S(t, T) + r(t, T) - y(t, T)])$$
$$= N(1 + \beta) r(t, T) - N\beta r_S(t, T) - N\beta y(t, T). \tag{III.2.50}$$

Thus we have:[72]

- an exposure of $-N\beta$ to the spot index;
- an exposure of $N(1 + \beta)$ to the discount rate of the same maturity as the future, with nominal sensitivity

$$PV01_r(t, T) = N(1 + \beta)\, \delta 01_r(t, T) \approx N(1 + \beta)\,(T - t)\, \exp(r(t, T)(T - t)) \times 10^{-4};$$

- an exposure of $-N\beta$ to the dividend yield on the equity portfolio of the same maturity as the future, with nominal sensitivity

$$PV01_y(t, T) = N\beta\delta 01_y(t, T) \approx N\beta(T - t)\, \exp(y(t, T)\,(T - t)) \times 10^{-4}.$$

The first exposure is likely to be much larger than the other two and, if the portfolio is denominated in foreign currency, another main exposure will be to the exchange rate. Finally, if we cannot buy exactly the right number of futures contracts there is a position risk that needs to be accounted for. The last example in our S&P 500 series illustrates these risks.

EXAMPLE III.2.13: HEDGING AN INTERNATIONAL STOCK PORTFOLIO

A UK investor invests £1 million in our S&P 500 index tracking portfolio, and the current $\$/£$ exchange rate is 1.8. Thus we have $1.8 million invested in the portfolio and it has a minimum variance hedge ratio of 0.9, just as before. It was shown in Example III.2.11

---

[72] As usual, we have used the approximation to the δ01 given in Section III.1.8.2.

that such an investor should sell 5 futures contracts to hedge the portfolio. Assume that the volatility of the $/£ rate is 10%. What are the risk factors of the hedged portfolio and the nominal sensitivities to these risk factors over a period of 1 day?

SOLUTION   In our solution we decompose the risks into three components due to tracking error, forex exposure and residual position risk.

Tracking error risk. Since the minimum variance hedge ratio on the S&P 500 index itself is likely to be near to 1, the portfolio's hedge ratio of 0.9 is probably due to the tracking error of the portfolio. That is, the portfolio does not return the same as the S&P 500 index. This introduces a type of *specific risk* on the portfolio, due to the use of a proxy for hedging. We call this the tracking error risk.

Using the risk decomposition described in Section IV.1.5.3, we have:

$$\text{Specific Risk} = (\text{Total Risk}^2 - \text{Systematic Risk}^2)^{1/2}. \qquad \text{(III.2.51)}$$

The total risk is given by the portfolio returns variance, i.e. $0.20^2 = 0.04$, because the portfolio volatility is 20%. The *systematic risk* is given by

$$\beta^2 \times \text{variance of futures returns} = 0.9^2 \times 0.18^2 = 0.02624.$$

Thus by (III.2.51) the specific risk on the portfolio, which in this case is due to a highly variable tracking error, is $\sqrt{0.04 - 0.02624} = 11.73\%$ per annum. Over a period of 1 day this scales to $0.1173/\sqrt{250} = 0.7418\%$, assuming 250 risk days per year. So in nominal terms and over a period of 1 day, the investor's specific risk of the portfolio is

$$£1m \times 0.007418 = £7418.$$

Forex risk. The forex risk has not been hedged as it was in Section III.2.6.1. With a volatility of 10% the daily standard deviation of the exchange rate is $0.1/\sqrt{250} = 0.6325\%$. Thus the daily forex risk of the portfolio is

$$£1m \times 0.006325 = £6325.$$

Position risk. The hedge is to sell 5 futures contracts, but according to the minimum variance hedge ratio we should be selling 5.0819 futures. The rounding in the number of futures contracts induces a small position risk where the risk factor is the futures return. The futures volatility is 18% and 1.16% of the position is not hedged, so the position risk in daily terms is $0.18 \times 0.0116/\sqrt{250} = 1.83$ bps. So the risk due to the rounding of the number of futures contracts, measured over a period of 1 day, is

$$£1m \times 0.000183 = £183.$$

The reason why we have enumerated the major risks and their nominal sensitivities in daily terms in the above example is to facilitate comparison with the basis risk on this same portfolio, which we calculated in Example III.2.12. From Example III.2.12 part (c) we know that the nominal basis risk due to fluctuations in the market price of the futures is $2811 or £1562. The risks due to dividends and interest rates calculated in Example III.2.12 parts (a) and (b) were very much lower.

We conclude that by far the largest residual risk of a stock portfolio that is hedged using an index futures contract is that arising from the tracking error of the portfolio. The forex risk is also large, but this may be hedged by taking a short position on a currency forward.[73] The next largest is the basis risk due to fluctuations in the market price of the futures contract.[74] These are the three major risks. The other three risk factors, which have a only a very minor impact, are the dividend risk, the interest rate risk and the residual position risk due to rounding the number of futures contracts. These risks are so small as to be more or less negligible, so they are often ignored.

III.2.6.3 Case Study: Hedging an Energy Futures Portfolio

This case study considers a hedging problem for a trader in futures on crude oil, heating oil and unleaded gasoline and on the crack spreads based on these energy commodities. We suppose that the trader has already mapped his current position to constant maturity futures, as explained in Section III.5.4.2.[75] First we characterize the major risk factors for the portfolio, and then we consider how he can rebalance this portfolio to reduce his risks relative to these key risk factors.

The Portfolio

Suppose that on 1 August 2006 a trader in energy futures holds long and short positions shown in Table III.2.6. Each futures contract is for 1000 barrels and the minus sign indicates a short position. Note that these positions could result from both straight futures trades and from positions on the two *crack spread* futures, i.e. unleaded gasoline–crude oil and heating oil–crude oil.

Table III.2.6   Number of futures contracts in an energy futures trading book

Maturity (months)	Crude oil	Heating oil	Unleaded gasoline
1	−100	70	20
2	180	−60	−60
3	−300	150	100
4	−400	200	250
5	250	−180	−100
6	−100	100	30

Figure III.2.17 shows a reconstructed price series for the portfolio, holding the positions constant at the values shown in Table III.2.6 and revaluing the portfolio using the historical

---

[73] However, we do not know the return on the portfolio so we do not know how much we should go short on the £/$ forward rate. If we only hedge the FX position overnight, then it would be reasonable to suppose that the daily return on the portfolio was 0, and hence we would take a short position of £1 million on the £/$ 1-day forward. But if we want to hedge the forex over a longer period such as 3 months, we would need to assume an expected return on the portfolio. Then the sterling position to be hedged would be equal to the expected portfolio value in 3 months' time, and the forex hedge ratio will depend on the correlation between the equity return and the forex return, as well as their volatilities.
[74] It is important to understand that it does not make sense to scale up basis risk using the square root of time rule because the basis is not an independent and identically distributed process.
[75] Constant maturity commodity futures are not tradable. They can be derived from the traded futures using linear interpolation. See Section III.2.2.4.

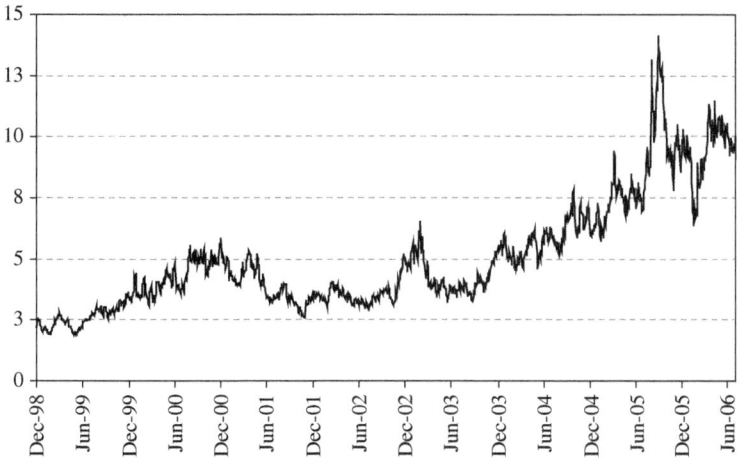

Figure III.2.17   Reconstructed price series for the portfolio

prices of the futures. Since the portfolio has short positions its value could become negative, hence we base our analysis on the portfolio P&L and not on portfolio returns. The current value of the portfolio is $10.025 million and its historical P&L volatility based on the reconstructed price series is extremely high, at over $3.5 million per annum. Concerned about this high volatility and the consequently the high probability of large losses, the trader decides to reduce the volatility of the portfolio returns by rebalancing his portfolio. Our question is, which futures should he trade, and how many contracts should he buy or sell?

The Risk Factors

Figures III.2.18–III.2.20 show how the daily prices of the constant maturity futures on all three products have evolved over a very long period. All prices spiked before the outbreak of the Gulf war in 1991, and since the war in Iraq in 2003 prices have risen tremendously. For instance, the crude oil futures prices rose from around $20 per barrel to nearly $80 per barrel in August 2006 and the prices of the futures on the refined products rose even more. The daily price fluctuations of futures of different maturities on each product are always very highly correlated, as are those on futures of different products.

We do not need to use thirty years of data for this case study; in fact looking back into the 1990s and beyond may give misleading results since energy markets have become much more volatile during the last few years. But we do need fairly high frequency data, because the trader needs to understand his short term risks. So we shall use daily data between 2 January 1999 and August 2006. In the spreadsheet for this case study we first calculate the average correlation of daily returns on each of the futures over the sample period. The correlation matrix is too large to be reported in the text, but Table III.2.7 shows some of these correlations.

The crude oil futures behave like a typical term structure, with the correlation being higher at the long end and decreasing as the maturity gap between the futures increases. All correlations are very high indeed. The same comments apply to heating oil and unleaded gasoline futures, and although their term structures are a little less highly correlated than

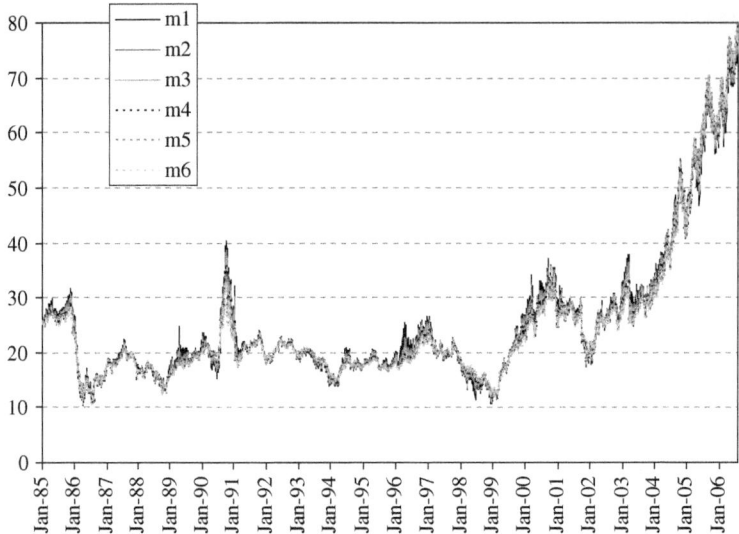

Figure III.2.18   NYMEX WTI crude oil constant maturity futures prices

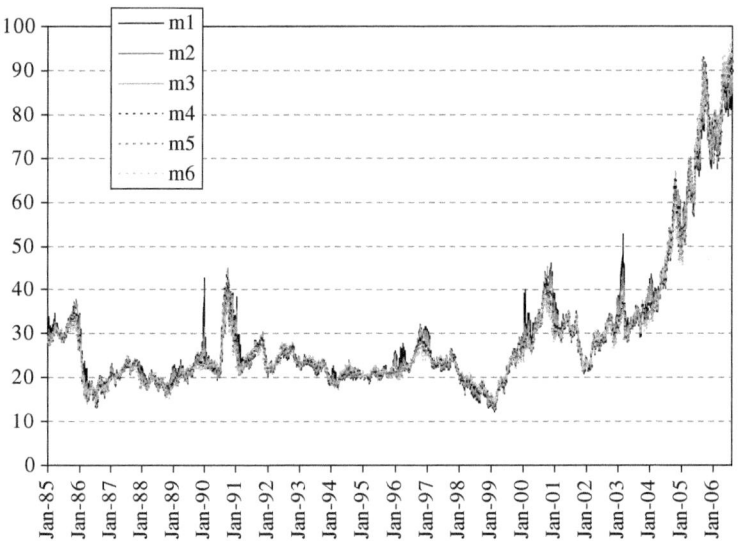

Figure III.2.19   NYMEX heating oil constant maturity futures prices

crude oil there is still a very high degree of correlation. The lower part of Table III.2.7 shows that the cross-correlations between futures on different products are lower than the correlations of futures on one of the products, but they are still very high. Note that the 1-month futures tend to have slightly lower correlations than futures of 2 months' maturity and longer.

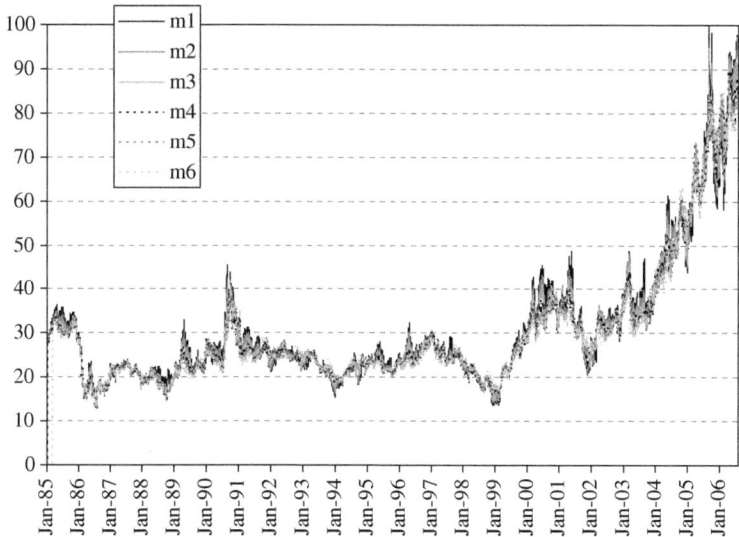

Figure III.2.20   NYMEX unleaded gasoline constant maturity futures prices

Table III.2.7   Daily correlations of futures prices at selected maturities

Correlations	m1–m2	m2–m3	m3–m4	m4–m5	m5–m6
Crude oil (CO)	0.972	0.994	0.997	0.998	0.998
Heating oil (HO)	0.946	0.986	0.986	0.991	0.991
Unleaded gasoline (UL)	0.918	0.951	0.951	0.947	0.949

Cross-correlations	m1	m2	m3	m4	m6
HO−CO	0.776	0.878	0.888	0.895	0.894
UL−CO	0.728	0.839	0.857	0.849	0.852
HO−UL	0.695	0.804	0.815	0.812	0.811

Identifying the Key Risk Factors

We have a total of 18 risk factors. But since they are so highly correlated we should perform a principal component analysis (PCA) to reduce the dimension of the risk factor space.[76] In the spreadsheet we apply PCA to the entire system of 18 risk factors. This way the principal component risk factors capture correlated movements across futures on different commodities, as well as within futures on the same commodity. The PCA may be applied to either the correlation or the covariance matrix of returns, with the latter accounting for any difference between the risk factor volatilities. In each commodity the 1-month futures have noticeably higher volatilities than the other futures, so we shall perform the PCA on the covariance matrix.

---

[76] See Section I.2.6 and Chapter II.2 for further details of principal component analysis.

Table III.2.8   Results of PCA on the futures returns covariance matrix

	86%	5%	3%	2%
WTI m1	0.2594	0.1326	0.3522	0.0562
WTI m2	0.2448	0.1183	0.3055	0.0387
WTI m3	0.2284	0.1159	0.2908	0.0303
WTI m4	0.2157	0.1133	0.2802	0.0255
WTI m5	0.2053	0.1112	0.2697	0.0225
WTI m6	0.1965	0.1086	0.2587	0.0183
HO m1	0.2750	0.2245	−0.5156	−0.2024
HO m2	0.2629	0.2342	−0.3045	−0.0457
HO m3	0.2449	0.2242	−0.2283	0.0654
HO m4	0.2316	0.1979	−0.1618	0.1777
HO m5	0.2210	0.1611	−0.1158	0.2479
HO m6	0.2126	0.1120	−0.0772	0.2676
UL m1	0.2835	−0.6028	−0.1512	0.5121
UL m2	0.2630	−0.3950	−0.0172	0.0412
UL m3	0.2390	−0.2952	0.0183	−0.2175
UL m4	0.2210	−0.2249	0.0066	−0.3559
UL m5	0.2094	−0.1452	0.0018	−0.4224
UL m6	0.2039	−0.0810	−0.0041	−0.4057

The results for the first four components from the PCA on the covariance matrix are displayed in Table III.2.8. The entries in Table III.2.8 are the eigenvectors corresponding to the first, second, third and fourth largest eigenvalues. The percentage of the total variation that is explained by each eigenvalue is shown in the first row of the table. Examining the eigenvalues and eigenvectors we deduce that, between January 1999 and August 2006:

- 86% of the historical variations were a similar and simultaneous shift and tilt in all three term structures;
- 5% of the historical variations were when the crude oil futures shift, the heating oil futures change convexity and the unleaded gasoline futures term structure tilts mostly at the short end;
- 3% of the historical variations were when the crude oil and heating oil futures shift and tilt in opposite directions and the unleaded gasoline futures term structure remains static at the short end;
- 2% of the historical variations were when the crude oil futures shift and tilt, and the short term heating oil futures and unleaded gasoline futures tilt in opposite directions.

The first four principal components are time series that represent the four key risk factors for *any* portfolios on these oil futures. The common trend principal component risk factor is much the most important, since 86% of the historical variation in these futures was due to movements of this type. Taking the first four components together captures 96% of the historical variations in these energy futures since January 1999.

Portfolio Sensitivity to Key Risk Factors

The principal component representation allows a close approximation of the portfolio in terms of its sensitivities to the four major risk factors. We first express the return on each futures using its principal component representation. For instance,

$$R_{m1}^{WTI} \approx 0.2594P_1 + 0.1326P_2 + 0.3522P_3 + 0.0562P_4,$$

where R_{m1}^{WTI} is the daily return on the 1-month crude oil futures and P_1, P_2, P_3 and P_4 are the first four principal components. Then we map the portfolio return to the principal component risk factors using the portfolio representation shown in Table III.2.6. This is done in the case study spreadsheet and we obtain:

$$P\&L = 2.7914P_1 - 4.2858P_2 - 17.0186P_3 - 5.56101P_3 \qquad \text{(III.2.52)}$$

where the coefficients are measured in millions of US dollars.

This representation tells that if the first principal component shifts up by 1% leaving the other components fixed then the portfolio will gain about 1% of $2.791 million, i.e. about $27,910. The first component is a common trend-tilt component, where all futures of the same maturity move by approximately the same amount.[77] The largest sensitivity of the portfolio is to the third principal component, where the crude oil and heating oil term structures shift and tilt in opposite directions. Looking at the coefficient in Table III.2.8 it is evident that a rise in price on the 1-month heating oil contract is the largest risk exposure of this portfolio. It is not easy to see this from the portfolio composition. Nevertheless, in the next section we shall confirm this by showing that selling the 1-month heating oil contract is the best hedge for the portfolio amongst all single contract futures hedges.

Hedging the Portfolio

We shall consider a partial hedge using a single futures contract and targeting a reduction on P&L volatility from over $3.5 million to less than $2.5 million per annum. For each of the futures contracts in turn, we calculate how many futures contracts of this type we need to sell to minimize the variance of the hedge portfolio P&L.

The results are summarized in Table III.2.9. For each commodity we first report the risk factor P&L volatility, and the correlation between this risk factor P&L and the portfolio P&L. Below this we show the number of contracts on the futures that should be sold to minimize the variance of the hedged portfolio's P&L. The futures having the highest correlation with the reconstructed portfolio P&L are the 1-month heating oil futures (P&L correlation = 0.746) and the corresponding minimum variance hedge ratio implies that a position equivalent to 145.45 contracts on the 1-month heating oil futures should be sold, and this trade effects the largest possible reduction in volatility compared with any other trade on a single futures contract. The result will be a portfolio with a historical P&L volatility of $2.389 million, compared with over $3.5 million without this hedge. Similarly, the 1% 10-day historical VaR of the portfolio is substantially reduced by this single futures hedge, from $2.076 million to $1.473 million. Other contracts can also reduce the P&L volatility considerably. For instance, selling a position that is equivalent to 179.24 on the 4-month futures on unleaded gasoline would reduce the P&L volatility to $2.411 million and the 1% 10-day VaR to $1.367 million. Clearly, hedging with several futures would reduce the portfolio risk even further.

---

[77] From Table III.2.7 we know that a 1% upward shift in the first component implies that the 1-month crude oil futures price increases by 0.2594%, the 2-month crude oil futures price increases by 0.2448%, and so on.

Table III.2.9   Minimum variance hedges to reduce to volatility of the futures portfolio

Risk factor	WTI m1	WTI m2	WTI m3	WTI m4	WTI m5	WTI m6
Risk factor P&L Volatility ($)	13.23	12.26	11.52	10.97	10.55	10.20
Correlation	0.411	0.441	0.440	0.440	0.440	0.441
No. contracts	111.44	128.88	137.10	143.72	149.56	155.17
Hedged portfolio P&L volatility ($)	3,269,509	3,219,570	3,219,902	3,221,064	3,221,055	3,218,688
1% 10 day historical VaR ($)	1,939,370	1,948,219	1,976,805	1,976,222	1,974,615	1,975,345

Risk factor	HO m1	HO m2	HO m3	HO m4	HO m5	HO m6
Risk factor P&L volatility ($)	**18.39**	16.79	15.70	14.86	14.22	13.67
Correlation	**0.746**	0.739	0.722	0.699	0.682	0.673
No. contracts	145.45	157.80	164.84	168.64	172.02	176.52
Hedged portfolio P&L volatility ($)	2,389,086	2,416,350	2,483,014	2,565,397	2,622,976	2,653,691
1% 10 day historical VaR ($)	1,472,834	1,509,869	1,588,319	1,725,051	1,791,145	1,852,938

Risk factor	UL m1	UL m2	UL m3	UL m4	UL m5	UL m6
Risk factor P&L volatility ($)	22.20	18.21	15.98	14.81	14.09	13.71
Correlation	0.661	0.679	0.703	0.740	0.682	0.682
No. contracts	106.82	133.81	157.67	179.24	173.56	178.55
Hedged portfolio P&L volatility ($)	2,690,058	2,631,691	2,552,091	2,411,291	2,622,860	2,621,616
1% 10 day historical VaR ($)	1,501,297	1,479,477	1,458,825	1,366,632	1,642,830	1,599,100

III.2.6.4   Hedging Bond Portfolios

A futures hedge of a bond portfolio is always a proxy hedge, because bond futures are always on notional bonds. Even if we want to hedge a single bond and this is the cheapest-to-deliver bond, the hedge ratio will not be 1. The change in the bond futures price is, however, closely related to the change in the price of the cheapest-to-deliver bond, and many bond traders assume that

$$F(t, T) - F(t - 1, T) \approx \frac{CTD(t) - CTD(t-1)}{CF_{CTD}},$$

where $F(t, T)$ is the price at time t of the bond futures that matures on date T, $CTD(t)$ is the price of the cheapest-to-deliver bond at time t and CF_{CTD} is the conversion factor for the cheapest-to-deliver bond.

With this approximation the CTD bond is almost perfectly correlated with the futures, and will have a P&L volatility that is CF_{CTD} times the volatility of the futures. Hence, the minimum variance hedge ratio (III.2.36), which gives a hedge with almost zero variance, is just

$$\beta^* = \frac{\mathrm{Cov}(\Delta F(t), \Delta CTD(t))}{V(\Delta F(t))} \approx \frac{CF_{CTD} \times \mathrm{Cov}(\Delta F(t), \Delta F(t))}{V(\Delta F(t))} = CF_{CTD}.$$

Now the number of bond futures required to hedge a principal of N_S invested in the cheapest-to-deliver bond is approximately equal to

$$n^* = \left(\frac{N_S}{N_F}\right) \times CF_{CTD}, \tag{III.2.53}$$

where N_F is the principal value of each futures contract. Bond futures contracts are specified in terms of point values, and the principal value N_F that is equivalent to a point value of P is 100P. For instance, US Treasury futures have a point value of $1000, meaning that if the futures price increases from 100 to 101 the exchange pays me $1000. The equivalent principal amount invested in the notional bond is therefore $100,000.

EXAMPLE III.2.14: HEDGING THE CHEAPEST TO DELIVER

I hold $500,000 of the US Treasury $4\frac{1}{2}\%$ November 2015 bond, which is currently the cheapest to deliver against the 10-year US Treasury futures contract expiring in December 2007. The conversion factor for this bond is given in Table III.2.2 as 0.9080. How many futures contracts should I sell to hedge this bond?

SOLUTION   Using (III.2.53) we have

$$n^* = \frac{500,000}{100,000} \times 0.9080 = 4.54.$$

So I should sell 5 contracts but there will be a large position risk since I am $(5 - 4.54)/4.54 = 10.13\%$ over-hedged. Thus, I have a position risk that is a little over 10% of the volatility of the P&L on the bond futures.

The approximation described above is sometimes used for other bonds in the delivery basket, and it could also be extended to similar bonds outside this basket. It is a very simple hedge since one only needs to know the conversion factor of the bond. But it cannot be extended to a portfolio of bonds. It is important to note that for any bond that is not the cheapest to deliver there is a basis risk that arises from the difference between the yield on the notional bond and the yield on the bond that is hedged. Denote by $\Delta y_B(t)$ the change in the yield of bond that is hedged from time 0, when the hedge is taken, to time t, when the hedge is closed. Similarly, let $\Delta y_F(t)$ denote the change in the notional bond yield over the period of the hedge. Now the minimum variance hedge ratio is not the conversion factor of the bond, CF_B but

$$\beta^* = \frac{\mathrm{Cov}(\Delta y_B(t), \Delta y_F(t))}{V(\Delta y_F(t))} \times CF_B. \tag{III.2.54}$$

The first term in (III.2.54) could, for instance, be calculated by OLS regression of the changes in the bond yield on the changes in the yield on the futures.

We now show that to hedge a portfolio of bonds with a single bond futures contract we can approximate the hedge ratio using the PV01 of the portfolio and of the futures. Knowing only the coupon and maturity of each bond in the portfolio and of the notional bond in the portfolio, it is simple to calculate these PV01s using the method described in Section III.1.8.2. We only need to know the continuously compounded zero coupon curve, so that we can discount the cash flows as in (III.1.59).

We denote the PV01 of the portfolio by $PV01_S$ and that of the bond futures by $PV01_F$. Suppose that the change in the zero coupon yield curve over the period of the hedge is a parallel shift. Then, since the PV01 calculation is based on the principal amount invested,

$$\frac{N_F \times \Delta F(t)}{N_S \times \Delta S(t)} = \frac{PV01_F}{PV01_S}, \tag{III.2.55}$$

where $\Delta S(t)$ denotes the change in price of our bond portfolio over the hedging period and N_S is the principal amount invested in this portfolio. In this case the number of contracts in the one-for-one hedge is just

$$n^* = \frac{\text{PV01}_S}{\text{PV01}_F}. \qquad (\text{III.2.56})$$

For instance, if I hold a portfolio of bonds with a PV01 of \$3000 and the PV01 of the bond futures is \$75, then I should sell 40 bond futures to hedge this portfolio. Alternatively, we could calculate the hedge using the value durations of the bond portfolio and the futures, noting the approximation between the PV01 and the value duration explained in Section III.1.8.1.

If we do not make the assumption that the zero coupon curve shifts parallel there is again a basis risk, arising from the difference between the yield on the notional bond and the yield on the portfolio that is hedged. Now the minimum variance hedge ratio is

$$\beta^* = \frac{\text{Cov}(\Delta y_B(t), \Delta y_F(t))}{V(\Delta y_F(t))} \times \frac{\text{PV01}_S}{\text{PV01}_F} \times \frac{N_F}{N_S}. \qquad (\text{III.2.57})$$

This approach to computing hedge ratios for bond portfolios is very flexible. In particular, instead of hedging with only one bond futures contract we can hedge with a portfolio of bond futures. Then we use the PV01 of this portfolio as the denominator in (III.2.57).

III.2.7   USING FUTURES FOR SHORT TERM HEDGING

If a portfolio is thought to be particularly risky, for instance if its systematic risk exceeds or is close to its limit, a trader may choose to hedge the portfolio over the very short term. For instance, he may hedge the portfolio overnight or over the weekend. When a spot position is hedged by its own futures contract and the contract is held until expiry the minimum variance hedge ratio is equal to the one-for-one hedge ratio. In fact whenever hedges are held for long periods there is virtually no difference between the minimum variance hedge ratio and the naïve hedge ratio. But when hedging over the very short term any less than perfect correlation between the spot and futures returns will result in a minimum variance hedge ratio that is different from 1 and it may be that minimum variance hedge ratios provide more efficient hedges than a naïve hedge.

Another situation in which minimum variance hedging may be superior to naïve hedging is when a trader implements a short term hedge for a portfolio containing several different assets using only a few futures contracts. In this case we have a proxy hedge where the correlation between the portfolio and the futures returns can be significantly less than 1, and again the minimum variance hedge ratio can be quite different from the naïve hedge ratio.

The question whether minimum variance hedge ratios are more efficient than naïve hedges for overnight hedging is a question that has been, for some obscure reason, of considerable interest to empirical financial econometricians. This section addresses the vast financial econometrics literature on minimum variance hedging with futures. The first subsection summarizes the complex econometric hedge ratios that are propounded by numerous academics. Then we survey the academic literature on the subject of regression based hedge ratios and comment on the circumstances when it may be possible to improve the efficiency of short term hedges using regression based minimum variance hedge ratios.

III.2.7.1   Regression Based Minimum Variance Hedge Ratios

We have already shown that minimum variance hedge ratios of the form (III.2.41), i.e. with

$$\tilde{\beta} = \varrho \frac{\sigma_S}{\sigma_F},$$

may be estimated by performing a simple linear regression by OLS. The regression model is

$$r_{St} = \alpha + \tilde{\beta} r_{Ft} + \varepsilon_t, \qquad (III.2.58)$$

where the dependent variable is the return on the portfolio to be hedged and the independent variable is the return on the hedging instrument.

Table III.2.10 reports the spot and futures daily returns volatilities and correlation for the stock indices discussed in Section III.2.4.2. Below these we calculate the OLS minimum variance futures hedge ratios for these indices, based on a hedging period of 1 day. As expected, the size of the minimum variance hedge ratio increases with the spot–futures correlation. When the spot and futures are very highly correlated the minimum variance hedge ratios are very close to 1.

Table III.2.10   Daily minimum variance hedge ratios, 2001–2006

Returns	NASD	S&P 500	FTSE 100	Hang Seng	Bovespa
Spot volatility	33.39%	17.42%	18.17%	18.24%	28.01%
Futures volatility	32.36%	17.50%	18.01%	20.22%	30.40%
Correlation	0.976	0.98	0.981	0.96	0.954
MV hedge ratio	1.007	0.975	0.990	0.866	0.879

It is also possible to use time varying estimates of (III.2.41) based on an exponentially weighted moving average models. These models are discussed in Section II.3.7, and we can define the EWMA minimum variance ratio in much the same way as the EWMA equity beta that was introduced in Section II.1.2.3. If λ denotes the smoothing constant the EWMA estimate of the minimum variance hedge ratio at time t is

$$\beta_t^\lambda = \frac{\mathrm{Cov}_\lambda (r_{St}, r_{Ft})}{V_\lambda (r_{Ft})}. \qquad (III.2.59)$$

Figure III.2.21 shows the EWMA minimum variance hedge ratios for crude oil that are based on the correlations shown in Figure III.2.3. The OLS minimum variance hedge ratio is 0.956 and this is roughly equal to the average of the EWMA hedge ratios over the sample period.

Time varying minimum variance hedge ratios may also be estimated using a bivariate *generalized autoregressive conditionally heteroscedastic* (GARCH) model. These models are introduced in Chapter II.4 and their application to estimating time varying portfolio betas was described in Section II.4.8.3. Their extension to time varying minimum variance hedge ratios is not entirely straightforward, since it is typical that the portfolio will be *cointegrated* with its hedging instrument.[78] For instance, we know from Section II.5.4.4 that a spot asset is cointegrated with its own futures. The implication of such cointegration is that the

---

[78] See Ghosh (1993).

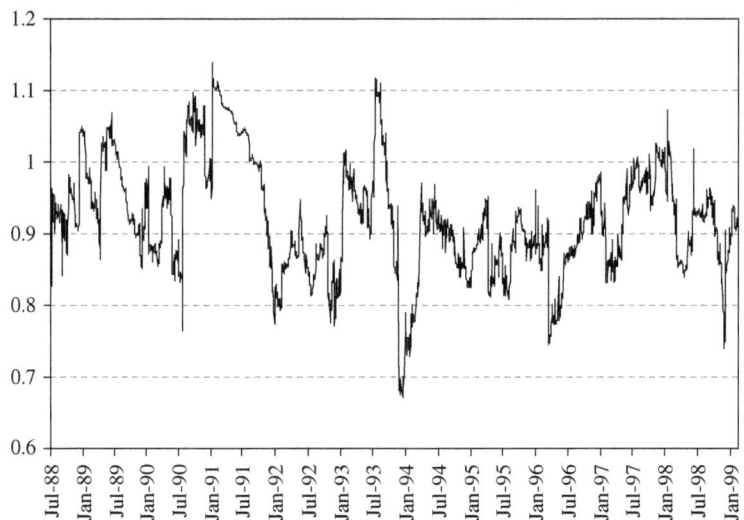

Figure III.2.21   EWMA minimum variance hedge ratios for crude oil

conditional mean equations in the bivariate GARCH model must take the form of an error correction mechanism.[79]

The disequilibrium term in the error correction mechanism will be closely approximated by the fair value of the basis. To see why, note that

$$\ln F^*(t, T) - \ln S(t) = (r - y)\,(T - t) = C(t, T),\ \text{say}$$

Although $C(t, T)$ will be stationary when the spot and futures are cointegrated, which they are when the basis is mean-reverting, it need not be the most stationary linear combination of the log of the market price of the futures and the log of the spot price. Nevertheless since the mispricing of the futures contract relative to its fair value is so small it is reasonable to assume the error correction term in the error correction model is equal to $C(t, T)$ when log returns rather than returns are used in the GARCH model.[80]

Introducing the notation

$$\mathbf{y}_t = \begin{pmatrix} r_{St} \\ r_{Ft} \end{pmatrix},\ \boldsymbol{\mu} = \begin{pmatrix} \mu_1 \\ \mu_2 \end{pmatrix},\ \boldsymbol{\pi} = \begin{pmatrix} \pi_1 \\ \pi_2 \end{pmatrix},\ \boldsymbol{\Gamma} = \begin{pmatrix} \Gamma_{11} & \Gamma_{12} \\ \Gamma_{21} & \Gamma_{22} \end{pmatrix}\ \text{and}\ \boldsymbol{\varepsilon}_t = \begin{pmatrix} \varepsilon_{1,t} \\ \varepsilon_{2,t} \end{pmatrix},$$

where the vector $\mathbf{y}$ contains log returns, we can write the conditional mean equations as

$$\mathbf{y}_t = \boldsymbol{\mu} + \boldsymbol{\Gamma}\mathbf{y}_{t-1} + \boldsymbol{\pi} C_{t-1} + \boldsymbol{\varepsilon}_t. \tag{III.2.60}$$

In the conditional bivariate GARCH framework we assume $\boldsymbol{\varepsilon}_t\,|I_{t-1} \sim N(\mathbf{0}, \mathbf{H}_t)$ where I_{t-1} denotes the information set at time $t-1$ and

---

[79] Further details are given in Section II.5.5.
[80] Since GARCH models are usually estimated on daily or higher frequency data, the log returns are very close to the returns.

$$\mathbf{H}_t = \begin{pmatrix} \sigma_{St}^2 & \sigma_{SFt} \\ \sigma_{SFt} & \sigma_{Ft}^2 \end{pmatrix},$$

where σ_{St} and σ_{Ft} are the conditional standard deviations of the portfolio and the hedging instrument and σ_{SFt} is their conditional covariance at time t. This matrix is called the *conditional covariance matrix*. The GARCH *minimum variance hedge ratio* at time t is then given by:

$$\tilde{\beta}_t = \frac{\sigma_{SFt}}{\sigma_{Ft}^2}.$$

Note that the GARCH model hedge ratio is time varying as well as its estimate. This should be compared with the EWMA hedge ratio (III.2.59), where the model hedge ratio is constant and only its estimate varies over time.

III.2.7.2 Academic Literature on Minimum Variance Hedging[81]

Much of the debate that followed Johnson's (1960) paper on mean–variance hedging concerned whether the minimum variance criterion is appropriate. This is only one of many possible objective functions in the mean–variance framework. Other utility functions, as in Cecchetti et al. (1988) or alternative hedging objectives may be applied. For instance: Howard and D'Antonio (1984) design the hedge to maximize the Sharpe ratio; Cheung et al. (1990), Lien and Luo (1993) and Lien and Shaffer (1999) minimize the mean Gini coefficient; and Eftekhari (1998) and Lien and Tse (1998, 2000) employ objectives that include minimization of the generalized semi-variance or higher lower partial moments.

The papers by Lien and Tse (2002) and Chen et al. (2003) are dedicated exclusively to reviewing the huge literature on futures hedging. Many papers consider minimum variance hedge ratio estimation based on an advanced econometric model with time varying minimum variance hedge ratios. Baillie and Myers (1991) concluded that the bivariate GARCH model provides a superior performance to other dynamic or constant hedges for commodities. Moschini and Myers (2002) also support the use of GARCH hedge ratios for commodities, and Chan and Young (2006) incorporate a jump component to the bivariate GARCH model to hedge the copper market, finding that this improves the hedge. Other more advanced models, such as the Markov switching GARCH of Lee and Yoder (2005), also appear useful for hedging commodity prices.

It is not only in commodity markets that advanced econometric models may produce more efficient minimum variance hedge ratios. For instance, Koutmos and Pericli (1999) and Bhattacharya et al. (2006) show that the cointegration GARCH model provides a powerful means of pricing and hedging mortgage backed securities. In fixed income markets the underlying and hedging contracts often differ, and the underlying is usually less liquid than the hedging instruments. And in commodity markets the basis may be extremely volatile and prices may not follow a random walk. In these circumstances advanced econometric models can be very useful for computing the most efficient hedge ratio.

However, the vast majority of applied econometric studies apply minimum variance hedge ratios to hedging stock indices, and the case for minimum variance hedging of stock indices is much less sound than it is for commodities, fixed income securities and indeed any asset

---

[81] This subsection and the next based on Alexander and Barbosa (2007) with kind permission of the *Journal of Portfolio Management*.

where the correlation between the underlying and the hedging instrument is far from perfect. Stock trading is now highly efficient on many exchanges and the basis risk on stock indices is usually very small indeed. Hence, it is not clear where the motivation for this enormous literature lies.[82]

Figlewski (1984) analysed the futures cross-hedging and hedging with the S&P 500 index and subsequent papers investigate the effect of dividend yield (Graham and Jennings, 1987), futures mispricing (Merrick, 1988), duration and expiration effects (Lindahl, 1992) and investment horizon (Geppert, 1995). Advanced econometric models can produce hedge ratios that vary excessively over time, as shown by Lien et al. (2002), Poomimars et al. (2003), Harris and Shen (2003), Choudhry (2003, 2004), Miffre (2004), Alizadeh and Nomikos (2004) and Yang and Allen (2005). Thus increased transactions costs could offset any potential gain in efficiency. So, even if basis risk is high enough to warrant the use of minimum variance hedge ratios, their costs may well be greater than their benefits. The papers by Garbade and Silber (1983), Myers and Thompson (1989) and Ghosh (1993) take cointegration and the lead–lag relationship between cash and futures prices into account. However, Lien (2004) has proved that the omission of the cointegration relationship should have minimal impact on hedging effectiveness. Kroner and Sultan (1993) and Miffre (2004) incorporate conditionality in the available information with error correction models.

Several other papers aim to demonstrate the superiority of sophisticated dynamic hedge ratios for hedging stock indices with futures. Park and Switzer (1995) show that a symmetric bivariate GARCH hedge ratio outperforms the constant hedge ratio for the S&P 500, Major Market index and Toronto 35 stock indices. Tong (1996) and Brooks et al. (2002) support this general result. Choudhry (2003) compares naïve, OLS and GARCH hedge ratios for several major stock indices and concludes that GARCH models perform the best. Floros and Vougas (2004) also find that GARCH hedge ratios perform better than OLS and error correction models for hedging the Greek stock index. However, Laws and Thompson (2005) apply OLS, GARCH and EWMA hedge ratios to index tracking portfolios and conclude that the EWMA method provides the best performance.

More recent papers investigate hedging efficiency using even more advanced econometric techniques for computing minimum variance hedge ratios. Alizadeh and Nomikos (2004) compare Markov switching GARCH models with traditional GARCH, error correction and OLS methods. They conclude that GARCH outperforms all other models. Dark (2004) examines the bivariate error correction GARCH and fractionally integrated GARCH models, finding that these produce ratios that are superior to the OLS and naïve hedge ratios, a result that is supported by Yang and Allen (2005). Finally, Lai et al. (2006) develop a copula threshold GARCH model to estimate optimal hedge ratios in the Hong Kong, Japan, Korea, Singapore and Taiwan indices, and their model improves on traditional OLS in three of the five markets.

However Poomimars et al. (2003) and Copeland and Zhu (2006) conclude that minimum variance hedging performance is similar for most econometric models. And Moosa (2003) says that

'although the theoretical arguments for why model specification does matter are elegant, the difference model specification makes for hedging performance seems to be negligible.

---

[82] We only mention a small fraction of the literature here. Sutcliffe (2005) gives a comprehensive review of the huge literature on hedging stock indices with futures.

What matters for the success or failure of a hedge is the correlation between the prices of the un-hedged position and the hedging instrument. Low correlation invariably produces insignificant results and ineffective hedges, whereas high correlation produces effective hedges irrespective of how the hedge ratio is measured.'

III.2.7.3   Short Term Hedging in Liquid Markets

In this section we question the wisdom of applying advanced econometric models to estimate minimum variance hedge ratios in liquid futures markets. The problem with these models, and particularly the bivariate GARCH models that have been so popular with econometricians, is that the minimum variance hedge ratios are extremely variable. If they were used to roll over a short term hedge the rebalancing costs would be enormous. To illustrate this for the case of the FTSE 100 index, Figure III.2.22 compares four different econometric minimum variance hedge ratios. The OLS hedge ratio is the most stable, followed by a similar hedge ratio labelled 'ECM' which is based on an error correction mechanism.[83] The time varying EWMA and GARCH hedge ratios are extremely variable and below we shall show that this additional sensitivity does not lead to a superior performance.

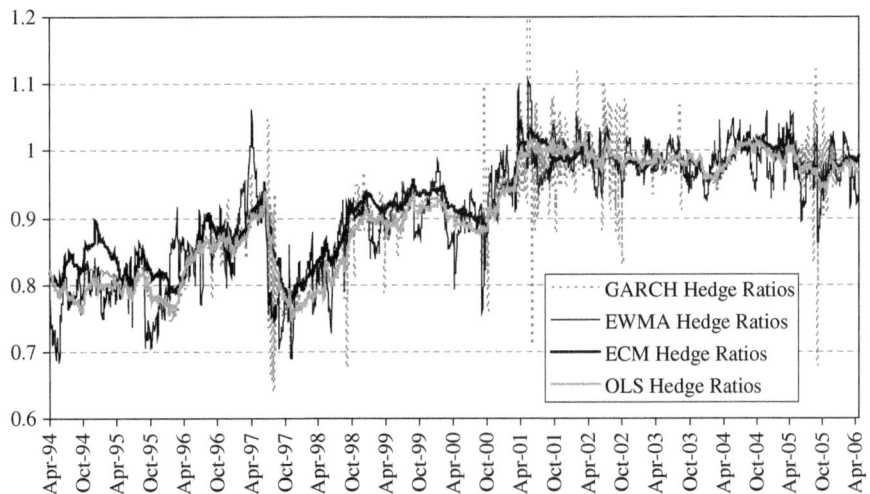

Figure III.2.22   Minimum variance hedge ratios for the FTSE 100 stock index

Alexander and Barbosa (2007) extend the Ederington methodology to use a time varying effectiveness measure. Figures III.2.23–III.2.25, all drawn on the same vertical scale, plot the differences between effectiveness measures given by four different minimum variance hedge ratios. For instance, a positive value on 'OLS–Naïve' indicates that the OLS minimum variance ratio performs better than the one-to-one ratio and a positive value on the 'ECM–OLS' indicates that the ECM hedge ratio outperforms the OLS hedge.[84]

---

[83] As explained in Section III.2.7.1, this captures the fact that the spot and the futures are cointegrated.

[84] The performance measures are based on a proper post-sample backtest, following the methodology described in Section II.8.5. Each day we estimate the hedge ratio to determine the futures position to be taken at the end of that day until the following day. The sample is then rolled 1 day, the hedge ratios re-estimated, and the hedge rebalanced and held until the end of the next day.

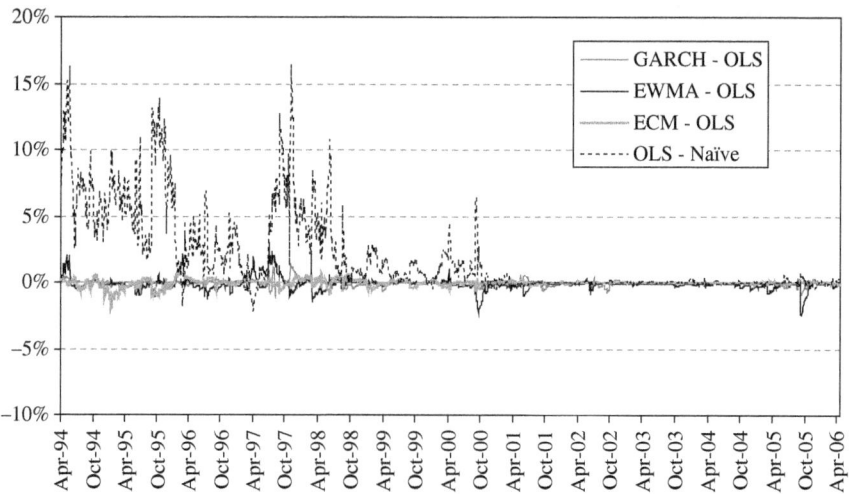

Figure III.2.23   Effectiveness of minimum variance hedging over time: FTSE 100

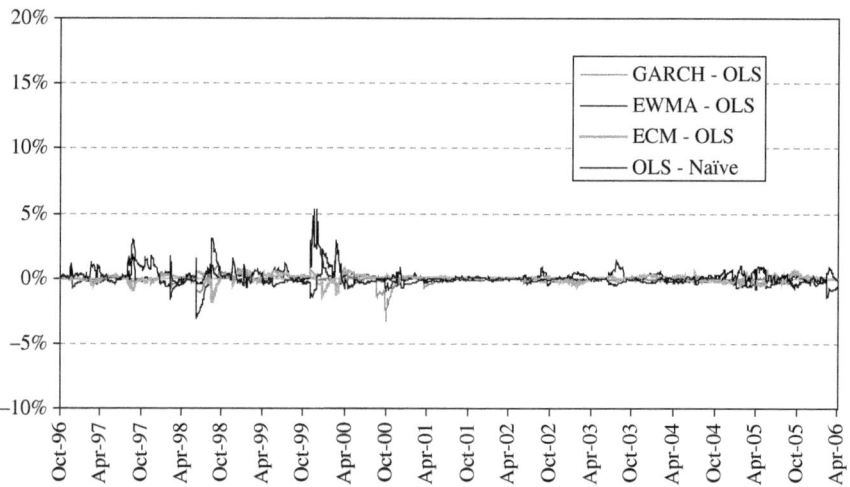

Figure III.2.24   Effectiveness of minimum variance hedging over time: NASDAQ

Figure III.2.23 for the FTSE 100 index shows very clearly that, when effectiveness is measured in a time varying framework, no significant variance reduction from minimum variance hedging beyond the variance reduction offered by the naïve hedge has been possible since 2000. Many other indices indicate very similar characteristics, i.e. since 2000 there is no significant variance reduction from minimum variance hedging.

The more efficient the market, the less important is a minimum variance hedge. For instance, Figure III.2.24 shows that the NASDAQ exchange is so efficient that minimum variance hedging has never been able to reduce variance significantly compared with the naïve hedge, except for a few short and isolated periods in the sample when there was exceptionally high volatility in technology stocks. By contrast, Figure III.2.25 shows that all minimum variance hedges can dramatically improve on the naïve hedge for the Hang Seng

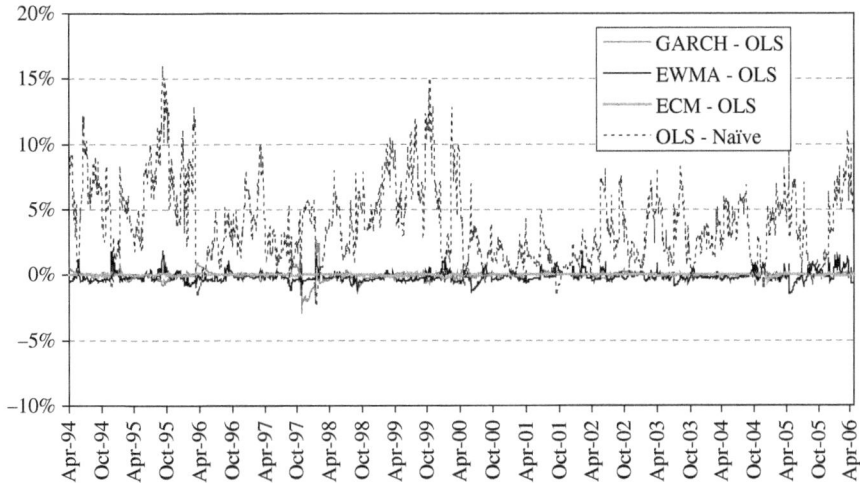

Figure III.2.25   Effectiveness of minimum variance hedging over time: Hang Seng

index, where trading is not nearly as efficient as it is in the older stock markets. However, simple OLS seems to be sufficient; the move to more complex econometric models offers little or no improvement on the OLS minimum variance hedge.

Based on these and many other results, Alexander and Barbosa (2007) conclude that minimum variance hedge ratios in liquid stock markets with efficient electronic trading platforms offer no discernable improvement on the naïve futures hedge, even for overnight hedging. However, in markets where trading is less efficient, such as in the Hang Seng composite index, simple econometric models may still provide hedge ratios with more efficient variance reduction than the naïve hedge. However, there is no evidence to suggest that complex econometric models such as GARCH can improve on a simple OLS regression for estimating minimum variance hedge ratios.

Time varying minimum variance hedge ratios estimated using GARCH or EWMA incorporate too much noise to be effective for hedging purposes and one is actually better off using OLS to estimate the minimum variance hedge ratio. The benefits of an active hedging strategy should be economically justifiable yet these models do not account for transactions costs, such as margins and commissions. When the costs of hedging are considered the case against time varying hedge ratios based on conditional covariances is strengthened even further. More than a decade ago Lence (1995) argued that sophisticated econometric models for estimating minimum variance hedge ratios provide negligible economic benefits and that the academic effort dedicated to estimate better minimum variance hedges 'has been a waste of resources'. Yet, at the time of writing, a considerable effort in academic research continues to be focused on this issue.

III.2.8 SUMMARY AND CONCLUSIONS

This chapter has provided a succinct introduction to pricing and trading futures and forwards, and using futures and forward contracts to form hedged portfolios. Futures and forward markets are the most actively traded of all derivative markets. The latest BIS estimates of the notional size of the main forward and futures markets are approximately: $30 trillion for bonds and interest rate futures; $250 trillion for interest rate forwards and swaps; $3 trillion for commodity futures; $3 trillion for commodity forwards and swaps; $1 trillion for stock index futures; $7 trillion for equity linked forwards and swaps; $200 billion for forex futures; and $20 trillion for forex forwards and swaps.[85]

Players in the futures markets are not just *hedgers*, i.e. investors wishing to lock in now some future value of their investment. Plenty of *speculators* operate in these markets because they can obtain a huge leverage of their positions. The main difference between these two types of financial instruments is that futures have a fixed *expiry date* and are traded on an exchange, whilst forwards usually have a fixed *term* and are traded OTC. The notional size of an investment in a futures contract is many times greater than the actual funds needed to make this investment, since investors only need to raise sufficient funds to cover their margin costs. And trading in forward markets is costless, until the trade is closed.

Bond, commodity and stock index futures contracts have been exchange traded for decades, but each market has very different characteristics. The exchange trading of futures has, of course, led to standardized contract specifications but the features of the underlying vary enormously. For instance, even within the relatively narrow category of *energy futures* each market has quite different characteristics. Energy futures prices are driven by the behaviour of hedgers and speculators and whilst the hedger's net demand often has strong seasonal characteristics, the speculator's net demand is usually influenced by political events. We have also described the new futures markets on volatility, credit spreads and real estate that recently began trading on Eurex and CME, and the futures on weather and pollution emissions allowances that are traded on new, specialized exchanges.

The ability to trade the spot and the futures leads to a *no arbitrage range* for the fair price of the futures or forward. The market price of a futures or forward deviates from the fair price because of the transactions costs associated with the arbitrage strategy. To improve liquidity and decrease transactions costs many futures exchanges are replacing open outcry trading with highly developed electronic trading systems. Now market prices of liquid futures rarely deviate from a narrow no arbitrage range. In fact, when futures or forward markets are very highly liquid (e.g. in major currencies) the bid–ask spread on the futures or forward is usually much smaller than this range. On the other hand the no arbitrage range will be:

- asymmetric when the spot cannot be sold short (e.g. in commodity markets),
- large if the spot is difficult to trade (e.g. in real estate index futures),
- approximate if the underlying cannot be traded (e.g. in bond futures).

The introduction of *exchange traded funds* or ETFs on stock indices has contributed to an increase in efficiency in stock index futures markets. ETFs can be used for arbitraging stock index futures and are traded just like a share. Since the early 1990s ETFs have been introduced on a very large number of stock indices, even those without futures, and where index futures exist the no arbitrage range has become very narrow indeed.

Financial futures (i.e. futures on a stock, stock index, bond, interest rate or exchange rate) are often more liquid than the corresponding cash market. Indeed, a cash market need not even exist. Where it does exist we usually find that the *price discovery* role is played by the

---

[85] Figures on futures as of June 2007, those on forwards and swaps as of December 2006.

futures. That is, a change in the futures price often leads a change in the spot price. Hence, the market prices of futures determine whether the *spot* price is fair, i.e. at its theoretical value, and not the other way around. And because futures are more liquid than the spot, these, not the spot, are the hedging instruments for most options.

The main component of *basis risk* in financial futures is the 'mispricing' as the futures price fluctuates within its no arbitrage range. There is little or no uncertainty on the dividend yields, coupon yields and interest rates that affect the fair value of the basis for financial futures. However, uncertainties about the fair value of the basis, and about carry costs and convenience yields in particular, lead to a large basis risk for commodities. For this reason we advocate mapping portfolios of commodities futures to *fixed maturity futures*. These are not traded instruments but they serve an extremely useful function as risk factors. A case study on energy futures has shown how they can be used to identify and hedge the key sources of risk for commodity traders.

Futures and forwards are used to hedge international exposures, and portfolios of bonds and stocks. This can remove a considerable amount of risk. But a small residual *position risk* remains because the optimal number of contracts in the hedge is usually not an integral number. Also, since buying a futures or forward contract locks in the *fair* value of the spot there are small residual risks arising from uncertainties about interest rates and dividend yields over the period of the hedge. A series of examples illustrating the hedging of a US stock portfolio by a UK investor shows that the systematic market risks due to uncertainties in equity prices and exchange rates can be hedged by taking futures positions on stock indices and exchange rates. We show that the residual risks after hedging are mainly due to tracking error and position risk.

It is usually optimal to employ a *hedge ratio* of 1, i.e. the value of the underlying position is exactly matched by the value of the futures position. The exceptions are when there is a maturity mismatch between the expiry date of the hedging instrument and the time period of the hedge, or when we need to use a proxy instrument for the hedge. For instance, when hedging a bond portfolio the number of contracts in the hedge is determined by the PV01s of the underlying portfolio and of the notional bonds in the hedging portfolio. But the hedging portfolio is a proxy instrument and because of this the optimal hedge ratio depends on the volatilities and correlation of the yields on the underlying and hedging portfolios.

A huge amount of academic research has been directed toward the problem of hedging with futures. Most academics call the one-for-one hedge ratio 'naïve' and their studies have focused on the use of econometric models to estimate a *minimum variance hedge ratio* when the hedge is placed over a very short horizon such as 1 day. Much of the literature has focused on the application of advanced GARCH and cointegration models to short term hedging of stock indices. However, this problem is not of central importance to practitioners, and empirical studies have shown that the basis risk on major stock indices is now so small that minimum variance hedges offer no improvement over the naïve hedge.

III.3

Options

III.3.1 INTRODUCTION

An option is a contract that gives the purchaser the right to enter into another contract during a particular period of time. We call it a *derivative* because it is a contract on another contract. The *underlying* contract is a security such as a stock or a bond, a financial asset such as a currency, or a commodity, or an interest rate.[1] The option contract that gives the right to buy the underlying is termed a *call option*, and the right to sell the underlying is termed a *put option*. Interest rate options give the purchaser the right to pay or receive an interest rate, and in the case of *swaptions* the underlying contract is a swap.

Options began trading in the seventeenth century, when the ability to purchase share options contributed to the South Sea bubble and options on tulip bulbs were traded in Amsterdam. The first exchange listed options were on the *Marché à Prime* in France. About 10% of trading on shares was carried out on this market, where shares were sold accompanied with a 3-month at-the-money put option.[2] The existence of this market prompted Louis Bachelier, in 1900, to derive a formula for the evaluation of options based on arithmetic Brownian motion.[3] The first independently traded exchange listed options were on commodities: e.g. gold options in Germany during the 1930s. But these options were not popular because of the difficulty of valuing them, plus the absence of margining requirements by the exchange.

Then in 1973 two important events occurred. First, the famous papers by Black and Scholes (1973) and Merton (1973) demonstrated how to value European options, and the celebrated *Black–Scholes–Merton formula* was based on geometric, rather than arithmetic Brownian motion. Secondly, in the same year the first modern options exchange started. The Chicago Board of Options Exchange (CBOE) issued six calls and six puts on US equities. This combination of a reliable pricing formula and a good exchange mechanism was a catalyst for extremely rapid growth in the options market.

Nowadays options are traded over the counter (OTC) and on exchanges. Many exchanges list standard options on equities, equity index futures, foreign exchange rates, notional bonds and interest rates, commodities and even 'alternative' investments. However, most exotic options are still traded OTC. The demand for options has grown so rapidly that at the time of writing the total notional value of exchange traded options was nearly US$65 trillion, and that of OTC options trades was over $62 trillion. The vast majority of options are traded in North America and Europe, and of these the majority are interest rate options. For instance, over $40 trillion notional of exchange traded options were traded on North

---

[1] The underlying contract for an option is always the instrument used to hedge the option position. For instance, the FTSE 100 index options are really options on the FTSE 100 index futures. Except in specific examples we use the term 'underlying contract' – or simply 'underlying' – and not 'underlying asset' because the hedging instrument for the option is not necessarily a financial asset. For instance, it could be an interest rate.

[2] See Section III.3.2.6 for the definition of the *moneyness* of an option.

[3] See Bachelier (2006).

American exchanges (of which \$35 trillion were in interest rate options) and over \$20 trillion notional were traded on European exchanges (of which over \$18 trillion were in interest rate options).[4] On the largest options exchange, the Chicago Mercantile Exchange (CME) and the Chicago Board of Trade (CBOT), trading volume is well over \$2 trillion per annum. Each month about 20 million options contracts are traded on the CME, a large majority of these being interest rate futures options where each contract is for \$100,000 notional of the underlying bond futures.

Who trades options and why are they traded? Some of the reasons are listed below:

- *Market makers* buy and sell options to make money on the bid–ask spread.
- *Hedgers* buy options to reduce risk. For instance, an out-of-the-money put on a share is cheap to buy and it provides a shareholder with an insurance against a substantial fall in the share price, because if the price crashes they can still sell the stock at the strike of the option.
- *Speculators* buy and sell options to gamble on the volatility of the underlying. Options are not used to hedge or to gamble on the underlying value itself, futures or forwards being preferred for this because they are far less expensive to trade than options.
- *Investment banks* and other providers of OTC options price them to make a profit after accounting for hedging costs. They hedge their positions by buying the underlying and buying and selling other options on the same underlying so that the portfolio is immune to small changes in the underlying price and its volatility.

The major aims of this chapter are to:

- introduce the characteristics of different types of options;
- understand the basic principles of option pricing;
- describe the trading strategies that are commonly used by investors and speculators;
- explain how providers of options hedge their risks;
- derive and interpret the Black–Scholes–Merton pricing model for standard options and clarify how it is used;
- explain how to price interest rate options and how to calibrate the LIBOR model;
- provide pricing models for European exotic options.

The outline of the chapter is as follows. The mathematical and economic foundations of options pricing are introduced in Section III.3.2. We introduce some elementary *stochastic calculus*, define the concepts of *measure* and *numeraire*, explain the principles of *hedging* and *no arbitrage* that allow us to price options in the *risk neutral* world, make the distinction between *market prices* and *model prices*, explain how to calibrate option pricing models and review the simple *binomial option pricing model*.

In Section III.3.3 we describe the general characteristics of *vanilla options*, which are standard (European or American) calls and puts. Amongst other things we derive the *put–call parity relationship* between prices of standard European calls and puts of the same strike and maturity, and define the *moneyness* of an option. We use the put–call parity relationship to derive a lower bound for the prices of American options, and explain when it may be optimal to exercise the option early. We finish with a brief overview of pricing methods for American options.

---

[4] Exchange traded figures are as of June 2007 and OTC figures are as of December 2006. Source: *BIS Quarterly Review*, Statistical Annex, September 2007. Available from http://www.bis.org.

Section III.3.4 defines the risk factors for options, emphasizing the sensitivity of option prices to the two main risk factors, which are the underlying price and its volatility. We introduce the *delta, gamma, vega* and other risk factor sensitivities, commonly called the 'Greeks', and explain how to hedge the risks of trading options, for instance by constructing portfolios that are delta–gamma–vega neutral. Then Section III.3.5 examines the strategies used by investors wishing to bet on the direction of underlying price movement or on the underlying volatility.

Section III.3.6 derives the *Black–Scholes–Merton partial differential equation* (PDE) that holds for the price of any claim on an underlying asset that follows geometric Brownian motion with constant volatility, and where the risk free interest rate and any dividend on the asset are also assumed to be constant. Then we focus on the case where the claim is a standard European option and derive and interpret the *Black–Scholes–Merton* (BSM) *formula* for the option price and its hedge ratios. We show how the BSM option price can be thought of as the amount that an option trader requires as compensation for writing the option and buying a replicating portfolio. A simple adjustment to BSM option prices that accounts for stochastic volatility is explained, and then Section III.3.7 discusses the properties of the BSM Greeks, providing numerical examples showing how to hedge an option against price and volatility risk.

In Section III.3.8 we consider interest rate options. After defining *caps, floors* and *swaptions* on fixed income securities, we derive their BSM prices when the underlying price of the asset (a bond) follows a geometric Brownian motion with constant volatility. Then we survey the family of mean-reverting interest rate models, including the LIBOR *model* which is a multifactor model where LIBOR or other market forward rates are assumed to be driven by correlated Brownian motions. The LIBOR model is used to hedge interest rate options books and to price exotic interest rate options such as Bermudan swaptions. A case study explains how to calibrate the LIBOR model using principal components analysis.

The Black–Scholes–Merton PDE has an analytic solution when the claim is a standard European call or put. The exact prices of other types of claims can usually only be obtained by solving the PDE using a numerical method. However, most of the standard *exotic options* have analytic prices or prices that can be approximated using an analytic formula, provided only that they are of European type. These formulae are given in Section III.3.9 and an Excel workbook provides several numerical examples of the application of these formulae, for many different types of European exotic options. Section III.3.10 summarizes and concludes.

III.3.2 FOUNDATIONS

The market price of a liquid traded option at any time prior to expiry is determined by the supply and demand for the option at that time, just like any other liquid traded asset. But when options are illiquid the price that is quoted in the market must be derived from a model. The most fundamental model for an option price is based on the assumption that the underlying asset price is lognormally distributed and thus follows a stochastic differential equation called a *geometric Brownian motion*. Equivalently, the log price – and also the log return – is normally distributed and follows an *arithmetic Brownian motion*. This section opens with a review of the characteristics of Brownian motion processes. Then we describe the concepts of *hedging* and *no arbitrage* that lead to the *risk neutral valuation* methodology for pricing options. We introduce the risk neutral *measure* and explain why the asset price is not a martingale under this measure. However, we can *change the numeraire* to the money market account, and then the price of a non-dividend paying asset becomes a martingale. The change of numeraire technique is useful in many circumstances, for instance when interest rates are stochastic or when pricing an exchange option.

For reasons that will become abundantly clear in the next chapter, we do not usually price options under the assumption that the price process is a geometric Brownian motion with constant volatility. Instead, we use a *stochastic* volatility in the option pricing model, and sometimes we assume there are other stochastic parameters, and/or a mean reversion in the drift, or a jump in the price and/or the volatility.[5] Hence the option pricing model typically contains several *parameters* that we *calibrate* by using the model to price liquid options (usually standard European calls and puts) and then changing the model parameters so that the model prices match the observed market prices. Then, with these calibrated parameters, we can use the model to price path-dependent and exotic options. However, if we are content to assume the price process is a geometric Brownian motion with constant volatility, European exotics have prices that are easy to derive, as we shall see in Section III.3.9.

A certain amount of formal language is necessary in this section, even though we have always tried to emphasize the concepts rather than the technicalities. Readers requiring a higher level of financial mathematics are recommended to consult the wonderful book by Baxter and Rennie (1996).

III.3.2.1   Arithmetic and Geometric Brownian Motion

Investors compare financial assets on the basis of their returns because returns are comparable whatever the price of the underlying asset. The simplest assumption we can make is that log returns are normally distributed; and if the log return over a time interval of length t is normally distributed then the future price at time t will have a lognormal distribution.[6] Another simplifying assumption is that the changes in price from one period to the next, i.e. the price increments, are independent.

To describe a lognormally distributed stochastic process in continuous time that has independent increments, we use a *geometric Brownian motion*. When $S(t)$ follows a geometric Brownian motion then we write

$$\frac{dS(t)}{S(t)} = \mu\, dt + \sigma\, dW(t), \tag{III.3.1}$$

where the parameters μ and σ are called the *drift* and the *volatility* of the process. We assume for the moment that these are constant. $W(t)$ is called a *Wiener process* or a *Brownian motion*. This is a continuous process whose increments $dW(t)$ are stationary, independent and normally distributed with zero expectation and variance equal to the time increment, dt.

If $\sigma = 0$ then (III.3.1) is an ordinary differential equation, called the standard *growth model*, which has the solution

$$S(t) = S(0)\exp(\mu t). \tag{III.3.2}$$

---

[5] An introduction to mean-reverting and jump models was provided in Section I.3.7.
[6] It also makes sense to assume that financial asset prices are represented by a lognormal variable rather than by a normal random variable, because lognormal variables cannot be negative. The lognormal distribution, and its relationship with the normal distribution, is described in Section I.3.3.5.

To see this, note that taking the first derivative of (III.3.2) gives

$$\frac{dS(t)}{dt} = \mu S(0)\exp(\mu t) = \mu S(t). \tag{III.3.3}$$

If $\sigma > 0$ then (III.3.1) is a *stochastic differential equation* (SDE), and it is often convenient to write it in an alternative form with $d\ln S(t)$ as the stochastic variable. To derive this alternative form we use *Itô's lemma,* which states that if f is any function of S and t then the SDE for the dynamics of f may be derived from the SDE for the dynamics of S as

$$df(S,t) = \left\{f_t(S,t) + \mu S(t)f_S(S,t) + \tfrac{1}{2}\sigma^2 S(t)^2 f_{SS}(S,t)\right\}dt + \sigma S(t)f_S(S,t)dW(t), \tag{III.3.4}$$

where the subscripts denote the partial derivatives with respect to S and t.[7]

Application of Itô's lemma with $f = \ln S$ shows that a continuous time representation of geometric Brownian motion that is equivalent to the geometric Brownian motion (III.3.1), but is translated into a process for *log* prices, is the *arithmetic Brownian motion,*

$$d\ln S(t) = \left(\mu - \tfrac{1}{2}\sigma^2\right)dt + \sigma\,dW(t). \tag{III.3.5}$$

This is a normally distributed process, because $dW(t)$ is normally distributed, with expectation $\left(\mu - \tfrac{1}{2}\sigma^2\right)dt$ and variance $\sigma^2 dt$.

Since

$$\int_0^t dW(s) = W(t) \tag{III.3.6}$$

the arithmetic Brownian motion (III.3.5) – and therefore also the geometric Brownian motion (III.3.1) – has the solution

$$\ln S(t) = \ln S(0) + \left(\mu - \tfrac{1}{2}\sigma^2\right)t + \sigma W(t). \tag{III.3.7}$$

Another way of writing (III.3.7) is, taking exponentials,

$$S(t) = S(0)\exp\left[\left(\mu - \tfrac{1}{2}\sigma^2\right)t + \sigma W(t)\right]. \tag{III.3.8}$$

---

[7] Itô's lemma is no more than a Taylor expansion, of first order with respect to t and second order with respect to S. Thus if the price process is $dS(t) = a(S,t)dt + b(S,t)dW(t)$ and if we drop the notation for dependence on t, or on S and t, for brevity, the general form of the lemma is simply a Taylor expansion of $f \equiv f(S,t)$. That is,

$$df \approx f_t dt + f_S\,dS + \tfrac{1}{2}f_{SS}\,dS^2$$

$$\approx f_t dt + f_S(a\,dt + b\,dW) + \tfrac{1}{2}f_{SS}(a\,dt + b\,dW)^2.$$

But W is a Wiener process, so $(dW)^2 = dt$ and, for the last term we ignore terms of order $(dt)^{3/2}$ and higher. Now collecting terms in dt and dW yields the general form of the lemma for price processes with no latent stochastic variables as

$$df \approx \left(f_t + af_S + \tfrac{1}{2}b^2 f_{SS}\right)dt + bf_S\,dW.$$

III.3.2.2   Risk Neutral Valuation

Option pricing is based, if possible, on a *no arbitrage* argument.[8] This goes as follows: if we can add other traded assets or instruments to an option so that the resulting portfolio is risk free, in other words if the option can be *perfectly hedged*, then the portfolio should return the risk free rate. Since it has no risk, this *risk free portfolio* will have the same value today for all investors, regardless of their attitude to risk.[9] And because the hedging instruments have market prices, which are the same for all investors, the option must also have the same value for all investors, in particular for a risk neutral investor.

A *risk neutral investor* is one who values any risky portfolio at its expected value, discounted at the risk free rate regardless of the risk. That is, a risk neutral investor requires no risk premium above the risk-free rate for holding a risky asset. For a risk neutral investor the value today of any asset that can be used to form a risk free portfolio is the expectation of a future value of this asset, including any benefits or costs accruing to the holder, discounted at the risk free rate.[10] The beliefs of a risk neutral investor about the future value of a risky asset are called a *risk neutral probability measure*.[11] A risk neutral probability measure is always such that the expected future value of a risky asset (cum dividends), discounted to today at the risk free rate, is equal to today's market value of this asset.

Measure is just another name for a probability distribution. The shape of this probability distribution depends on the asset and on the investor. A measure can have any expected value, volatility, skewness or kurtosis, since these depend on the investor's views. But the expected value of a probability measure for a risk neutral investor is unique. That is, all risk neutral investors have measures with the same expected value.

Actually there are only two types of probability measures that arise in finance theory and, for a given asset and investor, the two measures differ only by their expected values.[12] That is, each measure is just a *shift* of the other measure to a different expected value. The variance and higher moments are unchanged by a change of measure. The two measures are:

- the *physical measure* which has expectation determined by the investor's views about the future price of a risky asset;[13]
- the *risk neutral measure*, which is the physical measure shifted to have expectation equal to the current market value of the asset inflated at the risk free rate of return.

When perfect hedging is possible options are valued by setting up a risk free portfolio that has the same value for all investors, so we may as well value it for a risk neutral investor, since risk neutral investors value the portfolio at its expected value, discounted at the risk free rate and all such investors have measures with the same expected value. Put another way, when perfect hedging is possible options are valued under the risk neutral measure, not under any physical measure. This means that any objective or subjective views that an

---

[8] Following Ross (1976), Cox and Ross (1976) and Harrison and Kreps (1979).
[9] See Section I.6.2 for a formal definition of risk attitude.
[10] Here the asset price includes all the benefits associated with holding the asset. So we refer to the cum-dividend price of stock, for example. And if holding the asset incurs costs in addition to funding costs, such as carry cost for a commodity, then these must also be accounted for in the asset price.
[11] For our purposes an investor's beliefs are his subjective views about the distribution of a financial asset.
[12] In a complete, no-arbitrage market the measure defined by the price process is equivalent to a unique risk neutral measure, as explained below.
[13] The physical measure is also called the *real-world measure*. Sometimes we also distinguish between the *objective measure*, which is a physical measure where the investor's views are based on some historical sample, and the *subjective measure*, which is a physical measure where the expected value is set according to the investor's beliefs or subjective views.

investor has about the expected returns on the underlying asset are irrelevant when pricing an option on that asset.

Thus two 'typical' investors who have the same risk neutral measure will agree about the price of an option even though they may have different beliefs about the expected return on the underlying in the physical measure. Put another way, an investor's expected return on the underlying in the physical measure is irrelevant when pricing an option. All that matters is the risk of the underlying. And if the underlying has no risk, the option would have the same value as a forward contract.[14]

Breeden and Litzenberger (1978) showed that we can estimate a risk neutral measure from the market prices of traded options. This measure, which can be interpreted as the risk neutral measure of the 'typical' or 'average' risk neutral investor, is called the *market implied measure*.[15] For an asset price at time T the market implied measure is derived from the second derivatives of the market prices of all options with expiry date T with respect to the strike of these options.[16]

Harrison and Pliska (1981) proved that there is no possibility for arbitrage if and only if there is a risk neutral measure that is *equivalent* to the measure defined by the price process.[17] Moreover, this risk neutral measure is *unique* if the market is complete. The concept of a *complete market* was introduced by Harrison and Kreps (1979). It is a market in which it is possible to replicate the value of any option, whatever its pay-off function, with existing assets using a self-financing replicating portfolio.[18]

Harrison and Pliska's result is called the *fundamental theorem of arbitrage*. It means that, in a complete, no arbitrage market, all risk neutral investors have the *same* measure for each asset. In particular, they agree on the same volatility, skewness, kurtosis, etc. Of course, some investors may not be risk neutral, but risk attitude does not enter into the pricing of an option that can be hedged. In a complete, no-arbitrage market we price options under the unique risk neutral measure.

In Section III.2.3 we used hedging and the principle of no arbitrage to derive a *fair value* relationship between a spot price and the price of a forward contract. This led to a representation of the market spot price as the discounted fair value of the forward contract.[19] The fair price is the rational price demanded by a risk neutral investor. Hence, hedging and the principle of no arbitrage imply a unique risk neutral value for the price of a forward.

Similarly, hedging and the principle of no arbitrage imply a unique risk neutral price for an option. A no arbitrage argument can again be used, this time to derive a fair value relationship between the price of the option and the price of its underlying asset. But the expiry value of an option is uncertain because it depends on whether it is exercised (it may expire worthless)

[14] This is proved in Section III.3.6.5.
[15] The market implied measure is equivalent to the *state price density*, which for each state x gives the price of a security that pays 1, in present value terms, if the state falls between x and $x + dx$, and 0 otherwise. Such an elemental security is called an *Arrow–Debreu security* after the work of Debreu (1959) and Arrow (1964). They are elemental in the sense that any pay-off can be replicated using Arrow–Debreu securities.
[16] See Jackwerth and Rubinstein (1996) for a parametric approach to estimating this density, and Aït-Sahalia and Lo (1998) for a non-parametric approach.
[17] Two probability distributions are *equivalent* if they have the same *support*, in other words they are non-zero over the same range. That is, one distribution gives a non-zero probability for an event if and only if the other distribution has a non-zero probability for this same event. This is a very weak notion of equivalence and the terminology may be rather misleading since two 'equivalent' measures are not measures that give the same probabilities in the strict sense.
[18] See also Section III.3.6.1.
[19] This relationship should really be expressed as the fair spot price being the discounted market value of the forward contract. The forward is more liquid than the spot, and therefore it is the forward contract that we should use for the market price in the fair value relationship.

and the decision to exercise depends on the price of the underlying at the time when the option is exercised. Hence, the risk neutral price of an option depends on the entire risk neutral distribution of possible future prices for the underlying, and on the volatility in particular.

The *risk neutral valuation principle* states that the current price of any risky asset in a complete, no arbitrage economy is the discounted expected value of its future price, evaluated under the unique risk neutral measure. This principle underlies virtually all option pricing models used today.[20] We shall use it below when we review the binomial option pricing model. In this case the risk neutral valuation principle is used with the *delta hedging* form of no arbitrage pricing to construct a binomial tree of prices for any option using a binomial tree for the underlying price. And we shall use it again in Section III.3.6 when we derive the Black–Scholes–Merton partial differential equation under the assumption that the underlying price follows a geometric Brownian motion. Delta hedging leads to the construction of a position in the underlying asset and a bond called a *replicating portfolio* that is continuously rebalanced so that its value at any time is equal to the value of the option. Harrison and Kreps (1979) show that this replicating portfolio is *self-financing* and therefore, by no arbitrage, the initial value of the replicating portfolio must be equal to the value of the option.[21]

III.3.2.3   Numeraire and Measure

Numeraire is a French term that means 'cash' or 'currency'. For an *asset*, i.e. something that has a dollar (or any other currency) value, it is the unit of measurement. For an interest rate it is the unit of measurement for the principal on which interest accrues. A change of currency is one way to change the numeraire for that asset or interest rate.

A probability measure is defined with respect to a numeraire, which is the unit of measurement or unit of 'account' for the random variable. If we change the numeraire we change the measure, but only because the units are different. The new measure is *equivalent* to the old measure, in the rather weak sense of 'equivalent' defined in the previous subsection. We can use the price of any asset with strictly positive value as a numeraire.[22] For instance, we could use gold as the numeraire, or McDonald's burgers. If the price of an asset in gold is 1 troy ounce this means that it would cost us 1 troy ounce of gold to buy the asset. Equivalently, the asset would cost 300 McDonald's burgers, assuming we can buy 300 burgers for one ounce of gold. An asset has the same worth whatever numeraire is used. And the *relative* prices of traded assets are unchanged when we change the numeraire. That is, if the price of asset X in one numeraire is twice the price of asset Y, then the price of X is still twice the price of Y in any other numeraire.

There are two numeraires that are commonly used in finance, the money market numeraire and a risk free discount (zero coupon) bond.[23] The value of a numeraire changes over time. For instance, the *savings account* or *money market account* in US dollars is the price at time t of \$1 that was invested in the money market at time 0. That is, the numeraire for the money market account has value at time t given by

$$\beta(t) = \exp\left(\int_0^t r(s)\,ds\right),$$ (III.3.9)

---

[20] Although one should realize that many options are difficult to hedge perfectly.
[21] See Section III.3.6.5 for further details.
[22] It becomes messy if the asset pays dividends, so we try to avoid using such an asset as numeraire if possible.
[23] The problem with using the discount bond as numeraire is that it must have a maturity, which is tedious to deal with, so the money market numeraire is preferable. When the discount bond is used as numeraire we call this the *forward measure*.

where $r(t)$ is the risk free continuously compounded rate of return. However, the *discount bond* numeraire has value at time t given by

$$B(t, T) = E\left[\exp\left(-\int_t^T r(s)ds\right)\right],$$
(III.3.10)

where the expectation is taken under the risk neutral measure and T is the maturity of the instrument that we are hedging at time t.

Suppose $S(t)$ is the price of an asset that pays no dividends, and $S(t)$ follows the geometric Brownian motion

$$\frac{dS(t)}{S(t)} = r(t)dt + \sigma dW(t).$$
(III.3.11)

This gives the price of the asset in the risk neutral measure, but $S(t)$ is not a martingale under the risk neutral measure, because it has a non-zero drift. In other words, the risk neutral measure is not a *martingale measure* for $S(t)$. However, we can change the numeraire so that $S(t)$ becomes a martingale. In other words, we can change the measure for $S(t)$ to an equivalent measure that *is* a martingale.[24] In particular, if we price $S(t)$ in terms of the money market account, then its price becomes $\tilde{S}(t) = S(t)/\beta(t)$ and

$$\frac{d\tilde{S}(t)}{\tilde{S}(t)} = \sigma dW(t).$$
(III.3.12)

To see this that this is true, write (III.3.11) in the form

$$S(t) = S(0)\exp\left(\int_0^t r(s)ds - \tfrac{1}{2}\sigma^2 t + \sigma W(t)\right)$$
(III.3.13)

and then note that

$$\beta(t) = \beta(0)\exp\left(\int_0^t r(s)ds\right),$$

so

$$\tilde{S}(t) = \tilde{S}(0)\exp\left(-\tfrac{1}{2}\sigma^2 t + \sigma W(t)\right).$$

But[25]

$$E\left[\exp\left(-\tfrac{1}{2}\sigma^2 t + \sigma W(t)\right)\right] = \exp\left(-\tfrac{1}{2}\sigma^2 t\right) E\left[\exp\left(\sigma W(t)\right)\right]$$
$$= \exp\left(-\tfrac{1}{2}\sigma^2 t\right)\exp\left(\tfrac{1}{2}\sigma^2 t\right) = 1$$

Hence $E\left(\tilde{S}(t)\right) = \tilde{S}(0)$. This shows that $\tilde{S}(t)$, the price of the asset in the money market numeraire, *is* a martingale. This is useful, because if $r(t)$ is stochastic, it is very difficult to price a contingent claim under the risk neutral measure, but easy under its equivalent martingale measure, the money market measure.

Assume the original measure is a lognormal risk neutral measure, i.e. the probability distribution of the asset with price $S(t)$ at time t is a lognormal distribution. Now suppose that $N(t)$ is the price of any asset and $N(t) > 0$ at all times t. Then we can use $N(t)$ as the numeraire, but how is the new measure related to the original, risk neutral one? To answer this question we need to define some more notation. We denote the risk neutral measure

---

[24] In technical terms, we can find an *equivalent martingale measure*.
[25] Using the fact that $E(\exp(X)) = \exp\left(\mu + \tfrac{1}{2}\sigma^2\right)$, when $X \sim N(\mu, \sigma^2)$. Note that this fundamental result can be proved by direct integration or using (I.3.40), the mean of a lognormal variable, since $\exp(X)$ has a lognormal distribution.

by Q. This is standard, although a fuller notation would be $Q(S(t))$ if we conformed to our usual notation for a probability distribution.[26]

Measure theory has its roots in the French school of topology, rather than the classical statistical school, and the measure theory notation for a density is different from the classical notation. Since the risk neutral measure is lognormal, it is defined for a continuum of values of $S(t)$. Technically speaking, we say it has *continuous support*. Now if the measure (distribution) is Q then the probability that $S(t)$ takes a value within a small range dS is dQ, and as dS tends to zero, dQ tends to the *density function* associated with the measure. This construction is only valid if the measure has continuous support, but this is what we usually assume for prices of financial assets, even though prices do have a minimum tick size.

Assume we start from the lognormal risk neutral measure Q, where the price $S(t)$ is driven by the process (III.3.11), and that the new numeraire $N(t)$ is defined on a continuum of (strictly positive) values. Denote the rebased price by $\tilde{S}(t) = S(t)/N(t)$ and suppose this has measure $\tilde{Q}$. Then the two densities associated with these measures are related as

$$dQ = \frac{\tilde{S}(t)}{\tilde{S}(0)} d\tilde{Q}. \qquad (III.3.14)$$

This change of measure may be written in a form known as the *Radon–Nikodym derivative*,

$$\frac{d\tilde{Q}}{dQ} = \frac{N(t)/N(0)}{S(t)/S(0)}. \qquad (III.3.15)$$

III.3.2.4   Market Prices and Model Prices

When a trader first writes an option he prices it at a *premium* that corresponds to the price he believes he can charge. In a liquid market this premium is determined by supply and demand. If few other traders are writing similar options and demand from investors or speculators is high, then he can set a high premium for the option. Having checked the premium that the market can bear, the trader then determines whether he can make a profit on the deal, after deducting from the premium the costs of hedging his risks and, if the option is traded OTC, the risk capital required to cover any counterparty risk. Only if he expects the deal to make a reasonable profit would he decide to write the option.

There is a very large secondary market, particularly for exchanged traded options. The majority of investors (including speculators and hedgers) hold an exchange traded option for only a matter of days or weeks, but the option's time to expiry could easily be 6 months or more. Whilst options are issued with maturities of many months or even years, most of the trading is on short to medium term options that are near to 'at the money'. Options tend to lose liquidity when they get very close to expiry, especially when they are deep 'out of the money' or deep 'in the money'. The concept of moneyness of an option is defined in Section III.3.3 below. Because of this highly liquid secondary market it is important for the exchange to quote prices after the initial pricing of the issue. These market prices are set by market makers responding to demand and supply in the market.

So if both the issue price of the option and the option prices in the secondary market are set by economic forces, why do we need option pricing models? First, option writers should at least root the calculation of an initial premium for their issue on some sort of model. It might be a very basic theoretical model (e.g. the Black–Scholes–Merton model, described in

---

[26] In our usual notation we write $F(x)$ for a distribution function, with x being a possible value for the random variable X.

Section III.3.6), but option traders know that, in almost all markets, the assumptions made by a basic option pricing model will be incorrect. Hence, traders are likely to adjust the price obtained from a simple model, for instance they could use an *ad hoc* adjustment to account for uncertainty in volatility, as described in Section III.3.6.7. Secondly, when investors are buying and selling options in the secondary market, a model helps them decide whether or not the market price represents a fair deal. A model is particularly useful for pricing options that lack liquidity, when their exchange quotes are likely to be stale, perhaps several days old.

Thirdly, and perhaps most importantly, whilst the majority of exchange trading is on standard calls and puts, many other more complex options are traded in OTC markets. For these we really do need a good pricing model. To avoid the possibility of arbitrage, any pricing model that is used to price an exotic option should give European option prices that are consistent with the market prices of European calls and puts.[27] For this reason the parameters of an option pricing model are calibrated by equating the model prices of standard European calls and puts to the prices of these options that are observed in the market, as explained in the next section.

III.3.2.5   Parameters and Calibration

The simplest possible assumption about the stochastic process that drives the underlying price is that it is a geometric Brownian motion with constant volatility (see Section III.3.2.1). This is the assumption that underlies the Black–Scholes–Merton model, but it is not representative of the observed movements in returns in the real world. Thus during the last decade there has been a huge amount of research on numerous *stochastic volatility* option pricing models, some of which add jumps in the price and/or the volatility equations. These models assume that the volatility parameter is itself stochastic, so it becomes a latent (i.e. unobservable) risk factor.[28]

Sometimes we assume the mean is a *deterministic* function of time, so the mean of the asset price distribution at some fixed future point in time is just the risk free return from now until that time, less any benefits or plus any costs associated with holding the underlying. But some pricing models assume that the drift term has a mean-reverting component and/or that the interest rate or the dividend yield are stochastic.

Making a parameter into a risk factor introduces other parameters to the option pricing model, because these are required to describe the distribution of this new risk factor. For instance, the parameters of a typical stochastic volatility model include the *spot volatility*, the *long run volatility*, the *rate of volatility mean reversion*, the *volatility of volatility*, and the *price–volatility correlation*. In addition, we could include a *volatility risk premium*.[29]

When volatility is assumed to be the only stochastic parameter there are two risk factors in the option pricing model, the price and the volatility. To price the option we need to know their joint distribution at every point in time, unless it is a standard European option in which case we only need to know their joint distribution at the time of expiry. The easiest way to do this is to describe the evolution of each risk factor in continuous time using a pair

---

[27] In a complete market the pay-off to any option can be replicated using a portfolio of standard calls and puts, as shown in Section III.3.5.5, so arbitrage would be possible if the option price is not consistent with the market prices of standard calls and puts.

[28] See Section III.4.5 for a description of the most common types of stochastic volatility models.

[29] If investors have an expected return on volatility that is equal to the risk free rate then the volatility risk premium will be zero. But holding volatility risk may require compensation different from the risk free rate, in which case a volatility risk premium should be added as a parameter to the stochastic volatility model. In fact there is some evidence to suggest that the volatility risk premium is negative, i.e. investors are willing to pay to have volatility risk. See, for instance, Bakshi and Kapardia (2003). If true, the reason may be that volatility provides an excellent source of diversification, since it has a strong negative correlation with the underlying price.

of stochastic differential equations. The model parameters are the parameters in the price and volatility equations, and the price–volatility correlation.

The model parameters are *calibrated* by matching the model prices of standard European options to the observable market prices of these options. There are usually very many standard European options prices that are quoted in the market but an option pricing model typically has only a handful of parameters.[30] Hence, the model prices will not match every single market price exactly. The calibration of parameters is therefore based on a numerical method to minimize a root mean square error between the model price and the market price of every standard European option for which there is a market price.[31]

More precisely, we can calibrate the model parameters λ by applying a numerical method to the optimization problem:

$$\min_{\lambda} \sqrt{\sum_{K,T} w(K, T) \left(f^m(K, T) - f(K, T \mid \lambda) \right)^2}, \qquad (\text{III.3.16})$$

where $f^m(K, T)$ and $f(K, T \mid \lambda)$ denote the market and model prices of a European option with strike K and expiry time T, $w(K, T)$ is a weighting function (for instance, we might take it to be proportional to the option gamma, to place more weight on short term near at-the-money options) and the sum is taken over all options with *liquid* market prices. For an alternative calibration objective and a general discussion of calibration objectives, see Section III.4.5.

Most of the trading is on options that are near to at-the-money. The observed prices of deep in-the-money and out-of-the-money options may be stale if the market has moved since they were last traded. Therefore it is common to use only those options that are within 10% of the at-the-money to calibrate the model.

Once calibrated the option pricing model can be used to price exotic and path-dependent options. Traders may also use the model to dynamically hedge the risks of standard European options, although there is no clear evidence that this would be any better than using the Black–Scholes–Merton model for hedging. See Section III.4.6 for a discussion on this point.

III.3.2.6 Option Pricing: Review of the Binomial Model

Cox and Ross (1976) introduced a simple model for pricing an option in which the underlying asset price dynamics are governed by a *binomial tree* in which the price of an asset can move either upward or downward by a constant multiple, at each time step. They showed how to construct a binomial tree in which there can be no arbitrage, where the probability of an upward move (and therefore also the probability of a downward move) is constant throughout the tree.

We have already explained how to construct such a binomial tree in Section I.5.6.5. There we showed how to parameterize this tree so that it will discretize a geometric Brownian motion process for the underlying asset price with drift equal to the risk free rate of return, and we applied the binomial model to price an American as well as a European option. In this section we review the construction of the tree and its application to price an arbitrary option, using risk neutral valuation.

---

[30] For instance, on the S&P 500 index European options it is not unusual for 30 different strikes and for six or more different maturity dates to be actively quoted on CBOE.
[31] We may also calibrate using implied volatilities, as explained in the next chapter.

Figure III.3.1 depicts a binomial tree for the evolution of an underlying price. The tree begins at the initial node S, which represents the price of the underlying at the time that the option is priced. At the next point in time, an interval Δt later, the price can be either uS or dS, where $u > 1$ and $d < 1$. In order for the tree not to drift upward or downward, we require $u(dS) = d(uS) = S$, i.e. $u = d^{-1}$. At subsequent nodes, each covering the same time step Δt, the price can move either up or down by the same factors u and d. Figure III.3.1 illustrates a binomial tree with three steps. Typically we should discretize the underlying price process so that there are many steps in the tree, not just three. The more steps in the tree, the more accurate the price of the option.

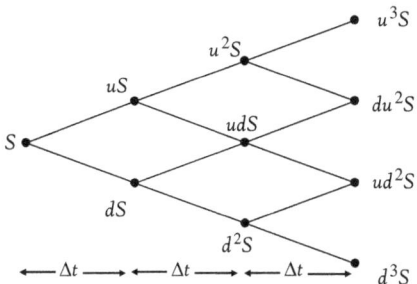

Figure III.3.1   Binomial tree with three steps

In a simple binomial tree we assume that the *transition probability*, i.e. the probability that the price moves up from one node to the next, is constant and we denote this by p. Consider the expected asset price after one time step. This is

$$E(S(\Delta t)) = puS(0) + (1-p)\, dS(0), \tag{III.3.17}$$

where $S(0) = S$. For risk neutral valuation we must choose p so that S grows at the risk free rate r, i.e.

$$E(S(\Delta t)) = S(0)\exp(r\Delta t). \tag{III.3.18}$$

How can we do this?

Also, in a simple binomial model for pricing an option we want to assume that the underlying price process follows a geometric Brownian motion with constant volatility. In this case the binomial option price will converge to the Black–Scholes–Merton model price as the number of time steps increases and time interval Δt gets smaller and smaller. So how should we choose not only p, but also u and d so that the discretization in a binomial tree will be consistent with the assumption that the asset price process follows a geometric Brownian motion with constant volatility σ and drift equal to the risk free rate of return?

In Section I.5.6 we proved that for this to be the case the parameters must satisfy two restrictions, which are

$$\exp(r\Delta t) = pu + (1-p)\, d \tag{III.3.19}$$

and

$$\exp(2r\Delta t + \sigma^2 \Delta t) = pu^2 + (1-p)\, d^2. \tag{III.3.20}$$

There are many possible parameterizations of the lattice that are consistent with (III.3.19) and (III.3.20). In Section I.5.6 we considered just two, including the parameterization of Cox et al. (1979) where

$$p = \frac{\exp(r\Delta t) - d}{u - d} \tag{III.3.21}$$

and

$$u = d^{-1} = \exp\left(\sigma\sqrt{\Delta t}\right). \tag{III.3.22}$$

With such a value for p the asset price will indeed grow at the risk free rate. To see this, substitute (III.3.21) into (III.3.17), giving

$$E(S(\Delta t)) = S(0)\left[\left(\frac{\exp(r\Delta t) - d}{u - d}\right)u + \left(\frac{u - \exp(r\Delta t)}{u - d}\right)d\right] = S(0)\exp(r\Delta t)$$

and so (III.3.18) holds.

In other words, when p is given by (III.3.21) it can be thought of as a *risk neutral probability*, and the additional condition (III.3.22) ensures that the volatility of the asset price process is σ. Furthermore, it can be shown that these two conditions ensure that the asset price will have a lognormal distribution, which is consistent with the assumption of geometric Brownian motion. See Section I.5.6 for further details.

Although many other parameterizations consistent with (III.3.19) and (III.3.20) are possible, the Cox et al. (1979) parameterization is often used because it can be shown that a risk neutral probability of the form (III.3.21) can be derived using a simple delta hedging form of no arbitrage argument. That is, we consider an option on S with price f and hedge this option by selling δ units of the underlying. The hedged portfolio has value $f - \delta S$ when the hedge is placed, which is at time 0. Now suppose that at time Δt the option value becomes either f_u or f_d, depending on whether the price moves up to uS or down to dS. Then if the portfolio is riskless it must have the same value whether the price moves up or down. That is,

$$f_u - \delta(uS) = f_d - \delta(dS).$$

In other words, we can obtain a riskless portfolio by setting the *hedge ratio* to be

$$\delta = \frac{f_u - f_d}{uS - dS}. \tag{III.3.23}$$

Now we apply a no arbitrage argument. The initial value of the portfolio is $f - \delta S$ and after one time step its value is $f_u - \delta(uS)$ which, in present value terms and discounted at the risk free rate, is

$$\exp(-r\Delta t)(f_u - \delta(uS)).$$

Hence, to avoid arbitrage we must have

$$\exp(-r\Delta t)(f_u - \delta(uS)) = f - \delta S,$$

and solving for f gives, after some calculations,

$$f = \exp(-r\Delta t)(pf_u + (1-p)f_d), \tag{III.3.24}$$

where p is given by (III.3.21). That is, the option price today is the discounted value of its expected price tomorrow. So this is an example of the risk neutral valuation principle.

Having parameterized the binomial tree we can use it to price any American or European option, knowing only its pay-off function. To price the option we use the tree for the underlying price to construct another tree for the price of the option, working backward from the terminal nodes and at every step applying the risk neutral valuation principle, so that there are no arbitrage opportunities. At the terminal nodes the price of the option is equal to its pay-off in each of the states. At any node just before the terminal nodes the price of the option is equal to its discounted expected value at the two succeeding terminal nodes, under the risk neutral measure. And in general,

$$f(t) = \exp(-r\Delta t) \left(pf_u(t + \Delta t) - (1 - p)f_d(t + \Delta t) \right). \qquad \text{(III.3.25)}$$

We use risk neutral valuation in the form (III.3.25) to fill in the values of the option at all the nodes immediately preceding the terminal nodes, and then we move progressively backward through the tree repeating this calculation until we reach the initial node. The current option price is then the price at this initial node.

We have already provided spreadsheets that use a binomial tree to price two types of option: a standard European option in Section I.5.6.3 and an American option in Section I.5.6.5.

III.3.3   CHARACTERISTICS OF VANILLA OPTIONS

First let us define some general terms and the notation we use. The *expiry date* of the option is the last day on which the option can be exercised, if the holder finds it profitable to do so. A *European option* can only be exercised on the day of expiry. The *strike* of the option, K, is the price at which the underlying is bought (for a call) or sold (for a put). The *maturity* of the option T is the time, measured in years, between the issue of the option and its expiry. An option is defined by its *pay-off function*. The pay-off to a European option is its value on the expiry date. This value depends on the expiry date, the strike of the option and any other characteristics of the option, as well as the price of the underlying at the expiry date, S_T. The pay-off to a *path-dependent* option also depends on the price of the underlying before the expiry date.

At any time t, with $0 \leq t \leq T$, the *residual time to maturity* is $T - t$, i.e. the time remaining until the expiry date, and we sometimes denote this by τ. The *price of the underlying* of an arbitrary option at time t is denoted $S(t)$. Sometimes we want to emphasize whether this is a spot price, a futures price or an interest rate. In that case, when the underlying is a futures contract we use $F(t, T)$ to denote the underlying price, and we use the notation $r(t)$ when the underlying is an interest rate.

We can summarize the material we will learn in this section as follows. There are two types of elementary options, which are called binary options and standard options. Both can be used to replicate the pay-offs of other options, and because we usually use standard calls and puts for portfolio replication they are the most actively traded type of option. The prices of standard European calls and puts are related by the *put–call parity* relationship. Standard European call and put options are characterized by their *strike* and *maturity* but it is often easier to replace the strike metric by the *moneyness* metric. An *American option* can be exercised at any time prior to the expiry date and a *Bermudan option* can also be exercised early, but only on certain specified dates before expiry. The *early exercise premium* means that the American option price is never less than its European counterpart, and the put–call parity relationship allows us to define a lower bound for the price of an American option. We shall illustrate the *early exercise boundary* graphically.

III.3.3.1 Elementary Options

In this subsection we introduce two types of elementary options. These options may be thought of as building blocks for other options. For instance, standard calls or puts can be used to replicate any continuous claim, as shown in Section III.3.5.5. A binary option has the simplest possible pay-off. A binary call pays 1 if the asset price is above a fixed level when the option is exercised, and 0 otherwise. In fact the four types of binary option, with their pay-off functions, are as follows:[32]

- A *binary call* pays 1 unit if $S(t) > K$ and 0 otherwise, so its pay-off is $1_{\{S(t)>K\}}$.
- A *binary put* pays 1 unit if $S(t) < K$ and 0 otherwise, so its pay-off is $1_{\{S(t)<K\}}$.
- A *cash-or-nothing* option has pay-off $K1_{\{S(t)>K\}}$ for a call and $K1_{\{S(t)<K\}}$ for a put.
- An *asset-or-nothing* option has pay-off $S(t)1_{\{S(t)>K\}}$ for a call and $S(t)1_{\{S(t)<K\}}$ for a put.

In the above, t is the time at which the option is exercised, so for an American option t can be anything between time 0 when the option is issued and time T when the option expires. But for a European option we must have $t = T$. Standard European options have pay-offs that depend only on the distribution of the underlying price at time T and not at any time prior to T.

Plain vanilla is the term usually applied to standard call and put options:

- A standard *call option* has pay-off $\max(S(t) - K, 0)$, also written $[S(t) - K]^+$,
- A standard *put option* has pay-off $\max(K - S(t), 0)$, also written $[K - S(t)]^+$.

The pay-offs to vanilla options are illustrated in Figure III.3.2, with the black line showing the call pay-off and the grey line showing the put pay-off, as a function of the underlying asset price.

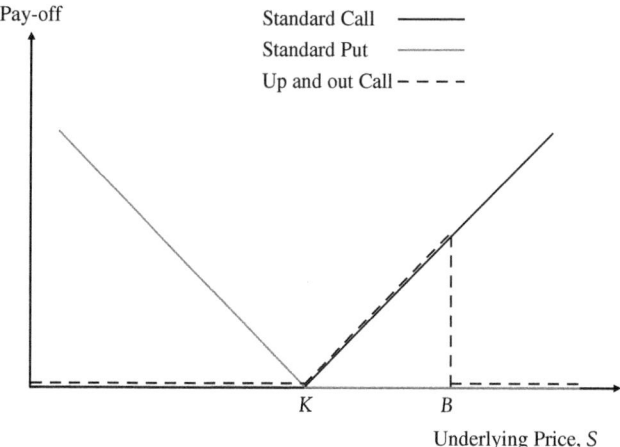

Figure III.3.2 Pay-offs to a standard call and put and an up and out barrier

Among the most liquid exotic options are *barrier options*. There are numerous different types of barrier options. For instance, the dotted line in Figure III.3.2 illustrates the pay-off

---

[32] The notation $1_{x>y}$ stands for the *indicator function*, which has the value 1 if $x > y$ and zero otherwise. More generally, the indicator function is 1_C where C can be any condition, and it takes the value 1 if and only if C holds.

to an *up and out European call*, $\max (S(T) - K, 0) \, 1_{\{S(t) < B, 0 \le t \le T\}}$. That is, the standard call pay-off is received if the underlying price remains below the barrier B throughout the life of the option and otherwise the pay-off is zero. In Section III.3.9 we list the pay-offs to other barriers and many other types of Exotic options. There we also quote and implement pricing formulae for European exotics when the underlying asset prices (and there is often more than one asset) follow geometric Brownian motion.

III.3.3.2   Put–Call Parity

The prices of European calls and puts are related by a simple rule that is derived using the no arbitrage principle. To derive this relationship we use the usual trick of comparing two different portfolios that have the same pay-off in all circumstances. The portfolios can contain a share and European call and put options with the same strike K and maturity T on this share. First assume the share pays no dividends and consider the following portfolios:

- *Portfolio I:* Buy one share and a European put on this share.
- *Portfolio II:* Buy a European call on the share with strike K and maturity T and lend an amount equal to the present value of the strike, discounted at the risk free interest rate r.

It is easy to see that both portfolios have the same pay-off when the options mature. If it turns out that $S(T) > K$ then both strategies pay $S(T)$ because:

- the put is worth nothing so portfolio I pays $S(T)$, and
- the call is worth $S(T) - K$ but you receive K from the pay-back on the loan.

If it turns out that $S(T) < K$ then both strategies pay K because:

- the put is worth $K - S(T)$ while the share has value $S(T)$, and
- the call is worth nothing but you still get K from the loan.

Thus both portfolios have the pay-off $\max (S(T), K)$. This means that the two portfolios must have the same value at *any* time t prior to the option's expiry date T. Otherwise it would be possible to make a risk free profit (i.e. an arbitrage) by shorting one portfolio and buying the other.

This no arbitrage argument implies that a standard European call price $C(K, T)$ and a standard European put price $P(K, T)$ of the same strike and maturity on the same underlying must satisfy the following relationship at any time t prior to the expiry date T:

$$P(S, t \,|\, K, T) + S(t) = C(S, t \,|\, K, T) + \exp(-r\,(T - t))\, K.$$

Now suppose the share pays dividends with continuous dividend yield y. Then a similar no arbitrage argument, but with portfolio I buying $\exp(-y\,(T - t))$ shares and reinvesting the dividends in the share, gives the relationship

$$P(S, t \,|\, K, T) + \exp(-y\,(T - t))\, S(t) = C(S, t \,|\, K, T) + \exp(-r\,(T - t))\, K$$

or, equivalently,

$$C(S, t \,|\, K, T) - P(S, t \,|\, K, T) = \exp(-y(T - t))\, S(t) - \exp(-r\,(T - t))\, K. \qquad \text{(III.3.26)}$$

The relationship (III.3.26) is the *put–call parity* relationship. It implies the following:

- Given the price of a European call it is simple to calculate the fair price of the corresponding put, and vice versa.
- If market prices do not satisfy this relationship there is, theoretically, an opportunity for arbitrage. However the trading costs may be too high for it to be possible to profit from the arbitrage.

The put–call parity relationship can also be used to derive lower bounds for prices of European options. Since the price of an option is never negative, (III.3.26) implies that

$$C(S,t \,|\, K,T) \ge \exp(-y(T-t))\, S(t) - \exp(-r(T-t))\, K \qquad \text{(III.3.27)}$$

and, similarly,

$$P(S,t \,|\, K,T) \ge \exp(-r(T-t))\, K - \exp(-y(T-t))\, S(t). \qquad \text{(III.3.28)}$$

III.3.3.3 Moneyness

Moneyness provides a measure of the *intrinsic value* of a vanilla call or put, i.e. the value of the option if it were exercised today. An option is said to be *at-the-money* (ATM) if the intrinsic value is zero, *in-the-money* (ITM) if the intrinsic value is positive and *out-of-the-money* (OTM) if the intrinsic value is negative. Of course, only an American option really has an intrinsic value, because a European option cannot be exercised before maturity.

There are many different definitions of moneyness with varying degrees of complexity. The simplest definition of moneyness at time t is just $S(t) - K$, but this cannot be used to compare options on different underlyings. If one underlying has price 1000 and it has an option with strike 900 the moneyness should be the same as for another option of strike 90 on an underlying with price 100. However, if we used this simple definition of moneyness, it would be 100 for the first option but 10 for the second option.

A slightly more advanced definition of moneyness that *can* be compared across different underlyings, is $S(t)/K$. But for a European option the strike price K only applies at time T, so we are not really comparing like with like. It would be better to discount the strike value to time t and use $S(t)/\exp(-r(T-t))\, K$ as a measure of moneyness. But we are still forgetting about costs or benefits that may be associated with the underlying. These do not accrue to (or cost) the holder of the option. It is the underlying *without* dividends or carry costs that the option refers to, and the price of this at time t is $\exp(-y(T-t))\, S(t)$, where y is the continuous dividend yield (or the net convenience yield, in the case of a commodity option).

This leads to a definition of the *moneyness* of an option at time t, as

$$M(t) = \frac{\exp(-y(T-t))\, S(t)}{\exp(-r(T-t))\, K}. \qquad \text{(III.3.29)}$$

Later we shall see that the expression

$$x(t) = \frac{\ln(M(t))}{\sigma\sqrt{T-t}} \qquad \text{(III.3.30)}$$

features prominently in the Black–Scholes–Merton formula.

The problem with using $M(t)$ or even $\ln(M(t))$ as a measure of moneyness is that it cannot always be used to compare options on different underlyings. For instance, crude oil has a very high volatility, so if the strike of an option is 10% above the current price the option may still have a high intrinsic value. By contrast, the euro–US dollar exchange rate has fairly low volatility, so if the strike of an option is 10% above the current exchange rate the option probably has a very small intrinsic value. The quantity (III.3.30) is actually a better measure of moneyness than $M(t)$ or $\ln(M(t))$ because it adjusts for the volatility of returns on the underlying.

Some authors go even further, using as the measure of moneyness[33]

$$d_2(t) = x(t) - \frac{1}{2}\sigma\sqrt{T-t} = \frac{\ln(M(t)) - \frac{1}{2}\sigma^2(T-t)}{\sigma\sqrt{T-t}}. \tag{III.3.31}$$

Cox and Ross (1976) prove that $\Phi(d_2)$ is the probability that $M(t) > 0$. In other words, $\Phi(d_2)$ is the probability that a call option is ITM at time t.

Table III.3.1 shows how the moneyness of vanilla calls and puts are related. We use the terms *deep ITM* and *deep OTM* to describe options whose moneyness has a high absolute value. There is very little trading on deep OTM and deep ITM options: most trading is on just OTM and near to ATM options, i.e. options with moneyness between 90% and 110%. Note that there is a symmetry between European calls and puts of the same strike: a call will be ITM to the same extent that the corresponding put is OTM, and conversely, but the OTM options tend to be more liquid because there is more 'optionality' in an OTM option. That is, ITM options behave more like the underlying asset than OTM options. Deep ITM options have a delta of almost 1 for a call, and almost -1 for a put (see the remarks following Figure III.3.5) which means that their prices change almost in line with those of the underlying contract.

Table III.3.1   Moneyness of vanilla puts and calls

	$M(t) < 1$ (i.e. $x(t) < 0$)	$M(t) = 1$ (i.e. $x(t) = 0$)	$M(t) > 1$ (i.e. $x(t) > 0$)
Call	OTM	ATM	ITM
Put	ITM	ATM	OTM

We end this section by remarking that the put–call parity relationship (III.3.26) may be written

$$C(S, t \,|\, K, T) - P(S, t \,|\, K, T) = (M(t) - 1)\exp(-r(T - t))\,K.$$

This shows that an OTM put will have a lower price than the ITM call of the same strike and maturity, and an OTM call will have a lower price than the ITM put of the same strike and maturity.

III.3.3.4 American Options

An *American option* has the same pay-off function as its European counterpart, but the pay-off relates to any time before expiry because the option can be exercised early. This early exercise feature is often included in new issues where market pricing may be unreliable. The

---

[33] Other authors refer to the *delta* of the option and its moneyness almost synonymously.

ability to exercise at any time and obtain the intrinsic value of the option gives investors added security, and thus boosts the demand for a new product. The *intrinsic value* of an American call at time t is $S(t) - K$ and that of an American put is $K - S(t)$, where K is the option strike and $S(t)$ is the underlying price at time t.

Before expiry the price of an American option is never less than the price of the corresponding European option, and as the expiry time approaches the two prices converge. The option to exercise early suggests that these options may command a higher price than their European counterpart. But, using the put–call parity relationship for standard European calls and puts, we can show that this is not always the case.

Consider an American call option with strike K and maturity T and denote its price by $C^A(S, t | K, T)$. Using the put–call parity relationship (III.3.27) and the fact that $C^A(S, t | K, T)$ can never be less than the European price, we have

$$C^A(S, t | K, T) \geq \exp(-y(T - t))\, S(t) - \exp(-r(T - t))\, K. \qquad \text{(III.3.32)}$$

But $\exp(-r(T - t)) \leq 1$, hence

$$C^A(S, t | K, T) \geq \exp(-y(T - t))\, S(t) - K. \qquad \text{(III.3.33)}$$

If there are no dividends then the right-hand side is the intrinsic value of the option, so it never pays to exercise a non-dividend paying American call early.

It also never pays to exercise an American call, or a put, on a forward contract *provided* that we do not have to pay the premium. This is the case when the options are *margined*, like futures contracts, and the settlement value for the option is determined by the difference between the initial and final option prices. When the option is on the forward price $F(t, T)$ and the option is margined the put–call parity relationship (III.3.26) for European options becomes

$$C^E(F, t | K, T) - P^E(F, t | K, T) = F(t, T) - K \qquad \text{(III.3.34)}$$

using the superscript E to denote the European option price. Hence

$$C^A(F, t | K, T) \geq C^E(F, t | K, T) \geq F(t, T) - K$$

and

$$P^A(F, t | K, T) \geq P^E(F, t | K, T) \geq K - F(t, T),$$

so in both cases we never gain by early exercise.

III.3.3.5   Early Exercise Boundary

For a given underlying the price of an American option is determined by the size of the dividend yield, as well as the risk free rate. For instance, if the dividends earned are greater than the interest accruing on the exercise price, an American call option will not be exercised early. Consider an American call option on S. We shall show that we can find some value of S such that it is optimal to exercise the option early whenever S is greater than this value. Similarly, for an American put option on S we can find some value of S such that is optimal to exercise early whenever S is less than this value. Such values, which are different for a call and a put, are called the *early exercise boundaries* for the American options.

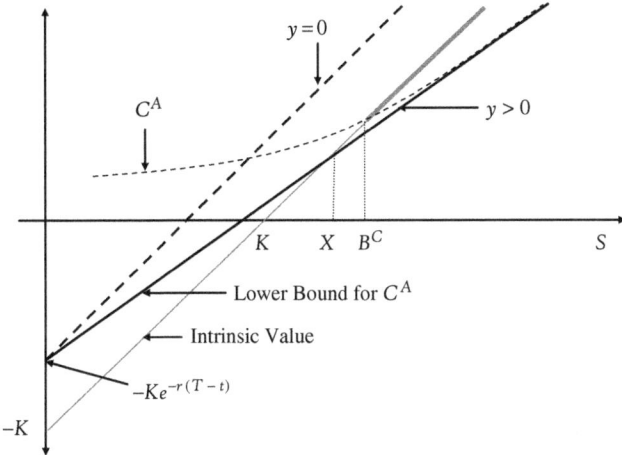

Figure III.3.3 Early exercise boundary for an American call

Figure III.3.3 illustrates the early exercise boundary for an American call. The right-hand side of (III.3.32) is the minimum value or lower bound for the American call price. This is depicted by the solid black line, as a function of $S(t)$. The line has intercept $-\exp(-r(T-t))K$ and slope $\exp(-y(T-t))$ so the slope is positive but less than 1 if $y > 0$. The grey line depicts the intrinsic value of the option. This is the line $S(t) - K$, so it passes through the point $(0, -K)$ and has a slope of 1. Consider the point marked X where the intrinsic value equals the minimum value of the call. When $S \geq X$ it could be optimal to exercise early. It is never optimal to exercise early when $S < X$. But the point X is *not* the early exercise boundary of the call, it is only the lower bound for the early exercise boundary. The early exercise boundary is a point $B^C \geq X$ such that it is optimal to exercise early if *and only if* $S \geq B^C$. This is the value of S at which the call price, shown by the dotted curve marked C^A, intersects the intrinsic value line.

As we increase the value of the dividend y the slope of the lower bound line decreases, so the point X and also the early exercise boundary move to the left. This shows that we are more likely to exercise an American call early when dividends are large. A third, dotted line is drawn in Figure III.3.3, corresponding to the lower bound line when $y = 0$. This line *never* intersects the line representing the intrinsic value, i.e. the minimum call value is always above the intrinsic value. Hence we never exercise a non-dividend paying American call early.

Figure III.3.4 illustrates the early exercise boundary for an American put. Using the put call parity relationship (III.3.27) and the fact that the American put price is never less than the European price, we have

$$P^A(S, t\,|K, T) \geq \exp(-r(T-t))K - \exp(-y(T-t))S(t).\qquad\text{(III.3.35)}$$

The solid black line in the figure represents the lower bound for the American put price, i.e. the right-hand side of (III.3.35). This line has intercept $\exp(-r(T-t))K$ and slope $-\exp(-y(T-t))$. The slope is between -1 and 0 if $y > 0$. The grey line depicts the intrinsic value of the option. This is the line $K - S(t)$, so it passes through the point $(0, K)$ and has a slope of -1. The point X marks the intersection of these two lines. When $S \leq X$, it could be optimal to exercise early. It is never optimal to exercise early when $S > X$.

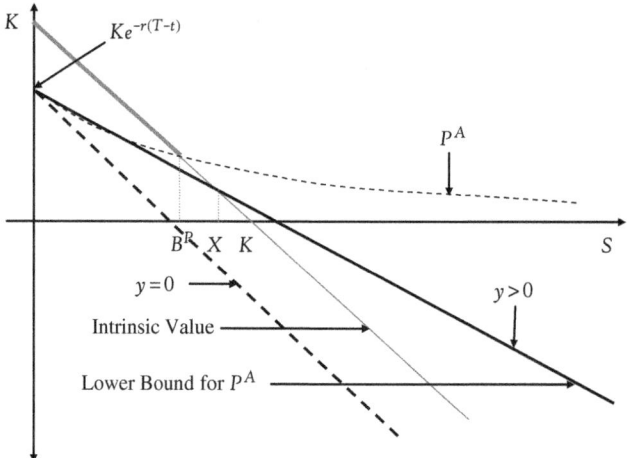

Figure III.3.4   Early exercise boundary for an American put

Again, the point X is *not* the early exercise boundary of the put, it is only its upper bound. The early exercise boundary is a point $B^P \leq X$ such that it is optimal to exercise early if *and only if* $S \leq B^P$. This is the value of S at which the put price, shown by the dotted curve marked P^A, intersects the intrinsic value line. Early exercise is possible, i.e. the solid grey line is there, whenever $r > 0$. And the line becomes longer as y decreases. Hence, we are more likely to exercise an American put early when dividends are low.

III.3.3.6   Pricing American Options

We can write the price of an American option as:

$$f^A(S, \sigma, r, y, t \,|\, K, T) = f^E(S, \sigma, r, y, t \,|\, K, T) + \pi(S, \sigma, r, y, t \,|\, K, T), \qquad \text{(III.3.36)}$$

where the first term on the right-hand side is the European option price and the second term is the non-negative *early exercise premium*. We know how to calculate the European price, using the BSM model, so one method of pricing American options is to calculate π. Barone-Adesi and Whaley (1987) suggested a useful approximation to this premium using the fact that, when it is small, it will satisfy the BSM PDE.

To price a standard American option with pay-off $\max\,(w(S(t) - K), 0)$, with $\omega = 1$ for a call and $\omega = -1$ for a put, Kim (1990) and Jacka (1991) apply *free boundary* pricing methods to drive an explicit expression for the early exercise premium:

$$\pi = \omega y S(t) \int_t^T \exp(-y(s-t))\,\Phi(\omega d_1)\,ds - \omega r K \int_t^T \exp(-r(s-t))\,\Phi(\omega d_2)\,ds, \qquad \text{(III.3.37)}$$

where

$$d_1 = \frac{\ln(S(t)/B(t))}{\sigma\sqrt{s-t}} + \tfrac{1}{2}\sigma\sqrt{s-t}, \quad d_2 = d_1 - \sigma\sqrt{s-t}$$

and $B(t)$ is the early exercise boundary. This boundary is allowed to vary with time, as the underlying price changes, hence the name 'free boundary'. This approach allows an

American option to be priced using numerical integration techniques. It may also be extended to other types of American options. For instance, Alexander and Venkatramanan (2007) derive the extension to American spread option pricing.

Two other numerical techniques for pricing American options are commonly used. The first is to price the option using a lattice or tree. The use of a binomial lattice to price a simple American option has already been described in Section I.5.6.5, and a simple Excel spreadsheet to implement the tree was provided there. The other common approach to pricing American options is Monte Carlo simulation. See Rogers (2002) for further details.

III.3.4   HEDGING OPTIONS

A *risk factor* for an asset is a random variable that influences the asset's price. Thus the underlying price and its volatility are two of the major risk factors of an option. In this section we introduce the option's sensitivities to its risk factors, also called the 'Greeks', and explain how they are used in strategies for dynamically hedging a single option against changes in the underlying price and its volatility.[34]

In the following we denote the price of an option on a single underlying with price S and volatility σ by g. To be more precise, we should write $g(S, \sigma, r, t, \ldots \,|K, T, \ldots)$ for the option price, where S and σ denote the price and the volatility of the underlying, r denotes the continuously compounded risk free interest rate, t is the time at which we price the option and the price is conditional on the strike K, maturity T and any other characteristics that enter the option pay-off. The underlying of the option can be a financial asset, a futures contract, an interest rate or an exchange rate. The option can be European or American and path-dependent or non-path-dependent. Hence, the following analysis is very general. The dots '$\ldots$' in the notation indicate that the option price can depend on other factors or parameters (e.g. a correlation) and the option's pay-off can have characteristics other than strike and maturity (e.g. a barrier, or several barriers). The first and second order sensitivities with respect to the underlying price are denoted by the Greek letters *delta* (δ) and *gamma* (γ). Sensitivities with respect to volatility are not denoted by Greek letters: *vega* and *volga* are the first two partial derivatives with respect to volatility and the cross price–volatility derivative is called *vanna*. Nevertheless it is still common to term option price sensitivities *the Greeks*.[35]

III.3.4.1   Delta

The first partial derivative of the option price respect to the underlying price is called the option 'delta'. That is,

$$\delta = \frac{\partial g}{\partial S} = g_S(S, \sigma, r, t, \ldots \,|K, T, \ldots).\qquad\text{(III.3.38)}$$

We use subscripts to denote the partial derivatives of the model's option price with respect to the risk factors. The delta is the *first order price sensitivity* of the model's option price,

---

[34] In a *static hedge* a single hedged position is taken at the time of issuing or purchasing the option and this position is held without rebalancing until the option expires or is sold. On the other hand, if the hedged position is rebalanced on a regular basis we have a *dynamic hedge*.

[35] There are also a number of different definitions of *position delta, value delta, dollar equivalent, value gamma* and so forth. We have therefore taken care to define precisely what we mean in this text by these different types of Greeks in Sections III.3.4.4–III.3.4.6.

i.e. its sensitivity to small changes in the price of the underlying contract. It is the partial derivative of an option price with respect to the underlying, so it gives the change in option price for a *one-unit* increase in the underlying price.

The model's option price at some time t is a function of the underlying price at that time, amongst other things. It may be represented as a curve, such as that depicted in the top graph in Figure III.3.5 , where the underlying price S is drawn along the horizontal axis. The value of the option delta is the slope of this curve at the point given by the underlying price. Delta differs according to the level of S. The more concave or convex the model's pricing function with respect to S, the more the delta will change when S changes, as shown in the lower graph in the figure.

A long position on a vanilla call or a short position on a vanilla put has a positive delta. A long position on a vanilla put or a short position on a vanilla call has a negative delta. Delta should be approximately 0 for a deep OTM option, because the model price should be near 0 and will not change much when the underlying price changes. For a deep ITM call option the delta should be near to 1 because the model price should be near $S - K$, and for a deep ITM put option the delta should be near to -1 because the model price should be near $K - S$. Hence, deep ITM options have price sensitivities that are similar to a long or short positions on the underlying, depending on whether the option is a call or a put.

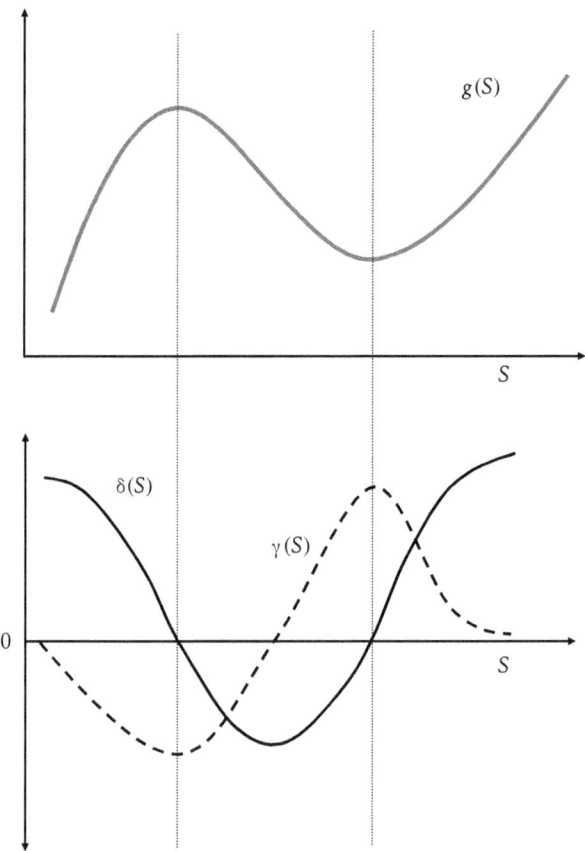

Figure III.3.5   Relationship between underlying price, delta and gamma

Complex calls and puts can have deltas that are positive or negative: for instance, a long position on an up-and-out barrier call option has a positive delta when S is just above the strike but negative delta when S is just below the barrier. The delta is a measure without units. For instance, a delta of 0.5, or 50%, implies that the model option price increases by 0.5 when the underlying increases by 1. Various modifications of delta and other Greeks will be used later on, and to be clear exactly which definition we mean we sometimes refer to the partial derivative g_S as the *percentage delta*.

III.3.4.2   Delta Hedging

A simple dynamic delta hedging strategy is to match each unit of the underlying that the option contracts to buy or sell with δ units of the underlying. Suppose a trader is short an option to buy N units of the underlying and the option price is g. Then the delta hedge is to buy δN units of the underlying. The quantity δN is the *position delta* of a single option, and the hedged portfolio has value

$$P = N(\delta S - g).\qquad\text{(III.3.39)}$$

The hedged portfolio is called *delta neutral* because its value will remain unchanged for small changes in the underlying. This is easy to see on differentiating (III.3.39) with respect to S and noting that $\delta = g_S$.

EXAMPLE III.3.1: A SIMPLE DELTA HEDGE

Suppose I write an equity call option with $\delta = 0.6$ to buy 1000 shares. If the share price is €100 and the option price per share €10, how many shares should I buy to make the position delta neutral?

SOLUTION   With $\delta = 0.6$ and $N = 1000$ the position delta is -600. Hence, I would delta hedge this position by buying 600 shares, and the value of this is $600 \times €100 = €60,000$. The total value of the underlying that the option contracts to buy is €10,000. So the total position has value €60,000 − €10,000 = €50,000. To see that the position is delta hedged, suppose the share price moves by a small amount, say it rises to €101. Then the option price moves up by approximately €0.6 because it has a delta of 0.6. Thus the value of my position is approximately unchanged, because $€(600 \times 101 - 1000 \times 10.6) = €50,000$.

III.3.4.3   Other Greeks

The Greeks are the risk factor sensitivities of the option price. They are partial derivatives of the model price of an option with respect to one or more of its risk factors. The popular names and definitions of the most common option price sensitivities are:

$$\text{Delta}\qquad g_S = \frac{\partial g}{\partial S} = \delta$$

$$\text{Gamma}\qquad g_{SS} = \frac{\partial^2 g}{\partial S^2} = \gamma$$

$$\text{Vega}\qquad g_\sigma = \frac{\partial g}{\partial \sigma} = \nu$$

$$\text{Volga}\qquad g_{\sigma\sigma} = \frac{\partial^2 g}{\partial \sigma^2} = \nu_0 \qquad\text{(III.3.40)}$$

$$\text{Vanna} \qquad g_{S\sigma} = \frac{\partial^2 g}{\partial S \partial \sigma} = \nu_a$$

$$\text{Theta} \qquad g_t = \frac{\partial g}{\partial t} = \theta$$

$$\text{Rho} \qquad g_r = \frac{\partial g}{\partial r} = \varrho.$$

In this section we discuss the general characteristics of each of these Greeks. Plenty of numerical examples of the Greeks based on the Black–Scholes–Merton pricing model will be given in Section III.3.7.

Gamma

The sensitivity of delta to changes in the underlying price is called the gamma of the pricing model. It is the first partial derivative of delta and the second partial derivative of the option price with respect to S. We refer to gamma as the model's *second order price sensitivity*. It is positive if and only if the pricing function is convex. This is the case in the Black–Scholes–Merton model. For deep ITM and deep OTM options delta will not change much for small changes in the underlying, hence gamma tends to be largest for near to ATM options. More generally, the gamma of an arbitrary option can be positive or negative, as shown for instance in the lower graph in Figure III.3.5.

Vega

The vega of an option is the partial derivative of the model price of the option with respect to the underlying volatility. It represents the absolute change in the model's option price for a *one-unit* change in volatility. A one-unit change in this case is 1%. For instance, if volatility is currently 20% a one-unit increase implies an increase to 21%.[36] The underlying volatility represents the uncertainty about future prices for the underlying contract, and an option's value stems entirely from this uncertainty. If there were no uncertainty we would trade the futures contract because it is much cheaper than an option (i.e. the bid–ask spread is lower). Hence, as the price uncertainty increases, so should the value of a vanilla option. For this reason many options have positive vega, and vega tends to increase with the option's maturity. For instance, the Black–Scholes–Merton vega for two options of different maturities is shown, as a function of the option's strike, in Figure III.3.22. However, barrier options, for example, can have a negative vega because an increase in volatility makes it more likely that the barrier will be breeched. And options on multiple underlyings can also have negative vegas because the model price will depend on the correlation between the underlyings as well as on their individual volatilities.

Volga

When the option price increases with the level of volatility the vega is positive and, if the option price is a convex increasing function, its second partial derivative with respect to

---

[36] Note that if volatility is represented as a decimal, i.e. 20% = 0.2, as is normally the case then the unit is 1, so vega would be a sensitivity to a 100% change in volatility. Hence it must be divided by 100 to obtain the sensitivity to a 1% change in volatility.

volatility will also be positive. We call this second order volatility sensitivity the option 'volga'. Volga tends to be highest for deep OTM and deep ITM vanilla options, and very near zero for ATM vanilla options. Volga is also higher for long-dated options than short-dated options, just like vega. The volga of the Black–Scholes–Merton model for a standard European option is illustrated in Figure III.3.23. It can be very small and negative for standard long term ATM options. For more complex options and different pricing models its value could also be negative.

Vanna

Vanna is the derivative of delta with respect to volatility, i.e. the cross-derivative of the model's option price with respect to volatility and underlying price. Vanna is near zero for an ATM standard European option priced by the Black–Scholes–Merton model. Standard OTM puts and ITM calls have positive vanna and ITM calls or OTM puts have negative vanna. Figure III.3.24 depicts the vanna for the Black–Scholes–Merton prices of vanilla European options.

Theta, Rho and Other Greeks

Delta, gamma, vega, vanna and volga are the most important Greeks for vanilla options because they correspond to the major risk factors, i.e. S and σ. However, two other first order sensitivities with respect to minor risk factors are given standard names: *theta*, the time sensitivity, is the partial derivative of the option price with respect to time; and *rho*, the interest rate sensitivity is the partial derivative of the option price with respect to the interest rate. Theta represents the change in the model's option price when its maturity reduces by 1 *day*. So just as we divide the vega by 100 when volatility is expressed in the form 0.2 for a 20% volatility, when the maturity of the option is expressed in years we must divide the theta by 365. Rho represents the sensitivity to interest rates and if the interest rate is expressed in the form 0.05 for a 5% rate we must divide by 100 to obtain the sensitivity to a 1% change in interest rates, rather than to a 100% change in interest rates. The Black–Scholes–Merton theta and rho are shown in Figures III.3.18 and III.3.19.

Other sensitivities may be necessary to hedge the risk an option. Multi-asset options in particular have many risk factors that need to be hedged. For instance, even with a simple spread option on two assets one has to consider sensitivities with respect to variations in two prices, two volatilities and one correlation.

III.3.4.4 Position Greeks

To hedge an option on a single underlying it convenient to work with position Greeks. Given an option on S, we define the option's position Greek as

$$\text{Position Greek} = \text{Percentage Greek} \times N, \qquad \text{(III.3.41)}$$

where the percentage Greek is the partial derivative of the option price as defined in (III.3.40) and N is the *position*, i.e. number of units of the underlying that the option contracts to buy or sell. Note that N is negative if we are *short* the option. We use the notation δ^p for the *position delta*, so for a single option with percentage delta δ the position delta is

$$\delta^p = \delta \times N. \qquad \text{(III.3.42)}$$

Similar definitions apply to the option's *position gamma, position vega, position theta, position rho*, etc. That is, the position Greek is just the product of the partial derivative and the position on the underlying.

Now consider a portfolio of options on a single underlying S. The *net position delta, gamma* and *theta* are the sum of the individual position Greeks. If all the options have the same maturity then the *net position rho* may also be obtained by summing the position rho of each option. More generally, the position rho is a *vector* of sensitivities with respect to a term structure of interest rates with maturities equal to the maturities of the options. Net position vega, vanna and volga are difficult to define. See Section III.5.6 for further details. We often work with position Greeks because:

- they tell us how much to buy or sell of the underlying asset and/or of other options to construct a *hedged portfolio* (see below);
- position Greeks are *additive*, but only for a single underlying.

EXAMPLE III.3.2: NET POSITION DELTA

We have a long call on 500 shares with a delta of $+0.6$, and a short position on a put with a delta of -0.25 on 1000 of the same shares. How many shares must we buy or sell so that the portfolio is delta neutral?

SOLUTION   The position delta of the long call is

$$+0.6 \times 500 = +300,$$

and the position delta of the short put is

$$-(-0.25) \times 1000 = +250.$$

Hence, the net position delta is $+550$ and we must short 550 shares for the book to be delta neutral.

Sometimes a net position Greek is expressed in percentage terms by dividing by the total number of shares, in this case 1500. So in this example the net position delta is $850/1500 = 0.567$. Notice that this is not equal to $0.6 - 0.25$. The percentage deltas do *not* add up but the position deltas *are* additive when all the options are on the same underlying.

III.3.4.5 Delta–Gamma Hedging

If the only source of risk is the uncertainty about variations in the underlying, it is theoretically possible to remove all uncertainty from options investments by delta hedging with the underlying. But since δ changes when either S or σ changes, the amount of the underlying required for delta neutrality changes over time. Hence, if delta hedging is to remove *all* uncertainty one has to assume *continuous rebalancing*, i.e. that one can rebalance the amount of the underlying held on a continuous basis. Another assumption is that there are *no transactions costs* when the hedge portfolio is rebalanced. Since neither assumption is realistic, delta hedging is not sufficient to remove all risk from option portfolios.

With discrete (e.g. daily) rebalancing of a dynamic delta hedge, a gamma hedge should be added to the portfolio if the option gamma is sufficiently large. A gamma hedge for a written option is implemented by buying another option on the same underlying, so that the gamma effects from the long and short options positions are offset. Then the net position delta from both options is calculated to hedge the net position with the underlying.

EXAMPLE III.3.3: A SIMPLE DELTA–GAMMA HEDGE

Suppose I have written 50 call options on a stock with $\delta = 0.6$ and $\gamma = 0.2$. There is another call option on the same stock that I can buy, currently with $\delta = 0.2$ and $\gamma = 0.1$. Both options are to buy 10 shares.

(a) How many options should I buy so that position is gamma neutral?
(b) How many shares should I buy or sell so that the total position is delta–gamma neutral?
(c) If the share price is €100, the written calls are priced at €10 and the other calls have price €2, what is the value of my hedged portfolio?
(d) If the share price changes to €95 and the delta and gamma of both calls are constant, show that the value of the hedged portfolio remains unchanged and decompose the change in value into delta and gamma components.

SOLUTION

(a) The written calls have position gamma $-50 \times 10 \times 0.2 = -100$. The other call has position gamma $10 \times 0.1 = 1$ per option. I must therefore buy 100 of these call options to make the portfolio gamma neutral.
(b) The written calls have position delta $-50 \times 10 \times 0.6 = -300$. The bought calls have position delta $100 \times 10 \times 0.2 = 200$. The net position delta is therefore $-300 + 200 = -100$. Hence, I must buy 100 shares to make the portfolio delta–gamma neutral.
(c) The value of the whole portfolio is $-50 \times €10 + 100 \times €2 + 100 \times €100 = €9700$.
(d) Suppose the stock price falls to €95, so we lose $100 \times €5 = €500$ on the share position. But we gain €250 on both the calls.

The changes in the value of each position are summarized in Table III.3.2.[37] Of course, these changes are only approximate if the delta and gamma are not constant. But when they are constant, as assumed, the change in the portfolio value will be 0, so the portfolio is delta–gamma hedged.

Table III.3.2   Example of delta–gamma hedged portfolio

Position	Delta price change	Gamma price change	Total price change
50 short calls	$-300 \times -€5 = €1500$	$\frac{1}{2} \times 5^2 \times -100 = -€1250$	€250
100 long calls	$200 \times -€5 = -€1000$	$\frac{1}{2} \times 5^2 \times 100 = €1250$	€250
100 long shares	$-€500$	N/A	$-€500$
Total portfolio	0	0	0

III.3.4.6   Delta–Gamma–Vega Hedging

Delta changes as the asset price and volatility change through time. If the portfolio cannot be rebalanced very frequently so that it is continually delta neutral, the gamma and vega

---

[37] Here we have multiplied the gamma price changes by ½ to be consistent with the delta–gamma approximation. The position deltas and gammas in the above example were additive, because the options have the same underlying stock. When the options are on different underlyings only the *value deltas and gammas* are additive: see Section III.5.5.2.

of the position become relevant. A delta–gamma–vega hedge is affected as follows. Before delta hedging with the underlying:

- Make the net gamma and net vega of the position zero by buying or selling two other call or put options on the same underlying.
- Then delta hedge the net position.

The gamma–vega neutral hedge requires the solution of two linear equations in two unknowns, as the following example demonstrates.

EXAMPLE III.3.4: A SIMPLE DELTA–GAMMA–VEGA HEDGE[38]

I have written 50 call options on a stock, with $\delta = 0.6$, $\gamma = 0.2$ and $v = 0.16$. There are two other options on the same stock that I can buy or sell: option 2 is a call option with $\delta = 0.2$, $\gamma = 0.1$ and $v = 0.1$; option 3 is a put option with $\delta = -0.8$, $\gamma = 0.3$ and $v = 0.2$. Each option is for 10 shares. How many of options 2 and 3 should I buy or sell to make the position gamma–vega neutral? How many shares should I buy or sell so that the total position is delta–gamma–vega neutral?

SOLUTION[39]   The Greeks for the 50 written calls and for a position of x option 2 and a position of y option 3 are summarized in Table III.3.3. As usual, each position Greek has been calculated by multiplying the number of shares the option contracts to buy or sell by the position in the option, and then also by the percentage option delta, gamma or vega.

Table III.3.3   Position Greeks

Option	No. Shares	Position	Position Delta	Position Gamma	Position Vega
Option 1	10	−50	−300	−100	−80
Option 2	10	x	$2x$	x	x
Option 3	10	y	$-8y$	$3y$	$2y$

We now find the positions x and y in options 2 and 3 that make the portfolio gamma and vega neutral. Gamma neutrality implies

$$-100 + x + 3y = 0,$$

while vega neutrality implies

$$-80 + x + 2y = 0.$$

Hence, we must solve the following linear equations for x and y:

$$x + 3y = 100$$
$$x + 2y = 80.$$

(III.3.43)

---

[38] We make no mention of the strike and maturities of the options used for gamma and vega hedging in this example. We start from knowledge of their Greeks alone. But note that it can be important to choose options for hedging that have a variety of different strikes and maturities. In the Black–Scholes–Merton model the Greeks are related, and unless we use options with different maturities as well as strikes the simultaneous linear equations have degenerate solutions!

[39] Changing the positions and the option's characteristics will alter the spreadsheet values for this example. The example above only explained how to implement a delta–gamma–vega hedge for a single option. To extend the method to portfolios of options on a single underlying, use the net position Greeks of the portfolio defined in Section III.3.4.4.

The solution is[40]

$$\begin{pmatrix} x \\ y \end{pmatrix} = \begin{pmatrix} 1 & 3 \\ 1 & 2 \end{pmatrix}^{-1} \begin{pmatrix} 100 \\ 80 \end{pmatrix} = \begin{pmatrix} 40 \\ 20 \end{pmatrix}.$$

Hence buy 40 of option 2 and 20 of option 3 to make the position gamma–vega neutral.

So far we have a portfolio with three options: short 50 of option 1, long 40 of option 2 and long 20 of option 3. Finally, we calculate the net delta for the portfolio of all three options to find the delta hedge. The net delta is

$$-300 + (40 \times 2) + (20 \times -8) = -300 + 80 - 160 = -380.$$

Hence, buying 380 shares and adding these to the portfolio makes it delta–gamma–vega neutral.

We end this section with an exercise for the reader. Extend the spreadsheet for Example III.3.4, using another option on the same underlying, to make a portfolio that is delta–gamma–vega–theta neutral. Or if you prefer, make the portfolio delta–gamma–vega–volga neutral. Either way this would involve the solution of three linear equations in three unknowns, which is easy to solve by inverting the matrix of coefficients as we did above. The spreadsheet for Example III.3.8 will help you find suitable values for the Greeks of each option, based on the Black–Scholes–Merton formula.

III.3.5   TRADING OPTIONS

Investors can use combinations of standard call and put options to speculate on the direction in which the underlying asset price moves, and/or to speculate on the volatility of the underlying asset. Portfolios of standard options of different strikes and maturities can replicate virtually any P&L profile. Hence, assuming traders are willing to write the options, investors can use option portfolios to bet on the underlying and/or its volatility.

III.3.5.1   Bull Strategies

Bull strategies are positions on options that will make a profit if the underlying price rises. The simplest bull strategy is to buy a call. This is a relatively expensive way to bet on direction because there is unlimited potential to profit from underlying price rises. If he is willing to forgo some of the upside potential the investor can sell the underlying, not to fully delta hedge the long call, but enough to cover the cost of the option premium. The combination of a long call and a short position on the underlying is a *covered call*.

Another bull strategy is to sell a put without hedging with the underlying – called a *naked put* – where profits will be made from the premium assuming the underlying price does not fall. But if the underlying price falls there is a huge potential for losses, limited only by the value of strike. Naked puts are very risky: if the underlying price jumps down the seller of the put has to buy the underlying at a price considerably higher than the market price, so losses from fulfilling the contract could be considerable.

---

[40] See Section I.2.2 for explanation, if needed.

Less expensive and less risky bull strategies can be designed according to P&L profiles that have limited profits and losses. An example of such a profile is shown in Figure III.3.6. This P&L could be replicated as follows:

- *Bull spread:* Buy a call at strike K_1 and sell a call of the same maturity at strike K_2.
- *Long collar:* Buy a put at strike K_1, sell a call of the same maturity at strike K_2 and cover the call with the underlying.

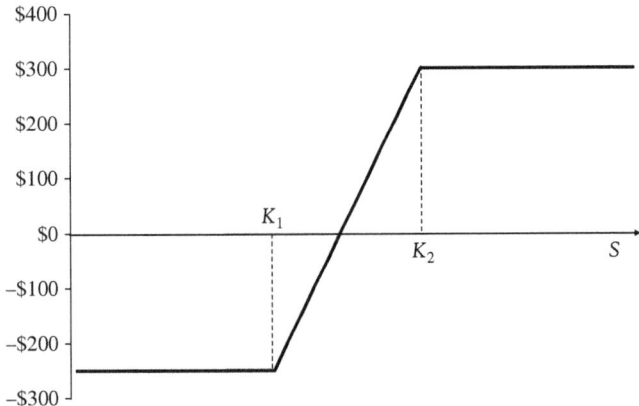

Figure III.3.6   Bull spread or long collar P&L

Collars are suitable for an investor who already holds the underlying but wants to place a bet that the price will move upward by selling a call and buying a put against his holding. Alternatively, an investor may simply wish to buy a low strike *protective put* against his underlying holding. The put provides insurance against substantial falls in the underlying price. But if this put is too expensive he can recover some of the cost by selling a call at a higher strike. However, this has the effect of limiting the upside potential if the underlying price rises.

III.3.5.2   Bear Strategies

Bear strategies are positions on options that will make a profit if the underlying price falls. The simplest bear strategy is to buy a put. This is a relatively expensive way to bet on direction because there is huge potential to profit from underlying price falls. If he is willing to forgo some of the upside potential the investor can sell the underlying, not to fully delta hedge the long put, but enough to cover the cost of the option premium. The combination of a long put and a short position on the underlying is a *covered put*.

Another bear strategy is to sell a call without hedging with the underlying – called a *naked call* – where profits will be made from the premium assuming the underlying price does not rise. But if the underlying price rises there is unlimited potential for losses. Naked calls are very risky: if the underlying price jumps up the seller of the call has to sell the underlying at a price considerably lower than the market price, so losses from fulfilling the contract could be considerable.

Less expensive and less risky bear strategies can be designed according to P&L profiles that have limited profits and losses. An example of such a profile is shown in Figure III.3.7. This P&L could be replicated as follows:

- *Bear spread:* Sell a put at strike K_1 and buy a put of the same maturity at strike K_2.
- *Short collar:* Sell a put at strike K_1, cover the put with the underlying and buy a call of the same maturity at strike K_2.

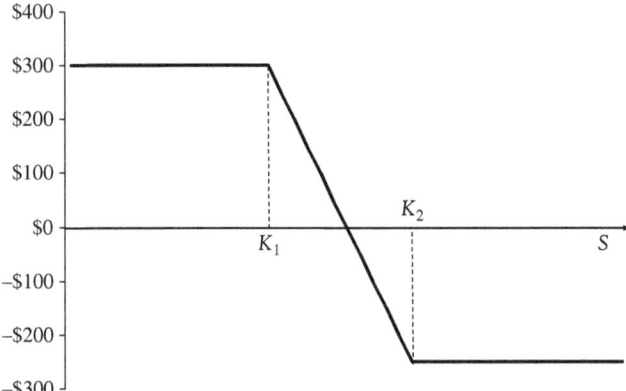

Figure III.3.7   Bear spread or short collar P&L

III.3.5.3   Other Spread Strategies

More complex views on the underlying price can be traded using options of different maturities. A *calendar spread strategy* (also known as a *time spread* or a *horizontal spread*) is a long-short position in two call options (or two put options) on the same underlying with the same strike but with different maturities. The value of a calendar spread strategy is simply the sum of the values of the options traded and this should not be confused with a *calendar spread option* (described in Section III.3.9.2). Calendar spreads can be bullish in the long term but bearish (or neutral) in the short term, or vice versa. For instance, selling a call with maturity T_1 and buying a call of the same strike with maturity T_2 is a bet that the underlying price will fall until time T_1, remain static until time T_2 and rise thereafter. Since the options in a calendar spread have different maturities, we cannot easily draw the P&L diagram.

An $X{:}1$ call *ratio spread* is to buy one call at a lower strike and sell X calls of the same maturity but at a higher strike. An $X{:}1$ put ratio spread is defined similarly, but using puts. The pay-off profiles of call and put ratio spreads are shown in Figures III.3.8 and III.3.9. The call ratio spread has limited potential for gains (a small profit is made if the underlying price changes little before expiry) but unlimited potential for losses if the underlying price rises too high. The put ratio spread also has limited potential for gains (a small profit is made if the underlying price changes little before expiry) but unlimited potential for losses if the underlying price falls too much. Finally, an $X{:}1$ *backspread* is a short position on a ratio spread. Hence, a call backspread is a bullish strategy and a put backspread is a bearish strategy.

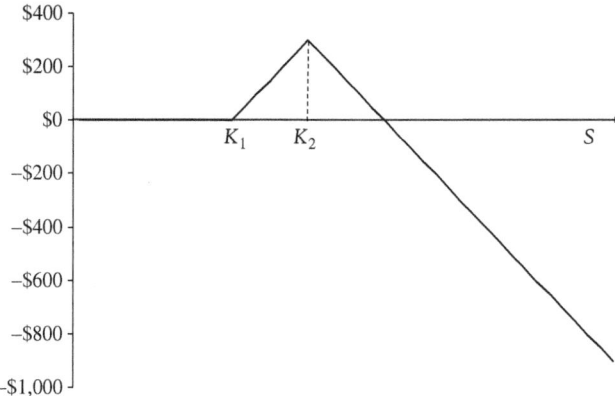

Figure III.3.8   P&L to 2:1 call ratio spread

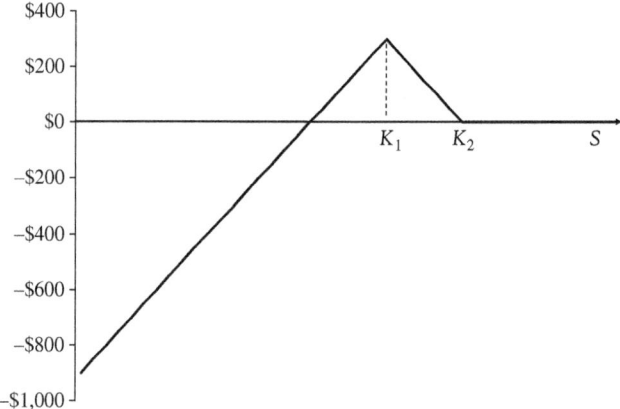

Figure III.3.9   P&L to 2:1 put ratio spread

III.3.5.4   Volatility Strategies

A standard trade on volatility is to buy a call and a put of the same strike K and the same maturity, a strategy known as the *straddle*. The P&L profile for a straddle is shown in Figure III.3.10. An ATM straddle is a volatility trade because it will make a small loss if the underlying price does not move much before the options expire, but it can make substantial gains if the price moves either up or down. A less expensive volatility trade is to buy a put with a lower strike and buy a call with a higher strike relative to the ATM strike, where again the two options have the same maturity. This is known as a *strangle* and its P&L profile is shown in Figure III.3.11.

Even less expensive volatility trades have limited potential for gain. A *butterfly* spread is a straddle with limited upside potential. Its P&L is shown in Figure III.3.12. This can be achieved by buying a straddle at strike K_2, selling a put at strike K_1 and selling a call at strike K_3. This is equivalent to a bull spread (buying a call at K_2, selling a call at K_3) plus a bear spread (selling a put at K_1, buying a put at K_2).

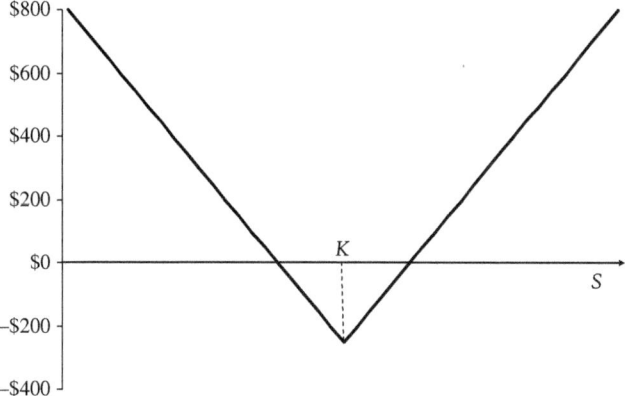

Figure III.3.10   Straddle P&L

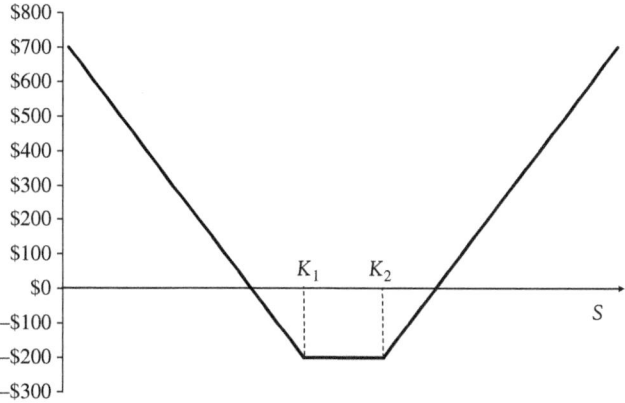

Figure III.3.11   Strangle P&L

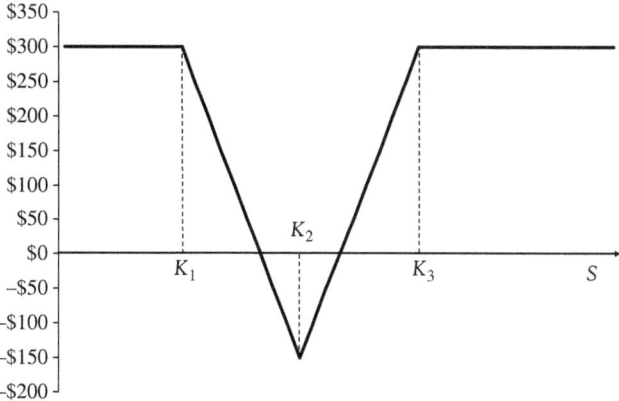

Figure III.3.12   P&L profile of butterfly spread

A *condor* is a strangle with limited upside potential. Its P&L is shown in Figure III.3.13. This can be achieved by buying a strangle at strikes K_2 and K_3 selling a put at strike K_1 and selling a call at strike K_4. This is equivalent to a bull spread (buying a call at K_3, selling a call at K_4) plus a bear spread (selling a put at K_1, buying a put at K_2).

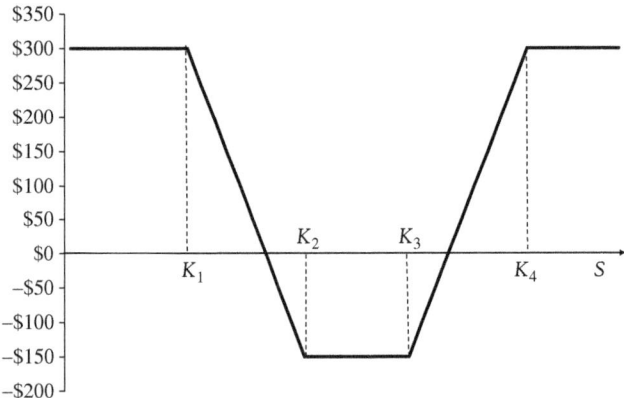

Figure III.3.13   P&L profile of condor

III.3.5.5   Replication of P&L Profiles

Any continuous P&L profile can be replicated using a series of vanilla call or put options. By forming a portfolio of vanilla options with weights that are proportional to the gamma of the options, the price of this *replicating portfolio* will approximate the price of the profile. To see this, first consider a simple case where we want to replicate the profile illustrated in Figure III.3.14. Here we shall build up the P&L profile from left to right, but one could also build from right to left, or indeed from centre out.

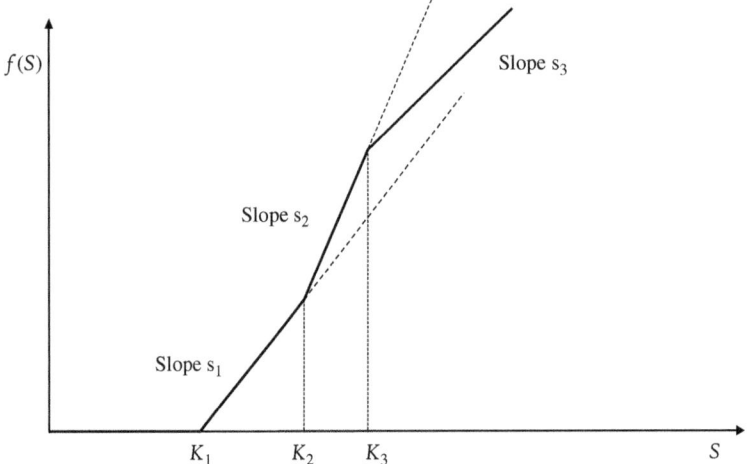

Figure III.3.14   Replicating a simple P&L profile

In Figure III.3.14 first consider the portion of the P&L between $S = 0$ and $S = K_2$. This can be replicated by purchasing s_1 calls with strike K_1, where s_1 is the slope of the segment between K_1 and K_2. Next, the portion from $S = K_2$ to $S = K_3$ can be replicated by adding to the portfolio $s_2 - s_1$ calls with strike K_2. In the diagram $s_2 > s_1$ but if $s_2 < s_1$ we would go short on these calls. Similarly the portion above $S = K_3$ can be replicated by adding to the portfolio $s_3 - s_2$ calls with strike K_3. And more generally, when there are n call options in the replication strategy, with prices $f(S, K_i)$, the replicating portfolio price is given by

$$P(S; K_1, \ldots, K_n) = \sum_{i=1}^{n} (s_i - s_{i-1}) f(S, K_i). \tag{III.3.44}$$

Although the profile depicted in Figure III.3.14 is not smooth the same principle applies to any continuous P&L profile: building from left the right, the number of calls purchased at strike K_i equals the *change in slope* of the profile between K_i and the previous strike K_{i-1}. But note that the change in slope is equal to the gamma $f_{SS}(S, K)$ of the option of strike K_i. So, if we could purchase options at a continuum of strikes, the price of the replicating portfolio would be

$$P(S) = \int_K f_{SS}(S, K) f(S, K) \, dK. \tag{III.3.45}$$

This is the continuous analogue of (III.3.44).

However, we can only purchase options at a discrete set of strikes $K_1, \ldots, K_n$ and the discrete approximation to (III.3.45) is

$$P(S; K_1, \ldots, K_n) = \sum_{i=1}^{n} \Delta K_i \times f_{SS}(S, K_i) \times f(S, K_i), \tag{III.3.46}$$

where ΔK_i is the interval between strikes, or alternatively $\Delta K_i = \frac{1}{2}(K_{i+1} - K_{i-1})$.[41]

The general principle to apply when replicating a profile, whether building from left to right, right to left, or from centre out, is that we weight each option by the product of its gamma and the increment in strike. Also, we do not have to use calls: short puts would work as well as long calls, and long puts could be used instead of short calls. Often we work from centre out and use the more liquid (i.e. OTM) options in the replicating portfolio. So we use calls for strikes below ATM and puts for strikes above ATM. This type of replicating strategy is used, for instance, in the construction of volatility indices – see Section III.4.7 for further details.

III.3.6   THE BLACK–SCHOLES–MERTON MODEL

This section explains the model for pricing standard European calls and puts that was developed by Black and Scholes (1973) and by Merton (1973). The assumptions of the model are stated and some intuition on the celebrated option pricing formula is provided. We go through the standard delta hedging argument to derive the Black–Scholes–Merton partial differential equation that is satisfied by an option price when the underlying follows a geometric Brownian motion. In the case of a standard European option this partial differential equation has an analytic solution, i.e. the *Black–Scholes–Merton formula*.

---

[41] The discrete approximation follows on noting that $\int_a^b g(x) \, dx \approx (b - a) \times g(a)$ for any integrable function g over a small interval $[a, b]$

III.3.6.1   Assumptions

The first assumption of the Black–Scholes–Merton model is about the stochastic process
for the price of the underlying contract. The original paper by Black and Scholes (1973)
assumes that the asset pays no dividends, that the risk free interest rate is a known constant
and that the price dynamics are governed by a *geometric Brownian motion*. In other words,
the underlying price S follows the stochastic differential equation of the form

$$\frac{dS(t)}{S(t)} = r\,dt + \sigma\,dW(t), \tag{III.3.47}$$

where $W(t)$ is a Wiener process.[42]

Using Itô's lemma we may write (III.3.47) in the equivalent form

$$d\ln S(t) = \left(r - \tfrac{1}{2}\sigma^2\right)dt + \sigma\,dW(t). \tag{III.3.48}$$

Since the increments $dW(t)$ are independent and normally distributed with zero mean and
variance dt, (III.3.48) implies that t-period log returns are independent and identically
normally distributed with mean $\left(r - \tfrac{1}{2}\sigma^2\right)t$ and standard deviation $\sigma\sqrt{t}$. We have shown in
Section I.3.3.5 that if the log return over a time interval of length t is normally distributed
then the future price at time t will have a lognormal distribution. Hence, the first assumption
of the BSM model, that the underlying asset price is generated by a geometric Brownian
motion with constant volatility, implies that the prices have a *lognormal distribution*.

The second assumption made by Black and Scholes was that the markets in which
the underlying and the option contracts are traded are *frictionless*: that is, it is possible
to buy and sell any amount at any time and without incurring transactions costs. This
assumption, combined with the assumption that the price follows the geometric Brownian
motion (III.3.47), was sufficient for Black and Scholes to apply the principle of no arbitrage
to derive a *partial differential equation* for the price of an option on S, which they showed
has an analytic solution when the option is a standard European call or put option.

In the same year Merton (1973) provided an alternative derivation of this partial differential
equation and extended it in several ways: to apply to assets that pay dividends; to include
the possibility of stochastic interest rates; and to value American options and barrier options.
However, in these cases it is not possible to derive an analytic solution to this partial
differential equation, except for a European option, and when both interest rates and dividend
yields are constant.

Black, Scholes and Merton used a no arbitrage argument to specific types of options in
a very restricted economy, where there is only an underlying asset and the option. It was
not until the path-breaking paper of Harrison and Kreps (1979) that the theory of option
pricing was placed on firm theoretical foundations. Harrison and Kreps asked: in what type
of market can we find a *unique* no arbitrage price of a general contingent claim? They
introduced the concept of a *complete market* as a market in which one can replicate the value
of any claim by trading the underlying and a risk free asset. Then they showed that the
market is complete and every contingent claim has a unique no arbitrage price if and only if
there is a unique *equivalent martingale measure*.[43] Moreover, there is a unique self-financing
portfolio that replicates the value of the claim.

---

[42] See Section III.3.2.1 for an introduction to geometric Brownian motion and Itô's lemma.
[43] That is, there is a unique measure, which is equivalent to the risk neutral measure, under which the asset price is a martingale.
See Section III.3.2.2 for further details.

III.3.6.2   Black–Scholes–Merton PDE

In this section we use the *risk neutral valuation principle* that was explained in Section III.3.2.2 to derive a partial differential equation (PDE) that must be satisfied by any claim on S when S follows a geometric Brownian motion

$$\frac{dS(t)}{S(t)} = \mu\,dt + \sigma\,dW(t) \tag{III.3.49}$$

with non-stochastic parameters μ and σ. Recall that, unlike the capital asset pricing model, investors do not have to share the same views about the expected return μ on the underlying. The BSM price is independent of these views. However, they all have to share the same view on the volatility σ of the underlying, i.e. that it is constant and that the underlying asset price is generated by a geometric Brownian motion process with this volatility.

Denote by $g(S, t)$ the price of an option on S at time t. We suppress the dependence of the option price on other variables (such as the option's strike and interest rates) since this is redundant in the following analysis. In other words, g is the price of any *contingent claim* on S – it may be European, American, exotic, or path-dependent. As usual, we denote the first partial derivative of this function with respect to S by delta, i.e.

$$\delta(S, t) = g_S(S, t). \tag{III.3.50}$$

We know from Section III.3.4.2 that a *delta hedged portfolio* is one with two assets, a short (or long) position of one unit of the option and a long (or short) position of delta units of the underlying asset. If we sell the option and buy delta units of the underlying, the value of the delta hedged portfolio is

$$\Pi(t) = g_S(S, t)S(t) - g(S, t). \tag{III.3.51}$$

So by (III.3.4) with $f \equiv g$, and assuming g_S is constant over the interval dt:[44]

$$d\Pi(t) = g_S(S, t)\{\mu S(t)dt + \sigma S(t)dW(t)\} - dg(S, t)$$
$$= \left\{-g_t(S, t) - \tfrac{1}{2}\sigma^2 S(t)^2 g_{SS}(S, t)\right\} dt. \tag{III.3.52}$$

Since there is no dW term in the portfolio price dynamics, the delta hedged portfolio is *risk free*. There is no stochastic term in the dynamics for the portfolio's price so the price is *known* at any time, now and in the future.

Risk neutral valuation implies that a risk free portfolio has a *net* return equal to the risk free rate, r. But holding the portfolio may earn income such as dividends at the rate y,[45] so if the net return is to be r the portfolio's price must grow at the rate $r - y$.[46] That is,

$$\frac{d\Pi(t)}{\Pi(t)} = (r - y)dt. \tag{III.3.53}$$

Combining the three equations (III.3.51) to (III.3.53) gives

$$\frac{-g_t(S, t) - \tfrac{1}{2}\sigma^2 S^2(t)g_{SS}(S, t)}{g_S(S, t)S(t) - g(S, t)}dt = (r - y)\,dt.$$

The above rearranges to give the *Black–Scholes–Merton* partial differential equation (PDE):

$$g_t(S, t) + (r - y) S(t)g_S (S, t) + \tfrac{1}{2}\sigma^2 S^2(t)g_{SS}(S, t) = (r - y)g(S, t). \tag{III.3.54}$$

This PDE may be more concisely expressed in terms of the option's Greeks and by dropping the dependence on S and t for brevity. This way the BSM PDE may be written in the equivalent form

$$\theta + \delta S(r - y) + \tfrac{1}{2}\gamma \sigma^2 S^2 = (r - y)g. \tag{III.3.55}$$

The solution to the BSM PDE gives the price of the claim.

The BSM PDE is one of the fundamental pillars of option pricing. It is satisfied by *every* European claim on a geometric Brownian motion when σ, r and y are non-stochastic.[47] The BSM PDE still holds if volatility is time-varying but has *deterministic* movements, as it is in the local volatility framework.[48] It also holds for an American claim, unless the price is in the early exercise region.

In the special case that volatility is constant and the claim is a European call or put the BSM PDE has an analytical solution which is called the Black–Scholes–Merton formula. We shall introduce and interpret this below. Otherwise, when volatility is not constant and/or we are pricing a different type of claim we usually need to use numerical methods to solve the PDE. A common approach to solving a PDE such as the BSM PDE is to use *finite differences*. These were introduced in Section I.5.5.

III.3.6.3   Is the Underlying the Spot or the Futures Contract?

Before we state the Black–Scholes–Merton formula for the price of a standard European option it is important to clarify the nature of the underlying contract for the option. In particular, if there is an exchange traded option on the spot price S with maturity T then there will also be an exchange traded futures contract on S with maturity T.[49] In this section we answer the following questions:

1. Is the option on S or is it on F, the price of the futures contract?
2. Does it matter whether the option is on S or on F? That is, is the price of the option the same whether it is on F or on S?

Regarding the first question, note that in the derivation of the BSM PDE we assumed that *the instrument used for hedging the option is also the underlying of the option*. So if the underlying of the option is *not* the hedging instrument then the option price will not be consistent with the BSM PDE. Futures contracts are almost costless to trade and are usually far more liquid than the spot asset. Futures can be sold short, traded on margin and are necessary to avoid squeezing the spot market. Hence futures, if they exist, are the preferred hedging instrument. This means that the option should be priced using the market price of the futures as the underlying.

The answer to the second question is a little more complex. The short answer is that it *will* matter which underlying is used to price the option, but only when the market price of the futures deviates from its fair value. To understand why this is the case we consider two

---

[47] See Section III.4.5.1 for the extension of this PDE to the case of stochastic volatility.
[48] See Section III.4.3 for further details.
[49] In OTC markets standard European options may exist without futures contracts.

pairs of price process: (a) for the market price of spot asset S and for the fair value of the futures based on this price, F^*; and (b) for the market price of the futures F and for the fair value of the spot based on this price, S^* .

(a) In a risk neutral world all assets have a net expected return equal to the risk free rate. Hence, the risk neutral drift μ of the process (III.3.49) is $r - y$ where r is the continuously compounded spot interest rate and y is the continuously compounded dividend yield (or, in the case of a commodity, y is the convenience yield minus the carry cost). Thus the price process for the spot asset is

$$\frac{dS(t)}{S(t)} = (r - y)\, dt + \sigma \, dW(t).$$ (III.3.56)

The price process for the fair value of the futures, F^*, can be derived directly from (III.3.56). Recall from Section II.3.3.2 that

$$F^*(t, T) = S(t) \exp((r - y)\,(T - t)).$$ (III.3.57)

Applying Itô's lemma to (III.3.57) when S follows (III.3.56) gives

$$\frac{dF^*(t, T)}{F^*(t, T)} = \sigma \, dW(t).$$ (III.3.58)

Hence, the fair value of the futures price is a martingale with the same volatility as the market price of the spot.

(b) Assume the market price of the futures is a martingale, i.e.[50]

$$\frac{dF(t, T)}{F(t, T)} = \sigma \, dW(t).$$ (III.3.59)

The no arbitrage relationship between the market price of the futures and the theoretical or 'fair' value of the spot is

$$S^*(t) = F(t, T) \exp((y - r)\,(T - t)).$$ (III.3.60)

Hence, by Itô's lemma, the market price of the futures follows (III.3.59) if and only if the fair value of the spot follows the geometric Brownian motion process:

$$\frac{dS^*(t)}{S^*(t)} = (r - y)\, dt + \sigma \, dW(t).$$ (III.3.61)

The answer to question 2 should now be clear. It is only in the case where $F = F^*$ (and so also $S = S^*$) that all four processes are equivalent. The market price of the futures contract is always equal to its fair value only when the basis risk is always zero. Hence, when there is no basis risk it makes no difference whether we price the option using the spot (i.e. based on the process (III.3.56)) or using the futures (i.e. based on the process (III.3.59)).

However, there is *always* basis risk, however small, until the futures contract expires. So it *does* matter which process is used to price the option. The size of the error induced by

---

[50] There is no reason to assume that a futures contract will have a drift, for reasons explained in Section III.2.1.

using the wrong underlying to price the option depends on the basis risk in the market. In Section III.4.2.2 we give an example where an option on the spot is priced off the futures and we consider the effect this has on the option price.

Almost all exchange traded bond and commodity options are on futures. Most exchange traded currency options are also on futures. But some options are on the spot, including exchange traded stock options and a few currency, bond, index and commodity options. When an option is on the spot there is a problem when we are uncertain about the value of the dividend yield y. We illustrate this problem with two examples.

Options on a Spot Equity Index

An option on a spot equity index should be priced using (III.3.56) but we do not know the dividend yield on the index. However, the basis risk on equity indices is usually very small, so it is standard practice to infer the value of the dividend yield by observing the market prices of the spot and futures, assuming the latter is at its fair price, and using the no arbitrage relationship (III.3.57) with $F^* = F$. In this case we are assuming there is *no basis risk*, in other words we assume that (III.3.56) and (III.3.59) are equivalent. Thus the option price can be obtained using either process. When there is no basis risk using (III.3.56) with a dividend yield that is inferred from the market price of the futures will give the *same* option price as that based on the futures process (III.3.59). But there will be a small error in the option price because there *is* a basis risk, albeit a small one.

Options on a Spot Commodity

An option on a spot commodity should be priced using (III.3.56), but here the convenience yield y is very uncertain and difficult to measure. Since spot commodities cannot be sold short, the spot price can move very far above the futures price and inferring y from an assumption that the basis risk is zero, as in the case of equity index options, is not justified. The only alternative is to include the uncertainty about y in the model, so that in addition to the price process (III.3.56) we have another stochastic process governing the dynamics of the convenience yield. See Alexander and Venkatramanan (2008a) for further details.

III.3.6.4   Black–Scholes–Merton Pricing Formula

The Black–Scholes–Merton formula gives the price of a standard European option at any time before the expiry date of the option. But this does *not* mean that market prices are based on the BSM formula! Market prices of all *liquid* options – and standard European options are the most liquid options of all – are based on supply and demand. So why do we need the BSM formula? First, we need it to price standard European options for which no market prices are available. But most traders in this position do not use the exact BSM model price, instead they adjust the price for uncertainties in volatility, and perhaps also in interest rates, using an approximation that we describe in Section III.3.6.7 below. Secondly, we use the BSM formula to derive an *implied volatility surface* corresponding to market prices of standard European calls and puts, as explained in Section III.4.2.

In this section we state the BSM formula for pricing options on (a) the spot, and (b) the futures. First it helps to summarize our notation as follows:

$f(S, \sigma, r, t \,|\, K, T)$ is the BSM option price when the option is on the spot price, $S(t)$

$f(F, \sigma, r, t \,|\, K, T)$ is the BSM option price when the option is on the futures price $F(t, T)$

σ	Volatility of the underlying process[51]
K	Strike of option
T	Option expiry date (fixed)
t	Time at which the option is priced (running)
r	Risk free interest rate of maturity $T - t$ (continuously compounded)
y	Dividend yield of maturity $T - t$ (continuously compounded)
ω	$\omega = 1$ for a call and $\omega = -1$ for a put
$\Phi(\cdot)$	Standard normal distribution function.

We now introduce two quantities that are closely related to the moneyness of the option:[52]

$$d_1 = \frac{\ln(F/K)}{\sigma\sqrt{T-t}} + \tfrac{1}{2}\sigma\sqrt{T-t}, \quad d_2 = d_1 - \sigma\sqrt{T-t}. \qquad \text{(III.3.62)}$$

Although the underlying spot and futures prices are stochastic processes we sometimes drop the notation for the explicit time dependence in S and F. To be more precise, we should of course write $F = F(t, T)$ for the market price of the futures expiring on date T and $S = S(t)$ for the market price of the spot at time t. Similarly, the risk free rate r, dividend yield y, d_1 and d_2 are also each a function of t and T. But we often suppress this dependence in the following, to keep the notation simple.

Finally, we can state the *Black–Scholes–Merton formula* as follows: for an option on the futures contract,

$$f(F, \sigma, r, t \,|\, K, T) = \omega \exp(-r(T-t))\left[F\Phi(\omega d_1) - K\Phi(\omega d_2)\right]; \qquad \text{(III.3.63)}$$

for an option on the spot that pays dividends with yield y,[53]

$$f(S, \sigma, r, t \,|\, K, T) = \omega\left[S\exp(-y(T-t))\Phi(\omega d_1) - K\exp(-r(T-t))\Phi(\omega d_2)\right]. \text{(III.3.64)}$$

Some authors assume the option is always priced at time $t = 0$ for simplicity. In this case the residual time to expiry, $T - t$, is replaced by T in the formulae above. But we prefer to distinguish between the time that the option is first issued, which is at time 0, and the subsequent pricing of the option at any time t between issue and expiry.

Sometimes we want to make clear in our notation whether the option is a call or a put. For instance, in Section III.3.3.2 we used abbreviated notations $C(S, t \,|\, K, T)$ and $P(S, t \,|\, K, T)$ for the prices of a call and a put. When the option is priced on the futures the BSM formulae may be written in the form:

$$\begin{aligned} C(F, t \,|\, K, T) &= \exp(-r(T-t))\left[F\Phi(d_1) - K\Phi(d_2)\right], \\ P(F, t \,|\, K, T) &= -\exp(-r(T-t))\left[F\Phi(-d_1) - K\Phi(-d_2)\right]. \end{aligned} \qquad \text{(III.3.65)}$$

---

[51] Note that σ, r and y are always in annual terms, and T is in years.

[52] When the option is on S then replace F/K by $Se^{-y(T-t)}/Ke^{-r(T-t)}$.

[53] A formula similar to (III.3.64) applies to a standard European option on a spot foreign exchange rate S, where now y is replaced by the foreign risk free interest rate and r is the domestic risk free interest rate.

Alternatively, when the options are priced on the spot:

$$C(S, t \,|\, K, T) = \exp(-y(T - t))S\Phi(d_1) - \exp(-r(T - t))K\Phi(d_2),$$
$$P(S, t \,|\, K, T) = -\exp(-y(T - t))S\Phi(-d_1) + \exp(-r(T - t))K\Phi(-d_2).$$
(III.3.66)

EXAMPLE III.3.5: BLACK–SCHOLES–MERTON CALL AND PUT PRICES

An underlying asset has price 1000 and the volatility is constant at 13% per annum. The dividend yield is zero and the risk free rate is 5%.

(a) Find the BSM price of a European call option of strike 1025 with 60 days to expiry.
(b) Find the price of the corresponding put and verify the put–call parity relationship.
(c) What would the BSM price of the options be if the volatility and interest rate remained the same but the underlying price was 100 and the strike was 102.5?

SOLUTION

(a) The BSM price is calculated in the spreadsheet for this example. It is 13.92 for the OTM call and 30.93 for the ITM put of the same strike.
(b) The difference between the put and call prices is $30.93 - 13.92 = 16.61$. The difference between the underlying price and the discounted strike is

$$1000 - \exp(-0.05 \times 60/365) \times 1025 = -16.61.$$

Of course put–call parity holds because these are model prices not market prices.
(c) If the underlying price and the strike price were each divided by 10, the option prices would also be divided by 10: they would be 1.392 for the call and 3.093 for the put.

Part (c) of the above example illustrates what Merton (1973) refers to as *constant returns to scale* or lack of *level illusion*. An option priced using the BSM model has the same value whether the underlying is measured in cents or dollars. That is, the price scales with the unit of measurement. Put another way, the BSM option prices are *scale invariant*.

III.3.6.5 Interpretation of the Black–Scholes–Merton Formula

In this section we interpret the BSM price of an option from the perspective of both the investor who buys the option and the trader who writes it. From the risk neutral investor's perspective the option price is the discounted expected benefit from buying the option. From the trader's perspective the option price is the discounted expected cost of writing the option.

First consider the investor's perspective. The risk neutral valuation principle states that the discounted value of an option at any time in the future is its value today. In particular, we verify that the BSM option price is the discounted expectation of the expiry pay-off by applying (III.3.63) with $\omega = 1$, i.e. for a call option on the futures.[54] A European call option on the futures has BSM price

$$f(F, \sigma, r, t \,|\, K, T) = \exp(-r(T - t))\,[F\Phi(d_1) - K\Phi(d_2)].$$
(III.3.67)

---

[54] A similar argument applies to put options and to options on the spot.

The expression inside the square bracket may be rewritten as

$$\left[F\frac{\Phi(d_1)}{\Phi(d_2)} - K\right]\Phi(d_2).$$ (III.3.68)

It can be shown that $\Phi(d_2)$ is the risk neutral probability that the call is ITM at expiry,[55] and that

$$F\frac{\Phi(d_1)}{\Phi(d_2)} = \text{conditional expectation of } F(T,T) \text{ given that } F(T,T) > K.$$

Hence, (III.3.68) is the expected pay-off at expiry. In other words, the BSM price (III.3.67) is indeed the expected pay-off to holding the option, discounted to today.

Suppose the underlying has no volatility. When $\sigma = 0$, $\Phi(d_1) = \Phi(d_2) = 1$ and so the BSM price is equal to

$$f(F, 0, r, t \,|\, K, T) = \exp(-r(T - t))\,[F - K].$$ (III.3.69)

This is the value of a forward contract to buy the underlying at K at time t. Although we have assumed that transactions costs are zero, in practice it is cheaper to trade a forward contract than to trade an option. So investors would not buy an option if the volatility of the underlying is zero.

More generally, the BSM price of a standard European option increases with the volatility of the underlying and with the maturity of the option. The BSM price of a standard European call or put option with a fixed strike K, now denoted f_{BSM}, is shown as a function of the forward price F in Figure III.3.15. Of course the option price depends on many parameters and on the strike and maturity of the option but we have here illustrated the BSM price of a European call option as a function *only* of F. The diagram is drawn assuming the interest rate and dividend yield are zero.[56] The expiry pay-off of the option is indicated by the solid black

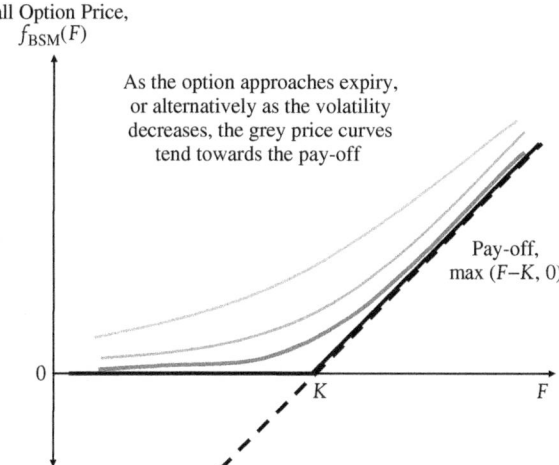

Figure III.3.15   Black–Scholes–Merton call option prices as a function of S

---

[55] See Cox and Ross (1976).
[56] If they were not both zero then the black line to which the grey curves converge needs to be drawn further to the left, so that it is parallel to the line shown here but crosses the horizontal axis at the point $\exp((r - y)(T - t))\,K$.

line and the value of a futures contract to buy the underlying at K is shown by the dotted black line. The price of the option is shown by a grey curve. Different curves are drawn to illustrate the BSM price as a function of F at different points in time and for different levels of the underlying volatility. As the time approaches the expiry time the curves tend to the option pay-off, and as the volatility decreases the curves again tend to the option pay-off. Hence, the BSM price of an option increases with both maturity and with volatility.

The BSM price of an option can also be thought of as the amount that an option trader requires as compensation for writing the option and buying a replicating portfolio. For a call option the *replicating portfolio* consists of buying δ units of the underlying asset. This quantity δ depends on the underlying price F and on the underlying volatility σ, amongst other things. For the moment, let us make explicit its dependence on F and time by denoting it $\delta(F, t)$. The portfolio delivers the value of the option at maturity, so the BSM price is the current cost of setting up the replicating portfolio.

To buy the underlying asset the trader uses the option premium and will usually also need to borrow money. He will do this by issuing a bond with the same expiry date as the option. Since we are in the risk neutral world where all investors require the (non-stochastic) risk free rate of return the value of one unit of the bond at time t, with $0 \leq t \leq T$, is

$$B(t, T) = \exp(-r(T-t)). \qquad \text{(III.3.70)}$$

Continuing with our example of pricing a European call option on the futures, the BSM option price, i.e. the value of the replicating portfolio at time t, may therefore be written

$$f(F, \sigma, r, t \,|\, K, T) = \delta(F, t) F(t, T) - \tilde{\delta}(B, t) B(t, T), \qquad \text{(III.3.71)}$$

where $\tilde{\delta}$ is the number of units of the bond that need to be sold to obtain enough funding to buy δ units of the futures. Comparison of (III.3.71) and (III.3.67) shows that:

$$\delta(F, t) = \exp(-r(T-t)) \, \Phi(d_1),$$
$$\tilde{\delta}(B, t) = \exp(-r(T-t)) \, K\Phi(d_2).$$

As the underlying price F changes over time, so does its delta. Thus the trader needs to rebalance his delta hedge on the underlying continually, to maintain delta neutrality at all times. This means that he also has to rebalance the position on the bond. But it is one of the pillars of option theory, proved by Harrison and Kreps (1979), that the replicating portfolio is a *self-financing portfolio*. That is, the value of the replicating portfolio *does not change* over time. The trader will derive no profit from the replicating portfolio and neither does he need to raise any further funds, since at any time t, with $0 \leq t \leq T$,

$$(\Delta\delta) F(t, T) = (\Delta\tilde{\delta}) B(t, T) \qquad \text{(III.3.72)}$$

where $\Delta\delta$ and $\Delta\tilde{\delta}$ are the changes in the deltas over any time interval $(t - \Delta t, t)$. Hence, the value of the option must be equal to the initial value of setting up the replicating portfolio.

This value is independent of the return on the underlying asset. That is, it does not matter whether the underlying price moves up or down when we are hedging. The only thing that influences the cost of hedging is the initial set-up cost of the self-financing replicating portfolio, and this depends on the volatility of the underlying, amongst other things, but not on the expected return on the underlying.

III.3.6.6   Implied Volatility

Option traders and investors do not believe the assumptions made by the BSM model. Markets are not complete and frictionless and the empirical distribution of the underlying price is, typically, too heavy-tailed for the price to be generated by a geometric Brownian motion. To explain why we know that market participants do not believe the assumptions made by the BSM model, consider the set of all traded European call and put options on a single underlying. We can observe the current price of the underlying S and we know that each option is determined by a different value for T and K. We can also observe the risk free rate r which, like any estimate of dividend yield or net convenience yield y, will be the same for all options of the same maturity. Likewise the volatility σ should also be the same for all the options, because they are all based on the same underlying. The volatility in the BSM formula is the volatility in the geometric Brownian motion price process (III.3.47) and since there is only one underlying price there can only be one σ. However, there is a difference between volatility and the other variables: S, r and y are observable in the market, but we cannot observe the volatility.

The *market implied volatility* of a standard European call or put option is the value of σ that is implicit in the market price of the option. We have observed values for the market price of the option and for S, r and y, and we know the strike K and maturity T of the option. Hence, we can find the value of the volatility so that the BSM model price (III.3.64) is equal to the observed market price. This value is the market implied volatility of the option.

If traders and investors believed the assumptions made by the BSM model then the implied volatility that is implicit in the observed market prices of all options should be the *same*. And this unique market implied volatility would be the volatility of the geometric Brownian motion process (III.3.47). But when we calculate the implied volatilities of different options on the same underlying we find that they are not the same. In fact certain ubiquitous features are evident when we plot a surface of implied volatilities as a function of the option's strikes and maturities. Understanding the characteristics of this *market implied volatility surface* lays the foundations for volatility analysis, a subject that is discussed in considerable detail in the next chapter. See Section III.4.2 in particular for further details on market implied volatilities.

III.3.6.7   Adjusting BSM Prices for Stochastic Volatility

We have emphasized that the market prices of liquid standard European options are, typically, *not* found using the BSM formula. These prices are set by market makers responding to demand and supply of the options in the market. But if the option is illiquid, traders need to use a model to price an option. Typically they will not use the BSM model or, if they do, they will adjust the BSM price to reflect their uncertainty about the model.

In order to use the BSM formula we need to have values for the current price of the underlying, the risk free return over the life of the option, any dividends or net convenience yields, and the volatility of the underlying until the option expires. The underlying price can be observed in the market, but we may hold considerable uncertainty about dividend or net convenience yields and may also believe that the risk free rate is stochastic. But the most uncertain input of all is the volatility of the underlying, particularly if we are pricing a long term option.

In the following we show how to adjust the BSM price for model uncertainty, on the assumption that only the volatility is uncertain. If the interest rates and/or the dividend yields or net convenience yield are also uncertain, then all this uncertainty will be captured by the uncertainty in the volatility since this is the only stochastic parameter in the following.

Suppose that a trader wishes to price an illiquid European option and he believes that volatility is not constant. Instead he believes volatility follows a stochastic process with some mean and variance, denoted $E(\sigma)$ and $V(\sigma)$ respectively. In this section we show how to use a second order Taylor expansion to see how volatility uncertainty leads to an adjustment for the BSM option price.

In our notation here we suppress the dependence of the option price on the underlying price S, since this adds nothing to the analysis. We simply write the trader's *adjusted* option price as $f(\sigma)$ considering it as a function of volatility alone. The option price based on the expected volatility, $f(E(\sigma))$, is the BSM option price, its first derivative $f'(E(\sigma))$ is the BSM vega, and the second derivative $f''(E(\sigma))$ is the BSM volga of the option.

Take a second order expansion of the trader's adjusted price about $E(\sigma)$:

$$f(\sigma) \approx f(E(\sigma)) + (\sigma - E(\sigma))f'(E(\sigma)) + \tfrac{1}{2}(\sigma - E(\sigma))^2 f''(E(\sigma)). \qquad \text{(III.3.73)}$$

Now take expectations of (III.3.73). This gives the expectation of the adjusted price as

$$E(f(\sigma)) \approx \text{BSM price} + \tfrac{1}{2}V(\sigma) \times \text{BSM volga}. \qquad \text{(III.3.74)}$$

If, furthermore, the trader wants some degree of confidence in these adjusted prices we need a measure of dispersion in the option price distribution. To first order only, and assuming the option is close to ATM so that f is approximately linear in σ,

$$f(\sigma) - E(f(\sigma)) \approx (\sigma - E(\sigma))f'(E(\sigma)).$$

Since $V(f(\sigma)) = E(f(\sigma) - E(f(\sigma)))^2$ the variance is approximately

$$V(f(\sigma)) \approx V(\sigma) \times \text{BSM vega}^2. \qquad \text{(III.3.75)}$$

A few remarks about the BSM vega and volga are worthwhile at this point. The price of a standard European option always increases with volatility, i.e. the BSM vega is always positive. See Figure III.3.21. But the volga depends on whether the price is a linear, convex or concave function of volatility, and this depends on the option's moneyness.

- ATM options are *approximately linearly increasing* with volatility so these options have a BSM volga that is close to zero.
- ITM and OTM options are *convex increasing functions* of volatility so these options have positive BSM volga.

An ATM option has a large vega but a very small, possibly even negative volga. Hence, (III.3.74) leads to very little adjustment of the option price to account for volatility uncertainty; however, our uncertainty about this adjusted price is, by (III.3.75), very high. Our uncertainty about this price increases with the BSM vega and $V(\sigma)$, both of which increase with the option's maturity. By contrast, a deep ITM or OTM option has a large volga but a very small vega. Hence, (III.3.74) leads to a large adjustment to the option price, particularly for long term options but by (III.3.75) we should be relatively certain about this adjusted price.

EXAMPLE III.3.6: ADJUSTING BSM PRICES FOR UNCERTAINTY IN VOLATILITY

What is the volatility uncertainty adjusted price of a 360-day standard European put option? Assume the risk free rate is zero, $S = 100$, $K = 85$, there are no dividends and that the option has an implied volatility of 20%. Draw a graph comparing the BSM price with the adjusted price, varying the strike of the option between 50 and 150. If the volatility of volatility is 30%, how certain are we of these adjusted prices?

SOLUTION   The spreadsheet calculates the BSM price, using the usual formula, as 2.1252. Then formula (III.3.74) above gives the price that is adjusted for our volatility uncertainty as 2.1638. The graph is also calculated in the spreadsheet for this example, and Figure III.3.16 plots the difference between the adjusted price and the BSM price, along with the standard error associated with our adjusted price. Since the BSM volga is almost zero for an ATM option, the trader should not adjust the BSM price of an ATM option when he believes volatility is stochastic. That is, under stochastic volatility the BSM prices of ATM options are fine. It is only the ITM and OTM options whose prices need adjusting when volatility is stochastic. The expression (III.3.74) indicates that the BSM prices of these options should be revised upward, because these options have positive volga. ATM options have greater vega than ITM and OTM options. Hence, whilst the adjusted price is very near the original price, the confidence in the adjusted price is lowest for ATM options. Readers may change the parameters in the spreadsheet to verify that the longer the maturity of the option, the greater the upward adjustment in price. Not only does the volga increase with maturity, the uncertainty in volatility, or the 'volatility of volatility' should also be greater over the long term.

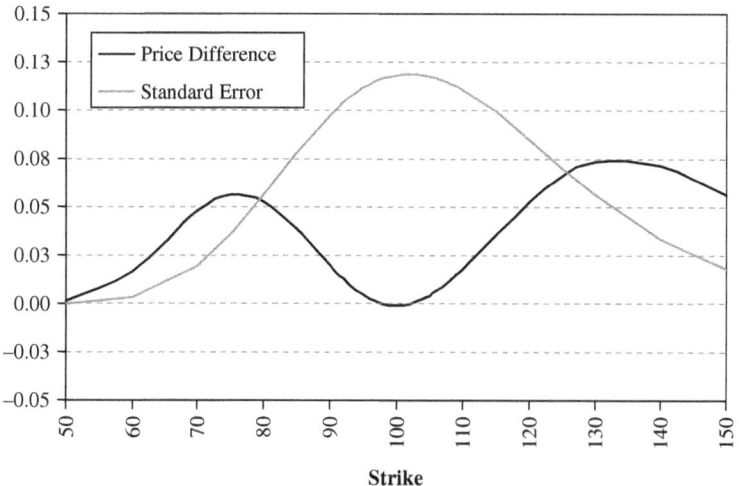

Figure III.3.16   Adjusting option prices for uncertainty in volatility

III.3.7 THE BLACK–SCHOLES–MERTON GREEKS

The Greeks of an option were defined in Section III.3.4 as the partial derivatives of the option's model price with respect to various risk factors. In general these partial derivatives are calculated using *finite differences*, which is a numerical method for differentiation. However, when we have a standard European option that is priced using the BSM model, we do not need to use finite differences because differentiation of (III.3.64) leads to *analytic* formulae for the BSM Greeks. Table III.3.4 summarizes the BSM Greeks for call and put options. This section examines the properties of the BSM Greeks and explains how they vary with the strike and maturity of the option.

Table III.3.4   Black–Scholes–Merton Greeks (with respect to a spot price)

Name	Formula	Sensitivity
Delta	$\omega \exp(-y(T-t))\,\Phi(\omega d_1)$	First order price
Gamma	$\dfrac{\exp(-y(T-t))\varphi(d_1)}{S\sigma\sqrt{T-t}}$	Second order price
Vega	$\exp(-y(T-t))\,S\varphi(d_1)\,\sqrt{T-t}$	First order volatility
Volga	$\exp(-y(T-t))\,S\varphi(d_1)\,\sqrt{T-t}\dfrac{d_1 d_2}{\sigma}$	Second order volatility
Vanna	$-\exp(-y(T-t))\,\varphi(d_1)\,\dfrac{d_2}{\sigma}$	Cross price–volatility
Rho	$\omega \exp(-r(T-t))\,K(T-t)\,\Phi(\omega d_2)$	Interest rate
Theta	$\omega\left[y\exp(-y(T-t))\,S\Phi(\omega d_1)\right.$ $\left.-r\exp(-r(T-t))\,K\Phi(\omega d_2)\right] - \dfrac{\exp(-y(T-t))\,\sigma S\varphi(d_1)}{2\sqrt{T-t}}$	Time

EXAMPLE III.3.7: BSM GREEKS

Calculate the BSM Greeks for a put option with strike 90 relative to an underlying price of 100 and maturity 150 days when the risk free rate is 5%, the dividend yield is 2% and the implied volatility of the option is 20% (or the market price of the option is 1.1636).

SOLUTION

Table III.3.5   BSM Greeks for a 150-day put option with strike 90

Option characteristics		BSM Greeks	
Volatility	20%	Delta	−0.1617
Risk free rate	5%	Gamma	0.0191
Dividend yield	2%	Theta	−0.0090
Option type	Put	Vega	0.1566
Strike	90	Rho	−0.1733
Maturity (days)	150	Vanna	−0.0104
Price	1.1636	Volga	0.6566

The formulae in Table III.3.4 are implemented in the spreadsheet for this example and the results are shown in Table III.3.5. We divide the theta given by the formula in Table III.3.4 by 365, so that it measures how much we could gain or lose when the option's maturity changes by 1 day, rather than by 1 year. Similarly vega and rho are divided by 100, so that they represent a sensitivity to a 1% absolute change in volatility or interest rates, not a 100% change.

III.3.7.1 Delta

The BSM delta is the derivative of the price with respect to underlying, i.e. the slope of the price lines in Figure III.3.15. For a call option on a spot price S it is

$$\delta_C\left(S, \sigma, r, y, t \,|\, K, T\right) = \exp(-y(T-t))\, \Phi(d_1),$$

where, substituting $F = S\exp((r-y)(T-t))$ in (III.3.62),

$$d_1 = \frac{\ln(S/K) + (r-y)(T-t)}{\sigma\sqrt{T-t}} + \frac{1}{2}\sigma\sqrt{T-t}.$$

This is always positive. It is near 0 when the call is deep OTM, around ½ for near ATM calls and approaches 1 for deep ITM calls. Similarly, for a put option, where

$$\delta_P\left(S, \sigma, r, y, t \,|\, K, T\right) = -\exp(-y(T-t))\, \Phi(-d_1),$$

the BSM delta is always negative. It is near 0 for deep OTM puts, around $-\frac{1}{2}$ for near ATM puts and approaches -1 for deep ITM puts.

Figure III.3.17 depicts the BSM delta for different call options (top graph) and different put options (bottom graph) as a function of the option's strikes and maturity.[57] Options of two different maturities are shown on each graph. We see that the deltas of short term

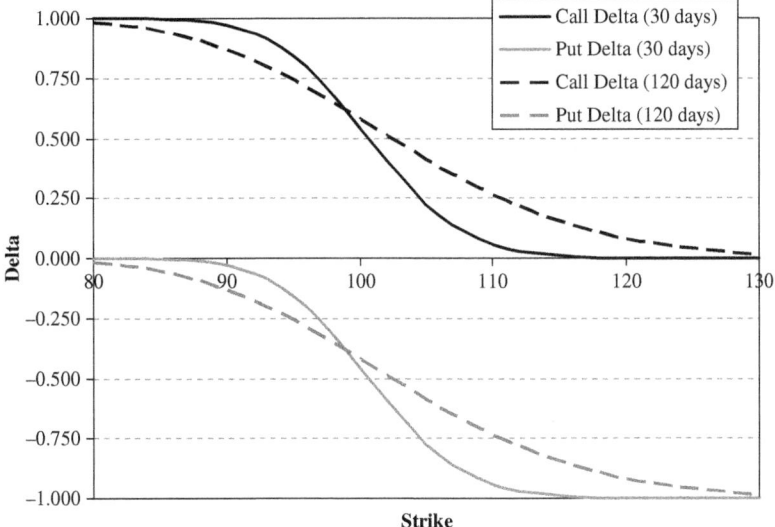

Figure III.3.17   BSM delta for options of different strike and maturity

---

[57] For all the graphs in this section we assume that the underlying is at 100, the volatility is 20%, the risk free rate is 5% and there are no dividends.

options (with maturity 30 days in this case) lie along a curve with a pronounced 'S' shape, but the deltas of longer term options (with maturity 120 days in this case) lie along a curve with much less curvature. Note that we could also plot the delta of a *single* option with a fixed strike, as a function of the underlying price. In this case the vanilla option's BSM delta will be an *increasing* 'S' shaped function of the underlying price.

Clearly the call and put curves in Figure III.3.17 are related. The relationship between the delta of a standard European call and a put of the same strike and maturity can be deduced from the put–call parity relationship (III.3.26). Using the subscripts C and P to distinguish between the call and put Greeks and differentiating (III.3.26) with respect to S yields

$$\delta_C(S, \sigma, r, y, t \,|\, K, T) - \delta_P(S, \sigma, r, y, t \,|\, K, T) = \exp(-y(T - t)). \qquad \text{(III.3.76)}$$

This relationship also follows directly from the definition of the BSM deltas and the fact that for any real x,

$$\Phi(x) + \Phi(-x) = 1. \qquad \text{(III.3.77)}$$

Hence, the difference between the delta of a call and the delta of the equivalent put does not depend on the option strike or maturity, it is the same for all options on S. In particular, in the absence of dividends, for any call and put of the same strike and maturity,

$$\{\text{BSM delta of call}\} - \{\text{BSM delta of put}\} = 1.$$

We remark that when the call and put options are on the futures the BSM deltas are given by

$$\delta_C(F, \sigma, r, t \,|\, K, T) = \exp(-r(T - t))\,\Phi(d_1),$$
$$\delta_P(F, \sigma, r, t \,|\, K, T) = -\exp(-r(T - t))\,\Phi(-d_1).$$

So again, the difference between deltas of any standard European call and put of the same strike and maturity is the same, and

$$\delta_C(F, \sigma, r, t \,|\, K, T) - \delta_P(F, \sigma, r, t \,|\, K, T) = \exp(-r(T - t)). \qquad \text{(III.3.78)}$$

III.3.7.2 Theta and Rho

Figures III.3.18 and III.3.19 illustrate the theta and rho of the same options as in Figure III.3.15 and again assume the underlying is at 100, the volatility is 20%, the risk free rate is 5% and there are no dividends. Note that the theta measures how much we could gain or lose in 1 day, merely due to a change in the maturity of the option. Hence, we divide the formula in Table III.3.5 by 365.

Figure III.3.18 shows that calls usually have negative theta but ITM puts can have positive theta. This can be seen from the BSM formula for theta when the divided yield is zero:

$$\theta_{\text{BSM}} = \begin{cases} -r\exp(-r(T - t))\,K\Phi(d_2) - \dfrac{1}{2}\dfrac{\sigma S\varphi(d_1)}{\sqrt{T - t}}, & \text{for a call,} \\[4mm] r\exp(-r(T - t))\,K\Phi(-d_2) - \dfrac{1}{2}\dfrac{\sigma S\varphi(d_1)}{\sqrt{T - t}}, & \text{for a put.} \end{cases} \qquad \text{(III.3.79)}$$

For high strike puts the first term in (III.3.79) is positive and larger than the second term.

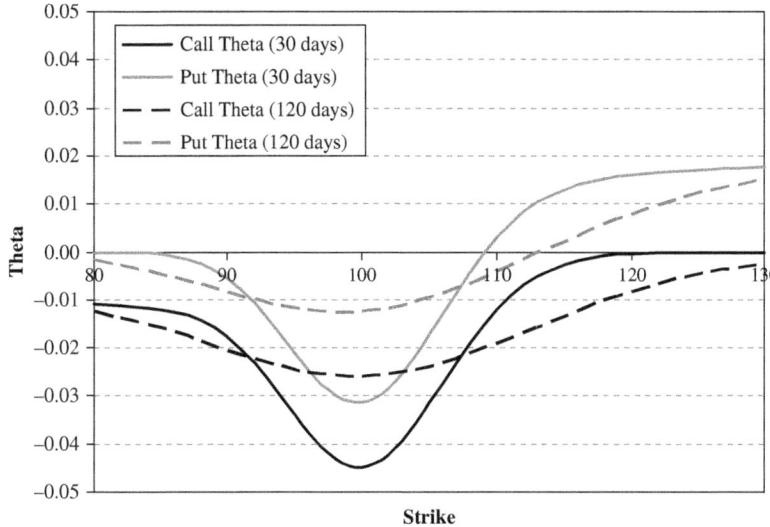

Figure III.3.18   BSM theta for options of different strike and maturity

Figure III.3.19 shows that the BSM rho is positive for a call and negative for a put. As the strike of the option increases the rho decreases. It also increases in absolute value with the maturity of the option.

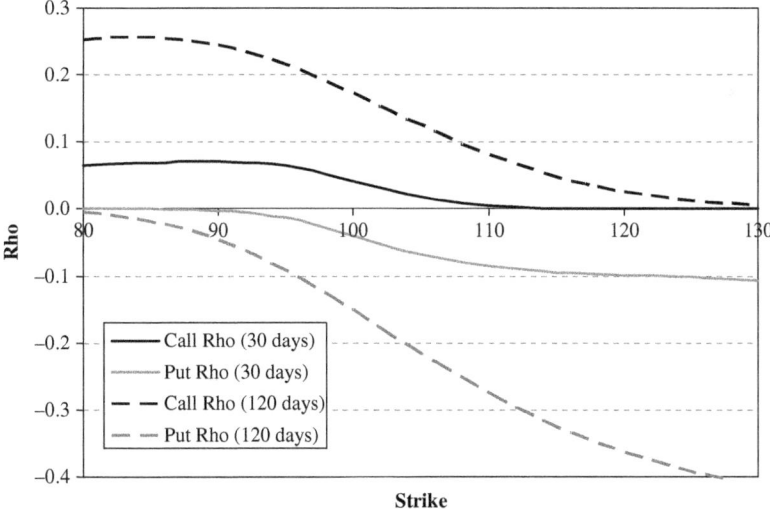

Figure III.3.19   BSM rho for options of different strike and maturity

III.3.7.3   Gamma

Differentiating (III.3.76) further with respect to S shows that the gamma is the *same* for European calls and puts of the same strike and maturity. Also the BSM delta of a call or a put is an increasing function of S, so the BSM gamma is never negative. When S is far above or far below the strike, so when the option strike is far away from the ATM strike, the price curve is close to linear. Hence, the gamma of a deep OTM or a deep ITM option is much smaller than the BSM gamma of an ATM option of the same strike and maturity.

The relationship between the gammas for options of different strikes and maturities is depicted in Figure III.3.20. We use the same scale for strikes and maturities as in the previous figures of this section. Considering all options of the same maturity, gamma will be greatest for the ATM option. And for two ATM options, the one that is closer to expiry has the greatest gamma.

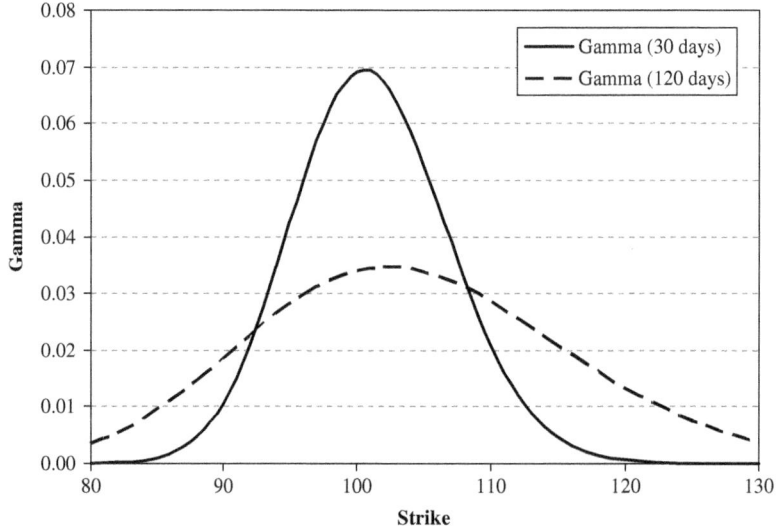

Figure III.3.20   BSM gamma for options of different strike and maturity

III.3.7.4   Vega, Vanna and Volga

If there were no uncertainty about the future evolution of the underlying contract there would be no point in trading options. Futures contracts would provide a much cheaper alternative. Hence, a standard European option price always increases with volatility, as shown in Figure III.3.21.

The vega of a standard European option is always positive, since the price of such an option always increases with the underlying volatility. Also, the put–call parity relationship tells us that a call and a put of the same strike and maturity have the *same* vega. This is because the right-hand side of (III.3.26) does not depend on σ. Figure III.3.22 illustrates the BSM vega of the same options as previously examined in this section. Considering all options of the same maturity, vega will be greatest for the ATM option. And for two ATM options, the one that is closer to expiry has the smallest vega.

We remark that an ATM vanilla option is almost linear in volatility, as seen in Figure III.3.21. Hence the volga, which measures the curvature of the option price as a function of volatility, will be near zero for an ATM option and it may be positive or negative. But ITM and OTM are convex monotonic increasing functions of volatility so their volga will

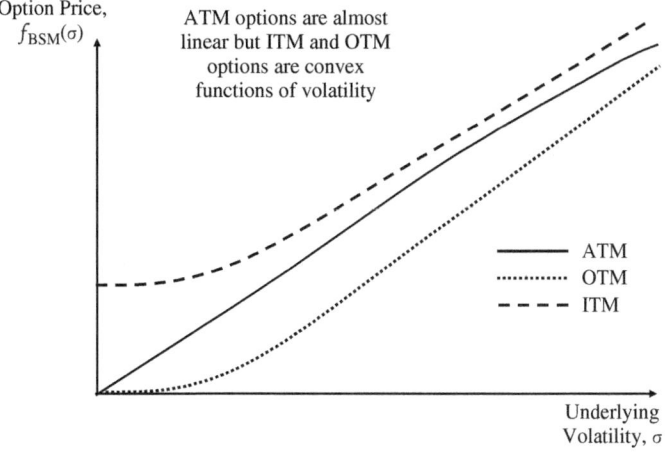

Figure III.3.21   Black–Scholes–Merton option prices as a function of volatility

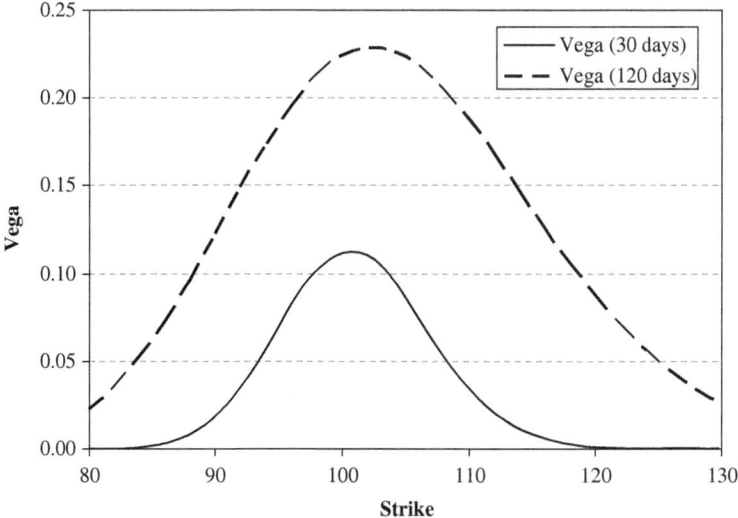

Figure III.3.22   BSM vega for options of different strike and maturity

be positive. The curvature also increases with maturity, hence volga increases with maturity. Figure III.3.23 shows the volga of the same options as considered in the previous figures. For the 120-day ATM option the volga is very slightly negative. Otherwise it increases as we move away from the ATM strike, and then decreases again for the very high and very low strike options. We see that volga has a very characteristic 'M' shape that is more pronounced in long term options.

Figure III.3.24 depicts the vanna of these options. It is positive for low strike options (ITM calls and OTM puts) and negative for high strike options (OTM calls and ITM puts). At very high or low strikes vanna starts to tend towards to zero, more rapidly so for short term options. Longer term options can have quite pronounced vanna even when deep ITM or deep OTM.

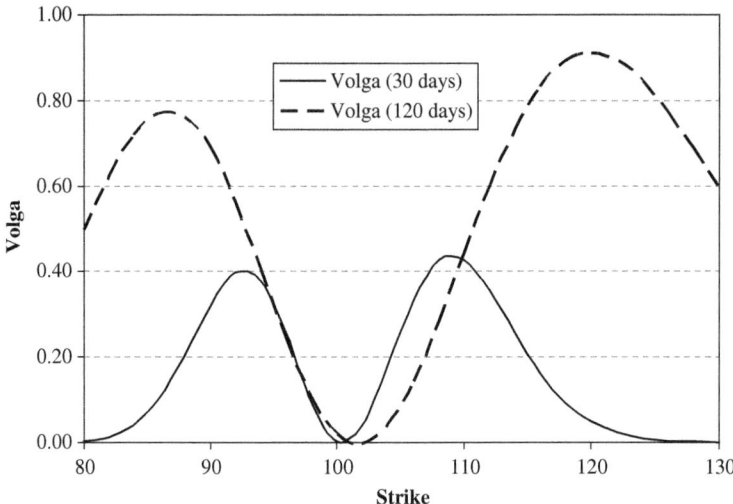

Figure III.3.23   BSM volga for options of different strike and maturity

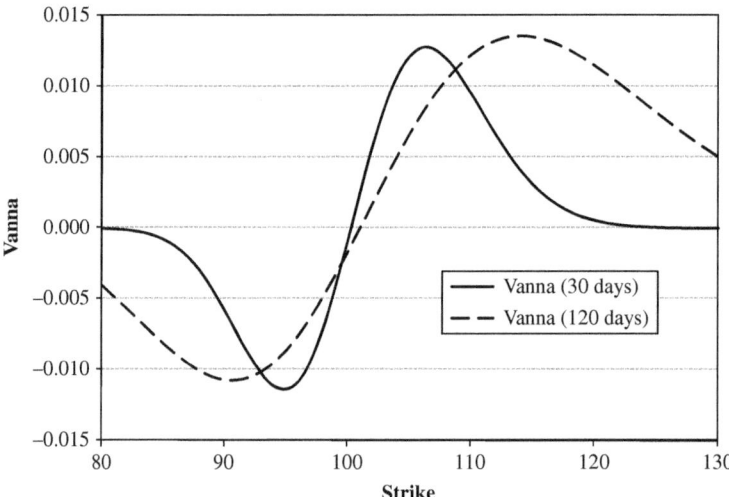

Figure III.3.24   BSM vanna for options of different strike and maturity

The following relationships between the BSM gamma, vega, volga and vanna follow immediately from Table III.3.4:

$$v(S, \sigma \,|K, T) = \sigma \, S^2 (T - t) \gamma(S, \sigma \,|K, T),$$

$$v_o(S, \sigma \,|K, T) = \left(\frac{d_1 d_2}{\sigma} \right) v(S, \sigma \,|K, T),$$

$$v_a(S, \sigma \,|K, T) = -\frac{v_o(S, \sigma \,|K, T)}{d_1 S \sqrt{T - t}}.$$

(III.3.80)

III.3.7.5   Static Hedges for Standard European Options

In this section we show by example that the Black–Scholes–Merton option price sensitivities can be used to form portfolios consisting of the underlying and options on the same underlying whose values are invariant under small changes in the underlying risk factors. Following our discussion in Section III.3.4.6, it is clear that when we hedge with n different options we need to solve a system of n linear equations in n unknowns. This is only possible if the coefficient matrix is invertible. Due to the relationships (III.3.80) between the BSM gamma, vega and volga of options with the same strike and maturity, the matrix is not invertible unless we choose options with three different maturities for gamma–vega–volga hedging.

EXAMPLE III.3.8: A DELTA–GAMMA–VEGA–VOLGA NEUTRAL FOREX OPTION PORTFOLIO

A trader plans to write 100 European calls on a foreign exchange rate, which is currently at 1.5 with a volatility of 15%. The strike and maturity of these call options are to be 1.6 and 70 days, respectively. In the secondary market he can trade several European options on the same forex rate and, including the calls he plans to write, the options available are summarized as follows:

	Type	Strike	Maturity
Option 1	Call	1.6	70
Option 2	Put	1.45	130
Option 3	Put	1.5	70
Option 4	Call	1.4	100

Assume the domestic and foreign risk free interest rates are 4% and 5% respectively and are the same for all maturities. Also assume that market prices of all the options are equal to their fair price based on the Black–Scholes–Merton model with a constant volatility of 15%.

(a) Calculate the fair price for these options and their delta, gamma, vega and volga according to the BSM formula.
(b) Calculate how many of options 2, 3 and 4 the trader should buy or sell to gamma–vega–volga hedge a short position of 100 in option 1.
(c) How many contracts on the spot forex rate should the trader buy or sell to delta hedge the portfolio obtained in (b)?

SOLUTION

(a) Recall that the foreign risk free interest rate takes the place of the dividend yield y in the BSM valuation of foreign exchange options. We have also assumed the risk free rates are the same for all maturities, so in the spreadsheet for this example we apply the BSM formula with $y=0.05$ and $r=0.04$. The results are summarized in the row headed 'Price' in Table III.3.6. The formulae for the BSM Greeks are given in Table III.3.4. Applying these in the spreadsheet gives the results shown in the other rows of Table III.3.6.

Table III.3.6 BSM prices and Greeks for some forex options

Options	1	2	3	4
Strike	1.6	1.45	1.5	1.4
Maturity (days)	70	130	70	100
Type	Call	Put	Put	Call
		BSM model		
Price	0.0082	0.0327	0.0404	0.1073
Delta	0.1638	−0.3506	−0.4985	0.8114
Gamma	2.5318	2.8098	4.0878	2.3253
Vega ($\times 100$)	0.1608	0.3259	0.2596	0.2092
Volga ($\times 100$)	1.0958	0.2452	−0.0004	0.9909

(b) We set up the linear equations that must be satisfied by the positions taken in these options for a gamma–vega–volga neutral portfolio, when we have written 100 of option 1: for gamma neutrality,

$$2.8098\, x_2 + 4.0878\, x_3 + 2.3253\, x_4 = 253.18;$$

for vega neutrality,

$$0.3259\, x_2 + 0.2596\, x_3 + 0.2092\, x_4 = 16.08;$$

and for volga neutrality,

$$0.2452\, x_2 - 0.0004\, x_3 + 0.9909\, x_4 = 109.58.$$

Here x_2, x_3 and x_4 are the positions in options 2, 3 and 4 and x_1, the position in option 1, is -100. The solution is given by:

$$\begin{pmatrix} 2.8098 & 4.0878 & 2.3253 \\ 0.3259 & 0.2596 & 0.2092 \\ 0.2452 & -0.0004 & 0.9909 \end{pmatrix}^{-1} \begin{pmatrix} 253.18 \\ 16.08 \\ 109.58 \end{pmatrix} = \begin{pmatrix} -51.46 \\ 27.15 \\ 123.32 \end{pmatrix}.$$

Hence we should sell 51 of option 2, buy 27 of option 3 and buy 123 of option 4 to obtain an approximately gamma–vega–volga neutral portfolio.

(c) With these positions, the portfolio with all four options has a position delta of:

$$(-100 \times 0.1638) - (51 \times -0.3506) + (27 \times -0.4985) + (123 \times 0.8114) = 87.84.$$

So we sell 88 spot forex contracts to obtain an approximately delta–gamma–vega–volga neutral portfolio.

III.3.8   INTEREST RATE OPTIONS

In this section we introduce options on forward rates, which are called *caps* (for call options) and *floors* (for put options), and options on swaps, which are called *swaptions*. These are all traded OTC. As in all OTC markets, prices of liquid options are set by supply and demand but less liquid options would be priced to cover the cost of hedging, plus the trader's premium and an add-on to cover any counterparty risk. In common with currency options and short term bond options, the price of an interest rate option is quoted in terms of its implied volatility. To obtain the option price we substitute the quoted volatility into the Black–Scholes–Merton formula. The BSM pricing formulae for interest rate options are given below.

When pricing and hedging interest rate options a more realistic process for the interest rate is usually assumed. In particular, a mean-reverting behaviour is often assumed in the drift. The most basic interest rate option models often assume there is only one factor, the instantaneous spot interest rate, which is assumed to drive the whole term structure of interest rates. That is, longer term interest rates are perfectly correlated with the short term rate. Only a brief description of these one-factor *short rate models* is given in this section, and we refer to James and Webber (2000) for a very complete treatment.

However, nowadays most traders price and hedge their interest rate options books using a more realistic model, which allows interest rates of different maturities to be highly correlated but not perfectly correlated. Heath, Jarrow and Morton (1992) introduced a multi-factor framework for pricing interest rate options where each instantaneous forward interest rate has its own diffusion process, and the Brownian motions driving these processes are highly but not perfectly correlated. Brace et al. (1997) adapted the Heath–Jarrow–Morton framework, replacing the instantaneous forward rates by the forward rates that are observed in the market. This multivariate lognormal forward rate model is called the *LIBOR model*, since the underlying variables are usually assumed to be the forward LIBOR rates. We shall see that the dynamics of the LIBOR model are most succinctly modelled using principal component analysis.

As well as hedging standard European interest rate options, the LIBOR model is used to price and hedge *Bermudan swaptions*, i.e. swaptions that may be exercised at a number of fixed early exercise dates. The issue of pricing and hedging of Bermudan swaptions in the LIBOR model framework is a complex one that is beyond the scope of this section, but we refer to Schoenmakers (2005) for further details.

III.3.8.1   Caplets and Floorlets

The simplest of all options in which the underlying contract is an interest rate is an option on a reference interest rate, e.g. 6-month LIBOR, or a constant maturity T-bill or swap rate. It is called a *caplet* if it is a European call on the reference rate or a *floorlet* if it is a European put on the reference rate. The seller of a caplet agrees to pay to the buyer the difference in interest rates accrued on a fixed notational amount N if the reference interest rate on a given date T (the maturity date of the caplet) *exceeds* a fixed level (the strike of the caplet). The seller of a floorlet agrees to pay to the buyer the difference in interest rates accrued on a fixed notational amount N if the reference interest rate on a given date T, the expiry date of the option, is *less* than a fixed level. The pay-off functions are

$$\text{Caplet Pay-off} = N\,m\,\max\left(R_m - K, 0\right),$$

$$\text{Floorlet Pay-off} = N\,m\,\max\left(K - R_m, 0\right),$$

(III.3.81)

where N is the notional amount on which interest is accrued, m is the fixed term of the spot rate R_m in years (e.g. $m = \frac{1}{2}$ for 6 month rates) and K is the interest rate representing the strike of the option.

Now suppose that we want to price the option at time t. In this book we use F_{nm} to denote an m-period discretely compounded forward interest rate starting n periods ahead, that is, n is the *term* and m is the *tenor* of the rate. Thus $F_{T-t,m}$ is the forward interest rate running for m periods starting at time T, as seen from time t. Similarly, R_{T-t} is the discretely compounded spot rate at time t which matures on date T. The relationship between the spot and forward rates was derived in Section III.1.2.4. The time line of forward rates and spot rates, as seen from time t, is depicted in Figure III.3.25.

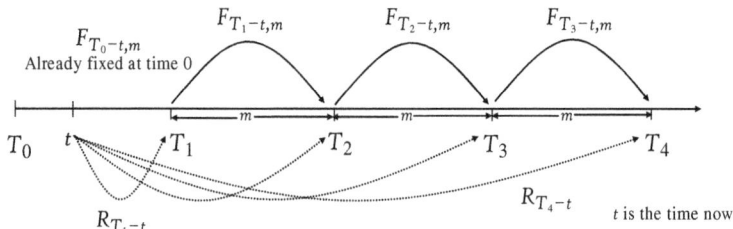

Figure III.3.25   Time line of spot and forward rates

We can apply the Black–Scholes–Merton model to price interest rate options under the assumption that the forward interest rate is a martingale, driven by a geometric Brownian motion with constant volatility σ. Then the BSM caplet and floorlet prices at time t are given by

$$\text{Caplet}\left(F_{T-t,m}, \sigma, r_{T-t+m}, t \,|\, K, T, N, m\right) = N\,m\exp\left(-r_{T-t+m}(T-t+m)\right)\left[F_{T-t,m}\Phi(d_1) - K\Phi(d_2)\right],$$

$$\text{Floorlet}\left(F_{T-t,m}, \sigma, r_{T-t+m}, t \,|\, K, T, N, m\right) = N\,m\exp\left(-r_{T-t+m}(T-t+m)\right)\left[-F_{T-t,m}\Phi(-d_1) + K\Phi(-d_2)\right],$$

$$(\text{III.3.82})$$

where r_{T-t+m} is the continuously compounded spot rate of maturity $T-t+m$ at time t, and

$$d_1 = \frac{\ln\left(F_{T-t,m}/K\right)}{\sigma\sqrt{T-t}} + \tfrac{1}{2}\sigma\sqrt{T-t} \quad \text{and} \quad d_2 = d_1 - \sigma\sqrt{T-t}. \qquad (\text{III.3.83})$$

III.3.8.2   Caps, Floors and their Implied Volatilities

A *cap* (*floor*) is a sequence of caplets (floorlets) based on the same nominal amount N and strike K. The buyer of a cap holds a portfolio of options, with different forward starting times and different maturity dates, where each caplet has the same strike K. Since each caplet pay-off is the excess of a fixed over a floating rate, the buyer of a cap is protecting himself against a future rise in interest rates. Similarly, the buyer of a floor holds a portfolio of options with pay-offs that are the excess of a floating rate over the fixed rate K, so he is buying protection against a future fall in interest rates.

The BSM price of a cap is just the sum of the BSM prices of the individual caplets in the cap; similarly, the BSM price of a floor is just the sum of the BSM prices of the individual floorlets in the floor. So if the payment dates are fixed at times $\{T_1, \ldots, T_n\}$ and $T_n = T$, the maturity of the cap, then the BSM price of a cap based on a notional of N is

$$f^{\text{Cap}}(K, T) = \sum_{i=1}^{n} \text{Caplet}\left(F_{T_i-t,m}, \sigma_i, r_{T_i-t+m}, t \,|\, K, T_i, N, m\right), \qquad (\text{III.3.84})$$

and similarly the BSM price of a floor is

$$f^{\text{Floor}}(K, T) = \sum_{i=1}^{n} \text{Floorlet}\left(F_{T_i-t,m}, \sigma_i, r_{T_i-t+m}, t \,|\, K, T_i, N, m\right), \qquad (\text{III.3.85})$$

where each caplet and floorlet has tenor m and their prices in the above are given by ((III.3.82)) with

$$d_{1i} = \frac{\ln\left(F_{T_i - t, m}/K\right)}{\sigma_i \sqrt{T_i - t}} + \tfrac{1}{2}\sigma_i \sqrt{T_i - t} \quad \text{and} \quad d_{2i} = d_{1i} - \sigma_i \sqrt{T_i - t} \,. \qquad \text{(III.3.86)}$$

We can use a standard bootstrapping method, similar to that use to derive forward rates from spot interest rates of different maturities, to derive prices of caplets that are implicit in market prices of caps of different maturities. Given each caplet price, we can 'back out' the implied volatility of the forward rate in (III.3.82). This is called the *caplet volatility*. The *cap implied volatility* is the constant volatility that, when used to price all caplets in the cap, gives the model price. See Section III.4.2.6. Since a cap is a sequence of caplets its price, according to the BSM model, will be determined by the current term structure of forward rates and a set of market implied caplet volatilities. The following example illustrates the method.

EXAMPLE III.3.9: PRICING A CAP

Consider a company that makes floating interest payments at LIBOR every 6 months on a $1 million loan, with the next payment due on 1 June 2009 and the last payment due on 1 January 2013. The company is concerned about interest rates rising in future so on 1 April 2009 purchases a cap with the following characteristics:

- Reference rate 6 month LIBOR
- Notional $1 million
- Strike 4%
- Maturity 3.5 years.

On 1 April 2009 the LIBOR spot curve and corresponding 6-month forward rates, and the 6-month caplet implied volatilities, are given in Table III.3.7. Calculate the BSM price of the cap, the BSM price of the corresponding floor and the cap implied volatility.

Table III.3.7 Forward rates (on 1 April 2009) and cash flow schedule for the cap

Maturity date	Spot LIBOR rates	Forward rates	Caplet volatility	Caplet maturity	Caplet pay-off
1 Jan 2010	4.15%	$F_{9,6} = 4.27\%$	$\sigma_1 = 8\%$	$T_2 = 9$ months	C_1
1 June 2010	4.25%	$F_{15,6} = 4.27\%$	$\sigma_2 = 9\%$	$T_2 = 15$ months	C_2
1 Jan 2011	4.32%	$F_{21,6} = 4.14\%$	$\sigma_3 = 8\%$	$T_3 = 21$ months	C_3
1 June 2011	4.35%	$F_{27,6} = 4.06\%$	$\sigma_4 = 7.5\%$	$T_4 = 27$ months	C_4
1 Jan 2012	4.37%	$F_{33,6} = 3.96\%$	$\sigma_5 = 7\%$	$T_5 = 33$ months	C_5
1 June 2012	4.38%				

SOLUTION   The cash flows on the cap $\{C_1, \ldots, C_5\}$ are pay-offs to a sequence of caplets. Note that there is no cash flow on 1 June 2009 because the interest rate payment for that date has already been fixed (at the 6-month forward rate on 1 January 2009). Each caplet pay-off is

$$C_i = \$1\text{m} \times \tfrac{1}{2} \times \max\left(F_{T_i, 6} - 4\%, 0\right),$$

where $F_{T_i,6}$ is the 6-month forward LIBOR rate starting T_i years from 1 April 2009. The price of the cap on 1 April 2009 is thus given using (III.3.84), (III.3.85) and (III.3.86) as

$$\$0.5m \times \sum_{i=1}^{5} \exp\left(-r_{T_i+\frac{1}{2}}(T_i+\frac{1}{2})\right)\left[F_{T_i,6}\Phi(d_{1i}) - 0.04\Phi(d_{2i})\right]$$

where $d_{1i} = \dfrac{\ln\left(F_{T_i,6}/0.04\right)}{\sigma_i\sqrt{T_i}} + \frac{1}{2}\sigma_i\sqrt{T_i}$ and $d_{2i} = d_1 - \sigma_i\sqrt{T_i}$.

The spreadsheet for this example computes the prices and sensitivities for each caplet and floorlet and these are shown in Table III.3.8. The calculations are based on the forward rate and caplet volatilities given in Table III.3.7. The BSM price of the cap (floor) is the sum of the caplet (floorlet) prices and the results are:

Cap price $= \$(1394.93 + 1545.31 + 1188.52 + 947.65 + 713.41) = \$5790,$

Floor price $= \$(128.13 + 301.72 + 545.29 + 671.01 + 890.33) = \$2536.5.$

The constant implied volatility for all caplets that gives the same price for the cap may be found using Excel Solver in the spreadsheet. The value is 7.875%. Note that the floor volatility is identical to the cap volatility.

Table III.3.8   Caplet and floorlet prices and sensitivities

Maturity (months)	9	15	21	27	33
Forward rates	4.27%	4.27%	4.14%	4.06%	3.96%
Implied volatilities	8.0%	9.0%	8.5%	7.5%	7.0%
Caplet price ($)	1,394.93	1,545.31	1,188.52	947.65	713.41
Floorlet price ($)	128.13	301.72	545.29	671.01	890.33
Caplet delta	0.833	0.757	0.643	0.577	0.488
Floorlet delta	−0.167	−0.243	−0.357	−0.423	−0.512
Gamma	84.471	72.939	80.105	85.668	86.764
Vega ($\times 10^4$)	0.9229	1.4949	2.0441	2.3858	2.6181

III.3.8.3   European Swaptions

A European swaption is an option to enter a swap on a specific date, the expiry date of the swaption, at a strike that is the fixed rate leg of the swap. In a *receiver swaption* the option buyer receives the fixed rate on the swap and pays the floating rate, and in a *payer swaption* the option buyer pays the fixed rate and receives the floating rate. For instance, a '3 into 2 payer swaption' is a 3-year option on a 2-year swap to pay fixed. A payer swaption provides protection against rising interest rates, just like a cap, but typically it will be cheaper than a cap of the same strike because there is only one option in the swaption whereas there are several caplets in a cap, some of which may be ITM and others OTM. The pay-offs are

$$\text{Payer swaption pay-off} = \max(V_L - V_K, 0),$$

$$\text{Receiver swaption pay-off} = \max(V_K - V_L, 0),$$

where V_K is the value of the fixed leg payments when the fixed rate is K, the strike of the swaption, and V_L is the value of the floating leg payments, at the maturity date T.

The *swaption volatility* is the implied volatility of the forward swap rate of maturity T. See Section III.4.2.7 for further details. It is related to the implied volatilities of the fixed and floating sides of the swap, denoted σ_K and σ_L, and their implied correlation, ϱ_{KL}, as

$$\sigma = \sqrt{\sigma_K^2 + \sigma_L^2 + 2\sigma_K \sigma_L \varrho_{KL}}. \tag{III.3.87}$$

Under the assumption that forward swap rates have a joint lognormal distribution a BSM formula can be used to determine the price of a swaption at time t as[58]

$$
\begin{aligned}
f^{\text{Payer}} &= PV_L \Phi(d_1) - PV_K \Phi(d_2), \\
f^{\text{Receiver}} &= -PV_L \Phi(-d_1) + PV_K \Phi(-d_2),
\end{aligned}
\tag{III.3.88}
$$

where

$$d_1 = \frac{\ln(PV_L/PV_K)}{\sigma\sqrt{T-t}} + \tfrac{1}{2}\sigma\sqrt{T-t}, \quad d_2 = d_1 - \sigma\sqrt{T-t}.$$

In the above PV_K and PV_L are values of the fixed and floating leg payments discounted to time t using the standard day count conventions: usually the fixed leg is discounted using the bond market convention and the floating leg follows the LIBOR convention.

The underlying of a cap (or floor) is a sequence of forward interest rates, but the pricing of a cap (or floor) takes no account of their correlation: the cap (floor) price is simply the sum of the individual caplet (floorlet) prices. On the other hand, the price of a swaption depends on the volatility of the swap rate, which is an average of forward rates. Thus volatility of the swap rate and hence also the price of a swaption *does* depend on the correlation between forward rates. For this reason, even though a swap is a sequence of forward rate agreements, there is no simple relationship between the prices of an option on a swap and the price of a series of options on forward rate agreements. That is, there is no simple relationship between the prices of caps, floors and swaptions. Assuming the forward rate correlation is less than 1, the swaption implied volatility will be lower than the cap implied volatility of the same strike. This is another reason why swaptions are cheaper than caps and floors.

III.3.8.4   Short Rate Models

The empirical behaviour of short term interest rates was discussed in Section III.1.4.4, using the 3-month US Treasury rate as an example. There we modelled the short term interest rate process using the stochastic differential equation

$$dr(t) = \varphi(\theta - r(t))\,dt + \sigma\, r(t)^\gamma\, dW. \tag{III.3.89}$$

The representation (III.3.89) has several advantages over a constant volatility geometric or arithmetic Brownian motion. In particular, the mean-reverting drift prevents the interest rate from becoming unreasonably large or small after a long period of time, and heteroscedastic volatility captures the fact that the volatility of interest rates may depend on the current level of the interest rate.

---

[58] This should be contrasted with the Black model for cap pricing where the assumption is that a geometric Brownian motion generates forward interest rates, not forward swap rates. The two assumptions are inconsistent because a forward swap is an approximately linear function of forward interest rates.

The model parameters have the following interpretation:

- θ is the long term average level of the interest rate. In some models this is assumed to be time varying, either deterministically or stochastically. If θ is itself stochastic we have a two-factor model such as that described in Section III.1.4.4.
- φ is the rate of mean reversion to this long term average level, and the characteristic time to mean-revert is φ^{-1}. Thus if the interest rate is quoted as an annual percentage then φ^{-1} is the time in years that is taken for one-half of the mean reversion following a market shock.
- σ is a constant that affects the volatility of the interest rate. However, the volatility is not constant unless $\gamma = 0$ (for an arithmetic process) or $\gamma = 1$ (for a geometric process).
- γ measures the degree of heteroscedasticity in interest rate volatility.[59] When

   o $\gamma = 0$ we have the *Vasicek process*, an arithmetic process with normally distributed interest rates;
   o $\gamma = 1$ we have a geometric process with lognormally distributed interest rates;
   o $\gamma = \frac{1}{2}$ we have the square root or *Cox–Ingersoll–Ross process*.

Numerous interest rate options pricing models based on a process of the form (III.3.89) for the *instantaneous* short rate, were proposed in a voluminous research literature, mainly during the 1980s and early 1990s. A single instantaneous short rate $r(t)$ will determine the entire term structure of spot interest rates via the relationship

$$\exp(-r_T T) = E\left(\exp\left(-\int_0^T r(s)\,ds \right) \right),$$

(III.3.90)

where r_T denotes the continuously compounded spot rate of maturity T. That is, the term structure of spot rates is given by

$$r_T = T^{-1} \ln\left(E\left(\exp\left(-\int_0^T r(s)\,ds \right) \right) \right)$$

(III.3.91)

for all $T > 0$.

However, most one-factor models do not capture realistic term structures for interest rates. In particular, they are unable to capture the 'hump' shape that we commonly observe where rates of maturities around 2 years are often higher than both short and long rates. For this reason various two- or three-factor models have been proposed that provide more flexible shapes for the term structure. Another reason for using more than one factor is that different mean-reverting cycles in interest rates can be captured, as explained in Section III.1.4.4.

Most models are designed for ease of calibration to market data. For instance, the model proposed by Longstaff and Schwartz (1992) has an analytic solution for bond option prices and is therefore easy to implement if bond option prices are the only market data used for calibration. However, we normally want to calibrate the model to all the liquid interest rate sensitive securities that are traded, including cap and swaption prices (or their implied volatilities). Most models need to be calibrated to these data using a binomial or trinomial tree. The calibration of interest rate models is a complex topic that is very well described,

---

[59] See Vasicek (1977) and Cox, Ingersol and Ross (1985).

along with a very extensive survey of the models, in the excellent book by James and Webber (2000).

III.3.8.5 LIBOR Model

To model the entire term structure of interest rates in a convincing way it is clear that interest rate models require more than one stochastic factor. However, the more factors in the model the more difficult the calibration becomes, in general. For instance, Heath, Jarrow and Morton (1992) introduced a framework for interest rate modelling where the instantaneous forward interest rates of different terms are assumed to follow correlated diffusion processes. But instantaneous forward rates are unobservable in the market and the model is extremely difficult to calibrate.[60] Even the models that have analytic solutions for bond option prices, such as that of Longstaff and Schwartz, need to resort to numerical methods of resolution to price an interest rate option or swaption, so calibration to cap and swaption volatility surfaces is generally a very difficult task.

For this reason many traders price and hedge interest rate options using a multivariate lognormal diffusion model for market forward rates, also called the *LIBOR model* or the *market model of interest rates*, introduced by Brace et al. (1997). A similar model introduced at the same time by Jamshidian (1997) uses swap rates instead of forward rates. Since the underlying variables are observable in the market, the calibration of these models is much easier than calibrating the Heath–Jarrow–Morton model. We now describe the LIBOR model, avoiding unnecessary complexities by assuming that year fractions between payment (or reset) dates are constant for all forward rates. We also assume the basic forward rate has a term of 6 months.

Denote by $f_i(t)$ the forward rate that applies between time t_i and time t_{i+1}. Then $f_i(t)$ is fixed at time t_i but is stochastic up to that point in time. Each forward rate has its own *natural measure*, which is the forward measure with numeraire equal to the value of a zero coupon bond maturing at date t_{i+1}.[61] Under its own natural measure each forward rate is a martingale and therefore has zero drift. So in the natural measure the lognormal forward rate model is

$$\frac{df_i(t)}{f_i(t)} = \sigma_i dB_i(t) \quad i = 1, \ldots, n; \; 0 < t < t_i,$$

$$E(dB_i(t), dB_k(t)) = \varrho_{ik} dt,$$

(III.3.92)

where n is the number of forward rates in the model. Here we have written each forward rate volatility and each pairwise correlation as a constant, but some authors assume the volatilities $\sigma_1(t), \ldots, \sigma_n(t)$ are deterministic functions of time, as are the forward rate correlations $\varrho_{ik}(t)$ for $i, k = 1, \ldots, n$.

To work with a single measure, rather than a different measure for each forward rate, Hull and White (2000) take as numeraire the discretely reinvested money market account and call this the *spot LIBOR measure*. In the spot LIBOR measure the appropriate rate for discounting an expected cash flow at time t_{i+1} to time t_i is the forward rate $f_i(t)$. This measure is not

---

[60] The tree is not even recombining unless all movements in interest rates are parallel shifts.
[61] See Section III.3.2.3 for further details about this measure.

only intuitive; it leads to a relatively tractable specification of the drift terms in the model. Under the spot LIBOR measure (III.3.92) becomes

$$\frac{df_i(t)}{f_i(t)} = \mu_i(t)\,dt + \sigma_i dW_i(t) \quad i = 1, \ldots, n;\, 0 < t < t_i,$$

$$\mu_i(t) = \sigma_i \sum_{k=m(t)}^{i} \frac{\varrho_{ik}\sigma_k f_k(t)}{1 + f_k(t)}, \tag{III.3.93}$$

$$E(dW_i(t), dW_k(t)) = \varrho_{ik} dt,$$

where $m(t)$ is the index of the accrual period, i.e. $t_{m(t)-1} < t < t_{m(t)}$.

Practitioners frequently use historical data as well as contemporaneous market data to calibrate the volatility and correlation parameters. Authors such as Rebonato (2004), Rebonato and Joshi (2002), Hull and White (2000) and Logstaff et al. (2001) advocate use of market data in the form of swaption volatilities to calibrate the volatilities of the forward rates, but base correlations on historical data because they are more stable than those calibrated to market data. Forward rate covariance matrices have a huge number of parameters, but parsimonious parameterizations have been suggested by Alexander (2003) and others. A popular technique is to set all but the two or three largest eigenvalues of the forward rate correlation matrix to zero, and to use historical data to calibrate the first three eigenvectors. The implication of zeroing eigenvalues is a transformation of the lognormal forward rate model into a model where each forward rate is driven by only two or three orthogonal factors.

For instance, the forward rate dynamics may be expressed in terms of only three uncorrelated stochastic processes that are common to all forward rates, as

$$\frac{df_i(t)}{f_i(t)} = \mu_i(t)\,dt + \lambda_{i1} dZ_1(t) + \lambda_{i2} dZ_2(t) + \lambda_{i3} dZ_3(t), \tag{III.3.94}$$

where dZ_1, dZ_2 and dZ_3 are uncorrelated Brownian motions. Then

$$\sigma_i dW_i(t) = \lambda_{i1} dZ_1(t) + \lambda_{i2} dZ_2(t) + \lambda_{i3} dZ_3(t).$$

So the forward rate covariances are completely determined by three *volatility components* for each forward rate, as:

$$\sigma_i^2 = \lambda_{i1}^2 + \lambda_{i2}^2 + \lambda_{i3}^2 \tag{III.3.95}$$

and

$$\varrho_{ik} = \frac{\lambda_{i1}\lambda_{k1} + \lambda_{i2}\lambda_{k2} + \lambda_{i3}\lambda_{k3}}{\sigma_i \sigma_k}. \tag{III.3.96}$$

Suppose the forward rate's implied volatilities $\sigma_1, \ldots, \sigma_n$ have been calibrated to the market. It remains to calibrate the parameters $\lambda_{i1}, \lambda_{i2}, \lambda_{i3}$ for $i = 1, \ldots, n$, i.e. three parameters for each forward rate. Often these are estimated via a *principal component analysis* of the empirical correlation matrix based on historical data on the forward rates.[62] So how, exactly, do we obtain the parameters $\lambda_{i1}, \lambda_{i2}, \lambda_{i3}$ from this principal component analysis? We set

$$\lambda_{ik} = M_i w_{ik} \Lambda_k^{1/2}, \quad k = 1, 2, 3, \tag{III.3.97}$$

---

[62] See Section I.2.6 and Chapter II.2 for further details on principal component analysis.

where Λ_k is the kth largest eigenvalue of the forward rate correlation matrix, w_{ik} is the ith element of the kth eigenvector of this matrix and, by (III.3.95)

$$M_i^2 = \frac{\sigma_i^2}{w_{i1}^2 \Lambda_1 + w_{i2}^2 \Lambda_2 + w_{i3}^2 \Lambda_3}.$$

One obvious limitation of the lognormal forward rate model is that empirical distributions of futures returns are too skewed and heavy tailed to be normal. Following Brigo and Mercurio (2001, 2002) a multi-dimensional extension by Brigo et al. (2004) provides smile consistent arbitrage free prices for multi-asset options. Remaining in a complete markets setting, they broaden the assumption of lognormality in the forward rate model to assume lognormal mixture dynamics for each of the underlying forward rates. That is, the risk neutral density of the forward rates is assumed to be a multivariate lognormal mixture density. The beauty of this approach is that the local volatility function is uniquely determined by the risk neutral price density. See Section III.4.3.4 for further details.

III.3.8.6   Case Study: Application of PCA to LIBOR Model Calibration

In this section we use historical data on UK forward rates to calibrate the LIBOR model on 1 November 2007. Daily data on UK LIBOR rates are available from the Bank of England.[63] Figure III.3.26 illustrates the forward rates of selected maturities from January 2005 to the October 2007. The Bank of England provides many years of data on 6-month forward rates from 6 months to 25 years ahead. But we should not use too long a historical period if we are to capture current market conditions. Also the LIBOR rates at the very long end are extremely variable, as is evident from Figure III.3.26, so the case study is based on forward rates from 1 to 20 years ahead, recorded daily from the beginning of January 2006 to the end of October 2007.

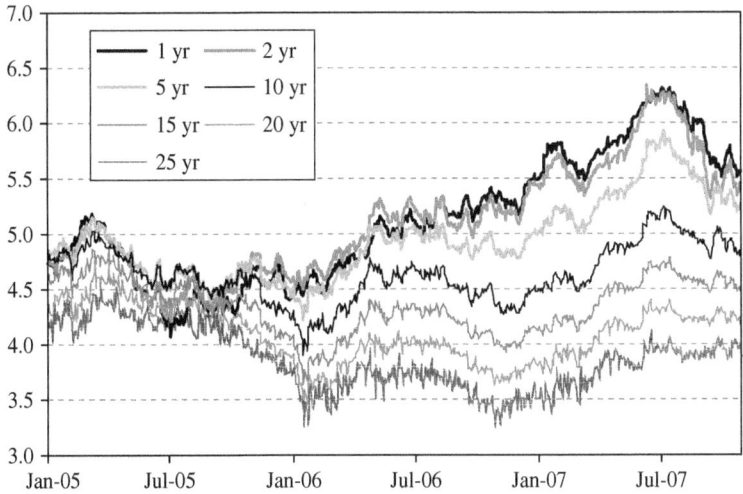

Figure III.3.26   Historical data on UK forward LIBOR rates

---

[63] See http://www.bankofengland.co.uk/statistics/yieldcurve/index.htm. Note that the extreme variability of very long term forward rates is due to yield curve calibration error, since few very long term instruments are available. See Section III.1.9.

We shall assume readers are familiar with principal component analysis. Otherwise, for further details about this statistical tool and its practical implementation, please refer to Chapter II.2, and to the case study on UK government spot curves in Section II.2.3 in particular.

Figures III.3.27 and III.3.28 depict the historical forward rate volatilities, in basis points per annum, and their correlations. The volatilities show the typical hump at the 1.5- to 2-year maturities, then another hump at 7 years, and then volatilities increase from 12.5 years to the long end. We remark that high volatility at the long end is mainly a result of calibration error in yield curve fitting. The correlations shown in Figure III.3.28 display a typical structure, with forward rate correlations being generally higher at the shorter end and correlations decreasing as the maturity gap increases. We remark that the shape of the forward rate correlation matrix is very sensitive to the method used to fit the yield curve, as demonstrated in Section III.1.9.5.

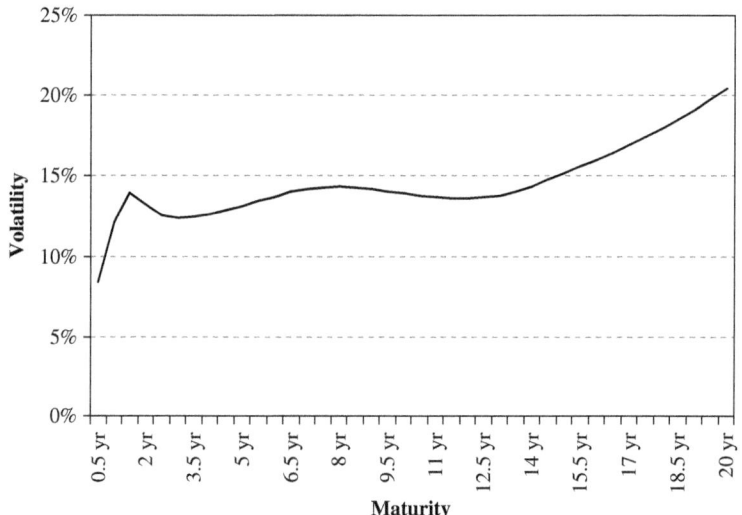

Figure III.3.27   Forward rate historical volatilities

Principal component analysis finds the eigenvalues and eigenvectors of the correlation matrix. Figure III.3.29 plots the first three eigenvectors as a function of the maturity of the rate. These display the typical 'trend', 'tilt' and 'curvature' features of any highly correlated term structure. The first eigenvalue is 29.42, the second is 5.77 and the third is 2.08. The sum of the eigenvalues is the dimension of the correlation matrix, i.e. 39. Hence, the trend component accounts for 29.42/39, i.e. over 75% of the common variation in forward LIBOR rates since January 2006. Adding a tilt component will explain over 90% of the variation, and the further addition of the curvature component explains over 95% of the total movements in LIBOR rates over the data period. The rest of the variation in LIBOR rates can be ascribed to unwanted 'noise' for the purposes of pricing and hedging options and swaptions today.

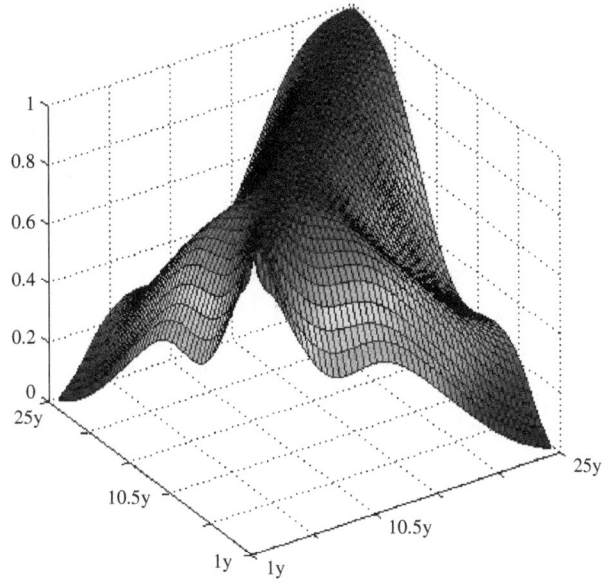

Figure III.3.28   Forward rate historical correlations. (See Plate 4)

The first three columns of Table III.3.9 show the eigenvectors that are plotted in Figure III.3.29, and in further columns we give the result of calculating the volatility factors according to (III.3.97). Since we do not have market data on implied forward rate volatilities we have used their historical values.

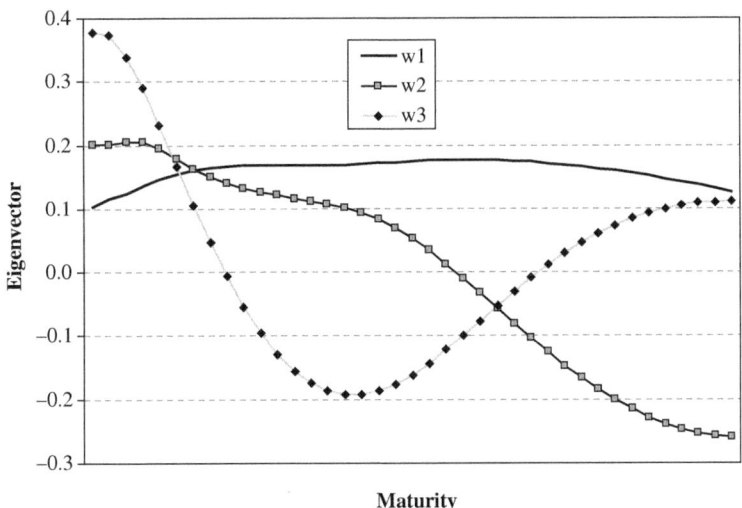

Figure III.3.29   The first three eigenvectors of the forward rate correlation matrix

Table III.3.9   Eigenvectors, volatilities and forward rate volatility factors

Eigenvectors	w_1	w_2	w_3	σ	M	λ_1	λ_2	λ_3
1 yr	0.1031	0.2003	0.3770	12.15%	13.26%	7.41%	2.31%	4.34%
1.5 yr	0.1155	0.2014	0.3728	13.99%	14.62%	9.16%	2.56%	4.73%
2 yr	0.1250	0.2056	0.3390	13.20%	13.59%	9.22%	2.43%	4.00%
2.5 yr	0.1363	0.2050	0.2901	12.55%	12.78%	9.45%	2.28%	3.22%
3 yr	0.1471	0.1944	0.2306	12.38%	12.60%	10.06%	2.13%	2.52%
3.5 yr	0.1550	0.1786	0.1671	12.47%	12.80%	10.76%	1.99%	1.86%
4 yr	0.1605	0.1629	0.1051	12.65%	13.09%	11.40%	1.85%	1.20%
4.5 yr	0.1643	0.1501	0.0472	12.88%	13.36%	11.91%	1.74%	0.55%
5 yr	0.1669	0.1403	−0.0062	13.14%	13.61%	12.32%	1.66%	−0.07%
5.5 yr	0.1682	0.1327	−0.0543	13.44%	13.85%	12.64%	1.60%	−0.65%
6 yr	0.1685	0.1266	−0.0956	13.73%	14.11%	12.90%	1.55%	−1.17%
6.5 yr	0.1683	0.1214	−0.1292	14.00%	14.34%	13.09%	1.51%	−1.61%
7 yr	0.1680	0.1169	−0.1552	14.20%	14.50%	13.21%	1.47%	−1.95%
7.5 yr	0.1680	0.1123	−0.1740	14.32%	14.57%	13.28%	1.42%	−2.20%
8 yr	0.1685	0.1073	−0.1863	14.36%	14.55%	13.29%	1.36%	−2.35%
8.5 yr	0.1694	0.1012	−0.1924	14.31%	14.45%	13.28%	1.27%	−2.41%
9 yr	0.1706	0.0933	−0.1926	14.20%	14.32%	13.25%	1.16%	−2.40%
9.5 yr	0.1720	0.0830	−0.1872	14.06%	14.18%	13.23%	1.02%	−2.31%
10 yr	0.1736	0.0698	−0.1768	13.91%	14.06%	13.24%	0.85%	−2.16%
10.5 yr	0.1751	0.0536	−0.1620	13.78%	13.97%	13.27%	0.65%	−1.97%
11yr	0.1764	0.0347	−0.1435	13.67%	13.91%	13.32%	0.42%	−1.73%
11.5 yr	0.1774	0.0135	−0.1222	13.61%	13.91%	13.38%	0.16%	−1.48%
12 yr	0.1778	−0.0093	−0.0993	13.61%	13.96%	13.46%	−0.11%	−1.20%
12.5 yr	0.1776	−0.0329	−0.0759	13.68%	14.06%	13.55%	−0.40%	−0.93%
13 yr	0.1769	−0.0567	−0.0528	13.83%	14.23%	13.65%	−0.70%	−0.65%
13.5 yr	0.1756	−0.0804	−0.0302	14.07%	14.46%	13.77%	−1.01%	−0.38%
14 yr	0.1739	−0.1036	−0.0087	14.39%	14.75%	13.91%	−1.33%	−0.11%
14.5 yr	0.1717	−0.1259	0.0115	14.77%	15.08%	14.04%	−1.65%	0.15%
15 yr	0.1691	−0.1470	0.0300	15.18%	15.43%	14.15%	−1.97%	0.40%
15.5 yr	0.1662	−0.1666	0.0466	15.59%	15.77%	14.22%	−2.28%	0.64%
16 yr	0.1631	−0.1846	0.0612	16.01%	16.12%	14.26%	−2.58%	0.86%
16.5 yr	0.1596	−0.2009	0.0739	16.45%	16.50%	14.28%	−2.88%	1.06%
17 yr	0.1558	−0.2154	0.0847	16.91%	16.93%	14.31%	−3.17%	1.25%
17.5 yr	0.1517	−0.2280	0.0936	17.41%	17.44%	14.36%	−3.45%	1.42%
18 yr	0.1473	−0.2385	0.1005	17.94%	18.05%	14.42%	−3.74%	1.58%
18.5 yr	0.1425	−0.2470	0.1056	18.52%	18.78%	14.51%	−4.03%	1.72%
19 yr	0.1374	−0.2533	0.1089	19.13%	19.62%	14.62%	−4.32%	1.86%
19.5 yr	0.1320	−0.2575	0.1106	19.76%	20.60%	14.74%	−4.61%	1.98%
20 yr	0.1264	−0.2598	0.1109	20.41%	21.70%	14.87%	−4.89%	2.09%

The volatility factors calculated in this table are drawn, as a function of the forward rate maturity, in Figure III.3.30. This shows that each volatility factor has an influence that is proportional to the eigenvalue to which it belongs, so the largest influence comes from the first volatility factor. They also inherit their structure as a function of the forward rates from the structure of the eigenvectors. Thus the first volatility factor is the largest, and is relatively constant over the forward rates, except that it is slightly smaller for the rates at the short end. The second and third volatility factors are smaller than the first, and these display the 'tilt' and 'curvature' features of their respective eigenvectors.

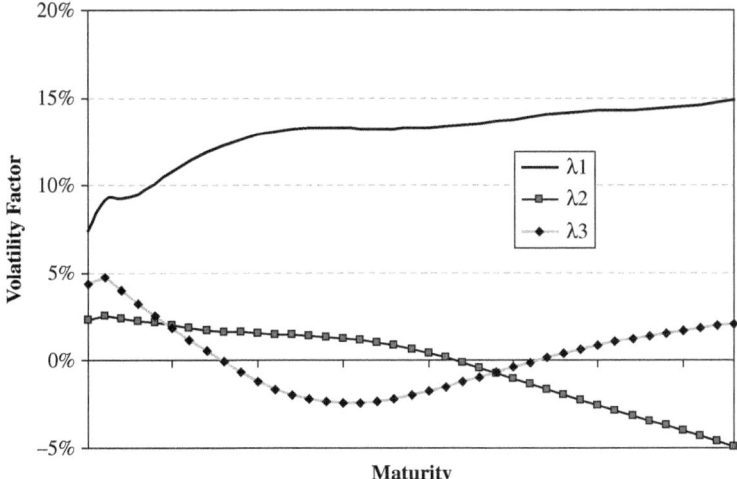

Figure III.3.30   Volatility factors

Of course, for the accurate calibration to market data we should have used cap volatilities for calibrating the forward rate volatilities and we may also consider using the swaption implied correlation matrix in the principal component analysis. However, whilst the implied volatilities are fairly stable over time, the implied correlations are not, and this is why we sometimes use historical data on forward rate correlations in the LIBOR model calibration.

III.3.9   PRICING EXOTIC OPTIONS

Exotic options are OTC contracts that have complex pay-offs depend on the distribution of the underlying price on and possibly before the expiry date. Some European exotic options have path-dependent pay-offs, and in this case the price of a European exotic option depends not only on the underlying price distribution at maturity, but also on the distribution of prices prior to maturity. For instance, the price of a barrier option depends on the probability that the underlying price hits the barrier at some time before maturity; the value of an Asian option depends on the underlying price during some averaging period prior to expiry; and a ladder option's value depends on the highest or lowest 'rung' in a ladder that the underlying price touched before expiry.

Under the assumption that the underlying asset or assets follow geometric Brownian motions with constant volatility, it is possible to derive a Black–Scholes–Merton type formula for the price (or in some cases the approximate price) of most European exotic options.[64] However, the BSM formula has no easy generalization to American options. Since the price

---

[64] From these is it usually possible to derive analytic formulae for the delta, gamma, vega and other risk factor sensitivities, using partial differentiation on the option price. Otherwise the sensitivities can be obtained using finite differences, as explained in Section I.5.5.2.

of an American option depends on whether the option is likely to be exercised early, the underlying price distribution at *every* point in time is needed to derive the option price. In the following we consider only European exotic options.

Many of the pricing formulae given in this section are based on those provided by my husband, Jacques Pézier, for the Reuters 2000 Analytics software.[65] These formulae are not derived, but they have been written directly into an Excel workbook which is intended for teaching purposes, i.e. without using VBA. As usual, anything in red is an input variable that may be changed by the reader and the resulting option prices are given in blue.[66]

We let S_i denote the price of the ith underlying asset at the time the option is priced. Except for the price at expiry, which is denoted $S_i(T)$ when we define the pay-offs, we shall suppress the dependence of the underlying prices on running time t, assuming that the option is priced at time $t = 0$.[67] Throughout we assume that underlying asset prices follow a geometric Brownian motion with constant volatility, where σ_i denotes the volatility of the ith underlying asset and its continuously compounded dividend yield is denoted y_i, if we do not assume that this is zero.

If the strike of the option is fixed this is denoted K, the option maturity is T and r is the continuously compounded risk free interest rate of maturity T. When the option is on a single asset there is no need for the subscript i, and when the option relates to two underlying assets ϱ denotes the correlation between the two geometric Brownian motions driving the asset prices. We express the prices of European options, both calls and puts in one formula, using the variable $\omega = 1$ for a call and $\omega = -1$ for a put.

III.3.9.1 Pay-offs to Exotic Options

The most liquid of all exotic options are barrier options. We have already met an *up-and-out call*, which has pay-off $\max(S(T) - K, 0) \, 1_{\{S(t) < B, 0 \le t \le T\}}$ that was illustrated by the dotted line in Figure III.3.2. That is, the standard call pay-off is received if the underlying price remains below the barrier B throughout the life of the option, and otherwise the pay-off is zero. Other single barrier options are 'up and in', 'down and out' and 'down and in', with the obvious pay-off functions. See Section III.3.9.10 for further details. *Multiple barrier options* have more complex pay-offs, which can knock in and out at barriers at different levels.

Other fairly common types of exotics include the following:

- *Asian options,* which are also fairly liquid. Here either the underlying contract value or the strike depends on an average taken over a pre-defined period. For example, an *average rate call* has the pay-off $\max(A(T) - K, 0)$, where $A(T)$ is an average of underlying prices taken at certain pre-defined times $t_1 < t_2 < \ldots < t_n \le T$.

- *Look-back options* with pay-off $\max(S(T) - S_{\min}, 0)$ for a call and $\max(S_{\min} - S(T), 0)$ for a put, where $S_{\min}$ is the minimum price of the underlying over the life of the option. *Look-forward options* have pay-off $\max(S_{\max} - K, 0)$ for a call and $\max(K - S_{\max}, 0)$ for a put, where $S_{\max}$ is the maximum price of the underlying over the life of the option.

---

[65] The latest version is Reuters 3000 Xtra. See http://about.reuters.com/productinfo/3000xtra. Since I modified these formulae considerably, any errors are my own responsibility.

[66] The only option price not coded in the spreadsheet for this section is the compounded option price in Section III.3.9.6, since this requires the bivariate normal distribution function which is not coded directly in Excel.

[67] To change the formulae to apply at an arbitrary time t, just replace T by $T - t$ in the formulae.

- *Forward start options* have a strike that is usually set as the ATM strike at some predetermined forward date.[68] A *cliquet option* is a series of forward start options.

- *Compound options* have a pay-off that depends on the value of another option (usually with a different expiry date) at time T.

- *Power options* have pay-offs that are homogeneous of degree greater than 1 in S and K: for instance, a quadratic call may have pay-off $\max(S(T) - K, 0)^2$.

We shall also be considering *multi-asset options*, i.e. exotic options on several underlying prices, including:

- *Spread options*, which have pay-off $\max(S_1(T) - S_2(T) - K, 0)$ for a call and $\min(S_1(T) - S_2(T) - K, 0)$ for a put.

- *'Best of'* options, with pay-off $\max(S_1(T), S_2(T), \ldots, S_n(T))$, and *'worst of'* options, with pay-off $\min(S_1(T), S_2(T), \ldots, S_n(T))$.

- *Rainbow options*, with pay-off $\max(S_1(T) - K, S_2(T) - K, \ldots, S_n(T) - K, 0)$ for a call and $\min(S_1(T) - K, S_2(T) - K, \ldots, S_n(T) - K, 0)$ for a put.

- *Quanto options*, with pay-off $\overline{X} \max(S(T) - K, 0)$ for a call and $\overline{X} \min(S(T) - K, 0)$ for a put, where $\overline{X}$ is a fixed domestic over foreign exchange rate and the underlying price and strike are in foreign currency.

- *Compo options*, with pay-off $\max(X(T)S(T) - K, 0)$ for a call and $\min(X(T)S(T) - K, 0)$ for a put, where X is a foreign exchange rate and the strike is in domestic currency.

- *Contingent options*, for instance with pay-off $\max(S_1(T) - K_1, 0) | S_2(T) > K_2$ for a call and $\min(S_1(T) - K_1, 0) | S_2(T) > K_2$ for a put.

III.3.9.2   Exchange Options and Best/Worst of Two Asset Options

Multi-asset options are not easily priced in general, but see Alexander and Venkatramanan (2008b) for a new recursive pricing approximation. The simplest case is where there are only two underlying assets both of which follow geometric Brownian motions with constant volatility. In this case we can use one of the prices as the numeraire and transform the pay-off so that it that depends only on the ratio of the two prices, and this price ratio will follow a geometric Brownian motion. Hence, a two-dimensional problem is effectively reduced to one dimension and the pricing formulae given below can easily be derived.

A European *exchange option* is an option to exchange asset 1 for asset 2 on some specified date, T years from now. The pay-off is $\max(S_1(T) - S_2(T), 0)$, where S_1 and S_2 are the asset prices. Margrabe (1978) derived the following formula for the exchange option price:

$$S_1 \exp(-y_1 T)\Phi(d_1) - S_2 \exp(-y_2 T)\Phi(d_2) \tag{III.3.98}$$

where y_1 and y_2 are the dividend yields on the two assets, and

$$d_1 = \frac{\ln(S_1/S_2) + (y_1 - y_2)T}{\sigma\sqrt{T}} + \tfrac{1}{2}\sigma\sqrt{T}, \quad d_2 = d_1 - \sigma\sqrt{T}$$

and

$$\sigma = \sqrt{\sigma_1^2 + \sigma_2^2 - 2\varrho\sigma_1\sigma_2}.$$

---

[68] See Section III.3.2.6 for the definition of at-the-money.

EXAMPLE III.3.10: EXCHANGE OPTION PRICE VS CORRELATION

How much is an option to exchange one asset for another 1 year from now worth, when both assets currently have the same price and volatility? Assume neither asset pays dividends. Show how the option price depends on the correlation between the two assets.

SOLUTION   In Figure III.3.31 we have set the asset volatilities equal to 25% and generated the graph by changing the correlation in the spreadsheet for the exchange option price. The current price of both assets was set to 100, so the option price is expressed as a percentage of the underlying price. The graph shows that the option increases in value as the behaviour of the assets diverges. Since they have the same volatility, they are essentially the same asset when the correlation is very near 1, hence the value of the option diminishes as correlation increases.

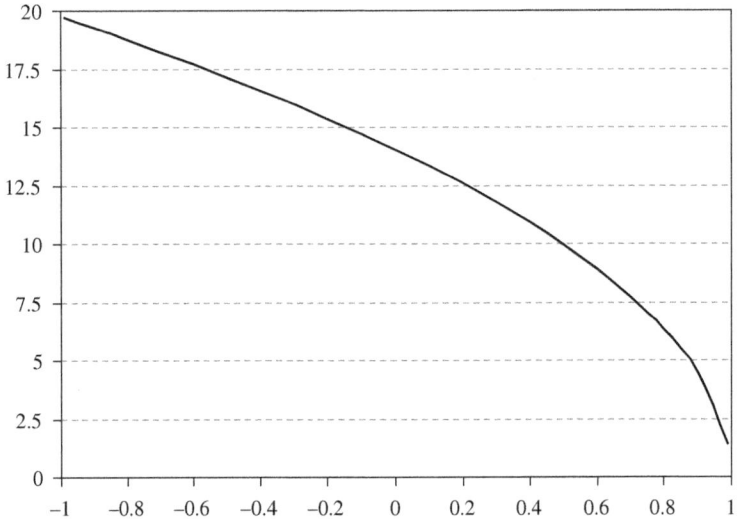

Figure III.3.31   Value of exchange option versus asset's correlation

The exchange option is related to the best-of-two-assets option, with pay-off $\max\left(S_1(T), S_2(T)\right)$ and the worst-of-two-assets option, with pay-off $\min\left(S_1(T), S_2(T)\right)$. With the same notation as above the price of such an option is

$$S_1 \exp(-y_1 T)\Phi(\omega d_1) + S_2 \exp(-y_2 T)\Phi(-\omega d_2), \tag{III.3.99}$$

where $\omega = 1$ for best of two assets and $\omega = -1$ for the worst of two assets.

EXAMPLE III.3.11: OPTIONS ON BEST OF TWO AND WORST OF TWO ASSETS

How much should you pay to receive a pay-off 1 year from now equal to the highest of two assets' prices? And how much should you pay to receive a pay-off equal to the lowest of two asset's prices? Assume that both assets currently have the same price and volatility and that neither asset pays a dividend. Again show how the option's prices depend on the correlation between the two assets.

SOLUTION   As in the previous example we set the current price of both assets equal to 100, so the option values are expressed as a percentage of the asset prices, and their volatilities are set at 25%. Table III.3.10 shows that the difference between the best of and worst of option prices diminishes as the behaviour of the assets becomes more similar, i.e. as the correlation increases. In fact as the correlation approaches $+1$, the prices of both options approach 100, the current value of the assets.

Table III.3.10 Best of/worst of option prices

Correlation	Best	Worst
-0.75	113.4901	81.50986
-0.5	117.1407	82.85931
-0.25	115.6675	84.33249
0	114.0316	85.96838
0.25	112.1675	87.83249
0.5	109.9476	90.05236
0.75	107.0432	92.9568

III.3.9.3 Spread Options

A spread option is an option on the spread between two underlying reference assets or futures. The spread option with maturity T and strike K has pay-off $\max(\omega(S(T) - K), 0)$, where $S(t) = S_1(t) - S_2(t)$ is the spread. And as usual, $\omega = 1$ for a call and $\omega = -1$ for a put. Several types of spread options are actively traded in energy markets:

- *Crack spread options*, where the two underlyings are futures of the same maturity on different energy products. The most common of these are the heating oil–crude oil and the natural gas–crude oil crack spreads which are listed on the NYMEX exchange.

- *Spark spread options*, which are similar to crack spread options but the spread is between the electricity futures and the crude oil futures of the same maturity. These are less liquid than crack spread options, and most of the trading is OTC.

- *Calendar spread options*, where the two assets are futures of different maturities on the same underlying. These are the most actively traded spread options listed on NYMEX.

It is worth noting that these options are of American type, but American spread options on futures have prices that are identical to the corresponding European spread options.[69] A spread option with zero strike is identical to an exchange option. Unfortunately, it is only in that case that we can reduce the dimension of two processes to one. When the spread option strike is not zero there is no exact analytic form for the price. However, a number of analytic approximations have been derived that are based on some form of dimension reduction. For instance, a very simple price approximation is

$$\omega \exp(-rT)\left(F\Phi(\omega d_1) - (M + K)\Phi(\omega d_2)\right) \tag{III.3.100}$$

where

$$d_1 = \frac{\ln(F/(M+K))}{\sigma\sqrt{T}} + \tfrac{1}{2}\sigma\sqrt{T}, \quad d_2 = d_1 - \sigma\sqrt{T},$$

---

[69] See Alexander and Venkatramanan (2007) for the proof.

$$\sigma = (M+S)^{-1}\left(\sigma_1^2 S_1^2 + \sigma_2^2 S_2^2 - 2\varrho\sigma_1\sigma_2 S_1 S_2\right)^{1/2},$$
$$F = (M+S)\exp((y_1 - y_2)T)$$

EXAMPLE III.3.12: PRICING A SPREAD OPTION

As in the previous examples, we set the current price of both assets equal to 100 and their volatilities σ_1 and σ_2 at 25%, assume both the risk free rate and the dividend yields are zero and set the option maturity to be 1 year. But this time we fix the correlation between the two assets at 0.5 and set the strike of the spread to be 10. How does the (*ad hoc*) choice of M in (III.3.100) affect the price of a spread put option?

SOLUTION   The current value of the spread S is zero and Σ is approximately 25%, so we need to set M to be 'very large' compared with 25%. But how large is 'very large'? As a rule of thumb, M needs to be approximately 100 times greater than the maximum of the underlying prices. So in our example, M needs to be about 10,000. Figure III.3.32 shows the value of the spread option as M increases from 100 to 5000. As M increases it appears to converge to a price of approximately 15.7656.

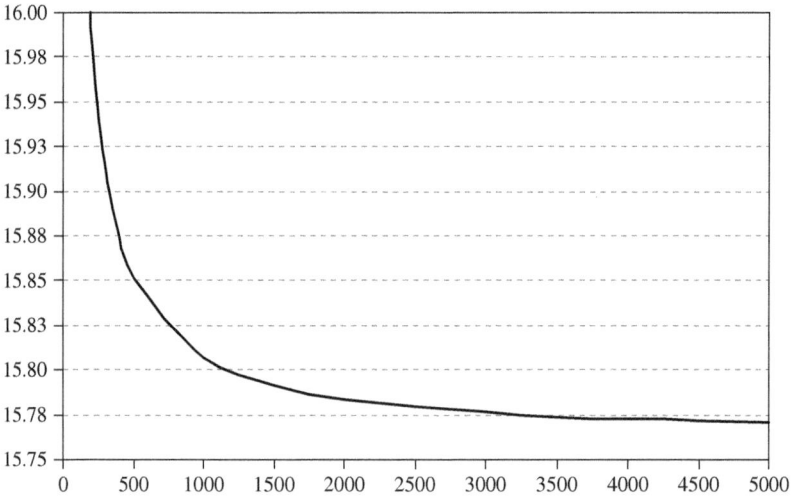

Figure III.3.32   Approximate price for a spread option as a function of M

The *ad hoc* choice of M is not the only problem with this approximation. Another is that traders seek to price spread options consistently with the prices of standard options on the legs of the spread, since this way they can use the spread option as a pure correlation trade. That is, they price a spread option in such a way that σ_1 and σ_2 are the implied volatilities of standard options: one on S_1 with strike K_1 and the other on S_2 with strike K_2, where $K_1 - K_2 = K$. However, there are infinitely many strike pairs $\{K_1, K_2\}$ such that $K_1 - K_2 = K$. Hence, another *ad hoc* choice arises as to which strike pair to choose, and this can have a great effect on the spread option price. This problem, which also arises when using other analytic approximations that are based on dimension reduction, is addressed by Alexander and Venkatramanan (2007), who derive a new analytic formula for pricing spread options that is free of such *ad hoc* choices.

III.3.9.4   Currency Protected Options

Currency protected options are options on foreign assets where the exchange rate risk is borne by the writer of the option. Hence, the buyer has a guaranteed pay-off in domestic currency. There are two types of currency protected options:

- In a *quanto option* the pay-off is calculated at a pre-determined domestic/foreign exchange rate $\overline{X}$: it is $\max\left(\omega\overline{X}\left(S(T)-K\right),0\right)$.

- In a *compo option* the asset price at expiry is translated into the domestic currency using the exchange rate at time T, but the strike is pre-determined in the domestic currency. Its pay-off is therefore $\max\left(\omega(X(T)S(T)-\overline{X}K),0\right)$.

Denote by σ_X and σ_S the volatilities of the exchange rate and the underlying asset respectively, and let ϱ denote their correlation. Then the price of a quanto option is

$$\omega\overline{X}\exp(-r_dT)\left(S\exp(gT)\Phi(\omega d_1)-K\Phi(\omega d_2)\right),$$

$$d_1=\frac{\ln(S/K)+gT}{\sigma_S\sqrt{T}}+\tfrac{1}{2}\sigma_S\sqrt{T},\quad d_2=d_1-\sigma_S\sqrt{T}, \tag{III.3.101}$$

$$g=r_f-y-\varrho\sigma_X\sigma_S,$$

where r_d and r_f are the domestic and foreign continuously compounded risk free rates of maturity T, both assumed constant. The price of a compo option is

$$\omega\exp(-r_dT)\left(XS\exp(gT)\Phi(\omega d_1)-\overline{X}K\Phi(\omega d_2)\right),$$

$$d_1=\frac{\ln(XS/\overline{X}K)+gT}{\sigma\sqrt{T}}+\tfrac{1}{2}\sigma\sqrt{T},\quad d_2=d_1-\sigma\sqrt{T},$$

$$\sigma=\sqrt{\sigma_X^2+\sigma_S^2+2\varrho\sigma_X\sigma_S}, \tag{III.3.102}$$

$$g=r_f-y.$$

where X is the current exchange rate, i.e. at the time the option is priced.

EXAMPLE III.3.13: COMPARISON OF QUANTO AND COMPO OPTION PRICES

Suppose the underlying asset is denominated in foreign currency, that the current asset price is 100 and the asset volatility is 25%. The exchange rate is currently at 1, and has a volatility of 10%. The correlation between the asset and the exchange rate is -0.2 and risk free rates are set to zero in both currencies. How does the price of a quanto put option compare with that of a compo put option? Assume the options have maturity 30 days, $\overline{X}=1.05$ and consider various strikes between 90 and 120.

SOLUTION   Figure III.3.33 shows the option prices as a function of strike: both are increasing with strike since the option is a put, and for every strike the compo price is always greater than the quanto price. By changing the parameters in the spreadsheet readers may verify that, for each strike, the compo put price is greater than (less than) the quanto put price if the fixed exchange rate is greater than (less than) the current exchange rate. The opposite is the case for a call: the compo call price is greater than (less than) the quanto call price of the same strike if the fixed exchange rate is less than (greater than) the current exchange rate.

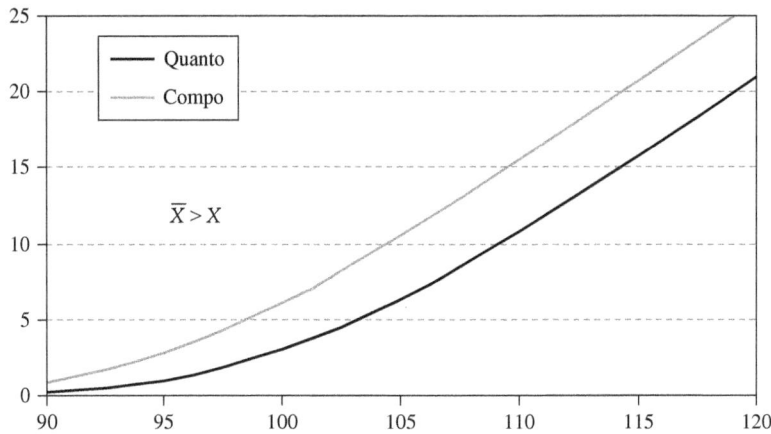

Figure III.3.33   Quanto versus compo put price as a function of strike

III.3.9.5   Power Options

The pay-off to a simple type of power option is $S^n(T)1_{\{S_T \geq K\}}$. The case $n = 0$ corresponds to the simple *binary option*. The price of the option is

$$\exp\left(\left(-r + \tfrac{1}{2}n(n+1)\sigma^2\right)T\right)F^n\Phi(d),$$

$$d = \frac{\ln(F/K)}{\sigma\sqrt{T}} + (n - \tfrac{1}{2})\sigma\sqrt{T}, \tag{III.3.103}$$

$$F = S\exp((r - y)T),$$

but if $n > 0$ this is only an approximation.

EXAMPLE III.3.14: PRICING A POWER OPTION

What is the approximate price of the option that pays the square root of the underlying asset price if that price exceeds 100? Assume the underlying asset is currently at 100 and has a volatility of 25% and that the risk free rate and dividend yield are both zero and the option has maturity 1 year.

SOLUTION   Since $F = S = 100$ and $n = \tfrac{1}{2}$ we have $d = 0$. Since $\Phi(0) = 0.5$ the approximate option price is $\exp\left(\tfrac{1}{2} \times \tfrac{1}{2} \times (\tfrac{1}{2} + 1) \times 0.25^2\right) \times 10 \times 0.5 = 5.1186$.

III.3.9.6   Chooser Options and Contingent Options

In a *chooser option* there is a choice at time T_1 to receive either a call or a put pay-off at time T_2, with $T_2 \geq T_1$. The call and put usually have the same strike, i.e. the pay-off is either $\max(S(T_2) - K, 0)$ or $\max(K - S(T_2), 0)$, depending on whether the call or the put is chosen. The price of the chooser is

$$C(K, T_2) + \exp(-y(T_2 - T_1))P(\exp((y - r)(T_2 - T_1))K, T_1), \tag{III.3.104}$$

where $C(K, T)$ and $P(K, T)$ are the standard BSM prices given by (III.3.65).

EXAMPLE III.3.15: PRICING A CHOOSER OPTION

Calculate the price of a chooser option, where the choice whether to receive a call or put is made 50 days before expiry, and the options mature 1 year from now. As usual, assume the underlying has price 100 and volatility 25%, that the risk free rate and dividends are zero and assume the options' strike is 100. How much does the chooser option's value increase or decrease as the choice time changes?

SOLUTION   The spreadsheet gives the option price as 19.19. With our choice of parameters the call and put options are ATM so the prices of the standard call and put are the same, i.e. 9.9476. However, the reader may easily change the parameters in the spreadsheet. In our case the price of the chooser converges to 9.9476 as the choice time T_1 decreases to zero. As T_1 increases to T_2, the option's maturity, the second term in (III.3.104) converges to $P(K, T_2)$, so the price of the chooser converges to $2 \times 9.9476 = 19.895$.

Figure III.3.34 illustrates the chooser option price as a function of choice time. This graph displays a general feature of chooser options, i.e. that their value decreases non-linearly as the choice time moves closer to the option's expiry date.

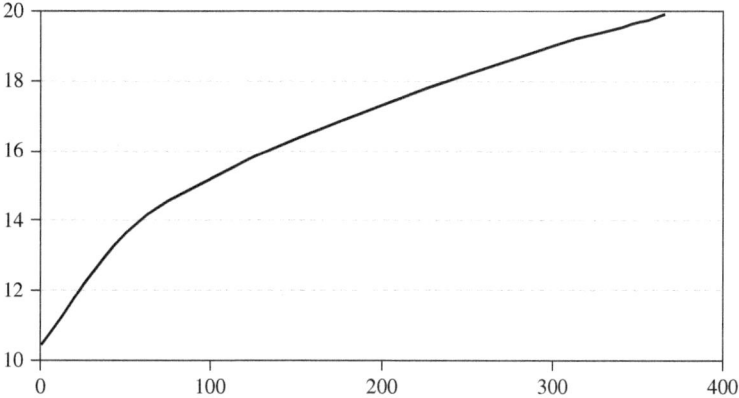

Figure III.3.34   Price of chooser versus choice time

There are many types of contingent options, where the pay-off is contingent on a certain event. A very simple type of contingent option is a standard option with a premium payment at expiry if and only if the option is ITM at expiry, i.e. if and only if $S(T) > K$ for a *contingent call* and if and only if $S(T) < K$ for a *contingent put*. If a fixed premium X has been set the option price is

$$\omega \exp(-rT) \left[F\Phi(\omega d_1) - (K + \omega X)\, \Phi(\omega d_2) \right],$$

$$d_1 = \frac{\ln(F/K)}{\sigma\sqrt{T}} + \tfrac{1}{2}\sigma\sqrt{T}, \quad d_2 = d_1 - \sigma\sqrt{T}, \qquad \text{(III.3.105)}$$

$$F = S \exp((r - y)\, T),$$

with $\omega = 1$ for a call and $\omega = -1$ for a put. At issue the trader writing the option can set the premium by setting this price to zero and backing out the fair value of the premium using a numerical method. In the spreadsheet for the contingent option this can be done using Excel's Goal Seek or Solver.

EXAMPLE III.3.16: FINDING THE FAIR PREMIUM FOR A CONTINGENT OPTION

What is the fair premium to set for a contingent call on the asset with price 100 and volatility 25%? Again set the risk free rate and dividends to zero, and the option to have strike 100 and maturity 1 year.

SOLUTION   In the spreadsheet we use Goal Seek to back out the premium by setting the option price to be zero. This gives 22.09.

III.3.9.7   Compound Options

A compound option is an option on an option. There are four types of compound option: a *call on a call*, a *put on a call*, a *call on a put* and a *put on a put*. Denote by K_1 the strike of the first option, which expires at time T_1, and denote by K_2 the strike of the second option, which expires at time T_2, with $T_2 \geq T_1$. The pay-off is made at time T_1 and refers to the value of the second option at this time. Denote the value of the second option at time T_1 by C_2 if it is a call or P_2 if it is a put. Then we can express the pay-offs as follows:

- compound option on a call, $\max(w(C_2 - K_1), 0)$;
- compound option on a put, $\max(w(P_2 - K_1), 0)$.

The price of a compound option depends on:

- the standard *bivariate* normal distribution function $\Phi(x, y; \varrho)$, where X and Y are standard normal variables with correlation ϱ;
- the underlying price S^* at which the second option has value at time T_1 equal to K_1.

Thus for a compound option on a call we find the price of the underlying S^* at which $C(K_2, T_2) = K_1$; and for a compound option on a put we find the price of the underlying S^* at which $P(K_2, T_2) = K_1$; there is no explicit formula of course, and S^* must be found using a numerical method such as Excel's Goal Seek or Solver.

Now we can express the price of a compound option as

$$\omega_1\omega_2(\exp(-yT_2)S\Phi(\omega_1\omega_2 x_1, \omega_2 y_1; \omega_1\varrho) - \exp(-rT_2)K_2\Phi(\omega_1\omega_2 x_2, \omega_2 y_2; \omega_1\varrho)$$
$$- \exp(-rT_1)K_1\Phi(\omega_1\omega_2 x_2))$$

where $\omega_i = 1$ if the ith option is a call and $\omega_i = -1$ if the ith option is a put, and

$$x_1 = \frac{\ln(F_1/S^*)}{\sigma\sqrt{T_1}} + \tfrac{1}{2}\sigma\sqrt{T_1}, \quad x_2 = x_1 - \sigma\sqrt{T_1},$$

$$y_1 = \frac{\ln(F_2/K_2)}{\sigma\sqrt{T_2}} + \tfrac{1}{2}\sigma\sqrt{T_2}, \quad y_2 = y_1 - \sigma\sqrt{T_2},$$

$$F_i = S\exp((r-y)T_i), \quad i = 1, 2,$$

$$\varrho = \sqrt{T_1/T_2}.$$

III.3.9.8   Capped Options and Ladder Options

A capped option has pay-off equal to that of a standard option but it is limited to a maximum value which is guaranteed as soon as the underlying price touches the cap level H. The pay-offs are:

- *capped call*, $\max\left(S(T) - K, 0\right) 1_{\{M(T)<H\}} + (H - K) 1_{\{M(T)\geq H\}}$,
- *capped put*, $\max\left(K - S(T), 0\right) 1_{\{m(T)>H\}} + (K - H) 1_{\{m(T)\leq H\}}$,

where $M(T)$ is the maximum achieved by the underlying price and $m(T)$ is the minimum achieved by the underlying price at any time on or before expiry.

Let $F = S\exp((r - y)T)$ and write

$$f(X; \omega) = \omega\exp(-rT)\left(F\Phi(\omega d_1) - X\Phi(\omega d_2)\right),$$

$$d_1 = \frac{\ln(F/X)}{\sigma\sqrt{T}} + \tfrac{1}{2}\sigma\sqrt{T}, \quad d_2 = d_1 - \sigma\sqrt{T}. \tag{III.3.106}$$

Also let $\lambda = 2\left(r - y\right)/\sigma^2$ and put $\omega = 1$ for a call and $\omega = -1$ for a put, as usual. Then:

- if $\omega H > \omega K$ and $\omega H > \omega S$ the price of a capped option is

$$f(K; \omega) - f(H; \omega) + \left(\frac{H}{S}\right)^{\lambda+1}\left(f(S^2 H^{-1}; -\omega) - f(K(S/H)^2; -\omega)\right), \tag{III.3.107}$$

- if $\omega H > \omega K$ and $\omega H \leq \omega S$ the price is

$$\omega\exp(-rT)(H - K), \tag{III.3.108}$$

- and if $\omega H \leq \omega K$ the option is worthless.

EXAMPLE III.3.17: PRICING A CAPPED CALL

How does the price of a 1-year capped call with strike 100 on an asset with price 100 and volatility 25% vary with the cap level? Again set the risk free rate and dividend yield to zero.

SOLUTION   If the cap level is at or below the strike of 100 the option has zero value. As the cap level increases the option price converges to the price of a standard call option, as shown in Figure III.3.35.

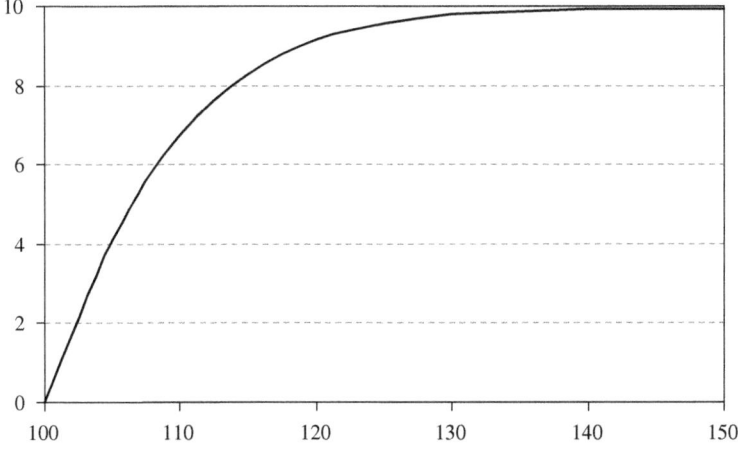

Figure III.3.35   Price of a capped call versus cap level

A more complex capped option is a *ladder option*. Here the pay-off depends on whether the underlying asset price touches one or more 'rungs' in a ladder. We suppose there are n rungs $\{H_1, \ldots, H_n\}$ such that:

- $K = H_0 < H_1 < H_2 < \ldots < H_n$ and H_m is the highest rung touched by a ladder call;
- $K = H_0 > H_1 > H_2 > \ldots > H_n$ and H_m is the lowest rung touched by a ladder put.

Using (III.3.106) we can write the price for the ladder option as:

$$\omega \exp(-rT)(H_m - K) + f(H_m; \omega) + \sum_{i=m+1}^{n} \left(\frac{H_i}{S}\right)^{\lambda+1} \left(f(S^2 H_i^{-1}; -\omega) - f(H_{i-1}(S/H_i)^2; -\omega)\right),$$

$$(III.3.109)$$

where f is given by (III.3.106). Note that the summation term disappears if $m = n$, i.e. if the highest (lowest) rung has been touched in a ladder call (put).

Ladder options with caps are those where the pay-off is guaranteed if the highest (lowest) rung has been touched in a ladder call (put). Their prices are:

$$\text{Ladder call with cap} = \text{Ladder call} - f(H_n; 1),$$

$$\text{Ladder put with cap} = \text{Ladder put} - f(H_n; -1).$$

$$(III.3.110)$$

III.3.9.9   Look-Back and Look-Forward Options

Denote by K the strike of the option and by $m(T)$ (or $M(T)$) the minimum (or maximum) of the underlying price between $t = 0$ and $t = T$. The pay-off functions for European look-back and look-forward options are:

$$\text{Look-back call, } \max(S(T) - m(T), 0);$$

$$\text{Look-back put, } \max(M(T) - S(T), 0);$$

$$\text{Look-forward call, } \max(M(T) - K, 0);$$

$$\text{Look-forward put, } \max(K - m(T), 0).$$

$$(III.3.111)$$

Denote by m (or M) the minimum (or maximum) of the underlying price that has been achieved since the option was written. So when we are pricing a new issue, $m = M = S$, but in general $m \leq S \leq M$. Also set $\lambda = 2(r - y)/\sigma^2$ where σ is the constant volatility in the geometric Brownian motion process for the underlying price, and set

$$d_{1X} = \frac{\ln(F/X)}{\sigma\sqrt{T}} + \tfrac{1}{2}\sigma\sqrt{T}, \quad d_{2X} = d_{1X} - \sigma\sqrt{T}, \quad d_{3X} = d_{1X} - \lambda\sigma\sqrt{T}, \qquad (III.3.112)$$

with $F = S\exp((r - y)T)$.

Assuming $\lambda \neq 0$, the option price is:[70]

$$\exp(-rT)\left(A + \omega_1\left(F\Phi(\omega_1 d_{1X}) - X\Phi(\omega_1 d_{2X}) + \omega_2\lambda^{-1}(F\Phi(\omega_1\omega_2 d_{1X}) - X^\lambda S^{1-\lambda}\Phi(\omega_1\omega_2 d_{3X})))\right)\right)$$

---

[70] Adjustments for the case $\lambda = 0$ are available on request.

where

$\omega_1 = 1$ for a call and $\omega_1 = -1$ for a put;

$\omega_2 = 1$ for a look-forward and $\omega_2 = -1$ for a look-back;

$X = m$ for a look-forward put with $K > m$ or a look-back call;

$X = M$ for a look-forward call with $K < M$ or a look-back put;

$X = K$ otherwise; and

$A = \max(\omega_1(X - K), 0)$ if $\omega_2 = 1$, $A = 0$ otherwise.

EXAMPLE III.3.18: PRICE OF A LOOK-FORWARD PUT

How does the price of a look-forward put option vary with the minimum price achieved so far? Assume the option has 180 days until expiry and strike 100, that the underlying price is currently at 100 and its volatility is 25%, and that the risk free rate is 5%.

SOLUTION   If the minimum price is well below the strike price of 100 the option already has a high intrinsic value. But even when the minimum price achieved so far is 100, the option is more valuable than a standard put option because of the potential for the asset price to fall considerably before the option matures. In our case the standard put option has price 5.76 but the look-forward put has more than double this value, as can be seen in Figure III.3.36.

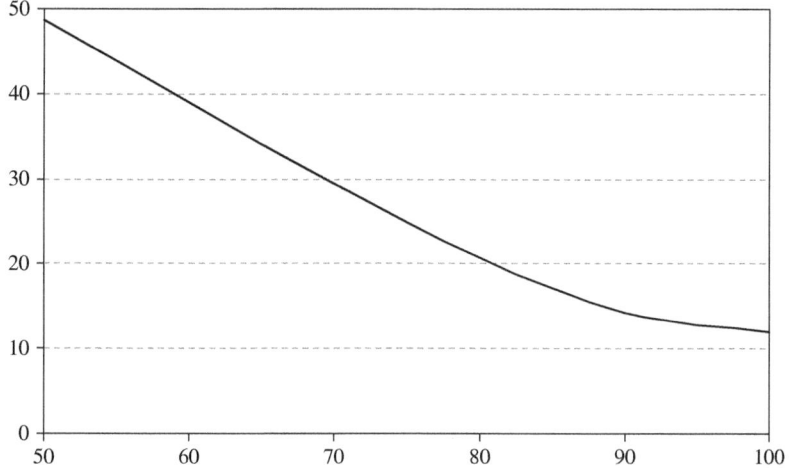

Figure III.3.36   Price of look-forward put option versus minimum price achieved so far

III.3.9.10   Barrier Options

There are two types of single barrier option: *knock-in barriers*, which only pay out if the underlying price has hit a certain barrier level B before expiry, and *knock-out barriers*, which only pay out if the underlying price has *not* hit a the barrier level B before expiry. Clearly the price of a knock-in barrier option price plus the price of the equivalent knock-out barrier option is the price of a standard option. Put another way, with the obvious notation:

$$C_{\text{in}}(K, B, T) + C_{\text{out}}(K, B, T) = C(K, T),$$

$$P_{\text{in}}(K, B, T) + P_{\text{out}}(K, B, T) = P(K, T), \tag{III.3.113}$$

where $C(K, T)$ and $P(K, T)$ are given by (III.3.65). Hence below we only quote the formulae for knock-in barriers, since the prices of the equivalent knock-out barriers follow from this relationship.

We shall consider the following barrier options: *down and in call, down and in put, up and in call, up and in put*. The following notation will be useful:

$$f(a, b, c; \omega) = \omega \exp(-rT) \left(\frac{B}{S}\right)^{2\lambda b} \left(F\Phi(\omega d) - \left(\frac{S}{B}\right)^{2b} K\Phi(\omega(d - \sigma\sqrt{T})) \right), \tag{III.3.114}$$

$$\lambda = \frac{r - y}{\sigma^2} + \frac{1}{2}, \quad d = \frac{a \ln(B/S) + b \ln(B/K) + c \ln(S/B)}{\sigma\sqrt{T}} + \lambda\sigma\sqrt{T}.$$

Down and in barrier options. We assume $S > B$, otherwise the price is equal to the price of a standard option. With f given by (III.3.114), the price of a down and in call is[71]

- $f(1, 1, 0; 1)$ if $K \geq B$,
- $f(0, 0, 1; 1) - f(0, 1, 0; 1)$ if $K < B$.

The price of a down and in put is

- $f(1, 1, 0; 1) + f(0, 0, 1; -1) - f(0, 1, 0; 1)$ if $K > B$,
- the same as that of a standard put if $K \leq B$.

Up and in barrier options. We assume $S < B$, otherwise the price is equal to the price of a standard option. With f given by (III.3.114) the price of an up and in put is

- $f(1, 1, 0; -1)$ if $K \leq B$,
- $f(0, 0, 1; -1) - f(0, 1, 0; -1)$ if $K > B$.

The price of an up and in call is

- $f(1, 1, 0; -1) + f(0, 0, 1; 1) - f(0, 1, 0; -1)$ if $K < B$,
- the same as that of a standard call if $K \geq B$.

EXAMPLE III.3.19: PRICES OF UP AND IN AND UP AND OUT BARRIER CALLS

Find the price of a 1-year up and in barrier call option with strike 100 and barrier 110 if the underlying is at 100 and has volatility 25%. Assume the risk free rate is zero and the underlying pays no dividends. How is this related to the corresponding up and out barrier call?

---

[71] These formulae are exact, but in practice the contracts have many specific conditions for hitting the barrier, and those conditions are not included here.

SOLUTION   Since the strike and current S are both less than the barrier level, we price the option by calculating $f(1, 1, 0; -1) + f(0, 0, 1; 1) - f(0, 1, 0; -1)$ with f given by (III.3.114). These values are given in the spreadsheet as

$$f(1, 1, 0; -1) = 3.1945, \quad f(0, 0, 1; 1) = 9.2539, \quad f(0, 1, 0; -1) = 2.5642.$$

The up and in barrier call price is thus 9.8842. Since the standard call price is 9.9476 the corresponding up and out call is only worth $9.9476 - 9.8842 = 0.0635$.

The high price of the up and in call and low price of the up and out call in this example reflect that fact that, with 1 year to expiry, the underlying has a very high chance of touching the barrier. The reader can verify that reducing the option's maturity increases the value of the up and out call and reduces that of the up and in call. However, the behaviour of a barrier option price with respect to maturity is not always monotonic. For instance, an up and out call tends to increase as the option maturity decreases because there is less chance that the option price will hit the barrier – but this effect is offset by the fact that standard option values increase with maturity. Figure III.3.37 shows the price of an up and out barrier option as a function of the option maturity.

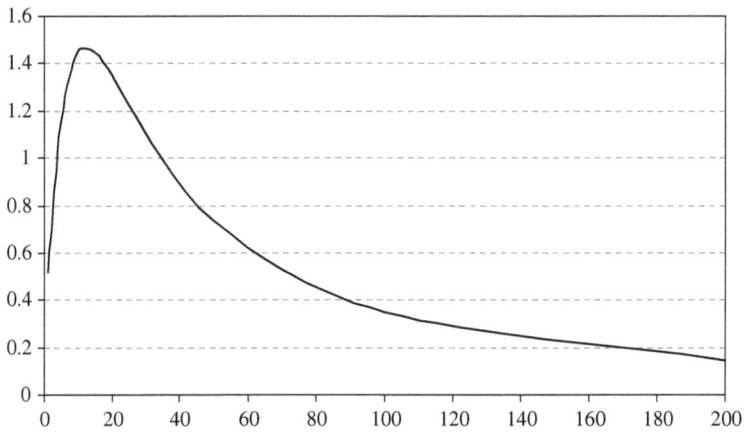

Figure III.3.37   Up and out barrier call price with respect to maturity

III.3.9.11   Asian Options

An Asian option is an option with an average strike, or based on an average price. There are four types of Asian options according to whether the average is geometric or arithmetic and depending on whether the average is for the value of the underlying (an *average price option*) or for the value of the strike (an *average strike option*). We use the following notation:

- The strike or forward price is some fraction π of the average price of the underlying, with $0 \leq \pi \leq 1$.
- Averages on the underlying price are taken on specified dates, at some specific points in time between time T_1 and time T_2, with $T_1 < T_2 \leq T$ where T is the maturity of the option.
- The averages on the underlying price are denoted G_{T_1,T_2} for a geometric average and A_{T_1,T_2} for an arithmetic average.

- $\lambda = T_2 / (T_2 - T_1)$; also for an average *price* option we set $T_2 = T$, noting that if $T_2 < T$ the average price has already been fixed by the time the option expires and the option pay-off can be calculated exactly.
- The growth rate on the asset is $g = r - y$.

Now we can define the pay-offs as:

$$\text{geometric average price option, } \max\left(\omega(\pi G(T_1, T_2) - K), 0\right),$$

$$\text{arithmetic average price option, } \max(\omega(\pi A(T_1, T_2) - K), 0),$$

$$\text{geometric average strike option, } \max\left(\omega(S_T - \pi G(T_1, T_2)), 0\right),$$

$$\text{arithmetic average strike option, } \max\left(\omega(S_T - \pi A(T_1, T_2)), 0\right),$$

where $\omega = 1$ for a call and $\omega = -1$ for a put. In each case we can express the approximate price as[72]

$$\omega \exp(-rT) \left(F\Phi(\omega d_1) - K\Phi(\omega d_2)\right), \tag{III.3.115}$$

where

$$d_1 = \frac{\ln(F/K)}{\sigma\sqrt{T^*}} + \tfrac{1}{2}\sigma\sqrt{T^*} \text{ and } d_2 = d_1 - \sigma\sqrt{T^*}. \tag{III.3.116}$$

The precise definition of F, K and T^* in the above formulae depends on the type of option and whether or not averaging has already begun. In the following we deal with several different cases separately.

Average price options

Here K is the ordinary option strike and

$$T^* = \begin{cases} \dfrac{2T_1 + T}{3}, & \text{if averaging has not started,} \\[2ex] \dfrac{T^3}{3(T - T_1)^2}, & \text{if averaging has started.} \end{cases} \tag{III.3.117}$$

The forward value F depends on the type of averaging:

(a) Geometric average
  If the averaging period has not yet begun,

$$F = \pi S \exp\left(\tfrac{1}{2}\left[(g - \tfrac{1}{2}\sigma^2)(T^* + T) + v_m^2\right]\right).$$

But if averaging has begun (i.e. $T_1 < 0$) and G is the value of the average so far,

$$F = \pi G^{(1-\lambda)} S^\lambda \exp\left(\tfrac{1}{2}\left[\lambda T(g - \tfrac{1}{2}\sigma^2) + v_m^2\right]\right).$$

(b) Arithmetic average
  If the averaging period has not yet begun

$$F = \pi S \exp(gT_1)(\exp(g(T - T_1)) - 1)/g(T - T_1).$$

---

[72] The approximation is necessary because these pricing formulae assume continuous or near continuous (e.g. daily) averaging between time T_1 and time T_2. The approximations to the *arithmetic* average option prices are the most approximate, because they are based on only a first order approximation to the price.

But if averaging has begun (i.e. $T^* < 0$) and A is the value of the average so far,

$$F = \pi \left[(1 - \lambda) A + \lambda S (\exp(gT) - 1) / g (T - T_1) \right].$$

Average strike options

The value F in (III.3.115) and (III.3.116) is just S, the current price of the underlying, and

$$T^* = \begin{cases} \dfrac{T - (T_1 + 2T_2)}{3}, & \text{if averaging has not yet started,} \\[2ex] T - \dfrac{2T_2 + T_1 - T_1^3(T_2 - T_1) - 2}{3}, & \text{if averaging has started but not finished,} \\[2ex] T, & \text{if averaging has finished.} \end{cases}$$

$$\text{(III.3.118)}$$

But the definition of the average strike K depends on the averaging as follows:

(a) Geometric average
   If the averaging period has not yet begun,

$$K = \pi S \exp\left(-\tfrac{1}{2} \left[\left(g + \tfrac{1}{2}\sigma^2\right)\left(T - \tfrac{1}{2}(T_1 + T_2)\right) - v_m^2 \right]\right).$$

But if averaging has begun (i.e. $T_1 < 0$) but is not completed and G is the value of the average so far, then

$$K = \pi G^{(1-\lambda)} S^\lambda \exp\left(-\tfrac{1}{2} \left[\left(g + \tfrac{1}{2}\sigma^2\right)\left(2T(T_2 - T_1)^{-1} - T_2^2\right) - v_m^2 \right]\right);$$

and if averaging has been completed (i.e. $T_2 < 0$) and G is the value of the average, then

$$K = \pi G \exp(-gT).$$

(b) Arithmetic average
   If the averaging period has not yet begun,

$$K = \pi S \exp(-g (T - T_2))(\exp(g(T_2 - T_1)) - 1) / g(T_2 - T_1).$$

But if averaging has begun (i.e. $T_1 < 0$) but is not completed and A is the value of the average so far, then

$$K = \pi (\lambda S + (1 - \lambda) A) \exp(-gT)\left(\exp(gT_2^2 / (T_2 - T_1)) - 1\right) / \left(gT_2^2 / (T_2 - T_1)\right);$$

and if averaging has been completed (i.e. $T_2 < 0$) and A is the value of the average, then

$$K = \pi A \exp(-gT).$$

The next examples are only two of many possible Asian options that can be priced using the formulae above. As with all the examples in this section, the spreadsheet can be used to price numerous variations on exotic options.

EXAMPLE III.3.20: PRICING A GEOMETRIC AVERAGE PRICE OPTION

Find the price of a geometric average price call option with 200 days remaining until expiry. Averaging began when the option was written 165 days ago, the average price so far is 100 and the forward price is 100% of this average. The current price of the underlying is also 100, as is the option strike, the volatility is 25% and the risk free rate is zero.

SOLUTION   The spreadsheet gives the option price as 2.4834. This is less expensive than a similar standard call option: with 200 days to expiry and strike 100 the standard call has value 7.3722.

EXAMPLE III.3.21: PRICING AN ARITHMETIC AVERAGE STRIKE OPTION

Find the price of an arithmetic average strike put option with 200 days remaining until expiry. Averaging began when the option was written 165 days ago, the average price so far is 100 and the average strike is 90% of this average. The current price of the underlying is also 100 the volatility is 25% and the risk free rate is zero.

SOLUTION   The spreadsheet gives the option price as 4.9334. This is more expensive than an equivalent standard put option: with 200 days to expiry and strike 90 the standard put has value 3.1046.

III.3.10   SUMMARY AND CONCLUSIONS

This chapter provides a comprehensive introduction to the pricing, hedging and trading of options. We have assumed not only that interest rates and dividend yields are non-stochastic, but also that volatility is constant, leaving until the next chapter the interesting subject of option pricing when volatility is *not* constant. In this chapter we have focused on the practical implementation of the concepts, using plenty of numerical examples and, whilst maintaining mathematical rigour, we avoid complex technical details where possible.

The chapter opens with a (relatively) non-technical discussion of the fundamental concepts for option pricing, including *Brownian motion, measure* and *numeraire*. We introduce the concepts of *hedging* and *no arbitrage pricing* that lay the foundations for the *risk neutral valuation principle*. When perfect hedging is possible options are priced under the *risk neutral measure*. The *fundamental theorem of arbitrage* implies that, in a *complete market*, all risk neutral investors have the same risk neutral measure for each asset. Of course, investors may have different risk attitudes, but risk attitude does not enter into the pricing of an option that can be perfectly hedged.

In a complete, no arbitrage market we price options under the unique risk neutral measure. Another argument that can be used to support the principle of risk neutral pricing is the ability to construct a *replicating portfolio* which is a *self-financing* portfolio containing the underlying asset and a bond in a complete, no arbitrage economy. Although the market prices of liquid options are set by supply and demand, in illiquid markets – and in OTC markets in particular – option prices are set equal to the set-up cost of the replicating portfolio with an add-on for the trader's premium and to cover the credit risk capital reserves.

Standard European and American calls and puts, which we call *vanilla options*, are the most commonly traded options. These are elementary options because they may be used to replicate any pay-off profile. A fundamental *put–call parity* relationship relates the prices of European calls and puts and, since the price of an American option is never less than its European counterpart, the put–call parity relationship can be used to derive lower bounds for the American option price. The *early exercise boundary* gives a range for the underlying price S for which it is optimal to exercise an American option early. This is related to the dividends on S and the risk free interest rate. American calls on non-dividend paying assets should never be exercised early, and as the dividend yield increases from zero so does the likelihood of early exercise. Early exercise for an American put is possible provided the risk free rate is positive, and becomes more likely when dividends are low.

The major *risk factors* of an option are the price of the underlying and its volatility. Secondary risk factors include interest rates, dividend yields or net carry costs, and time. Multi-asset options such as basket options or spread options also have correlation between two underlying prices as a risk factor. The *hedge ratios* of an option are its sensitivities to changes in risk factors: the *delta* and *gamma* are the first and second order price sensitivities and the *vega* and *volga* are the first and second order volatility sensitivities. Other Greeks represent sensitivities to minor risk factors and factor combinations, such as the second order price–volatility sensitivity *vanna*. Other cross-sensitivities may be used when the option relates to multiple assets (e.g. a spread option).

An option's *position Greeks* are used to hedge the option against movements in the underlying risk factors, and the most important risk factors to hedge against are the underlying price and its volatility. Simple linear algebra is used to derive the quantities of other options on the underlying needed to gamma–vega hedge the option or, more generally, to form a *gamma–vega–vanna–volga–theta–rho* neutral portfolio of options. Then we find the quantity of the underlying asset to buy or sell to make this portfolio *delta neutral*.

Trading strategies that reflect the investor's views about the future evolution of asset prices can be constructed by forming simple portfolios of options on the same underlying asset. Some of these strategies, such as *bull, bear* or *ratio spreads* and *collars*, are directional bets and others, such as *straddles, strangles, butterflies* and *condors*, are bets on the volatility of the underlying.

The Black–Scholes–Merton (BSM) model assumes that the underlying price process is a *geometric Brownian motion* with constant volatility. A consequence of this assumption is that the log returns on the underlying have a normal distribution, or equivalently that the underlying price has a *lognormal distribution*. The BSM model also assumes that markets are *complete* (i.e. that one can replicate the value of any claim by trading the underlying and a risk free asset) and *frictionless* (i.e. that it is possible to buy and sell any amount at any time without incurring transactions costs). The *BSM partial derivative equation* can be applied to find the price of any contingent claim, but the celebrated *Black–Scholes–Merton pricing formula* only applies to the special case of a standard European call or put option.

Since the market prices of any liquid option are set by supply and demand, the Black–Scholes–Merton model merely provides a translation of the market price into the *market implied volatility* of the option. This is the (constant) volatility of the price process that is consistent with the observed market price of the option. If traders believed in the BSM model assumptions the implied volatility would be the same for every option on the same underlying. The empirical fact that the implied volatility is *not* constant shows that traders and investors do not believe in the BSM assumptions. In particular, they do not believe that the underlying price process is a geometric Brownian motion with constant volatility. For this reason, if they need to use a model to price an option they will not use the BSM model or, if they do, they will adjust the BSM price to reflect their uncertainty about the model, especially to reflect their belief that the volatility is not constant.

It is easy to use the Black–Scholes–Merton formula to derive analytic expressions for the delta, gamma and other Greeks of standard European calls and puts. We have provided examples of computing the BSM Greeks and have used these to derive hedged portfolios containing several options and the underlying asset. More generally, the Greeks of other options, or the Greeks of European calls and puts that are priced using a different pricing model, are estimated using finite difference methods.

The most commonly traded interest rate options are options on a sequence of forward rates (*caps* and *floors*) and options to enter a swap (*swaptions*). If these options are of European type then a version of the BSM formula applies. However, it is more realistic to price interest rate options using a *short rate model*, or an interest rate option pricing model with two or more stochastic factors. This is because interest rates are not well represented by a geometric Brownian motion with constant volatility. In particular, most models assume the instantaneous spot rate is a *mean-reverting, heteroscedastic process*.

Many interest rate options are *American*, so they can be exercised at any time. These options can be priced using their relationship with the price of their European counterpart. For instance, we can use an approximation to the *early exercise premium*, or calculate this using numerical integration. However, Bermudan options, which can be exercised on several fixed dates prior to expiry, are more difficult to price and there is an active market in *Bermudan swaptions*. The pricing and hedging of these options, and the risk management of most interest rate option portfolios today, is usually set in the framework of a multivariate forward rate model called the *LIBOR model*. This model is easier to calibrate than many other interest rate models because it is based on observable forward rates (often LIBOR rates) rather an unobservable instantaneous spot or forward rates. We have provided a case study that illustrates the calibration methodology.

It is usually possible to price a European-type exotic option under the assumption that the underlying asset(s) follow geometric Brownian motions with constant volatility. Sometimes approximate formulae are required, such as for *Asian options* where the pay-off depends on an average of the underlying prices prior to expiry, and for *spread options* with non-zero strike where the option relates to more than two underlying assets. Under the correlated geometric Brownian motions assumption we have provided pricing formulae for European exotic options, including *barriers, Asians, look-backs, spreads, choosers, exchange options, ladders* and *currency protected options*. The formulae have been implemented in interactive Excel spreadsheets, despite being extremely complex in some cases. VBA code has not been used so that the formulae are completely transparent for teaching purposes.

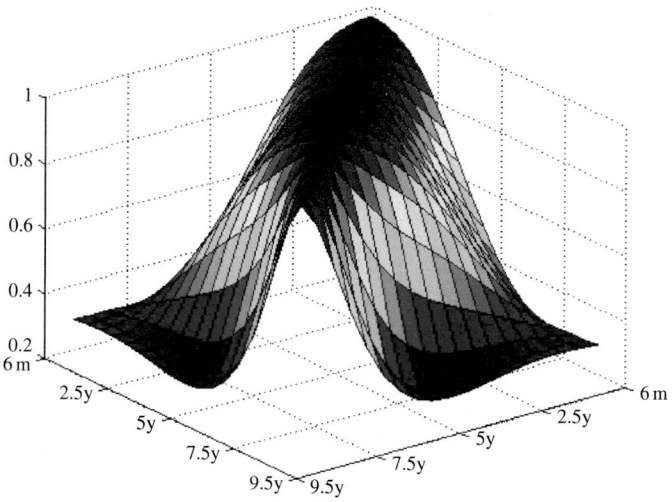

Plate 1 Forward rate correlation estimates (Svensson model). (See Figure III.1.16)

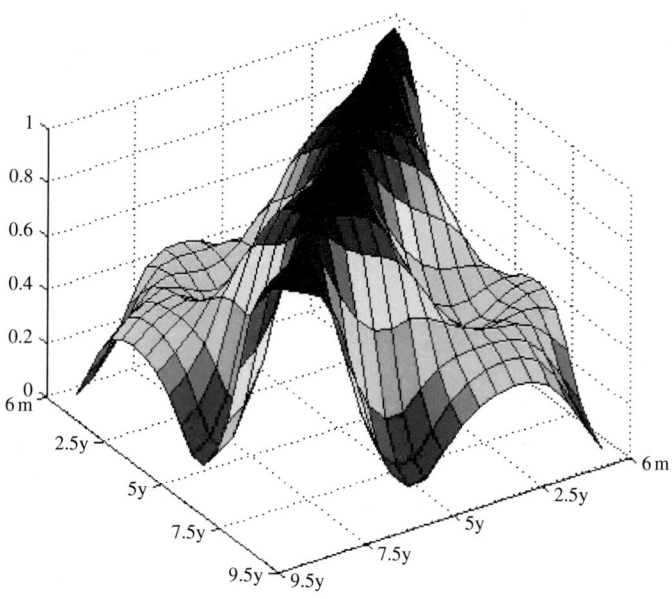

Plate 2 Forward rate correlation estimates (B-spline model). (See Figure III.1.17)

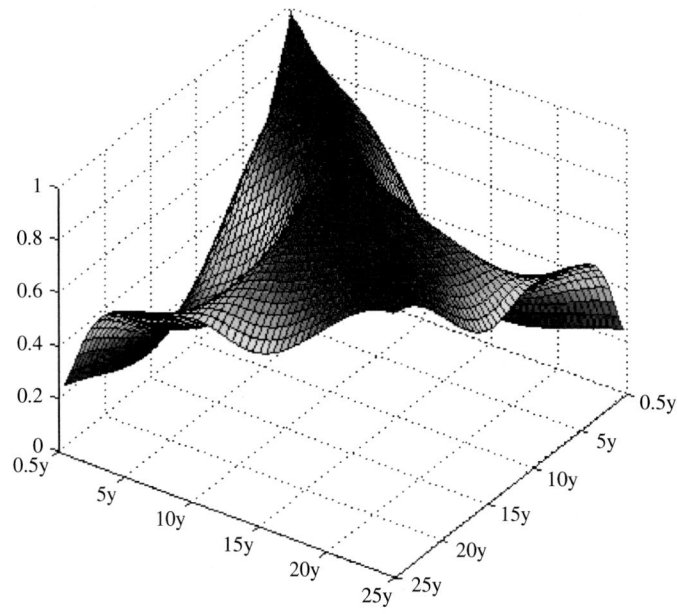

Plate 3 Bank of England forward curve – correlations. (See Figure III.1.19)

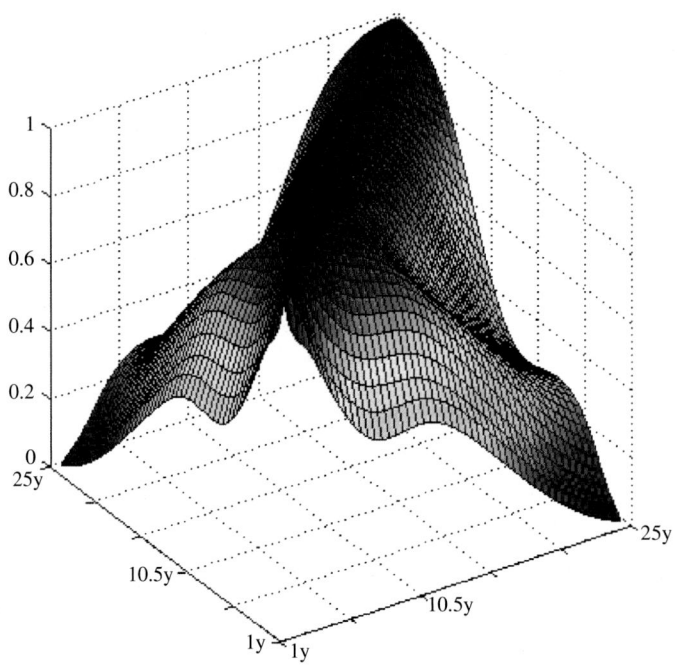

Plate 4 Forward rate historical correlations. (See Figure III.3.28)

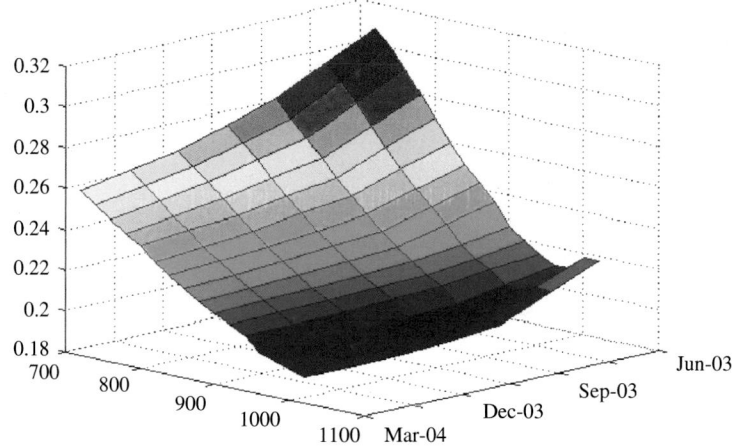

Plate 5 S&P 500 Implied volatility surface. (See Figure III.4.6)

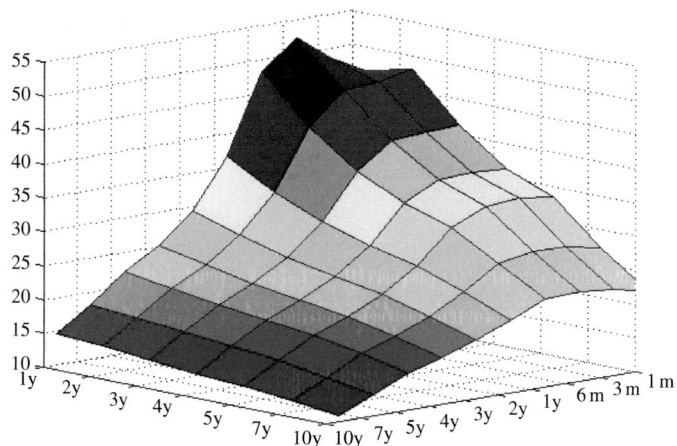

Plate 6 A swaption volatility surface. (See Figure III.4.7)

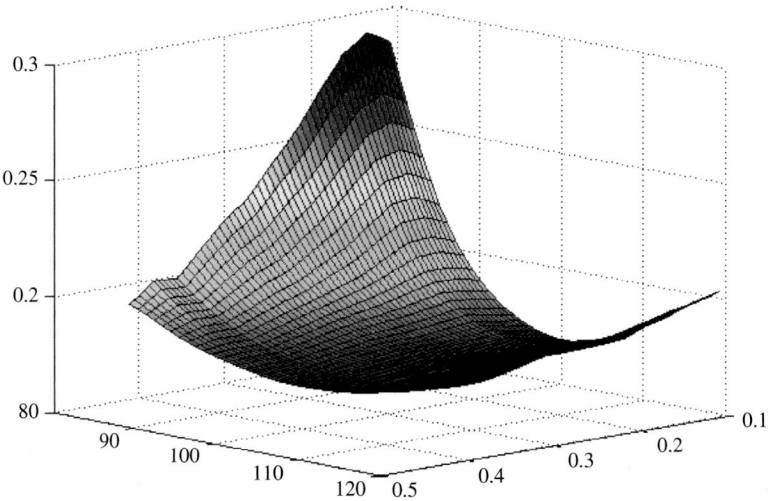

Plate 7 Implied volatility surface for the option prices in Table III.4.4 (the horizontal axes here are strike K (84–120) and maturity T (40–150 days)). (See Figure III.4.8)

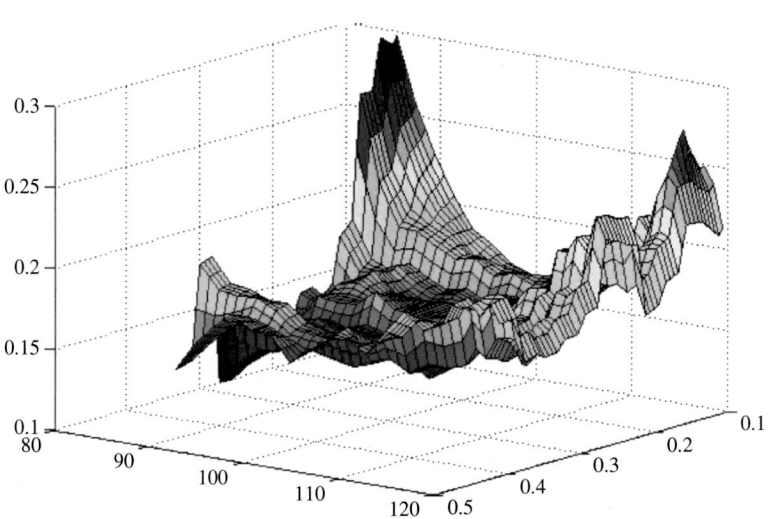

Plate 8 Local volatility surface for the option prices in Table III.4.4 (the horizontal axes here are price S (84–120) and future time t (40–150 days)). (See Figure III.4.9)

III.4

Volatility

III.4.1 INTRODUCTION

A set of standard European options of different strikes and maturities on the same underlying has two related volatility surfaces: the implied volatility surface and the local volatility surface. When we use the market prices of options to derive these surfaces we call them the *market implied volatility* surface and the *market local volatility* surface. When we use option prices based on a stochastic volatility model we call them the *model implied volatility* surface and the *model local volatility* surface.[1]

Implied volatility is a transformation of a standard European option price. It is the volatility that, when input into the Black–Scholes–Merton (BSM) formula, yields the price of the option. In other words, it is the constant volatility of the underlying process that is implicit in the price of the option. For this reason some authors refer to implied volatility as *implicit volatility*.

The BSM *model* implied volatilities are constant. And if the assumptions of the BSM model were valid then all options on the same underlying would have the same *market* implied volatility. However, traders do not believe in these assumptions, hence the market prices of options yield a surface of market implied volatilities, by strike (or moneyness) and maturity of the option, that is *not* flat. In particular, the market implied volatility of all options of the same maturity but different strikes has a skewed smile shape when plotted as a function of the strike (or moneyness) of the options. This is called the (market) *volatility smile*. And the market implied volatility of all options of the same strike (or moneyness) but different maturities converges to the long term implied volatility when plotted as a function of maturity. This is called the (market) *term structure* of implied volatility.

An implied volatility is a deterministic function of the price of a standard European option (the transformation that is implicitly specified by the BSM formula). Thus a dynamic model of implied volatility is also a dynamic model of the option price and hedge ratios. If we can forecast market implied volatility successfully then we can also forecast the market price of the option and hedge the option accurately. Hence, practitioners spend considerable resources on developing models of market implied volatility dynamics.

The BSM model assumes that volatility is constant. But volatility changes stochastically over time. Since the early 1990s a huge number of *stochastic volatility* models have been developed in the academic literature, but many practitioners (perhaps even most, currently) employ the model of Heston (1993) because it is relatively easy to calibrate. The parameters of a stochastic volatility model are calibrated to the market implied volatility surface, since the aim of these models is to price exotic options consistently with the market prices of

---

[1] When we use the term *implied volatility* without prefixing it with 'market' or 'model' we refer to the market implied volatility. Similarly, the term *local volatility* without the 'market' or 'model' prefix refers to the market local volatility.

standard European options. Hence, the *model* implied volatility surface should be very close to the market implied volatility surface at the time of calibration. However, the *dynamics* of the model implied volatility surface that are predicted by the model may be quite different from the empirical dynamics of the market implied volatility surface. It is important to choose a stochastic volatility model that has intuitive and realistic dynamics for its implied volatility surface, otherwise the model's delta and gamma will be highly inaccurate. However, in this chapter we shall prove that this is virtually impossible in some markets, such as equities.

Dupire (1994) pioneered an alternative approach to pricing exotic options consistently with market prices of standard European options. He proved that for every set of market prices for options on the same underlying there is a unique *market local volatility* surface that 'locks in' the forward volatilities associated with these prices in the same way that forward interest rates are 'locked in' by the market prices of fixed income securities. As we mentioned above, there are two volatility surfaces associated with a set of market (or model) option prices on a given underlying – the implied volatility surface and the local volatility surface – and each surface can be transformed into the other. We use the BSM equation to transform option prices into implied volatilities, but we use *Dupire's equation* to transform the prices of all the options on the same underlying into a *local volatility* surface. This surface is a 'dual' of the implied volatility surface, in the sense that each surface can be derived from the other, via integration or differentiation.

There is no doubt that the empirical behaviour of the underlying asset price, and of the market option price, depends on the asset class. For instance, a negative volatility skew, where the implied volatility is much higher for low strike options than it is for high strike options, is most pronounced in short term equity options. As a result of this skew, the market implied risk neutral measure for log returns that is derived from option prices, using the Breeden and Litzenberger (1978) result, will be highly non-normal. However, by the central limit theorem, if the log returns on the underlying are drawn from an independent and identically distributed (i.i.d.) process, the distribution of h-period log returns will converge quite rapidly to the normal distribution. Under the i.i.d. assumption a negative skew should not be evident in options of longer maturities. But it is. Hence, log returns are not i.i.d. and one of the reasons for this is that their volatility is not constant.[2]

Currency options have fairly symmetric smiles (or, put another way, log returns on forex positions have fairly symmetrical distributions) and again the smile persists into very long maturities, contradicting the i.i.d. log returns assumption that leads to the central limit theorem. In this case it is not only stochastic (or at least non-constant) volatility that induces a long term smile, but also stochastic interest rates. Commodity options sometimes have negative skews and sometimes positive skews, interest rate options appear to have negative skews but volatility options (of which we shall learn more in this chapter) may have positive skews, and in these cases the underlying prices may even be mean reverting processes. And structured products can have underlyings with more or less any type of distributional characteristics.

This diversity of characteristics by asset class has motivated some practitioners to adopt what they call a *building block* approach but which I call the *Heath Robinson* approach

---

[2] Their skewness and kurtosis are also not constant. See Alexander and Lazar (2008).

to option pricing.[3] For instance, to price an option on a volatility index such as the Vix option, a trader might take a mean-reverting arithmetic jump volatility process that itself has a geometric stochastic volatility (a stochastic 'vol-of-vol'), and calibrate the parameters so as to match the model implied volatility characteristics with the empirically observed characteristics of the market implied volatility of the Vix. The Heath Robinson approach does, of course, entail many parameters and *any* model with many parameters can fit more or less anything, irrespective of the characteristics of the process. The problem is that the Heath Robinson approach is lacking a general framework; the choice of mean-reversion/price jumps/volatility jumps/arithmetic/geometric/stochastic vol-of-vol/etc., is completely *ad hoc*. In short, we learn nothing of theoretical value from this approach; we just end up with a model that seems to fit the market data reasonable well. However, Carr et al. (2007) and Eberlein and Madan (2008) have recently introduced a generalized approach to option pricing, using a process from the class of *Sato processes* for the underlying price. Using such a process they are able to fit an implied volatility surface that has empirical characteristics of virtually any type, using only four parameters![4]

With so many different option pricing models it has been difficult to draw conclusions about which model is best for hedging. However, recently Alexander and Nogueira (2007a) showed that any stochastic volatility and/or jump process that is appropriate for pricing options on tradable assets must have a *scale invariant* property. That is, the model's option price scales with the units of price measurement, and the model's implied and local volatilities remain invariant under a change of scale in the price dimension. As a corollary they showed that all the price sensitivities of virtually any contingent claim are identical; that is, it does not matter which stochastic volatility and/or jump model is used, the price sensitivities of a standard European option, a barrier option, an Asian option or virtually any other traded option are *model free*.[5] Since we must use some form of scale invariant pricing model for options on a tradable asset, the only differences between the deltas and gammas of two competing models are empirical; that is, differences in hedge ratios from different models arise only because the models do not fit the market data equally well!

The price of an option depends primarily on the price of the underlying and the implied volatility, so an option trade is a trade on both. Certain trading strategies, such as an at-the-money (ATM) straddle, attempt to isolate the volatility component so that the trade is sensitive only to this and not to the underlying price. But trading options is an expensive way to trade volatility. For this reason the Chicago Board Options Exchange (CBOE) in the US

---

[3] William Heath Robinson (1872–1944) was a British artist with a penchant for drawing improbable inventions and machines; machines which work even though they are simply propped up with anything useful that comes to hand. A 'Heath Robinson invention' is, to my mind, an invention that works remarkably well, even though it is not built on sound engineering principles.

[4] A *Sato process* is a self-similar, additive process. Self-similar processes are continuous processes corresponding to the stable laws that were introduced in Section I.3.3.11. More precisely, $S(t)$ is a self-similar process if and only if $S(at)$ has the same distribution as $a^\gamma S(t)$ for all $a > 0$, and some $\gamma \geq 0$. To understand the importance of Sato processes, note that the normal distribution is not the only limit law distribution, i.e. it is not the *only* distribution that can be obtained when we sum up independent variables. If the variables are identically distributed their limiting distribution is indeed normal (this is the central limit theorem). However, suppose they are not identically distributed but still independent, and we sum up a finite number n of such random variables, obtaining a random variable S_n. If there are scaling constants a_n and b_n such that the random variable $X_n = a_n S_n + b_n$ converges in distribution to that of a random variable X as $n \to \infty$, then X is a *class L* random variable, and its distribution is a *limit law distribution*. Sato (1991) showed that X is *class L* if and only if X is *self-decomposable*, i.e. X has the same distribution as $cX + Z^c$, for any constant c, with $0 < c < 1$ and Z^c being independent of X. Such random variables are *infinitely divisible* (i.e. they have the same distribution as a sum of i.i.d. variables) and they also have unimodal distributions, hence class L (i.e. self-decomposable) random variables make an ideal choice for modelling log returns. Self-similar, additive processes are called Sato processes because it was Sato who proved that such processes have self-decomposable laws (and self-decomposable laws have self-similar, additive processes).

[5] The only exception being options, if they exist, whose pay-off functions are not homogeneous of some degree in the price dimension.

and Eurex in Europe now trade futures on volatility indices on several major international stock indices. A *volatility index* of maturity T is a single number that represents an average implied volatility over the whole smile of maturity T. Under standard assumptions on underlying price dynamics it is equal to the *variance swap* rate of maturity T. Variance swaps have been actively traded in over-the-counter (OTC) markets for over a decade, but the only way to trade a volatility index is to buy all the options used to construct it. However, futures on 30-day volatility indices have been traded on the exchanges since 2003, and in 2006 the CBOE also introduced European options on the 30-day S&P 500 volatility index, the Vix.

The major aims of this chapter are to:

- explain how to model the market implied and market local volatility surfaces;
- discuss the properties of model implied and model local volatility surfaces;
- introduce several stochastic volatility and jump models and explain why they should be scale invariant, for pricing options on tradable assets;
- explain why it does not matter which scale invariant model we use for dynamic delta–gamma hedging of virtually any claim;
- introduce minimum variance hedge ratios, and consider whether they are also model free;
- show how to construct an implied volatility index and describe their empirical characteristics;
- describe the market and the characteristics of variance swaps, volatility futures and volatility options.

The outline of this chapter is as follows. Section III.4.2 introduces market implied volatility and describes its characteristics, and Section III.4.3 introduces market local volatility and its relationship with market implied volatility. Here we also discuss the use of parametric deterministic volatility functions for pricing and hedging options. Section III.4.4 presents a long case study, which develops a dynamic model of the market implied volatility surface based on principal component analysis and uses this to estimate price hedge ratios that are adjusted for implied volatility dynamics.

Section III.4.5 provides a brief overview of stochastic volatility models. After deriving the stochastic volatility partial differential equation (PDE) and interpreting the variance risk premium as the market price of volatility risk, we explain how to derive the model implied and local volatility surfaces corresponding to any stochastic volatility model. Thereafter we describe several stochastic volatility models in detail, discussing their characteristics and their applications to options pricing and, in Section III.4.6, to hedging. Section III.4.6 includes a discussion of the implications of scale invariance for hedging options, advocating the use of *minimum variance hedge ratios* instead of the standard 'Merton' partial derivatives. All sensible models for tradable assets are scale invariant and hence have the same Merton delta and gamma, but the minimum variance hedge ratios are not the same as the Merton hedge ratios when volatility is correlated with the underlying price. Minimum variance hedging is shown to improve the hedging performance, compared with the use of Merton hedge ratios, when volatility is stochastic and correlated with the underlying price.

Section III.4.7 introduces variance and volatility swaps, the use of variance swaps for pure volatility trades, and the behaviour of the variance risk premium. Then we explain how to construct a volatility index term structure using as an example the Vftse, a volatility index that is not currently quoted on any exchange. The strange relationship between a volatility index and its futures contract is explained and we finish the section with some remarks on the pricing of Vix options. Section III.4.8 summarizes and concludes.

III.4.2   IMPLIED VOLATILITY

The *market implied volatility* of a standard European option, or just the *implied volatility* for short, is the volatility of the underlying that gives the market price of the option when used in the Black–Scholes–Merton formula. If put – call parity holds on market prices then a call and a put of the same strike and maturity will have the same implied volatility.[6] Hence, in this chapter we shall denote the market implied volatility of a call option *or* a put option with strike K and maturity T by $\theta^m(K, T)$.[7]

In this section we show how to obtain the implied volatility from the market price of an option, and we describe the properties of market implied volatilities. We discuss the features of implied volatility in different markets and give reasons why the volatility smile is observed.[8] The presence of the volatility smile has motivated the development of many new option pricing models, such as stochastic volatility models and models based on jumps in prices and volatilities: these models are better able to explain why options are transacted at the prices that we observe.

III.4.2.1   'Backing Out' Implied Volatility from a Market Price

Set the market price $f^m(K, T)$ of a standard European call or put option with strike K and maturity T equal to the BSM model price.[9] That is, assuming the option is priced from the market price of the futures F, set

$$f^m(K, T) = \omega \exp(-r(T - t)) [F\Phi(\omega d_1) - K\Phi(\omega d_2)],$$
$$d_1 = \frac{\ln(F/K)}{\sigma\sqrt{T-t}} + \tfrac{1}{2}\sigma\sqrt{T-t} \quad \text{and} \quad d_2 = d_1 - \sigma\sqrt{T-t}, \tag{III.4.1}$$

where $\omega = 1$ for a call and $\omega = -1$ for a put, and $\Phi(.)$ is the standard normal distribution function.[10]

We know K and T, and we can observe the market price of the option and of the futures, and the risk free interest rate r. Hence we can ask, what is the value of σ that satisfies equation (III.4.1)? It is straightforward to find this value using Excel. The following example illustrates the method.

EXAMPLE III.4.1: BACKING OUT IMPLIED VOLATILITY

A simple European put option with strike 105 and maturity 75 days has a market price of 7.5 when the underlying is at 100. If the underlying contract pays no dividends and the 75-day risk free interest rate is 4.5% per annum, find the market implied volatility of the option.

---

[6] This follows from the fact that the right-hand side of the put–call parity relationship does not depend on volatility. See Section III.3.3.2.
[7] This notation for implied volatility should not be confused with the option's time sensitivity, also denoted theta. We use this notation, which is standard in the volatility theory literature, only in this chapter simply because it is easier to make a clear distinction between implied volatility (θ) and the process volatility (σ). However, in the next chapter, on portfolio mapping, we will need to use the option's theta *as well as* implied volatility in the Taylor expansions for the P&L of an option, so then we use σ for the implied volatility – and this is also standard in the portfolio mapping literature!
[8] The volatility smile is also called the *volatility skew* or *smirk*, or even *sneer* (in the US), particularly when it is very asymmetric.
[9] Of course, the market price is set by supply and demand, but it still depends on the time t at which it is made and on the underlying price F at this time, although we do not make this dependence explicit at the moment.
[10] We could also assume the option is priced from the spot price, including the dividend yield in the BSM formula as in Section III.6.3.4.

SOLUTION   The spreadsheet for this example gives the solution 28.4%. It uses the Excel Solver, although Goal Seek could also be used. These are simple optimization routines that can be used to find the maximum or minimum value of a given function, or to find the value of a variable so that the function value is zero.[11] We set up an objective function that is the difference between the model price and the market price of the option and use the Solver to set the objective functions value to zero, as shown in Figure III.4.1.

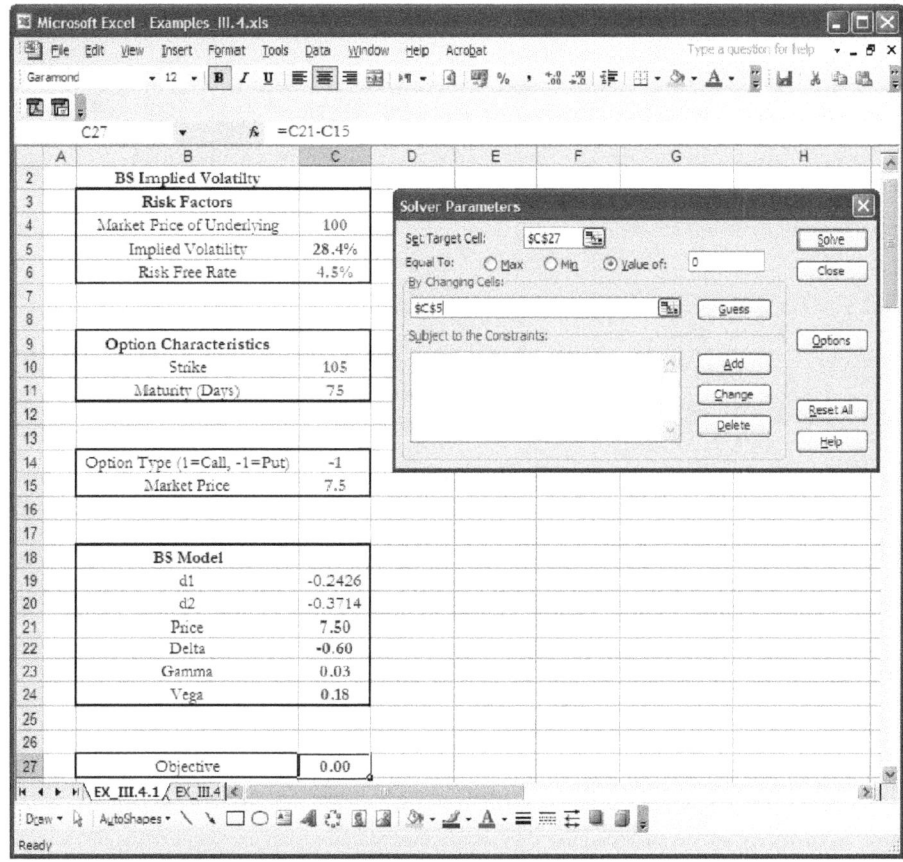

Figure III.4.1   Solver setting for backing out implied volatility

The objective in cell c27 is the difference between the model price of the option in cell c21 and the market price of the option in cell c15. When the implied volatility in cell c5 is 25% the objective is not zero. Run the Solver as shown in the figure.[12] This sets the objective to zero and yields an implied volatility of 28.4% at which the model price is 7.5, the same as the market price.

---

[11] See Sections I.5.2 and I.5.4.
[12] This is a highly non-linear optimization problem and the Solver will not always converge to the correct solution. If this occurs, change the starting value for the implied volatility in cell c5.

In all option pricing models, including the BSM model, the volatility σ is the diffusion coefficient in the price process. The essential difference between the BSM model and stochastic volatility pricing models is that the BSM model assumes σ is constant, whilst stochastic volatility models assume that σ is stochastic and is driven by a second diffusion process. When we calculate an implied volatility we obtain just *one* number. So if the data generation process has stochastic volatility, the number we get for implied volatility represents an *average* of the process volatility over the life of the option.

III.4.2.2 Equity Index Volatility Skew

According to the BSM model, volatility is constant. Hence, if the BSM model is correct the implied volatility should not change over time. Moreover, all European options on the same underlying with different strikes K and maturities T should have the same implied volatility (because there is only one price process and only one σ in this process). So if market makers believe that the BSM model is correct they should set the prices of all standard European options on the same underlying according to the BSM model based on the *same* implied volatility. That is, when the market implied volatility is backed out from these market prices we should obtain a surface which is completely flat. But we do not. Market prices of different options on the same underlying have different implied volatilities.

EXAMPLE III.4.2: EQUITY INDEX IMPLIED VOLATILITIES

On 19 January 2005 the closing price of the FTSE 100 index future was 4805.5 and the closing market prices of European calls and puts on the March index, for strikes between 4525 and 5225, are given in Table III.4.1. The maturity of these options was 58 days and the 58-day LIBOR rate was 4.85%. Find the implied volatility for each of these options.

Table III.4.1 Market prices of March options on FTSE 100 index: Closing prices on 19 January 2005

Strike	4525	4625	4725	4825	4925	5025	5125	5225
Call price	291	203.5	126	66	28.5	10	3	0.5
Put price	13.5	25	46.5	86	147.5	228.5	320.5	417.5

Figure III.4.2 shows the implied volatilities of call and put options based on the market prices shown in Table III.4.1. The spreadsheet for this figure calculates the model prices of these options using (III.4.1) and then, by repeated use of the Solver, the implied volatilities are backed out from the market prices. This way we generate the implied volatilities shown in the figure. Clearly the market does not believe in the BSM model. If traders set prices according to this model the implied volatility should be the same for all options.

Under put–call parity every call and put of the same strike and maturity would have the same implied volatility. Hence, put–call parity does not appear to hold for the option prices given in Table III.4.1. But not all options are actively traded at any point in time. The price that is quoted corresponds to the last trade on the option, and if the underlying price has changed substantially since that trade the quoted price is not an accurate representation of the current price the option would trade at. In particular, the prices of the deep out-of-the-money (OTM) options in Table III.4.1 could be stale, since these are less actively traded than other

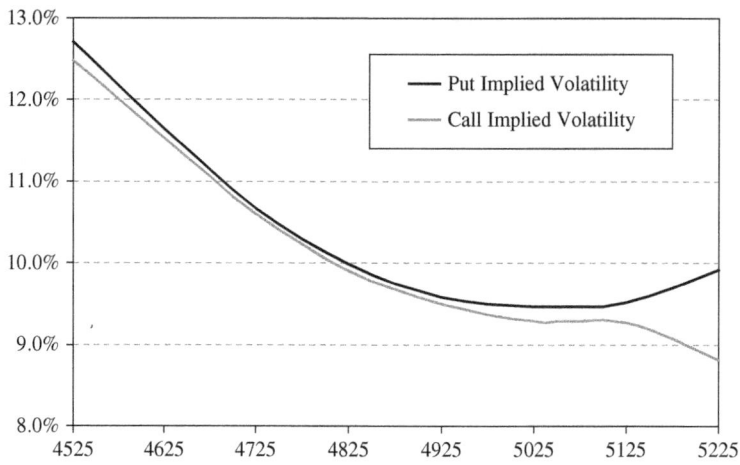

Figure III.4.2   Implied volatility skew of March 2005 FTSE 100 index future options

options. In particular, the 5225 call may be very illiquid since it has the minimum possible price (0.5), which is a sign of a stale quote with a very small trade.

A second reason why put–call parity does not appear to hold on these FTSE 100 index options may be because the Excel spreadsheet prices the options on the spot index from the market price of the futures. As explained in Section III.3.6.3, we have used the futures because we do not know the dividend yield for the index. The correct underlying price is the current price, but we have based our price on the futures price process and we know that this is only equivalent to the current price process when there is no basis risk. There is a basis risk on the FTSE 100, albeit rather small, so the market price of the futures may not have been at its theoretical value. Moreover, the futures market closes shortly after the spot market in London, so the closing market price of the futures may be different from its theoretical value at the time when the spot market closed. In summary, the BSM formula (III.4.1) is not equivalent to the correct BSM formula when the underlying is the spot. If we knew the dividend yield on the index we would have used this formula but we do not, and that is why we have priced the option from the market price of the futures.

In the above example it does not make much difference whether we price the options on the spot or the futures, as the spot and futures prices on the FTSE 100 index are always very similar. But this type of consideration becomes very important when pricing options for which the spot and futures can be very different, such as options on volatility indices. See Section III.4.4.8 for further details.

In Figure III.4.2 it is remarkable that the implied volatility is so much higher for low strike options. That is, it is much higher for out-of-the money (OTM) puts and in-the-money (ITM) calls than it is for OTM calls and ITM puts. Why should this be so? A deep OTM put equity option is an insurance against a dramatic fall in the share price. When an investor already holds the share then buying a deep OTM put option is a very cheap way to limit the loss potential, because he knows that he can sell the share on a certain date at a certain price – the strike price of the option. Deep OTM options are not expensive. The 4525 put in Table III.4.1 had a market price of only 13.5. This is very low – but it would be even lower if all the options had been priced using the ATM volatility!

How can a trader charge market prices for OTM put options that are so much greater than their BSM model price? The reason is that individual investors are risk averse and that institutional investors have stringent capital requirements. Both types of investors are prepared to pay a high premium for the insurance value of OTM put options, especially during periods of high uncertainty in the market. Traders know this so they add a premium to the BSM price of OTM options. Moreover, the traders themselves have capital requirements and they would not be prepared to write the option unless they could charge a substantial price, because of the high risk they accept. Now when we back out the implied volatility from these high market prices, we have to match the BSM price to the model price and the only way this can be done is to increase the volatility – that is the only factor that we are free to change in the BSM model.

On the other hand, the market prices of OTM call options are sometimes lower than the BSM prices based on the ATM volatility. Traders may need to charge quite a low premium for these options because many investors believe there is less chance that the option will end up ITM than is predicted by the BSM model. This is clearly the case in Example III.4.2, where the call with strike 5225 had a market price of only 0.5, whereas the BSM price based on the ATM volatility of 9.5% is 1.26.

There are other factors that contribute to the volatility smile or skew:

- When a trader writes an option he needs to hedge the risk he accepts (using the underlying and other options on the same underlying) and the costs of hedging will be factored into the trader's premium. This premium can be considerable, especially for long term options. Assuming hedging costs are the same for all strikes, the percentage increase in premium for factoring in the hedging cost will be much higher for lower priced options than for higher price options. Therefore, the increase in implied volatility that results from factoring in the hedging costs will be much greater for OTM calls and puts, and hence the smile effect is augmented.
- In equity options a trader may also factor in a credit risk premium to the price he quotes, to compensate for the default risk on the share. The probability of default during the life of the option increases with the option's maturity so the credit risk premium will be greater for options with longer maturities. And, just as for hedging costs, if the credit risk premium is the same for all strikes then it will have the greatest impact on the implied volatilities of OTM calls and puts. So credit risks increase the smile effect especially at longer maturities.

In summary, in equity markets the implied volatility of OTM puts is much higher than the volatility of OTM calls. This feature is known as the *negative skew* because it goes hand in hand with a negatively skewed log price density.[13] The BSM model assumes the price process is geometric Brownian motion and from this it follows that the risk neutral log price density is normal. But the premiums traders charge for equity options correspond to a log price density that has a heavier lower tail and a lighter upper tail than the normal density. In other words, the market believes that a large price fall is more likely and a large price rise is less likely than assumed in the BSM model. Part of this belief is fuelled by a pessimism that is particularly obvious after market crashes. Indeed, the skew is usually more pronounced in

---

[13] Because the market implied density may be derived by taking the second partial derivative with respect to strike of all option prices of the same maturity, a result proved by Breeden and Litzenberger (1978).

index options than it is in individual share options. A large fall in the index price means that many shares have price falls. This is bad news for the whole economy and may precipitate further price falls. Investors holding portfolios of equities will seek to limit losses in a market crash scenario by purchasing an OTM put on the index, and will be prepared to pay a very substantial premium for this insurance. This high demand for OTM puts pushes up their prices, and hence we observe a pronounced negative skew in index options.

III.4.2.3   Smiles and Skews in Other Markets

Implied volatilities in currency, commodity and bond markets also display characteristic features, although these are often less pronounced than they are in equities. We describe some of these features below.[14]

Currency Markets

Implied volatilities of options on foreign exchange rates have a more symmetric *smile* appearance, where the implied volatilities of both low strike and high strike options tend to be higher than the ATM volatility. The smile is skewed, but not as much as in equity or commodity options, and the skew can go either way. To see why, suppose the value of a foreign currency falls in domestic terms. This is bad news for holders of the foreign currency but equally good news for holders of the domestic currency. Conversely, if the foreign currency becomes more valuable in domestic terms, the gain by holders of the foreign currency is matched by losses to holders of the domestic currency. Hence, there is an approximately equal demand for OTM puts and OTM calls on foreign exchange rates, and traders will not distinguish between the insurance values of different options in their premiums as they do for other options. An example of a currency smile was given in Figure I.5.8, and this is fairly symmetric. Readers are recommended to consult Section I.5.3.2 for further information on the interpolation methods used to construct realistic currency smiles from the relatively few implied volatility quotes given in the market.

Commodity Markets

Commodity options often exhibit a very pronounced upward skew, i.e. the implied volatility of high strike options is greater than it is for low strike options. The implied volatility of commodity options tends to increases with strike and the risk neutral log price density is positively skewed. The skew in the log price density arises because price rises in commodities are bad news for investors, and can lead to an increased volatility. So there is a positive correlation between price changes and volatility changes, and because of this the upper tail of the price density will be heavier than the lower tail.

However, the implied volatility in some commodity markets, and in energy markets in particular, is often very high and variable and there are times when the skew can be negatively sloped. For instance, some skews for the crude oil options traded on NYMEX are shown in Figure III.4.3. These varied considerably from day to day over a 2-week period in March

---

[14] Since strike and moneyness are simply different metrics for measuring how far volatility deviates from the at-the-money volatility, we may also ask how the implied volatility at different moneyness varies with moneyness rather than strike. That is, the implied volatility skew can be drawn with moneyness along the horizontal axis instead of the strike, and similar features will be apparent.

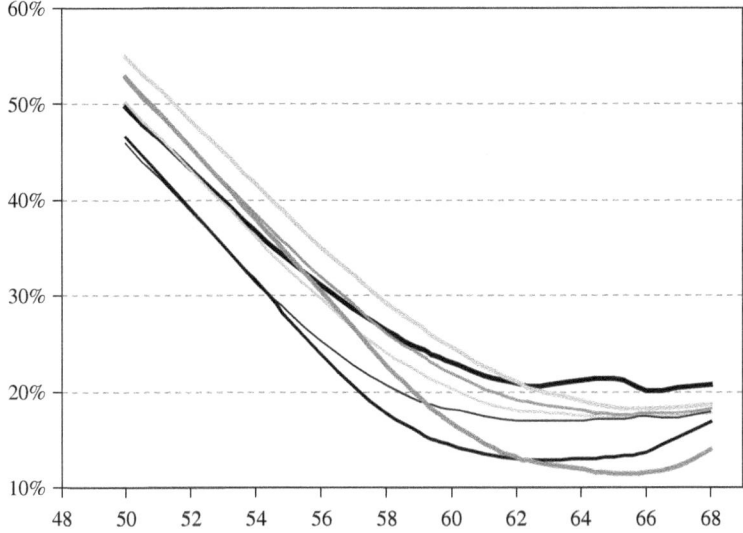

Figure III.4.3   Volatility skews on crude oil options in March 2006

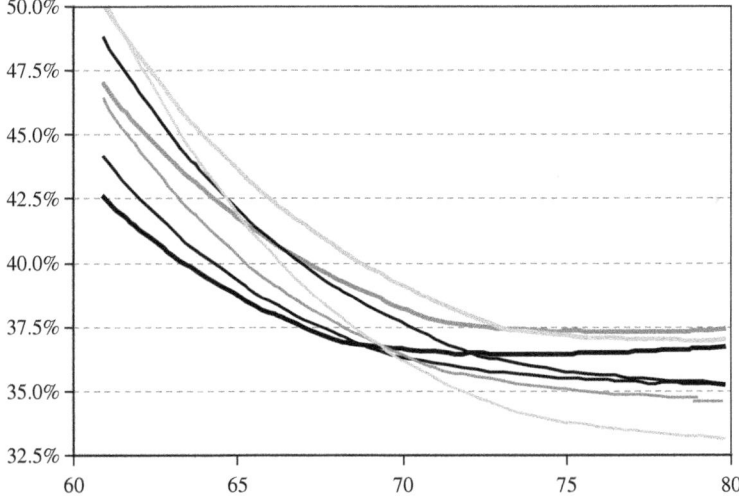

Figure III.4.4   Volatility skews on natural gas options in March 2006

2006, but they all have negative slope. The skews on NYMEX natural gas options shown in Figure III.4.4 varied even more during the same period, and again the skews are negative.

A possible explanation for this is that oil and gas prices had been trending downward for many months and by March 2006 many energy producers were buying OTM puts to protect themselves against further price falls. This unusually high demand for OTM puts pushed up their market prices considerably so that low strike volatilities were, unusually, higher than high strike volatilities as seen in the figures.

Fixed Income Markets

Negative sloping implied volatility skews may also be observed on caps and floors. That is, ITM caps may have a higher implied volatility than OTM caps, and the opposite may be the case with floors. Jarrow et al. (2007) provide an extensive empirical analysis of caps that are written on 3-month US LIBOR rates, in which the implied volatility skew is consistently negatively sloped over ten different strikes. Their data period covers a little over 3 years, from August 2000 to September 2003, and the skews became more pronounced after 11 September 2001. Since any smile in cap volatilities is inconsistent with the lognormal forward rate model, the authors develop an extension of the LIBOR model to include stochastic volatility and jumps in forward rates. Their pricing and hedging results suggest that stochastic volatility alone, without jumps in forward rates, is insufficient to capture the observed market behaviour.

Interest rates in the US were falling steadily during this period, so option traders may have expected a further fall in interest rates to be more likely than a rise. If this is the case, the distribution of interest rate changes will have had a negative skew, which is consistent with the behaviour of cap implied volatilities observed by Jarrow et al. However, the negative skew could also be an artefact of using a lognormal forward rate model rather than an arithmetic Brownian to model forward rates. In the lognormal model the implied volatilities are measured in percentage terms, whereas in an arithmetic model volatility is measured in absolute (basis point) terms. A negative skew on percentage volatilities may not translate into a negative skew on absolute volatilities, so it could be that the negative skews that Jarrow et al. observed were a result of using a geometric rather than an arithmetic process for interest rates.

III.4.2.4   Term Structures of Implied Volatilities

Until now we have examined how implied volatility varies across options having the same maturity but different strikes (or equivalently, with different moneyness). In this section we ask how the implied volatility of a fixed strike (or fixed moneyness) option behaves as a function of maturity. For instance, we may consider all options of different maturities with zero log moneyness. This is the *at-the-money term structure of implied volatilities*.

Volatility in financial markets comes in clusters, with periods of high volatility being interspersed with periods of low volatility. There are many behavioural explanations of this phenomenon. For instance, in equity markets a large and sudden fall in share price will increase the debt–equity ratio, i.e. the firm will instantly become more highly leveraged. This makes its future more uncertain and hence volatility tends to increase dramatically following a large fall in share price. The effect is not symmetric because large and sudden share price rises are rare, and even if they do occur this would be good news for the shareholders, so volatility should decrease. A similar asymmetric volatility response is often observed in commodity markets. This time it can be a large price *increase* that precipitates the more volatile response, since consumers and producers may be very uncertain of the economic effect. As a result speculative investments increase and the volatility increases.

Volatility clustering has the effect of inducing a downward sloping term structure of implied volatility during relatively volatile periods, and an upward sloping term structure in relatively tranquil times. If volatility clustering is asymmetric, as it is in equity markets, then downward sloping term structures tend to be steeper than the upward sloping ones. The opposite is generally the case in commodity markets.

Figure III.4.5 depicts two equity volatility term structures, one during a volatile period and the other during a tranquil period. In this example the 1-month volatility ranged from less than 8% during the tranquil period to almost 11% in the volatile period, whereas the 1-year volatility changed very little. Long term volatilities usually tend to vary less than short term volatilities.

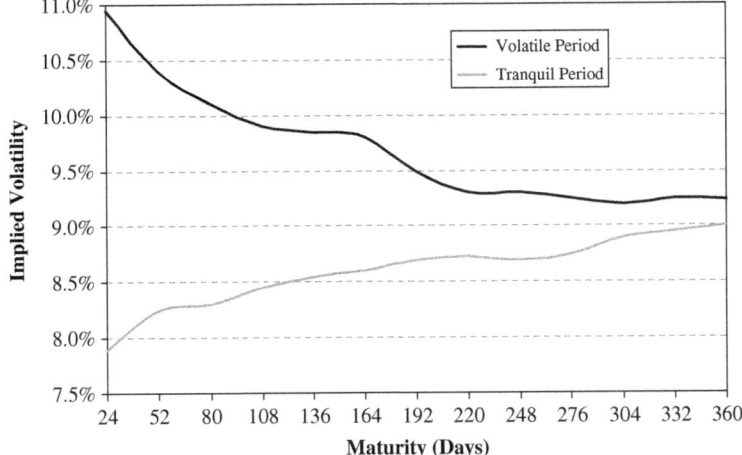

Figure III.4.5   Equity implied volatility term structures

III.4.2.5   Implied Volatility Surfaces

Putting together the implied volatilities of all options on the same underlying gives a surface called the *implied volatility surface*. In equity, currency and commodity markets the implied volatility surface refers to implied volatilities of options with different strikes and different maturities. For instance, Table III.4.2 gives the implied volatility surface of S&P 500 index options on 1 April 2003, and the surface is depicted in Figure III.4.6.

The last traded prices of far OTM options and long dated options are frequently stale, as these options are much less liquid than short dated ATM options. For this reason we often use a smoothing method such as cubic splines to extrapolate into the edges of the surface and to interpolate around any bad points.[15]

Table III.4.2   S&P 500 implied volatilities, 1 April 2003

Option expiry	Option strike															
	700	725	750	775	800	825	850	875	900	925	950	975	1025	1050	1075	1100
Jun-03	30.81	30.04	29.05	28.00	27.05	25.96	25.01	24.26	23.53	22.47	21.94	21.48	21.07	21.10	21.75	21.74
Sep-03	28.38	27.58	26.82	25.99	25.13	24.41	23.68	23.03	22.40	21.87	21.34	20.97	20.26	20.08	19.88	19.71
Dec-03	26.94	26.33	25.69	25.04	24.41	23.80	23.19	22.66	22.12	21.60	21.20	20.75	20.09	19.81	19.57	19.35
Mar-04	26.07	25.52	24.97	24.43	24.02	23.35	22.85	22.35	21.90	21.50	21.09	20.72	20.05	19.80	19.57	19.31

---

[15] More details and Excel examples on cubic spline smoothing algorithms are given in Section I.4.3.3.

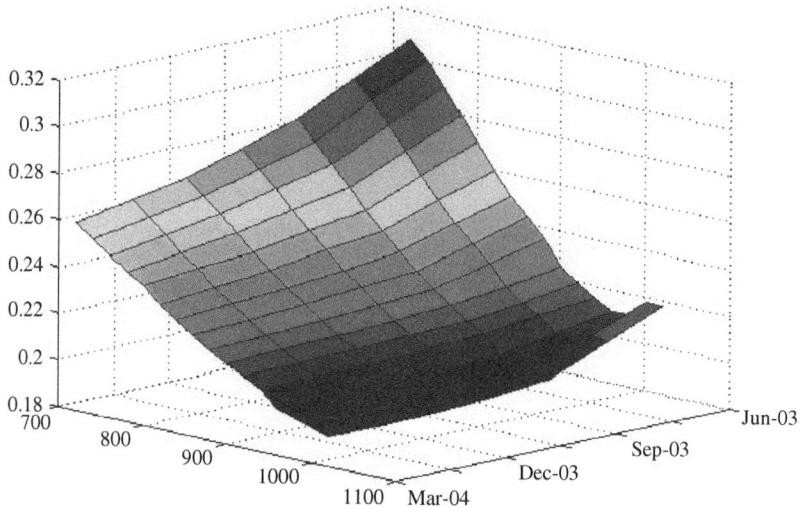

Figure III.4.6   S&P 500 implied volatility surface. (See Plate 5)

III.4.2.6   Cap and Caplet Volatilities

The ATM volatility term structures for interest rate options typically have a 'humped' shape, where volatilities that are implied from market prices of short term ATM caps are lower than those implied from caps of about 18 months' to 2 years' maturity. We know from Section III.3.8.2 that the BSM cap price is the sum of its component caplet prices. By assuming the caplet volatility is the same for all caplets we can find a single *flat volatility* that is implicit in the observed market price of a cap. A numerical example was given in the previous chapter (Example III.3.9).

When the underlying is a *single* instrument that follows a geometric Brownian motion, the average variance of log returns over a period $T = T_1 + T_2$ is the sum of the average variance over period T_1 plus the average variance over period T_2. The additivity of *variances* is a consequence of the independent increments in geometric Brownian motion. So, if a single underlying follows a geometric Brownian motion, variances are additive and we can back out the forward implied volatilities that are implicit in a term structure of implied volatilities. That is, given a set $\theta(T_i)$ of market implied volatilities of different maturities $\{T_1, \ldots, T_n\}$, we can find a set of forward implied volatilities $\theta^F(T_i, T_{i+1})$ using the following algorithm.

Variance Iteration

Set $\theta^F(0, T_1) = \theta(T_1)$, and then solve for $\theta^F(T_1, T_2)$ using

$$\theta(T_2)^2 = T_2^{-1}\big(T_1\theta^F(0, T_1)^2 + (T_2 - T_1)\theta^F(T_1, T_2)^2\big)$$

and then for $\theta^F(T_2, T_3)$ using

$$\theta(T_3)^2 = T_3^{-1}\big(T_1\theta^F(0, T_1)^2 + (T_2 - T_1)\theta^F(T_1, T_2)^2 + (T_3 - T_2)\theta^F(T_2, T_3)^2\big)$$

and so on.

Now consider the relationship between a term structure of implied volatilities of caps and a term structure of implied volatilities of the component caplets.[16] The problem with using a straightforward iteration on variances as above is that the underlying forward rate *changes* for every caplet in the cap. A cap does *not* have a single stochastic process for the underlying and therefore a standard iteration on variances such as that described above is not an appropriate method for backing out the caplet implied volatility from a term structure of cap implied volatilities.

In fact, the iteration should be performed on the *vega weighted* volatilities of the caplets. This is because we can approximate every flat cap volatility as the vega weighted sum of its caplet volatilities. To see why, consider the BSM price f^{Cap} of a cap with some fixed strike and maturity.[17] By (III.3.84),

$$f^{\text{Cap}} = \sum_{i=1}^{n} C_i(\sigma_i),$$

where C_i is the price of the ith caplet and σ_i is the volatility of the ith forward rate, i.e. the volatility of the underlying of the ith caplet.[18] Let $v_i(\theta)$ denote the vega of the ith caplet evaluated at some volatility θ. We can apply a first order Taylor expansion to the cap price, obtaining the approximation

$$f^{\text{Cap}}(\theta) \approx \sum_{i=1}^{n}(C_i(\theta) + (\sigma_i - \theta)\, v_i(\theta)). \qquad (\text{III.4.2})$$

Now suppose that θ is the implied volatility of the cap. This is a *flat* volatility, i.e.

$$f^{\text{Cap}}(\theta) = \sum_{i=1}^{n} C_i(\theta).$$

Hence, at the flat volatility, the forward rate volatilities satisfy

$$\sum_{i=1}^{n}(\sigma_i - \theta)\, v_i(\theta) \approx 0,$$

from which it follows that

$$\theta \approx \frac{\sum_{i=1}^{n} \sigma_i v_i(\theta)}{\sum_{i=1}^{n} v_i(\theta)}.$$

Thus, using more precise notation, the flat cap volatility for a cap with strike K and maturity T is approximately equal to

---

[16] Since each fixed strike caplet in the cap with strike K has a *different moneyness*, how can we fix the strike of an ATM cap? We normally take the current value of the swap rate of the same maturity as the cap, so the different caplets in an ATM cap are only approximately ATM.

[17] We drop the explicit mention of the dependence of implied volatilities on strike and maturity for ease of notation.

[18] Again, we have dropped dependence of this on the forward rate and other variables for ease of notation.

$$\theta^{\text{Cap}}(K, T) \approx \sum_{i=1}^{n} \omega_i(K)\, \sigma_i, \tag{III.4.3}$$

where the weights $\omega_i(K)$ are proportional to the vegas of the caplets with strike K in the cap of strike K. Therefore we can find a set of caplet implied volatilities from a term structure of cap implied volatilities using the following algorithm:

Vega Weighted Volatility Iteration

Set

$$\theta^{\text{Caplet}}(K, 0, T_1) = \theta^{\text{Cap}}(K, T_1),$$

and then solve for $\theta^{\text{Caplet}}(K, T_1, T_2)$ using

$$\theta^{\text{Cap}}(K, T_2) = \frac{\nu_1(K)\, \theta^{\text{Caplet}}(K, 0, T_1) + \nu_2(K)\, \theta^{\text{Caplet}}(K, T_1, T_2)}{\nu_1(K) + \nu_2(K)}$$

and then solve for $\theta^{\text{Caplet}}(K, T_2, T_3)$ using

$$\theta^{\text{Cap}}(K, T_2) = \frac{\nu_1(K)\, \theta^{\text{Caplet}}(K, 0, T_1) + \nu_2(K)\, \theta^{\text{Caplet}}(K, T_1, T_2) + \nu_3(K)\, \theta^{\text{Caplet}}(K, T_2, T_3)}{\nu_1(K) + \nu_2(K) + \nu_3(K)},$$

and so on.

Vega weighting has the effect of increasing caplet volatility term structures at the long end, compared to the volatility iteration applied with equal weights on the volatilities. We remark that variance iteration often leads to negative caplet volatilities at the long end. See Alexander (2003) for empirical examples that support these remarks.

III.4.2.7   Swaption Volatilities

In Swaption markets the implied volatility surface refers to ATM implied volatilities only, for options of different maturities to enter swaps of different tenors. This is called the *swaption implied volatility surface*. It is used to calibrate interest rate option models and the LIBOR model in particular, since this is the standard model for pricing the American and Bermudan swaptions that are actively traded in OTC markets.

Table III.4.3 shows the swaption implied volatility surface for pay-fixed US LIBOR European swaptions on 5 March 2004. Figure III.4.7 depicts this surface, with the maturity of the swaption shown on one horizontal axis and the tenor of the swaption shown on the other. This surface displays the typical structure of a swaption volatility surface, where short tenor and short maturity swaptions have higher volatility than long tenor and/or long maturity swaptions. Also, the swaptions with short tenors exhibit typical 'humped' shape, where volatility is highest for swaptions with maturity between 1 and 2 years.

Table III.4.3 ATM swaption implied volatilities for US LIBOR swaptions, 5 March 2004

Swap tenor	Swaption maturity									
	1mth	3mth	6mth	1yr	2yr	3yr	4yr	5yr	7yr	10yr
1yr	48.5	51	54.9	50.8	39.3	31.9	27.7	24.6	20.7	17.2
2yr	49.9	48.9	48.5	43.9	35.2	29.8	26.2	23.6	20.1	16.7
3yr	43.1	43	42.5	38.9	32.3	27.9	24.8	22.6	19.3	16
4yr	38	38.4	38.2	35.6	30.2	26.4	23.7	21.6	18.6	15.4
5yr	35.2	35.9	35.5	33.3	28.5	25.2	22.7	20.8	17.9	14.9
7yr	29.2	30.2	30.4	29.4	26	23.3	21.2	19.5	16.8	14.2
10yr	24.2	25.3	25.8	25.6	23.3	21.2	19.4	17.9	15.6	13.3

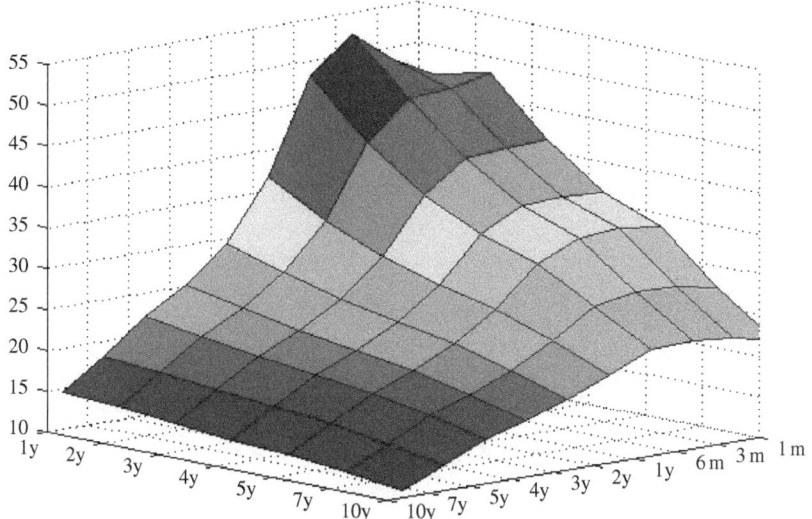

Figure III.4.7   A swaption volatility surface. (See Plate 6)

III.4.3   LOCAL VOLATILITY

The market prices of standard European options have another volatility surface which is called the (market) local volatility surface, or the *local volatility surface* for short.[19] The local volatility surface uses the option prices to 'lock in' the *forward volatilities* of the underlying, which are a function of the underlying asset price and time.[20] This section formally defines the concept of forward volatility in the context of a *binomial tree*. Then we state the result of

---

[19] In Section III.4.6 we distinguish between *market* local volatility and *model* local volatility, where the model prices of standard European options are used in place of the market prices.

[20] In this sense, forward volatilities may be thought of as a two-dimensional analogue of forward interest rates: forward interest rates are 'locked in' by the current market prices of bonds (and swaps and FRAs and any other instruments that are used to derive the current yield curve). Similarly, forward volatilities are 'locked in' by the current market prices of options.

Dupire (1994) that explains how a unique local volatility surface can be calibrated to market prices of standard European options. Finally, we describe some of the more popular types of parameterization of the local volatility surface.

III.4.3.1   Forward Volatility

The *forward volatility* $\sigma(S, t)$ is the volatility at some future point in time t if the underlying price takes value S at this time. The easiest way to visualize forward volatility is in the context of an *implied lattice* or, following Derman and Kani (1994) and Rubinstein (1994), an *implied tree*. Denote by $S(t)$ the price of the underlying asset at time t, with $0 < t < T$, with 0 being the current time and T being the maximum maturity of the market prices of standard European options on S. We can model the evolution of the underlying price process at discrete time intervals between time 0 and time T using a binomial lattice or tree, as explained in Sections I.5.6 and III.3.2.6. A three-step binomial tree was depicted in Figure III.3.1. More generally, a binomial tree has n steps, each over a time interval $\Delta t = T/n$, and in each interval there can be either an upward move from S to uS with probability p or a downward move from S to dS with probability $1 - p$. In Section I.5.6 we drew a four-step tree, where $u = 1.25$ and $d = u^{-1} = 0.8$.

Recall from Sections I.5.6 and III.3.2.6 that there are several ways to parameterize the tree so that the price process would, in the limit as $\Delta t \to 0$, be a geometric Brownian motion with drift equal to the risk free rate r and a constant volatility σ. A popular choice is the *Cox – Ingersoll – Ross parameterization* where

$$p = \frac{e^{r\Delta t} - d}{u - d}, \quad u = d^{-1} = e^{\sigma\sqrt{\Delta t}}. \tag{III.4.4}$$

Since we parameterize the tree to be consistent with constant volatility geometric Brownian motion, the volatility is *constant at every node in the tree*. For instance, under (III.4.4) we have

$$\sigma = \frac{\ln u}{\sqrt{\Delta t}} = -\frac{\ln d}{\sqrt{\Delta t}}. \tag{III.4.5}$$

Now suppose we parameterize the tree so that the volatility depends on the node that we are at. The forward volatility $\sigma(S, m\Delta t)$ is the volatility at the node $(S, m\Delta t)$, i.e. at the node at time $m\Delta t$ when the price is at S. When the volatility varies between different nodes in the tree, the tree can still recombine, but the size of the up moves and the down moves will no longer be constant throughout the tree.

The lattice example is very restricting, since the forward time must be a multiple of Δt and the possible values of S are very limited. However, the definition of forward volatility extends beyond a lattice. Indeed, we can forget the lattice and simply redefine the risk neutral price process as[21]

$$\frac{dS(t)}{S(t)} = (r - y)\, dt + \sigma(S, t)\, dW. \tag{III.4.6}$$

---

[21] We also assume the underlying pays dividends (or incurs carry costs) with yield y, so that the total rate of return is r.

Here the forward volatility $\sigma(S, t)$ is the *instantaneous volatility* of the price process at some future time t when the underlying price is S at this time, and the local volatility surface is the surface of all forward volatilities for different S and t.[22]

III.4.3.2 Dupire's Equation

Dupire (1994, 1996) derived a famous equation that allows the unique forward volatilities in (III.4.6) to be calibrated from the market prices of standard European options on S. Dupire's equation is to local volatility as the BSM model is to implied volatility. That is, using Dupire's equation we can 'back out' the unique local volatility surface from the market (or model) prices of options.

Let $C(K, T)$ denote the market price of a standard European call option on S with strike K and maturity T. Use subscripts to denote partial derivatives, i.e.

$$C_T(K, T) = \frac{\partial C(K, T)}{\partial T}, \quad C_K(K, T) = \frac{\partial C(K, T)}{\partial K} \text{ and } C_{KK}(K, T) = \frac{\partial^2 C(K, T)}{\partial K^2}. \quad \text{(III.4.7)}$$

Dupire's equation gives the *local variance* as

$$\sigma^2(S, t)\big|_{t=T, S=K} = \frac{2(C_T(K, T) + (r - y)KC_K(K, T) + yC(K, T))}{K^2 C_{KK}(K, T)}, \quad \text{(III.4.8)}$$

and the *local volatility* $\sigma(S, t)$ is the square root of this. This is the *unique*, deterministic forward volatility in (III.4.6) that is consistent with the market prices of standard European options on S.

How do we calibrate the local volatility given by Dupire's equation? We estimate the values of the derivatives (III.4.7) using the market prices of the liquid call and put options as follows:

1. Smooth and extrapolate the market prices so that they properly cover all strikes and all maturities – and use put–call parity to infer the prices of illiquid calls (puts) from those of the more liquid puts (calls) with the same strike and maturity;
2. Apply finite differences, as explained in Section I.5.5, to approximate the derivatives (III.4.7) and use these values in (III.4.8).

EXAMPLE III.4.3: CALIBRATION OF A LOCAL VOLATILITY SURFACE

Given the call option prices given in Table III.4.4, calculate the implied volatility surface and calibrate the local volatility surface.[23] Assume the spot underlying price is 100, the risk free rate is 4% and the dividend yield is zero for all maturities. How sensitive are these surfaces to the current price of the underlying, holding the option prices fixed?

---

[22] Gyöngy (1986) proves that for every Itô process with stochastic coefficients there is a process with deterministic coefficients that has the same marginal distribution for every t. As explained by Alexander and Nogueira (2008), a special case of Gyöngy's result allows one to find a unique set of forward volatilities in (III.4.6) that are consistent with the arbitrage-free market prices of standard European options.
[23] These prices are not market prices – they were simulated using the normal mixture GARCH model described in Section II.4.4.3. Many thanks to my ex PhD student Leonardo Nogueira of the Banco Central do Brasil and the ICMA Centre, and to Stamatis Leontsinis (a current PhD student) for providing this exercise for a workshop in the ICMA Centre's Volatility Analysis MSc module. Also many thanks to another of my PhD students, Joydeep Lahiri, for drawing the Matlab graphs throughout these volumes.

Table III.4.4   Call option prices

Strike	Maturity (days)											
	40	50	60	70	80	90	100	110	120	130	140	150
80	20.372	20.495	20.611	20.690	20.800	20.916	20.972	21.063	21.166	21.220	21.329	21.408
82	18.383	18.510	18.632	18.716	18.832	18.956	19.019	19.118	19.228	19.291	19.409	19.498
84	16.396	16.528	16.660	16.751	16.876	17.010	17.081	17.191	17.311	17.383	17.511	17.611
86	14.414	14.557	14.700	14.803	14.937	15.085	15.170	15.290	15.425	15.506	15.645	15.758
88	12.445	12.602	12.760	12.882	13.029	13.195	13.299	13.431	13.580	13.675	13.827	13.957
90	10.501	10.681	10.860	11.010	11.178	11.362	11.490	11.634	11.801	11.911	12.077	12.226
92	8.605	8.818	9.030	9.206	9.404	9.605	9.760	9.924	10.107	10.230	10.413	10.580
94	6.794	7.051	7.303	7.508	7.729	7.953	8.140	8.319	8.520	8.659	8.852	9.032
96	5.128	5.426	5.720	5.950	6.194	6.441	6.656	6.847	7.059	7.209	7.411	7.604
98	3.666	4.001	4.328	4.576	4.836	5.100	5.325	5.529	5.739	5.904	6.114	6.309
100	2.473	2.820	3.151	3.415	3.676	3.945	4.171	4.384	4.585	4.758	4.970	5.171
102	1.577	1.898	2.215	2.479	2.721	2.981	3.202	3.413	3.609	3.780	3.985	4.186
104	0.960	1.228	1.502	1.743	1.969	2.208	2.414	2.615	2.797	2.963	3.145	3.345
106	0.560	0.768	0.993	1.194	1.396	1.612	1.793	1.974	2.137	2.292	2.456	2.645
108	0.324	0.469	0.645	0.806	0.969	1.157	1.317	1.475	1.620	1.753	1.899	2.079
110	0.185	0.285	0.410	0.535	0.662	0.823	0.958	1.096	1.222	1.337	1.461	1.624
112	0.103	0.171	0.260	0.351	0.449	0.580	0.697	0.810	0.919	1.019	1.119	1.260
114	0.057	0.102	0.166	0.232	0.306	0.408	0.506	0.598	0.688	0.771	0.856	0.976
116	0.032	0.061	0.108	0.153	0.208	0.289	0.370	0.443	0.511	0.581	0.654	0.756
118	0.018	0.039	0.071	0.100	0.142	0.204	0.271	0.330	0.381	0.439	0.501	0.584
120	0.010	0.024	0.047	0.064	0.097	0.145	0.201	0.246	0.287	0.334	0.383	0.451

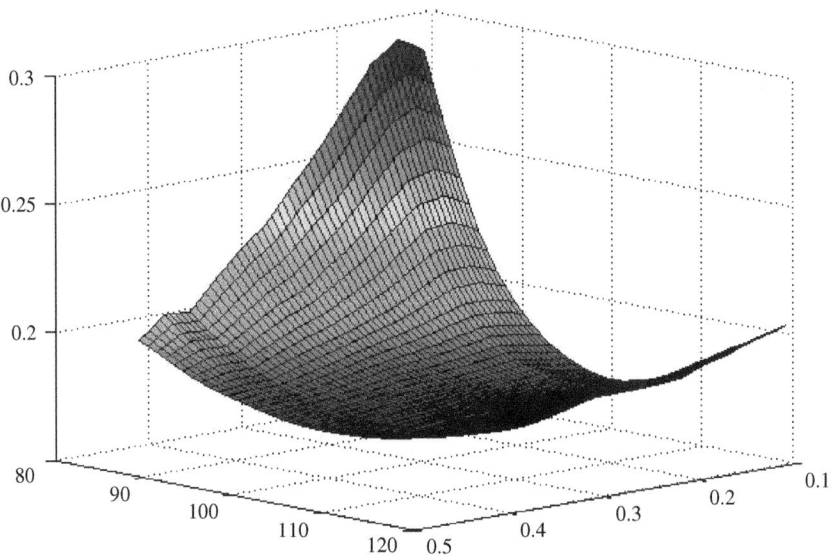

Figure III.4.8   Implied volatility surface for the option prices in Table III.4.4 (the horizontal axes here are strike K (84–120) and maturity T (40–150 days)). (See Plate 7)

SOLUTION   The implied volatility surface is backed out from the option prices using the numerical algorithm described in Example III.4.1 and the result is displayed in Figure III.4.8. Note that the spreadsheet for this example does not actually calculate these implied volatilities, but they can be obtained using the spreadsheet for Example III.4.1. For instance, the call option price with strike 100 and maturity 40 days is 2.473175 and the spreadsheet for Example III.4.1 gives the implied volatility for this strike and maturity as

$$\theta(100, 40 \,|S_0 = 100) = 17.06\%.$$

It is important to note that the implied volatility is very sensitive to the current price of the underlying. For instance, if the current price S_0 were 101 instead of 100, and the option prices *remained* as they are in Table III.4.4, then the implied volatility would be different. In fact,

$$\theta(100, 40 \,|S_0 = 101) = 12.51\%.$$

For this reason (i.e. that the surface moves with S) we say that the implied volatility surface has the *floating smile* property.

To find the local volatility surface we calculate the first partial derivatives of the option prices with respect to time, and the first and second partial derivatives of the option prices with respect to strike, using finite differences. Then we use Dupire's equation to calculate the local volatility surface, and this is shown in Figure III.4.9.

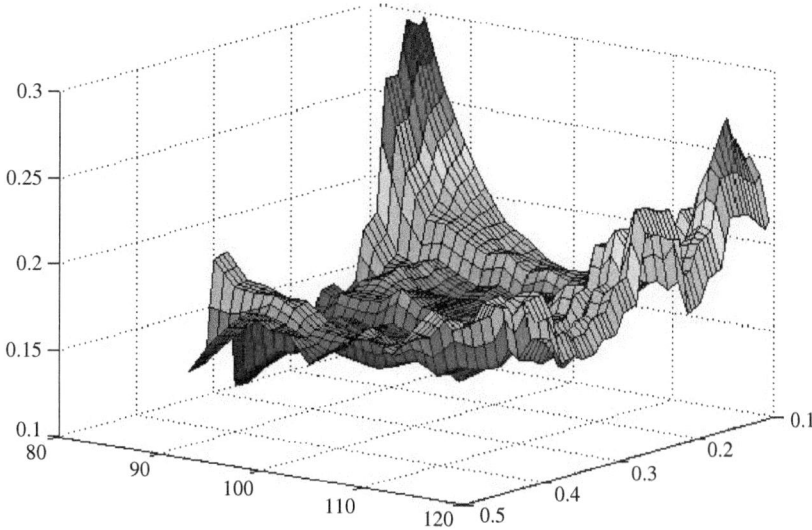

Figure III.4.9   Local volatility surface for the option prices in Table III.4.4 (the horizontal axes here are price S (84–120) and future time t (40–150 days)). (See Plate 8)

What would this local volatility surfaces look like if the current price of the underlying were not 100, but 101, given the same options prices as in Table III.4.4? Unlike the implied volatility surface, the local volatility surface would not change, since there is nothing in Dupire's equation relating to the current price of the underlying. The forward volatility at the point $S = 100$ and $t = 40$ days is 16.87%, as can be seen in the spreadsheet. But this is the *same* whether the current underlying price is 100 or 101 given the option prices in the table remain unchanged.

That is:

$$\sigma(100, 40 \,|\, S_0 = 100) = \sigma(100, 40 \,|\, S_0 = 101) = 16.87\%.$$

In other words, the local volatility surface that is obtained using Dupire's equation is a *fixed* surface. That is, it has the *static smile* property, in contrast to the floating smile property of the implied volatility surface. The forward volatilities in the local volatility surface are 'locked in' by the current prices of the options, as if they will be realized with certainty.

However, it is highly unlikely that the forward volatility will be realized. That is, in 40 days' time, even if the underlying price were still at 100, it is highly unlikely that the 40-day realized volatility would be 16.87%. In fact, the local volatility surface moves each time it is recalibrated, in just the same way that forward interest rates change over time.

III.4.3.3   Parametric Models of Local Volatility

The local volatility surface that we derived in Figure III.4.9 is quite irregular, even though the implied volatilities in Figure III.4.8 were smooth and quite well behaved. In fact readers may see in the spreadsheet for Example III.4.3 that it was not possible to calculate feasible values from Dupire's equation near the lower boundary of S and this is why only the values above 84 were shown in the figure.

In practice, the local volatilities that are calibrated directly to market data are highly sensitive to small movements in option prices. Hence the local volatility surface can be very 'spiky' and it can also jump about a lot from day to day. Although a certain amount of smoothing is possible using regularization methods proposed by Avallaneda et. al. (1997) and Bouchouev and Isakov (1997, 1999), it is very difficult to apply the directly calibrated market local volatility in the price process (III.4.6) because the option prices and hedge ratios change considerably every time the volatilities are recalibrated.

For these reasons practitioners often parameterize the local volatility surface. A number of different approaches have been proposed in the literature, including:

- cubic polynomials (e.g. Dumas et al., 1998);
- piecewise quadratic functions (e.g. Beaglehole and Chebanier, 2002);
- cubic splines (e.g. Coleman et al., 1999);
- hyperbolic trigonometric functions (e.g. Brown and Randall, 1999);
- Hermite polynomials (e.g. McIntyre, 2001).

Whilst these all represent useful developments in the local volatility literature, the problem for practitioners is how to choose the 'best' functional form for their purposes. Also, they do not lead to a closed form solution for standard European option prices; instead these prices must be found by numerical solution of the BSM PDE, with the parametric form for local volatility in place of the constant volatility.

It is important to note that some of these parameterizations do not preserve the static property of market local volatility. For instance, the quadratic parameterization

$$\sigma(S, t) = AS(t)^2 + BS(t) + C\exp(Dt), \tag{III.4.9}$$

where A, B, C and D are constants, has the same *static smile* property that market local volatility has, but the parameterization

$$\sigma(S, t) = \tilde{A}\left(\frac{S(t)}{S(0)}\right)^2 + \tilde{B}\left(\frac{S(t)}{S(0)}\right) + C\exp(Dt), \tag{III.4.10}$$

where $S(0)$ is the current price, has the *floating smile* property.[24] So (III.4.10) is not a 'true' local volatility function in the sense of Dupire (1994, 1996). A misunderstanding of this point has led to considerable confusion in the recent literature.[25]

But a price process of the form

$$\frac{dS(t)}{S(t)} = (r - y)\, dt + \sigma(S, t)\, dW$$

will give the *same* option prices when we use (III.4.9) as it does when we use (III.4.10) for the local volatility. This is because we can set

$$\tilde{A} = AS(0)^2, \quad \tilde{B} = BS(0) \qquad \qquad \text{(III.4.11)}$$

and, since $S(0)$ is observed, (III.4.11) is just another way of writing (III.4.9). In fact we can always reparameterize a floating smile model to become a static smile model, simply by scaling certain parameters by the current price. This is important because, whilst a single calibration of the model will give the same option prices, the *dynamics* of the option prices – and the dynamics of the model implied volatilities – are very different in the two models. A consequence of this is that the two models (III.4.9) and (III.4.10) will have very different hedging properties. We shall return to this discussion in Section III.4.6.

To summarize our discussion, it is confusing to refer to a deterministic volatility function $\sigma(S, t)$ that has the *floating smile* property as a local volatility function, because local volatility has the *static smile* property. Later we explain why we refer to deterministic volatility functions with the floating smile property as *scale invariant deterministic volatility* functions. True local volatility functions, such as those used in Dumas et al. (1998) and Coleman et al. (1999), have the *static smile* property.

III.4.3.4   Lognormal Mixture Diffusion

The lognormal mixture diffusion, introduced by Brigo and Mercurio (2002), is a geometric price diffusion with a scale invariant deterministic volatility function that is based on the assumption that the price density is a mixture of lognormal distributions. Thus the model is a natural extension of the Black–Scholes–Merton model, in which the price distribution is of course lognormal. In the following we describe the simplest possible log normal mixture process, i.e. there are only two lognormals in the mixture that are generated by constant volatilities.

Let $X(t) = \ln S(t)$ be the log price and assume that

$$\frac{dS(t)}{S(t)} = (r - y)\, dt + \sigma(S, t)\, dW(t).$$

Then we have, by Itô's lemma,

$$dX(t) = \left(r - y - \tfrac{1}{2}\, \tilde{\sigma}(X, t)^2 \right) dt + \tilde{\sigma}(X, t)\, dW(t), \qquad \qquad \text{(III.4.12)}$$

where $\tilde{\sigma}(X, t) = \sigma(\exp(X), t)$.

---

[24] This is a special case of a general result proved by Alexander and Nogueira (2007a). See also Alexander and Nogueira (2007b) for further details.

[25] See Hagan *et al.* (2002). We remark that the critique applied to local volatility in that paper does not apply to *true* local volatility, only those parametric models with the floating smile property. On the other hand, Hagen's critique *does* apply to almost all stochastic volatility models. The SABR stochastic local volatility introduced in that paper is an exception only because they use a *non-scale-invariant* form. See Section III.4.6.1 for further details.

Suppose that the distributions of the log prices with dynamics given by (III.4.12) are not normal, as they would be in the constant volatility case. Instead we assume that the distribution of the log price $X(t)$ for any $t > 0$ is a mixture of two normal distributions. More specifically, we let $X(t)$ have distribution function

$$F_t(x) = \pi\, \Phi\left(\frac{x - \mu_1 t}{\sigma_1 \sqrt{t}}\right) + (1 - \pi)\, \Phi\left(\frac{x - \mu_2 t}{\sigma_2 \sqrt{t}}\right), \tag{III.4.13}$$

where Φ is the standard normal distribution function. In other words, the density function of X at time t is a mixture of two normal density functions φ_1 and φ_2 which have different means and variances. Specifically, the density function for X may be written[26]

$$f_t(x\,|\,\pi, \mu_1, \mu_2, \sigma_1, \sigma_2) = \pi\varphi_1(x, t) + (1 - \pi)\,\varphi_2(x, t), \tag{III.4.14}$$

where

$$\mu_i = r - y - \tfrac{1}{2}\sigma_i^2, \quad \text{for } i = 1, 2, \tag{III.4.15}$$

and

$$\varphi_i(x, t) = \frac{d}{dx}\, \Phi\left(\frac{x - \mu_i t}{\sigma_i \sqrt{t}}\right), \quad i = 1, 2. \tag{III.4.16}$$

Then Brigo and Mercurio (2002) showed that there is a unique local volatility function in (III.4.12) and this may be written

$$\tilde{\sigma}(X, t)^2 = \tilde{\pi}(X, t)\,\sigma_1^2 + (1 - \tilde{\pi}(X, t))\,\sigma_2^2, \tag{III.4.17}$$

where

$$\tilde{\pi}(X, t) = \frac{\pi\varphi_1(X, t)}{\pi\varphi_1(X, t) + (1 - \pi)\,\varphi_2(X, t)}. \tag{III.4.18}$$

The definition of $\tilde{\pi}(X, t)$ in (III.4.18) is a ratio of two density functions, derived from the Radon–Nikodym derivative.[27] The intuition behind this is that, for every observation x on X, the weight that the local volatility at x assigns to the variance σ_1 is proportional to the likelihood of x being drawn from φ_1 rather than φ_2.

Since market completeness is preserved in this framework, no-arbitrage pricing is possible and we can obtain the price of any option as the discounted expectation of its pay-off under the risk neutral measure. Since the model assumes a normal mixture log price distribution, i.e. a lognormal mixture price distribution, this expectation can be expressed as a weighted average of expectations under lognormal densities. In particular, the lognormal mixture price of a standard European option is a weighted average of BSM option prices. This makes the lognormal mixture diffusion model very easy to calibrate.

For a standard European call or put option with strike K and maturity T, when the underlying is at S the lognormal mixture option price is given by

$$f^{\mathrm{LNM}}(S, \pi, \sigma_1, \sigma_2, t\,|\,K, T) = \pi f^{\mathrm{BSM}}(S, \sigma_1, t\,|\,K, T) + (1 - \pi)f^{\mathrm{BSM}}(S, \sigma_2, t\,|\,K, T). \tag{III.4.19}$$

---

[26] See Section I.3.3.6 for further details on normal mixture distributions.
[27] See Section III.3.2.3.

EXAMPLE III.4.4: CALIBRATING A SIMPLE LOGNORMAL MIXTURE DIFFUSION

Use the European call price data given in Table III.4.5 to calibrate a lognormal mixture option pricing model, where log prices are assumed to have a mixture of two zero mean normal distributions with constant volatility. The options maturity is 90 days, the underlying price is 100 and the risk free rate and dividend yield are assumed to be zero for simplicity.

Table III.4.5   Market prices of standard European call options

Strike	80	82	84	86	88	90	92
Market price	21	18.5	16.25	14.25	12.3	10.4	8.5
Strike	94	96	98	100	102	104	106
Market price	6.7	5	3.6	2.45	1.7	1.1	0.76
Strike	108	110	112	114	116	118	120
Market price	0.56	0.45	0.39	0.35	0.32	0.3	0.25

SOLUTION   Before calibrating the model, we need to think about the calibration objective. In Section III.3.2.5 we introduce a general calibration objective, which in this example where all options have the same maturity may be written

$$\min_{\pi, \sigma_1, \sigma_2} \sqrt{\sum_K w(K) \left(f^m(K) - f^{\mathrm{LNM}}(K \mid \pi, \sigma_1, \sigma_2) \right)^2}, \tag{III.4.20}$$

where $f^m(K)$ and $f^{\mathrm{LNM}}(K \mid \pi, \sigma_1, \sigma_2)$ denote the market and lognormal mixture model prices of the option with strike K, and $w(K)$ is some weighting function. We want to place more weight in the calibration on the more liquid options, which are those that are closest to the ATM strike. Deep OTM options may be rather illiquid and therefore have unreliable prices. Thus a common way to weight the calibration objective so that it is not overly sensitive to these prices is to use the BSM gamma of the options, and we do that in the spreadsheet for this example. For reasons that will presently become clear, the BSM gamma of each option is based on the weighted average of the volatilities, i.e. on

$$\sigma = \pi \sigma_1 + (1 - \pi) \sigma_2. \tag{III.4.21}$$

We set up the problem using the Excel Solver, and the result is the following values for the calibrated parameters: $\sigma_1 = 59.32\%$, $\sigma_2 = 9.94\%$, $\pi = 5.21\%$ and $\sigma = 12.51\%$.

Hedging standard European options is also straightforward in the lognormal mixture model, since differentiating (III.4.19) with respect to S implies that the lognormal mixture delta is just a weighted sum of two BSM deltas, and similarly for the gamma.

EXAMPLE III.4.5: DELTA AND GAMMA FROM LOGNORMAL MIXTURE MODEL

Using the lognormal mixture model that was calibrated in the previous example, find the delta and the gamma for each option in the calibration set, first based on the BSM model and then based on the lognormal mixture model. Use a graph to compare these deltas and gammas.

SOLUTION   To understand the characteristics of lognormal mixture delta and gamma we must first examine the characteristics of the market price data. To this end, Figure III.4.10 shows the market implied volatility smile, and these volatilities are calculated in the spreadsheet using Excel Goal Seek. It is clear that the smile is fairly symmetric with a minimum at the ATM strike of 100. We now show that this symmetry is inherited by the lognormal mixture deltas and gammas.

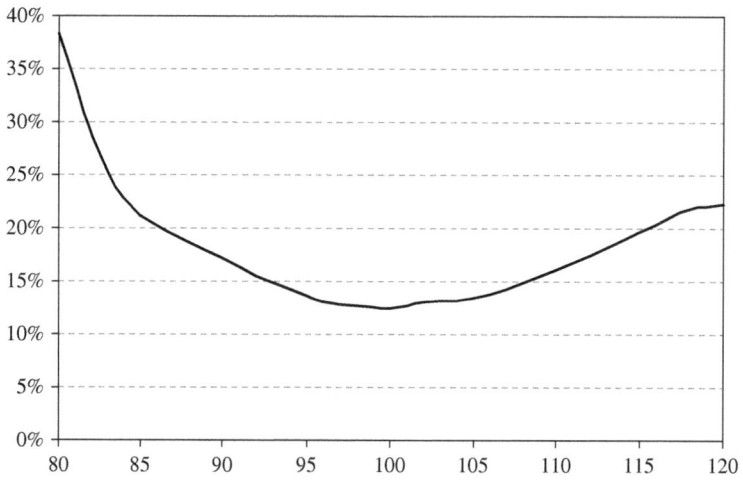

Figure III.4.10   Market implied volatilities

The lognormal mixture delta and gamma for each option are calculated using

$$\delta_{\mathrm{LNM}}(K) = 5.21\% \times \delta_{\mathrm{BSM}}(59.32\%, K) + 94.79\% \times \delta_{\mathrm{BSM}}(9.94\%, K),$$

$$\gamma_{\mathrm{LNM}}(K) = 5.21\% \times \gamma_{\mathrm{BSM}}(59.32\%, K) + 94.79\% \times \gamma_{\mathrm{BSM}}(9.94\%, K),$$

and these are compared with the BSM delta and gamma based on the average volatility (III.4.21), i.e. with $\delta_{\mathrm{BSM}}(12.51\%, K)$ and $\gamma_{\mathrm{BSM}}(12.51\%, K)$. We use the formulae given in Section III.3.7 for the BSM delta and gamma. The resulting graphs are shown in Figures III.4.11 and III.4.12.

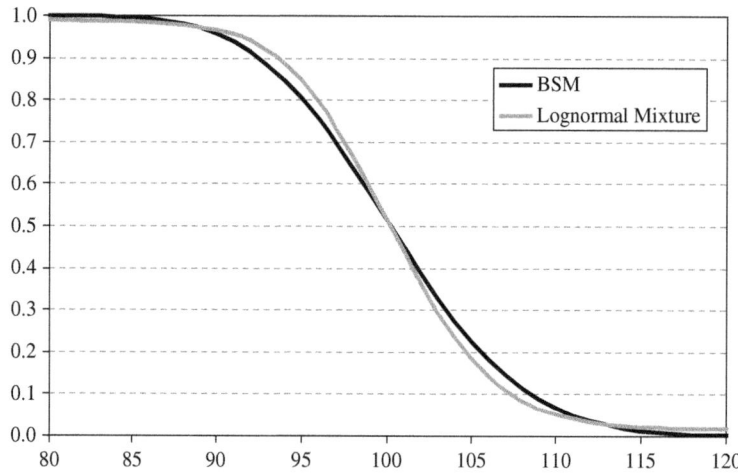

Figure III.4.11   Comparison of lognormal mixture and BSM deltas

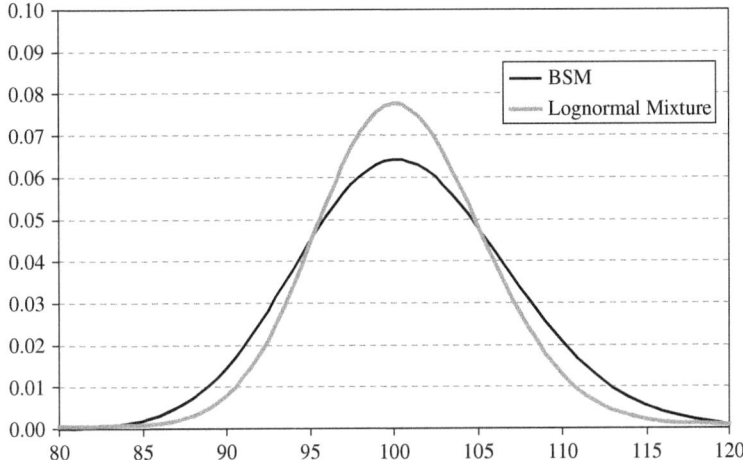

Figure III.4.12 Comparison of lognormal mixture and BSM gammas

The two deltas are equal at the ATM strike, and presently we shall understand why this is so. For strikes less than the ATM strike the smile slopes downward and the lognormal mixture deltas are greater than the BSM deltas for these options, until we reach very low strikes where the lognormal mixture deltas are less than the BSM deltas. For strikes above the ATM strike the smile slopes upward and the lognormal mixture deltas are less than the BSM deltas, until we reach very high strikes where the lognormal mixture deltas are greater than the BSM deltas.

The shape of the gamma is inherited from the log price density function, as well as the market implied volatility skew. Hence the lognormal mixture model, being based on a leptokurtic density, has a gamma curve with a higher peak and heavier tails than the BSM gamma curve. However, if the market implied volatility smile were more skewed then this feature would also be reflected in the gammas.

The vega of the lognormal mixture model is not so straightforward to define. In the lognormal mixture model, and indeed in *any* model where there are several parameters in the volatility function, the option price is not a function of a single volatility.[28] Hence, the only way that we can define a *single* vega for the lognormal mixture model is to link σ_1 and σ_2 to another independent variable, say $\sigma*$, and then we can define the vega with respect to this variable. For instance, suppose we put

$$\sigma_i = \omega_i \sigma*, \quad i = 1, 2.$$

Then differentiating (III.4.19) with respect to $\sigma*$ gives

$$\frac{\partial f_{\text{LNM}}}{\partial \sigma*} = \pi \omega_1 \nu_{\text{BSM}}(\sigma_1) + (1 - \pi) \omega_2 \nu_{\text{BSM}}(\sigma_2), \tag{III.4.22}$$

where $\nu_{\text{BSM}}(\sigma_i)$ is the BSM vega evaluated at σ_i for $i = 1, 2$.

---

[28] For instance, in mean-reverting stochastic volatility models, the option price is a function of both spot volatility and long term volatility.

In the above example we compared deltas and gammas from the lognormal mixture model with the deltas and gammas of the BSM model based on the *average volatility* and *not* the BSM model deltas and gammas based on the square root of the average variance. This is because it is the volatility and not the variance that is the basic parameter of an option pricing model. In fact the lognormal mixture model can be thought of as a very simple model of a trader's uncertainty in volatility. It is not a stochastic volatility model, but it can be thought of as a simple distribution over volatility where volatility can take value σ_1 with probability π and value σ_2 with probability $1 - \pi$. Then the average volatility (III.4.21) is the expected volatility in this framework.

In Section III.3.6.7 we described, in general terms, how traders adjust their BSM prices to account for uncertainty in volatility. There we assumed that it was volatility, not variance, that was the basic parameter on which option traders form their beliefs. Thus in (III.3.74) we identified the BSM price as the price based on the expected volatility, and not the price based on the square root of the expected variance. If we believed that the option price were based on expected variance rather than the expected volatility, then we would conclude that the BSM model cannot even price short term ATM options (indeed this is exactly the conclusion that was drawn by Hull and White, 1987).

The BSM volga at the average volatility σ given by (III.4.21) drives the difference between the lognormal mixture option price and the BSM price.[29] To keep the notation very simple, denote the two BSM prices on the right-hand side of (III.4.19) by $f^{BSM}(\sigma_1)$ and $f^{BSM}(\sigma_2)$. Then, applying a second order Taylor expansion,[30]

$$f^{BSM}(\sigma_i) \approx f^{BSM}(\sigma) + (\sigma_i - \sigma)\, \nu_{BSM}(\sigma) + \tfrac{1}{2}(\sigma_i - \sigma)^2 v_{BSM}(\sigma), \quad i = 1, 2,$$

where $\nu_{BSM}(\sigma)$ is the BSM vega and $v_{BSM}(\sigma)$ is the BSM volga evaluated at σ. Hence, the lognormal mixture option price may be written

$$\begin{aligned}
f^{LNM}(\pi, \sigma_1, \sigma_2) &= \pi f^{BSM}(\sigma_1) + (1 - \pi) f^{BSM}(\sigma_2) \\
&\approx f^{BSM}(\sigma) + [\pi(\sigma_1 - \sigma) + (1 - \pi)(\sigma_2 - \sigma)]\, \nu_{BSM}(\sigma) \\
&\quad + \tfrac{1}{2}\left[\pi(\sigma_1 - \sigma)^2 + (1 - \pi)(\sigma_2 - \sigma)^2\right] v_{BSM}(\sigma)
\end{aligned}$$

or, using (III.4.21)

$$f^{LNM}(\pi, \sigma_1, \sigma_2) \approx f^{BSM}(\sigma) + \tfrac{1}{2}\left[\pi\sigma_1^2 + (1 - \pi)\sigma_2^2 - \sigma^2\right] v_{BSM}(\sigma). \tag{III.4.23}$$

The term in the square bracket above is not zero, because σ is the average volatility, not the average variance. By (III.4.21),

$$\sigma^2 < \pi\sigma_1^2 + (1 - \pi)\sigma_2^2$$

so the term in the square brackets in (III.4.23) is positive. The BSM volga is illustrated in Section III.3.7.4. It is very small for near ATM options, positive for ITM and OTM options, and converges towards zero at extremely high or low strikes.

Hence, the approximation (III.4.23) shows that the lognormal mixture price will be similar to the BSM price based on the average volatility for an ATM option, but greater than the BSM price based on the average volatility for ITM or OTM options. This way, the lognormal

---

[29] The BSM volga is illustrated in Section III.3.7.4.
[30] Taylor expansions are introduced and illustrated in Section I.1.6.

mixture model provides a simple way for traders to adjust BSM option prices to account for uncertainty in volatility, as explained in Section III.3.6.7. Instead of the *ad hoc* adjustment described there, traders may calibrate the parameters π, σ_1 and σ_2 to option prices, set $\sigma = \pi\sigma_1 + (1-\pi)\sigma_2$ and then use (III.4.23).

In the above we have assumed there are only two normal distributions for the log prices, with zero means and constant volatilities. But the theoretical analysis can be extended to more than two component distributions, and with non-zero means. Still, the constant volatility assumption implies that there is no term structure in option prices, so the smile surface is like a cylinder with a constant curvature. The curvature does not fade with maturity, as we usually find in market smile surfaces. However, to capture the features of the market smile the lognormal mixture model can be extended to a simple stochastic volatility model, where the persistence of the skew into longer maturities is determined by uncertainty over long term volatility, as explained in Alexander (2004).

III.4.4 MODELLING THE DYNAMICS OF IMPLIED VOLATILITY

Section III.4.3.2 gave a practical example that demonstrated the sensitivity of the implied volatility surface to changes in the underlying price. Example III.4.3 shows that the implied volatility surface changes when the underlying price changes, even if the option prices remain fixed. That is,

$$\frac{\partial\theta}{\partial S} = \theta_S \neq 0. \tag{III.4.24}$$

For the time being we shall continue to use the notation $\theta = \theta(K, T)$ for simplicity, but since implied volatility depends on the current price of the underlying, later on we shall need to use a fuller notation for the implied volatility of a standard European option with strike K and maturity T, i.e. $\theta(K, T \,|\, S)$ rather than $\theta(K, T)$.[31] We shall also be careful to distinguish between market implied volatilities, i.e. the volatilities that are implicit in the market prices of standard European options, and model implied volatilities, i.e. the volatilities that are implicit in the model prices of standard European options. We use the superscript m to make it clear when we are specifically referring to market implied volatility.

In the first part of this section we describe the *sticky models* of implied volatility that were introduced by Derman (1999) to explain the regime behaviour in equity index volatility. After summarizing the properties of these models we apply principal component analysis to model the dynamics of market implied volatilities and discuss the applications of this approach to dynamic delta hedging of option portfolios.

III.4.4.1 Sticky Models

We assume, for simplicity and without loss of generality, that the risk free rate and dividend yield are both zero. We also fix the maturity of the options and drop the variable T from our notation.[32] We now consider a simple time and space discretization in the form of a tree. At each node in the tree the range of the price movements depends on a forward volatility. The

---

[31] Or even $\theta(K, T \,|\, S, t)$ if we wish to emphasize the time at which it is measured.
[32] However, note that the coefficient β in (III.4.25) depends on the options' maturity.

object of the sticky models is to parameterize these forward volatilities using only the current market implied volatility surface. Suppose we are now at time $t = 0$ when the underlying price is S_0 and the instantaneous volatility of the price process (i.e. the spot volatility) is σ_0. We denote the implied volatility of strike K by $\theta(K|S_0, \sigma_0)$.

Derman (1999) proposed three different linear parameterizations of implied volatility that are appropriate in three different equity index market regimes. These parameterizations are labelled *sticky strike*, *sticky delta* and *sticky tree*. In each sticky model,

$$\theta(K|S_0, \sigma_0) = \theta(S|S_0, \sigma_0) - \beta(K - S), \qquad (\text{III.4.25})$$

where $\beta > 0$, S_0 denotes the current price and σ_0 denotes the process volatility at time $t = 0$, i.e. at the root of the tree. Differentiating with respect to S gives

$$\theta_S(K|S_0, \sigma_0) - \theta_S(S|S_0, \sigma_0) = \beta. \qquad (\text{III.4.26})$$

On the left-hand side we have the *fixed strike spread* over ATM volatility and (III.4.26) shows that spreads at different strikes move parallel to each other when S changes. Their movements are perfectly correlated with each other and with S.[33] Since $\beta > 0$ they all increase by the same amount when S increases.

Derman specified three possibilities for parameterizing the ATM implied volatility as follows:

$$\theta(S|S_0, \sigma_0) = \begin{cases} \sigma_0 - \beta(S - S_0), & \text{in sticky strike,} \\ \sigma_0, & \text{in sticky delta,} \\ \sigma_0 - 2\beta(S - S_0), & \text{in sticky tree.} \end{cases} \qquad (\text{III.4.27})$$

Hence

$$\theta_S(S|S_0, \sigma_0) = \begin{cases} -\beta, & \text{in sticky strike,} \\ 0, & \text{in sticky delta,} \\ -2\beta, & \text{in sticky tree.} \end{cases} \qquad (\text{III.4.28})$$

Since $\beta > 0$, ATM volatility decreases when S increases, in the sticky strike and sticky tree regimes, and the sensitivity to S is twice as large in the sticky tree regime as in the sticky delta regime. And ATM volatility is independent of S in the sticky delta regime, so the smile must move with S in this regime. In other words, the sticky delta model is a floating smile model (we shall discuss this further below).

In Section III.3.2.6 we explained how a binomial tree may be used to price options. The tree for the underlying price S is used to construct another tree for an option price, so one tree for S is used to generate many different trees, one for each option. Derman (1999) used the linear parameterizations of implied volatility skews defined above to construct a binomial tree for S, where the local volatility at any given node is determined by the implied volatility surface. Each sticky model corresponds to a different type of tree for modelling the evolution of S. However, the problem with the sticky strike and sticky delta models is that each option has to have a *different* tree for S. Thus we need to model the evolution of S simultaneously in many trees with different volatilities!

In the sticky strike and sticky delta models the local volatilities are constant at each node of every tree for S, but there are different local volatilities in each tree. In the sticky strike

---

[33] Put another way, a principal component representation has only one component.

model the local volatility in each tree for S depends on the strike of the option being priced. When S changes the root of the tree is changed from S_0 to the new level of S. The same tree is still used to price the option. Each option has its own constant volatility tree for the underlying price.

In the sticky delta model the local volatility depends on the moneyness of the option.[34] Now there is a different price tree for every moneyness. We must move to a different constant volatility tree for the underlying price S whenever S moves, because the moneyness of the option changes. Put another way, the sticky delta model is a model where the local volatility surface *floats* around with S. It is not a 'true' local volatility in the sense of Dupire. The sticky delta model is a *floating smile* model, like the lognormal mixture model. All stochastic volatility models that are appropriate for pricing options on tradable assets are *also* floating smile models, as we shall show in Section III.4.6.

It is only in the sticky tree model that there is a single, static tree for S that can be used to price every option. The tree can have different local volatilities at each node and it remains static as S moves. When S changes we simply move to a different node in the tree.[35] Thus the sticky tree model is a true local volatility model in the sense of Dupire.

III.4.4.2   Case Study I: Principal Component Analysis of Implied Volatilities

The implied volatility surface moves in a highly correlated fashion when the underlying price changes, like a two-dimensional version of the yield curve. Thus a practical approach to modelling movements in implied volatilities can focus on a principal component analysis (PCA) of implied volatilities. This section demonstrates how PCA can be used to model the dynamics of the smile and how to develop a hedging model based on this analysis.[36]

Early applications of PCA to the equity implied volatility skew include Derman and Kamal (1997), Skiadopoulos et al. (1998) and Fengler et al. (2003), the latter paper applying common PCA to the entire volatility surface. Alexander (2001) shows that PCA is more effectively applied to *spreads* of implied volatility over the ATM volatility, rather than to implied volatilities directly. Not only is the choice of spreads rather than levels empirically justified by a significant increase in the variation explained by PCA, if Derman's sticky models are empirically justified then, by (III.4.25), there should be a much higher correlation between the daily changes in fixed strike spreads over ATM volatility than between the daily changes in the levels of fixed strike volatility.

We use daily closing prices on the FTSE 100 index options from 2 January 1998 until 31 March 1999 obtained from LIFFE. We have chosen this period because it covers the three regimes of equity markets identified by Derman: a *stable trending* market, a *range bounded* market and a *market crash*. First the market prices are converted to implied volatilities, and then the volatilities are interpolated to obtain time series of volatilities of a fixed maturity of 1 month. Figure III.4.13 illustrates 60 different fixed strike volatilities, the ATM volatility (shown by the bold grey line) and the FTSE 100 index on the right-hand scale (shown by the bold black line). Since the index has a pronounced negative skew the low strike volatilities are greater than the high strike volatilities.

---

[34] A crude definition of moneyness $(K - S)$ suffices when we use the simple linear sticky models (III.4.25)–(III.4.28).
[35] Just as we do in the standard, constant volatility binomial trees introduced in Section III.3.2.6.
[36] The principles of PCA are explained and illustrated in Section I.2.6 and in chapter II.2 and several practical applications are discussed in other chapters of *Market Risk Analysis*.

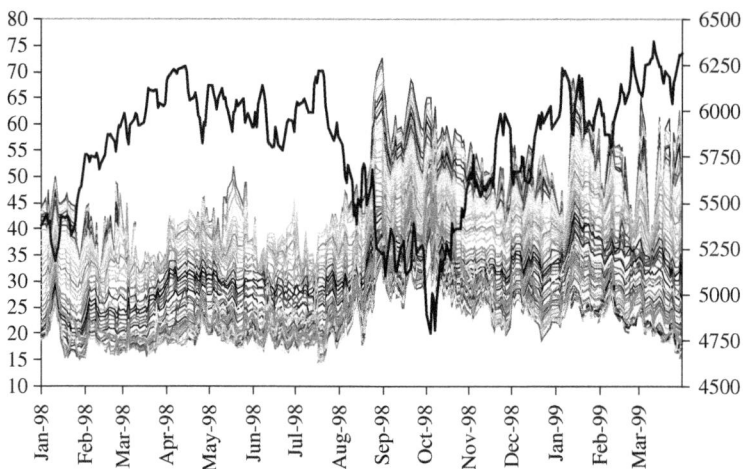

Figure III.4.13   One-month implied volatilities, ATM volatility and the FTSE 100 index

We can identify the three regimes of equity index markets from the figure:

- The period from February to mid April 1998 was characterized by a stable trending market, and during this time the ATM implied volatility remained relatively constant. Given the properties (III.4.28), we can identify the stable trending regime with the sticky delta model.
- The period from mid April to July 1998 was characterized by a range bounded market and during this time the ATM implied volatility has a small negative correlation with the index. Given the properties (III.4.28), we can identify the range bounded regime with the sticky strike model.
- Between August 1998 and January 1999 the ATM volatility first increased sharply as the index crashed and then decreased sharply during the recovery period. The correlation between ATM volatility and the index was large and negative in this period, and we therefore identify the crash and recovery regime with the sticky tree model.

We remark that from January to March 1999 it is unclear whether the volatility remained in the crash regime or moved to the range bounded regime. ATM volatility was still very sensitive to movements in the index, but an additional feature of *tilting skew* is very pronounced. That is, when the index falls the low strike volatilities increase much more than the high strike volatilities so the skew becomes much steeper, and when the index increases the skew flattens out. Put another way, the *range* of the skew (i.e. difference between the low strike volatility and the high strike volatility) is inversely proportional to the index change. When the index moves down the range increases and when it moves up the range narrows.

Figure III.4.14 presents the same data as in Figure III.4.13, but here we graph the fixed strike spreads over ATM volatility on the left-hand scale and the ATM spread is shown as the grey line at zero on this scale. The tilting skew is still evident, particularly at the end of the data period. We remark that tilting skews are not captured by the linear sticky model parameterizations described in the previous section. If (III.4.25) were valid we would need only one principal component to describe the dynamics of fixed strike spreads, but the strong empirical evidence of tilting skew justifies the inclusion of at least one – and possibly

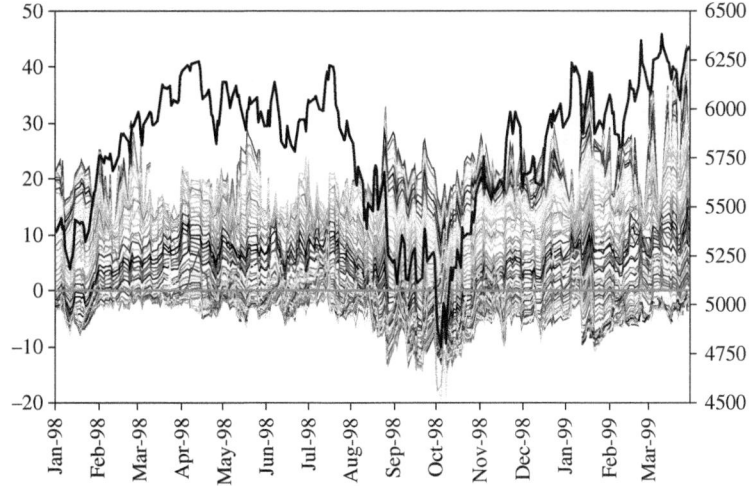

Figure III.4.14   Fixed strike spreads over ATM volatility and the FTSE 100 index

two – more components in the PCA. Hence, we now perform a PCA of daily changes in fixed strike spreads and interpret the results.

The spreadsheet for this case study takes as the input to the PCA the daily changes in fixed strike spreads over ATM volatility, on all strikes up to 6225, from 1 September 1998 until 31 March 1999. We shall compare the results of applying PCA to (a) the covariance matrix and (b) the correlation matrix.[37] The first five eigenvalues are presented in Table III.4.6.

Table III.4.6   Eigenvalues

	1	2	3	4	5
Covariance matrix					
Eigenvalue	184.26	41.11	14.75	5.55	3.27
Variation explained	69.87%	15.59%	5.59%	2.10%	1.24%
Cumulative variation	69.87%	85.46%	91.05%	93.16%	94.40%
Correlation matrix					
Eigenvalue	24.26	10.82	4.64	1.35	0.88
Variation explained	53.91%	24.05%	10.31%	3.01%	1.95%
Cumulative variation	53.91%	77.97%	88.28%	91.28%	93.24%

Turning first to the eigenvalue analysis, applying PCA to the covariance matrix achieves a better result than applying PCA to the correlation matrix. The first component in particular explains almost 70% of the variation in the covariance matrix but less than 55% of the

---

[37] When choosing the data for PCA we need a fairly short data period (unlike cointegration) to capture the current market circumstances. On the other hand, with up to 60 implied volatilities trading at some times, we need to take enough data for a robust estimation of the covariance or correlation matrix. For instance, the reader can verify the results of applying PCA to data on all 60 strikes between 1 February and 31 March 1999 are not useful. The data on the very high strike volatilities may be unreliable, since these options were very sparsely traded, and the period of 45 days is rather short. In our case study here we take 6 months of data.

variation in the correlation matrix. Thus a large proportion of the movements in fixed strike spreads are parallel, as the linear sticky models assume, but 30% of the variation comes from tilts in the term structure and non-linear movements. Together the first three components explain over 90% of the variation in the covariance matrix, but we need four components to capture movements to a similar degree in the correlation matrix.

The first three eigenvectors of the covariance matrix are shown in Figure III.4.15. The first two eigenvectors of the covariance matrix are similar in shape: *both* capture a tilting skew movement where high strike spreads move parallel but low strike spreads tilt. The third component reflects a strong change in convexity of the fixed strike spreads.

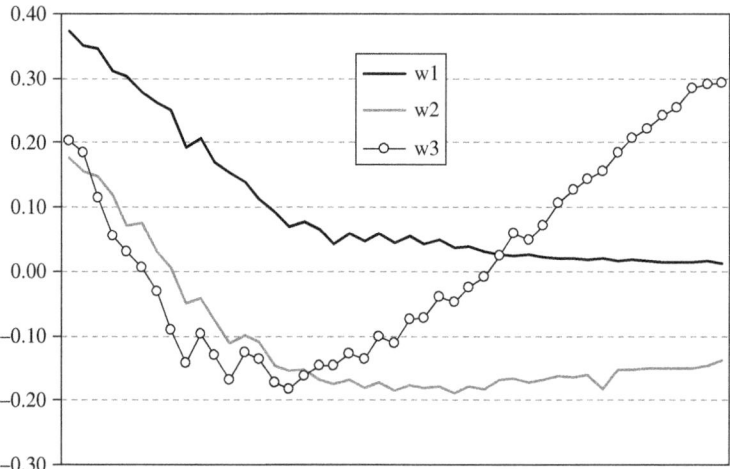

Figure III.4.15   Eigenvectors (covariance)

These eigenvectors should be contrasted with the first three eigenvectors of the correlation matrix shown in Figure III.4.16. Here the first eigenvector captures a parallel shift. But we know from Table III.4.6 that this accounts for little more than 50% of the movements in fixed strike spreads. The second and third components have the traditional tilt and curvature interpretation. The oscillation in all three eigenvectors in the mid strike range points to the possibility of stale data at *25 strikes, with more trading on the *75 strikes.[38]

We shall proceed with the PCA from the covariance matrix, since the results are slightly better than those based on the correlation matrix. A three principal component representation of the fixed strike spreads is given by

$$\Delta(\theta(K) - \theta(S))_t \approx \omega_{K1}P_{1t} + \omega_{K2}P_{2t} + \omega_{K3}P_{2t}, \qquad \text{(III.4.29)}$$

where ω_{Ki} is the Kth element of the ith eigenvector of the covariance matrix and P_1, P_2 and P_3 are the principal components that are obtained from the covariance matrix. The time series of the first three principal components P_1, P_2 and P_3 are shown in Figure III.4.17. An excessive volatility at the end of the period, from March 1999 onward, is apparent.

---

[38] The 4925, 5025, 5125 and 5225 strikes have much lower correlations with other strikes than the 4975, 5075, 5175 and 5275 strikes.

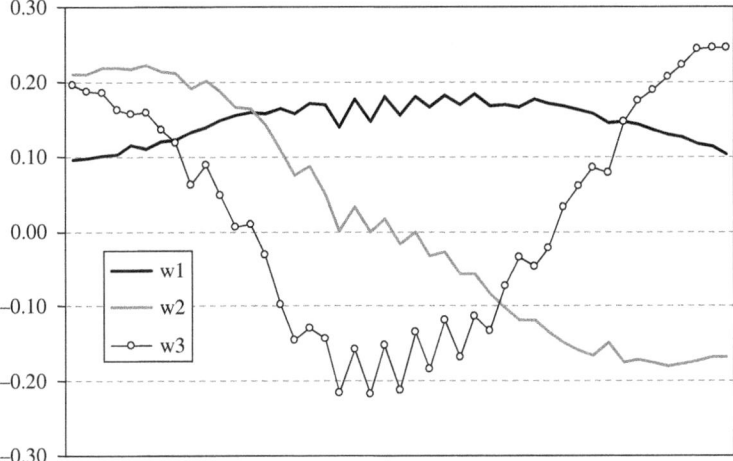

Figure III.4.16   Eigenvectors (correlation)

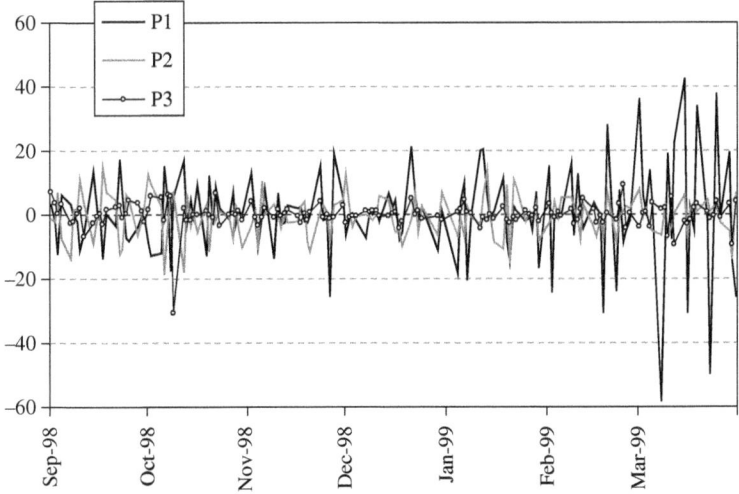

Figure III.4.17   First three principal components

III.4.4.3   Case Study II: Modelling the ATM Volatility–Index Relationship

The PCA described in the previous section provides us with an adequate model on which to base the dynamics of the fixed strike spreads, i.e. the model (III.4.29). But we have not yet modelled the relationship between S and the ATM volatility, here denoted simply $\theta(S)$. We now define and estimate such a model. When combined with (III.4.29) the model will allow us to predict movements in implied volatilities of all strikes conditional on some assumed change in the index. Armed with such a model the trader can find, for any x, where the skew will be if the index moves by x points.

Derman (1999) hypothesizes that the relationship between the ATM volatility and the underlying price undergoes regime switches, with three different equity market regimes. In this case a *Markov switching* model of the form

$$Y_t = \alpha^s + \beta^s R_t + \varepsilon_t^s, \quad s = 1, 2, 3,$$ (III.4.30)

will be appropriate, where

$$Y_t = \Delta\theta(S)_t = \theta(S)_t - \theta(S)_{t-1},$$

$$R_t = \frac{S_t - S_{t-1}}{S_{t-1}} = \frac{\Delta S_t}{S_{t-1}},$$ (III.4.31)

and the coefficients and the error process all depend on the current state s.

Alternatively, we could assume that instead of abrupt switches between regimes the sensitivity of implied volatility to the index return, i.e. the coefficient β in (III.4.30), does change over time but evolves smoothly. In this case the appropriate model is

$$Y_t = \alpha_t + \beta_t R_t + \varepsilon_t,$$ (III.4.32)

where the time varying coefficients can be estimated by the *Kalman filter* or a *bivariate GARCH* model.

Unfortunately Markov switching, the Kalman filter and bivariate GARCH cannot be done in Excel without special add-ins or VBA code. For this reason only we shall proceed with a crude approximation of the relationship (III.4.32) using the exponentially weighted moving average (EWMA) beta method described in Section II.3.7. That is, we set:

$$\hat{\beta}_t^\lambda = \frac{\text{Cov}_\lambda(Y_t, R_t)}{V_\lambda(R_t)},$$ (III.4.33)

where the covariance and variance are estimated using EWMA with the same value of the smoothing constant λ. We also make the simplifying assumption that $\alpha_t = 0$ so that the ATM implied volatility changes only when the index changes. Figure III.4.18 displays the result for $\lambda = 0.95$.[39] The estimated value of beta (i.e. the sensitivity of ATM implied volatility to index returns) at each point in time is marked on the figure by the bold black line and measured on the left-hand scale. A return sensitivity of -1 on this scale implies a 1% absolute rise in ATM volatility when the index falls by 1%.[40]

Dividing the *volatility returns sensitivity* (III.4.33) by yesterday's index price provides an estimate of the *volatility price sensitivity* of ATM volatility, i.e. an estimate of the partial derivative $\theta_S(S)$. This is shown by the grey line in Figure III.4.18 and it is measured on the right-hand scale. As expected, the relationship between ATM volatility and the index is negative. A price sensitivity of -1 on this scale implies a 1% absolute rise in ATM volatility when the index falls by 100 points.

The returns and price sensitivity graphs in Figure III.4.18 are very similar to each other and also very similar to the time series of the FTSE 100 index shown in Figures III.4.13 and III.4.14. It appears that the sensitivity of implied volatility to the index grows stronger when the index is falling and weaker when the index recovers.

Unfortunately, there is nothing in the model (III.4.32) to capture any asymmetry in the relationship between implied volatility and the index. The change in volatility is of the same

---

[39] The problem with EWMA models is that the choice of λ is subjective. A lower value of λ makes the estimates more time sensitive.
[40] For instance, the ATM volatility would increase from 20% to 21%.

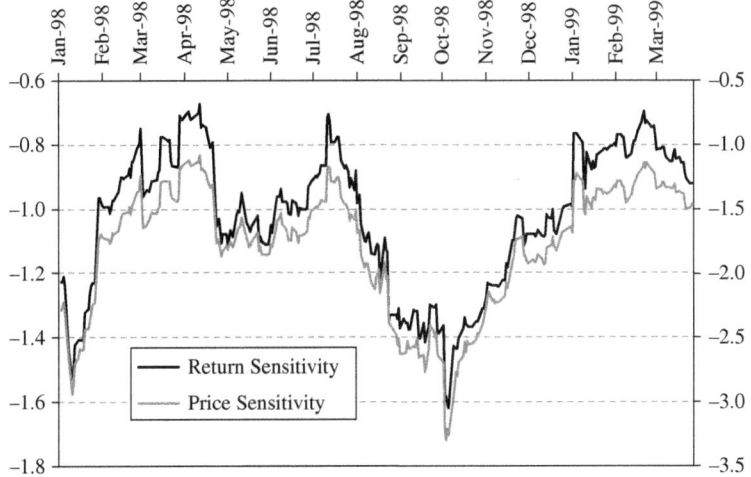

Figure III.4.18   ATM implied volatility sensitivity to FTSE index

magnitude – it just has a different sign when the index falls or rises. A simple *asymmetric* model for the relationship between index price and volatility is

$$Y_t = \beta^+ R_t^+ + \beta^- R_t^- + \varepsilon_t, \qquad\qquad (\text{III.4.34})$$

where R_t^+ is the set of positive index returns and R_t^- is the set of negative index returns. The up and down beta coefficients, β^+ and β^-, are assumed constant over the sample and hence may be estimated by ordinary least squares. This is done in the spreadsheet for this case study, and we obtain

$$\hat{\beta}^+ = -0.935 \text{ and } \hat{\beta}^+ = -1.414.$$

That is, when the index increases by 1% the ATM volatility decreases absolutely by 0.935% on average and when the index decreases by 1% the ATM volatility increases absolutely by 1.414% on average.

We may also capture the time varying nature of the asymmetric relationship between index price and volatility by extending (III.4.32) to the quadratic model

$$Y_t = \beta_t R_t + \gamma_t R_t^2 + \varepsilon_t. \qquad\qquad (\text{III.4.35})$$

In the spreadsheet we estimate the EWMA coefficients as

$$\begin{pmatrix} \hat{\beta}_t \\ \hat{\gamma}_t \end{pmatrix} = \mathbf{V}_\lambda^{-1} \mathbf{C}_\lambda, \qquad\qquad (\text{III.4.36})$$

with

$$\mathbf{V}_\lambda = \begin{pmatrix} V_\lambda(R_t) & 0 \\ 0 & V_\lambda(R_t^2) \end{pmatrix} \quad \text{and} \quad \mathbf{C}_\lambda = \begin{pmatrix} \mathrm{Cov}_\lambda(Y_t, R_t) \\ \mathrm{Cov}_\lambda(Y_t, R_t^2) \end{pmatrix}$$

assuming $\mathrm{Cov}_\lambda(R_t, R_t^2)$ is equal to its unconditional value of zero. The up and down returns sensitivities are derived from (III.4.36) and shown in Figure III.4.19.[41]

---

[41] The smoothing constant λ was chosen, as usual arbitrarily, as 0.97 in this figure.

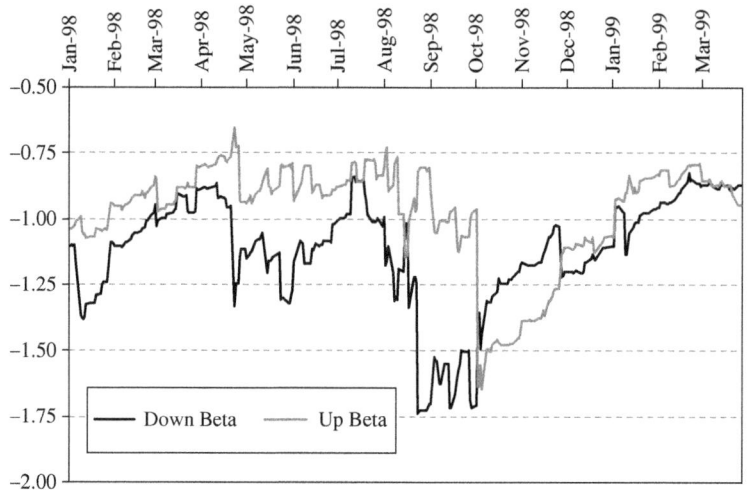

Figure III.4.19   Up and down returns sensitivities in the quadratic EWMA model

At the time of the market crash in August 1998 the sensitivity of ATM volatility to falls in the index, as measured by the down market beta, suddenly became much stronger. From a 1.25% increase in volatility for a 1% fall in the index it jumped to a 1.75% increase in volatility for a 1% fall in the index in the space of a few days. The sensitivities to index falls are greater than the sensitivities to index rises except during the recovery period of the crash. At the beginning of October 1998, as the index began to recover from the crash, the sensitivity of ATM volatility to increases in the index, as measured by the up market beta, was actually greater than its sensitivity to decreases in the index at this time.

III.4.4.4   Case Study III: Modelling the Skew Sensitivities

In this section we put the results of the previous two sections together to calculate the sensitivity of fixed strike volatilities to changes in the index. The return sensitivities shown in Figure III.4.20 are obtained by combining the symmetric return sensitivities β_t shown by the black line in Figure III.4.18 with the principal component model (III.4.29). Thus

$$X_{Kt} = \beta_t R_t + \omega_{K1} P_{1t} + \omega_{K2} P_{2t} + \omega_{K3} P_{2t},\qquad\text{(III.4.37)}$$

where $X_{Kt} = \Delta\theta(K)_t$ is the change in fixed strike volatility. To complete the model we assume each principal component is linearly related to the index returns as[42]

$$P_{it} = \delta_i R_t + \varepsilon_{it}.\qquad\text{(III.4.38)}$$

Then the total return sensitivity of the volatility with strike K at time t is

$$\theta_S(K)_t = \beta_t + \omega_{1K}\delta_1 + \omega_{2K}\delta_2 + \omega_{3K}\delta_3.\qquad\text{(III.4.39)}$$

---

[42] We make this assumption here only for simplicity. Since the principal components are uncorrelated by construction, only one of the three δ_i will be significant. Alexander (2001) uses a time varying framework for (III.4.38). Since the principal components are only *un*conditionally uncorrelated, they have non-zero conditional correlation.

For instance, on 1 October 1998 we find that a 1% fall in the index would have been accompanied by an increase of about 1% in the 5025 strike volatility but an increase of 1.65% in the 4025 strike volatility.[43] These returns sensitivities can be converted to index price sensitivities as in the previous section.

The sensitivity of fixed strike volatilities to changes in the index price on 1 October 1998 is shown in Figure III.4.20. At this time a 100-point fall in the index would have been accompanied by the 5025 strike volatility increasing absolutely by 1.88% but the 4025 strike volatility would increase absolutely by 3.17%.

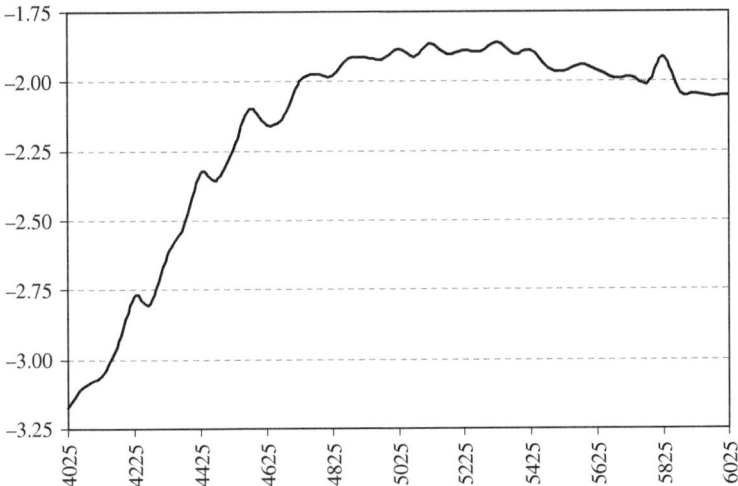

Figure III.4.20   Fixed strike price sensitivities of 1-month FTSE 100 options on 1 October 1998

This last case study has demonstrated that an analysis based on three principal components of the fixed strike spreads over ATM volatility is a flexible and practical approach to modelling skew sensitivities to changes in the underlying price. It captures tilts and changes in curvature of the skew when the index moves, as well as parallel shifts. However, since we have not used one of the asymmetric models of ATM index sensitivities from case study II, the model implemented in this third case study predicts a symmetric response when the index changes. The extension of this study to an asymmetric model for skew dynamics is left to the intrepid reader!

III.4.4.5   Applications of Implied Volatility Dynamics to Hedging Options

In the Black–Scholes–Merton world where volatility is constant none of the features that we have discussed above would be observed. The BSM *model* implied volatilities are constant and do not depend on the underlying price, but the market implied volatilities are *very* sensitive to changes in S, as we have seen above. How should we incorporate this information into the delta?

---

[43] Again, these are in absolute terms, so a 1% absolute rise is a rise from 20% to 21%, for example.

For a standard European option with strike K and maturity T we define:

$$f^{BSM}(S, \theta^m \,|\, K, T)$$ BSM option price

$$\delta_{BSM}(K, T\,|\,S) = f_S^{BSM} = \frac{\partial f^{BSM}(S, \theta^m \,|\, K, T)}{\partial S}$$ BSM delta

$$\nu_{BSM}(K, T\,|\,S) = f_{\theta^m}^{BSM} = \frac{\partial f^{BSM}(S, \theta^m \,|\, K, T)}{\partial \theta^m}$$ BSM vega

$$\theta^m = \theta^m(K, T\,|\,S)$$ market implied volatility

$$\theta_S^m = \frac{\partial \theta^m(K, T\,|\,S)}{\partial S}$$ volatility price sensitivity.

The aim of the case studies above was to explain how to estimate the volatility price sensitivity of implied volatilities of different strikes.[44] Indeed, Figure III.4.20 graphs the curve $\theta_S^m(K, T\,|\,S)$ for strikes ranging from $K = 4025$ to $K = 6025$ on the FTSE index options and for $T = 1$ month. In this section we explain how this *volatility price sensitivity curve* – or, more generally, a whole surface $\theta_S^m(K, T\,|\,S)$ for different K *and* T – can be used to improve the accuracy of delta hedging.

The *market delta* of an option is the sensitivity of the market price of the option with respect to S. It cannot be captured by a continuous time model, it can only be estimated empirically by observing the movements of market prices of options over time. However, when we calibrate the market implied volatility we equate $f^{BSM}(S, \theta^m \,|\, K, T)$ to the market price, i.e. we set

$$f^m(K, T) \equiv f^{BSM}(S, \theta^m \,|\, K, T). \tag{III.4.40}$$

So the market implied volatility depends on S because the BSM price depends on S. Differentiating (III.4.40) with respect to S, applying the chain rule, gives

$$\delta^m(K, T) = \delta_{BSM}(K, T\,|\,S) + \nu_{BSM}(K, T\,|\,S)\,\theta_S^m(K, T\,|\,S). \tag{III.4.41}$$

This defines the 'market delta' as an *adjusted* BSM delta where the adjustment term depends on the BSM vega and the market implied volatility price sensitivity. The BSM vega is positive and when the skew is negative we also find $\theta_S^m(K, T\,|\,S) < 0$, as in our case study of equity index options (i.e. we observed a negative correlation between the equity index implied volatility and the index). To account for this negative correlation we should *reduce* the BSM delta, by an amount that depends on the vega and the market implied volatility price sensitivity.

The adjustment of the BSM delta in (III.4.41) depends crucially on the market implied volatility price sensitivity $\theta_S^m(K, T\,|\,S)$. In equity markets this is very strong and negative, as we have seen in the case studies above, and bond option implied volatilities also have a negative relationship with bond prices (and a positive relationship with interest rates); but in commodity and currency options markets the market implied volatility price sensitivity can be positive for some liquid strikes. Hence, in these markets the market deltas obtained using (III.4.41) may be greater than the BSM deltas.

---

[44] And of different maturities, although in the case studies above we only considered the volatilities with 1-month maturity.

EXAMPLE III.4.6: ADJUSTING DELTA FOR SKEW DYNAMICS

Calculate the BSM position delta of FTSE 100 index options with strikes between 4025 and 6025 and maturity 1 month on 1 October 1998. Each FTSE 100 option is for £10 per point and on 1 October 1998 the index was at 5054. So the position size is £50,540. Then consider the volatility price sensitivity curve for these options that was estimated in case study III above and shown in Figure III.4.20. Use this curve to *adjust* the BSM position deltas for the dependence of the volatility skew on S. How different is the adjusted position delta from the standard BSM delta?

SOLUTION   The spreadsheet for this example first calculates the BSM delta and BSM vega using the formulae given in Section III.3.7. Then we apply the formula (III.4.41) to find the adjusted 'market' delta, $\delta_m(K, 1\text{mth})$ for each strike K. The position delta is the delta multiplied by £50,540. The difference between the two position deltas is shown in Figure III.4.21.

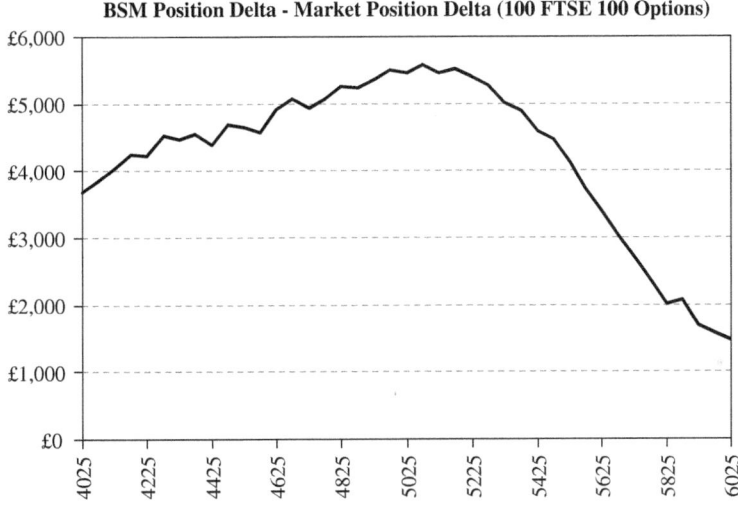

BSM Position Delta - Market Position Delta (100 FTSE 100 Options)

Figure III.4.21   Comparison of BSM and adjusted 'market' position deltas

Overall the BSM deltas, which fail to account for the dynamics of the skew and its correlation with index price changes, lead to substantial over-hedging, especially for ATM options. For instance, a position of 1000 options with a strike of 5025 has a BSM delta that is £54,510 too high. This is approximately the same as over-hedging by one FTSE 100 futures contract.

We conclude that the modelling approach presented in this section provides a practical and *model free* method for adjusting delta hedge ratios to account for skew dynamics.[45] We have shown that failing to account for the relationship between market implied volatility and underlying price changes when calculating hedge ratios can lead to very inaccurate hedging.

---

[45] Model free in the sense that the results do not depend on any stochastic volatility model.

III.4.5   STOCHASTIC VOLATILITY MODELS

The BSM model is the benchmark by which market prices of standard European options are measured. In currency markets the prices of options are even quoted in terms of their BSM volatility rather than their price.[46] The BSM model makes the assumption that the underlying price has a lognormal distribution and constant volatility but, since the market implied volatility surface is not flat, this assumption is clearly not believed by traders. Historically the log returns on most financial assets are not normally distributed, they are leptokurtic and skewed. Moreover, volatility is not constant. The log returns distribution changes randomly over time, so its volatility is stochastic.

There is an enormous literature on models that relax the assumptions made by the BSM model so that the price process is no longer assumed to follow a geometric Brownian motion with constant volatility. The aim of these models is to price OTC options that may have exotic and/or path-dependent pay-offs so that their prices are consistent with the market prices of standard European options. This precludes the possibility of arbitrage between an exotic option and a replicating portfolio of standard calls and puts.

Hence, the market prices of European options are used to calibrate the model parameters. We may calibrate the model by changing the parameters so that the model prices of European options are set equal to, or as close as possible to, the market prices, as described in Section III.3.2.5. Alternatively, the model's parameters may be calibrated by fitting the model implied volatilities to the market implied volatility smile. That is, instead of (III.3.16) the calibration objective may be

$$\min_{\lambda} \sqrt{\sum_{K,T} w(K,T) \left(\theta^m(K,T) - \theta(K,T\,|\boldsymbol{\lambda})\right)^2}, \qquad (III.4.42)$$

where $\theta^m(K,T)$ and $\theta(K,T\,|\boldsymbol{\lambda})$ denote the market and model implied volatilities of a European option with strike K and expiry time T and $w(K,T)$ is some weighting function that ensures that more weight is placed on the options with more reliable prices.

Three main strands of research into option pricing models have been developed: *stochastic volatility* where the variance or volatility of the price process is stochastic; *local volatility* where volatility is a parametric deterministic function of time and the asset price; and *jump* or *Lévy models* where jumps in the price or volatility or both are allowed. There are also hybrid models, which combine stochastic and local volatilities (Hagan et al., 2000; Alexander and Nogueira, 2004, 2008), stochastic volatility and jumps (Bates, 1996; Bakshi et al., 1997; Andersen et al., 2002) or local volatility and jumps (Andersen and Andreasen, 2000; Carr et al., 2004). For general review papers covering many of these models, see Jackwerth (1999), Skiadopoulos (2001), Psychoyios et al. (2003), Bates (2003) and Cont and Tankov (2004).

The aim of this section is to describe some general properties of stochastic volatility models. Then we review in detail a few specific stochastic volatility models that are currently very popular amongst option traders, such as the GARCH, Heston and SABR models, and models with jumps.

---

[46] The BSM formula may be modified to price other European options, even those with path-dependent pay-offs, as we have seen in the previous chapter.

III.4.5.1   Stochastic Volatility PDE

Suppose a price $S(t)$ is driven by a geometric Brownian motion but that volatility $\sigma(t)$ is stochastic and driven by its own Brownian motion that is correlated with the Brownian motion driving the price process. We write

$$\frac{dS(t)}{S(t)} = (r - y)\,dt + \sigma\,(t)\,dW_1(t),$$
(III.4.43)

$$d\sigma(t) = \alpha(\sigma, t)\,dt + \beta(\sigma, t)\,dW_2(t)$$

and, using $\langle\cdot, \cdot\rangle$ to denote the *quadratic covariation*, we have[47]

$$\langle dW_1(t), dW_2(t)\rangle = \varrho\,dt.$$
(III.4.44)

The property (III.4.44) implies a non-zero constant *price–volatility correlation* ϱ between the log returns on the underlying and the changes in volatility.

When volatility is stochastic there are two sources of risk that must be hedged, the price risk and the volatility risk. In this subsection we set up a risk free portfolio just as in the constant volatility case, but now the portfolio contains three assets: the underlying asset with price S and *two* options on S. The second option is needed to hedge the second source of uncertainty. In the following we write the price of a general claim on S as $g(S, \sigma)$, thus making explicit its dependence on the volatility σ but ignoring the other variables and parameters that may affect the option price.

We set up a portfolio with price Π consisting of a short position of one unit in an option with price $g_1(S, \sigma)$, a long position of δ_1 units of the underlying with price S and a position of δ_2 units in another option on S. Denoting the price of the second option by $g_2(S, \sigma)$, we may write down the price of the portfolio as

$$\Pi(S, \sigma) = \delta_1 S + \delta_2 g_2(S, \sigma) - g_1(S, \sigma).$$
(III.4.45)

To eliminate both sources of uncertainty we must choose δ_1 and δ_2 in such as way that the price remains constant with respect to changes in both the price S and the volatility σ.

Differentiating (III.4.45) with respect to S and σ and setting to zero gives two first order conditions that are easily solved, namely

$$\Pi_S(S, \sigma) = 0:$$

$$g_{1S}(S, \sigma) = \delta_1 + \delta_2 g_{2S}(S, \sigma) \Rightarrow \delta_1 = g_{1S}(S, \sigma) - \delta_2 g_{2S}(S, \sigma)$$

and

$$\Pi_\sigma(S, \sigma) = 0:$$

$$g_{1\sigma}(S, \sigma) = \delta_2 g_{2\sigma}(S, \sigma) \Rightarrow \delta_2 = \frac{g_{1\sigma}(S, \sigma)}{g_{2\sigma}(S, \sigma)}.$$

Substituting these values for δ_1 and δ_2 back into (III.4.45) yields

$$\Pi(S, \sigma) = (g_{1S}(S, \sigma)S - g_1(S, \sigma)) - \frac{g_{1\sigma}(S, \sigma)}{g_{2\sigma}(S, \sigma)}(g_{2S}(S, \sigma)S - g_2(S, \sigma))$$
(III.4.46)

---

[47] Quadratic covariance is the continuous time equivalent of the instantaneous covariance operator. Hence, if W is a Brownian motion then $\langle dW, dW\rangle = V(dW) = dt$ and for two Brownian motions W_1 and W_2 the instantaneous covariance between the increments is $\langle dW_1, dW_2\rangle = \varrho V(dW_1)^{1/2} V(dW_2)^{1/2} = \varrho\,dt$. We may also write $\langle dW_1, dW_2\rangle$ as $\mathrm{Cov}(dW_1, dW_2)$ or as $\mathrm{E}(dW_1, dW_2)$, as in Section III.3.8.5.

This portfolio will be risk free so it must earn a *net* return equal to the risk free rate, r. Since holding the portfolio may earn income such as dividends or incur costs such as carry costs at the rate y, the portfolio's price must grow at the rate $r - y$.[48] We assume both r and y are constant and set

$$\frac{d\Pi(S, \sigma)}{\Pi(S, \sigma)} = (r - y)\,dt. \tag{III.4.47}$$

Now, just as in the constant volatility case, we apply Itô's lemma to (III.4.46) using the approximation that δ_1 and δ_2 are unchanged over a small time interval dt. Then we use the resulting total derivative in (III.4.46) and (III.4.47) to derive a PDE that must be satisfied by every claim. However, we have only one condition (III.4.47) from which to derive the values of two unknowns, i.e. $g_1(S, \sigma)$ and $g_2(S, \sigma)$. So there are infinitely many solutions.

We resolve this problem by introducing a parameter corresponding to a premium that investors demand for holding the risky asset called volatility. This is called the *volatility risk premium* or the *market price of volatility risk* and is here denoted λ. The resulting PDE for the price of the claim may be written

$$g_t + (r - y)\,Sg_S + \tfrac{1}{2}\sigma^2 S^2 g_{SS} + \left\{(\alpha - \lambda\beta)\,g_\sigma + \alpha\,\varrho\,\sigma\,S\,g_{S\sigma} + \tfrac{1}{2}\beta^2 g_{\sigma\sigma}\right\} = (r - y)\,g, \tag{III.4.48}$$

where g can be either $g_1(S, \sigma)$ or $g_2(S, \sigma)$ and we have dropped the dependence on variables from our notation for simplicity. If volatility were constant the term

$$(\alpha - \lambda\beta)\,g_\sigma + \alpha\,\varrho\,\sigma\,S\,g_{S\sigma} + \tfrac{1}{2}\beta^2 g_{\sigma\sigma}$$

would be zero and the PDE would reduce to the BSM PDE (III.3.54). When volatility is not constant the general solution to (III.4.48) may be written in the form of the stochastic volatility model (III.4.43).

The presence of a volatility risk premium in the stochastic volatility PDE (III.4.48) indicates that we are in an *incomplete market*. That is, it is not possible to replicate the value of every claim with a self-financing portfolio.[49] Then the price of a claim is not unique. Different investors have different claim prices depending on their risk attitude. However, it is possible to complete the market by adding all options on a tradable asset, so that we can observe the price of the second option instead of having to solve for it. In this case, there should be no volatility risk premium.

We shall see below that the volatility risk premium appears as a parameter in the drift term of the volatility or variance diffusion in parametric stochastic volatility models. For instance, in the Heston model the volatility risk premium affects the rate of mean reversion. When the price–volatility correlation is positive, most investors have a positive volatility risk premium and the mean reversion speed is slow, and when the price–volatility correlation is negative, most investors have a negative volatility risk premium and mean reversion is rapid.[50] To see why this is intuitive, suppose that we are modelling the equity index price and volatility processes with the Heston model. The price–volatility correlation in equity indices is large and negative, so when the index falls volatility is high. Suppose all investors have the same negative volatility risk premium – which means they like to hold volatility. Then after a market fall investors will buy the index, because of the high volatility it adds to their portfolio, so the index price rises again and volatility will come down very quickly, i.e. the mean reversion rate will be rapid. But if investors had the same positive volatility

---

[48] So y will be negative if holding the portfolio incurs costs.
[49] See Section III.3.2.2 for further details on complete markets.
[50] This follows from (III.4.63).

risk premium, they would not buy into high volatility and therefore it would take longer to mean revert.

When we calibrate a stochastic volatility model to market data on option prices we often assume the market has been completed (by adding all options on S to the tradable assets) and so the volatility risk premium is zero. If we do not assume it is zero, we usually find that the volatility risk premium is negative, i.e. that investors appear to like to hold volatility. This makes sense, for the same reason as the variance risk premium that is calculated from the market prices of variance swaps is usually negative. Investors are usually prepared to accept low or even negative returns for holding volatility because the negative correlation between prices and volatility makes volatility a wonderful diversification instrument. Hence, returns on volatility do not need to be high for volatility to be an attractive asset.

III.4.5.2   Properties of Stochastic Volatility

This subsection discusses some general properties of stochastic volatility and in particular its connection with the implied volatility smile or skew, mean reversion in stochastic volatility and a standard discretization of the continuous time mean-reverting stochastic volatility process.

Price–Volatility Correlation and the Smile or Skew

Variance is the second moment about the mean. Thus variance captures the degree of uncertainty about the mean of a distribution. In our case the distribution in question is the distribution of log returns on the underlying contract and we use the square root of the variance, i.e. the volatility, as our metric for uncertainty about the future price.

Kurtosis is the fourth moment about the mean. We can think of kurtosis as measuring the degree of uncertainty about the variance of a distribution. In our case we use excess kurtosis as a metric for uncertainty about the volatility of log returns. If the excess kurtosis is zero, the returns are normal and future asset prices have a lognormal distribution. This is the Black–Scholes–Merton world, where the price process volatility is assumed to be constant. But if the excess kurtosis is positive the volatility is not constant and the degree of excess kurtosis is a metric for our uncertainty about volatility.

Put another way, when volatility is stochastic the log price distribution will have heavier tails than the normal distribution. Thus the implied volatility that is backed out from model option prices in a stochastic volatility model will exhibit a smile. To be more precise, suppose we use a stochastic volatility model to price several standard European calls and puts on the same underlying and with different strikes but the same maturity. Treating these model prices like market prices we can back out the implied volatility from them, by inverting the BSM formula.[51] When these model implied volatilities are plotted as a function of strike we see the following features that depend on the price–volatility correlation ϱ:

- symmetric smile when $\varrho = 0$, e.g. in some currency markets;
- negative skew when $\varrho < 0$, e.g. in equity markets;
- positive skew when $\varrho > 0$, e.g. in some commodity markets.

To understand the effect of non-zero price–volatility correlation on the skew, let us assume the correlation is negative, as is typically the case in equity markets. When the price decreases

---

[51] See Section III.4.5.3 below for more information on model implied volatilities.

the volatility increases. Hence, we could obtain some excessively low returns, and the lower tail of the log returns distribution will be long and thin.[52] But when the price increases the volatility decreases and so there is not much potential for excessively large positive returns, and the upper tail of the log returns distribution will be light. Hence, a negative correlation induces a negative skew in the log returns distribution. And a negatively skewed log returns distribution is paired with a negatively skewed implied volatility smile. A similar argument explains why a positive implied volatility skew is associated with positive price–volatility correlation.

Stochastic Variance versus Stochastic Volatility

Most of the stochastic volatility models that are commonly used today are specified in terms of variance rather than volatility. But a stochastic volatility process can be written using *either* volatility or variance as the dependent variable.[53] To see this, start with a stochastic variance equation of the form

$$dV(t) = \ldots dt + \xi V(t)^\alpha dB(t), \tag{III.4.49}$$

where $B(t)$ is a Brownian motion and $V(t)$ is the variance. The process (III.4.49) is very general: the drift term has not (yet) been made specific and the parameter α can be anything, to allow for arithmetic, geometric or heteroscedastic dynamics.

Now consider a second order Taylor expansion of the form

$$df(x) = f_x dx + \tfrac{1}{2} f_{xx} (dx)^2 + \ldots$$

and apply this to $f(V) = V^{1/2} = \sigma$. This gives

$$d\sigma(t) = \tfrac{1}{2} V(t)^{-1/2} dV(t) - \tfrac{1}{8} V(t)^{-3/2} (dV(t))^2 + \ldots.$$

We can ignore terms of higher order than dt and $(dV)^2$ has order dt so we can put this part into our unspecified drift. Hence, the stochastic variance process (III.4.49) may be written in the form of a stochastic volatility process of the form

$$d\sigma(t) = \ldots dt + \tfrac{1}{2} \xi \sigma(t)^{(2\alpha-1)} dB(t).$$

And vice versa, any stochastic volatility equation has a stochastic variance counterpart. The process

$$d\sigma(t) = \ldots dt + \zeta \sigma(t)^\beta dB(t) \tag{III.4.50}$$

may also be written variance as a stochastic variance equation

$$dV(t) = \ldots dt + 2\zeta V(t)^{(\beta+1)/2} dB(t).$$

Interestingly, the Heston model that we describe below and which is the most popular form of stochastic volatility model because it is easier to calibrate than many others, specifies a variance process of the form (III.4.49) with $\alpha = 1/2$ and so the equivalent volatility process is an arithmetic process with constant volatility.

---

[52] This is what we mean by a heavy tail, and is the reason why the term 'fat tails' is a misnomer.
[53] As it is in Heston (1993).

Orthogonalization of the Brownian Motions

Suppose we have two correlated Brownian motions with constant correlation ϱ. That is,

$$\langle dW_1(t), dW_2(t) \rangle = \varrho\, dt. \tag{III.4.51}$$

Instead of specifying (III.4.51) as a third equation in the stochastic volatility model we can introduce another Brownian $Z(t)$ that is *uncorrelated* with $W_1(t)$ and such that

$$dW_2(t) = \varrho\, dW_1(t) + \sqrt{1 - \varrho^2}\, dZ(t). \tag{III.4.52}$$

Then $W_2(t)$ is another Brownian motion, which has variance dt because (dropping time dependence for brevity)

$$\langle dW_2, dW_2 \rangle = \varrho^2 \langle dW_1, dW_1 \rangle + \left(1 - \varrho^2\right) \langle dZ, dZ \rangle = \varrho^2 dt + \left(1 - \varrho^2\right) dt = dt,$$

and has correlation $\varrho\, dt$ with W_1,

$$\langle dW_1, dW_2 \rangle = \left\langle dW_1, \varrho\, dW_1 + \sqrt{1 - \varrho^2} dZ \right\rangle = \varrho\, dt \quad \text{since } \langle dZ, dW_1 \rangle = 0.$$

In the following we shall use the form (III.4.52) rather than (III.4.51) to specify stochastic volatility models, and we always assume $\langle dW(t), dZ(t) \rangle = 0$.

Mean Reversion in Volatility

The empirical fact that volatility comes in clusters means that volatility term structures converge to a long term average level. Thus most (but not all) stochastic volatility models assume that the drift in the diffusion process for volatility is specified in such a way that volatility can never drift too far away from its long term average.

In fact we shall see below that the majority of models may be written in the form:

$$\frac{dS(t)}{S(t)} = (r - y)\, dt + \sqrt{V(t)} dW(t),$$

$$dV(t) = \varphi(m - V(t))\, dt + \xi V(t)^\alpha \left(\varrho\, dW(t) + \sqrt{1 - \varrho^2}\, dZ(t) \right). \tag{III.4.53}$$

In (III.4.53) the variance diffusion is said to have a *mean-reverting* drift, and the drift parameters have the following interpretation:

- The parameter m is the long term average level to which the variance converges.
- The parameter φ denotes the *rate of mean reversion*. This governs the time taken for the drift term to 'pull' volatility towards its long term average. The rate must be positive, otherwise the process would explode, and φ^{-1} is called the characteristic time to mean-revert.[54] Thus the greater is φ, the more rapid the mean reversion. If there is a non-zero volatility risk premium in the model then φ will be a function of this premium. See, for instance, the Heston model in Section III.4.5.5 below.

To see why the variance process in (III.4.53) has a mean reversion, consider only the drift term. Ignoring the stochastic part, we have

$$dV(t) = \varphi(m - V(t))\, dt.$$

---

[54] For instance, if $\varphi = 6$ then the process takes one sixth of a year, i.e. 2 months, (assuming V is annualized) for half the mean-reversion effect following a market shock.

In other words,

$$\frac{dV(t)}{dt} = \varphi(m - V(t)) .$$

This ordinary differential equation has a simple exponential solution:

$$V(t) = V(0) \exp(-\varphi t) + m. \qquad (III.4.54)$$

The variance at time zero $V(0)$ is called the *spot variance* or the *instantaneous variance*. So if the spot variance is greater than the long term variance, i.e. if $V(0) > m$, then (in the absence of the stochastic part) variance is exponentially declining with time, as shown in Figure III.4.22.[55] Note that the spot variance is a parameter of the stochastic volatility model that requires calibrating, along with the long term variance m and the rate of mean reversion φ.

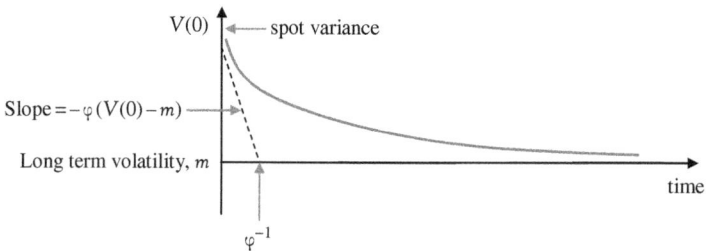

Figure III.4.22   Mean reversion in variance

The parameter α in (III.4.53) must be positive otherwise the variance could become negative. Two of the most popular stochastic volatility models do not leave α as a free parameter to be calibrated to the data. Instead, for good reasons which we shall discuss below, they specify a value for α. In the Heston model $\alpha = \frac{1}{2}$ and in the GARCH diffusions $\alpha = 1$.

Discretization of Stochastic Volatility Processes[56]

A standard 'Euler' discretization of a continuous process of the form

$$dV(t) = \varphi(m - V(t)) \, dt + \xi V(t)^\alpha dB(t)$$

uses forward differences, writing

$$\Delta V_t = \varphi(m - V_t) + \varepsilon_{t+1}, \quad \varepsilon_t \,|I_t \sim N\left(0, \sigma_t^2\right),$$

where Δ denotes the forward difference operator, i.e. $\Delta V_t = V_{t+1} - V_t$. The above can be written as

$$V_t = m\varphi + (1 - \varphi) V_{t-1} + \varepsilon_t, \qquad (III.4.55)$$

which is a first order autoregressive process with conditionally heteroscedastic errors. Since $\varphi > 0$, the process will be stationary provided that $\varphi < 2$.[57]

---

[55] Figure III.4.22 ignores the stochastic component of the variance processes. Adding this introduces uncertainty around the exponential trajectory shown here and periodically large shocks to the variance would take variance from its previous course onto another mean reverting course.

[56] See also Section II.5.3.7.

[57] See Section II.5.2.1.

Alternatively we could use backward differences, setting

$$\Delta V_t = \varphi(m - V_t) + \varepsilon_t, \quad \varepsilon_t \, | I_t \sim N\left(0, \sigma_t^2\right),$$

where $\Delta V_t = V_t - V_{t-1}$. The above discretization can be rearranged as

$$(1 + \varphi)\, V_t = m\varphi + V_{t-1} + \varepsilon_t$$

or

$$V_t = \alpha + \beta V_{t-1} + \eta_t, \qquad (\text{III.4.56})$$

where $\eta_t = (1 + \varphi)^{-1} \varepsilon_t$ and

$$\alpha = m\varphi(1 + \varphi)^{-1}, \quad \beta = (1 + \varphi)^{-1}, \quad \tilde{\sigma}_t = (1 + \varphi)^{-1} \sigma_t.$$

This is again a first order autoregressive process with conditionally heteroscedastic errors and now, since $\beta = (1 + \varphi)^{-1}$ with $\varphi > 0$, this process is always stationary. However, the problem with using backward differences is that now the mean reversion parameter affects the volatility, which is a nuisance. A forward difference discretization based on (III.4.55) is normally used in practice, since it is easier to infer the values of φ and m directly without estimating the parameters of the error process.[58]

III.4.5.3   Model Implied Volatility Surface

A standard European call or put can be priced, under the assumption of constant volatility, using the Black–Scholes–Merton formula. And we can invert this formula to obtain the implied volatility of the option as explained in Section III.4.2. That is, we set $f^m(K, T) \equiv f^{\mathrm{BSM}}(K, T)$ where K and T are the strike and maturity of the option, $f^m(K, T)$ is the market price of the option and $f^{\mathrm{BSM}}(K, T)$ is the price given by the BSM formula. More precisely, we find the market implied volatility $\theta^m(K, T\,|S)$ using the identity

$$f^m(K, T) \equiv f^{\mathrm{BSM}}(K, T\,|S, \theta^m(K, T\,|S)). \qquad (\text{III.4.57})$$

Here we make explicit the fact that the BSM price is a function of the underlying and the volatility as well as the strike and maturity of the option.

We may also use the price of a standard European call or put given by a stochastic volatility model to back out the *model* implied volatility. Thus we set $f(K, T) \equiv f^{\mathrm{BSM}}(K, T)$, where $f(K, T)$ is the stochastic volatility *model* price of the option. Using more precise notation we find the stochastic volatility *model implied volatility* $\theta(K, T\,|S, \boldsymbol{\lambda})$ from the relationship

$$f(K, T\,|S, \sigma, \boldsymbol{\lambda}) \equiv f^{\mathrm{BSM}}(K, T\,|S, \theta(K, T\,|S, \boldsymbol{\lambda})), \qquad (\text{III.4.58})$$

where both S and σ are stochastic processes and the vector $\boldsymbol{\lambda}$ denotes the model parameters. So the model implied volatility is a single number that represents a sort of average of the process volatility over the life of the option when the current price of the underlying is S.[59]

Stochastic volatility models are calibrated to the liquid market prices of standard European calls and puts (and then used to hedge these options, and to price and hedge exotic and/or path-dependent options on the same underlying). Hence, the stochastic volatility model prices of standard European calls and puts are approximately equal to their market prices, which

---

[58] It is necessary to ensure that a simulation of a stochastic volatility process does not produce negative variances. For this reason the forward difference discretization is usually adjusted. See Section III.4.5.5 for further details.

[59] In fact, the model *implied variance* (i.e. the square of the model implied volatility) is the continuous average of the expected instantaneous process variance $E(V(t))$ where the expectation is taken under some probability measure. See Gatheral (2006: 26–31) for further details about this measure, which depends on the BSM gamma, and a precise derivation.

are determined by traders and market makers responding to supply and demand. The more parameters in the model, the closer the model prices will be to the market prices.

Similarly, the stochastic volatility model implied volatilities should be close to the market implied volatilities. In fact, as mentioned above, we often use the weighted root mean square error between the model and the market implied volatilities as the model calibration objective. If the model has enough parameters, the differences between the market smile and the model smile will be very small at the time of calibration.

However, unfortunately, in all stochastic volatility models for equities (and any other tradable assets) the model smile dynamics, resulting from a movement in the underlying price alone, contradict the observed dynamics of the market smile. The standard (partial derivative) delta ignores the indirect effect that price movements have on volatility in stochastic volatility models where price and volatility are correlated. So, according to the standard delta, as soon as the underlying price moves the model smile and the market smile move in opposite directions.

We justify this remark later, but for now will only support it with some mathematics. In Section III.4.4.5 we used the chain rule to derive the relationship (III.4.41) which defines what I call the *market delta* of a standard European option as an adjusted BSM delta, where the sign of the adjustment term depends on the partial derivative of the market implied volatility with respect to S. The market implied volatility is here denoted $\theta^m(K, T|S)$ to distinguish it now from the model implied volatility. Exactly the same argument as in Section III.4.4.5 may be used to derive the stochastic volatility model delta of a standard European option as an adjusted BSM delta if we assume the model is well calibrated so that $\theta(K, T|S, \lambda) = \theta^m(K, T|S)$. Applying the chain rule to (III.4.58) gives

$$\delta_{\mathrm{SV}}(K, T|S) = \delta_{\mathrm{BSM}}(K, T|S) + \nu_{\mathrm{BSM}}(K, T|S)\theta_S(K, T|S, \lambda), \qquad (\text{III.4.59})$$

where

$$\theta_S(K, T|S, \lambda) = \frac{\partial \theta(K, T|S, \lambda)}{\partial S} \qquad (\text{III.4.60})$$

is the sensitivity of the model implied volatility to changes in the underlying price.

Since the BSM vega is positive the sign of the adjustment term in (III.4.59) depends on the sign of the volatility price sensitivity $\theta_S(K, T|S, \lambda)$. If it has the same sign as $\theta_S^m(K, T|S)$, i.e. if the market smile and the model smile move in the same directions in response to a move in S, then the model delta will be similar to the market delta.

In equity markets (and in many other markets, except currencies and some commodities) the price–volatility correlation is negative. So typically, $\theta_S^m(K, T|S) < 0$. Hence we want to have

$$\theta_S(K, T|S, \lambda) < 0,$$

otherwise the stochastic volatility model will not be capturing the empirically observed movements in market implied volatilities properly. However, we shall see in Section III.4.6 that in stochastic volatility models for any tradable asset $\theta_S(K, T|S, \lambda) > 0$ whenever the implied volatility smile has a negative slope, and $\theta_S(K, T|S, \lambda) < 0$ whenever the implied volatility smile has a positive slope. Thus in equity markets, where there is a pronounced negative skew, the stochastic volatility model delta will be *greater* than the BSM delta. whereas the market delta is *less* than the BSM delta. Since there is evidence that BSM delta already over-hedges in the face of a negative skew readers are advised not to apply the standard stochastic volatility model delta to hedge equity options.[60] We shall return to this topic in Section III.4.6 with more constructive advice on hedging options.

---

[60] See for instance Coleman et al. (2001).

III.4.5.4   Model Local Volatility Surface

The model implied volatility surface $\theta(K, T | S, \lambda)$ is specific to a particular instrument, i.e. a standard European option. It makes no sense to talk about implied volatility outside the context of pricing such an option. Indeed, the model implied volatility surface is just a transformation of the surface of stochastic volatility model prices of standard European options. However, there is another volatility surface that is associated with a stochastic volatility model that is free of any assumption about the instrument to which it applies, and this is the model local volatility surface.

The stochastic volatility model local volatility surface is the set of forward volatilities $\sigma(S, t | S_0, \sigma_0)$ for all possible prices S at all future times t that are implicit in the stochastic volatility model prices of options when the current price is S_0 and the spot volatility is σ_0. To interpret what this surface means, suppose the current price is at 100 and consider two scenarios:

1. The price in 1 month's time is 100.
2. The price in 1 month's time is 200.

What are your expectations about the volatility at $t = 1$ month under each scenario? Clearly you would expect volatility to be greater conditional on the future price being 200 than conditional on the future price being 100.

Following Dupire (1996) and Derman and Kani (1998), we define the local volatility surface that is implied by a stochastic volatility $\sigma(t)$ at a given time t when the price is $S(t)$ to be the square root of the risk neutral expectation of the variance at time t. That is,

$$\sigma(S, t) = \sqrt{E(\sigma^2(t) | S(t) = S)}. \qquad (III.4.61)$$

Or, to be more precise about the dependence on the current price and spot volatility,

$$\sigma(S, t | S_0, \sigma_0) = \sqrt{E(\sigma^2(t) | S(t) = S, S(0) = S_0, \sigma(0) = \sigma_0)}.$$

Figure III.4.23 illustrates the local volatility surface when volatility is stochastic and the current price and volatility of the underlying are at S_0 and σ_0, respectively, as marked on the figure at $t_0 = 0$. The important point is that the instantaneous volatility $\sigma(t)$ at some future

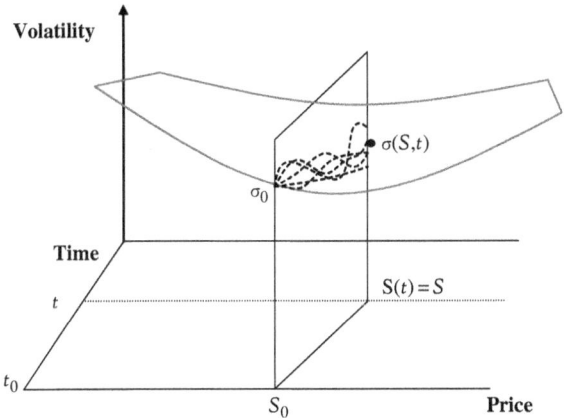

Figure III.4.23   Local volatility surface belonging to a stochastic volatility model

time t has a distribution, because it is stochastic. The figure depicts a few possible paths for volatility, all starting from the spot volatility σ_0, and each path brings the underlying price to the value S at time t. Hence, all the paths are in the plane indicated by the vertical pane. Now the local volatility $\sigma(S, t)$, which is marked by the black dot, and is defined by (III.4.61) is a type of average value of the instantaneous volatility values $\sigma(t)$ at time t, where the average is taken over all paths that lead to $S(t) = S$.

In Figure III.4.23 we show a smile-shaped local volatility surface. A symmetric smile in local volatility results when there is no price–volatility correlation in the model. Then we expect volatility to be equally high whether the price has doubled or halved by some time in the future. But if the price–volatility correlation were negative then we would expect volatility to be greater conditional on the future price being lower than the current price than conditional on the future price being higher than the current price. Hence, negative price–volatility correlation induces a negative skew in the local volatility surface, and similarly positive price–volatility correlation induces a positive skew in the local volatility surface. Hence, the local volatility surface has similar characteristics to the model implied volatility surface. Indeed, Dupire (1996) expresses the *model implied variance* (i.e. the square of the model implied volatility) as a gamma-weighted average of the *local variance* (i.e. the square of the model local volatility).

III.4.5.5   Heston Model

The stochastic volatility model introduced by Heston (1993) is a mean-reverting process with non-zero price–volatility correlation:

$$\frac{dS(t)}{S(t)} = (r - y)dt + \sqrt{V(t)}dW(t),$$

$$dV(t) = \varphi(m - V(t))\,dt + \xi\sqrt{V(t)}(\varrho dW(t) + \sqrt{1 - \varrho^2}\,dZ(t)),$$

(III.4.62)

with $\langle dW(t), dZ(t)\rangle = 0$. Adding a volatility risk premium λ requires modification of the mean revision rate parameter to

$$\tilde{\varphi} = \lambda\varrho\xi + \sqrt{\varphi^2 - \lambda(1 + \lambda)\xi^2}.$$

(III.4.63)

Hence, if $\lambda = 0$ as in (III.4.62) the rate of mean reversion is $\tilde{\varphi} = \varphi$.

Figure III.4.24 depicts one simulation of the Heston volatility and underlying price S over 1000 days based on the (annual) parameters shown in Table III.4.7.[61] The Heston volatility is shown on the left-hand scale and the corresponding asset price is shown on the right-hand scale. The current price is 100, the spot volatility is 20% and the long run volatility to which volatility tends to mean-revert is 15%. With our choice of parameters the characteristic time of mean reversion is about 60 days. Notice how the volatility increases when the price falls due to the negative price–volatility correlation that we have chosen. Readers may like to simulate other price and volatility paths using the Excel spreadsheet on the website.

---

[61] In continuous time a stochastic volatility can never be zero. This is why we usually assume that the vol-of-vol is proportional to $V(t)$, so as $V(t)$ decreases so does its variation. However in a simple discretization of a stochastic volatility model an uncommonly large and negative increment in volatility may send the volatility to zero, or even to become negative. The spreadsheet used to construct Figure III.4.25 uses a simple but very crude trick to eliminate the possibility that the volatility becomes zero or negative. However, when using Heston simulations in practice it is important to apply a more sophisticated discretization scheme. The *Milstein discretization scheme*, described for instance in Gatheral (2006) is generally preferred.

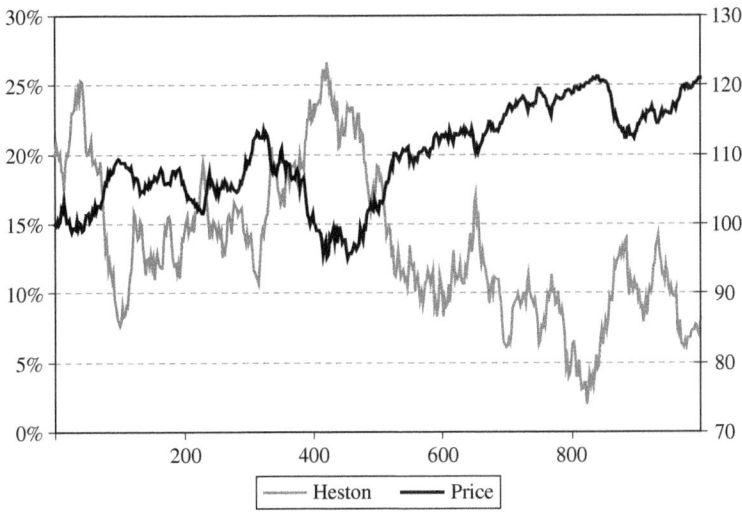

Figure III.4.24   Simulation of price and Heston volatility

Table III.4.7   Parameters chosen for Heston model simulation

Parameter	Notation	Value
Discount rate	r	5%
Mean reversion (with zero λ)	φ	6
Long run volatility	$m^{1/2}$	15%
Spot volatility	$V(0)^{1/2}$	20%
Vol-of-vol	ξ	35%
Price–volatility correlation	ϱ	−0.75
Volatility risk premium	λ	−1

In Section III.4.5.2 we showed that, if we rewrite the Heston model in terms of volatility rather than variance, the diffusion coefficient in the volatility equation is a constant, ξ. It is also possible to show that the Heston model local variance is approximately linear in log moneyness. See Gatheral (2006: 31–33) for the proof. So it has some very tractable properties. But the main reason for the huge popularity of the Heston model is that, compared with some other stochastic volatility models with mean reversion and price–volatility correlation, it is relatively simple to calibrate.

Heston (1993) shows that the model (III.4.62) has a closed-form solution for the price at time t of a standard European call option on the futures, with price $F(t, T)$ of the form

$$f(F(t, T), \sigma, r, t \mid K, T) = \exp(-r(T - t))[F(t, T)P_1 - KP_2].$$
(III.4.64)

This is similar to the BSM formula, with $P_i = P_i(S, T, t, \sigma, r)$ replacing the standard normal distribution values $\Phi(d_i)$ for $i = 1, 2$. In fact the expression inside the square bracket may be rewritten as

$$\left[F(t, T)\frac{P_1}{P_2} - K\right]P_2,$$
(III.4.65)

where P_2 is the risk neutral probability that the call is ITM at expiry and $F(t, T)P_1/P_2$ is the conditional expectation of $F(T, T)$ given that $F(T, T) > K$.

Unfortunately the functions P_1 and P_2 are based on the Fourier transform, and their evaluation requires the use of numerical integration which is beyond the mathematical scope of the text. However, Matlab code for calibration of the Heston model and several other volatility models is provided on the website.[62]

III.4.5.6 GARCH Diffusions

An options trader has a vast array of possible volatility models to choose from. The criteria for choosing a model can include its in-sample or out-of-sample fit to option prices, its ability to hedge accurately and, perhaps more than anything, the ease with which the model can be calibrated. However, the *micro-econometric foundations* of stochastic models are seldom considered. A great advantage of generalized autoregressive conditional heteroscedasticity (GARCH) diffusions is that they do have a solid micro-econometric foundation.

Since the path-breaking papers by Engle (1982) and Bollerslev (1986) literally thousands of papers have been published on the ability of GARCH models to capture the empirical characteristics of the statistical volatility of financial asset returns.[63] However, surprisingly little work has been done on the specification of a variance diffusion corresponding to the different type of GARCH models.

In this section we discuss the continuous time diffusion limit of the standard symmetric GARCH model,

$$\ln\left(\frac{S_t}{S_{t-1}}\right) = c + \varepsilon_t, \quad \varepsilon_t \,|I_t \sim N(0, \sigma_t^2),$$

$$\sigma_t^2 = \omega + \alpha\,\varepsilon_{t-1}^2 + \beta\,\sigma_{t-1}^2,$$

(III.4.66)

where I_t denotes the *information set*, which is the discrete finance term for the filtration of all past prices and volatilities up to time t.

Nelson (1990) derived the diffusion limit of (III.4.66) as

$$\frac{dS(t)}{S(t)} = (r - y)\,dt + \sqrt{V(t)}dW(t),$$

$$dV(t) = \varphi(m - V(t))\,dt + \sqrt{2}\,\alpha V(t)\,dZ(t),$$

(III.4.67)

where $\langle dW(t), dZ(t)\rangle = 0$, and

$$\varphi = 1 - \alpha - \beta \text{ and } m = \varphi^{-1}\omega.$$

For reasons that will be apparent later, we call the model (III.4.67) the *strong GARCH diffusion*. There are four major problems with the strong GARCH diffusion:

1. The GARCH model (III.4.66) is not *time aggregating*. This means that if we generate a GARCH process at one discrete time frequency and then resample the process at another frequency the result is *not* another GARCH process. Lack of time aggregation is a real problem because one has to assume time aggregation to derive the continuous limit of any model, and without time aggregation it makes no sense to derive a continuous limit.

---

[62] Many thanks to my PhD student Andreas Kaeck for providing this code.
[63] GARCH models are covered in considerable detail in Chapter II.4.

2. The form (III.4.67) for the limit only arises when one is prepared to make a specific assumption about the convergence behaviour of the GARCH parameters and other assumptions lead to different (not necessarily stochastic) limits.[64]
3. Any discretization of (III.4.67) is not a GARCH model.
4. The fact that the Brownian motions are independent means that (III.4.67) has very limited applicability, because very few financial markets have zero price–volatility correlation, i.e. symmetric volatility smiles.

Having spent many years researching and developing GARCH models before turning my attention to wider problems in volatility analysis, I personally found the Nelson diffusion limit very disappointing. It seemed unbelievable to me that such a powerful discrete time volatility model would have such a limit. This motivated my research, with Emese Lazar, to review the continuous limit of the standard symmetric GARCH model and to derive proper continuous limits for the best possible GARCH models, i.e. Markov switching GARCH models. In this section we describe the *weak GARCH diffusion* derived by Alexander and Lazar (2005) and in Section III.4.5.8 we state the continuous version of the Markov switching GARCH model.

Alexander and Lazar (2005) derive the *weak GARCH diffusion* as the limit of weak GARCH:

$$\frac{dS(t)}{S(t)} = (r - y)\, dt + \sqrt{V(t)}dW(t),$$

$$dV(t) = \varphi(m - V(t))\, dt + \sqrt{\eta - 1}\, \alpha V(t)\, (\varrho dW(t) + \sqrt{1 - \varrho^2}\, dZ(t)), \qquad \text{(III.4.68)}$$

where $\langle dW(t), dZ(t) \rangle = 0$, and

$$\varphi = 1 - \alpha - \beta, \quad m = \varphi^{-1}\omega, \quad \varrho = \tau(\eta - 1)^{-1/2} \qquad \text{(III.4.69)}$$

and τ and η are the skewness and kurtosis of the log returns.

We remark that when the log returns are assumed to be normally distributed, (III.4.68) reduces to Nelson's GARCH diffusion. But stochastic volatility introduces positive excess kurtosis into the log returns distribution and, if the log returns are also skewed the price–volatility correlation ϱ will be non-zero. The weak GARCH diffusion limit is very intuitive since, from our discussion in Section III.4.5.2 above, we do expect leptokurtosis to be associated with the diffusion parameter in the volatility process (i.e. the 'vol-of-vol') and skewness to be associated with the price–volatility correlation.

Moreover, the limit (III.4.68) has *none* of the four problems associated with strong GARCH diffusion that we outlined above:

1. The limit is based on a time aggregating or 'weak' version of (III.4.66) which also makes more general distributional assumptions.
2. It is not necessary to make any assumption about the convergence behaviour – the convergence of the parameters is implied by the model.
3. The standard Euler discretization of (III.4.68) is the weak version of (III.4.66).
4. The Brownian motions are correlated.

---

[64] For instance, Corradi (2000) makes a different assumption about the rate of convergence for α and obtains a deterministic volatility model as the limit. She also proved property 3.

The weak GARCH parameter α determines the reaction to market shocks, i.e. the vol-of-vol; the parameter β determines the persistence in volatility after a shock and these, together with the parameter ω determine the speed of mean reversion and the long run GARCH volatility. In discrete time these parameters must be estimated on high frequency data and often daily data are used. The corresponding annualized value of any one of these parameters depends on the time aggregation properties of the parameter. In Alexander and Lazar (2005) it is shown that ω and α should be annualized using the square root of time, i.e. we multiply daily parameter estimates by $\sqrt{365}$. The other convergence criterion is on $\theta = 1 - \alpha - \beta$ and this converges with time, not its square root, so we multiply it by 365 to obtain the annual equivalent, i.e. $\varphi = 365 \times \theta$.

We now compare the simulated volatility paths based on GARCH diffusion models with comparable volatility paths based on the Heston model. We shall use the Heston model parameters shown in Table III.4.7. What are the corresponding GARCH parameters? We can easily set the spot volatility to be the same for all models, i.e. 20%, but we need to determine the appropriate choice of GARCH model parameters so that the vol-of-vol is 35%, the mean reversion rate is 6 (i.e. the characteristic time to mean revert is 2 months), the long run volatility is 15% and, in the weak GARCH models, the price–volatility correlation is −0.75.

EXAMPLE III.4.7: GARCH ANNUAL AND DAILY PARAMETERS

Find the strong GARCH diffusion parameters that correspond, approximately, to the Heston model parameters in Table III.4.7. Find the corresponding daily GARCH parameters ω, α and β.

SOLUTION   So that the diffusion coefficients are equal, the annual value of α which is used in the strong GARCH diffusion should be such that

$$\sqrt{2}\alpha V(t) = \xi\sqrt{V(t)},$$

with $\xi = 0.35$, as in Table III.4.7. Of course this cannot hold for all t because volatility is stochastic, so to find a constant value for α we set

$$\alpha = \frac{\xi}{\sqrt{2V(0)}} = \frac{0.35}{\sqrt{2} \times 0.2} = 1.237.$$

This corresponds to a daily GARCH reaction parameter equal to

$$(365)^{-1/2} \times 1.237 = 0.06477.$$

Then we set $\theta = \varphi/365$ and $\beta = 1 - \alpha - \theta$. The results are summarized in Table III.4.8.

Table III.4.8   Parameters used in simulations

Heston parameters		Value	GARCH parameters	Annual	Daily
Long run volatility	$m^{1/2}$	15%	ω	2.8×10^{-5}	1.5×10^{-6}
Spot volatility	$V(0)^{1/2}$	20%	α	1.2374	0.06477
Vol-of-vol	ξ	35%	β		0.91879
Mean reversion	φ	6	θ		0.01644

The daily parameters shown in the table lie within the normal ranges. For daily data the GARCH reaction parameter α usually ranges between about 0.05 (for a market that is relatively stable) and about 0.1 (for a market that is jumpy or nervous). The GARCH persistence parameter β usually ranges between 0.85 and 0.98, with lower values being associated with higher α. GARCH volatilities with relatively high α and relatively low β are more 'spiky' than those with relatively low α and relatively high β. In other words, high α which is often associated with a low β produces GARCH volatilities with a high vol-of-vol.

Figure III.4.25 compares the simulations from four volatility diffusions, with all four volatility paths based on the same random numbers. In other words, all four simulations are driven by the same realizations for the Brownian motions $W(t)$ and $Z(t)$. The simulations are based on the Heston model, the strong GARCH diffusion, the weak GARCH diffusion with a shallow skew, and the weak GARCH diffusion with a deep skew. The strong GARCH parameters are set as in Table III.4.8. In both the weak GARCH models we assume that the price–volatility correlation is −0.75 but in the strong GARCH of course, the price–volatility correlation is zero. We remark that in the weak GARCH diffusion there are infinitely many possible choices of skewness and kurtosis that give a price–volatility correlation of −0.75. For the weak GARCH diffusion with shallow skew we assume the kurtosis is 5 and the skewness is −1.5, and for the weak GARCH diffusion with deep skew we assume the kurtosis is 7 and the skewness is −1.837.[65]

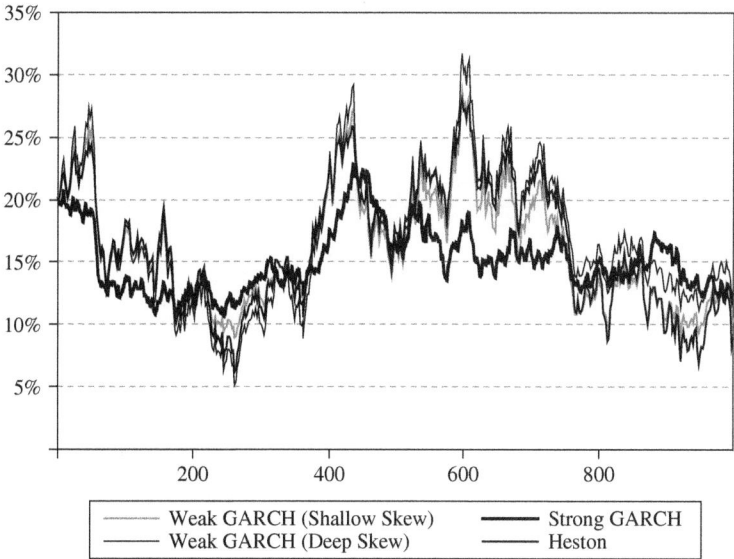

Figure III.4.25   Comparison of GARCH and Heston volatility simulations

The strong GARCH volatility is very different from the Heston volatility in every simulation, not just the one shown in Figure III.4.25.[66] This is primarily because the price–volatility correlation is zero in the strong GARCH process. The two weak GARCH model simulations are always

---

[65] As for Figure III.4.24 we have used a crude method to ensure the discretization always has positive variance.
[66] This figure was generated using the last spreadsheet, labelled 'Weak GARCH', in the workbook SV_Simulations.xls.

closer to the Heston model simulations, but which of the two weak GARCH simulations is closest to the Heston model depends on the simulations. Readers can verify this by pressing F9 in the spreadsheet for this figure.

Calibration of GARCH diffusions is not as easy as in the Heston model because there is no closed form for the price of a European option. Instead GARCH prices for European options are calculated, using risk neutral valuation, by simulating the underlying price distribution at expiry, using this distribution to find the expected value of the pay-off and then discounting the expected pay-off to today. The next example is designed purely to illustrate the method. Of course, using only 20 simulations is totally inadequate in practice. At least 10,000 simulations are required for reasonable accuracy.

EXAMPLE III.4.8: GARCH OPTION PRICING

Use the parameter values above to simulate 20 possible values for S in 30 days using (a) the Heston model; (b) the strong GARCH diffusion with $\alpha = 1$ and (c) the weak GARCH diffusion with $\eta = 5$ and $\tau = -1.5$. Start with $S = 100$ and use the simulated 30-day price distribution to estimate the price of a standard European put on S with strike $K = 102$.

SOLUTION   The spreadsheet for this example simulates prices over 30 days and the price on the 30th day is shown in Table III.4.9, along with the put option pay-off corresponding to each price. Taking the discounted average of the pay-offs gives the option prices as 1.8098 for the Heston model, 2.0155 for the strong GARCH and 1.7800 for the weak GARCH. It is left as an exercise to the reader to repeat the above for a realistic number of simulations (i.e. several thousand).

Table III.4.9   Simulated underlying prices under different stochastic volatility models

Simulation no.	Prices			Pay-offs		
	Heston	Strong	Weak	Heston	Strong	Weak
1	103.41	103.02	103.40	0.00	0.00	0.00
2	109.27	110.43	109.16	0.00	0.00	0.00
3	97.47	97.02	97.52	4.53	4.98	4.48
4	97.68	97.50	97.75	4.32	4.50	4.25
5	96.20	95.90	96.16	5.80	6.10	5.84
6	99.07	98.78	99.25	2.93	3.22	2.75
7	103.36	103.22	103.35	0.00	0.00	0.00
8	103.12	102.69	103.19	0.00	0.00	0.00
9	104.97	104.94	104.87	0.00	0.00	0.00
10	109.76	111.35	109.56	0.00	0.00	0.00
11	100.14	99.77	100.22	1.86	2.23	1.78
12	97.51	97.30	97.62	4.49	4.70	4.38
13	101.94	101.51	101.92	0.06	0.49	0.08
14	102.01	101.74	102.03	0.00	0.26	0.00
15	97.18	96.96	97.31	4.82	5.04	4.69
16	100.80	100.43	100.76	1.20	1.57	1.24
17	97.61	97.53	97.71	4.39	4.47	4.29
18	105.60	105.17	105.56	0.00	0.00	0.00
19	100.89	100.40	100.89	1.11	1.60	1.11
20	101.47	101.01	101.44	0.53	0.99	0.56

The empirical results presented in Section III.4.6.4 below will show that the Heston model does not fit the market prices of short maturity options very well. However, the weak GARCH diffusion has parameters that are specifically designed to capture the characteristics of short term market implied skews. Hence, there are two main advantages of the weak GARCH diffusion over the Heston model:

- Only the weak GARCH diffusion has a firm micro-econometric foundation.
- Two additional parameters in the weak GARCH diffusion correspond to the skewness and kurtosis in the log price density. These should allow for a better fit to market data and to short term options in particular.

Of course, the main disadvantage of the weak GARCH diffusion is that, as yet, no simple calibration method has been derived.

Another difference between the weak GARCH diffusion and the Heston model is that, if variance is regarded as a tradable asset, then it should be modelled using a scale invariant process (as we show in Section III.4.6). The weak GARCH diffusion is scale invariant, but the Heston model is not.

III.4.5.7   CEV and SABR Models

The *constant elasticity of variance* (CEV) price process introduced by Cox (1975) is

$$dS(t) = (r - y)S(t)dt + \alpha S(t)^\beta dW(t). \tag{III.4.70}$$

This is not a stochastic volatility model. In fact, it is a parametric deterministic volatility model since there is only one Brownian motion driving both the price and the volatility. In other words, the volatility and the price are perfectly correlated.

Figure III.4.26 shows three simulations of the CEV price process, based on the same random numbers, for $\alpha = 20\%$ and for $\beta = 0.75$, $\beta = 1$ and $\beta = 1.25$ (and assuming zero drift).

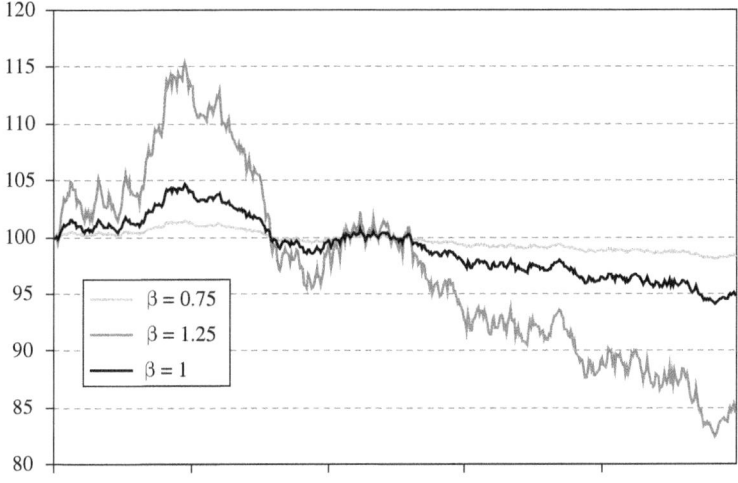

Figure III.4.26   Simulations from CEV processes

The case where $\beta = 1$ corresponds to geometric Brownian motion. As β decreases below 1 the process becomes less and less volatile and as β increases above 1 the process becomes more and more volatile. Eventually the price will hit zero and when it does the process has zero volatility so the price will remain at zero! There is another problem with the CEV model: the α parameter – which is supposed to be constant – usually fluctuates wildly as the model is recalibrated from day to day.

The CEV is therefore not a good model, nevertheless we mention it here because it forms the basis of a stochastic volatility model that has recently become popular amongst practitioners. The 'stochastic-$\alpha\beta\varrho$' or SABR model of Hagan *et al.* (2002) uses the CEV functional form for the dynamics of the forward price F with maturity equal to the option that is being priced, but it allows the α parameter to be stochastic and driven by a correlated diffusion as follows:

$$dF(t) = \alpha(t)F(t)^{\beta}dW(t).$$

$$d\alpha(t) = v\alpha(t)(\varrho dW(t) + \sqrt{1 - \varrho^2}\, dZ(t)). \qquad \text{(III.4.71)}$$

$$\langle dW(t), dZ(t) \rangle = 0.$$

Figure III.4.27 shows a simulation of the forward price process generated by a SABR model, along with the stochastic volatility parameter α, on the right-hand scale with $\alpha(0) = 1$, $v = 25\%$, $\beta = 0.75$ and $\varrho = -0.75$. The SABR model has a lognormally distributed rather than chi-squared distributed variance, and the fact that there is no mean reversion in volatility may adversely effect on the pricing of long term options.

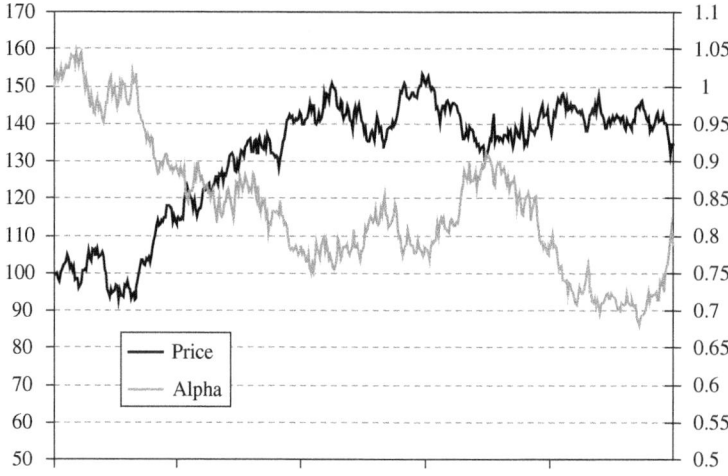

Figure III.4.27   SABR price and alpha

The CEV and its stochastic volatility extension, the SABR model, are relatively straightforward to calibrate using the non-central chi-squared extension of Schroder (1989) and Andreas Kaeck's Matlab calibration code for this is included on the website. The CEV and SABR models have an unusual property, that the price is generated by a process which is *not* scale invariant unless $\beta = 1$. However, they can be reparameterized into a scale invariant form, as we shall presently explain. This has important implications for hedging, as we shall see in Section III.4.6 below.

III.4.5.8 Jumps in Prices and in Stochastic Volatility

A diffusion process is not necessarily the best representation for a price process. Prices of individual stocks often jump on important news events, commodity prices jump due to perceived imbalances between demand and supply, and energy prices (electricity prices in particular) exhibit spikes, even in forward prices of several months' maturity.

Merton (1976) added a Poisson jump process to the price process that is uncorrelated with the Brownian motion driving the price. In a Poisson process $q(t)$, during an interval of length dt the probability of a jump is λdt and the probability of no jump is $(1 - \lambda)dt$. The process has a single parameter λ which corresponds to the expected number of jumps per annum, assuming t is measured in years. The constant λ is called the *jump intensity* or *hazard rate*.[67] Jumps in a process affect the drift. If the expected size of each jump is μ_J then the expected return (per annum) due to the jump alone is $\lambda\mu_J$. Hence, a risk neutral drift term must be equal to the risk free rate r less the dividend yield y as usual, but now we must also subtract the expected return due to the jump, in order that the net return is the risk free rate.

Merton's jump diffusion adds a single jump process to a geometric Brownian price process as follows:

$$\frac{dS(t)}{S(t)} = (r - y - \lambda\mu_J)dt + \sigma dW(t) + J(t)dq(t). \tag{III.4.72}$$

This model has an analytic solution for prices of European options if the jump size $J(t)$ has a lognormal distribution. Then Merton (1976) shows that the price of a standard European option is a Poisson distributed sum of Black–Scholes–Merton option prices.

It is convenient to express $J(t)$ as a percentage of the price at time t. Since no downward jump can be greater that 100% of the price, we have $J(t) > -1$. So when the jump size is lognormally distributed we assume:

$$\ln(1 + J(t)) \sim N(\ln(1 + \mu_J) - \tfrac{1}{2}\sigma_J^2, \sigma_J^2). \tag{III.4.73}$$

Figure III.4.28 simulates a price path from a lognormal jump diffusion with $\lambda = 6$, $\mu_J = 5\%$ and $\sigma_J = 20\%$. The realizations of the jump process, and of the geometric Brownian motion price path based on the same random numbers but when there are no jumps, are also shown in the figure.

Bakshi et al. (1997) extend Merton's jump diffusion process so that the diffusion coefficient is stochastic and follows Heston's stochastic volatility diffusion. In the *Heston jump* model a quasi-analytic solution for the price of a standard European option is obtain using a Fourier transform technique and Andreas Kaeck has again kindly provided the Matlab calibration code on the website.

Eraker et al. (2003) and Broadie et al. (2007) consider whether the introduction of a jump in the stochastic volatility process, as well as in the price process, is important for improving the fit of the option pricing model. The standard motivation for introducing jumps into the volatility process is the apparent inability of stochastic volatility models to fit the extreme skew that is sometimes observed in very short term implied volatilities. Implied volatilities,

---

[67] See Section I.3.7.4 for further details.

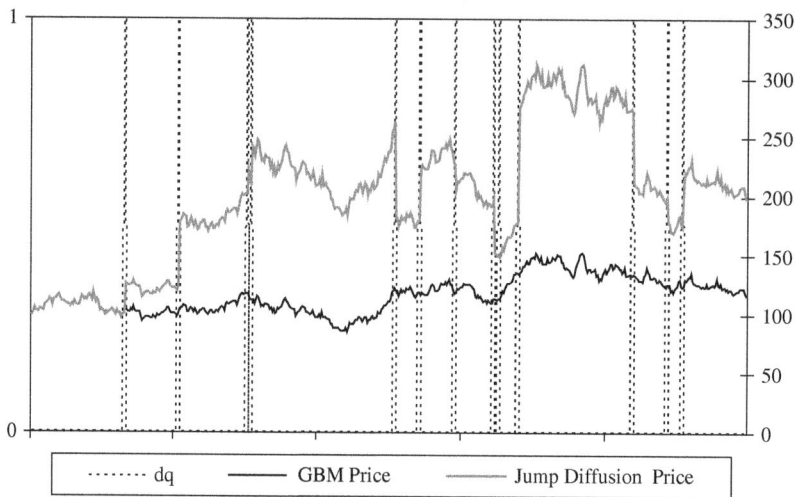

Figure III.4.28   Simulation from Merton's lognormal jump diffusion

especially those on stocks and commodities, are renowned for exhibiting discrete jumps, both upward and downward. Sometimes jumps in volatility, particularly in short term volatility, are related to jumps in prices, but volatility jumps may also be observed simply when the market is 'nervous' and undecided about direction. Hence, in this *double jump* stochastic volatility model the timing and size of the volatility jump need not be correlated with the timing and size of the price jump. At present there appears to be conflicting evidence on whether the double jump model fits better than the stochastic volatility model with a jump only in the price process, the evidence from Eraker et al. (2003) and Broadie et al. (2007) contradicting that from Gatheral (2006: 66–73).

To introduce jumps in volatility just because we need jumps to fit the smile is a somewhat Heath Robinson approach to volatility modelling. But there is an alternative motivation for introducing a jump in the volatility process, and this is that a volatility process with jumps is the continuous version of the queen of GARCH models – the Markov switching GARCH. In Section II.4.7 we introduced Markov switching GARCH and compared the simulated volatility processes based on several different GARCH models. We demonstrated that the most realistic volatility clustering behaviour is generated by Markov switching GARCH. No other GARCH model, not even asymmetric normal mixture GARCH, is able to capture the volatility clustering characteristics that we observe in financial markets nearly as well as the Markov switching GARCH.

Single volatility state GARCH models do have some volatility clustering, but it is not sufficiently pronounced to capture the real-life behaviour of most financial assets. Moreover, single state GARCH models have no time variation in conditional skewness and kurtosis, even though aggregate returns from GARCH models do have a term structure of skewness and kurtosis. But in implied densities the skew can be very extreme at short maturities, and the skew at longer maturities is stronger than single-volatility-state models would predict.[68] Furthermore, there is by now a considerable body of empirical evidence

---

[68] See Alexander and Lazar (2008a) and references therein.

that Markov switching GARCH models fit historical returns better and forecast statistical volatility more accurately than any other type of GARCH model.[69]

For all these reasons we should expect the continuous time version of the Markov switching GARCH model to lead to a superior specification for a stochastic volatility model. Alexander and Lazar (2008b) show that the Markov switching GARCH model, where volatility switches at a random time between a high volatility and a low volatility state, has a new type of jump volatility process as continuous time version. Specifically, denoting the volatility state at time t by $s(t)$:[70]

$$\frac{dS(t)}{S(t)} = \left(\mu_1 1_{\{s(t)=1\}} + \mu_2 1_{\{s(t)=2\}}\right) dt + \sqrt{V(t)}\, dW(t),$$

$$dV_i(t) = \varphi_i(m_i - V_i(t))\, dt + \sqrt{2}\alpha_i V_i(t) dW_i(t), \quad i = 1, 2, \qquad \text{(III.4.74)}$$

$$dV(t) = dV_1(t)\, 1_{\{s(t)=1\}} + dV_2(t)\, 1_{\{s(t)=2\}} + dJ(t),$$

$$\langle dW_i(t),\ dW(t)\rangle = \rho_i dt$$

$$dJ(t) = \begin{cases} 0, & \text{if there is no switch of volatility state at time } t, \\ V_i(t) - V_j(t), & \text{if the volatility state switches from state } i \text{ to state } j \text{ at time } t. \end{cases}$$

The model is not complete until we have described the evolution of the conditional probability of being in volatility state i at time t, i.e. the process for $p_i(t)$. At any point in time, we have $0 \le p_1(t), p_2(t) \le 1$ and $p_1(t) = 1 - p_2(t)$. Furthermore,

$$p_1(t) = \pi_{11} p_1(t) + (1 - \pi_{22}) p_2(t),$$

$$p_2(t) = (1 - \pi_{11}) p_1(t) + \pi_{22} p_2(t),$$

where π_{ii} is the unconditional probability of remaining in volatility state i, for $i = 1, 2$.

III.4.6   SCALE INVARIANCE AND HEDGING

A multitude of models for option pricing have been developed in recent years and the academic literature is enormous. For comprehensive reviews, see Jackwerth, 1999; Skiadopoulos, 2001; Bates, 2003; Psychoyios et al., 2003; Cont and Tankov, 2004. Given the huge variety of volatility models currently available, a number of research papers have attempted to identify the best model (e.g. Bakshi et al., 1997, Dumas et al., 1998, Das and Sundaram, 1999; Buraschi and Jackwerth, 2001; Andersen et al., 2002; Wilkens, 2005). The Heston model is easier to calibrate than other stochastic volatility models and is very popular for this reason, but is it the 'best' parametric form for the volatility or variance diffusion?

To answer this question we must define what we mean by 'best'. The best model could be the one with the smallest calibration errors, although in that case we would always prefer

---

[69] See Section II.4.4.4.
[70] The diffusion coefficients in the volatility process are again related to the skewness and kurtosis of the returns.

models with many parameters over models with few parameters. The more parameters there are in the model, the better the fit to market data. Alternatively, the best model could be the one with the smallest out of sample predictions errors. This is a criterion used by Bakshi et al. (1997), for instance. In that case the best model is the one that provides the best predictions of future prices. Thus the best pricing model will perform well if it:

- provides a good fit to current market data on option prices or volatilities;
- forecasts future market prices or volatilities more accurately than other models;
- has stable parameters when recalibrated over time, so the model prices of exotic and path-dependent options do not jump from day to day.

However the purpose of the model is also to hedge options since hedging costs are factored into the price of most new deals. It may be that a good pricing model turns out to be a bad hedging model, or vice versa. But the choice of a model often depends on its ability to price and hedge simultaneously.

Some recent developments on the hedge ratios derived from pricing models for options on tradable assets show that the price hedge ratios of almost all options, derived from most of the models that we use today, *are the same*! For instance, the following models all have the same deltas and the same gammas:

- Heston's stochastic volatility model;
- Hull and White's stochastic volatility model;
- virtually any other variance or volatility diffusion;
- the lognormal mixture diffusion;
- many other parametric deterministic volatility models;
- models based on Lévy processes;
- models with jumps in price and/or volatility;
- standard LIBOR models, with or without stochastic volatility and jumps.

If two models appear to have different deltas and gammas, this is only due to calibration error. That is, the two models do not have identical fits to the market smile. Moreover, the delta and gamma here refer to the price hedge ratios of virtually any American or European option.

The above applies to options on tradable assets. But if the underlying is an interest rate, then the hedge ratios from the LIBOR model with constant volatility are theoretically the same as those we obtain when using stochastic volatility in the LIBOR model. The only differences that may be observed in practice are because two models may not fit market data equally well. We therefore call this the *model free hedge ratio* property.

This section begins with a precise definition of *scale invariance* and, after showing that the vast majority of option pricing models that we use today are scale invariant, we explain why they should be used for pricing all options on tradable assets. We also show that their price hedge ratios are model free for virtually any type of option.

Then we describe the unfortunate implications of scale invariance for hedging. We explain the concept of *locally risk minimizing*, also called *minimum variance*, hedge ratios. Providing the formulae to calculate minimum variance delta and gamma hedge ratios, we show that these are only different from the standard, model free hedge ratios when the price–volatility correlation is non-zero. For instance, in the BSM model and the stochastic volatility models of Hull and White (1987) and Nelson (1990) the minimum variance hedge ratios are the same as the standard hedge ratios. Finally, we present some empirical results comparing the hedging performance of several standard models for S&P 500 index options.

III.4.6.1 Scale Invariance and Change of Numeraire

Merton (1973) called a price process *scale invariant* if and only if the marginal distribution of returns is independent of the price level. That is, if we scale the price and everything else in the price dimension such as the strike of the option or barriers by the *same* multiplicative factor u, then the option price is also scaled by the same factor u. The way that Merton put it was that it does not matter whether the underlying asset is measured in cents or dollars; this will not affect the price of the option.

But the scale invariance property is *not* equivalent to a change of numeraire. A numeraire is a unit of currency, so changing the numeraire changes the unit of measure for the price of every asset in the economy, including the discount bond. A change of numeraire also changes the drift in the price process, as seen in Section III.3.2.3. But scale invariance is weaker than a change of numeraire. We only change the unit of measurement of the price, and everything else in the price dimension, and we do not change the discount rate or the drift in the price process (unless the drift depends on S). So scale invariance captures only one aspect of the change in numeraire.

However, if a model is not scale invariant, then its option prices relative to the underlying asset are not invariant under a change of numeraire. That is, when a model is not scale invariant, the option price expressed as a percentage of the underlying price would be different when we change the numeraire. When an option is on a tradable asset, both the underlying and the option are tradable. Hence their relative price should be invariant under a change of numeraire. This means that we should always use a scale invariant model to price an option on a tradable asset.

III.4.6.2 Definition of Scale Invariance

It is obvious whether a model is scale invariant or not, assuming one can specify the returns distribution. But Alexander and Nogueira (2007a) show that we do not actually need to specify the returns distribution in order to classify an option pricing model as scale invariant or otherwise. We show that the process can be driven by Brownian motions with/without jumps, and stochastic volatility with/without jumps, and/or Lévy processes – the driving processes are immaterial. The only thing that matters for scale invariance is that the process must depend *only* on the *relative* price and time. More precisely, we must be able to write the process in the form

$$\frac{dS(t)}{S(t)} = \text{function of} \left[\frac{S(t)}{S(0)} \right] \text{ and time.} \tag{III.4.75}$$

So, for example a stochastic volatility process can be correlated with the price process and have mean reversion and jumps in volatility and jumps in price and it will be scale invariant if and only if condition (III.4.75) holds.

As mentioned in the introduction to this section, almost all the option pricing models we use today are scale invariant. The addition of a mean reversion and/or a jump does not affect the scale invariance. However, an *arithmetic* Brownian price process (with or without mean reversion and jumps), such as those that are commonly used to price interest rate options, is *not* scale invariant. This is acceptable, since interest rates are not tradable assets, and hence the price of an interest rate option relative to the underlying interest rate need not be invariant under a change of numeraire.

Another example is the CEV process (III.4.70) and its extension to the SABR model (III.4.71). These are *not* scale invariant unless $\beta \neq 1$. Nevertheless we can write them in a scale invariant form through a simple reparameterization. For instance, setting $\tilde{\alpha} = \alpha S(0)^{\beta-1}$ gives an alternative form for the CEV model as

$$\frac{dS(t)}{S(t)} = (r - y)dt + \tilde{\alpha}\left(\frac{S(t)}{S(0)}\right)^{\beta-1} dW(t). \qquad (\text{III.4.76})$$

And setting $\tilde{\alpha} = \alpha F(0)^{\beta-1}$ in the SABR model, we have the scale invariant form

$$\frac{dF(t)}{F(t)} = \tilde{\alpha}\left(\frac{F(t)}{F(0)}\right)^{\beta-1} dW(t),$$

$$d\tilde{\alpha}(t) = \tilde{v}\tilde{\alpha}(t)\left(\varrho dW(t) + \sqrt{1 - \varrho^2}\, dZ(t)\right). \qquad (\text{III.4.77})$$

$$\langle dW(t), dZ(t) \rangle = 0.$$

The argument in the previous section, that options on tradable assets should be priced using a scale invariant model, implies that the CEV and SABR models should be applied in their scale invariant form, at least when pricing options on tradable assets. To illustrate this Alexander and Nogueira (2007b) compare two model prices of a simple barrier option, one based on the process (III.4.76) and the other based on the non-scale-invariant form of the CEV model, (III.4.70). The option price is expressed as a percentage of the underlying price. If we change the price measurement scale the model price of the option does not change when we use process (III.4.76), but it *does* change, because the barrier is hit, when we use process (III.4.70).

III.4.6.3 Scale Invariance and Homogeneity

Alexander and Nogueira (2007a) show that virtually every stochastic volatility model in which the price process is written in geometric rather than arithmetic form has the *model free* hedge ratio property, and that the model free property is equivalent to a *floating smile* property. Moreover, the results extend to virtually every American or European contingent claim. We only require that the option's pay-off is *homogeneous* of some degree in the underlying price, the strike of the option and in any other option characteristic such as a barrier. Then the delta and gamma are model free.

That is, for an American or European option to have the model free hedge ratio property, the pay-off function of the option $p(S, K, B, \dots)$ must have the property that

$$p(uS, uK, uB, \dots) = u^k p(S, K, B, \dots) \qquad (\text{III.4.78})$$

for any positive real number u. The constant k is called the *degree of homogeneity* of the function. Most claims are homogeneous of degree 1, but binary options and the log contract are homogeneous of degree 0 and power options can be homogeneous of degree greater than 1.

Let $\theta(K, T | S, t)$ denote the implied volatility of a standard European option with strike K and maturity T, and denote by $\sigma(K, T | S, t) = \sigma(S, t)|_{t=T,\ S=K}$ the local volatility for forward price $S(T) = K$ and time T. Both the implied and the local volatility are seen from time t, when $S(t) = S$. Alexander and Nogueira (2007a) prove that the following properties are equivalent for all T and K:

- S is generated by a scale invariant process,
- $\theta(K, T \mid S, t) = \theta(uK, T \mid uS, t)$,
- $\sigma(K, T \mid S, t) = \sigma(uK, T \mid uS, t)$,

where u is any positive real number. Hence the implied and local volatility surfaces are invariant under a change of scale in the price dimension.

The problem with models that are not scale invariant is that the model implied and local volatilities do not have this property, i.e. they are not *homogeneous of degree zero* in the price dimension. In other words, if you change the units in which the price is measured, then the volatility is changed.

On the other hand, when the local volatility is homogeneous of degree 0 in the price dimension, so the model is scale invariant, then the model local volatility *also* has the floating smile property.[71] To prove this result, suppose we calibrate the model twice, first at time 0 and then again at time $t > 0$.

For some $t \geq 0$ write the local volatility at the point $(S(t), t)$ that is calibrated at time $t_1 \leq t$ as $\sigma(S(t), t \mid S(t_1), t_1)$. Such a point, calibrated at time 0 is depicted in Figure III.4.29. A static local volatility surface requires

$$\sigma\left(S(t), t \mid S(0), 0\right) = \sigma\left(S(t), t \mid S(t), t\right) \qquad \text{(III.4.79)}$$

for all t. We now show that if the model is scale invariant then the only way that (III.4.79) can hold is when the local volatility is completely flat in the price dimension.

Since we can write any price $S(t)$ as $cS(0)$ for some $c > 0$, we have, by the homogeneity property of scale invariant models,

$$\sigma\left(S(t), t \mid S(0), 0\right) = \sigma\left(cS(0), t \mid S(0), 0\right) = \sigma\left(c, t \mid 1, 0\right) \qquad \text{(III.4.80)}$$

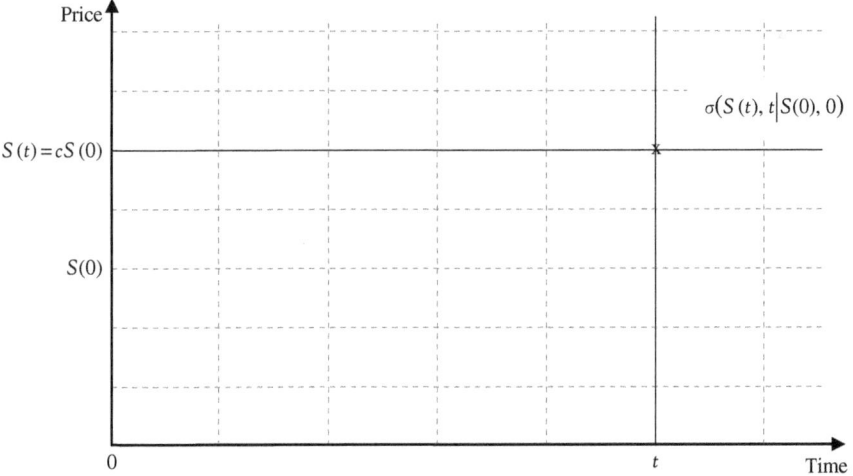

Figure III.4.29   Why scale invariance models have floating local volatility smiles

[71] The exception is the BSM model, which is a scale invariant model where the model and local volatilities are constant. However, all scale invariant stochastic volatility models have the floating smile property.

if the model is scale invariant. Now move to calibration time t, where (III.4.79) would hold if the local volatility surface is static. But at calibration time t, the homogeneity property implies $\sigma(S(t), t | S(t), t) = \sigma(1, t | 1, t)$. So if the surface is static then

$$\sigma(1, t | 1, t) = \sigma(c, t | 1, 0),$$

and this must hold for all $c > 0$ and $t \geq 0$. Since the right hand side of the above is the same function of t for all $c > 0$, the local volatility surface must be flat in the price dimension. But no model, scale invariant or otherwise, has flat local volatilities except the BSM model.

We now apply *Euler's homogeneous function theorem* to

$$\theta(K, T | S, t) = \theta(uK, T | uS, t). \tag{III.4.81}$$

Euler's theorem states that if

$$h(ux_1, \ldots, ux_n) = u^k h(x_1, \ldots, x_n). \tag{III.4.82}$$

so that h is a homogeneous function of degree k, then

$$\sum_{i=1}^{n} x_i h_i(x_1, \ldots, x_n) = k h(x_1, \ldots, x_n) \tag{III.4.83}$$

where

$$h_i(x_1, \ldots, x_n) = \frac{\partial h(x_1, \ldots, x_n)}{\partial x_i}.$$

The theorem is easy prove by differentiating (III.4.82) with respect to u and then setting $u = 1$. It is also easy to prove, just by differentiating (III.4.82) with respect to x_i, that if a function is homogeneous of degree k then all its partial derivatives are homogeneous of degree $k - 1$.

Applying the theorem to (III.4.81) gives

$$S \theta_S(K, T | S, t) + K \theta_K(K, T | S, t) = 0.$$

Turning this around yields the following expression for the model implied volatility's sensitivity to changes in the underlying price:

$$\theta_S(K, T | S, t) = -\frac{K}{S} \theta_K(K, T | S, t). \tag{III.4.84}$$

The relationship (III.4.84) proves that the model implied volatility is model free. Since the model is calibrated to market implied volatilities, when the calibration is close we will have $\theta(K, T | S, t) \approx \theta^m(K, T | S, t)$ and so

$$\theta_S(K, T | S, t) \approx -\frac{K}{S} \theta_K^m(K, T | S, t), \tag{III.4.85}$$

where $\theta_K^m(k, t | S, t)$ is the slope of the market implied volatility smile. So the only difference between different models arises from calibration errors.

III.4.6.4 Model Free Price Hedge Ratios

Following Merton (1973), Bates (2005) assumed that the price process is scale invariant and then showed that if the *price* of an option at every time on and before expiry is homogeneous of degree 1 in the underlying asset and exercise price, then the option's delta and gamma are model free. Alexander and Nogueira (2007a) extend this result to all American and

European contingent claims with a *pay-off function* that is homogeneous of some degree in the price dimension. As mentioned above, virtually every claim has a pay-off function that is homogeneous of some degree.

Suppose the claim has maturity T and its pay-off function $p(S, \mathbf{K})$ depends on the underlying price S and a vector of characteristics $\mathbf{K}$. We assume that

$$p(uS, u\mathbf{K}) = u^k p(S, \mathbf{K}),$$

i.e. that the pay-off is homogeneous of degree k, and we denote the price of the claim at time t when the underlying is at S by $g = g(\mathbf{K}, T|S, t)$. We also assume that S is generated by a scale invariant process.

Then *all* partial derivatives of the claim price with respect to S at any time $t < T$ are given by linear combinations of g and its partial derivatives with respect to $\mathbf{K}$, and, in particular,

$$
\begin{aligned}
g_S &= S^{-1}(kg - \mathbf{K}' g_{\mathbf{K}}), \\
g_{SS} &= S^{-2}\left[(k-1)(kg - 2\mathbf{K}' g_{\mathbf{K}}) + \mathbf{K}' g_{\mathbf{K}\mathbf{K}} \mathbf{K}\right],
\end{aligned}
\tag{III.4.86}
$$

where $g_{\mathbf{K}}$ is the gradient vector of first partial derivatives of the claim price with respect to the elements of $\mathbf{K}$ and $g_{\mathbf{K}\mathbf{K}}$ is the Hessian matrix of second partial derivatives.

If the claim is traded the claim price g is observable, and if a variety of claims with different strikes and other characteristics are traded then we can estimate the values of the gradient vector and Hessian matrix in (III.4.86) directly from market data. Hence, all the terms on the right-hand side of (III.4.86) are observable in the market. This means that model free deltas and gammas can be obtained directly from market data on the options: we do not need to use an option pricing model at all!

A simple case of the model free hedge ratio formula arises when $\mathbf{K} = K$, i.e. the only claim characteristic is a strike. Then (III.4.86) becomes

$$
\begin{aligned}
g_S &= S^{-1}(kg - Kg_K), \\
g_{SS} &= S^{-2}\left(k(k-1)g - 2K(k-1)g_K + K^2 g_{KK}\right).
\end{aligned}
\tag{III.4.87}
$$

A special case of (III.4.87) in the case where the claim is a standard American or European option was derived by Bates (2005) as follows. Vanilla options have pay-offs that are homogeneous of degree 1 in the underlying price and strike. Merton (1973) showed that when such options are priced under a scale invariant process their prices at any time prior to expiry are also homogeneous of degree 1. Thus, with our usual notation f for the price of a vanilla option,

$$f(uK, T|uS, t) = uf(K, T|S, t). \tag{III.4.88}$$

Applying Euler's homogeneous function theorem yields

$$f = Sf_S + Kf_K,$$

dropping the dependence on parameters, and this may be rewritten in the form

$$f_S = S^{-1}(f - Kf_K). \tag{III.4.89}$$

Moreover, since f is homogeneous of degree 1, f_S and f_K must be homogeneous of degree 0, and hence

$$
\begin{aligned}
Sf_{SS} + Kf_{SK} &= 0, \\
Sf_{KS} + Kf_{KK} &= 0,
\end{aligned}
$$

from which it follows that

$$f_{SS} = \left(\frac{K}{S}\right)^2 f_{KK}. \tag{III.4.90}$$

The model free delta (III.4.89) and gamma (III.4.90) are a special case of (III.4.87) for the case of a vanilla option.

An alternative form of the model free result (III.4.89) that only applies to a vanilla option is to use the model free implied volatility sensitivity (III.4.85) in formula (III.4.59). Thus

$$\delta(K, T \,|\, S, t) \approx \delta_{BSM}(K, T \,|\, S, t) - \nu_{BSM}(K, T \,|\, S, t) \frac{K}{S} \theta_K^m(K, T \,|\, S, t), \tag{III.4.91}$$

where $\delta(K, T \,|\, S, t) \equiv f_S(K, T \,|\, S, t)$ is the model free delta of a scale invariant model and the approximation is the result of calibration error. This shows that the model free delta will be greater than the BSM delta of a vanilla option when the market implied volatility skew has a negative slope, i.e. when $\theta_K^m(K, T \,|\, S, t) < 0$ and less than the BSM delta of a vanilla option when the market implied volatility skew has a positive slope, i.e. when $\theta_K^m(K, T \,|\, S, t) > 0$.

When the hedge ratios for standard European puts and calls that are derived from different scale invariant models appear to differ, this can only be because either or both of the models are not well calibrated. For instance, consider two scale invariant models: the lognormal mixture diffusion with two volatility components and the Heston model. The first model has only three parameters whilst the second has five (or six, including the volatility risk premium). So the Heston model often fits the market prices of standard European options better than the lognormal mixture diffusion. And any differences that are observed between the hedge ratios of the Heston model and those of the lognormal mixture diffusion model are only because of their different quality of fit to the smile.

It is important to understand that the Black–Scholes–Merton model *is* scale invariant, but the BSM hedge ratios are often very different from the hedge ratios derived from other scale invariant models. Why should this be so? Unless the skew is flat we cannot fit *all* vanilla option prices with a single volatility parameter. In other words, the BSM model provides a terrible fit to market data and this is why its hedge ratios differ from those of other scale invariant models that are usually well calibrated to the smile.

However, when we use the BSM model in practice we 'tweak' the model so that it fits the smile exactly. That is, we change the volatility, which is supposed to be constant, so that there is a zero calibration error. If we did the same with other scale invariant volatility models, for instance, letting the spot volatility be strike dependent, then they would also fit the smile exactly.

Finally, we emphasize that the model free result (III.4.86) applies to *all* homogeneous claims on tradable assets, and that it can be extended to third and fourth order price hedge ratios, if desired. The practical application of this formula to derive model free hedge ratios directly from market data does, however, depend on the options having observable market prices. But amongst the many exotic options that are traded today, most are in fairly illiquid OTC markets and only barrier options and Asian options have liquid prices. For other types of exotic options we cannot infer the model free hedge ratios from observable prices, so we need to calibrate a model (to the observable prices of standard European options) and use this model to derive prices for the exotic claim. Then the hedge ratios can be derived using formula (III.4.86). It should not matter which scale invariant model we use to hedge the option, provided it calibrates to standard European calls and puts well. In particular, we need the calibrated parameters to be stable over time and the errors in calibration to be consistently small.

III.4.6.5   Minimum Variance Hedging

Does the model free property of scale invariant models mean that there is no point in trying out different stochastic volatility and jump models for hedging? Our theoretical results above have proved that all (sensible) models for tradable have the same hedge ratios. In this subsection we introduce the *minimum variance* delta and gamma, which are different from the usual delta and gamma in scale invariant models with non-zero price–volatility correlation. So the minimum variance hedge ratios are the same as the standard hedge ratios in the BSM model, and also in stochastic volatility models with zero price–volatility correlation such as the Hull and White (1987) and Stein and Stein (1991) models and the strong GARCH diffusion. But in other stochastic volatility models, and in deterministic volatility models such as the lognormal mixture diffusion (where the price and volatility are perfectly correlated), the minimum variance hedge ratios are different from the standard hedge ratio.

When volatility is stochastic and/or there are jumps in price or volatility, the market is incomplete. In a complete market we can find a self-financing portfolio that provides a perfect hedge for any claim.[72] But if we can find a replicating portfolio in an incomplete market it will not be self-financing. In this case investors will seek to minimize the uncertainty about the cost of replication. The cost at time t is the difference between the value of the replicating portfolio at time t and the cumulative profit or loss on the replicating portfolio up to time t. It is only when this cost is zero that the replicating portfolio is self-financing. The *local risk minimizing* replicating portfolio, introduced by Schweizer (1991), is the portfolio for which the local variance of the cost process of a non-self-financing replicating portfolio is minimized. The hedge ratios in a local risk minimizing replicating portfolio are called *minimum variance* hedge ratios.

The *minimum variance delta* is the amount of the underlying asset that minimizes the instantaneous variance of a delta hedged portfolio. The *minimum variance gamma* is the amount of another option on the underlying asset that minimizes the instantaneous variance of a delta–gamma hedged portfolio. The minimum variance delta accounts for the *total* effect of a change in the underlying price, including the indirect effect of the price change on the volatility (or any other parameter that is correlated with the underlying price). Similarly the minimum variance gamma can be thought of as a *total* second derivative of the option price with respect to the underlying asset price, including the indirect effect of the price change on the volatility.[73]

El Karoui et al. (1997) show that one can compute the minimum variance hedge ratios by completing the market with a pure volatility derivative, finding the replicating portfolio in the completed market and then projecting this onto the original market. One of the most accessible accounts of minimum variance delta hedging is given by Poulsen et al. (2007). These authors also demonstrate, via simulations and empirically,[74] that minimum variance deltas provide a better hedging performance than standard deltas and that the minimum

---

[72] See Section III.3.6.5.
[73] See Alexander and Nogueira (2007a) for further details.
[74] Using data on S&P 500 index options, Eurostoxx 50 options and USD/EUR options with up to 1 year to expiry.

variance deltas may *also* have a model free property. That is, their empirical tests indicate that it does not seem to matter which scale invariant model is used for minimum variance delta hedging.

We now derive formulae for the minimum variance delta and gamma within a general class of stochastic volatility models.[75] Consider the model

$$dS(t) = \ldots \, dt + S(t)^{\beta} x\left(V(t)\right) dW(t),$$

$$dV(t) = \ldots \, dt + y(V(t)) \, dB(t), \tag{III.4.92}$$

$$\langle dW(t), dB(t) \rangle = \varrho dt.$$

The notation $\ldots \, dt$ is used simply because the drift term does not affect the result, provided it has no stochastic latent variables. So the process could be arithmetic or geometric and there may or may not be mean reversion in the drift.

In the following we shall, for brevity, drop the dependence on volatility and time, and also set

$$m \equiv m(V(t)) = \frac{y(V(t))}{x(V(t))}.$$

Application of Itô's lemma to $x \equiv x(V(t))$ and $y \equiv y(V(t))$ gives

$$dx = \ldots \, dt + x_V y dB,$$

$$dy = \ldots \, dt + y_V y dB.$$

Let $g \equiv g(S, V)$ be any claim on S, so again by Itô's lemma,

$$dg = \ldots \, dt + g_S S^{\beta} x dW + g_V y dB.$$

The minimum variance delta and gamma are defined as:

$$\delta_{MV} = \frac{\langle dg, dS \rangle}{\langle dS, dS \rangle} \quad \text{and} \quad \gamma_{MV} = \frac{\langle d\delta_{MV}, dS \rangle}{\langle dS, dS \rangle}.$$

Since $\langle dS, dS \rangle = (S^{\beta} x)^2 \, dt$, $\langle dW, dS \rangle = S^{\beta} x dt$ and $\langle dB, dS \rangle = S^{\beta} x \varrho dt$, we have

$$\delta_{MV} = \frac{\langle dg, dS \rangle}{\langle dS, dS \rangle} = \frac{g_S (S^{\beta} x)^2 + g_V y S^{\beta} x \varrho}{(S^{\beta} x)^2}.$$

That is,[76]

$$\delta^{MV} = g_S + g_V S^{-\beta} m \varrho. \tag{III.4.93}$$

Intuitively, this resembles a total derivative of the claim price with respect to S, i.e.

$$\delta^{MV} = \frac{dg}{dS} = g_S + \frac{dV}{dS} g_V$$

with

$$\frac{dg}{dS} \equiv \frac{\langle dg, dS \rangle}{\langle dS, dS \rangle} = \frac{\mathrm{Cov}_t(dg, dS)}{\mathrm{Var}_t(dS)} \quad \text{and} \quad \frac{dV}{dS} \equiv \frac{\langle dV, dS \rangle}{\langle dS, dS \rangle} = \frac{\mathrm{Cov}_t(dV, dS)}{\mathrm{Var}_t(dS)}.$$

---

[75] But see Poulsen et al. (2007) for comments on this 'deceptively simple' derivation and a more exact approach.

[76] This formula for the minimum variance delta is used by Poulsen et al. based on results from El Karoui et al. Also a general formula for the minimum variance delta of jump diffusion models with stochastic volatility is given in Grünwald and Trautman (1996), and Lee (2001) derives a simple approximation to the minimum variance delta simply by changing the minus sign to a plus sign in (III.4.91).

It may also be shown that the minimum variance gamma of the general stochastic volatility model (III.4.92) is [77]

$$\gamma^{MV} = g_{SS} + \varrho S^{-\beta} m \big(\varrho S^{-\beta} m g_{VV} + 2g_{SV} - S^{-1}\beta g_V + \varrho S^{-\beta} m_V g_V \big). \tag{III.4.94}$$

From (III.4.93) and (III.4.94) it is immediately apparent that the minimum variance delta and gamma are the same as the standard delta and gamma when the price – volatility correlation ϱ is zero.

III.4.6.6   Minimum Variance Hedge Ratios in Specific Models

The minimum variance delta and gamma for some specific models, including deterministic volatility models and the Heston and SABR models, are derived by Alexander and Nogueira (2007a, 2007b). In the Heston model, i.e. the model

$$\frac{dS}{S} = (r - y)\, dt + \sqrt{V} dW,$$

$$dV = \varphi(m - V)\, dt + \xi\sqrt{V}\Big(\varrho dW + \sqrt{1-\varrho^2}\, dZ \Big), \tag{III.4.95}$$

we have $\beta = 1$ and $m = \xi$, using the general notation defined in (III.4.92). Hence, using (III.4.93),

$$\delta^{MV} = g_S + \varrho S^{-1} \xi g_V. \tag{III.4.96}$$

Thus the only model-dependent part of the hedge ratio is the second term on the right-hand side. In the case of equity options, when ϱ is typically negative, the Heston minimum variance delta will be less than the model free delta g_S when g_V is positive. This implies that the model free delta over-hedges vanilla equity options relative to the minimum variance delta, and should be less efficient for pure delta hedging. Alexander and Nogueira (2007a) also show that the minimum variance gamma in the Heston model is

$$\gamma^{MV} = g_{SS} + \varrho S^{-1} \xi \big(S^{-1}\varrho \xi g_{VV} + 2g_{SV} - S^{-1}g_V \big) \tag{III.4.97}$$

which is a special case of (III.4.94), as can easily be verified.
    In the SABR model, i.e.

$$dF = \alpha F^\beta dW,$$

$$d\alpha = v\alpha \Big(\varrho dW + \sqrt{1-\varrho^2}\, dZ \Big), \tag{III.4.98}$$

$m = v$ and β remains a parameter, hence

$$\delta^{MV} = g_F + \varrho F^{-\beta} v g_V \tag{III.4.99}$$

and

$$\gamma^{MV} = g_{FF} + \varrho F^{-\beta} v \big(F^{-\beta}\varrho v g_{VV} + 2g_{FV} - F^{-1}\beta g_V \big), \tag{III.4.100}$$

as also given in Alexander and Nogueira (2007b) . On the right-hand side of (III.4.99) and (III.4.100) g_F and g_{FF} are the standard delta and gamma of the SABR model with respect to F, and note that they are not model-free because the model is not scale invariant.

---

[77] The proof is omitted since it is rather lengthy, but see a forthcoming ICMA Centre discussion paper on this subject.

Bakshi et al. (1997) derive the minimum variance delta of the Heston jump model:

$$\frac{dS(t)}{S(t)} = \left(r - y - \lambda\mu_J\right)dt + \sqrt{V(t)}dW(t) + J(t)dq(t),$$

$$dV(t) = \varphi(m - V(t))\,dt + \xi\sqrt{V(t)}\left(\varrho dW(t) + \sqrt{1 - \varrho^2}\,dZ(t)\right).$$

$$\langle dW(t), dZ(t)\rangle = 0,$$ (III.4.101)

$$\ln(1 + J(t)) \sim N\left(\ln(1 + \mu_J) - \tfrac{1}{2}\sigma_J^2, \sigma_J^2\right).$$

Since the jumps are lognormally distributed, the instantaneous variance of the jump component $J(t)dq(t)$ is

$$V_J(t)dt = \lambda\left(\mu_J^2 + \exp(\sigma_J^2 - 1)\left(1 + \mu_J^2\right)\right).$$ (III.4.102)

Bakshi et al. show that the minimum variance delta for a claim with price

$$g = g(K, T \,|\, S(t), V(t), J(t) \ldots)$$

is

$$\delta^{MV}(t) = \psi(t)\left(g_S + S(t)^{-1}\left(\varrho\xi g_V + \lambda\Lambda(t)\right)\right),$$ (III.4.103)

where
$$\psi(t) = \frac{V(t)}{V(t) + V_J(t)}$$ (III.4.104)

is the proportion of the total instantaneous variance that is due to the diffusion and $\Lambda(t)$ is a positive adjustment term that means that if the jump risk premium λ is not zero we must increase our holding of the underlying for the additional hedge against jump risk. In the absence of jumps the hedge ratio reduces to (III.4.96). See the appendix to Bakshi et al. (1997) for the precise specification of $\Lambda(t)$, which is rather complex.

III.4.6.7 Empirical Results

In this subsection the Heston (1993) model is used as a representative scale invariant model. Its delta and gamma are model free but if the price – volatility correlation is non-zero, the minimum variance delta (III.4.96) and gamma (III.4.97) will be different from the model-free hedge ratios. The SABR model (Hagan et al., 2002) is used as a representative model that is not scale invariant, and the BSM model is used as a benchmark (but with exact calibration! – see the discussion on page 296).

The empirical results, which are abstracts from those used in Alexander and Nogueira (2007a, 2007b), study the hedging performance of the June 2004 European call options on the S&P 500 index, using daily close prices from 16 January 2004 to 15 June 2004 for up to 34 different strikes on any day. Only the strikes within ±10% of the current index level were used for the model's calibration each day, but all strikes were used for the hedging strategies. Each model was calibrated daily by minimizing the root mean square error between the model implied volatilities and the market implied volatilities of the options used in the calibration set. For the BSM model, the deltas and gammas are obtained directly from the market data and there is no need for model calibrations.[78]

The delta hedge strategy consists of one delta hedged short call on each available strike, rebalanced daily. The delta–gamma hedge strategy again consists of a short call on each strike, but this time an amount of the 1125 option, which is closest to ATM in general over the period, is bought. This way the gamma on each option is set to zero and then we delta hedge the portfolio. The portfolio is rebalanced daily, assuming zero transaction costs.

Table III.4.10 reports some results obtained from the two hedging strategies. The table shows the standard deviation of the hedging errors, expressed as a percentage of the standard deviation of the hedging errors from the BSM model. The options are grouped into moneyness buckets, as shown in the first row of the table, and the second row reports the number of options that were hedged in each moneyness group.

Table III.4.10 Standard deviation of hedging errors relative to standard deviation of BSM hedging errors: S&P 500 June 2004 options

Moneyness (and below this, number of options)									
0.90–0.95		0.95–1.00		1.00–1.05		1.05–1.10		1.10–1.15	
141		476		435		217		55	
Delta hedging									
SABR^{MV}	64.7%	SABR^{MV}	76.0%	Heston^{MV}	84.5%	SABR^{MV}	89.3%	Heston^{MV}	93.1%
Heston^{MV}	65.7%	Heston^{MV}	78.2%	SABR^{MV}	85.8%	Heston^{MV}	89.6%	SABR^{MV}	95.9%
SABR	107.9%	SABR	128.3%	SABR	143.4%	SABR	134.4%	SABR	119.6%
Heston	130.2%	Heston	153.1%	Heston	161.8%	Heston	148.6%	Heston	130.9%
Delta–gamma hedging									
Heston^{MV}	89.5%	SABR^{MV}	95.0%	Heston^{MV}	123.7%	Heston^{MV}	99.3%	Heston^{MV}	87.1%
SABR^{MV}	98.6%	Heston^{MV}	101.3%	SABR^{MV}	140.7%	SABR^{MV}	117.6%	SABR^{MV}	100.6%
SABR	108.7%	SABR	125.0%	SABR	158.7%	SABR	171.5%	SABR	135.4%
Heston	159.8%	Heston	144.3%	Heston	168.8%	Heston	180.2%	Heston	143.9%

The minimum variance hedge ratios perform better than the standard hedge ratios for all options, and it is not possible to decide which of the two models gives the more accurate minimum variance hedge ratios. But note that neither of these minimum variance hedge can improve on the performance of the 'BSM model' for delta–gamma hedging ATM options. The scale invariant (i.e. Heston) model provides the least accurate hedge ratios for all options, and the error standard deviation is between 30% and 80% greater than the BSM error standard deviation! This is because the scale invariant delta is significantly higher than the BSM model delta, except for very high strike options when the skew levels out and may even have a positive slope.

---

[78] Since we allow the BSM volatility to be strike dependent, this is not really the BSM model, and to be honest it is not really a fair test of the other models if we only allow the BSM model to have a strike dependent parameters. As Dilip Madan has kindly pointed out, to be fair in a hedging race with the 'BSM model' (calibrated exactly in this way) we should allow all the models to have their spot volatility parameters 'tweaked' so that there is no calibration error. (But then, the Heston standard hedge ratios would be identical to the BSM hedge ratios, although the minimum variance hedge ratios would not be the same. The BSM minimum variance hedge ratios are the same as the standard hedge ratios.)

Figures III.4.30 and III.4.31 show the distribution functions of the errors for each model, with that of the BSM model hedging errors shown by the bold black line. The steeper the 'S' shape, the lower the standard deviation of the error distribution. For the delta hedge there is a clear distinction between the error distributions resulting from the five hedging models, except for the Heston and SABR minimum variance delta hedges, which appear to be almost identical. For delta–gamma hedging it is impossible to distinguish between the hedging performance of the BSM model and the Heston and SABR models with minimum variance

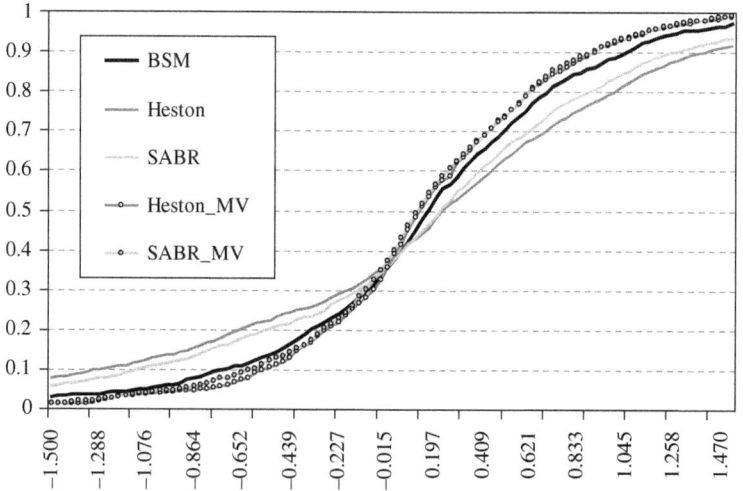

Figure III.4.30   Comparison of hedging error distributions: delta hedge

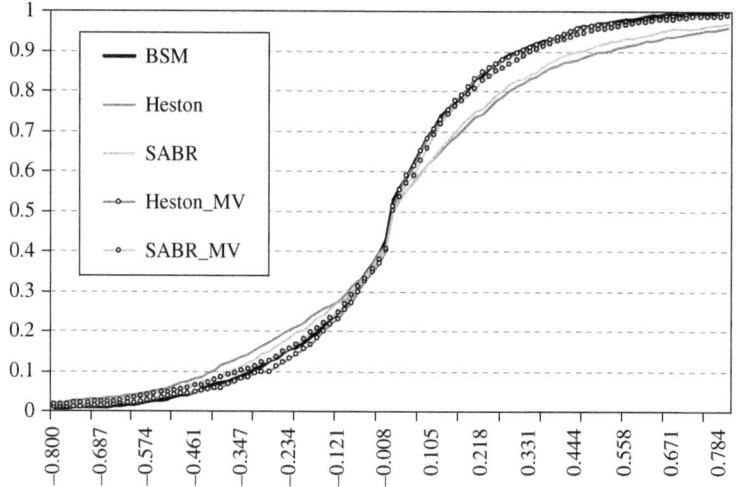

Figure III.4.31   Comparison of hedging error distributions: delta–gamma hedge

delta and gamma hedge ratios. However, the scale invariant model (Heston) and the non-scale invariant model (SABR) have error standard deviation distributions that are significantly different from the other distributions, according to Kolmogorov–Smirnoff tests.[79]

III.4.7   TRADING VOLATILITY

There are many reasons to trade volatility as an asset class in its own right. For instance, equity volatility is strongly negatively correlated with the equity price so adding volatility to an equity portfolio provides investors with excellent diversification. By the same token, holding volatility in an equity portfolio provides insurance against market crashes, since volatility tends to increase markedly at such time. Trading forward volatility via calendar spreads provides a vega hedge for forward start and cliquet options. Arbitrage traders and hedge funds may take positions on different volatilities of the same maturities, and speculative investors may simply make a bet on future volatility.

An option is a trade on both the price of the underlying and the implied volatility. Some options trading strategies, such as an ATM straddle, attempt to isolate the volatility component so that the trade is a pure directional trade on volatility. But options are expensive to trade and options strategies for trading volatility require frequent rebalancing. For instance, whilst an ATM straddle is a pure volatility trade at inception, as soon as the underlying price moves it is no longer ATM, and straddles that are not ATM are directional trades, i.e. they have pay-offs that are sensitive to the direction of movement of the underlying price.

During the last few years *variance swaps* and instruments based on *volatility indices* have become popular for trading pure volatility. A volatility index of maturity T is a single number that represents the entire volatility smile of maturity T. That is, the volatility index is a type of average implied volatility over all strikes of traded options with the same maturity on the underlying asset. Equity index volatility indices are calculated using the market prices of all standard European options on the index. The formula is based on an approximation of the index by the *variance swap rate*.

We begin this section by describing a variance swap and explaining the relationship between the variance swap rate and *realized variance*. The difference between the realized variance and the square of the variance swap rate is called the *variance risk premium* and we describe the characteristics of this premium. Thereafter we derive the formula for a volatility index and describe the characteristics of the equity index volatilities that are quoted on the Chicago Board Options Exchange (CBOE) in the US and on the Eurex exchange in Europe. Note that equity volatility indices are not traded, but the CBOE and Eurex have recently started trading futures on volatility indices. In section III.4.7.8 we emphasize that, unlike most other futures contracts, the spot volatility is *not* the underlying of the futures. In June 2006 the CBOE launched standard European options on the S&P 500 volatility index, Vix. These are not heavily traded at present and the market prices of Vix options appear to be

---

[79] See Section I.3.5.7 for further details on Kolmogorov–Smirnoff tests.

very high. We conclude the section by proposing some reasons why this should be the case. I would like to thank my PhD student Stamatis Leontsinis for his great help with all the empirical results in this section.

III.4.7.1   Variance Swaps and Volatility Swaps

A *variance swap* of maturity T is an OTC contract that exchanges a variable rate, i.e. the *realized variance* from initiation of the swap until date T, with a fixed strike for the swap. The strike is the square of the *variance swap rate* which sets the initial value of the swap to zero. Variance swap rates are always quoted as an *annualized volatility* and so an annualized realized variance is used to calculate the pay-off to a variance swap. Formally, the pay-off to a variance swap is given by

$$\text{Variance Swap Pay-off} = \left(RV_{0,T} - K_T^2\right) \times pv, \qquad (\text{III.4.105})$$

where $RV_{0,T}$ is the annualized realized variance, the strike K_T is the variance swap rate and pv is the point value.

The annualized realized variance is calculated at expiry of the swap and the calculation method is defined in the OTC contact. Usually it is based on a geometric Brownian motion for the underlying asset price with constant volatility, so we take an annualized *equally weighted average of the squared daily log returns* over the life of the swap. Term sheets for variance swaps vary on whether to use an actual/365 or a business days/252 day-count convention. In the latter case

$$RV_{0,T} = \frac{252}{T^e} \sum_{t=1}^{T^e} \ln\left(\frac{P_t}{P_{t-1}}\right)^2, \qquad (\text{III.4.106})$$

where P_t is the price of the underlying index, and T^e is the number of scheduled trading days between inception of the swap on day 0 zero and its expiry on day T. The square root of (III.4.106) is called the *realized volatility*.

A *volatility swap* has a pay-off that is not quadratic but linear in realized volatility:

$$\text{Volatility Swap Pay-off} = \left(\sqrt{RV_{0,T}} - K_T\right) \times pv. \qquad (\text{III.4.107})$$

However, there is much less trading on volatility swaps than on variance swaps. One reason for this is that the variance swap pay-off (III.4.105) is a *convex* function of volatility, and purchasing a convex pay-off is always better than its linear alternative. If realized volatility is above the value that was expected when setting the variance swap rate, the gains from being long the variance swap are greater than the gains from a long position on a volatility swap with the same strike. But if realized volatility is less than the value that was expected when setting the variance swap rate, the loss to the buyer of a variance swap is less than the loss to the buyer of a volatility swap with the same strike.

EXAMPLE III.4.9: EXPECTED PAY-OFF TO A VARIANCE SWAP

Suppose the 30-day variance swap rate is 20% and the expected 30-day realized variance is 18%, both quoted as annual volatilities. What is the expected pay-off to a short position of $100 per basis point on this swap?

SOLUTION   The point value of $100 per basis point is the same as $10,000 per percentage point. Hence the expected pay-off is $\left(20^2 - 18^2\right) \times \$10,000 = \$760,000$.

Indicative quotes for variance swap rates on the major equity indices are provided by Bloomberg. Daily data from Bloomberg on 30-day variance swap rates between February 2006 and June 2007 are shown in Figure III.4.32. Periods of high market volatility are apparent in May–June 2006 and in March 2007. In May 2006 equities fell on the back of a commodity crisis and in March 2007 they fell on concerns about the Chinese economy.

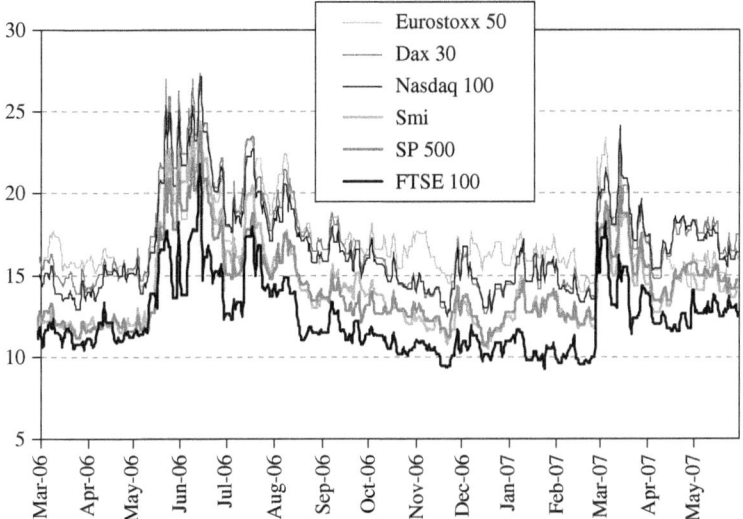

Figure III.4.32   Bloomberg variance swap rates

Suppose a variance swap is entered at time 0 and matures at time T. How do we *mark to market* the fair value of variance swap rate at time t with $0 < t < T$? We use the discounted expected pay-off to the variance swap where the realized variance term is decomposed into two terms: a fraction that is already observed and the remaining fraction that is equal to the square of the variance swap rate at time t with the residual term to maturity $T - t$. That is,

$$PV_{t,T} = \exp(-r(T - t)) \left[\frac{t}{T} RV_{0,t} + \frac{(T - t)}{T} K_{t,T}^2 - K_{0,T}^2 \right] \times pv, \qquad (III.4.108)$$

where r is the discount rate and $K_{t,T}$ is the variance swap rate at time t for a swap that matures at time T.

EXAMPLE III.4.10: MARKING A VARIANCE SWAP TO MARKET

Consider a 6-month variance swap issued 2 months ago with a strike of 25% and a point value of $1000 per percentage point. The realized volatility over the past 2 months was 20% and today's 4-month variance swap rate is 22%. What is the mark-to-market value of the variance swap? You may assume the discount rate is zero for simplicity.

SOLUTION

$$PV_{t,T} = \left[\frac{2}{6} 20^2 + \frac{4}{6} 22^2 - 25^2 \right] \times \$1000 = -\$169,000.$$

III.4.7.2   Trading Forward Volatility

Calendar spreads on variance swap rates of different maturities allow one to trade *forward* volatility. But unlike trading forward interest rates we do not take equal and opposite positions in the calendar spread on variance swaps. The following example explains why.

EXAMPLE III.4.11: CALENDAR SPREADS ON VARIANCE SWAPS

Consider the following spread trade on a variance swap:

- sell N per percentage point on the 30-day variance swap at a rate of 15%;
- buy M per percentage point on the 120-day variance swap at a rate of 18%.

What should N and M be for this position to trade 90-day realized variance 30 days forward?

SOLUTION   Under the assumption that log returns are independent and identically distributed,

$$RV_{30,120} = \frac{120 \times RV_{0,120} - 30 \times RV_{0,30}}{90} = \frac{1}{3}\left(4RV_{0,120} - RV_{0,30}\right). \qquad \text{(III.4.109)}$$

Hence, our short position on the 120-day variance swap needs to be four times as large as our position on the 30-day variance swap for the spread to be a trade on the 90-day realized variance 30 days forward. That is, $M = 4N$. The case where $N = 10,000$ is depicted in Figure III.4.33.

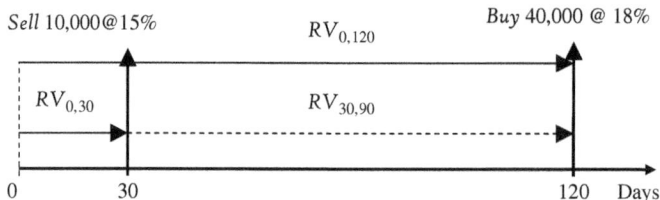

Figure III.4.33   Calendar spread on variance swap rates

When $N = 10,000$ the pay-off to our position is given by:

$$\text{Pay-off} = \left(RV_{0,30} - 15^2\right) \times (-10,000) + \left(RV_{0,120} - 18^2\right) \times 40,000$$
$$= \left(15^2 \times 10,000 - 18^2 \times 40,000\right) + \left(4 \times RV_{0,120} - RV_{0,30}\right) \times 10,000$$
$$= -10.71\text{m} + RV_{30,90} \times 30,000 = \left(RV_{30,90} - 18.8944^2\right) \times 30,000.$$

If it turns out that

$$RV_{30,90} = \frac{120 \times 18^2 - 30 \times 15^2}{90} = 18.8944^2,$$

then the pay-off will be zero. But if the realized variance is greater than this then one would make a profit on the position and if it is less than this one makes a loss. For instance, if the realized volatility between time $t = 30$ and $t = 120$ is 19% then one makes a profit of $-\$10.71\text{m} + 19^2 \times 30,000 = \$120,000$.

III.4.7.3   Variance Risk Premium

The *variance risk premium* of maturity T is the difference between the realized variance of maturity T and the square of the associated variance swap rate. Since the realized variance is forward looking the variance risk premium can only be measured *ex post*. However, a statistical forecast of the realized variance can be used to predict and therefore trade on the variance risk premium. The expected variance risk premium is the expected pay-off to a long position on the variance swap.

Figure III.4.34 shows the variance risk premiums that are computed from the *ex post* realized variance and the variance swap rates shown in Figure III.4.32.[80] variance It is important to emphasize that we cannot know a variance risk premium in advance, we can only forecast it or calculate it ex post. For instance, in Figure III.4.33 the variance risk premium of 7.1693 on the FTSE 100 on 11 May 2006 was calculated using FTSE 100 returns over the period from 11 May 2006 to 10 June 2006. Hence, anyone entering a variance swap on 11 May 2006 would *not* know that the variance risk premium was so very high on that day.

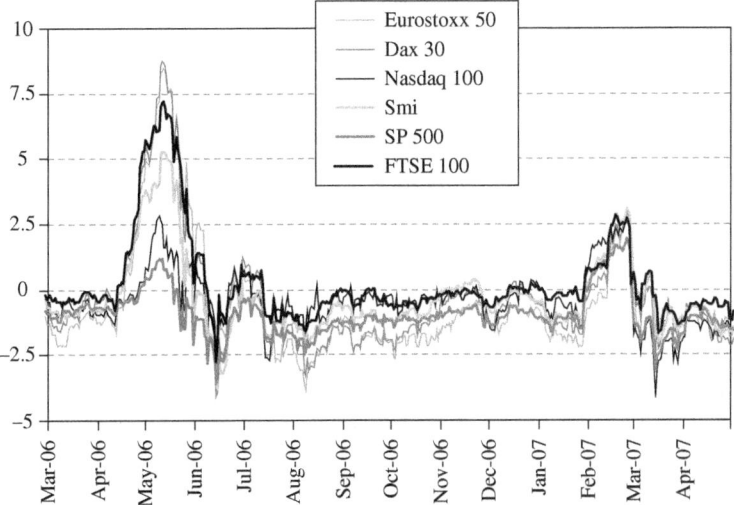

Figure III.4.34   Ex post 30-day variance risk premia

The variance risk premium is usually slightly negative. Hence, it usually pays to go short on a variance swap. This explains why many banks are happy to sell variance swaps to investors and other volatility traders. However, before a period of high market volatility, such as those in May–June 2006 and March 2007, the variance risk premium becomes very large and positive. To give some idea of the money that could be lost when writing a variance swap, if you took a short position of just \$1 per basis point on a 30-day variance swap on the FTSE 100 on 11 May 2006, then you would have lost

$$(29.46^2 - 12.29^2) \times 100 = \$71,693!$$

---

[80] Note that we end the series 30 days earlier than the series in Figure III.4.32, since the realized variance is forward looking over the next 30 days. Also, the series shown are $(RV_{0,30} - K_{30}^2)/100$, so they represent the dollar pay-off to 1 cent per percentage point. Multiply by 10,000 to obtain the pay-off to \$1 per basis point, for instance.

III.4.7.4   Construction of a Volatility Index

Variance swap rates are set by traders in OTC markets. But volatility indices are not traded, so how do we know their prices? A volatility index of maturity T for the underlying price S is constructed from the market prices of standard European options on S of maturity T. It is based on a formula that approximates the variance swap rate as the value of a certain portfolio of these options. Hence, a volatility index is an approximation to the variance swap rate of the same maturity. But since variance swap rates are fixed in OTC markets and the volatility index is constructed by an exchange using market prices of standard European calls and puts, differences between variance swap rates and volatility indices do arise.[81]

We now derive the formula used to construct a volatility index.[82] Neuberger (1994) showed that if the underlying price S follows a geometric Brownian motion then the realized variance can be replicated as the expected pay-off to a short position on the log contract. The *log contract* of maturity T is defined by the pay-off $\ln(S(T)/S(0))$, where $S(0)$ is the underlying price today, i.e. at the inception of the contract. Hence the expected pay-off to a *short* position on this contract is

$$LC(T) = -E\left[\ln\left(\frac{S(T)}{S(0)}\right)\right],\tag{III.4.110}$$

Assume for simplicity that the underlying asset pays no dividends and its price follows a standard geometric Brownian motion with risk neutral drift r and constant volatility σ.[83] By Itô's lemma we can write the stochastic differential equation for the price as

$$d\ln S(t) = \left(r - \tfrac{1}{2}\sigma^2\right)dt + \sigma\, dW(t).\tag{III.4.111}$$

Integration from 0 to T gives

$$\ln\left(\frac{S(T)}{S(0)}\right) = rT - \tfrac{1}{2}\int_0^T \sigma^2\, dt + \int_0^T \sigma\, dW(t).\tag{III.4.112}$$

Rearranging the above gives

$$T^{-1}\int_0^T \sigma^2\, dt = 2r - 2T^{-1}\ln\left(\frac{S(T)}{S(0)}\right) + 2T^{-1}\int_0^T \sigma\, dW(t).\tag{III.4.113}$$

Take expectations of (III.4.113) under the risk neutral measure:

$$E\left[T^{-1}\int_0^T \sigma^2 dt\right] = 2r - 2T^{-1}E\left[\ln\left(\frac{S(T)}{S(0)}\right)\right] = 2r + 2T^{-1}LC(T).\tag{III.4.114}$$

The variance swap rate is the fair value for the swap. Hence, before annualization,

$$K_T^2 = E\left[T^{-1}\int_0^T \sigma^2 dt\right] = 2r + 2T^{-1}LC(T).\tag{III.4.115}$$

---

[81] And variance swaps rates also differ across banks.
[82] More detailed descriptions are given in Demeterfi et al. (1999) and Carr and Wu (2007).
[83] The risk free rate r is assumed constant. We can also include a constant dividend yield here by replacing r with $r - y$.

Thus we can estimate the variance swap rate by replicating the expected pay-off $LC(T)$ to a short position on the log contract with maturity T.

In Section III.3.5.5 we showed how to replicate any continuous profile on S by holding a portfolio of vanilla calls (or puts) on S with different strikes $\{K_1, \ldots, K_m\}$ and with weights determined by (a) the difference between successive strikes and (b) the gamma of the profile. The strikes should cover the whole range of available strikes and the more strikes chosen the better the replication.

Denote by $f(K_i, T)$ the standard European call or put option of strike K_i and maturity T that is used in the replication of the short log contract. Since the gamma of the short log contract is S^{-2}, the replication of the short log contract in present value terms is achieved with a portfolio having price $\sum_i \Delta K_i K_i^{-2} f(K_i, T)$, where $\Delta K_i = \frac{1}{2}(K_{i+1} - K_{i-1})$. But $LC(T)$ is *not* expressed in present value terms, hence

$$LC(T) \approx \exp(rT) \sum_i \frac{\Delta K_i}{K_i^2} f(K_i, T). \tag{III.4.116}$$

And the variance swap rate (before annualization) is therefore approximated as

$$K_T \approx \left[2T^{-1} \sum_i \frac{\Delta K_i}{K_i^2} \exp(rT) f(K_i, T) \right]^{1/2}. \tag{III.4.117}$$

This is the basis of the formula used to construct the main equity index volatility indices.

III.4.7.5   Effect of the Skew

The construction of a volatility index is based on the prices of options of all strikes of a given maturity. Hence the value of the volatility index, and so also the fair value of a variance swap, is sensitive to the implied volatility skew. The steeper the skew, the higher the variance swap rate and the volatility index. The value of a volatility index depends on the implied volatilities of options of all strikes, including the deep OTM options that may have stale prices. Alexander and Leontsinis (2008) investigate the sensitivity of the volatility index to (a) the minimum price for the options used in the calculation and (b) the normal strike range of the options used. The volatility index is robust to small increases in the minimum price and to small reductions in the strike range. The index is, however, quite sensitive to the prices of deep OTM options. In particular, if the values of low strike options increase and the skew becomes steeper this can have a significant impact on the mark-to-market value of a variance swap.

Demeterfi *et al.* (1999) derived an approximation for the effect of the skew on the variance swap rate under the assumption that the skew is linear in strike. Assuming a linear skew of the form (III.4.25) they derived the approximation

$$K_T^2 \approx \theta(S \exp(rT)) \left(1 + 3T + \beta^2\right), \tag{III.4.118}$$

where β is the slope of the skew in (III.4.25) and $\theta(S \exp(rT))$ is the ATM forward volatility of maturity T.

III.4.7.6   Term Structures of Volatility Indices

Alexander and Leontsinis (2008) apply the annualized form of (III.4.117) to construct volatility indices of different maturities. In this section we discuss the properties of the term structure of the Vftse index, i.e. the volatility index on the FTSE 100 options. At the time of writing it is not quoted on any exchange. For the period from January 2004 to December 2006 daily data on the 30-day Vftse index and the FTSE 100 are shown in Figure III.4.35. Over the 3 years shown in the figure, the Vftse 30 index had an average value of a little over 13% as the FTSE 100 trended upward in generally stable circumstances. However, traders were clearly nervous that the long bull trend on the FTSE 100 would reverse. Between 11 May 2006 and 14 June 2006 a 500-point drop in the index precipitated a 12% rise in the Vftse 30 index. This is equivalent to an absolute volatility sensitivity to a 100-point fall in the index of −2.4%, averaged across the skew.

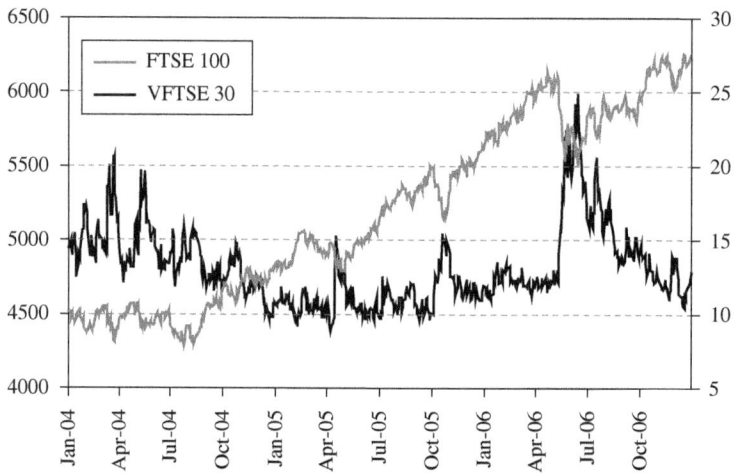

Figure III.4.35   Vftse 30 and the FTSE 100 index

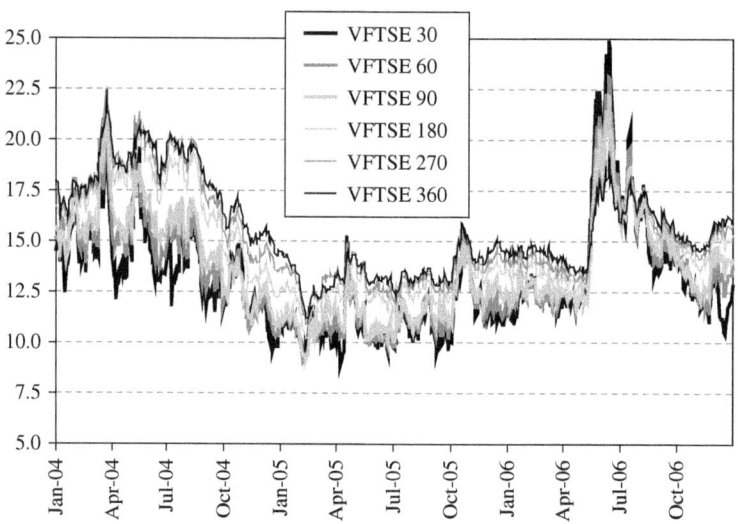

Figure III.4.36   Term structures of FTSE 100 implied volatility indices during 2005

The Vftse indices of maturities $T = 30, 60, 90, 180, 270$ and 360 days during the year 2005 are shown in Figure III.4.36. Taking a vertical slice through the graph at date t will give the Vftse term structure on that date. The typical pattern of an upward sloping term structure is apparent most of the time, but when the FTSE index becomes more volatile the term structure flattens. During exceptionally volatile periods the term structure even slopes downwards. For instance, Figure III.4.37 shows that the Vftse term structure was downward sloping on 14 June 2006.

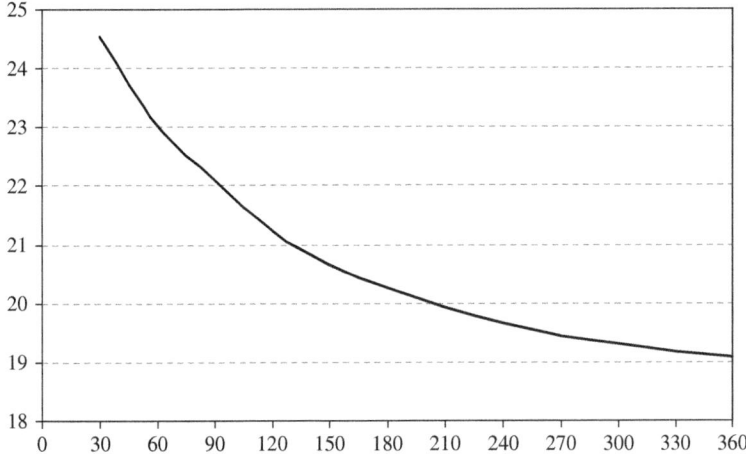

Figure III.4.37   Vftse term structure on 14 June 2006

III.4.7.7   Vix and Other Volatility Indices

Since the derivation of the formula (III.4.117) many volatility indices that are equivalent to stock index variance swap rates have been quoted on the CBOE and European exchanges such as the SWX Swiss Exchange and the Deutsche Börse. The standard maturity for each volatility index is 30 days and the names of the indices are listed in Table III.4.11.[84]

Time series data on these indices are available from the exchanges and from standard data vendors such as Bloomberg. Figure III.4.38 shows some of these indices, over the period from February 2001 to June 2007. Obviously Vxn, the volatility on the technology stock index Nasdaq, was excessively high during the years 2001 and 2002 and it remains marginally higher than the other indices on average. The European stock indices are more volatile in general than US indices, and react more to unexpected events such as 11 September 2001. However, at the time of writing volatility was lower than during the winter of 2002–2003, when the war in Iraq made investors extremely nervous. Even during the sub-prime mortgage crisis in August 2007 (not shown in the figure) the volatility indices reached only 30–35%, with the lowest volatility of 30% being on the Vix. As usual, the US sneezes and Europe catches a cold!

---

[84] CBOE and Eurex publish the precise details of the constructions they use on http://cfe.cboe.com/education/vixprimer/About.aspx and http://www.eurexchange.com/documents/publications/vol_en.html.

Table III.4.11   Volatility indices on CBOE and Eurex[85]

Equity index	Volatility index
S&P 500	Vix
Eurostoxx 50	Vstoxx
Dax	Vdax
DJ 30	Vxd
Nasdaq 100	Vxn
Smi (Switzerland)	Vsmi
Cac (France)	Vcac
Atx (Austria)	Vatx

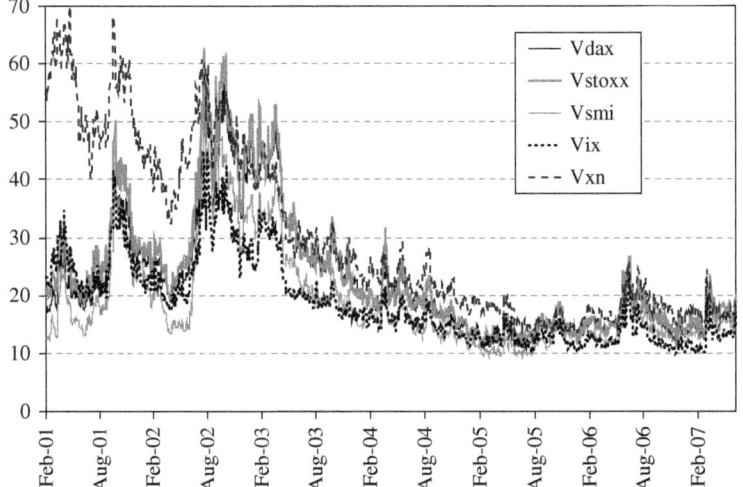

Figure III.4.38   Volatility indices, daily historical data

III.4.7.8   Volatility Index Futures

The only way to trade the spot volatility index is to buy all the options in (III.4.117) and continually rebalance, which is very difficult, time-consuming, approximate and expensive. However, all the equity index volatility indices in Table III.4.11 now have exchange traded futures contracts, except the Vcac and Vatx indices which are anyway not based on the variance swap formula (III.4.117).

At the time of writing all futures contracts are on 30-day volatility indices. Volatility index futures, like variance swaps, can be used to arbitrage the spread between two correlated volatility indices. For instance, in Section II.5.5.3 we explain how to trade the spread between the 30-day Vdax and 30-day Vstoxx futures. Whilst the spot volatility index and its futures are not cointegrated, for reasons explained below, volatility index futures on different indices but with the same maturity date *are* cointegrated. For example the Vix–Vxd futures spread

---

[85] At the time of writing there is no index on FTSE 100 on any exchange, and the Vcac and Vatx volatility indices are calculated using an old methodology, i.e. they are not based on (III.4.117).

is highly mean-reverting, as is the Vdax–Vstoxx futures spread and their mean-reverting characteristics were captured using impulse response in an error correction model framework.

Volatility index futures allow exchanges to offer pure trades on implied volatility. The CBOE has even constructed a new index, called the Varb-X benchmark index, which is based on selling Vix volatility futures and rolling over each position as it expires. The index did not do well during the sub-prime mortgage crises, losing about 7% of its value in the space of just 2 weeks, but before then it was showing a steady gain with a very low volatility. This is because implied volatility is usually too expensive relative to realized volatility. In other words, the variance risk premium is usually negative, as we have demonstrated in Figure III.4.34. However, we have seen in Section III.4.7.3 that when the market becomes highly volatile a considerable sum can be lost by shorting a variance swap – or, equivalently, by shorting the volatility index futures.

It is crucial to understand that volatility index futures behave quite differently from spot volatility indices. The spot and futures on a volatility index are not cointegrated, i.e. they are not 'tied together' by a mean-reverting spread.[86] This is in stark contrast to the usual spot–futures relationship on equity indices. Usually the basis is very rapidly mean reverting and the spot and futures are tied together through no arbitrage activities of market makers. But there is no such thing as spot–futures arbitrage on volatility indices.

Consider, for example, the Vix July 2009 futures contract during its lifetime. The contract is cash settled on 15 July 2007 at a special opening quote on the spot Vix when the market opens on 15 July 2007. Thus the underlying contract for the futures always refers to options expiring on 14 August 2009. Yet at any time *before* 15 July 2007 the spot Vix relates to a *different* underlying! For instance on 9 April 2009 the spot Vix refers to all options maturing on 5 May 2009.[87]

Since the volatility index futures contracts refer to an underlying at a fixed point in time (i.e. at the maturity of the futures) they are less variable than spot volatility indices. To illustrate this point, Figure III.4.39 shows a simple GARCH estimate of the Vix volatility compared with a similar estimate of the Vix futures volatility. Both estimates are obtained in the Excel spreadsheet for this figure using the GARCH Solver algorithm given with the spreadsheets for Chapter II.4.[88] The estimated GARCH parameters are shown in Table III.4.12.

Both volatilities are generally much higher, more reactive and less persistent than equity index GARCH volatilities. The Vix spot volatility is much greater than that of the Vix futures: it averages over 130% over the sample whilst the Vix futures volatility averages less than 80%. The Vix spot volatility is highly reactive to the market and the effect of a shock dies away; the Vix futures volatility is also highly reactive to market shocks but the effects last only a few days.

Notice the effects of the fall in the S&P 500 index between 11 May and 14 June 2006. As the index started to fall the Vix and the Vix futures volatilities began to increase. Although the S&P 500 index started to recover in mid June, option traders were obviously rather nervous, and the implied volatility index remained highly volatile until August 2006, which is long after the time that the statistical volatility based on S&P 500 returns returned to normal.

---

[86] See Chapter II.5 on cointegration.
[87] Since no S&P 500 options expire on 5 May 2009, the Vix is calculated by interpolating between two indices, one based on the April options and the other based on the May options.
[88] We emphasize that this is merely for illustrative purposes – Solver is not an industrial strength optimizer for GARCH. Readers requiring more information are referred to Volume III Chapter 4, on GARCH.

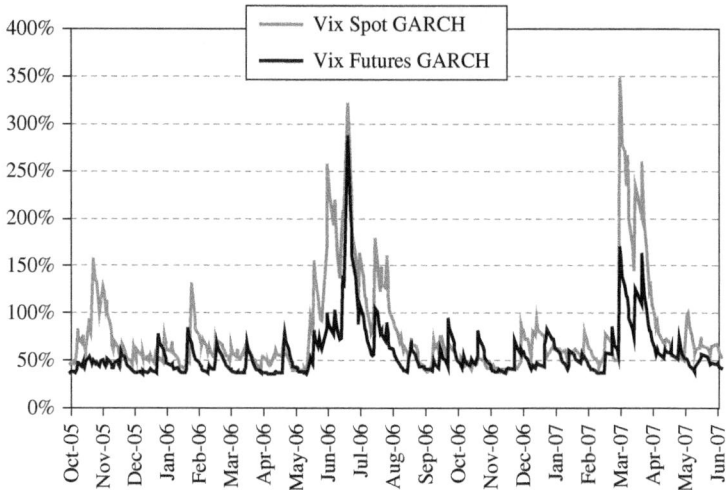

Figure III.4.39   Comparison of Vix volatility and Vix futures volatility

Table III.4.12   GARCH parameter estimates for volatility of Vix spot and Vix futures

Parameter	Vix spot GARCH	Vix futures GARCH
ω	0.050000	0.032952
α	0.1550	0.2333
β	0.8165	0.7138
$\alpha + \beta$	0.9715	0.9472
Average volatility	132.51%	78.98%

III.4.7.9   Options on Volatility Indices

Options on volatility indices are traded in OTC markets. Also, standard European calls and puts on the Vix were launched on the CBOE in June 2006, but at the time of writing they remain fairly illiquid. The market implied volatility surface for Vix 30 options traded on 30 May 2007 is shown in Figure III.4.40. The two horizontal axes are the strike of the options – between 10% and 35% – and the maturity of the futures contract. Notice the (rather unusual) *positive* skew where high strike short maturity options have a higher volatility than low strike short maturity options. But the skew flattens in the longer term.

Figure III.4.41 illustrates the skew on 30 May 2007 for the Vix options maturing between 16 June 2007 and 17 May 2008. Note that the short term implied volatilities are positively skewed and much higher than the volatilities of long term options. The average volatility shown Figure III.4.40 for the near term Vix options was over 100%, yet the GARCH volatility of the spot Vix on 30th May 2007 was only 68%. And the GARCH volatility of the Vix futures was 46%. Hence, short term Vix options appear to be very highly priced at the time of writing. Even the long term options are over priced relative to the Vix futures GARCH volatility.

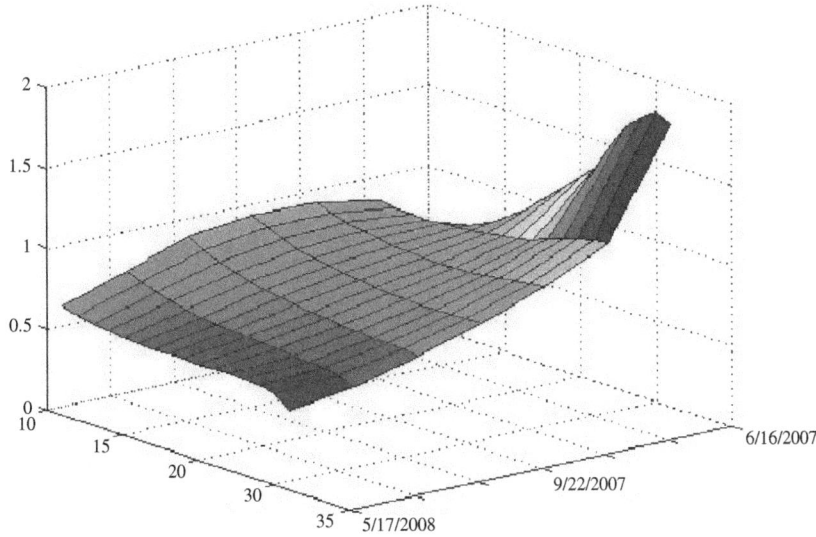

Figure III.4.40 The Vix smile surface on 30 May 2007

It is important to note that even though the options are on the spot Vix they should be priced using the Vix futures and *not* using the spot Vix. The spot Vix and the Vix futures are the same when the option expires, and options should always be priced using the *hedging instrument* which in this case is the Vix futures.

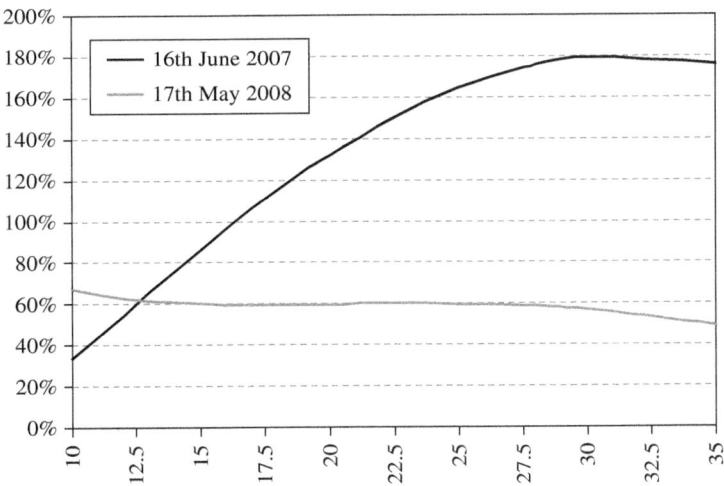

Figure III.4.41 Skews in Vix options

III.4.7.10   Using Realized Volatility Forecasts to Trade Volatility

When a realized volatility forecast is used for trading variance swaps, signals to buy or sell may be obtained by comparing the realized volatility forecast with the implied volatility index. A considerable body of recent academic research has focused on using high frequency data to forecast realized volatility, and a review of this literature along with a description of the models used is given in Section II.7.7.3.

The realized volatility forecasting model must be thoroughly tested, for instance following an operational backtest procedure that is explained in Section II.8.5.2. For example, we could do the following:

1. Take a very long time series on the returns for which we are forecasting realized volatility. If we are considering trading a variance swap on the FTSE 100 index, we could take a long time series of high frequency log returns on the FTSE 100 index.
2. Take a fixed number of observations in the estimation sample.
3. Estimate all the realized volatility forecasting models that are being tested using the observations in the estimation sample. Then use each model to forecast the realized volatility over the next h days, where h is the maturity of the variance swap.
4. Compute the difference between the forecast of the realized volatility and the realized volatility that is calculated ex post. This is the prediction error.
5. Roll the estimation sample forward h days, return to step 3 and repeat until the entire sample is exhausted.

A long position on a variance swap is long realized volatility, so the pay off is less than expected when the forecast is higher than the ex post realized volatility, i.e. the prediction error is positive. A short position on a variance swap is short realized volatility, so the pay-off to issuing a variance swap is less than expected when the prediction error is negative, i.e. the forecast is lower than the ex post realized volatility. Thus to take account of whether we intend to go long or short the variance swap we should use an *asymmetric* risk metric, or risk adjusted performance metric, on the prediction errors.[89] But the decision whether to buy a variance swap often depends on factors other than profit. The diversification potential of adding volatility to a portfolio more than justifies a negative return on this asset provided the risk is not too large. We may also need to constrain the trading strategy to limit the potential for losing vast amounts. For instance, the Varb-X benchmark places a limit on the number of contracts sold so that we cannot lose more than $1 million if the volatility futures price increases by 25 points between the sale of the contract and expiry.

III.4.8 SUMMARY AND CONCLUSION

The *market implied volatility* of a European call or put option is the volatility that should be input to the Black–Scholes–Merton (BSM) formula so that the (observed) market price of the option equals the BSM model price. If traders set prices according to the BSM model all options would have the same implied volatility irrespective of the strike or maturity of the option. But the market prices of options are set by supply and demand, traders charging the prices they believe customers will pay, and we almost always observe that different options on the same underlying have different implied volatilities.

Option traders do not set prices according to the BSM model. Instead market makers and investors believe that there is a greater chance that out-of-the-money options will end up in

---

[89] See Section I.6.5.6.

the model than the BSM model would predict. That is, log returns on the underlying asset are not normally distributed, as assumed by the BSM model, but have a *leptokurtic* distribution. Also the pronounced implied volatility skew, which is negatively sloped in many markets and especially in equity markets, indicates that the implied density of log returns is not only leptokurtic, but also highly *skewed*.

For this reason the BSM model is not appropriate for option pricing or hedging. It is, however, used to transform the price of a standard European option into an implied volatility. In fact in some markets, e.g. currency markets, standard options are quoted in terms of their implied volatilities rather than their prices. The reason for this is that implied volatilities tend to be more stable than the option prices themselves. By the same token many quants prefer to calibrate their models, for all classes of underlying, to the implied volatility surface rather than to the surface of option prices. When model prices for illiquid European calls and puts are required, some traders apply an adjustment to the BSM price to reflect their uncertainty about volatility.

Using model prices in the same way as market prices, we can construct a *model implied volatility* surface by finding a single volatility that, when input to the BSM formula, equates the model price of an option with its BSM price. This single volatility represents a type of *average* of the process volatility – which is assumed to be time-varying and often stochastic – over the life of the option. Since models are calibrated to the market prices (or implied volatilities) of standard European options, at the time of calibration the model implied volatility should be very close to the market implied volatility. However, and very unfortunately, the dynamics of model implied volatilities are usually very different from those market implied volatilities. For instance, in equity index markets the market implied volatility usually increases when the underlying index decreases. However, when the implied volatility surface has a negative skew (which is almost always the case in equity index markets) all *scale invariant* volatility models will have *positive* model implied volatility sensitivity to the underlying price. Hence, scale invariant models predict skew dynamics that are counter-intuitive, at least in equity markets. So, one problem that volatility theorists now have to address is that all sensible models for volatility (including all stochastic volatility models, and including those with jumps) are scale invariant!

Thus it turns out that the model implied volatility surface is not model-specific, but it *is* instrument-specific. An implied volatility surface only exists in the context of a standard European option. By contrast, the local volatility surface, which is the other volatility surface that is associated with market or model option prices, is *not* instrument-specific. Dupire's equation allows one to calibrate a unique market local volatility surface from market prices of standard European options. However, the local volatility function $\sigma(S, t)$ of a stochastic volatility model does not require standard European options for its definition. It is simply the square root of the risk neutral expectation of the stochastic variance at time t given that the underlying asset price is S at that time.

There is considerable confusion in the literature about what does and does not constitute a local volatility model. In Bruno Dupire's sense, local volatility is the forward volatility that is *locked in* by the current prices of standard European options, just as a forward interest rate is locked in by the current prices of bonds. Hence, in a true local volatility model the local volatility surface must be static. It should not float about as the price of the underlying changes. Nevertheless many parametric specifications of deterministic volatility functions are termed 'local volatility' models in the literature. This is rather confusing, because many of these have the *floating smile* property, which is actually a characteristic of *all* stochastic volatility models for tradable assets! Some parametric deterministic volatility functions, such as the *lognormal mixture diffusion* of Brigo and Mercurio (2002), have the floating smile property and others, such as the cubic polynomial form of Dumas et al. (1998) have the *static smile* property. Only those parametric forms with the static smile property are capturing local volatility in the sense that Dupire intended.

In fact, the floating smile property is common to *all* scale invariant processes, i.e. processes in which the returns distribution is independent of the price measurement scale. The class of scale invariant processes is very large, and includes almost all the stochastic volatility models that we use today, including the Heston model, the LIBOR model and most models with jumps in price and/or volatility. This is as it should be, since any option on a tradable asset *should* be priced using a scale invariant process, otherwise the price of the option relative to the underlying asset price is not invariant under a change of numeraire. The problem is that, scale invariant processes have undesirable hedging properties, because the floating smile property commonly yields counterintuitive dynamics for the implied volatility skew.

Amongst the plethora of option pricing models that are commonly used today there are only a few exceptions to scale invariance: the mean-reverting arithmetic Brownian motions that are commonly used to model short rates; the CEV model of Cox (1975) and its stochastic volatility extension, the SABR model of Hagan et al. (2002);[90] and the parametric local volatility models such as that of Dumas et al. (1998). Given our comment above, these models should only be used for pricing non-tradable assets.

The dynamics of implied volatility need to account for regime-specific behaviour as it moves between high and low volatility regimes. Emanuel Derman hypothesized three *volatility regimes* for equity index implied volatility that rule in stable trending markets, sideways markets, and crash markets. The fixed strike volatility spreads over at-the-money volatility are the same in all three regimes, but the correlation between at-the-money volatility and the underlying price varies according to the regime. It is zero when the market is stable and trading, negative in sideways markets and very negative in crash markets. To model the dynamics of the implied volatility surface we have presented a case study that applies principal component analysis to daily fixed strike volatility spreads over at-the-money volatility in the FTSE 100 index. Subsequently we used this model to estimate delta hedge ratios that take account of the dynamics of market implied volatilities. In equity markets these deltas are considerably less than the BSM delta (as are the minimum variance deltas that we derive).

Since the mid 1990s many different stochastic volatility models have been proposed in the literature. By far the most popular model, due to its ease of calibration, is the *Heston model*. This is the mean-reverting square root variance process introduced by Heston (1993). The equivalent process, when written in terms of volatility rather than variance, is an arithmetic process with *constant* vol-of-vol.

One approach to developing a stochastic volatility model is simply to specify a process that has meaningful properties. For instance, all stochastic volatility models should allow for non-zero price–volatility correlation. Also, jumps in price, and maybe also in volatility, may be thought to be important. Another approach is to take the discrete time volatility models that are known to provide the best estimates and forecasts of the process volatility, i.e. the GARCH processes. Unfortunately the *strong GARCH diffusion* derived by Nelson (1990) has zero price–volatility correlation. However, Alexander and Lazar (2005) highlight

[90] Although they are scale invariant if $\beta = 1$.

a number of problems with the strong GARCH diffusion and derive a new continuous limit of GARCH called the *weak GARCH diffusion*. This model is very flexible, having two more parameters than the strong GARCH diffusion, and it also has very intuitive properties: the vol-of-vol depends on the kurtosis of the price distribution, i.e. the extent of the smile, and the price–volatility correlation is related to the skewness in the distribution and the extent of the skew. These properties are intuitive since it is the uncertainty of volatility that produces the smile effect and price–volatility correlation augments the skew.

A symmetric, single state GARCH model is the 'plain vanilla' version of a GARCH process. There are almost as many versions of GARCH models in discrete time as there are stochastic volatility processes in continuous time. However, the diffusion limit of vanilla GARCH can be extended, and of particular interest is the continuous version of asymmetric Markov switching GARCH models. These models generally provide a much better fit to historical returns than standard symmetric GARCH, and these are the only models that properly capture the 'bursts' of volatility that we frequently observe in financial markets. The continuous version of Markov switching GARCH has a jump in the volatility process, but it is not a Poisson jump. Instead, in the *Markov switching GARCH diffusion* the volatility switches between two volatility diffusion processes at random times, with the switching probability being determined by a Markovian transition matrix.

A great variety of stochastic volatility, deterministic volatility and jump models have been developed in recent years. The models have parameters that are calibrated to market prices of vanilla calls and puts, or equivalently to the implied volatility smile surface, and the calibrated model is used to price and hedge other options consistently with the smile. However, most option pricing models used today are scale invariant, as mentioned above, and in that case it makes no difference which model we use to hedge the price risk of the option, the result will be the same. Theoretically the price hedge ratios for *any* American or European homogeneous claim with an observable price (such as a barrier or an Asian option as well as a standard call or put) are independent of the scale invariant model used. That is, the delta is the *same*, whether we use

- Heston diffusion
- Merton's jump diffusion
- GARCH diffusion
- Heston diffusion with jump in volatility or price
- lognormal mixture diffusion

or any other scale invariant model. And the gamma and higher order price sensitivities also have this *model free* property. The only differences that we may observe in practice are because some models fit market data better than others!

However, when volatility is stochastic we are in an incomplete market, where replicating portfolios (if they exist as all) are not self-financing. Therefore, we seek a replicating portfolio that will minimize the uncertainty about the cost of replication. We call *locally risk minimizing strategies* those that are specifically designed to minimize the instantaneous variance of the hedged portfolio returns. The quantity of the underlying asset in a locally risk minimizing delta hedged portfolio is called the *minimum variance delta*, and the quantity of an option in a locally risk minimizing delta–gamma hedged portfolio is called the *minimum variance gamma*. There is mounting empirical evidence that minimum variance hedge ratios provide better hedges to standard options in incomplete markets, especially when the skew is negative. By contrast, with a negative skew the scale invariant delta and delta–gamma hedges perform worse than the BSM model hedges, in the sense that the hedged portfolio P&L has a higher standard deviation in out-of-sample tests.

An option trade is a trade on both the direction of the underlying and the direction of volatility. By contrast a *variance swap*, i.e. a swap between a floating rate (the realized volatility) and a fixed rate (the variance swap rate) is a pure volatility trade. Variance swaps have a convex pay-off that makes them more attractive to buyers of realized volatility than their volatility swap counterparts. There are numerous trading applications of variance swaps including spread trades on forward volatility and on the spread between volatilities on different underlyings. They also provide a natural diversification for long equity investors, since there is a strong negative correlation between their pay-offs and returns on equities.

Variance and volatility swaps are traded OTC, but recently the CBOE and Eurex have introduced futures contracts on equity index *volatility indices*. These volatility indices are constructed from market prices of standard European options based on a formula that relates the volatility index to the variance swap rate. However, their futures are not related to the spot volatility indices in the same way as simple financial futures because the futures contract is based on an underlying that is *not* the spot index. For this reason considerable care should be taken to use the futures price and not the spot price when pricing and hedging *options on volatility indices*. Only the S&P 500 volatility index, the Vix, has exchanged traded options at the time of writing and these are not very liquid. However, there are numerous reasons to trade pure volatility as an asset class in its own right and trading volumes on both futures and options on volatility indices are growing very rapidly.

Portfolio Mapping

III.5.1 INTRODUCTION

The first four chapters of this book covered the analysis of three broad categories of financial instrument: interest rate sensitive instruments, futures/forwards, options, and volatility swaps. We focused on the characteristics of the individual instruments and of the market in general but rarely discussed how to analyse large portfolios of these instruments. In this chapter we describe how to map large portfolios of financial instruments to their risk factors. Since the portfolio risk factors and their risk factor sensitivities are quite different in each case, we treat each of the main categories of instruments separately.

Interest rate sensitive instruments without embedded options include loans, cash and futures positions on fixed coupon bonds, floating rate notes, forward rate agreements (FRAs) and vanilla interest rate swaps. The positions on these instruments can be characterized by a *cash flow*, i.e. a series of cash payments $\left\{C_{T_1}, \ldots, C_{T_n}\right\}$ at times T_i for $i = 1, 2, \ldots, n$. Large portfolios of similar types of instruments have cash flows that occur at numerous different times in the future. For this reason the market risk of such portfolios is usually analysed by mapping all the cash flows to a fixed, finite set of zero coupon yields at standard maturities such as 1 month, 2 months, and so on up to the maximum maturity of the instruments. Such a set of discount rates is a set of *risk factors* for the portfolio. To understand these cash flow mappings is the first aim of this chapter.

Mapping a portfolio of loans, bonds, notes, FRAs or swaps to a finite set of zero coupon yields requires calculation of the net sensitivities of the portfolio to each of these risk factors. These sensitivities represent the change in the present value of the portfolio corresponding to a change in one of the risk factors, and they are measured by the *present value of a basis point move* (PV01). Then a change in the portfolio value will be a linear function of changes in the risk factors. For this reason we call such a portfolio a *linear portfolio*. All the non-linearity in the relationship between portfolio value and the risk factors is subsumed into the risk factor sensitivities. These sensitivities are held constant when we study the risk of the portfolio.

Mapping portfolios containing futures and/or forwards is straightforward. We can use the spot price, a discount curve and the basis as the risk factors, but the basis risk may be difficult to model. In financial futures the basis risk is usually fairly small, but in commodity markets it is large and highly uncertain. In this case we may prefer to use a set of *constant maturity futures* as risk factors. We explain how the principles of cash flow mapping are applied in this case.

A very substantial portion of this chapter concerns the mapping of option portfolios to their major risk factors via *Taylor approximations*. There are two major types of risk factors for option portfolios, the underlying asset prices (or interest rates, if the option is on interest rates) and their implied volatility surfaces. Minor risk factors include the discount curve and time. We begin by focusing on the mapping to underlying prices. The value of an option portfolio is a non-linear function of the underlying assets prices and so (at least) a second order Taylor approximation must be used. This is called a *delta–gamma approximation.* The *delta* of the portfolio with respect to an underlying asset price S is the change in portfolio value when S changes by one unit, leaving the other underlying asset prices constant. It is calculated as the first partial derivative of the portfolio's value with respect to S. The *gamma* of the portfolio is the change in the delta, or the second partial derivative of the portfolio's value with respect to S.

Netting deltas and gammas over all the underlying assets in a portfolio requires the use of value Greeks. Then the delta–gamma approximation is based on the *value delta* and the *value gamma*.[1] Position Greeks are *not* additive over different underlyings, but value Greeks are. If a portfolio has many different underlying assets the multivariate delta–gamma approximation can become quite complex as we shall see below. However, we can reduce the number of asset price risk factors using a *price beta mapping*. Here several underlying assets are mapped to a single index or reference asset. In this case the value delta and value gamma with respect to the index price will depend on the sensitivity (beta) of the asset with respect to the index.

Next we consider mapping of option portfolios to interest rate and time risk factors. Under risk neutral valuation the price of an option is the discounted expected value of its pay-off, and so it will depend on the risk free interest rate of the same maturity as the option. Thus a portfolio of options with different maturities has a curve of discount rates as risk factors. Since the delta and gamma of the portfolio are expressed in value terms, so must the interest rate sensitivity vector *rho* also be expressed in value terms. The value of an option increases with its maturity, i.e. long term options are more valuable than short term options with the same moneyness and the same implied volatility. Hence the option value changes over time, *cateris paribus*. The time sensitivity of an option portfolio, i.e. the *theta*, is likewise expressed in value terms.

Portfolios of options have a very large number of volatility risk factors. Even a portfolio where all the options are on a *single* underlying asset has one implied volatility risk factor for each option. Thus it is important to find ways to reduce the dimension of the volatility risk factor space. Volatility indices of different maturities are a natural choice as reference volatility risk factors. For volatility risk factor mapping we advocate a *volatility beta* mapping that is similar to price beta mapping. Volatility beta mapping is illustrated with a case study that uses the Vftse term structure as the reference volatilities.

Options traders usually operate under limits on their net value delta, gamma and vega and sometimes also on their net value theta and rho. By mapping an option portfolio to its risk factors, traders can assess their positions relative to their limits and hence identify the risks that need to be hedged. However, more and more banks are replacing the traditional sensitivity limits by limits based on the value at risk of the portfolio.

The outline of this chapter is as follows. Section III.5.2 introduces the general concepts of portfolio risk factors and the sensitivity of a portfolio to its risk factors. Then we specify the major types of risk factors of various categories of financial instruments including cash and futures or forward portfolios on equities, bonds, currencies and commodities and portfolios of options on these different types of assets. Section III.5.3 examines different ways to map a large series of cash flows to a set of constant maturity interest rates. It is important to keep such things as present value, duration, volatility and PV01 *invariant* under the cash flow mapping. Section III.5.4 covers risk factor mapping of futures and forward portfolios.

---

[1] These are called the *dollar delta* and *dollar gamma* by some authors.

In the case of commodity portfolios we extend the cash flow mapping methodologies that are normally applied to cash flows on interest rate sensitive instruments to a portfolio of commodity futures. Then in Sections III.5.5 and III.5.6 we deal with risk factor mappings for option portfolios. This is a little more technical than mapping cash portfolios. We require some knowledge of matrix algebra to understand multivariate delta–gamma mapping, and statistical techniques such as regression and principal component analysis are often used to reduce the dimension of the risk factor space.

III.5.2   RISK FACTORS AND RISK FACTOR SENSITIVITIES

The traditional approach to risk measurement in banks is to decompose the irreducible or undiversifiable risk of a portfolio into two parts: the risk due to the volatility of a market *risk factor* and the risk due to the portfolio's *sensitivity* to this risk factor. The portfolio's sensitivity to a risk factor only assesses the risk relative to factors: it ignores the risk of the factor itself.

Risk factor sensitivities are difficult to aggregate, unless they are expressed in value terms. Even then, it is difficult to compare sensitivities across different activities. For instance, the duration or PV01 of a bond portfolio cannot be compared with the beta of a stock portfolio. Hence, risk factors and their sensitivities must be described separately for each asset type:

- Interest rate sensitive portfolios have interest rate and credit spread risk factors and duration or present value of basis point (PV01) sensitivities.
- Equity portfolios usually have indices as risk factors and equity betas as sensitivities.
- Futures and forwards have interest rate risk factors with present value of basis point sensitivities, in addition to the risk factors of the corresponding spot position.
- Option portfolios have many risk factors, the main ones being the underlying assets and the asset's implied volatility surfaces. Sensitivities to risk factors are called the portfolio Greeks.

III.5.2.1   Interest Rate Sensitive Portfolios

Portfolios of domestic loans, cash positions on fixed coupon bonds, FRAs or interest rate swaps have a set of zero coupon market interest rates of different maturities as risk factors. For transactions between banks the usual benchmark is a LIBOR curve, which is based on swap rates at the long end, and we shall call this the *zero curve* for short. The risk factors are the spot rates of some constant maturities such as {1 day, 1 week, 1 month, 2 months, 3 months, . . . , 60 months, $5^{1}/_{2}$ years, 6 years, . . . , 25 years}.

Interest rate sensitive portfolios with international exposures are mapped to zero curves in various currencies. Even though currency *forwards* are commonly used to hedge the exchange rate risk in international portfolios, the portfolio risk factors are the spot zero curve for each currency and the spot exchange rates only. This is because the fair value of the forward exchange rates can be derived from the spot exchange rates and the zero curve in the foreign currency.

In Section III.1.8 we introduced the *present value of a basis point move*, commonly denoted PV01 or PVBP, as the sensitivity of a cash flow to a small change in market interest rates. It is distinguished from the dollar duration, which is a bond price sensitivity to a change in its own yield, precisely by the fact that the risk factors are the *market* interest rates. So, if we use PV01 rather than duration as the risk factor sensitivity, all bonds in the same currency will share the same risk factor curve. Indeed, all cash flow portfolios, whatever interest rate sensitive securities they contain, may be mapped to a single zero curve, provided we use the PV01 vector of the cash flows as the sensitivity vector.

From its definition in Section III.1.8.1 we know that the PV01 is measured in discounted, absolute terms. Hence, the risk factor mapping produces variations in the discounted P&L of the portfolio corresponding to an *absolute* basis point change in each interest rate. The risk factor mapping is *linear*.[2] That is, the discounted P&L is a weighted sum of absolute changes in interest rates with weights given by the PV01 vector. All the non-linearity in the relationship between the portfolio price and interest rates has been subsumed into this vector. Thus in the following we shall estimate the risk and return on the portfolio using matrix methods.

Using the same notation as in Section III.1.8.1, denote by

$$\mathbf{c} = \left(C_{T_1}, \ldots, C_{T_n}\right)' \quad \text{and} \quad \mathbf{r} = \left(R_{T_1}, \ldots, R_{T_n}\right)'$$

the mapped cash flow vector,[3] *not* expressed in present value terms, and the discretely compounded market interest rates at these maturities. Suppose that the interest rate R_{T_i} of maturity T_i changes by a small amount ΔR_{T_i}, say, a few basis points. The PV01 at this maturity is the increase in present value of the cash flow when the interest rate falls by one basis point. So we can approximate the change in present value of the mapped cash flow at maturity T_i as $\Delta PV \approx -\text{PV01}_{T_i} \times \Delta R_{T_i}$. Now suppose all interest rates change, but they can change by different amounts, and denote the vector of interest rate changes (in basis points) as $\Delta \mathbf{r} = \left(\Delta R_{T_1}, \ldots, \Delta R_{T_n}\right)'$. Then the portfolio's P&L is the net change in present value of the entire cash flow, i.e.

$$\Delta PV \approx -\sum_{i=1}^{n} \text{PV01}_{T_i} \times \Delta R_{T_i}, \tag{III.5.1}$$

and this may be written in matrix form as

$$\Delta PV \approx -\mathbf{p}'\Delta \mathbf{r}, \tag{III.5.2}$$

where $\mathbf{p} = \left(\text{PV01}_{T_1}, \ldots, \text{PV01}_{T_n}\right)'$.

Hence knowing the risk factor sensitivities, i.e. the PV01 vector $\mathbf{p}$, we have an expression for the discounted P&L of the portfolio as a linear function of *any* absolute changes in interest rates.[4] Furthermore, if $\Delta \mathbf{r}$ has mean $\boldsymbol{\mu}$ and covariance matrix $\mathbf{V}$ then, based on the linear approximation (III.5.2), the mean of the discounted P&L is $-\mathbf{p}'\boldsymbol{\mu}$ and its variance is $\mathbf{p}'\mathbf{V}\mathbf{p}$. Since the returns $\Delta \mathbf{r}$ are measured in basis points we also express their volatilities and correlations in basis points.

III.5.2.2 Equity Portfolios

Chapter II.1, which focused exclusively on equity portfolios, explained how the asset pricing theory described in Chapter I.6 is used to represent the return on a stock with a linear model, i.e. to represent the stock return as a weighted sum of several risk factor returns. Cash equity portfolios can have *fundamental* or *statistical* risk factors. Fundamental risk factors would

---

[2] We use such a risk factor mapping only when the portfolio contains no options.
[3] Details on how to map the cash flow are given in Section III.5.3. below.
[4] Since each PV01 is expressed in present value terms, (III.5.1) and (III.5.2) are also expressed in present value terms.

normally include a broad market index and possibly also style, industry or sector factors. But we may choose to use statistical factors instead, for instance the APT software uses principal components of the equity universe as risk factors.

Equity portfolios with positions in individual stock futures or stock index futures will have the dividend yield curve and the discount curve as additional risk factors. In the absence of dividends the fair value of a long domestic equity futures position is equivalent to the spot position plus a long zero coupon bond position, with maturity equal to the maturity of the future. Hence, the domestic discount curve is a risk factor. The dividend yield on the equity also affects the difference between spot and futures prices, because futures do not pay dividends.

The weights in the linear risk factor model, which are called the *risk factor betas*, measure the sensitivity of the stock returns to changes in the risk factors. The *market beta* of a risky asset represents the asset return's sensitivity to changes in the market return. We may also estimate the *portfolio beta* with respect to any risk factor and the market portfolio beta in particular, as a weighted sum of the stock betas where this time the weights are the portfolio weights, i.e. the percentage of the portfolio value that is invested in each stock. Suppose there are k stocks in the universe and let $\beta = (\beta_1, \ldots, \beta_k)'$ denote the betas of these stocks with respect to the given risk factor, assuming for simplicity there is just one factor. If the portfolio weights are $\mathbf{w} = (w_1, \ldots, w_k)'$ then the net portfolio beta with respect to the market risk factor is the weighted sum of the stock betas, i.e.

$$\beta = \mathbf{w}'\beta = \sum_{i=1}^{k} w_i \beta_i.$$

Stock betas are usually estimated by a regression factor model, based on either time series or cross-sectional data depending on the type of risk factors in the model.[5] The beta of an existing portfolio may also be estimated directly, using a regression factor model. The independent variables are the returns on the risk factors and the dependent variable is the return on the stock, or the return on the portfolio. Hence, an equity portfolio beta represents the percentage change in portfolio value when one of the risk factors' values changes by 1% and the values other risk factors remain constant. Multiplying the beta vector by the current value of the portfolio gives a set of *value betas* for each risk factor, from which we can drive the absolute change in portfolio value when one of the risk factors changes.

The regression model that is used to estimate stock betas has a residual return term that is specific to each stock. This is called the *idiosyncratic return*, or *stock-specific return*. Using the portfolio weights, the weighted sum of the idiosyncratic returns gives the portfolio-specific return.[6] Or it can be calculated by a direct regression for the portfolio returns. If these portfolio's specific returns are large and variable then the idiosyncratic risk of the portfolio will be high. In that case the factor model is not capturing the risk of the portfolio very well. This is likely to occur if the risk factors are not well chosen, if there are too few risk factors or if those that are used are not significant for the stocks that are heavily weighted in the portfolio. A good factor model will use a set of risk factors that is able to capture most of the variation in a large, diversified portfolio.

---

[5] See Section II.1.3 for further details of the application of multiple regression to equity portfolio analysis.
[6] But the variance of the portfolio's specific return is not the weighted sum of the variances of the stock-specific returns. See Section II.1.3.1.

In Section II.1.2.5 we showed that factor models allow the total variance of a stock portfolio to be decomposed into three different sources of risk, i.e. the:

- risk factor sensitivities, as measured by the risk factor betas;
- risk of the factors themselves, which is represented by the risk factor covariance matrix;
- idiosyncratic or reducible risk, which is represented by the variance of the residual returns.

The first two sources of risk combine to give the *undiversifiable risk*, also called the *irreducible risk* or the *systematic risk*. Thus an equity beta captures only part of the total risk in a portfolio. It ignores the irreducible risk arising from its factor volatility and it ignores the reducible risk that could theoretically be reduced to zero by holding a large and diversified portfolio.

Chapter II.1 described many types of multi-factor regression models that are used for both asset management and risk management. But the aims of asset management and risk management are quite different, so the factor models are applied in very different ways.

Factor Models in Asset Management

Asset managers use such models to select stocks and make allocations that maximize utility or some risk adjusted performance metric over a long horizon. They base allocations on the expectation and variance of discounted returns, i.e. the excess return over the risk free rate. Since their investment horizon is several months or more, it is important to take account of this risk free rate and to discount the returns to today.

An asset manager will normally use a factor model representation for each stock in his universe to calculate its beta with respect to each factor. Then he considers the feasible allocations to various stocks, taking account of his client's preferences such as no short sales, or that 50% of the portfolio value must be held in UK stocks. For each potential portfolio, the net portfolio beta with respect to each risk factor is obtained as a weighted sum of the stock betas, based on the assumed portfolio weights. The asset manager then uses the factor model representation to decide on the optimal allocation using the investor's utility function, or some risk adjusted performance metric such as the Sharpe ratio.[7] Since his investment horizon can be several months or longer, he will use a long term estimate of betas for each stock in the universe of possible investments. These betas are typically based on ordinary least squares (OLS) regression using 3–5 years of monthly data. The aim is to find the 'optimal' portfolio weights that define the portfolio with the best risk *and return* characteristics.

Factor Models in Risk Management

The risk manager's focus is quite different. He does not choose optimal allocations. He is concerned with the risk but not the return on an existing portfolio. He uses the factor model as a risk model for the whole portfolio, not as a returns model for each of the stocks. Moreover, his risk horizon is, at least initially, over a few days only. The discounting of returns to present value terms and adjustment for any non-zero expected excess return is insignificant over very short risk horizons. It is only when the risk horizon is 1 month or more that it becomes important for the risk manager to base his risk factor returns and

---

[7] See Section I.6.5.

sensitivities on excess returns over the risk free rate. So often risk managers ignore the discounting of returns distributions as they know it will have negligible effect on the risk when measured over a very short risk horizon.

Usually he is not interested in the individual factor models for each stock in the portfolio, where the betas are estimated using a long period of weekly or monthly data. Unless he seeks a decomposition of risk into risks due to various sub-portfolios, the risk manager only needs to model the returns on the portfolio as a whole. He is only interested in the portfolio betas, the risk of the factors (including their correlations) and the portfolio-specific risk. The best way to estimate these is to re-create an artificial price history for his portfolio using the current portfolio weights and composition. The risk manager needs to monitor risks on a day-to-day basis, so he should *assume that the factor model's betas can vary over time*. Typically he will use daily data on the portfolio price history and employ a time varying estimation technique to estimate the portfolio's betas.[8] Only in this way will he be properly capturing the day-to-day variation in the portfolio's risk.

III.5.2.3   International Exposures

The relative sensitivity of an international cash flow to the spot foreign exchange (forex) rate is 1. For instance, if a UK bank invests £1 million in European securities when the EUR/GBP rate is 0.68, the value of the position in euros is (approximately) €1,470,588. If the forex rate increases by 1% to 0.6868 then the sterling value of €1,470,588 is exactly £1.01 million. Thus the relative change in portfolio value is 1%, and the absolute change is £1m × 1% = £10,000.

Holdings in any foreign securities and derivatives have a forex risk that is usually managed using the currency forward market. As explained in Section III.2.3.4, a forex forward position is equivalent to a spot currency position plus a long and a short zero coupon bond position in the two currencies, with maturity equal to the maturity of the futures. Hence, whenever there is an international exposure both the domestic zero curve and the foreign zero curve become risk factors.

The absolute sensitivity of an exposure to a zero curve (and to dividend yields) is obtained using the PV01. For example, if a UK bank uses a 1-month forward forex rate to invest £1 million in European securities, we have cash flows at the 1-month vertex of +£1m on the foreign curve and −£1m on the domestic curve. The PV01 of these cash flows gives the sensitivity to changes in foreign and domestic interest rates at the 1-month maturity.

International interest rate exposures are of two types: those where the payments depend on foreign instruments but are made in domestic currency and those where cash flows also occur in foreign currencies. The first type includes *differential swaps*, i.e. interest rate swaps between domestic and foreign interest rates, when the notional is denominated in the domestic currency. The second type includes portfolios containing foreign bonds, loans made in foreign currencies and differential swaps denominated in the foreign currency. The mapping of cash flows to foreign zero coupon rates and the computation of PV01 sensitivities follows the same basic principles as for domestic exposures. But now for each vertex in the cash flow map we have an additional sensitivity to the forward forex rate. But this sensitivity translates into sensitivity on the spot forex rate and the domestic and foreign zero coupon rates. In general, therefore, international interest rate exposures

---

[8] Such as an exponentially weighted moving average (EWMA) or generalized autoregressive conditional heteroscedasticity (GARCH). See Section II.1.2.3 for further details.

have the spot forex rate and the zero coupon curves in domestic and foreign currencies as risk factors.

The spot forex and interest rate risk in futures/forward positions is often managed separately from the risk of the underlying asset. For instance, the equity desk will primarily be concerned with the risk of spot exposures to stocks in local currency and the commodity desk is primarily concerned with the term structure of commodity futures prices in local currency. Whilst a complete picture of their risks would include forex and interest rate risk, it is not efficient for the equity and commodity desks to manage these risks on a stand-alone basis. The fixed income and forex desks are better equipped to manage these risks and they can net them with similar forex and interest rate risks taken elsewhere in the firm.

III.5.2.4   Commodity Portfolios

Commodity futures and forwards may also be modelled using spot prices and an equivalent interest rate risk component. Indeed, all futures or forwards positions introduce zero coupon spot interest rates as risk factors, in addition to the spot price. But it is not always prudent to use spot prices and the zero curve as risk factors for commodities because this ignores fluctuations in convenience yields and carry costs,[9] which are an important component of commodity basis risk.

Unpredictable variations in demand and supply, as well as uncertainties in carry costs, play a very important role in determining the basis risk for some commodities, and the difference between the spot price and the futures prices can become rather large and variable. For instance, during cold snaps in winter months demand for energy commodities can peak sharply and the spot price can shoot up as storage is depleted. The prompt futures price may be much less affected than the spot price, especially if the cold snap is not expected to last long.

We can map each position on a commodity futures or forward contract to a position on a *constant maturity* near term futures contract and a forward interest rate. This is preferable to expressing the position as a spot price plus spot interest rate position, because commodity spot prices can become substantially decoupled from the futures prices. Since the commodity basis is not easy to predict it may be preferable to map commodity portfolios to a whole term structure of constant maturity futures. Constant maturity commodity futures are not tradable instruments, but since we only want to measure the risk of a commodity futures portfolio there is no reason why we should not construct these series and use them as risk factors for commodity portfolios.[10]

III.5.2.5   Option Portfolios

The value of an option portfolio is sensitive to variations in the underlying asset prices and the implied volatilities of every option in the portfolio. Also, to capture the time value of an option the zero coupon rate of maturity equal to that of the option must be included as a risk factor, just as it would be for a position on a futures or forward contract. But the most important distinction between option portfolios and positions on futures or forwards is that the *volatility* affects an option price but it does not affect the price of a futures or forward contract.

---

[9] The main components of carry costs are storage, transportation and insurance costs.
[10] See Section III.2.2.4 for further details.

Each option in a portfolio has its own *implied volatility* as a risk factor. Even when all options in the portfolio are on the same underlying asset, the implied volatility is different for each option, i.e. it depends on the strike and the maturity of the option.[11] Hence, the entire volatility surface for each underlying price is a risk factor.[12] A large option portfolio will typically contain options of different strikes and maturity on several different underlying assets, and for each asset we need its whole implied volatility surface for risk factors.

Option portfolios are mapped to risk factors using *Taylor approximation*. The sensitivities to the price risk factors are called *delta* and *gamma*, and the sensitivities to the volatility risk factors are called *vega*. We often express the delta, gamma and vega in value terms, so that the risk factor sensitivities are additive across different portfolios. There are also minor risk factors, each having its own Greek.[13]

Why do we use Taylor approximation? In large option portfolios containing complex positions the risk manager's challenge is to produce a model that estimates the trader's risk at the push of a button, based on many different possible values for the portfolio. This cannot be done with full revaluation of each complex option price, at least using the numerical methods normally employed in option pricing models. But the Taylor approximation allows one to generate thousands of hypothetical values for the portfolio very quickly.

How do we choose the risk factors in the Taylor approximation? For a small portfolio of options on a single underlying asset, we should use at least the underlying asset price and its implied volatility surface. But when we have a large portfolio of options on several underlyings there can be many price risk factors and for each of these we have an entire surface of volatility risk factors, so efforts must be made to reduce their number. Individual stock options share the broad market index as a common risk factor. Thus for stock option portfolios we often chose equity indices rather than individual stocks as price risk factors. Then sensitivities are calculated by multiplying the option delta by the equity beta before weighting and summing to obtain the net position or value delta. A similar method applies to the gamma – see Section III.5.5.5 for further details.

Careful consideration needs to be given to the choice of volatility risk factors. The primary exposure is to an entire volatility smile surface for each underlying of the options contracts, but the technological demands of using so many volatility risk factors are impractical. Whenever the underlying asset is mapped to a price risk factor that is common to other options in the portfolio we do not need to use a different implied volatility for every option. Some banks use *vega bucketing* techniques for volatility risk, described in Section III.5.6.3, but these can produce a high degree of specific volatility risk. For this reason Section III.5.6.4 introduces an alternative to vega bucketing that is designed to reduce specific volatility risk whilst not allowing the number of volatility risk factors to grow too large.

The Taylor expansion technique allows one to approximate the P&L of an option portfolio as a sum of risk factor sensitivities weighted by the portfolio's net value delta, gamma, vega and possibly other Greeks. The portfolio mapping provided by the Taylor expansion allows

---

[11] But vanilla puts and a calls of the same strike and maturity should have the same implied volatility, by the put–call parity relationship.

[12] The situation is similar to that of interest rates, where the whole zero curve is used as risk factor, but with volatility we have two dimensions: the volatilities of different maturities *and* of different strikes.

[13] Minor risk factors include interest rates and time. The risk factor sensitivities are called *theta* (with respect to time) and *rho* (with respect to interest rates). But these are often minor compared with the price and volatility risk factors, and the theta risk often offsets the gamma risk. It is only for very short-dated options that theta can be important. See Section III.3.4.3.

one to decompose the total risk of the portfolio (as measured by the variance of the P&L) into three distinct sources, i.e. the:

- risk factor sensitivities, as measured by the relevant Greek;
- risk of the factors themselves, which can be represented by a risk factor covariance matrix;
- idiosyncratic risk, which is the risk that is ignored by truncating the Taylor expansion at the first or second order term.

III.5.2.6 Orthogonalization of Risk Factors

It is important to isolate the effect of the individual variations in risk factors on the portfolio returns. This allows the risk analyst to identify the important sources of risk, and to request that traders hedge these risks if deemed appropriate by management. Yet in many cases the factors are some highly collinear; that is, their returns are highly correlated. This is certainly true for a zero curve, for a term structure of commodity futures prices, and for implied volatility risk factors in option portfolios.

Hence, large portfolios that have many risk factors also tend to have some highly collinear risk factors. Because of this it helps to transform each collinear system of risk factors into a few uncorrelated risk factors. For instance, in equity portfolios where potential risk factors include various market, sector, industry and style indices, we may not choose to include them all in the factor model that is used for risk assessment because their correlation would mask their individual effects.[14] Instead we could take the market index that is relevant to the universe of stocks that can be traded, and then as possible additional risk factors the differences between this index value and the values of other types of indices. Similarly, instead of using both the 3-month and the 12-month interest rates as risk factors, one could use the 3-month rate and the 3-month to 12-month spread, the spread being relatively uncorrelated with the 3-month rate. The same comment is relevant to futures prices of different maturities on the same commodity.

However, since the list of risk factors for a large portfolio can be very long, it should be stressed that *principal component analysis* provides a much better method for obtaining an uncorrelated risk factor representation for any high collinear system. Indeed, we have had reason to apply this technique several times earlier in this volume and in the other volumes of *Market Risk Analysis*. Not only will the principal component risk factors have zero correlation, but also the technique will greatly reduce the dimension of the risk factor set. Only a few principal components are needed, yet one can capture most of the variation in the entire system. Moreover, what variation remains can usefully be ignored as it can be ascribed merely to 'noise' that is not important for modelling the risk of the portfolio. We present in Section III.5.7 a case study illustrating the application of principal components to reduce the number of volatility risk factors.

III.5.2.7 Nominal versus Percentage Risk Factors and Sensitivities

In this section we have shown how every portfolio has a representation called a risk factor mapping in which the portfolio return is related to the returns on certain risk factors. The

---

[14] This is called multicollinearity – see Sections I.4.4.8 and II.1.4.2.

mapping is linear except when we have an option portfolio. The risk factor sensitivities are the coefficients of the risk factor returns in the representation.

The risk factor returns can be measured in either nominal or relative terms. For instance, interest rate and volatility risk factor changes are usually taken to be nominal changes, but changes in equity indices, exchange rates and commodity futures are usually measured in relative terms, i.e. we use percentage or log returns. The exception is when we have long and short positions in the portfolio and a risk measure (such as historical value at risk) is based on a historical series of portfolio prices. In a long-short portfolio the concept of relative return does not make sense and so instead we use nominal returns, i.e. the portfolio P&L.

For the broad asset classes and position types discussed in this section, Table III.5.1 summarizes the risk factors.

Table III.5.1 Fundamental risk factors by position type and broad asset class

Position type	Asset class		
	Interest rate sensitive instruments	Equities	Commodities
Cash	Risk free curve and credit spread curve	Broad market indices, sector/industry indices, style indices; or principal components	Spot prices
Futures, forwards		Constant maturity index futures; or spot prices plus risk free curve and dividend yields	Constant maturity futures; or spot prices plus risk free curve and carry costs
Options	Price risk factors as for the futures/forward positions above; one implied volatility index or surface for each of the price risk factors		
International exposures	Spot forex rates and domestic and foreign risk free curve		

Risk factor sensitivities may also be calculated in nominal or relative terms. For instance, an equity beta is a sensitivity that is often expressed in relative terms, whereas the present value of a basis point (PV01) is measured in nominal terms. It is a simple matter to convert a relative sensitivity measure into nominal terms: one simply multiplies the relative sensitivity measure by the current value of the exposure to that risk factor.

It is helpful to summarize the cases where nominal or relative risk factor changes and risk factor sensitivities are usually applied.

(i) Interest rate risk factors: Use basis point changes in discount rates and credit spreads, and the risk factor sensitivities (PV01) produce discounted nominal returns on the portfolio.

(ii) Risk factors for tradable assets (equity indices, exchange rates, constant maturity commodity futures):

(a) if the risk factors always have positive values, use relative returns on the risk factors and the risk factor sensitivities (e.g. equity betas) produce relative returns on the portfolio;

(b) if the risk factors can take negative values (e.g. spreads) use changes in the risk factors and the nominal risk factor sensitivities (e.g. exposure to constant maturity spread) produce nominal returns on the portfolio.

(iii) Option portfolios: Use a Taylor approximation for the risk factor mapping and

(a) if sensitivities are value Greeks then use relative returns on the risk factors, and the mapping produces nominal returns on the portfolio;

(b) if sensitivities are position Greeks then use changes in the risk factors, and the mapping again produces nominal returns on the portfolio.

III.5.3 CASH FLOW MAPPING

In very large portfolios of interest rate sensitive instruments cash payments can occur at more or less any time between now and time T, the maturity date of the longest instrument. Hence the risk factors are an entire zero curve, i.e. each t-maturity interest rate for all t from 0 to T. However, for the purposes of market risk assessment we normally map the cash flow on such portfolios to a finite set of standard maturities along the curve. The zero coupon interest rates at these standard maturities are sometimes called *key rates*. But in the context of cash flow mapping, we refer to this finite set of market interest rates as the *vertices* of the cash flow map. The more vertices chosen, the closer together they will be and hence the more representative will the mapped cash flow be of the original cash flow. On the other hand, the chosen interest rates should be of maturities that are relatively liquid because it is standard to use some historical data on the risk factors to analyse their possible variations. It is this consideration more than anything that can limit the choice to just a few vertices. Having chosen the vertices we now consider the problem of mapping all the portfolio's cash flows to these vertices. There are numerous ways in which one can answer this question, some of which are quite complex and involve mapping to non-adjacent vertices.[15]

III.5.3.1 Present Value Invariant and Duration Invariant Maps

We first consider three simple mappings that use only the two adjacent vertices. Suppose the original cash flow is at time T, where $T_1 < T < T_2$ with T_1 and T_2 being the two adjacent vertices, and suppose the original cash flow has a *present value* of €1. Let €x_1 of the cash flow be mapped to the T_1-maturity interest rate, and €x_2 be mapped to the T_2-maturity interest rate. Note that x_1 and x_2 are in present value terms and the simple mappings described in this section have the same conditions, whether we use continuous or discrete compounding.[16]

We do not absolutely require that $x_1 + x_2 = 1$, i.e. the present value of the mapped cash flow does not need to be the same as the present value of the mapped cash flow, but it

---

[15] See Henrard (2000) for further details.

[16] For the equivalent problem without discounting the amount €$\exp(rT)$ is mapped to amounts €$\exp(r_1 x_1) x_1$ and €$\exp(r_2 x_2) x_2$. Or in discrete time, assuming the maturities are integer numbers of years for ease of notation, we map €$(1+R)^T$ to amounts €$(1+R_1)^{T_1} x_1$ and €$(1+R_2)^{T_2} x_2$ where R, R_1 and R_2 are the discretely compounded zero coupon interest rates at the three maturities.

is unusual for this condition not to be applied. Assuming we want the present value to be preserved by the mapping, then

$$x_1 + x_2 = 1. \tag{III.5.3}$$

The Macaulay duration of the original cash flow, i.e. a single cash flow at time T, is just T. But that of the mapped cash flow is $(x_1 T_1 + x_2 T_2)(x_1 + x_2)^{-1}$. So for the Macaulay duration to be invariant under the mapping, we must have

$$x_1 T_1 + x_2 T_2 = (x_1 + x_2) T. \tag{III.5.4}$$

Taken alone, neither (III.5.3) nor (III.5.4) has a unique solution. There are an infinite number of pairs (x_1, x_2) that satisfy just one of these conditions. But, taken together, we can find a unique solution for (x_1, x_2) as illustrated in the following example.

EXAMPLE III.5.1: DURATION AND PRESENT VALUE INVARIANT CASH FLOW MAPS

Find a duration and present value invariant mapping of a cash flow in 1 year and 65 days with present value $1 million, when it is mapped to the 12-month and 18-month vertices. Assume the day count convention is actual/360.

SOLUTION   We write $x_1 = x$, $x_2 = 1 - x$ so that (III.5.3) is satisfied. Then (III.5.4) becomes

$$x = (T_2 - T)(T_2 - T_1)^{-1}. \tag{III.5.5}$$

The day count convention is actual/360 so $T_1 = 360$, $T = 425$ and $T_2 = 540$. Hence,

$$x = (540 - 425)/180 = 0.638889.$$

That is, $638,889 is mapped to the 12-month vertex and $361,111 is mapped to the 18-month vertex, in present value terms.

III.5.3.2   PV01 Invariant Cash Flow Maps

The PV01 invariant condition for a cash flow map depends on whether we use discrete or continuous compounding of interest. Consider a single cash flow at time T with a present value of $1. Denote by r_T and R_T the zero coupon rate at maturity T under continuous and under discrete compounding, respectively. Normally the maturity T is not a standard maturity for the curve, so the interest rate at this maturity must be calculated using a zero curve interpolation technique such as the Svensson model or cubic splines (see Section III.1.9).

Suppose we map this cash flow to a set of fixed vertices at standard maturities $\{T_1, \ldots, T_n\}$. Note that we no longer require that the cash flow be mapped to adjacent vertices. Let the discretely compounded interest rates at these maturities be $\{R_{T_1}, \ldots, R_{T_n}\}$ and let $\{r_{T_1}, \ldots, r_{T_n}\}$ be the continuously compounded rates at the same maturities.

Table III.5.2 sets out the mapping in both continuous and discrete terms. In the last row of the table we have used the approximation to PV01 given in Section III.1.8.2, under both continuous and discrete compounding. Also, to keep the discrete compounding notation simple, we assume that all maturities are integers. Otherwise we would have to use more complex notation, as described in Section III.1.2.2.

Thus a present value of $1 received at time T has a non-discounted value of $\$\exp(rT)$ under continuous compounding which has an approximate PV01 of $\$T \times 10^{-4}$. If a present

Table III.5.2   PV01 invariant cash flow mapping

	Continuous compounding		Discrete compounding	
	Original	Mapped to vertex	Original	Mapped to vertex
Present value	1	x_i	1	x_i
Non-discounted value	$\exp(rT)$	$x_i \exp(rT_i)$	$(1+R)^T$	$x_i(1+R_i)^{T_i}$
PV01 $\times 10^4$	T	xT_i	$T(1+R)^{-1}$	$x_iT_i(1+R_i)^{-1}$

value of $\$x_i$ is mapped to vertex i at maturity T_i where the interest rates or r_i (continuously compounded) and R_i (discretely compounded), then its non-discounted value and PV01 are calculated similarly. The calculation is slightly more complex under discrete compounding because $\$1$ has a non-discounted value of $\$(1+R)^T$ under continuous compounding at the vertex T, which has an approximate PV01 of $\$T(1+R)^{-1} \times 10^{-4}$.

It follows from this table that the PV01 invariant condition for a cash flow map under continuous compounding is

$$\sum_{i=1}^{n} x_i T_i = T, \qquad (\text{III.5.6})$$

and under discrete compounding is

$$\sum_{i=1}^{n} \frac{x_i T_i}{(1+R_i)} = \frac{T}{(1+R)}. \qquad (\text{III.5.7})$$

Note that a present value and duration invariant mapping always satisfies the PV01 invariance condition (III.5.6) under continuous compounding, but it does not always satisfy (III.5.7) if we have discrete compounding.

The advantage of using the continuous compounding condition is that zero coupon rates at the vertices of the cash flow map do not need to be known for continuously compounded PV01 invariant mapping. However, they do need to be known for discretely compounded PV01 invariant mapping. Moreover since the conditions imposed on the present value and duration invariant map no longer ensure PV01 invariance, the PV01 invariance under discrete compounding would need to be imposed as an additional condition.

III.5.3.3   Volatility Invariant Maps

Let us begin with an example where, again, we map a single cash flow with present value $\$1$ to two standard vertices. Let the volatilities of the interest rates of maturities T_1, T and T_2 be σ_1, σ and σ_2 and the correlation between the changes in interest rates of maturities T_1 and T_2 be ϱ. Normally we will know the volatilities at the standard vertices and their correlation, but we would not know the volatility at T. This can be obtained by linearly interpolating between the variances at adjacent vertices (see the example below).

If we want the mapped cash flow to have the same volatility as the original cash flow, then

$$x_1^2 \sigma_1^2 + x_2^2 \sigma_2^2 + 2x_1 x_2\, \rho\, \sigma_1 \sigma_2 = \sigma^2. \qquad (\text{III.5.8})$$

Again there is no unique solution for (x_1, x_2). However, if we combine (III.5.8) with one of the previous conditions we can solve for (x_1, x_2).

EXAMPLE III.5.2: MAPPING CASH FLOWS TO PRESERVE VOLATILITY

Again consider the cash flow and mapping vertices in Example III.5.1, and now suppose the interest rate volatilities are 75 bp for the 12-month and 90 bp for the 18-month rate and that the correlation is 0.75. Find a cash flow mapping that preserves:

(a) the volatility and present value;
(b) the volatility and duration;
(c) the volatility and PV01.

SOLUTION   Before we start, we do not know the volatility of the 1 year 65 day interest rate. We infer it by interpolating between $\sigma_1 = 75$ bp and $\sigma_2 = 90$ bp as follows:

$$\sigma = \sqrt{0.638889 \times 0.75^2 + 0.361111 \times 0.90^2} = 80.7388 \text{bp}.$$

(a) Again write $x_1 = x$, $x_2 = 1 - x$ so that (III.5.3) is satisfied. Now find x as the solution to $\sigma^2 = x^2\sigma_1^2 + (1 - x)^2 \sigma_2^2 + 2x(1 - x)\,\varrho\,\sigma_1\sigma_2$, i.e.

$$0.65188 = 0.5625x^2 + 0.81\,(1 - x)^2 + 1.0125\,x\,(1 - x).$$

Collecting terms,

$$0.36x^2 - 0.6075x + 0.158125 = 0.$$

There are two roots: 0.321564 and 1.365936. If we require both mapped cash flows to be positive we take the first root, so $x = 0.321564$. It follows that to keep the volatility of the mapped cash flow the same as the volatility of the pre-mapped cash flow, we must map $321,564 to the 12-month vertex and $678,436 to the 18-month vertex, in present value terms.

(b) We need to solve the equations

$$360x_1 + 540x_2 = 425\,(x_1 + x_2) \Rightarrow 13x_1 = 23x_2,$$
$$0.65188 = 0.5625x_1^2 + 0.81x_2^2 + 1.0125x_1x_2.$$

A solution is $x_1 = 0.683944$ and $x_2 = 0.386577$. Hence we map $683,944 to the 12-month vertex and $386,577 to the 18-month vertex, in present value terms. However, now the present value of the mapped cash flow is no longer $1 million, but $1,070,521.

(c) We need to solve the equations

$$360x_1 + 540x_2 = 425,$$
$$0.65188 = 0.5625x_1^2 + 0.81x_2^2 + 1.0125x_1x_2.$$

A solution is $x_1 = 0.893542$ and $x_2 = 0.191342$. Hence, in present value terms we map $893,542 to the 12-month vertex and $191,342 to the 18-month vertex. But again, the present value of the mapped cash flow is no longer $1 million, but $1,084,884.

III.5.3.4 Complex Cash Flow Maps

When a cash flow mapping is used as the basis for portfolio risk calculations we need to keep volatility, present value, duration and PV01 all constant under the mapping. This was impossible in the previous section because we only considered methods for mapping to two vertices. The vertices were assumed to be adjacent to the vertex at T in our numerical examples, but they need not have been. The real problem was that the constraint of mapping to only two vertices implied that only two properties of the cash flow could remain invariant under the mapping. In this section we show by example how all the above properties can remain invariant by mapping cash flows to three different vertices.

First we summarize the constraints we want to place on the cash flow map $\{x_1, \ldots, x_n\}$ to a fixed set of vertices at maturities $\{T_1, \ldots, T_n\}$ as follows:

Present Value Invariance

$$\sum_{i=1}^{n} x_i = 1 \tag{III.5.9}$$

Duration Invariance

$$\sum_{i=1}^{n} x_i T_i = T \sum_{i=1}^{n} x_i \tag{III.5.10}$$

PV01 Invariance (continuous compounding)

$$\sum_{i=1}^{n} x_i T_i = T \tag{III.5.11}$$

Volatility Invariance

$$\mathbf{x}'\mathbf{V}\mathbf{x} = \sigma^2 \tag{III.5.12}$$

In (III.5.12) $\mathbf{V}$ is the covariance matrix of the interest rates at the vertices in the mapping set, $\mathbf{x}$ is the vector of present values of mapped cash flow amounts, i.e. $\mathbf{x} = (x_1, \ldots, x_n)'$, and σ is the volatility of the interest rate at the maturity T. Note that if we impose present value invariance, then duration invariance and PV01 invariance are equivalent.

EXAMPLE III.5.3: A PRESENT VALUE, PV01 AND VOLATILITY INVARIANT CASH FLOW MAP

Map a cash flow in 1 year and 65 days map with present value \$1 million to the 6-month, 12-month and 18-month vertices when the day count convention is actual/360 and the volatilities and correlations of the continuously compounded interest rates at the vertices in the mapping set are given in Table III.5.3. The mapping should keep present value, PV01 and volatility invariant.

Table III.5.3 Volatilities and correlations of the mapping set

Correlations	6 month	12 month	18 month	Volatilities (bp)
6 month	1	0.8	0.7	60
12 month	0.8	1	0.75	75
18 month	0.7	0.75	1	90

SOLUTION   We shall find the vector x using the Excel Solver. First we set up the constraints (III.5.9) and (III.5.10) for the given values $T_1 = 180$, $T_2 = 360$, $T_3 = 540$ and $T = 425$. We know that if these are satisfied then so is (III.5.11). Then in the Solver we use the objective $\left[x'Vx - \sigma^2\right]$ with the covariance matrix

$$V = \begin{pmatrix} 0.36 & 0.36 & 0.378 \\ 0.36 & 0.5625 & 0.50625 \\ 0.378 & 0.50625 & 0.81 \end{pmatrix}.$$

where σ is interpolated as in the previous example. The solution is not unique because the volatility constraint is quadratic. One solution is

$$(x_1, x_2, x_3) = (-0.227054, 1.092997, 0.134057).$$

Hence $-\$227,054$ is mapped to the 6-month vertex, $\$1,092,997$ is mapped to the 12-month vertex and $\$134,057$ is mapped to the 18-month vertex, in present value terms. This mapping keeps present value, duration, PV01 and volatility invariant.

III.5.4   APPLICATIONS OF CASH FLOW MAPPING TO MARKET RISK MANAGEMENT

Here we consider just two of the many practical examples where market risk analysts can use cash flow mapping to manage the market risk of portfolios. First we consider portfolios of interest rate sensitive instruments. Since the notional size of the global swaps market is approximately five times that of the global bond market, the largest component of these portfolios are likely to be interest rates swaps. In Section III.1.7.3 we showed that a fixed for floating swap, which is a sequence of FRAs, can be modelled as a principal payment plus a long position on a bond with coupon equal to the swap rate. To account for netting, e.g. where equal and opposite exposures are taken by different desks in the same firm, we should model the markets risk of very large interest rate sensitive portfolios, containing all positions in fixed and floating coupon bonds, FRAs and swaps. In Section III.5.4.1 we explain how to use the mapped cash flows on such a portfolio to decide on an optimal hedging strategy.

If basis risk is small, forwards and futures are best expressed using the cash price as the main underlying risk factor, and each futures or forward exposure then yields an exposure to the constant maturity zero coupon interest rate. This interest rate exposure should then be managed along with other interest rate sensitive exposures, as above. But when basis risk is large and unpredictable, as it is in many commodity portfolios, risk management can focus on mappings to a set of constant maturity futures. In fact, we have already provided an example of this in action, in a case study in Section III.2.6.3. In Section III.5.4.2 we explain how to construct constant maturity commodity futures and how to map portfolios containing many commodity futures or forward positions with different expiry dates.

III.5.4.1   Risk Management of Interest Rate Sensitive Portfolios

We model the market risk of a single vanilla swap by modelling the interest rate risk of a sequence of expected cash flows at regularly spaced payment dates, starting at the next but one payment date and lasting until the maturity of the swap.[17] For any given set of expected cash flows, the interest rate risk arises from our uncertainty about the present value of these cash flows in the future. That is, whilst we know the discount curve today and can therefore calculate the present value of the expected cash flows with certainty, we do not know the discount curve tomorrow, so the present value of the expected cash flows tomorrow is uncertain.

Consider a vanilla fixed for floating interest rate swap. In Section III.1.5.7 we showed that there is no interest rate risk on the floating leg payments after the first payment date. The only interest rate risk is that on a single cash flow at the first payment date, equal to $N(1 + \tau R)$ where N is the notional, τ is the year fraction before the next payment and R is the interest rate that was fixed at the last payment date. The interest rate risk arises because the present value of $N(1 + \tau R)$ will fluctuate as spot rates change. We also showed that market risk of the fixed leg is equivalent to the market risk of a bond with coupon equal to the swap rate.

Hence, the buyer of a pay fixed receive floating vanilla interest rate swap should model his market risk on this position as the risk of a positive cash flow of $N(1 + \tau R)$ and the risk of a short position on bond with coupon equal to the swap rate and maturity equal to the swap maturity. For this reason, the interest rate risk management of swaps and FRAs is often performed together with that of bond portfolios. A large portfolio of such instruments can have positive or negative cash flows at virtually any point in time until the maturity of the longest swap or bond in the portfolio. Using the cash flow mapping methods described in the previous section, we can map all these cash flows to a set of 'key' constant maturity interest rates at a fixed set of vertices.

In the risk management of a large, complex portfolio containing non-vanilla swaps and illiquid bonds (without embedded options) we often assume that the key rates are at 6 months, 1 year, 18 months, 2 years, . . . , T years. It is normal to take 6-month intervals between the key rates because many of the most liquid vanilla swaps are semi-annual. Interest rate risk management of these portfolios should, at every point in time during a trading day, find some portfolio of liquid instruments, including vanilla swaps, FRNs and FRAs, that has a mapped cash flow equal to the mapped cash flow on the complex portfolio. This way the complex portfolio is replicated using liquid instruments and, by adding long or short positions in such instruments to the portfolio, we can change the interest rate risk of the portfolio as we choose. For instance, we could hedge the portfolio by taking the opposite position on each of the liquid instruments to that in the replicating portfolio.

III.5.4.2   Mapping Portfolios of Commodity Futures

Historical series on constant maturity futures prices may be constructed using the simple *concatenation* method described in Section III.2.2.4. To calculate the time t value of a constant maturity futures series of maturity T we take, if possible, two futures contracts with expiry dates either side of T and use linear interpolation on their prices. For instance, suppose we wish to construct a 3-month futures series when the maturity dates are 16 March, 16 June, 16 September and 16 December. On 1 September we use the September and the December contracts, with prices P_1 and P_2 respectively. The number of days between the

---

[17] The payments are set one period in advance, i.e. the payment at the next payment date will have been fixed at the previous payment date.

September contract expiry date and our 3-month expiry date (which is 1 December on 1 September) is 76 and the time interval between the December contract expiry date and our expiry date is 15 days. Hence, the concatenated price is

$$\frac{15 \times P_1 + 76 \times P_2}{91}.$$

We can continue to use the September and December contract prices in the construction of the 1-month futures price. For instance, on 12 September, our 3-month expiry date is 12 December, so the concatenated price would be

$$\frac{4 \times P_1 + 87 \times P_2}{91},$$

where P_1 and P_2 are now the prices of the September and December futures contracts on 12 September.

Since prices can behave oddly a few days before expiry, we should drop the September contract from our calculations after 12 September, and instead take the 3-month maturity contract price to be equal to the December contract price for a few days. However, on 17 September we can start using linear interpolation between the December and March futures prices as above, but now with the December contract being the shorter one. As time moves on we decrease the weight of the December price in our calculation of the concatenated futures price and increase the weight on the March futures price.

We now give an example that demonstrates how to map a commodity futures portfolio to a set constant maturity futures or forwards. The mapping is a simple adaptation of the cash flow mapping methods that were described for interest rate sensitive portfolios in Section III.5.3.

EXAMPLE III.5.4: MAPPING COMMODITY FUTURES OR FORWARD POSITIONS

Suppose we have just two forward positions on a commodity: a long position with present value $2 million in 1 month and 10 days and a short position with present value $1 million in 1 month and 20 days. How should we map these to equivalent positions at the 1-month and 2-month maturity?

SOLUTION Suppose there are 30 days in a month. We could simply use linear interpolation and map $2/3 \times 2 - 1/3 \times 1 = \$1$ million to the 1-month vertex and $1/3 \times 2 - 2/3 \times 1 = \$0$ to the 2-month vertex. But we know from Section III.5.3.3 that this will change the volatility of the portfolio. Instead we can use a present value and volatility invariant map, depicted in Figure III.5.1. For this we need to know the volatilities of the 1-month and 2-month futures and their correlation – suppose the volatilities are 30% and 27% as shown and the correlation is 0.95. Using linear interpolation on the variances we infer the volatilities of 29.03% for the 1 month 10 day position and 28.04% for the 1 month 20 day position.

For the mapped position to have the same volatility as the original position, the proportion x of the long position of $2 million at 1 month 10 days that is mapped to the 1-month future must satisfy

$$29.03^2 = 30^2 \times x^2 + 27^2 \times (1-x)^2 + 2 \times 0.95 \times 30 \times 27 \times x \times (1-x).$$

This quadratic equation has one solution between 0 and 1, i.e. $x = 0.762092$. Similarly, the proportion y of the short position of $1 million at 1 month 20 days that is mapped to the 1-month future must satisfy

$$28.04^2 = 30^2 \times y^2 + 27^2 \times (1-y)^2 + 2 \times 0.95 \times 30 \times 27 \times y \times (1-y),$$

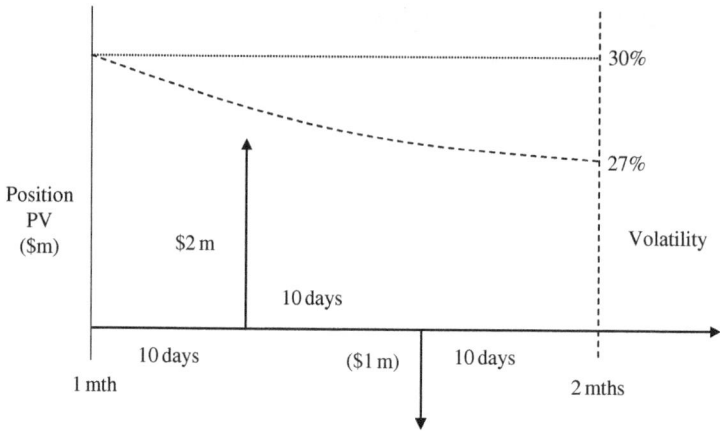

Figure III.5.1 A volatility invariant commodity futures or forwards mapping

and solving this gives $y = 0.464239$. Thus in total we must map

$$0.762069 \times \$2,000,000 - 0.464239 \times \$1,000,000 = -\$1,059,945$$

to the 1-month future, and

$$0.237908 \times \$2,000,000 - 0.535761 \times \$1,000,000 = -\$59,945$$

to the 2-month future. This way the present value and the volatility of the mapped position is the same as the volatility of the unmapped position.

The availability of historical data on constant maturity futures prices has greatly facilitated the computation of value at risk for commodity portfolios. Moreover, commodity futures often have very highly correlated term structures, and this indicates that principal component analysis will be an effective method for reducing the dimension of the risk factor space. A practical example of using PCA to reduce the risk factor space, and of finding the portfolio's sensitivities relative to the new (principal component) risk factors, is given in Section III.5.7.4 below.

III.5.5 MAPPING AN OPTION PORTFOLIO TO PRICE RISK FACTORS

To value an option portfolio today we need to price every option. If the options are actively traded in the market we can price them by observing the current market price, i.e. by *marking to market*. Otherwise we have to use a model to price, i.e. *marking to model*. For a mark-to-model price we use an analytic formula for the price whenever possible. For exotic or path-dependent options without analytic prices either we use approximate prices (see Section III.3.9) or their price is given by a numerical solution to a stochastic differential equation.

When our purpose is not to value but to assess the risk of an option portfolio we have to forecast possible values for the portfolio in the future. There are several reasons why we use risk factor mapping for this purpose. First, the total portfolio risk can be attributed to different sources, so that traders and risk managers identify their most risky exposures. Second, traders have traditionally operated under different limits that relate to different risk factors. And thirdly, it is relatively quick to approximate a portfolio's *value at risk* (VaR) using such a mapping. If the portfolio contains complex path-dependent options that have no analytic price it is a lengthy business to revalue the portfolio exactly for many thousands of risk factor scenarios, which is necessary for estimating its VaR. However, the risk factor mapping allows the portfolio value change to be measured using a simple non-linear function, simulating thousands of portfolio prices under the assumption that the factor sensitivities are constant.

Risk factor sensitivities provide an estimate for the change in value of the portfolio when an underlying risk factor changes by a small amount. They provide an estimate of the portfolio risk relative to each of its risk factors, but ignore the risk of the factors themselves. The purpose is to allow traders to hedge the portfolio against changes in certain risk factors.

Risk factor mapping of an option portfolio is based on Taylor expansion. The mathematical foundations of Taylor expansion are described in Section I.1.6. In the next subsection we simply review why Taylor expansions are useful for risk measurement and explain how they are implemented in general, non-mathematical terms. Later subsections define an option portfolio's net sensitivities with respect to movements in underlying asset prices, interest rates and time. We assume readers are already familiar with the definitions of the 'Greeks' for individual options given in Section III.3.4 and the characteristics of the Black–Scholes–Merton (BSM) Greeks discussed in Section III.3.7.

III.5.5.1   Taylor Expansions

A Taylor expansion may be used as a local approximation to the change in the value of an option portfolio as a function of small changes in its risk factors. The major risk factors of an option portfolio are prices and implied volatilities. The price risk factors are prices of the underlying contracts. An underlying contract could be a stock, an index, a bond, an interest rate, a commodity futures or a foreign exchange rate. Then each option in the portfolio has its own implied volatility as a risk factor. Minor risk factors include interest rates, dividends or carry costs and time.

The risk factor sensitivities in the Taylor expansion are collectively called the portfolio's Greeks. If all the options in the portfolio are on the same underlying we can use *net position Greeks* and absolute returns on all risk factors in the expansion. But, as we shall see below, if the portfolio contains options on different underlyings we must use the portfolio's net *value Greeks* and the price risk factor returns are then measured in relative terms in the Taylor expansion.[18]

Analytic methods for computing Greeks may exist, depending on the assumed underlying price process and the type of option. For instance, if the option is a standard European call or put and the underlying price process follows geometric Brownian motion with constant volatility then the Greeks are given by the formulae in Section III.3.7. Otherwise we can calculate the Greeks using the finite difference method explained in Section I.5.5.2. This is time-consuming, even with the powerful computers used today. It can take several minutes to calculate the net portfolio Greeks of a large and complex option portfolio because it requires complete revaluation of all the options in the portfolio for different values of the underlying risk factors. Moreover, the value of the Greeks will change whenever one

---

[18] In the following we sometimes refer to absolute returns as, simply 'changes' in risk factor values and relative returns as, simply, 'returns' on the risk factors.

of the underlying risk factors changes.[19] It is quite possible that by the time the value of the Greek has been computed the underlying price will have changed, so the computed value will no longer relevant! In this case the most that a trader of such a portfolio could hope for is to have the Greeks updated on a regular basis, perhaps every 10 minutes.

When traders operate under VaR limits they need to have a quick and accurate assessment of the impact of a proposed trade on the VaR. If the trade would bring them over the VaR limit they cannot make the trade. The exact calculation of VaR for a large portfolio of complex options can be a major computational task that cannot normally be performed in a few seconds. It requires revaluing the options in the portfolio not a few times, as when computing the Greeks in the Taylor expansion, but many thousands of times. This could take several hours, by which time the opportunity to trade may have passed. By contrast, it is quick and fairly accurate to measure the effect of a relatively small trade on an option portfolio VaR using its Taylor approximation.

III.5.5.2   Value Delta and Value Gamma

When mapping option portfolios we often use *value Greeks* rather than percentage Greeks or position Greeks for risk factor sensitivities. This is because only the value Greeks are additive over different underlyings. This section defines the value delta and value gamma for a portfolio of options and describes how to calculate them.

We first introduce the *point value* (*pv*) of an option, i.e. the value of the underlying contract per point. It gives the profit and loss from trading the option as

$$P\&L = \Delta g \times pv, \qquad (III.5.13)$$

where Δg is the change in the option price. For example, exchange traded options on the FTSE 100 index have a point value of £10. So if an option is bought at 50 and sold at 55 then the profit is £10 × 5 = £50. The point value can also be used to convert the underlying price S of the FTSE 100 index, which has no units of measurement, into a notional equivalent. The 'point' for FTSE 100 options and futures is a point on the FTSE 100 index. So if, say, the index stands at 6500 then an option or futures on the FTSE 100 index is on a notional value of £10 × 6500 = £ 65,000.[20]

The *value delta*, also termed the *dollar delta*, is the position delta multiplied by the price S and the point value. As defined in Section III.3.3.4, the position delta is the ordinary delta (i.e. the partial derivative with respect to S) times N, the number of units of the underlying that the option contracts to trade. Hence, for a single option we may write the value delta as

$$\delta^{\$} = \delta^{P} \times S \times pv = \delta \times N \times S \times pv. \qquad (III.5.14)$$

The value delta divided by 100 represents the sensitivity of the nominal value of the position to a 1% change in the underlying price. It is the value of a position in the underlying that has the same profit (or loss) as the option portfolio when S changes by 1%. For this reason some people call (III.5.14) the *delta equivalent*.

---

[19] For instance, consider an ATM option with a delta of 0.5 when $S = 100$. Suppose that S moves to 110. Now the option is no longer ATM so its delta will no longer be 0.5.
[20] The point value of options and futures on the S&P 500 index is $250. Further examples of point values for exchange traded options (or futures) are provided in Table III.5.4.

When the portfolio contains options on different underlyings, even position deltas are not additive. But value deltas in the same currency are always additive. The following example illustrates.

EXAMPLE III.5.5: VALUE DELTA OF A PORTFOLIO WITH MULTIPLE UNDERLYING ASSETS

We have two short calls on a UK stock X, which has share price of 50 pence and four short puts on UK stock Y, which has share price of 75 pence. The call has a delta of $+0.5$, and the put has a delta of -0.6. The point value of each option is £10 per penny. What is the value delta of this portfolio?

SOLUTION

- The value delta of the two short calls on stock X is

$$-0.5 \times 2 \times 50 \times £10 = -£500.$$

  This means that if the price of share X rises by 1% we would lose approximately £5 on this position.
- The value delta of the four short puts on stock Y is

$$0.6 \times 4 \times 75 \times £10 = £1800.$$

  This means that if the price of share Y rises by 1% we gain approximately £18 on this position.

The value delta of the portfolio is $-£500 + £1800 = £1300$. This means that if the prices of *both* shares rise by 1% then we would gain approximately £13 on the total position.

There appear to be some slightly different definitions of the *value gamma*.[21] We define the value gamma as

$$\gamma^{\$} = \gamma \times N \times S^2 \times pv, \qquad (III.5.15)$$

i.e. the value gamma is the position gamma multiplied by the square of the underlying price, and this is converted into value terms by multiplying by the point value.

Like value deltas, value gammas are additive across options on different underlyings. Table III.5.4 illustrates portfolios containing some standard exchange traded option contracts. We state the point value for options and futures on S. We assume $\delta = \frac{1}{2}$ for all underlyings but the gamma differs because it depends on the level of S. A typical gamma value for each underlying is shown in the table. This is based on a portfolio with a short time to expiry, so that the gamma effects are large. We use an assumed value for the underlying contract price S to compute the value delta and gamma using (III.5.14) and (III.5.15).

Other value Greeks are simple to define. The *value theta* and *value rho* (also called *dollar theta* and *dollar rho*) are the product of the position theta (or rho) and the point value. We could also define the *value vega* as the product of the position vega and the point value – except that we have not yet defined the position vega. The concept of position vega is difficult, so we shall leave this until Section III.5.6.

---

[21] Another common definition includes the factor of $\frac{1}{2}$. This is to be consistent with the delta–gamma approximations (III.5.16)–(III.5.18).

Table III.5.4   Value deltas and gammas

	FTSE 100	US bond future	UK share	€/$ forex rate	Crude oil futures
Units for S	–	$1	1p	€1	$1
Point value	£10	$1,000	£10	€100,000	$1,000
Delta	0.5	0.5	0.5	0.5	0.5
Gamma	0.002	0.12	0.15	10	0.15
S	6000	105	80	1.3	80
Value delta	£30,000	$52,500	£400	€65,000	$40,000
Value gamma	£720,000	$1,323,000	£9,600	€1,690,000	$960,000

III.5.5.3   Delta–Gamma Approximation: Single Underlying

Here we consider how to map a portfolio of options on a single underlying to its price risk factor. The *delta–gamma approximation* is a quadratic risk factor mapping that captures the non-linearity of the pay-off profile for option portfolios. When all the options in the portfolio are on the same underlying, with price S, it may be written

$$\Delta P(S) \approx \delta^P \Delta S + \tfrac{1}{2}\gamma^P(\Delta S)^2, \tag{III.5.16}$$

where δ^P and γ^P are the net position delta and gamma of the portfolio.

Figure III.5.2 illustrates how the delta–gamma approximation depends on the current value of the underlying, because the values of delta and gamma will depend on the current value of S. At the point A shown to the left of the graph, and in a 'local' region around A, i.e. for values of S near to the value of S at A, the portfolio price change can be approximated by a quadratic function. The delta–gamma approximation to the change in portfolio value at the point A is illustrated with the curve shown by the dotted line. At point B and in a small region around B, we can approximate the change in portfolio price by a different (but still quadratic) form, using the delta–gamma approximation at that value of S.

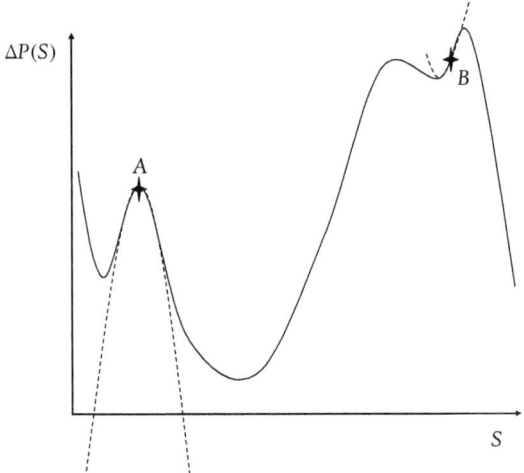

Figure III.5.2   Delta–gamma approximation

Multiplying both sides of (III.5.16) by the point value of the underlying gives an expression for the P&L of the option portfolio that is equivalent to (III.5.16), but this time giving the change in value expressed as a quadratic function of the underlying asset's *returns*. We have

$$\text{P\&L} \approx \left[\delta^P \Delta S + \tfrac{1}{2}\gamma^P (\Delta S)^2\right] \times pv. \tag{III.5.17}$$

Hence if $\delta^\$$ and $\gamma^\$$ denote the *value delta* and *value gamma* defined by (III.5.14) and (III.5.15) above, then (III.5.17) may be written

$$\text{P\&L} \approx \delta^\$ R + \tfrac{1}{2}\gamma^\$ R^2, \tag{III.5.18}$$

where $R = \Delta S/S$ is the return on the underlying.

We now consider two examples of the application of (III.5.18) to a portfolio of options on the same underlying. These options need not be 'vanilla' options, i.e. simple European calls and puts. We only need to know the delta and the gamma of each option.

EXAMPLE III.5.6: DELTA–GAMMA APPROXIMATION WITH SINGLE UNDERLYING

We have a short call on 3000 shares and a short put on 6000 shares of the same UK stock. When the stock has a share price of 50 pence the call has $\delta = 0.3$ and $\gamma = 0.2$ and the put has $\delta = -0.4$ and $\gamma = 0.3$. The point value is £10 per penny. Use the delta–gamma approximation (III.5.18) to estimate the change in the portfolio value if the share price falls to 48 pence.

SOLUTION The net position delta and gamma are:

$$\delta^P = -0.3 \times 3000 + 0.4 \times 6000 = -900 + 2400 = 1500,$$
$$\gamma^P = -0.2 \times 3000 - 0.3 \times 6000 = -600 - 1800 = -2400.$$

Hence by (III.5.16) the approximate change in the portfolio price when the share price falls by 2 pence is

$$\Delta P \approx 1500 \times (-2) - \tfrac{1}{2} \times 2400 \times (-2)^2 = -7800,$$

and the approximate change in the portfolio value is therefore

$$\text{P\&L} \approx -7800 \times £10 = -£78,000.$$

This is relative to a delta equivalent notional value given by the value delta, i.e.

$$\delta^\$ = 1500 \times 50 \times £10 = £750,000.$$

Hence when the share price falls by 2 pence, i.e. by 4%, the portfolio value would fall by approximately 10%. This is because the portfolio has a large *negative* gamma. In fact the portfolio value would also fall if the share price rose by 2%!

EXAMPLE III.5.7: DELTA–GAMMA APPROXIMATION FOR AN S&P 500 OPTION PORTFOLIO

A portfolio of options on the S&P 500 index has a delta of –0.5 and a gamma of 0.01 when the index is at 1200. Find the value delta and the value gamma of the portfolio and hence approximate the change in portfolio value if the S&P 500 index (a) increases by 1% and (b) decreases by 1%.

SOLUTION   The point value of futures and options on the S&P 500 index is $250. Hence

$$\delta^\$ = -0.5 \times 1200 \times \$250 = -\$150,000,$$

$$\gamma^\$ = 0.01 \times 1200^2 \times \$250 = \$3,600,000.$$

According to the value delta, if the S&P 500 index increased by 1% we would lose $1500 on the portfolio and if the index decreased by 1% we would gain $1500. But this is only a linear approximation. Using the quadratic approximation (III.5.18), which is a better approximation, we have:

$$R = +0.01 \Rightarrow P\&L = -\$150,000 \times 0.01 + \tfrac{1}{2} \times \$3,600,000 \times 0.01^2$$

$$= -\$1500 + \$180 = -\$1320,$$

$$R = -0.01 \Rightarrow P\&L = \$150,000 \times 0.01 + \tfrac{1}{2} \times \$3,600,000 \times 0.01^2$$

$$= \$1500 + \$180 = \$1680.$$

Hence if the S&P 500 index increased by 1% we would only lose $1320 on the portfolio and if the index decreased by 1% we would gain $1680. Clearly, having a positive gamma on an option portfolio is a good thing.

III.5.5.4   Effect of Gamma on Portfolio Risk

Table III.5.5 extends Table III.5.4, showing the delta-only approximation and the delta–gamma approximation (III.5.18) to each portfolio P&L when the underlying increases by 1% and when it decreases by 1%.

Table III.5.5   Delta–gamma approximation (1% change in S)

		FTSE 100	US bond future	UK share	€/$ forex rate	Crude oil
Value delta		£30,000	$52,500	£400	€65,000	$40,000
Value gamma		£720,000	$1,323,000	£9,600	€1,690,000	$960,000
1% ↑	Delta	£300	$525.00	£4.00	€300	$400.0
	Delta–gamma	£336	$591.15	£4.48	€336	$448.0
1% ↓	Delta	−£300	−$525.00	−£4.00	−€300	−$400.0
	Delta–gamma	−£264	−$458.85	−£3.52	−€264	−$352.0

In Table III.5.5 all the portfolios have positive gamma, hence

- the upside gains from a 1% price increase are augmented, and
- the downside losses from a 1% price decrease are diminished.

Indeed all portfolios with *positive gamma* have less price risk than those with negative gamma, irrespective of the sign on delta.

Figure III.5.3 shows a grey curve which represents the value of a simple European call option as a function of the underlying asset price. The delta approximation to the change in price is depicted by the straight line and the delta–gamma approximation is depicted by the dotted curve. A call option has positive gamma, hence when S moves the price of the option changes less under the delta–gamma approximation than under the delta-only approximation. In the figure we suppose the current price is at S_1 and then it moves up to S_2. Then:

- under the delta-only (i.e. linear) approximation shown by the straight dot-dashed line, the value of the option changes from f_1 to f_2 (delta only);
- under the delta–gamma approximation shown by the curved dotted line, the value of the option changes from f_1 to f_2 (delta–gamma).

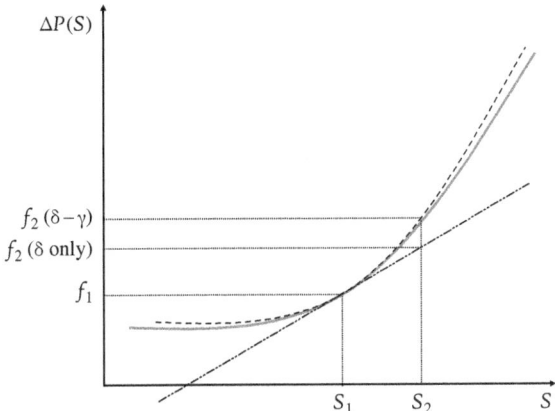

Figure III.5.3   Effect of positive gamma

Hence with a positive gamma the upward price moves are enhanced and the downward price moves are diminished. The opposite is the case for portfolio with negative gamma. For instance, a similar figure but with a negative delta and a negative gamma (from going short this option) would show that the upside gains from a 1% price decrease are diminished, and the downside losses from a 1% price increase are augmented, compared with the delta-only approximation.

III.5.5.5   Price Beta Mapping

Now consider the case where we have a portfolio of options on different securities but, rather than using each individual security price as a risk factor, we choose one (or more) indices to use as risk factors. For simplicity assume the portfolio contains only two options, each on a different security, and the two securities have prices S_1 and S_2. Then the portfolio has a delta–gamma representation

$$\Delta P \approx \delta_1^P \Delta S_1 + \tfrac{1}{2}\gamma_1^P (\Delta S_1)^2 + \delta_2^P \Delta S_2 + \tfrac{1}{2}\gamma_2^P (\Delta S_2)^2, \tag{III.5.19}$$

where the deltas and gammas are the position deltas and gammas with respect to each security price. How do we convert this to a delta–gamma representation of the form (III.5.16) where S is the price of an index?

The conversion of a delta and a gamma with respect to the security price into a delta and a gamma with respect to the index price is equivalent to a change of scale. We assume that the *percentage* return on security i is related to the *percentage* return on the index as

$$\frac{\Delta S_i}{S_i} = \beta_i \frac{\Delta S}{S}. \tag{III.5.20}$$

In other words, we can estimate the betas above using the *single index model*[22]

$$R_i = \beta_i R + \varepsilon_i. \tag{III.5.21}$$

From Section I.2.1 we know that in the case of OLS regression,

$$\beta_i = \frac{\text{Cov}(R_i, R)}{V(R)}. \tag{III.5.22}$$

Estimates of the covariance and variance on the right-hand side may be based, for instance, on a sample of historical returns on each underlying and on the index.

Substituting (III.5.20) in (III.5.19) gives

$$\Delta P \approx \left[\delta_1^P \beta_1 \left(\frac{S_1}{S} \right) + \delta_2^P \beta_2 \left(\frac{S_2}{S} \right) \right] \Delta S + \frac{1}{2} \left[\gamma_1^P \beta_1^2 \left(\frac{S_1}{S} \right)^2 + \gamma_2^P \beta_2^2 \left(\frac{S_2}{S} \right)^2 \right] (\Delta S)^2. \tag{III.5.23}$$

More generally, when there are options on n securities in the portfolio, the *net position delta* and *net position gamma* are obtained as

$$\delta^P = \sum_{i=1}^{n} \delta_i^P \beta_i \left(\frac{S_i}{S} \right), \tag{III.5.24}$$

$$\gamma^P = \sum_{i=1}^{n} \gamma_i^P \beta_i^2 \left(\frac{S_i}{S} \right)^2, \tag{III.5.25}$$

where δ_i^P and γ_i^P denote the net position delta and gamma of the options on the ith securities and β_i denotes the ith market beta. With these net position Greeks we have

$$\Delta P \approx \delta^P \Delta S + \frac{1}{2} \gamma^P (\Delta S)^2. \tag{III.5.26}$$

It is usually the case that the point value of the securities options is the same as the point value of the index options. For instance, in the FTSE 100 index both index options and stock options have a point value of £10. Since the value delta of the ith stock option is $\delta_i^\$ = \delta_i^P \times S_i \times pv$ and the value gamma is $\gamma_i^\$ = \gamma_i^P \times S_i^2 \times pv$, the relationships (III.5.24) and (III.5.25) imply that the value delta and value gamma of the portfolio are given by

$$\delta^\$ = \sum_{i=1}^{n} \delta_i^\$ \beta_i, \tag{III.5.27}$$

$$\gamma^\$ = \sum_{i=1}^{n} \gamma_i^\$ \beta_i^2. \tag{III.5.28}$$

Hence, we obtain the net value delta of the portfolio by weighting the value delta by the equity beta for each security and then summing over all securities in the portfolio. Similarly, we obtain the net value gamma of the portfolio by weighting each value gamma by the square of the corresponding equity beta and again summing over all securities. With these net value Greeks we have the usual delta–gamma approximation, i.e.

$$\text{P\&L} \approx \delta^\$ R + \frac{1}{2} \gamma^\$ R^2, \tag{III.5.29}$$

where R is now the return on the index.

---

[22] See Chapter II.1.2.1.

EXAMPLE III.5.8: DELTA–GAMMA MAPPING TO A SINGLE UNDERLYING

Consider a portfolio with two stock options, one on American Express (Amex) and the other on Cisco Systems. The share prices are currently $50 and $20 respectively, and the point value of the stocks and the S&P 100 index options is $250. The regression betas of Amex and Cisco with respect to the S&P 100 index were found, using OLS, in Example II.1.2. These were 1.24 for Amex and 1.76 for Cisco. On the Amex stock we have 30 long calls with $\delta = 0.5$ and $\gamma = 0.2$, and on the Cisco stock we have 40 long calls with $\delta = 0.25$ and $\gamma = 0.1$. Estimate the portfolio's value delta and value gamma with respect to the S&P 100 index, which currently stands at 600. Hence, use the delta–gamma approximation (III.5.29) with the S&P 100 index as the risk factor to estimate the change in portfolio value if the S&P 100 index rises by 1%.

SOLUTION   The spreadsheet for this example computes the result in two equivalent ways:

- Use the stock betas to estimate the expected returns on the stocks when the index returns 1%, convert these returns into stock prices changes (of $0.62 for Amex and $0.35 for Cisco) and then use the position delta and gamma for each stock to calculate the change in price of each options position. Add these two option price changes and multiply by the point value to obtain the P&L of the portfolio. The result is a gain of $3473.
- Calculate the value delta and value gamma of each option. The Amex option has a value delta of $187,500 and a value gamma of $1,875,000; the Cisco option has a value delta of $50,000 and a value gamma of $800,000. Then calculate the net value delta and gamma with respect to the index using (III.5.27) and (III.5.28). We obtain $32,500 for the net value delta and $5,361,080 for the net value gamma. Then apply these in the delta–gamma approximation (III.5.29) with $R = 1\%$ and the result is a gain of $3473, as before.

The same result is obtained either way. The reason we may prefer to use the second approach, i.e. use the net value deltas and gamma with respect to an index, is that traders' limits on stock options are usually set in these terms.

III.5.5.6   Delta–Gamma Approximation: Several Underlyings

Here we consider portfolios of options on several underlying assets and derive a quadratic mapping for the change in portfolio value. Let the underlying assets have prices $S_1, \ldots, S_n$ and let

$$\Delta S = (\Delta S_1, \ldots, \Delta S_n)'$$

be the vector of changes in underlying prices. Consider the net position deltas and gammas of the portfolio, i.e. the ordinary partial derivatives of the portfolio price P with respect to the underlying prices. Using subscripts to denote partial differentiation, these may be written

$$\delta_P = \begin{pmatrix} P_{S_1} \\ \vdots \\ P_{S_n} \end{pmatrix}, \quad \Gamma_P = \begin{pmatrix} P_{S_1 S_1} & \cdots & P_{S_1 S_n} \\ \vdots & \ddots & \vdots \\ P_{S_n S_1} & \cdots & P_{S_n S_n} \end{pmatrix}. \tag{III.5.30}$$

Note that we do not assume that the gamma matrix is diagonal, i.e. the delta with respect to the ith asset may change when the kth asset price changes, even when the ith asset price does not change. We call this the *cross-gamma* effect.

With this notation a multivariate second order Taylor approximation to the change in portfolio value may be written

$$\Delta P \approx \boldsymbol{\delta}_p' \Delta \mathbf{S} + \tfrac{1}{2} \Delta \mathbf{S}' \boldsymbol{\Gamma}_p \Delta \mathbf{S}, \qquad (\text{III.5.31})$$

but this cannot be extended to an expression for the P&L of the portfolio. That is because we cannot write $P\&L = \Delta P \times pv$ as before, because different underlyings have different point values for their options and futures.

So let pv_i be the point value for options on the ith asset. Then we can define the *value delta vector* and the *value gamma matrix* as

$$\boldsymbol{\delta}_\$ = \left(\delta_1^\$, \ldots, \delta_n^\$ \right)', \quad \boldsymbol{\Gamma}_\$ = \left(\gamma_{ij}^\$ \right), \qquad (\text{III.5.32})$$

where

$$\delta_i^\$ = P_{S_i} \times S_i \times pv_i \qquad (\text{III.5.33})$$

and

$$\gamma_{ij}^\$ = P_{S_i S_j} \times S_i \times S_j \times \sqrt{pv_i pv_j}. \qquad (\text{III.5.34})$$

That is, the value delta vector is the vector of value deltas on each underlying and the value gamma matrix has the value gammas with respect to each underlying along its diagonal. The definition (III.5.34) extends the definition of value gamma to value cross-gammas with respect to two underlying assets with (possibly) different point values.

Now we can write the *multivariate delta–gamma approximation* to the portfolio P&L as

$$P\&L \approx \boldsymbol{\delta}_\$' \mathbf{R} + \tfrac{1}{2} \mathbf{R}' \boldsymbol{\Gamma}_\$ \mathbf{R}, \qquad (\text{III.5.35})$$

where $\mathbf{R} = (R_1, \ldots, R_n)'$ is the vector of the underlying asset returns.

EXAMPLE III.5.9: DELTA–GAMMA APPROXIMATION FOR A PORTFOLIO OF BOND AND STOCK OPTIONS

A bank holds positions in bond and stock options. The bond option portfolio has a position delta of 10, a position gamma of 2.5, a point value of $1000 and a delta equivalent of $1 million. The stock option portfolio has a position delta of 20, a position gamma of 0.5, a point value of $250 and a delta equivalent of $5 million. The cross-gamma between bonds and equities is -0.15. What is the delta–gamma approximation to the portfolio's P&L corresponding to a return on bonds of -1% and a return on equities of $+1\%$?

SOLUTION   First we use the fact that the delta equivalent is the value delta, to infer values for S_1 and S_2 to use in (III.5.33) and (III.5.34). We have

$$S_1 = \frac{\$1,000,000}{10 \times \$1000} = 100 \quad \text{and} \quad S_2 = \frac{\$5,000,000}{20 \times \$250} = 1000.$$

We can calculate the value gamma matrix as follows:

$$\boldsymbol{\Gamma}_\$ = \begin{pmatrix} 2.5 \times 100^2 \times 1000 & -0.15 \times 100 \times 1000 \times \sqrt{1000 \times 250} \\ -0.15 \times 100 \times 1000 \times \sqrt{1000 \times 250} & 0.5 \times 1000^2 \times 250 \end{pmatrix}$$

$$= \begin{pmatrix} 25 & -7.5 \\ 7.5 & 125 \end{pmatrix} \times \$1\text{m}.$$

Now we use this and the value deltas (the delta equivalents) in (III.5.35) to obtain the delta–gamma approximation to the portfolio's P&L in millions of dollars as

$$\text{P\&L} \approx (1, 5) \begin{pmatrix} -0.01 \\ +0.01 \end{pmatrix} + \tfrac{1}{2} (-0.01, +0.01) \begin{pmatrix} 25 & -7.5 \\ -7.5 & 125 \end{pmatrix} \begin{pmatrix} -0.01 \\ +0.01 \end{pmatrix} = 0.04825.$$

Thus if bond prices fall by 1% and equity prices increase by 1% the portfolio will make a gain of approximately $48,250.

III.5.5.7   Including Time and Interest Rates Sensitivities

Taylor expansion methods apply to all option portfolios, including those containing options on multiple assets or interest rates. The more risk factors included in the expansion and the higher the order of approximation for each risk factor, the more accurate the representation of the portfolio's P&L due to small changes in the risk factors.

Up to this point we have been using a delta–gamma approximation whilst ignoring the effect of time on the portfolio value.[23] We have asked what the portfolio value would be if the underlying price moves, but have not associated this price movement with any time period. However, price changes do not happen instantly, they take place over time. And over time the value of an option portfolio will change, even when the underlying price or volatility remains static. To capture this effect we include the portfolio's time sensitivity, i.e. the theta of the portfolio, in the Taylor expansion. This yields the *delta–gamma–theta approximation* to the change in portfolio price:

$$\Delta P \approx \theta^P \Delta t + \delta^P \Delta S + \tfrac{1}{2} \gamma^P (\Delta S)^2, \tag{III.5.36}$$

where δ^P, γ^P and θ^P denote the portfolio's net position delta, gamma and theta.

Another common form of Taylor approximation to the change in value of a single option introduces further Greeks (and their respective risk factor changes) into the expansion. The *delta–gamma–theta–rho approximation* to the change in portfolio price is

$$\Delta P \approx \theta^P \Delta t + \delta^P \Delta S + \tfrac{1}{2} \gamma^P (\Delta S)^2 + \boldsymbol{\pi}'_p \Delta \mathbf{r}, \tag{III.5.37}$$

where $\mathbf{r}$ is a vector of discount rates with maturities equal to those of the options and $\boldsymbol{\pi}_p$ is the position rho vector.[24]

The general expression for the delta–gamma–theta–rho approximation for the P&L of a portfolio of options, possibly on different underlyings, is

$$\text{P\&L} \approx \theta^\$ \Delta t + \delta'_\$ \mathbf{R} + \tfrac{1}{2} \mathbf{R}' \Gamma_\$ \mathbf{R} + \boldsymbol{\pi}'_\$ \Delta \mathbf{r}, \tag{III.5.38}$$

where the value delta and gamma are defined in the previous subsection. The *value theta* $\theta^\$$ is the sum of each position theta multiplied by the point value of the option. The *value rho* vector $\boldsymbol{\pi}_\$$ is calculated similarly, as the sum of each position rho multiplied by the point value of the option. Note that there is a curve of interest rate risk factors $\mathbf{r}$ unless all the options in the portfolio have the same maturity.

---

[23] And, indeed, ignoring the need to discount the P&L to today's terms if it is measured over a risk horizon of months rather than days or weeks.
[24] We use the notation π for the sensitivity to interest rates, rather than ϱ, because the notation ϱ is used to denote the correlation between risk factors.

EXAMPLE III.5.10: DELTA–GAMMA–THETA–RHO APPROXIMATION

Consider the portfolio of standard European options defined in Table III.5.6 with the risk free zero coupon interest rate and dividend zero curves shown in Table III.5.7.[25] Assume the market price of the underlying asset is 100. Find a delta–gamma–vega–theta–rho approximation for the portfolio's P&L.

Table III.5.6   A portfolio with four options

Option name	A	B	C	D
Option type	Put	Call	Call	Put
Strike	95.0	105.00	100.0	85.0
Maturity (days)	30	60	90	180
Market price	0.5363	1.1897	3.4899	0.2203

Table III.5.7   Curves for valuing the four options of Table III.5.6

Maturity (days)	30	60	90	180
Risk free rate	4.0%	3.8%	3.7%	3.6%
Dividend yield	2.0%	2.2%	2.5%	2.3%

SOLUTION   The spreadsheet for this example calculates the delta, gamma, theta and rho of each option using the BSM formulae given Section III.3.7. The results are shown in Table III.5.8. The net position delta, gamma and theta are calculated by summing the product of the position and the option sensitivity over all options, giving the results in the right-hand column of the table. Note that theta is normally expressed per day, so the formula for theta given in Table III.3.4 is divided by 365 in the spreadsheet. The position rho must be calculated for each option separately since they each have different interest rate risk factor.

Table III.5.8   Option price sensitivities

Option Name	A	B	C	D		
Delta	−0.1703	0.2746	0.5275	−0.0483	Position delta	−0.6024
Gamma	0.0442	0.0456	0.0468	0.0095	Position gamma	0.0532
Theta	−0.0232	−0.0213	−0.0199	−0.0027	Position theta	−0.0269
Rho	−0.0144	0.0432	0.1215	−0.0249		
Position rho	−0.0433	−0.1727	0.2429	−0.0249		

Hence the portfolio delta–gamma–theta–rho approximation may be written:[26]

$$\Delta P \approx -0.0269\Delta t - 0.6024\Delta S + 0.0532(\Delta S)^2 + \left(-0.0433, \ -0.1727, \ 0.2429, \ -0.0249\right)\begin{pmatrix} \Delta r_{30} \\ \Delta r_{60} \\ \Delta r_{90} \\ \Delta r_{180} \end{pmatrix}.$$

---

[25] In the spreadsheet we input the market implied volatilities of the options and then find the market prices from these.
[26] Since all the options are on the same underlying they all have the same point value and so the given approximation for the price change can be translated into an approximation for the value change, i.e. the P&L of the portfolio, if we multiply the right hand side by this point value.

Occasionally traders are given theta and rho limits, but this practice is less common now that the traditional sensitivity based limits are being replaced by VaR limits in major banks. Interest rates and time are only minor risk factors for most option portfolios, with a few notable exceptions such as shorted dated straddles. Otherwise, sensitivities to interest rates and time are usually small relative to the price and implied volatility sensitivities.

III.5.6 MAPPING IMPLIED VOLATILITY

In this section an option price is regarded as a function of two risk factors: a single underlying price S and its volatility σ. We assume that the price process does not have a stochastic volatility because in this case the 'vega' of the option is not clearly defined. In fact with stochastic volatility the volatility sensitivity depends on the option price sensitivities to the *parameters* of the stochastic volatility process. Hence, in the following changes in volatility are assumed to be deterministic.

Implied volatilities are very important risk factors for option portfolios. The vega of an option increases with maturity, and prices of long dated options in particular are very sensitive to small differences in the volatility of the underlying asset during the life of the option. For instance, the BSM price of a 1–year at-the-money (ATM) vanilla call is approximately 7.4% of the underlying when volatility is 20%.[27] But if volatility were 21%, the option price would increase to approximately 7.8% of the underlying. That is, a 5% relative increase in implied volatility leads to approximately a 5% relative increase in price of a 1-year ATM call.

In this section we first discuss the problems that arise when we try to extend the Taylor expansions that were introduced above to include volatility as a risk factor. The remainder of this section addresses these problems, recommending a *volatility beta mapping* approach that is similar to the price beta mapping described in Section III.5.5.5.

III.5.6.1 Vega Risk in Option Portfolios

Denote the price of a general option on S by $g(S, \sigma)$.[28] The change in option price with respect to changes in the volatility is often approximated to first order only. Then the price change of a single option is represented via its *delta–gamma–vega* approximation, and we write

$$\Delta g \approx \delta \Delta S + \tfrac{1}{2}\gamma(\Delta S)^2 + v\Delta\sigma. \tag{III.5.39}$$

We want to apply an expansion such as this to a portfolio of options.[29] If the options are all on the same underlying we can extend the approximation (III.5.37) to a *delta–gamma–vega–theta–rho approximation* of the form

$$\Delta P \approx \theta^P \Delta t + \delta^P \Delta S + \tfrac{1}{2}\gamma^P(\Delta S)^2 + \pi'_P \Delta \mathbf{r} + v'_P \Delta \boldsymbol{\sigma} \tag{III.5.40}$$

---

[27] Ignoring discounting and taking the definition of an ATM call to be that the delta is 0.5.
[28] Throughout these volumes we use the notation f for a standard European option and g for an arbitrary option that may or may not be a standard European call or put.
[29] We use the notation σ rather than θ for a market implied volatility in this section because the notation θ is used for the time sensitivity.

where $\boldsymbol{\sigma}$ is the vector of implied volatilities, one for each option. For instance, the portfolio of Example III.5.10 has the representation

$$\Delta P \approx -0.0269\Delta t - 0.6024\Delta S + 0.0532\,(\Delta S)^2$$

$$+ (0.0726, 0.1349, 0.1963, 0.0703)\begin{pmatrix}\Delta\sigma_{95,30}\\ \Delta\sigma_{105,60}\\ \Delta\sigma_{100,90}\\ \Delta\sigma_{85,180}\end{pmatrix} + (-0.0433, -0.1727, 0.2429, -0.0249)\begin{pmatrix}\Delta r_{30}\\ \Delta r_{60}\\ \Delta r_{90}\\ \Delta r_{180}\end{pmatrix}.$$

More generally, for options on several underlyings we require the portfolio's value delta, value gamma *and* value vega. We know how obtain the net position delta and gamma, and the value delta and gamma. But how do we obtain the net position vega and the value vega? The problem is that each option vega represents the sensitivity of the option value to its *own* implied volatility, and the implied volatility differs according to the strike and maturity of each option.

A typical portfolio will contain hundreds of options, of various strikes and maturities on different underlyings. This means that there many different implied volatilities that arise as risk factors. It is simply not feasible to have one volatility risk factor for every option, so somehow the delta–gamma–vega approximations for option portfolios have to find a way to reduce the number of volatility risk factors. We shall discuss this problem in subsections III.5.6.3 and III.5.6.4.

III.5.6.2 Second Order Approximations: Vanna and Volga

In the previous subsection we approximated the change in an option price $g(S, \sigma)$ with respect to changes in the volatility to *first order* only. However, a second order bivariate Taylor expansion of $g(S, \sigma)$ actually has two first order terms and three second order terms in these risk factors.

The *delta–gamma–vega–volga–vanna approximation* to the change in option price is

$$\Delta g = g(S+\varepsilon_S, \sigma+\varepsilon_\sigma) - g(S, \sigma) \approx \varepsilon_S\delta + \tfrac{1}{2}\varepsilon_S^2\gamma + \varepsilon_\sigma\nu + \tfrac{1}{2}\varepsilon_\sigma^2\eta\nu_o + \varepsilon_S\varepsilon_\sigma\nu_a. \qquad \text{(III.5.41)}$$

As above we use the subscript notation for partial derivatives with respect to the risk factors, i.e. $[\delta = g_S(S, \sigma), \gamma = g_{SS}(S, \sigma), \nu = g_\sigma(S, \sigma), \nu_o = g_{\sigma\sigma}(S, \sigma)$ and $\nu_a = g_{S\sigma}(S, \sigma)]$. Here volga, denoted ν_o, is the second order volatility sensitivity and vanna, denoted ν_a, is the second order price–volatility sensitivity. Another way of expressing (III.5.41) is to write, using the usual notation,

$$\Delta P \approx \delta\Delta S + \tfrac{1}{2}\gamma(\Delta S)^2 + \nu\,\Delta\sigma + \tfrac{1}{2}\nu_o(\Delta\sigma)^2 + \nu_a\Delta S\Delta\sigma. \qquad \text{(III.5.42)}$$

The vanna and volga are related to the vega as in (III.3.80). For instance, the vanna and volga sensitivities for the options in Example III.5.10 are calculated in that spreadsheet.

It is important to note that (III.5.42) only applies to a portfolio with *one* option. It is possible to generalize (III.5.42) to portfolios of options, as we have done for the first order mapping in (III.5.45) and (III.5.46). But how should we define the volatility risk factors and how would we compute their risk factor sensitivities? The following subsections offer some answers.

Before addressing these questions we remark that Taylor expansions for multi-asset option prices depend on two or more underlying prices and their volatilities *and correlations*. For instance, the change in price of a spread option may be approximated by expanding to second order with respect to the prices and to first order with respect to the volatilities and correlation ϱ of the two price returns:

$$\Delta P \approx \delta_1 \Delta S_1 + \delta_2 \Delta S_2 + \tfrac{1}{2} \left[\gamma_{11} (\Delta S_1)^2 + 2\gamma_{12} (\Delta S_1 \Delta S_2) + \gamma_{22} (\Delta S_2)^2 \right]$$
$$+ \nu_1 \Delta \sigma_1 + \nu_2 \Delta \sigma_2 + \psi \Delta \varrho, \qquad \text{(III.5.43)}$$

where, dropping the dependence of g on the risk factors to shorten the notation, we have $\delta_1 = g_{S_1}$, $\delta_2 = g_{S_2}$, $\gamma_{11} = g_{S_1 S_1}$, $\gamma_{12} = g_{S_1 S_2}$, $\gamma_{22} = g_{S_2 S_2}$, $\nu_1 = g_{\sigma_1}$, $\nu_2 = g_{\sigma_2}$, $\psi = g_\varrho$. In value terms, the change in price on the spread option is therefore approximated as

$$\Delta P \approx \boldsymbol{\delta}_\$ ' \mathbf{R} + \tfrac{1}{2} \mathbf{R}' \boldsymbol{\Gamma}_\$ \mathbf{R} + \boldsymbol{\nu}_\$' \Delta \boldsymbol{\sigma} + \psi_\$ \Delta \varrho, \qquad \text{(III.5.44)}$$

where the risk factor changes are

$$\mathbf{R} = \begin{pmatrix} \Delta S_1 / S_1 \\ \Delta S_2 / S_2 \end{pmatrix}, \quad \Delta \boldsymbol{\sigma} = \begin{pmatrix} \Delta \sigma_1 \\ \Delta \sigma_2 \end{pmatrix},$$

and their value sensitivities are

$$\boldsymbol{\delta}_\$ = \begin{pmatrix} \delta_1 \\ \delta_2 \end{pmatrix} \times S \times pv, \quad \boldsymbol{\Gamma}_\$ = \begin{pmatrix} \gamma_{11} & \gamma_{12} \\ \gamma_{12} & \gamma_{22} \end{pmatrix} \times S^2 \times pv, \quad \boldsymbol{\nu}_\$ = \begin{pmatrix} \nu_1 \\ \nu_2 \end{pmatrix} \times pv, \quad \psi_\$ = \psi \times pv.$$

III.5.6.3   Vega Bucketing

Suppose we want a *delta–gamma–vega–theta–rho* approximation for a portfolio of options on a single underlying. Denoting the portfolio price by P, such an approximation would take the form

$$\Delta P \approx \theta^P \Delta t + \delta^P \Delta S + \tfrac{1}{2} \gamma^P (\Delta S)^2 + \boldsymbol{\pi}_p' \Delta \mathbf{r} + \boldsymbol{\nu}_p' \Delta \boldsymbol{\sigma}, \qquad \text{(III.5.45)}$$

where $\boldsymbol{\sigma}$ is a vector of volatility risk factors and the vector $\boldsymbol{\nu}_P$ is the *net position vega*. More generally, a delta–gamma–vega–theta–rho approximation for a general portfolio of options on several underlyings is

$$\Delta P \approx \theta^\$ \Delta t + \boldsymbol{\delta}_\$' \mathbf{R} + \tfrac{1}{2} \mathbf{R}' \boldsymbol{\Gamma}_\$ \mathbf{R} + \boldsymbol{\pi}_\$' \Delta \mathbf{r} + \boldsymbol{\nu}_\$' \Delta \boldsymbol{\sigma}, \qquad \text{(III.5.46)}$$

where the vector $\boldsymbol{\nu}_\$$ is the net *value vega*, also called the *dollar vega*.

But how are the position vega in (III.5.45) and the value vega in (III.5.46) defined? Some banks employ a crude approach called *vega bucketing*. Here all the options on the *same* underlying with similar maturities are grouped together into a single maturity 'bucket'. The volatility risk factor for a given bucket is usually taken as the ATM implied volatility of the average maturity in the bucket. The sensitivity to this ATM volatility, i.e. the net position vega for that bucket and price risk factor, is calculated as the sum of the position vegas of all options in that bucket. The net value vega is simply the net position vega multiplied by the point value for that underlying.

For instance, all GBP/USD options with maturity up to 2 months could be put into the first bucket, with the 1-month ATM volatility on GBP/USD as the reference volatility; the next bucket could consist of all GBP/USD options with maturity between 2 and 4 months, with the 3-month ATM volatility on GBP/USD as the reference volatility; and so on.

This approach gives the trader a perspective on his volatility exposure, according to maturity, and it may be useful for traders who always deal in options on the same underlying. But it assumes that the implied volatilities of all options in the same bucket are perfectly correlated with the risk factor for that bucket, which is clearly not the case. Also vega bucketing becomes rather unwieldy for a large portfolio where there are many different underlying assets and with several volatility buckets for each underlying.

III.5.6.4   Volatility Beta Mapping

A simple alternative to vega bucketing which turns out to be very practical for risk assessment is to choose a small set of reference volatility risk factors for each price risk factor in the option portfolio. In the following, to keep the analysis simple, we assume that only one reference volatility risk factor is chosen for each underlying. It is straightforward to generalize this to several reference volatilities, usually a term structure of ATM volatilities or volatility indices (if they exist) for each underlying.

For instance, suppose the portfolio contains US and UK stock options. Then it is natural to choose broad market indices such as the FTSE 100 and the S&P 500 as the two price risk factors, S_1 and S_2. In that case the two volatility risk factors σ_1 and σ_2 could be two curves of ATM index implied volatilities, one for the FTSE 100 and the other for the S&P 500 index. If all the UK option implied volatilities are represented by a *single* reference volatility risk factor, its maturity should be similar to the average maturity of the UK stock options. For instance, we might take the 3-month FTSE 100 ATM volatility for σ_1. Similarly, the S&P 500 ATM volatility should have a maturity roughly equal to the average maturity of the US stock options. For instance, we might take the 6-month S&P 500 ATM volatility for σ_2.[30]

How do we obtain the net position vegas and the value vegas with respect to these volatility risk factors? For each option we first calculate a *volatility beta* with respect to the reference volatility risk factor, and for this we need some historical data on implied volatilities. Then we can use an OLS regression of the changes in the option's implied volatility on the absolute changes in the risk factor volatility. Note that we use the absolute changes, not the changes in the logarithm of the volatilities, since it is the absolute change in the implied volatility that appears in the delta–gamma–vega representation.[31]

The partial derivative of an option price with respect to volatility gives the absolute change in option price for a 1% absolute change in volatility.[32] Thus to obtain the *net position vega* for a portfolio of options the volatility beta of each option is multiplied by the position vega of the option and these are summed. That is, the net position vega is approximated as

$$v^P \approx \sum_{i=1}^{n} v_i \times \beta_i^v \times N_i, \qquad (III.5.47)$$

[30] Ignoring the forex risk.
[31] Alternatively, a more sensitive approach than OLS is to construct a time series of time varying volatility beta estimates, e.g. using EWMA or GARCH, and take the beta that is forecast for the current risk horizon. In EWMA this would be the last (i.e. current) estimate, and in GARCH it would be constructed using the GARCH covariance and variance forecasts over the risk horizon.
[32] If volatility is quoted in percentage points, e.g. 20 refers to a volatility of 0.2 (20%), we must divide the partial derivative by 100.

where N_i denotes the number of units of the underlying that the ith option contracts to buy or sell and β_i^{ν} is the volatility beta of the ith option.[33] The *value vega* is sum of the position vegas multiplied by the point value of the options.[34]

Remark on Dimension Reduction

Suppose there are n_i options on the ith underlying, for $i = 1, \ldots, k$. Thus there are n_i implied volatility risk factors for each underlying i, and this could be very large number indeed. Suppose $n_i = 100$ for some underlying asset. The volatility beta mapping allows one to map these 100 implied volatility risk factors to just m_i risk factors of representative maturities. For instance, we may take a term structure of $m_i = 10$ different ATM volatilities. However, when the number of underlyings is large we still have $k \times m_i$ volatility risk factors to contend with. For instance, with $k = 5$ underlyings, $n_i = 100$ options in each, and a term structure of $m_i = 10$ reference volatilities, we have reduced the dimension of the volatility risk factor space from 500 to 50. The next section presents a case study that illustrates how to take the volatility beta mapping methodology one step further, using principal components of the reference volatility term structure.

III.5.7 CASE STUDY: VOLATILITY RISK IN FTSE 100 OPTIONS

This study illustrates the volatility mapping of a simple portfolio of European options on the FTSE 100 index. We take a single volatility risk factor and compute the net position vega with respect to this risk factor using the volatility beta mapping described in the previous section.[35]

III.5.7.1 Estimating the Volatility Betas

Suppose that on 31 December 2005 a trader has a portfolio of simple European options on the FTSE 100 with the structure shown in Table III.5.9. Each option is for £10 per index point on the FTSE 100. The closing price of the FTSE 100 index on 30 December 2005 was 5618.8.

The continuously compounded interest rate and dividend yield data are given in Table III.5.10, the dividend yields being derived from the futures prices in Table III.5.9, and the calculations of the BSM vega and net value vega are contained in the spreadsheet for this case study. The net position vega shown in the last column is the product of the BSM vega and the value of the contracts in the underlying.

---

[33] The net position vega (III.5.47) and its associated value vega represent the volatility sensitivity to an *absolute* change of 1% in the reference implied volatility. Hence, if the reference volatility increases from 20% to 21% we would use a 1% rise (not a 5% rise) in the reference volatility to find the approximate change in portfolio value, according to the net position vega.
[34] Note that vega is already in the correct units of measurement of the underlying price. Hence, we do not need to multiply by the price of the underlying contract to obtain the value vega.
[35] For large portfolios and for portfolios of options on several underlyings, it may be preferable to apply the volatility beta method using several volatility risk factors because this reduces the model risk. In that case we compute a net vega with respect to each reference volatility.

Table III.5.9   A portfolio of options on FTSE 100

Name	Type	Strike	Maturity	Futures prices	Number of options
Option A	Long call	4925	1 month	5628	200
Option B	Long put	5725	3 month	5618	100
Option C	Long put	5475	5 month	5625	50

Table III.5.10   Net vega of the options in Table III.5.9

Name	Implied volatility	LIBOR	Dividend	BSM vega	Net value vega
Option A	19.50%	4.41%	2.45%	0.363	£726
Option B	10.55%	4.36%	4.42%	10.376	£10,376
Option C	11.57%	4.31%	4.04%	13.031	£6,515

We now take some time series data on implied volatilities of the relevant strikes and maturities and choose the 3-month ATM volatility on the FTSE 100 for the volatility risk factor. The data were obtained from Euronext LIFFE. Since options have fixed expiry dates, the time series of constant maturity implied volatilities were found by linearly interpolating between the implied variances of the two adjacent maturities. These data are shown in Figure III.5.4. Note that option A is very in-the-money by the end of the sample, with a strike of 4925 when the 1 month futures price was 5628 on 30 December 2005. Thus it has a much higher implied volatility than the other two options during the latter part of the sample.

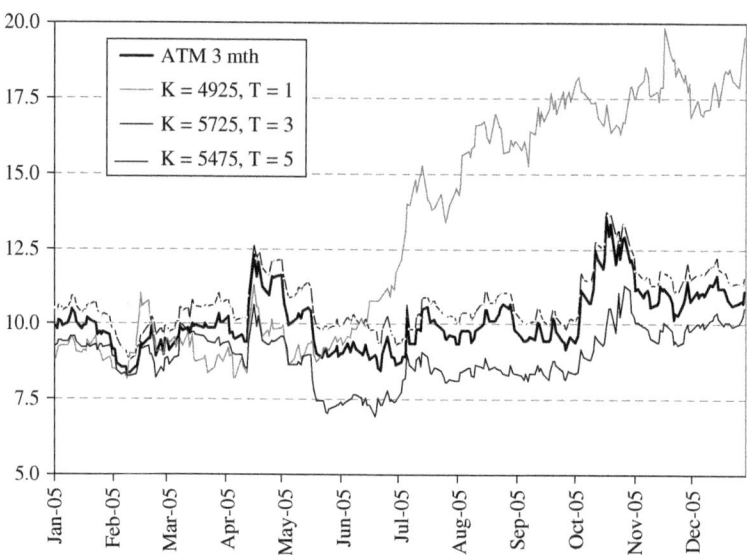

Figure III.5.4   Three-month ATM and fixed strike implied volatilities of the FTSE 100 index

Using these data, we now estimate exponentially weighted moving average (EWMA) volatility betas with respect to the 3-month ATM volatility on the FTSE 100, following the

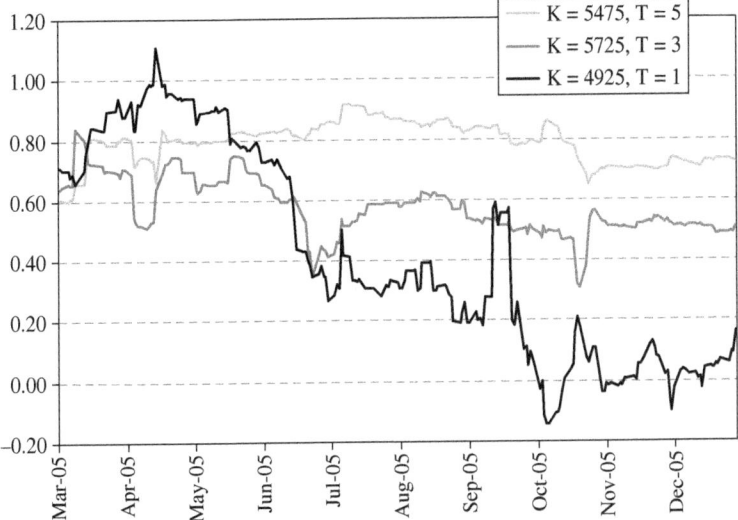

Figure III.5.5   EWMA volatility betas ($\lambda = 0.95$) with respect to the 3-month ATM implied volatilities of the FTSE 100 index

method described in Section II.1.2.3. A value of 0.95 was chosen for the smoothing constant, and the resulting betas are shown in Figure III.5.5. The volatility beta of option A decreases as this option moves further way from ATM over time. The same is true for the other two options, although the effect is less noticeable in the figure.

Given the values of the volatility betas on 30 December 2005, Table III.5.11 shows the net value vega of the portfolio with respect to the reference implied volatility. This is based on formula (III.5.47). In the table we compare the net position vega based on these EWMA volatility betas, with the OLS volatility betas that are computed using the ratio of equally weighted average covariance and variance estimates, using (a) 1 year and (b) 3 months of data. We also show the EWMA net value vegas for different values of the smoothing constant.

Table III.5.11   Net value vega on 3-month FTSE 100 ATM volatility

	Value vega	OLS (1 year)	OLS (3 months)	EWMA ($\lambda = 0.99$)	EWMA ($\lambda = 0.98$)	EWMA ($\lambda = 0.95$)
Option A	£726	0.373	0.039	0.179	0.117	0.162
Option B	£10,376	0.565	0.488	0.522	0.513	0.508
Option C	£6,515	0.770	0.700	0.748	0.733	0.723
Net value vega		£11,143	£9,717	£10,426	£10,180	£10,104

The net value vega provides an approximation to the increase in portfolio value when the 3-month ATM volatility of the FTSE 100 increases by 1%, but the price of the FTSE 100 futures remains fixed. The estimates in Table III.5.11 differ considerably, so there is a substantial error due to *model risk*. But at least, with a proper model, we can quantify this risk.

III.5.7.2   Model Risk of Volatility Mapping

The use of one volatility risk factor for each price risk factor has the great advantage that it considerably reduces the number of volatility risk factors in the multivariate delta–gamma–vega approximation to the portfolio's P&L. We no longer need to use a different implied volatility for each option in the portfolio as a risk factor, and in our risk factor mapping we have the same number of volatility factors as we have price risk factors.

However, the differences in our results above when different estimations are used, indicate a substantial model risk with the volatility beta approach. Firstly, the volatility beta that is used to weight the option vega in the net (position or dollar) vega only captures the systematic part of the volatility risk. An option's implied volatility will not be perfectly correlated with the risk factor volatility. The lower the correlation between the option's implied volatility and the risk factor volatility, the greater the specific volatility risk, i.e. the volatility risk that is being ignored by this approach. Hence, taking only one risk factor volatility for each price risk factor means that a certain amount of specific volatility risk is introduced to the delta–gamma–vega approximation.

Secondly, it is may be difficult to obtain time series data on constant maturity, fixed strike options. When the options are on major stock indices or foreign exchange rates such data should be relatively easy to obtain, as we have done above, but for options on other underlyings, e.g. for an option on an individual stock, it may be quite a challenge to obtain a time series of recent implied volatilities from which to estimate the volatility beta.[36]

Thirdly, the estimate of the volatility beta will depend on the data used and on the estimation methodology. The case study in the previous section employed time series data on the reference volatility and all the implied volatilities in the portfolio, applying OLS regression to obtain the volatility beta for each option. But the OLS estimate depended very much on the sample period used in the regression. Also, we could have estimated the beta using a different statistical technique, for instance have also estimated EWMA volatility betas. These reflect the current market conditions better than the OLS betas but the choice of smoothing constant is *ad hoc*.

The reader must appreciate that a limitation of *any* vega netting method is that it introduces significant model risk to the risk model. The vega bucketing method has more model risk than the volatility beta approach to netting vega, and one of the major problems with vega bucketing is that its model risk is impossible to quantify. However, we can quantify and control the model risk using the volatility beta mapping approach. To reduce the model risk we may consider the following:

- The OLS estimates are based on an arbitrary data period and the EWMA estimates are based on an *ad hoc* choice of smoothing constant. But a bivariate GARCH model of the hedge ratio circumvents this type of model risk because there are statistical tests for choosing the best model and obtaining optimal parameter estimates.
- The volatility beta approach described above could capture more specific volatility risk if *more than one* volatility risk factor were used for each price risk factor, as described in the next subsection.

---

[36] However, daily historical data on listed options are available from exchanges.

III.5.7.3   Mapping to Term Structures of Volatility Indices

Term structures of volatility indices provide a highly correlated curve of volatility risk factors, in much the same way as market interest rates constitute a curve of risk factors for cash flow portfolios. Hence, volatility indices of different maturities are ideal volatility risk factors when vegas are netted using volatility beta mapping.

Suppose that a portfolio of options with various maturities up to 2 years has been mapped to a single price risk factor, the Eurostoxx 50 index. Then instead of using only the 30-day Vstoxx index as volatility risk factor we might prefer to use all the available Vstoxx volatility indices as volatility risk factors, i.e. with maturities 1, 2, 3, 6, 9, 12, 18 and 24 months. Note that each stock option should be mapped to only one of these factors, otherwise high collinearity between these risk factors will make it difficult to identify the different volatility betas of an option. Hence, we might map all options with maturity up to 1.5 months to the 1-month Vstoxx index, all options with maturity 1.5–2.5 months to the 2-month Vstoxx index, and so on.

This type of mapping reduces the model risk associated with volatility mapping in two ways:

- *Matching strikes.* A volatility index at a given maturity is the square root of a weighted average of implied variances at that maturity, with weights being inversely proportional to the square of the strike of the option. Thus, rather than just the ATM volatility, the volatility index captures the whole volatility smile.
- *Matching maturities.* Specific risk may be significant when, for instance, a 1-month option is mapped to a 6-month ATM volatility risk factor. But here we use a term structure of volatility indices at a set of standard maturities.

III.5.7.4   Using PCA with Volatility Betas

Suppose that we have performed a volatility beta mapping to a term structure of volatility indices, as outlined in the previous section. We have a set of highly collinear volatility risk factors for our portfolio, and we know the net position vega or value vega with respect to each of these risk factors. At this stage it becomes natural to use principal component analysis (PCA) to reduce the large collinear set of volatility risk factors to a smaller and orthogonal set of risk factors.

The general PCA approach should be very familiar to readers now, since it has been used in many of the case studies included in *Market Risk Analysis*, albeit for different purposes. In this section we:

(i) obtain historical data on the term structure of reference implied volatilities;
(ii) obtain the equally weighted covariance matrix of the one-period changes in these implied volatilities;
(iii) find the first three eigenvectors of this matrix and hence obtain the first three principal components which are the new reference volatility risk factors;
(iv) multiply the value vega by the implied volatility factor weight;
(v) sum up over all options (and adjust for any normalization in the PCA) to obtain the net vega with respect to the jth volatility risk factor, for $j = 1, 2, 3$.

This process will be illustrated by considering the term structure of Vftse implied volatility indices measured daily from 3 January 2006 to 30 December 2006, and shown in

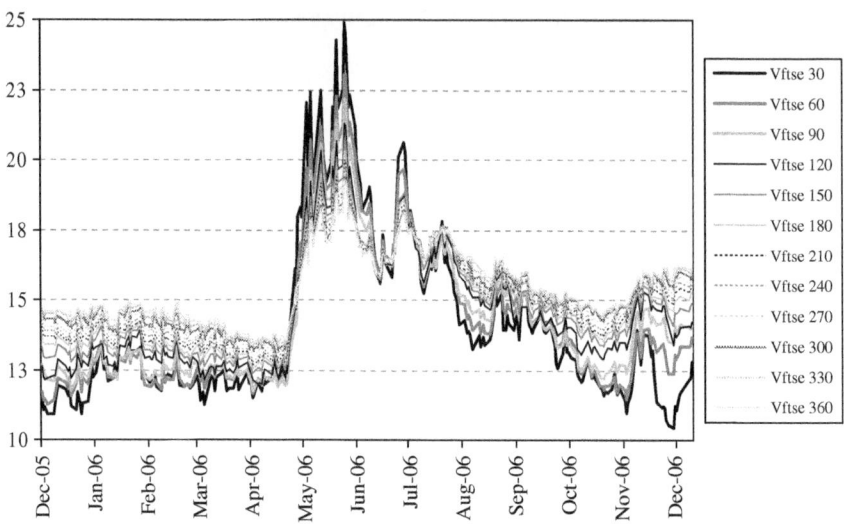

Figure III.5.6   Vftse term structure during 2006

Figure III.5.6. The volatility term structure is sloping upward most of the time, except during the period of high volatility during May 2006 when the FTSE 100 index fell dramatically before returning to a long upward trend.

Table III.5.12   Net vegas, eigenvalues and normalized eigenvectors

| | | Eigenvalues | | | | |
	1	2	3	4	5	6
Value	2.52	0.09	0.03	0.02	0.01	0.01
% Variation explained	93.72%	3.39%	1.18%	0.65%	0.55%	0.22%
Cumulative variation	93.72%	97.11%	98.29%	98.95%	99.49%	99.72%

| Portfolio Net value vegas | | Eigenvectors | | | | |
	w1	w2	w3	w4	w5	w6
£1,025	Vftse 30	0.5114	0.7133	0.3324	0.0453	0.3278	0.0922
£575	Vftse 60	0.3863	0.1817	−0.1499	−0.3151	−0.6714	−0.3295
£1,000	Vftse 90	0.3370	0.0000	−0.4081	0.1373	−0.3409	0.5551
£1,500	Vftse 120	0.3190	−0.1521	−0.5116	0.3797	0.3467	0.0213
£1,350	Vftse 150	0.2862	−0.1708	−0.2297	0.0371	0.2338	−0.3554
£1,450	Vftse 180	0.2575	−0.2108	−0.0347	−0.2668	0.1813	−0.3217
£1,800	Vftse 210	0.2325	−0.2593	0.0687	−0.3984	0.1804	−0.0523
£1,775	Vftse 240	0.2083	−0.2840	0.1828	−0.3411	0.1036	0.2742
£2,050	Vftse 270	0.1907	−0.2785	0.2498	−0.1035	0.0004	0.3400
£2,450	Vftse 300	0.1798	−0.2532	0.3149	0.1578	−0.1174	0.1975
£2,125	Vftse 330	0.1750	−0.2093	0.3188	0.3824	−0.1726	−0.1222
£2,225	Vftse 360	0.1703	−0.1678	0.2889	0.4541	−0.1757	−0.3116

Table III.5.12 reports the first six eigenvalues and the corresponding (normalized) eigenvectors of the covariance matrix on the absolute changes in the volatility indices.

The eigenvalues tell us that the first three principal components together explain over 98% of the total variation, and with six components we could explain almost 100% of the variation in the FTSE volatility indices.

Figure III.5.7 depicts the first three eigenvectors in Table III.5.12. They display the usual 'trend–tilt–curvature' features that we expect in any highly correlated ordered system, except that the first component does not represent a parallel shift: rather, the short term volatilities move more than the long term volatilities.

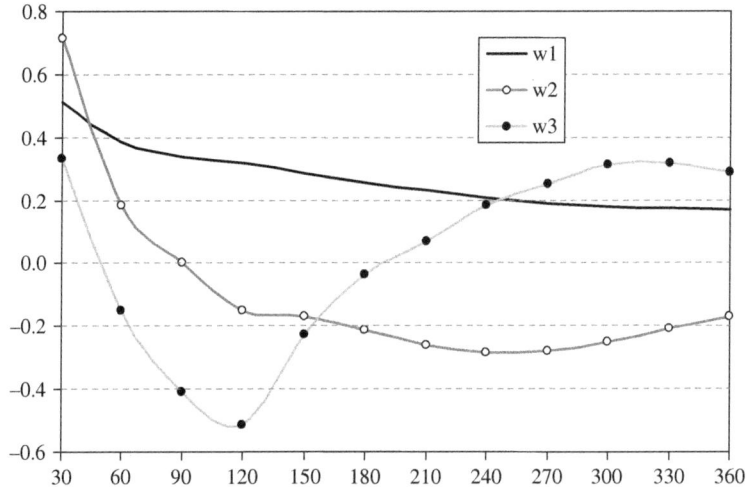

Figure III.5.7   Factor weights on the first three principal components

Now consider a large portfolio of options on UK stocks (or stock indices) that has already been mapped to the Vftse indices using the volatility beta methodology explained above. The value vegas of the portfolio with respect to each reference volatility risk factor are assumed known, and these are given in the first column of Table III.5.12. We now use the eigenvectors on the first three principal components to compute a net value vega with respect to the first three principal component risk factors. The net vega with respect to the ith PC is the dot product $\mathbf{w}'_i \mathbf{v}$, where $\mathbf{w}_i$ is the ith eigenvector and $\mathbf{v}$ is the vector of value vegas with respect to the Vftse indices.

Using this dot product the value vega with respect to P_1, the first principal component, is £4692, as shown in the spreadsheet for this case study.[37] The vegas with respect to the other components are calculated similarly, giving the following vega mapping of the option portfolio P&L due to volatility risk factors alone:

$$P\&L = 4692\,P_1 - 2909\,P_2 + 1770\,P_3. \tag{III.5.48}$$

The above P&L gives the change in portfolio value when the principal components change by 1%. For instance, if the first component, corresponding to a roughly parallel shift in volatility indices of all maturities, increased by 1% but the other principal components and the underlying price remained fixed then the portfolio value would increase by £4692.

---

[37] Note that there is no requirement that the vega with respect to a principal component implied volatility factor be positive. Indeed in the above the sensitivities with respect to the second PC is negative.

III.5.8   SUMMARY AND CONCLUSIONS

This chapter began by providing an overview of the risk factors and risk factor sensitivities of portfolios containing different types of assets and financial instruments. Since equity portfolios require many econometric techniques for their analysis, they were best dealt with in Volume II. As a result there were two distinct aims in this chapter. The first was to cover the analysis of portfolios that can be represented by a sequence of cash flows, including portfolios of loans, bonds, notes, FRAs and swaps, and the interest rate component of futures and forward positions. The second was to explain how we map large portfolios of options to their main risk factors.

Cash flows on a large portfolio of interest rate sensitive instruments occur at many different times in the future. To analyse the risk characteristics of the portfolio we map its cash flows to an equivalent set of cash flows occurring at a fixed set of times in the future, which we call the *vertices* of the cash flow map. The portfolio's risk factors are the interest rates at these maturities, and we use constant maturity interest rate time series data to assess the risk of the portfolio. The portfolio's sensitivities to the risk factors are summarized by a PV01 vector, representing the PV01 of the mapped cash flow at each vertex.

There are a number of different ways to map cash flows. It is normal to ensure that the present value of the mapped cash flows is the same as the present value of the original cash flows. In addition, a cash flow mapping can keep the duration, PV01 and volatility of the portfolio invariant. We showed that if present value and duration are kept constant under the cash flow map, then so is the PV01. The mapped cash flow provides a linear representation of a portfolio of interest rate sensitive instruments as a weighted sum of its risk factors, with weights given by the PV01 vector and the risk factors being a set of constant maturity zero coupon market interest rates. Note that the PV01 vector has captured the non-linearity in the price–yield relationship. Since the PV01 vector is the basis point sensitivity to absolute changes in interest rates, we measure the volatility of absolute changes in zero coupon rates in basis point terms. Their covariance matrix is also expressed in basis point terms.

Option portfolio mapping consists of representing the portfolio P&L as the change in a risk factor multiplied by the risk factor's sensitivity, summed over all risk factors. Option traders require mapping of their portfolios to assess their risks relative to the major risk factors, especially with respect to the underlying price and the volatility. Very often they operate under strict limits on their net delta, gamma and vega relative to the underlying prices or indices and the reference volatilities of their trading universe. Traders operating under such limits use the mappings described in this chapter to assess the effect of a trade on their limits.

Some traders operate under a value-at-risk limit rather than individual limits on their net risk factor sensitivities. Sensitivity limits only measure the risk relative to the risk factor and not the risk of the factor itself. Also, individual delta, gamma and vega limits do not take into account the correlation between the price and the volatility risk factors. By contrast, VaR limits *do* account for the volatilities and correlations of the risk factors, and this is the reason for their growing popularity. Traders operating under VaR limits need to know the VaR impact of a proposed trade, and they need to know this very quickly before the opportunity to trade has passed. But complete revaluation of the portfolio VaR may take too much time. Large portfolios can have a huge number of risk factors. To measure the risk of such a portfolio almost always requires simulations and the time taken for these simulations increases enormously as the number of risk factors grows. Therefore we must find ways to reduce the number of risk factors with the minimum possible loss of accuracy to develop a risk measurement framework for large portfolios.

To approximate the P&L of a portfolio of options, possibly on several different underlyings, one has to aggregate the option's sensitivities or 'Greeks'. When the portfolio has only one underlying price risk factor the *position* Greeks are additive. But when the portfolio has more than one underlying price risk factor only the *value* Greeks are additive. Also when value Greeks are used in the risk factor mapping the P&L of the portfolio is expressed in terms of *percentage* returns on price risk factors but *absolute* returns on volatility and interest rates.

Portfolios of stock options have one underlying price risk factor for each stock. But it is possible to reduce the number of underlying price risk factors to a single index price risk factor by employing a beta mapping methodology. Either the stock betas are taken from equity analysis, or historical data on a stock return and on the index returns are used to estimate the stock's beta, as described in Section II.1.2. The stock beta can then be used to transform the delta and gamma of each stock into a delta and gamma relative to the index price. We have provided an example of implementing this method for a portfolio of stock options but there is no reason why a similar methodology should not be applied to other option portfolios such as portfolios of bond options.

Every single option has its own implied volatility as a risk factor! To reduce the dimension of the volatility risk factor space, in this chapter we show how to use a 'reference' term structure of volatilities, such as ATM volatilities or volatility indices of different maturities, for the risk factors, and how to compute the vegas with respect to this reference term structure using volatility beta mapping. This technique is very similar to the price beta mapping of stock option portfolios. A detailed case study explained how to implement a volatility beta mapping for a portfolio of options. These options can be European or American and may have complex path dependencies. All we need to know are the Greeks of each option. By contrast with the crude *vega bucketing* techniques employed by some institutions, the volatility beta mapping approach has the advantage that both the model risk and the specific risk associated with the mapping can be assessed and managed.

The mapping of an option portfolio to its risk factors should be contrasted with the mapping of a linear portfolio (i.e. a portfolio of cash or futures in shares, bonds and swaps, forex rates or commodities) to its risk factors. The P&L distribution of a linear portfolio can be computed directly from a current weighted historical series on P&L, and the primary aim of risk factor mapping is to stress-test portfolios and to allocate capital. However, the 'Greeks' approximations that we use to map option portfolios are not applicable when risk factor values change by more than a small amount. Hence, they are of questionable validity for stress testing. The main uses of option portfolio mapping via Taylor approximations are for monitoring traders' limits, to facilitate fast risk limit calculations and to attribute risk to different sources.

References

Aït-Sahalia, Y. and Lo, A. (1998) Nonparametric estimation of state-price densities implicit in financial asset prices. *Journal of Finance* 53, 499–547.

Alexander, C. (2001) *Market Models: A Guide to Data Analysis*. John Wiley & Sons, Ltd, Chichester

Alexander, C. (2003) Common correlation and calibrating the lognormal forward rate model. *Wilmott*, March, 68–78.

Alexander, C. (2004) Normal mixture diffusion with uncertain volatility: Modelling short and long term smile effects. *Journal of Banking and Finance* 28(12), 2957–2980.

Alexander, C. and Barbosa, A. (2007) Effectiveness of minimum variance hedging. *Journal of Portfolio Management* 33(2), 46–59

Alexander, C. and Barbosa, A. (2008) Hedging exchange traded funds. *Journal of Banking and Finance* 32(2), 326–337.

Alexander, C. and Lazar, E. (2005) On the continuous limit of GARCH. ICMA Centre Discussion Papers in Finance DP2005-13.

Alexander, C. and Lazar, E. (2008a) Asymmetries and volatility regimes in the European equity markets. Revised version of ICMA Centre Discussion Papers in Finance DP2005-14.

Alexander, C. and Lazar, E. (2008b) Markov switching GARCH diffusion. ICMA Centre Discussion Papers in Finance DP2008-01.

Alexander, C. and Leontsinis, S. (2008) The Vftse term structure and applications to vega mapping. ICMA Centre Discussion Papers in Finance.

Alexander, C. and Lvov, D. (2003) Statistical properties of forward Libor rates. ICMA Centre Discussion Papers in Finance DP2003-03.

Alexander, C. and Nogueira, L. (2004) Hedging with stochastic and local volatility. ICMA Discussion Papers in Finance 2004-11.

Alexander, C. and Nogueira, L. (2007a) Model-free hedge ratios and scale invariant models. *Journal of Banking and Finance* 31(6), 1839–1861.

Alexander, C. and Nogueira, L. (2007b) Price hedge ratios for homogeneous claims on tradable assets. *Quantitative Finance* 7(5), 473–479.

Alexander, C. and Nogueira, L. (2008) Stochastic local volatility. ICMA Discussion Papers in Finance DP2008-02.

Alexander, C. and Venkatramanan, A. (2007) Analytic approximations for spread options. ICMA Centre Discussion Papers in Finance DP2007-11.

Alexander, C. and Venkatramanan, A. (2008a) Commodity options. In F.J. Fabozzi, R. Füss and D.G. Kaiser (eds), *Handbook of Commodity Investing*. John Wiley & Sons, Ltd, Chichester. To appear.

Alexander, C. and Venkatramanan, A. (2008b) Analytic approximations for multi-asset options. ICMA Centre Discussion Papers in Finance.

Alizadeh, A. and Nomikos, N. (2004) A Markov regime switching approach for hedging stock indices. *Journal of Futures Markets* 24(7), 649–674.

Altıntığ, Z.A. and Butler, A.W. (2005) Are they still called late? The effect of notice period on calls of convertible bonds. *Journal of Applied Corporate Finance* 11, 337–350.

Andersen, L. and Buffum, D. (2004) Calibration and implementation of convertible bond models. *Journal of Computational Finance* 7(2), 1–34.

Andersen, L.B.G. and Andreasen, J. (2000) Jump-diffusion processes: Volatility smile fitting and numerical methods For option pricing. *Review of Derivatives Research* 4(3), 231–262.

Andersen, T.G., Benzoni, L. and Lund, J. (2002) An empirical investigation of continuous-time equity return models. *Journal of Finance* 57(3), 1239–1284.

Anderson, R.W. and Danthine, J.P. (1981) Cross hedging. *Journal of Political Economy* 89(6), 1182–1196.

Andreson, N. and Sleath, J. (1999) New estimates of the UK real and nominal yield curves. *Bank of England Quarterly Bulletin* 39, 384–392.

Arrow, K. (1964) The role of securities in the optimal allocation of risk bearing. *Review of Economic Studies* 31, 91–96.

Asquith, P. and Mullins, D. (1991) Convertible debt: corporate call policy and voluntary conversion. *Journal of Finance* 46, 1273–1289.

Asquith, P. (1995) Convertible bonds are not called late. *Journal of Finance* 50, 1273–1289.

Avellaneda, M., Friedman, C., Holmes, R. and Samperi, D. (1997) Calibrating volatility surfaces via relative entropy minimization. *Applied Mathematical Finance* 4, 37–64.

Ayache, E., Forsyth, P.A. and Vetzal, K.R. (2003) Valuation of convertible bonds with credit risk. *Journal of Derivatives* 11(1), 9–29.

Bachelier, L. (2006) *Louis Bachelier's Theory of Speculation: The Origins of Modern Finance*, translation and introduction by M. Davis and A. Etheridge. Princeton University Press, Princeton, NJ.

Baillie, R. and Myers, R. (1991) Bivariate GARCH estimation of the optimal commodity futures hedge. *Journal of Applied Econometrics* 6(2), 109–124.

Bakshi, G and Kapadia, N. (2003) Delta-hedged gains and the negative market volatility risk premium. *Review of Financial Studies* 16(2) , 527–566.

Bakshi, G., Cao, C. and Chen, Z. (1997) Empirical performance of alternative option pricing models. *Journal of Finance* 52, 2003–2049.

Bates, D.S. (1996) Jumps and stochastic volatility: Exchange rate processes implicit in Deutsche Mark options. *Review of Financial Studies* 9, 69–107.

Bates, D.S. (2003) Empirical option pricing: A retrospection. *Journal of Econometrics* 116, 387–404.

Bates, D.S. (2005) Hedging the smirk. *Financial Research Letters* 2(4), 195–200.

Baxter, M. and Rennie, A. (1996) *Financial Calculus: An Introduction to Derivative Pricing*. Cambridge University Press, Cambridge.

Beaglehole, D., Chebanier, A. (2002) Mean Reversion with a Smile. *Risk*, 15(4), 95–98.

Bermudez, A. and N. Webber. (2003) An asset based model of defaultable convertible bonds with endogenised recovery. Working Paper, Cass Business School, City University, London.

Bhattacharya, A., Sekhar, A. and Fabozzi, F. (2006) Incorporating the dynamic link between mortgage and treasury markets in pricing and hedging MBS. *Journal of Fixed Income* 16(2).

Black, F. and Scholes, M. (1973) The pricing of options and corporate liabilities. *Journal of Political Economy* 81, 637–659.

Bollerslev, T. (1986) Generalised autoregressive conditional heteroscedasticity. *Journal of Econometrics* 31, 307–327.

Bouchouev, I. and Isakov, V. (1997) The inverse problem of option pricing. *Inverse Problems*, 13(5), L11–17.

Bouchouev, I. and Isakov, V. (1999) Uniqueness, stability and numerical methods for the inverse problem that arises in financial markets. *Inverse Problems*, 15, 95–116.

Brace, A., Gatarek, D. and Musiela, M. (1997) The market model of interest rate dynamics. *Mathematical Finance*, 7, 127–155.

Breeden, D. and Litzenberger, R. (1978) Prices of state-contingent claims implicit in option prices. *Journal of Business*, 51, 621–651.

Brigo, D. and Mercurio, F. (2001) *Interest Rate Models: Theory and Practice*. Springer-Verlag, Berlin.

Brigo, D. and Mercurio, F. (2002) Lognormal-mixture dynamics and calibration to market volatility smiles. *International Journal of Theoretical and Applied Finance* 5(4), 427–446.

Brigo, D., Mercurio, F. and Rapisarda, F. (2004) Connecting univariate smiles and basket dynamics. Available from http://citeseer.ist.psu.edu/669984.html (accessed December 2007).

Broadie, M., Chrenov, M. and Johannes, M. (2007) Model specification and risk premia: Evidence from futures options. *Journal of Finance* 62(3), 1453–1490.

Brooks, C., Henry, O.T. and Persand, G. (2002) The effect of asymmetries on optimal hedge ratios. *Journal of Business* 75, 333–352.

Brown, G. and Randall, C. (1999) If the skew fits. *Risk* 12(4), 62–65.

Buraschi, A. and Jackwerth, J. (2001) The price of a smile: Hedging and spanning in option markets. *Review of Financial Studies* 14, 495–527.

Butler, A. (2002) Revisiting optimal call policy for convertibles. *Financial Analysts Journal* 58(1), 50–55.

Campbell, C., Ederington, L. and Vankudre, P. (1991) Tax shields, sample selection bias, and the information content of convertible bond calls. *Journal of Finance* 46, 1291–1324.

Carr, P. and Wu, L. (2007) Variance risk premia. *Review of Financial Studies*. Forthcoming

Carr, P., Geman, H., Madan, D. and Yor, M. (2004) From local volatility to local Lévy models. *Quantitative Finance* 4, 581–588.

Carr, P., Geman, H., Madan, D. and Yor, M. (2007) Self decomposability and option pricing. *Mathematical Finance* 17(1), 31–57.

Cecchetti, S.G., Cumby, R.E. and Figlewski, S. (1988) Estimation of optimal futures hedge. *Review of Economics and Statistics* 70, 623–630.

Chan, W. and D. Young. (2006) Jumping Hedges: An Examination of Movements in Copper Spot and Futures Markets. The *Journal of Futures Markets* 26. 2. 169–188.

Chen, F. and C. Sutcliffe. (2007) Better Cross Hedges with Composite Hedging? Hedging Equity Portfoloios Using Financial and Commodity Futures. *ICMA Discussion Papers in Finance*, DP2007-04

Chen, S., Lee, C. and Shrestha, K. (2003) Futures hedge ratios: A review. *Quarterly Review of Economics and Finance*, 43, 433–465.

Cheung, C. S., Kwan, C. C. Y. and Yip, P. C. Y. (1990) The hedging effectiveness of options and futures: A mean-Gini approach. *Journal of Futures Markets* 10, 61–74.

Choudhry, T. (2004) The hedging effectiveness of constant and time-varying hedge ratios using three Pacific Basin stock futures. *International Review of Economics and Finance* 13, 371–385.

Choudhry, M. (2005) *Corporate Bond Markets: Instruments and Applications*. John Wiley & Sons (Asia) Pte Ltd, Singapore.

Choudhry, M. (2006) *An Introduction to Bond Markets*, 3rd edition. John Wiley & Sons, Ltd, Chichester.

Choudhry, T. (2003) Short-run derivations and optimal hedge ratio: Evidence from stock futures. *Journal of Multinational Financial Management* 13(2), 171–192.

Chu, Q.C. and Hsieh, W.G. (2002) Pricing efficiency of the S&P 500 index market: Evidence from the Standard & Poors depositary receipts. *Journal of Futures Markets* 22, 877–900.

Chu, Q.C., Hsieh, W.G. and Tse, Y. (1999) Price discovery on the S&P 500 index markets: An analysis of spot index, index futures, and SPDRs. *International Review of Financial Analysis* 8, 21–34.

Coleman, T. F., Li, Y. and Verma, A. (1999) Reconstructing the unknown local volatility function. *Journal of Computational Finance* 2(3), 77–102.

Coleman, T., Kim, Y., Li, Y. and Verma, A. (2001) Dynamic hedging with a deterministic local volatility function model. *Journal of Risk* 4(1), 63–89.

Constantinides, G.M. and Grundy, B.D. (1987) Call and conversion of convertible corporate bonds: Theory and evidence. Working Paper, Graduate School of Business, University of Chicago.

Cont, R. and Tankov, P. (2004) *Financial Modelling with Jump Processes*. Chapman & Hall/CRC, Boca Raton, FL.

Copeland, L. and Zhu, Y. (2006) Hedging effectiveness in the index futures market. Working Paper, Cardiff Business School.

Corradi, V. (2000) Reconsidering the continuous time limit of the GARCH(1,1) process. *Journal of Econometrics* 96, 145–153.

Cox, J.C. (1975) Notes on option pricing I: Constant elasticity of variance diffusions. Working Paper, Stanford University.

Cox, J., Ingersoll, J. and Ross, S. (1985) A theory of the term structure of interest rates. *Econometrica* 53, 385–407.

Cox J. and Ross, S. (1976) The valuation of options for alternative stochastic processes. *Journal of Financial Economics*, 3, 145–166.

Cox, J.C., Ross, S.A. and Rubinstein, M. (1979) Option pricing: A simplified approach. *Journal of Financial Economics* 7, 229–263.

Cremers, J.-H., Kritzman, M. and Page, S. (2004) Portfolio formation with higher moments and plausible utility. Revere Street Working Paper Series in Financial Economics 272-12.

Dark, J. (2004) Long term hedging of the Australian All Ordinaries index using a bivariate error correction FIGARCH model. Business and Economics Working Paper 2004-07, Monash University.

Das, S. and Sundaram, R. (1999) Of smiles and smirks: A term-structure perspective. *Journal of Financial and Quantitative Analysis* 34, 211–230.

Davis, M. and Lischka, F.R. (1999) Convertible bonds with market risk and credit risk. Research Report, Tokyo-Mitsubishi International PLC.

Debreu, G. (1959) *Theory of Value*. John Wiley & Sons, Inc., New York.

Demeterfi, K., Derman, E., Kamal, A. and Zou, J. (1999) More than you ever wanted to know about volatility swaps. Goldman Sachs Quantitative Research Notes.

Derman, E. (1994) Valuing convertible bonds as derivatives. Quantitative Strategies Research Notes, Goldman Sachs, New York.

Derman, E. (1999) Volatility regimes. *Risk* 12(4), 55–59.

Derman, E. and Kani, I. (1994) Riding on a smile. *Risk*, 7(2), 32–39

Derman, E. and Kani, I. (1998) Stochastic implied trees: Arbitrage pricing with stochastic term and strike structure of volatility. *International Journal of Theoretical and Applied Finance* 1(1), 61–110.

Derman, E. and Kamal, M. (1997) The patterns of change in implied index volatilities. Quantitative Strategies Research Notes, Goldman Sachs.

Dumas, B., Fleming, F. and Whaley, R. (1998) Implied volatility functions: Empirical tests. *Journal of Finance* 53(6), 2059–2106.

Dunn, K. and Eades, K. (1984) Voluntary conversion of convertible securities and the optimal call strategy. *Journal of Financial Economics* 23, 273–301.

Dupire, B. (1994) Pricing with a smile. *Risk*, 7(1), 18–20

Dupire, B. (1996) A unified theory of volatility. Working Paper, later published in P. Carr (ed.), *Derivatives Pricing: The Classic Collection*. Risk Books, London (2004).

Eberlein, E. and Madan, D. (2008) Sato processes and the valuation of structured products. *Quantitative Finance*. To appear.

Ederington L.H. (1979) The hedging performance of the new futures market. *Journal of Finance* 34(1), 157–170.

Eftekhari, B. (1998) Lower partial moment hedge ratios. *Applied Financial Economics* 8, 645–652.

El Karoui, N., Peng, S. and Quenez, M. (1997) Backward stochastic differential equations in finance. *Mathematical Finance* 7, 1–71.

Engle, R.F. (1982). Autoregressive conditional heteroscedasticity with estimates of the variance of UK inflation. *Econometrica* 50, 987–1007.

Eraker, B., Johannes, M. and Polson, N. (2003) The impact of jumps in volatility and returns. *Journal of Finance* 58(3), 1269–1300.

Fabozzi, F. (2002) *The Handbook of Financial Instruments*. John Wiley & Sons, Inc., New York.

Fabozzi, F. (ed.) (2005) *Handbook of Fixed Income Securities*, 7th edition. McGraw-Hill, New York.

Fengler, M., Härdle, W. and Villa, C. (2003) The dynamics of implied volatilities: A common principal component approach. *Review of Derivatives Research* 6, 179–202.

Figlewski, S. (1984) Hedging performance and basis risk in stock index futures. *Journal of Finance* 39, 657–669.

Fisher, M., Nychka, D. and Zervos, D. (1995) Fitting the term structure of interest rates with smoothing splines. Finance and Economics Discussion Series 95-1, Federal Reserve Board.

Flavell, R. (2002) *Swaps and Other Derivatives*. John Wiley & Sons, Ltd, Chichester.

Floros, C. and Vougas, D. (2004) Hedge ratios in Greek stock index futures market. *Applied Financial Economics* 14(15), 1125–1136.

Garbade, K.D. and Silber, W.L. (1983) Price movement and price discovery in futures and cash markets. *Review of Economics and Statistics* 65, 289–297.

Gatheral, J. (2006) *The Volatility Surface: A Practitioner's Guide*. John Wiley & Sons, Inc., Hoboken, NJ.

Geppert, J.M. (1995) A statistical model for the relationship between futures contract hedging effectiveness and investment horizon length. *Journal of Futures Markets* 15(7), 507–536.

Ghosh, A. (1993) Cointegration and error correction models: Intertemporal causality between index and futures prices. *Journal of Futures Markets* 13(2), 193–198.

Graham, D. and Jennings, R. (1987) Systematic risk, dividend yield and the hedging performance of stock index futures. *Journal of Futures Markets* 7(1), 1–13.

Grau, A.J., Forsyth, P.A. and Vetzal, K.R. (2003) Convertible bonds with call notice periods. Working Paper, University of Waterloo.

Grimwood, R. and Hodges, S. (2002) The valuation of convertible bonds: A study of alternative pricing models. Preprint, Financial Options Research Centre, Warwick Business School.

Grünwald, B. and Trautmann, S. (1996) Option hedging in the presence of jump risk. Mimeo. Available from http://citeseer.ist.psu.edu/286064.html.

Gurkaynak, R.S., Sack, B. and Wright, J.H. (2006) The U.S. Treasury yield curve: 1961 to the present. Federal Reserve Board Finance and Economics Discussion Series 2006-28.

Gyöngy, I. (1986) Mimicking the one-dimensional marginal distributions of processes having an Itô differential. *Probability Theory and Related Fields* 71, 501–516.

Hagan, P.S., Kumar, D., Lesniewski, A. and Woodward, D. (2002) Managing smile risk. *Wilmott* (September), 84–108.

Harris, M. and Raviv, A. (1985) A sequential model of convertible debt call policy. *Journal of Finance* 40, 1263–1282.

Harris, R. and Shen, J. (2003) Robust estimation of the optimal hedge ratio. *Journal of Futures Markets* 23(8), 799–816.

Harrison, J. M. and Kreps, D. (1979) Martingales and arbitrage in multiperiod securities markets. *Journal of Economic Theory* 20, 381–408.

Harrison, M. and Pliska, S. (1981) Martingales and stochastic integrals in the theory of continuous trading. *Stochastic Processes and Applications* 11, 215–260.

Harvey, C., Liechty, J., Liechty, M. and Muller, P. (2004) Portfolio selection with higher moments. Working Paper 70, Fuqua School of Business, Duke University.

Heath, D., Jarrow, R. and Morton, A. (1992) Bond pricing and the term structure of interest rates: A new methodology for contingent claims valuation. *Econometrica* 60, 77–105.

Henrard, M. (2000) Comparison of cash flow maps for value at risk. *Journal of Risk* 3(1), 57–71.

Heston, S. (1993) A closed form solution for options with stochastic volatility with applications to bond and currency options. *Review of Financial Studies* 6(2), 327–343.

Howard, C.T. and D'Antonio, L.J. (1984) A risk-return measure of hedging effectiveness. *Journal of Financial and Quantitative Analysis* 19, 101–112.

Howard, C.T. and D'Antonio, L.J. (1987) A risk-return measure of hedging effectiveness: A reply. *Journal of Financial and Quantitative Analysis* 22(3), 377–381.

Hull, J. (2008) *Options, Futures, and Other Derivatives*, 7th edition. Prentice Hall. To appear.

Hull, J. and White, A. (1987) The pricing of options on assets with stochastic volatilities. *Journal of Finance*, 42(2), 281–300.

Hull, J. and White, A. (1990) Pricing interest rate derivative securities. *Review of Financial Studies* 3, 573–592.

Hull, J. and White, A. (2000) The essentials of the LMM. *Risk* 13(12), 126–129.

Ingersoll, J.E. (1977a) A contingent claim valuation of convertible securities. *Journal of Financial Economics* 4, 289–322.

Ingersoll, J.E. (1977b) An examination of corporate call policies on convertible securities. *Journal of Finance* 32, 463–478.

Jacka. S. (1991) Optimal stopping and the American put. *Mathematical Finance* 1(1), 14.

Jackwerth, J.C. (1999) Option-implied risk-neutral distributions and implied binomial trees: A literature review. *Journal of Derivatives* 7, 66–82.

Jackwerth, J.C. and Rubinstein, M. (1996) Recovering probability distributions from contemporary security prices. *Journal of Finance* 51, 1611–1631.

James, J. and Webber, N. (2000) *Interest Rate Modelling*. John Wiley & Sons, Ltd, Chichester.

James, P. (2003) *Option Theory*. John Wiley & Sons, Ltd, Chichester..

Jamshidian, F. (1997) Libor and swap market models and measures. *Finance and Stochastics* 1, 293–330

Jarrow, R., Li, H. and Zhao, F. (2007) Interest rate caps smile too! But can the Libor market models capture the smile? *Journal of Finance*, 62(1), 345–382.

Johnson L.L. (1960 . The theory of hedging and speculation in commodity futures. *Review of Economic Studies* 27(3), 139–151.

Kim, I. (1990) The analytic valuation of American options. *Review of Financial Studies* 3(4), 547–72.

Koutmos, G. and Pericli, A. (1999) Hedging GNMA mortgage-backed securities with T-note futures: Dynamic versus static hedging. *Real Estate Economics* 27(2), 335–363.

Kroner, K.F. and Sultan, J. (1993) Time varying distribution and dynamic hedging with foreign currency futures. *Journal of Financial and Quantitative Analysis* 28, 535–551.

Lai, Y.H, Chen, C.W. and Gerlach, R. (2006) Optimal dynamic hedging using copula-threshold-GARCH models. Presented at the International Conference on Time Series Econometrics, Finance and Risk, Perth, Western Australia.

Lancaster, P. and Salkauskas, K. (1986) *Curve and Surface Fitting: An Introduction*. Academic Press, London.

Landskroner, Y. and Raviv, A. (2003a) Pricing inflation-linked and foreign-currency linked convertible bonds with credit risk. Working Paper, Hebrew University and Stern School of Business, New York University.

Landskroner, Y. and Raviv, A. (2003b) Credit spreads implied by convertible bonds prices. Working paper, Hebrew University and Stern School of Business, New York University.

Laws, J. and Thompson, J. (2005) Hedging effectiveness of stock index futures. *European Journal of Operational Research* 163, 177–191.

Lee, H.T. and Yoder, J. (2005) A bivariate Markov regime switching GARCH approach to estimate time varying minimum variance hedge ratios. Working Paper 05, School of Economics Sciences, Washington State University.

Lee, R.W. (2001) Implied and local volatilities under stochastic volatility. *International Journal of Theoretical and Applied Finance* 4(1), 45–89.

Lence, S.H. (1995) The economic value of minimum-variance hedges. *American Journal of Economic Surveys* 16(3), 357–396.

Lien, D. (2004) Cointegration and the optimal hedge ratio: The general case. *Quarterly Review of Economics and Finance* 44, 654–658.

Lien, D. (2005) The use and abuse of the hedging effectiveness measure. *International Review of Financial Analysis* 14(2), 277–282.

Lien, D. (2006) Estimation bias of futures hedging performance: A note. *Journal of Futures Markets* 26(8), 835–841.

Lien, D. and Luo, X. (1993) Estimating the extended mean-Gini coefficient for futures hedging. *Journal of Futures Markets* 13, 665–676.

Lien, D., and Shaffer, D. R. (1999) Note on estimating the minimum extended Gini hedge ratio. *Journal of Futures Markets* 19, 101–113.

Lien, D. and Tse, Y. K. (1998) Hedging time-varying downside risk. *Journal of Futures Markets* 18, 705–722.

Lien, D., and Tse, Y. K. (2000) Hedging downside risk with futures contracts. *Applied Financial Economics* 10, 163–170.

Lien, D. and Tse, Y. (2002) Some recent developments in futures hedging. *Journal of Economic Surveys* 16(3), 357–396.

Lien, D.D., Tse, Y.K. and Tsui, A.K.C. (2002) Evaluating the hedging performance of the constant correlation GARCH model. *Applied Financial Economics* 12(11), 791–798.

Lindahl, M. (1992) Minimum variance hedge ratios for stock index futures: Duration and expiration effects. *Journal of Futures Markets* 12(1), 33–53.

Longstaff, F. A. and Schwartz, E. S. (1992) A two factor interest rate model and contingent claims valuation. *Journal of Fixed Income* 2(3), 16–23.

Longstaff, F., Santa-Clara, P. and Schwartz, E. (2001) The relative valuation of caps and swaptions: Theory and empirical evidence. *Journal of Finance* 56(6), 2067–2109.

Margrabe, W. (1978) The value of an option to exchange one asset for another. *Journal of Finance* 33, 177–186.

McConnell, J.J. and Schwartz, E.S. (1986) LYON taming. *Journal of Finance* 41(3), 561–577.

McCulloch, J.H. (1975) The tax adjusted yield curve. *Journal of Finance* 30(3), 811–830.

McIntyre, M. (2001) Performance of Dupire's implied diffusion approach under sparse and incomplete data. *Journal of Computational Finance* 4(4), 33–84.

Merrick, J.J. (1988) Hedging with mispriced futures. *Journal of Financial and Quantitative Analysis* 23(4), 451–464.

Merton, R. (1973) Theory of rational option pricing. *Bell Journal of Economics and Management Science* 4(1), 141–183.

Merton, R. C. (1976) Option pricing when underlying stock returns are discontinuous. *Journal of Financial Economics* 3, 125–144.

Miffre, J. (2004) Conditional OLS minimum variance hedge ratios. *Journal of Futures Markets* 24(10), 945–964.

Mikkelson, W.H. (1985) Capital structure change and decrease in stock holder wealth: A cross-sectional study of convertible security calls. In B.M. Friedman (ed.), *Corporate Capital Structure in the United States*, pp. 265–296. University of Chicago Press, Chicago.

Miron, P. and Swannell, P. (1991) *Pricing and Hedging Swaps*. Euromoney, London.

Moosa, I. (2003) The sensitivity of optimal hedge ratio to model specification. *Finance Letters* 1, 15–20.

Moschini, G. and Myers, R. (2002) Testing for constant hedge ratios in commodity markets: A multivariate GARCH approach. *Journal of Empirical Finance*, 9, 589–603.

Myers, R. and Thompson, S. (1989) Generalized optimal hedge ratio estimation. *American Journal of Agricultural Economics* 71, 858–868.

Neftci, S. (2000) *An Introduction to the Mathematics of Financial Derivatives*. Second Edition. Academic Press, San Diego.

Nelson, C.R. and Siegel, A.F. (1987) Parsimonious modelling of yield curves. *Journal of Business* 60(4), 473–489.

Nelson, D.B. (1990) ARCH models as diffusion approximations. *Journal of Econometrics* 45, 7–38.

Neuberger, A. (1994) The log contract. *Journal of Portfolio Management* 20(2), 74–80.

Park, T.H. and Switzer, L.N. (1995) Time-varying distributions and the optimal hedge ratios for stock index futures. *Applied Financial Economics* 5, 131–137.

Patton, A. (2004) On the out of sample importance of skewness and asymmetric dependence for asset allocation. *Journal of Financial Econometrics* 2, 130–168.

Poomimars, P., Cadle, J. and Theobald, M. (2003) Futures hedging using dynamic models of the variance/covariance structure. *Journal of Futures Markets* 23(3), 241–260.

Poulsen, R., Schenk-Hoppé, K. and Ewald, C.-O. (2007) Risk minimization in stochastic volatility models: Model risk and empirical performance. Working paper. Available from SSRN.

Psychoyios, D., Skiadopoulos, G. and Alexakis, P. (2003) A review of stochastic volatility processes: Properties and implications. *Journal of Risk Finance* 4(3), 43–60.

Rebonato, R (2004) *Volatility and Correlation*, 2nd edition. John Wiley & Sons, Ltd, Chichester.

Rebonato, R. and Joshi, M. (2002) A joint empirical and theoretical investigation of the modes of deformation of swaption matrices: Implications for model choice. *International Journal of Theoretical and Applied Finance,* 5(7), 667–694.

Rogers, L. (2002) Monte Carlo valuation of American options. *Mathematical Finance* 12, 271–286.

Ross, S. (1976) Options and efficiency. *Quarterly Journal of Economics* 90, 75–89.

Rubinstein, M. (1994) Implied binomial trees. *Journal of Finance* 49(3), 771–818.

Sato, K. (1991) Self similar processes with independent increments. *Probability Theory and Related Fields* 89, 285–300.

Schoenmakers, J. (2005) *Robust Libor Modelling and Pricing of Derivative Products.* Chapman & Hall/CRC, Boca Raton, FL.

Schroder, M. (1989) Computing the constant elasticity of variance option pricing formula. *Journal of Finance* 44(1), 211–219.

Schweizer, M. (1991) Option hedging for semimartingales. *Stochastic Processes and their Applications* 37, 339–363.

Skiadopoulos, G. (2001) Volatility smile-consistent option models: A survey. *International Journal of Theoretical and Applied Finance,* 4(3), 403–438.

Skiadopoulos, G., Hodges, S. and Clewlow, L. (1998) The dynamics of implied volatility surfaces. Financial Options Research Centre Preprint 1998/86, Warwick Business School.

Steely, J.M. (1991) Estimating the gilt-edged term structure: Basis splines and confidence intervals. *Journal of Business Finance and Accounting* 18(4), 512–529.

Stein, E. and Stein, J. (1991) Stock price distributions with stochastic volatility: An analytic approach. *Review of Financial Studies* 4(4), 727–752.

Stein J.L. (1961) The simultaneous determination of spot and futures prices. *American Economic Review* 51, 1012–1025.

Sutcliffe, C. (2005) *Stock Index Futures*, 3rd edition. Ashgate, Aldershot.

Svensson, L. (1994) Estimating and interpreting forward interest rates: Sweden 1992–94. International Monetary Fund Working Paper 114.

Svensson, L. (1995) Estimating forward interest rates with the extended Nelson and Siegel method. *Sveriges Riksbank Quarterly Review* 1995(3), 13.

Switzer, L.N., Varson, P.L. and Zghidi, S. (2000) Standard & Poors depository receipts and the performance of the S&P 500 index futures market. *Journal of Futures Markets* 20, 705–716.

Takahashi, A., Kobayashi, T. and Nakagawa, N. (2001) Pricing convertible bonds with default risk: A Duffie-Singleton approach. *Journal of Fixed Income* 11(3), 20–29.

Tong, S. (1996) An examination of dynamic hedging. *Journal of International Money and Finance* 15, 19–35.

Tsiveriotis, K. and Fernandes, C. (1998) Valuing convertible bonds with credit risk. *Journal of Fixed Income* 8(2), 95–102.

Vasick, O. (1977) An equilibrium characterisation of the term structure. *Journal of Financial Economics* 5, 177–188

Waggoner, D. (1997) Spline methods for extracting interest rate curves from coupon bond prices. Working Paper 97-10, Federal Reserve Bank of Atlanta.

Wilkens, S. (2005) Option pricing based on mixtures of distributions: Evidence from the Eurex index and interest rate futures options market. *Derivatives Use, Trading and Regulation* 11(3), 213–231.

Wilmott, P (2006) *Paul Wilmott on Quantitative Finance,* 3 volumes. John Wiley & Sons, Ltd, Chichester.

Yang, W. and Allen, D.E. (2005) Multivariate GARCH hedge ratios and hedging effectiveness in Australian futures markets. *Accounting and Finance* 45, 301–321.

Yigitbaşıoğlu, A. and Alexander, C. (2006) Pricing and hedging convertible bonds: Delayed calls and uncertain volatility. *International Journal of Theoretical and Applied Finance* 9(2), 415–437.

Index